MANAGING PROFESSIONALS IN INNOVATIVE ORGANIZATIONS

MANAGING PROFESSIONALS IN INNOVATIVE ORGANIZATIONS

A Collection of Readings

Edited by **Ralph Katz**

BALLINGER PUBLISHING COMPANY
Cambridge, Massachusetts
A Subsidiary of Harper & Row, Publishers, Inc.

International Standard Book Number: 0-88730-351-X

Library of Congress Catalog Card Number: 88-24201

Printed in the United States of America

Library of Congress Cataloging-in-Publication Data

Katz, Ralph.
 Managing professionals in innovative organizations.

 Includes bibliographies and index.
 1. High technology industries—Personnel management. 2. Technicians in industry. I. Katz, Ralph.
 HD62.37.M37 1988   658.3   88-24201
 ISBN 0-88730-351-X (pbk.)

Table of Contents

Introduction

More than ever before, organizations competing in a world of rapid technological change are faced with the challenges of "dualism," that is, operating effectively today while also innovating for tomorrow. These organizations not only have to manage the economic and market successes of their current products but they must also be concerned with their ability to introduce into next generation products those technical advances, designs, services, and manufacturing processes that will sustain their future competitiveness. Technology-based companies, no matter how they are organized, must find ways to satisfy both sets of concerns.

Now, it would be very comforting if everyone in an organization agreed on how to provide for this dualism, but such consensus is rare. Amid the diverse pressures of daily job requirements and rewards, managers representing different business units and departmental areas usually disagree on the relative merits of allocating already scarce resources and talents among the range of activities that might benefit "today's" versus "tomorrow's" products. Furthermore, management theory has essentially no well-established principles for structuring organizations and managing professionals to accommodate these conflicting challenges. Classical management theory deals primarily with the efficient utilization and production of the company's existing assets and product offerings. The principles of high task specialization, unity of command and direction, high division of labor, and the equality of authority and responsibility all address the problems of structuring work systems and information flows in clear, repetitive ways to resolve familiar problems and to facilitate productivity and control through formal lines of authority and job standardization. What is missing is a comparable set of principles, concepts, or guidelines that would reveal how to manage professionals and organize innovative activities within a functioning organizational environment such that new developmental efforts not only take place but take place in a more timely and efficient manner!

The need to manage technology-based innovation expeditiously is not new. The ability to develop and use new technology has long been a cornerstone of economic growth and industrialization. More recently, however, the diversification and decentralization of businesses, the growth of international competition, the faster rates at which new technologies are generated worldwide, and the dramatic reduction of lead times for new product developments and technological life cycles have all placed greater pressures on the firm to expand both its commitment to and its competence in managing technological innovation and organizational change. In particular, the ways in which a company's professional personnel and resources are allocated, positioned, and more generally managed will have a strong bearing on that firm's ability to compete successfully in tomorrow's more global economy. Thus, decision-makers in organizations today require those managerial skills and perspectives necessary to enhance the innovation process and to bring technological advances to the marketplace. They must acquire substantial knowledge not only in managing and directing the technological and market developments themselves but also in utilizing and directing the professionals involved in these developmental efforts. They must be able to understand, inspire, and guide professional technical employees and integrate them with the marketing, manufacturing, and financial functions of the organization. The need for executive leadership in managing both innovation and people has never been greater.

Managing Professionals in Innovative Organizations, offers a comprehensive view of the many varied problems and possible solutions associated with managing technical professionals during the innovation process. This collection is not intended to span the gamut of issues involved in the management of technology and innovation per se. Rather, it focuses on managing and coordinating the creative and organizational roles of professional specialists, in general, and engineers and scientists, in particular. Many of the articles discuss how internal work environments can be structured and designed to provide technical professionals the kinds of opportunities, experiences, and managerial leadership that will enable them to contribute in a significant way to their organization's innovation process. The articles presented here represent the current thinking of a large number of researchers and practitioners seeking richer understanding of the difficult interplay between the specialized knowledge and skills of the creative technical professional and the realistic pressures and constraints required by the responsible organization.

The articles in this book will appeal to several audiences. The book was developed for students in advanced undergraduate or graduate courses on the leadership and management of individual professionals and project teams within an innovative or change process. While texts are available in the areas of new product development, strategic management, strategic management of technology, R&D management, entrepreneurism, and new venture management, this book focuses explicitly on the more individual and group-related roles and activities performed by professional managers and specialists within these strategic and innovative processes. At MIT and Northeastern, our course in managing professionals has been extremely well received and has greatly enhanced students' perspectives for grappling with a host of individual, group, and organizational issues found in both large and small innovative settings.

This collection of readings can also be used as a complementary text for any course that emphasizes product, process, organizational, or technological innovation. It could be used in behavioral courses on issues of leadership, organizational behavior, change, project management, or strategic management; or it could be used in courses on the management of innovation per se such as R&D management, technology management, new product development, engineering management, or innovation management. Another audience is managers attending workshop-type programs in the aforementioned areas who want background readings on the special concerns and problems of organizational and functional leaders within innovative companies. Finally, this book is not limited to managers of engineers and scientists. Instead, the issues, problems, and concepts covered in this collection apply to a wide range of professionals including those involved in new products or services, organizational or technological changes, organizational or environmental uncertainties, or any situation involving the development or application of specialized knowledge or abilities.

Managing Professionals in Innovative Or-

ganizations is organized into six sections. Section I looks at a number of issues associated with the performances of individual professionals. Chapter 1 examines the problem of motivation, emphasizing the importance of designing energizing and challenging work environments as well as the significant influence that various sources of creative tension can have on these environments. The chapter also cautions against generalizing across all types of professionals, pointing out critical differences and interrelationships not only between science and technology but also between their respective constituents. Chapter 2 presents a variety of studies and methodologies for examining problems of managing and measuring the productive performances of professionals within organizations, especially at different career stages and between product generations. While Chapter 1 focuses mainly on creative performance, Chapter 2 discusses improving individual productivity.

Section II discusses the critical roles that professionals must carry out within innovation and technological change in order to improve the new product development process. Chapter 3 presents a general model for conceptualizing the innovation process and discusses the different technical, managerial, and entrepreneurial roles that professionals can and should play at particular times within this process. The chapter also describes problems associated with each of these roles in the context of the mainstream of the business or as part of a new business venture. Chapter 4 distinguishes between managers and leaders and highlights the important elements of each role. It also describes the many problems professionals encounter during the difficult transition from functional specialist to functional manager.

Sections III and IV cover a set of topics relating to the management of creative and high performing individuals and teams. In particular, Section III looks at how individuals and their project or functional teams work with new or creative ideas. Chapter 5 describes obstacles to

and alternatives for structuring and managing constructive roles for creative professionals within ongoing organizations. Chapter 6 then looks at the creative roles that different groups of professionals can play within their organizational surroundings. Chapter 7 rounds out the picture with its discussion on maintaining creative performance over time, especially if the teams becomes increasingly cohesive and insular, form pockets of stability, or erect intergroup barriers that lead to uncooperative cross-functional relationships.

The articles in Section V illustrate just how powerfully organizational cultures, boundaries, technologies, and structures can influence the attitudes, behaviors, and performances of professionals within the innovation process. Chapter 8 focuses on the powerful effects that cultures can have as these cultures are formed through the many informal interactions and shared understandings that take place within a given organizational setting. Chapter 9 goes on to describe how difficult it then becomes to communicate effectively and consequently transfer ideas and technology across organizational boundaries that represent distinct "technical cultures." Chapter 9 also emphasizes the key role of "gatekeeper" in overcoming this difficulty. The papers in Chapter 10 discuss the strong positive and negative effects that alternative organizational structures and processes can have on the overall effectiveness and contribution of professionals within particular designs and climates.

Finally, Section VI discusses a number of issues from a human resource management point of view. Specifically, Chapter 11 describes several career development models for professionals and points out the strengths and weaknesses of the dual-ladder promotional system. Chapter 12 covers a broad range of personnel-related issues and policies, including compensation and appraisal, recruiting, idea-generating programs, and the problems involved in managing a diverse professional work force.

Clearly, no book could cover every topic associated with managing professionals; nor could it cover each included topic with the depth and nuance that could be achieved in a volume dedicated completely to that topic. Nevertheless, it is my hope that the articles in this book will be illuminating and useful to those readers who must deal with or manage innovation or change—that it will increase their sensitivity to the issues they will face as they work with various professional teams and individuals and give them some tools for handling these kinds of issues.

SECTION
I

Managing and Motivating Professional Performance

ISSUES IN MOTIVATING PROFESSIONALS

Distinguishing Engineers from Scientists

Thomas J. Allen

Engineers are not scientists. Few would contest this statement, and yet the failure to recognize the distinction has created untold confusion in the literature. Despite the fact that they should be the last to commit such an egregious error, social scientists studying the behavior of scientists and engineers seldom distinguish properly between the two groups. The social science literature is replete with studies of "scientists," who upon closer examination turn out to be engineers. Worse still, in many studies the populations are mixed, and no attempt is made to distinguish between the two subsets.[1] Many social scientists still view the two groups as essentially the same and feel no need to distinguish between them. This sort of error has led to an unbelievable amount of confusion over the nature of the populations that have been studied and over the applicability of research results to specific real-life situations. A common practice is to use the term *scientist* throughout a presentation, preceded by a disclaimer to the effect that "for ease of presentation, the term *scientist* will be assumed to include both engineers and scientists."

This approach totally neglects the vast differences between the two professions. One might almost as readily lump physicians with fishermen. Managers are not immune from this problem either. Many managers of R&D fail to recognize the true differences and often assume differences that are really non-existent.

At this point, many readers will accuse the author of magnifying what they may consider a trivial issue. But it is just that failure to recognize the distinction that has resulted in so much misdirected policy. In the field of information science, it has often resulted in heavy investments in solutions to the wrong problem. Engineers differ from scientists in their professional activity, their attitudes, their orientations, and even in their typical family background. To interpret the results of research, it is essential to know whether those results were derived from the study of engineers or of scientists because the behavior of the two is so different.

One area in which distinctions are very marked is technical communication. Engineers and scientists communicate about their work in very different ways. The reasons for this are many. Not only are the two groups socialized into entirely different subcultures but their educational processes are vastly different, and there

---

[1] A broader discussion of these issues can be found in Allen (1984).

is a considerable amount of evidence to show that they differ in personality characteristics and family backgrounds as well. Krulee and Nadler (1960) contrast the values and career orientation of science and engineering undergraduates in the following ways:

> [Students] choosing science have additional objectives that distinguish them from those preparing for careers in engineering and management. The science students place a higher value on independence and on learning for its own sake, while, by way of contrast, more students in the other curricula are concerned with success and professional preparation. Many students in engineering and management expect their families to be more important than their careers as major sources of satisfactions, but the reverse pattern is more typical for science students. Moreover, there is a sense in which the science students tend to value education as an end in itself, while the others value it as a means to an end.

Note that Krulee and Nadler do not distinguish between engineering students and students in management. There is considerable evidence to show that many engineering students see the profession as a transitional phase in a career leading to higher levels of management. There is evidence also that many of them are successful in accomplishing their long-term objectives (Schein & Bailyn, 1975). Krulee and Nadler go on to describe the orientations of engineering students:

> Engineering students are less concerned than those in science with what one does in a given position and more concerned with the certainty of the rewards to be obtained. It is significant that they place less emphasis on independence, career satisfactions, and the inherent interest their specialty holds for them, and place more value on success, family life, and avoiding a low-level job. On the whole, one suspects that these students want above all for themselves and their families some minimum status and a reasonable degree of economic success. They are prepared to sacrifice some of their independence and opportunities for

innovation in order to realize their primary objectives. They are more willing to accept positions which will involve them in complex organizational responsibilities and they assume that success in such positions will depend upon practical knowledge, administrative ability and human relations skills.

In the same vein, Ritti (1971) finds a marked contrast between the work goals of scientists and engineers after graduation (Table 1). Ritti draws the following three general conclusions from the data of his study:

> First, the notion of a basic conflict in goals between management and the professional is misapplied to engineers. If the goals of the business require meeting schedules, developing products that will be successful in the marketplace, and helping the company expand its activities, then the goals of engineering specialists are very much in line with these ends.
>
> Second, engineers do not have the goals of scientists. And evidently they never had the goals of scientists. While publication of results and professional autonomy are clearly valued goals of Ph.D. scientists, they are just as clearly the least valued goals of the baccalaureate engineer. The reasons for this difference can be found in the work functions of engineers as opposed to research scientists. Furthermore, both groups desire career development or advancement but for the engineer advancement is tied to activities within the company, while for the scientist advancement is dependent upon the reputation established outside the company.

The type of person who is attracted to a career in engineering is fundamentally quite different from the type who pursues a scientific career. On top of all of this lies the most important difference: level of education. Engineers are generally educated to the baccalaureate level; some go on to a Master of Science degree; some have no college degree at all. The scientist is almost always assumed to have a doctorate. The long,

4

TABLE 1. *Work Goals of Research Scientists and Engineers*

Work goal: How important is it to you to—	Percentage Indicating Goal Is "Very Important"	
	Scientists[a] (N = 33)	Engineers[a] (N = 4,582)
have the opportunity to explore new ideas on technology or systems	b	61
have the opportunity to help the company increase its profit	28	69
gain knowledge of company management policies and practices	19	60
participate in decisions that affect the future business of the company	6	41
work on projects that have a direct impact on the business success of your company	b	47
advance to a policy-making position in management	6	32
work on projects you yourself have originated	75	32
establish your reputation outside the company as an authority in your field	84	29
publish articles in technical journals	88	15
be judged only on the basis of your *technical* contributions	b	13

[a]The relative size of the two samples reflects the size of the two populations in one very large, very technology-intensive firm.

[b]This item is not included in survey of this group (from Ritti, 1971).

complex process of academic socialization that is involved in reaching this stage is bound to result in a person who differs considerably in his life-view. These differences in values and attitudes toward work will almost certainly be reflected in the behavior of the individuals. To treat both professions as one and then to search for consistencies in behavior and outlook is almost certain to produce error and confusion of results.

THE NATURE OF TECHNOLOGY

The differences between science and technology lie not only in the kinds of people who are attracted to them; they are basic to the nature of the activities themselves. Both science and technology develop in a cumulative manner, with each new advance building on and being a product of vast quantities of work that have gone before. In science all of the work up to any point can be found permanently recorded in literature, which serves as a repository for all scientific knowledge. The cumulative nature of science can be demonstrated quite clearly (Price, 1965a, 1970) by the way in which citations among scientific journal articles cluster and form a regular pattern of development over time.

A journal system has been developed in most technologies that in many ways emulates the system originally developed by scientists; yet the literature published in the majority of these journals lacks, as Price (1965b, 1970) has shown, one of the fundamental characteristics of the scientific literature: it does not cumulate or build upon itself as does the scientific literature. Citations to previous papers or patents are fewer and

5

are more often to the author's own work. Publication occupies a position of less importance than it does in science where it serves to document the end product and establish priority. Because published information is at best secondary to the actual utilization of the technical innovation, this archival function is not as essential to ensure the technologist that he is properly credited by future generations. The names of Wilbur and Orville Wright are not remembered because they published papers. The technologist's principal legacy to posterity is encoded in physical, not verbal, structure. Consequently, the technologist publishes less and devotes less time to reading than do scientists.

Information is transferred in technology primarily through personal contact. Even in this, however, the technologist differs markedly from the scientist. Scientists working at the frontier of a particular specialty know each other and associate together in what Derek Price has called "invisible colleges." They keep track of one another's work through visits, seminars, and small invitational conferences, supplemented by an informal exchange of written material long before it reaches archival publication. Technologists, on the other hand, keep abreast of their field by close association with co-workers in their own organization. They are limited in forming invisible colleges by the imposition of organizational barriers.

BUREAUCRATIC ORGANIZATION

Unlike scientists, the vast majority of technologists are employed by organizations with a well-defined mission (profit, national defense, space exploration, pollution abatement, and so forth). Mission-oriented organizations necessarily demand of their technologists a degree of identification unknown in most scientific circles. This organizational identification works in two ways

to exclude the technologist from informal communication channels outside his organization. First, he is inhibited by the requirements that he work only on problems that are of interest to his employer, and second, he must refrain from early disclosure of the results of his research in order to maintain his employer's advantage over competitors. Both of these constraints violate the strong scientific norms that underlie and form the basis of the invisible college. The first of these norms demands that science be free to choose its own problems and that the community of colleagues be the only judges of the relative importance of possible areas of investigation, and the second is that the substantive findings of research are to be fully assigned and communicated to the entire research community. The industrial organization, by preventing its employers from adhering to these two norms, impedes the formation by technologists of anything resembling an invisible college.

Impact of "Localism" on Communication

What is the effect of this enforced "localism" on the communication patterns of engineers? Because proprietary information must be protected to preserve the firm's position in a highly competitive marketplace, free communication among engineers of different organizations is greatly inhibited. It is always amusing to observe engineers from different companies interacting in the hallways and cocktail lounges at conventions of professional engineering societies. Each one is trying to draw the maximum amount of information from his competitors while giving up as little as possible of his own information in return. Often the winner in this bargaining situation is the person with the strongest physical constitution.

Another result of the concern over divulging proprietary information will be observed in looking at an engineer's reading habits. A good proportion of the truly important information generated in an industrial laboratory cannot be published in the open literature because it is considered proprietary and must be protected. It is, however, published within the organization, and, for this reason, the informal documentation system of his parent organization is an important source of information for the engineer.

The Effect of Turnover

It is this author's suspicion that much of the proprietary protectionism in industry is far overplayed. Despite all of the organizational efforts to prevent it, the state of the art in a technology propagates quite rapidly. Either there are too many martinis consumed at engineering conventions or some other mechanism is at work. This other mechanism may well be the itinerant engineer, who passes through quite a number of organizations over the course of a career. Shapero (1968) makes this point very strongly and musters evidence in support of it. He points to the finding by the Engineering Manpower Commission of the Engineers' Joint Council that the turnover in industries classified as "aircraft and parts," "communications," "electrical-electronics," "instruments," and "R&D" is over 12 percent. He goes on to say that his own "limited data . . . indicate that the turnover rates of [engineers and scientists] are considerably higher than 12 percent in many defense R&D establishments." Turnover, both voluntary and as a result of layoffs, has at times certainly been far in excess of 12 percent. And for certain years in individual firms it has been far more than 25 percent. Studies that we have done in Ireland (Allen & Cooney, 1973) and Sweden (Allen & DeMeyer, 1982) show that turnover is the principal stimulus for inter-firm or inter-organizational communication.

Each time that an engineer leaves an employer, voluntarily or otherwise, he carries some knowledge of the employer's operations, experience, and current technology with him. We are gradually coming to realize that human beings are the most effective carriers of information and that the best way to transfer information between organizations or social systems is to physically transfer a human carrier. Roberts's studies (Roberts and Wainer, 1967) marshal impressive evidence for the effective transfer of space technology from quasi- academic institutions to the industrial sector and eventually to commercial application in those instances in which technologists left university laboratories to establish their own businesses. This finding is especially impressive in view of the general failure to find evidence of successful transfer of space technology by any other mechanism, despite the fact that many techniques have been tried and a substantial amount of money has been invested in promoting the transfer.

This certainly makes sense. Ideas have no real existence outside of the minds of people. Ideas can be represented in verbal or graphic form, but such representation is necessarily incomplete and cannot be easily structured to fit new situations. The human brain has a capacity for flexibly restructuring information in a manner that has never been approached by even the most sophisticated computer programs. For truly effective transfer of technical information, we must make use of this human ability to recode and restructure information so that it fits into new contexts and situations. Consequently, the best way to transfer technical information is to move a human carrier. The high turnover among engineers results in a heavy migration from organization to organization and is therefore a very effective mechanism for disseminating technology throughout an industry and often to other industries. Every time an engineer changes jobs he brings with him a record of his experiences on the former job and a great amount of what his former organization considers "proprietary" information. Now, of course, the information is usually quite perishable, and its value decays rapidly with time. But a continual flow of engineers among the firms of an industry ensures that no

7

single firm is very far behind in knowledge of what its competitors are doing. So the mere existence of high turnover among R&D personnel vitiates much of the protectionism accorded proprietary information.

As for turnover itself, it is well known that most organizations attempt to minimize it. Actually, however, a certain amount of turnover may be not only desirable but absolutely essential to the survival of a technical organization, although just what the optimum turnover level is for an organization is a question that remains to be answered. It will vary from one situation to the next and is highly dependent upon the rate at which the organization's technical staff is growing. After all, it is the influx of new engineers that is most beneficial to the organization, not the exodus of old ones. When growth rate is high, turnover can be low. An organization that is not growing should welcome or encourage turnover. The Engineers' Joint Council figure of 12 percent may even be below the optimum for some organizations. Despite the costs of hiring and processing new personnel, an organization might desire an even higher level of turnover. Although it is impossible to place a price tag on the new state-of-the-art information that is brought in by new employees, it may very well more than counterbalance the costs of hiring. This would be true at least to the point where turnover becomes disruptive to the morale and functioning of the organization.

COMMUNICATION PATTERNS IN SCIENCE AND TECHNOLOGY

Scientists all share a common concern and responsibility for processing information, which is the essence of scientific activity. As physical systems consume and transform *energy,* so too does the system of science consume, transform, produce, and exchange *information.* Scientists talk to one another, they read each other's papers, and most important, they publish scientific papers, their principal tangible product. Both the input and output of this system we call science are in the form of information. Each of the components, whether individual investigations or projects, consume and produce information. Furthermore, whether written or oral, this information is always in the form of human language. Scientific information is, or can be, nearly always encoded in a verbal form.

Technology is also an ardent consumer of information. The engineer must first have information in order to understand and formulate the problem confronting him. Then he must have additional information from either external sources or memory in order to develop possible solutions to his problem. Just like his counterpart in science, the technologist requires verbal information in order to perform his work. At this level, there is a very strong similarity between the information input requirements of both scientists and technologists.

It is only when we turn to the nature of the outputs of scientific and technological activity that really striking differences appear. These, as will be seen, imply very real and important second-order differences in the nature of the information input requirements.

Technology consumes information, transforms it, and produces a product in a form that can still be regarded as information bearing. The information, however, is no longer in a verbal form. Whereas science both consumes and produces information in the form of human language, engineers transform information from this verbal format to a physically encoded form. They produce physical hardware in the form of products or processes.

The scientist's principal goal is a published paper. The technologist's goal is to produce some physical change in the world. This difference in orientation, and the subsequent difference in the nature of the products of the two, has profound implications for those concerned with supplying information to either of the two activities.

The information-processing system of science has an inherent compatibility between input and output. Both are in verbal form (Figure 1). The output of one stage, therefore, is in the form in which it will be required for the next stage. The problem of supplying information to the scientist thus becomes one of systematically collecting and organizing these outputs and making them accessible to other scientists to employ in their work.

In technology, on the other hand, there is a fundamental and inherent incompatibility between input and output. Because outputs are in form basically different from inputs, they usually cannot serve directly as inputs to the next stage. The physically encoded format of the output makes it very difficult to retrieve the information necessary for further developments. That is not to say that this is impossible: technologists frequently analyze a competitor's product in order to retrieve information; competing nations often attempt to capture one another's weapon systems in order to analyze them for their information content. This is a difficult and uncertain process, however. It would be much simpler if the information were directly available in verbal form. As a consequence, attempts are made to decode or understand physically encoded information only when one party to the exchange is unavailable or unwilling to cooperate. Then an attempt is made to understand how the problems were approached by analyzing the physical product. In cases where the technologists responsible for the product are available and cooperative, this strategy is seldom used. It is much more effective to communicate with them directly, thereby obtaining the necessary information in a verbal form.

A question that arises concerning the documentation produced in the course of most technological projects is why it cannot serve to meet the information needs of subsequent stages in technological development. The answer is that it is not quite compatible with other input require-

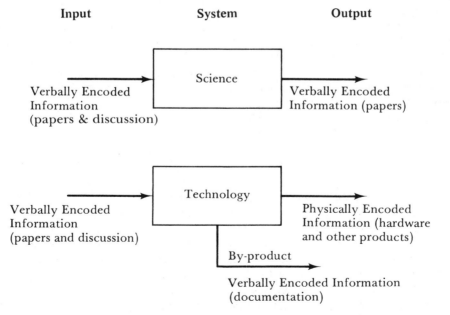

FIGURE 1. *Information Processing in Science and Technology*

ments although it meets the requirements of verbal structure. First, as seen in Figure 1, it is merely a by-product. The direct output is still physical, consequently it is incomplete. It generally assumes a considerable knowledge of what went into the physical product. Those unacquainted with the actual development therefore require some human intervention to supplement and interpret the information contained in this documentation. Thus, technological documentation is often most useful only when the author is directly available to explain and supplement its content.

Now if all of this is true, it leads to an interesting conclusion: whereas the provision of information in science involves the gathering, organizing, and distribution of publications, the situation in technology is very different. The technologist must obtain his information either through the very difficult task of decoding and translating physically encoded information or by relying upon direct personal contact and communication with other technologists. His reliance upon the written word will be much less than that of the scientist. Thus, there are very different solutions to the problems of improving the dissemination and availability of information in the two domains. If, for example, one were to develop an optimum system for communication in science, there is no reason to suspect that it would be at all appropriate for technology. It is essential that we bear these distinctions in mind while exploring the nature of the communication processes in technology. Much has been written about scientific information flow; we may even understand something about it. One must be extremely cautious, however, in extrapolating or attempting to apply this understanding of science to the situation in technology.

The difference between communication patterns in science and technology is amply illustrated by the data originally reported by Allen (1984). Among a sample of nineteen projects, seventeen were clearly developmental in their nature. The remaining two had clear-cut goals, but these were directed toward an increased understanding of a particular set of phenomena. While the information generated by these two teams would eventually be used to develop new hardware, this was not the immediate goal of the teams, who were far more interested in the phenomena than in the application. For this reason, their work can be considered to be much more scientific than technological in nature.

A comparison of the two scientific projects with the seventeen technological projects (Table 2) shows a marked disparity in the use of eight information channels. The scientists engaged in the phenomena-oriented project concentrated their attention heavily upon the literature and upon colleagues outside their laboratory organization. The engineers spread their attention more evenly over the channels and received ideas from two sources unused by the scientists. The customer (in this case, a government laboratory) suggested a substantial number of ideas, demonstrating the importance of the marketplace for technologists. Vendors are another important channel in technology because they are important potential suppliers of components or subsystems, and they provide information that they hope will stimulate future business. Involvement in the marketplace, either through the customer or potential vendors, exerts a significant influence upon the communication system, providing channels for the exchange of information in two directions and connecting buyers and sellers through both the procurement and marketing functions of the organization.

The extent to which scientists and engineers differ in the degree to which they use oral and written channels can be seen even more clearly in comparing the way in which they allocate their time (Table 3). A comparison of time spent using literature or talking by the engineers working on twelve technological projects and the scientists of the two phenomena-oriented research projects shows the scientists devoting 75 percent more of their time to communication. Most of this increased communication time is given to the liter-

TABLE 2. *Sources of Messages Resulting in Technical Ideas Considered during the Course of Nineteen Projects**

Channel	Seventeen Technological Projects		Two Scientific Research Projects	
	Number of Messages Produced	Percentage of Total	Number of Messages Produced	Percentage of Total
Literature	53	8	18	51
Vendors	101	14	0	0
Customer	132	19	0	0
Other sources external to the laboratory	67	9	5	14
Laboratory technical staff	44	6	1	3
Company research programs	37	5	1	3
Analysis and experimentation	216	31	3	9
Previous personal experience	56	8	7	20

*From Allen (1984).

ature. Both the engineers and scientists spent about 10 percent of their overall time discussing technical matters with colleagues, but the engineers spent more time in personal contact than in reading.

This comparison is quite revealing. Despite all the discussion of informal contact and invisible colleges among scientists (and scientists do make extensive use of personal contacts), it is the engineer who is more dependent upon colleagues. The difference between communication behavior of scientists and engineers is not simply quantitative, however. The persons contacted by scientists are very different from those contacted by engineers, and the relationship between the engineer and those with whom he communicates is vastly different from the relationship that exists among scientists. In written channels, too, there are significant differences. The literature used by scientists differs qualitatively from that used by engineers. And the engineer not only reads different journals, but, as discussed in Allen (1984), he uses the literature for entirely different purposes.

TABLE 3. *A Comparison of Engineers' and Scientists' Allocation of Time in Communication*

Channel	Proportion of Time Spent During:	
	Twelve Technological Problems	Two Scientific Projects
Literature use	7.9%	18.2%
Total time in communication	16.4	28.6
Total time reported (man-hours)	20,185	1,580

THE RELATION BETWEEN SCIENCE AND TECHNOLOGY

Given the vast differences between science and technology, how do the two relate to each other?

This is a question that has intrigued a number of researchers in recent years. It is generally assumed that the two are in some way related, and in fact national financing of scientific activity is normally justified on the basis of its eventual benefits to technology. Is there any basis for this, and what, if any, is the relation of science to technology? How are the results of scientific activity incorporated into technological developments? To what extent is technology dependent upon science? What are the time lags involved?

The Process of Normal Science

Kuhn (1962) describes three classes of problems that are normally undertaken in science:

1. The determination of significant facts that the research paradigm has shown to be particularly revealing of the nature of things.[2]
2. The determination of facts, which (in contrast with problems of the first class) may, themselves, be of little interest, but which can be compared directly with predictions made by the research paradigm.
3. Empirical work undertaken to articulate the paradigm theory.

The first two of these—the precise determination and extension to other situations of facts and constants that the paradigm especially values (for example, stellar position and magnitude, specific gravities, wave lengths, boiling points) since they have been used in solving paradigmatic problems, and the test of hypotheses derived from the central body of theory—will not concern us here. These are the normally accepted concerns of science, but the third-listed function is probably the most important, and I shall address myself to this category of activity that comprises empirical work undertaken to extend and complete the central body of theory. It may, itself, be subdivided into three classes of activity (Kuhn, 1970):[2]

1. The determination of physical constants (gravitational constants; Avogadro's Number; Joule's Coefficient; etc.).
2. The development of quantitative laws. (Boyle's, Coulomb's, and Ohm's Laws).
3. Experiments designed to choose among alternative ways to applying the paradigm to new areas of interest.

Within the third class lie problems that have resulted from difficulties encountered during the course of scientific research or during the process of technological advance. This, as we shall see, is a form of scientific activity of extreme interest and importance.

The Dependence of Technology on Science

Despite the long-held belief in a continuous progression from basic research through applied research to development, empirical investigation has found little support for such a situation. It is becoming generally accepted that technology builds upon itself and advances quite independently of any link with the scientific frontier, and often without any necessity for an understanding of the basic science which underlies it. Price (1965b), a strong advocate of this position, cites Toynbee's view that

> physical science and industrialism may be conceived as a pair of dancers, both of whom know their steps and have an ear for the rhythm of the music. If the partner who has been leading chooses to change parts and to follow instead, there is perhaps no reason to expect that he will dance less correctly than before.

Price goes on to marshal evidence refuting the idea of technology as something "growing out of" science and to make the claim that communication between the two is at best a "weak interaction." Communication between the two is restricted almost completely to that which takes place through the process of education.

Singer (1959), in setting the scene for his history of scientific thought, describes science as the activity or process of knowledge making. He stresses that "science . . . is no static body of knowledge but rather an active process that can be followed through the ages." It is a stream of human activity devoted to building a store of knowledge and can be traced back to the beginning of recorded history. Science can thereby be represented as a stream of events over time cumulating in a body of knowledge. There are two other streams of human activity that operate parallel to science and that function both as contributors to scientific development and as beneficiaries of scientific accomplishment. First there is the activity we have labeled "technology." This is a stream of human activity oriented toward incorporating human knowledge into physical hardware, which will eventually meet with some human use. Then there is a much more general

form of human activity in which the ideas of science and the hardware of technology are actually put to some use in the stream of human affairs. This last stream we will label *utilization* (Figure 2).

The activities of technology and of utilization in commerce, industry, welfare, and war, while at various times in close harness with science, have developed for the most part independently. Science builds on prior science; technology builds on prior technology; and utilization grows and spreads in response to needs and benefits.

The familiar notion of science providing the basis upon which technology is built to be later utilized in commerce or industry has been shown by the historians of science to have only a limited basis in historical fact. Civilizations have often emphasized activity in one or two of these areas to the exclusion of the others. The Greeks, for example, were very active in science, but they were relatively little concerned with the practical

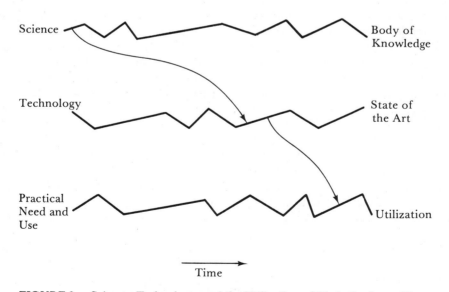

FIGURE 2. *Science, Technology, and the Utilization of Their Products, Showing the Normal Progression from One to the Other*

applications or implications of their discoveries. The Romans, in contrast, developed a highly practical civilization, which was greatly concerned with the building of artifices to aid in coping with the physical and social environment. They devoted much effort to the construction of roads and aqueducts and of improvement of armor and weapons without much concurrent increase in their understanding of the natural basis of their developments. History shows quite independent paths through the succeeding centuries to the present time. The three streams appear now in rapid parallel growth; an increased emphasis in one is usually accompanied by an increase in the other two. It is probable that the streams are more closely coupled now than they have been historically, but the delays encountered in any of the communication paths between them remain substantial.

The Flow of Information Between Science and Technology

Over the past ten years several studies have attempted to trace the flow of information from science to technology. In one of the earlier of these, Price (1965b), after investigating citation patterns in both scientific and technological journals, concluded that science and technology progress quite independently of one another. Technology, in this sense, builds upon its own prior developments and advances in a manner independent of any link with the current scientific frontier and often without any necessity for an understanding of the basic science underlying it.

Price's hypothesis certainly appears valid in light of more recent evidence. There is little support for direct communication between science and technology. The two do advance quite independently, and much of technology develops without a complete understanding of the science upon which it is built.

Project Hindsight was the first of a series of attempts to trace technological advances back to their scientific origins. Within the twenty-year horizon of its backward search, Hindsight was able to find very little contribution from basic science (Sherwin and Isenson, 1967). In most cases, the trail ran cold before reaching any activity that could be considered basic research. In Isenson's words, "It would appear that most advances in the technological state of the art are based on no more recent advances than Ohm's Law or Maxwell's equations."

Project TRACES (IIT Research Institute, 1968), partially in response to the Hindsight results, succeeded in tracing the origins of six technological innovations back to the underlying basic sciences but only after extending the time horizon well beyond twenty years. In a follow-up, Battelle (1973) investigators found similar lags in five more innovations. In yet another study, Langrish found little support for a strong science-technology interaction. Langrish wisely avoided the problem of differentiating science from technology. He categorized research by the type of institution in which it was conducted—industry, university, or government establishment. In tracing eighty-four award-winning innovations to their origins, he found that "the role of university as a source of ideas for [industrial] innovation is fairly small" (Langrish, 1971) and that "university science and industrial technology are two quite separate activities which occasionally come into contact with each other" (Langrish, 1969). He argued very strongly that most university basic research is totally irrelevant to societal needs and can be only partially justified for its contributions through training of students.

Gibbons and Johnston (1973) attempted to refute the Langrish hypothesis. They presented data from thirty relatively small-scale technological advances and found that approximately one-sixth of the information needed in problem solving came from scientific sources. Furthermore, they claimed greater currency in the scientific information that was used. The mean age of the scientific journals they cited was 12.2 years. This is not quite twenty, but with publication lags, it can safely be concluded that the work was fourteen or fifteen years old at the time of use. They showed considerable use of personal contact with university scientists, but nearly half of these were for the purpose of either referral to other sources of information or to determine the existence of specialized facilities or services. So, while Gibbons and Johnston may raise some doubt over the Price-Langrish hypothesis, the contrary evidence is hardly compelling.

The evidence, in fact, is very convincing that the normal path from science to technology is, at best, one that requires a great amount of time. There are certainly very long delays in the system, but it should not be assumed that the delays are always necessarily there. Occasionally, technology is forced to forfeit some of its independence. This happens when its advance is impeded by a lack of understanding of the scientific basis of the phenomena with which it is dealing. The call then goes out for help. Often a very interesting basic research problem can result, and scientists can be attracted to it. In this way, science often discovers voids in its knowledge of areas that have long since been bypassed by the research front. Science must, so to speak, backtrack a bit and increase its understanding of an area previously bypassed or neglected.

Morton (1965) described several examples in which technology has defined important problems for scientific investigation. He pointed out that progress in electron tube technology at one time appeared to have reached an upper limit of a few megacycles in frequency response. With the rapidly increasing amount of radio frequency communication, it was clearly desirable to extend the range of usable frequencies above that limit to increase the number of channels available to communicators and to allow the use of larger band widths, thereby increasing the amount of information per unit of time that could be transmitted. This difficulty forced the realization that electron tube technology had advanced without a real understanding of the principles involved. It did this largely by "cut and try" methods,

manipulating the geometry of the elements and the composition of the cathode materials with little real understanding of the fundamental physics underlying the results. This block to the advance of a burgeoning technology forced a return to basic classical physics and a more detailed study of the interactions of free electrons and electromagnetic waves. The return allowed scientists to fill a gap in their understanding and subsequently permitted the development of such microwave amplifiers as the magnetron, klystron, and traveling wave tube. To quote Morton (1965, p. 64), "The important lesson to be learned from the vigorous past of electronics is not that it was always close to the *new frontiers* of basic science. Rather, it was the conscious or unconscious recognition of *relevant* physical phenomenon and materials, *old or new* which could fulfill a critical need or break an anticipated technological barrier." Note that there was first of all communication of a problem from technology to science, followed by a relatively easy transfer of scientific results back to the technologists. The two conditions are clearly related. When technology is the source of the problem, technologists are ready and capable of understanding the solution and putting it to work.

Additional support for this idea is provided by Project Hindsight (Sherwin and Isenson, 1967). While in most cases, Hindsight was unable to find any contribution to technology from basic science, it is the exception to this discontinuity between science and technology that chiefly concerns us at the present. Isenson reports[3] that he discovered exceptions to his general finding and that these exceptions are usually characterized by a situation in which, similar to Morton, technology has advanced to a limit at which an understanding is required of the basic physical science involved. Thus technology defines a problem for science. When this problem is attacked and resolved by scientists, its solution is passed immediately into technology. A close coupling thus exists for at least an isolated point in time, and the researchers of Project Hindsight were able to trace the record back from an improved system in what we have labeled the "utilization stream" through an advance in the technological state of the art to the closure of a gap in the body of scientific knowledge. To distinguish this latter form of research from "frontier science," I propose calling it "technology-pull" science.

Technology-pull science is by its nature directly responsive to technological need, and the advance of technology is often contingent upon the pursuit of such science. So when the connection between science and technology is of this form, little delay is encountered in the transfer of information (Figure 3). Communication is rapid and direct, and the long delays of the normal

transfer process are circumvented. The transfer from technology-pull science can be further accelerated by including in the technological development team former scientists or individuals whose training was in science. The advantages of such a strategy were clearly demonstrated during World War II when many scientists became engineers, at least temporarily, and were very effective in implementing the results of fundamental research.

A similar phenomenon is occurring at the present time in genetic engineering. Molecular biologists have been attracted by the potential economic benefits into what is now becoming a new technology. These former basic research scien-

FIGURE 3.   *Science, Technology, and the Utilization of Their Products, Showing Communication Paths Among the Three Streams ([a] The normal process of assimilation of scientific results into technology. [b] Recognized need for a device, technique, or scientific understanding. [c] The normal process of adoption of technology for use. [d] Technological need for understanding of physical phenomena and its response [from Marquis and Allen, 1966])*

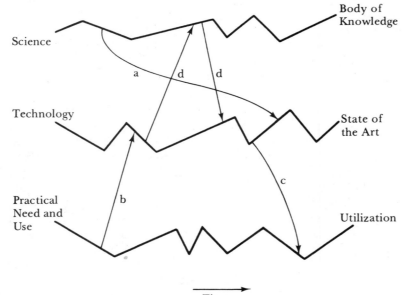

tists both carry with them substantial scientific knowledge and retain informal ties to the scientific community.

The point to be made is that at least a segment of basic science is not conducted at what is called the "frontier" of knowledge. Technology—and often investigation in a different scientific area—will raise problems that attract investigators to an area that has been worked on before. The investigation then proceeds, looking perhaps from a somewhat different vantage at items that had not previously been deemed important phenomena. That such investigations are searching in what had been considered secure territory makes them no less fundamental in their nature. To draw upon the National Science Foundation's definition of basic research, because these researchers are being directed back

over old ground does not mean that their primary aim cannot be "a fuller knowledge or understanding of the subject under study, rather than a practical application" (National Science Foundation, 1965).

A second element can be added to Price's hypothesis. While technology and science in general may progress quite independently of each other, there very probably are some technologies that are more closely connected with science than others. For example, electronics technology is more closely related to frontier work in physics than say, mechanical technology. Nuclear technology should be more closely coupled to the advance of physical knowledge than either of these two. And of course, genetic engineering still retains a very close association with its parent science. There is some evidence to support this variance in the na-

TABLE 4. *Citations From Engineering Journals to Other Technological and Scientific Journals*

	Proportion of References[a] Citing:			
	Technological Journals	Scientific Journals	Ratio of Technological to Scientific Citations	Total Number of Citations
Journal of Applied Mechanics[b]	38.7%	6.4%	6.05	1,172
Burton's (1959b) data for mechanical engineering journals[c]	62.0	19.7	3.15	1,278
Burton's (1959a) data for chemical engineering journals[c]	55.1	27.4	2.01	1,741
Burton's (1959c) data for metallurgical engineering journals[c]	62.4	31.8	1.96	2,639
IEEE Transactions on Electron Devices[d]	43.4	25.0	1.74	865
Nuclear Science and Engineering[e]	18.3	19.8	.93	1,669

[a]References to books, unpublished reports, and unclassified journals constitute the remainder.
[b]January through December 1965.
[c]January through December 1957. The values shown result from a reanalysis of the original data. Proportions shown for the Burton data are based on a count which does not include books or unpublished reports. Hence, they are somewhat larger in absolute magnitude compared with the other proportions; thus the ratios are the only comparable figures.
[d]January through October 1965.
[e]January through December 1965.
From Marquis and Allen (1966)

ture of the coupling. The engineering fields examined in Table 4 show the ratio of technological to scientific citations to range from about six to one to less than one to one. The data clearly indicate that a wide variation exists in the degree to which technologies are coupled to their respective sciences.

NOTES

1. Even Pelz and Andrews (1966), who are careful to preserve the distinction throughout most of their book, a study of 1,300 engineers and scientists, chose *Scientists in Organizations* as its title, forgetting the majority of their sample.
2. Kuhn's term "research paradigm" refers to a body of scientific theory and evidence whose "achievement [is] sufficiently unprecedented to attract an enduring group of adherents away from competing modes. Simultaneously, it [is] sufficiently open ended to leave all sorts of problems for . . . practitioners to resolve."
3. Personal communication, April 22, 1966.

REFERENCES

Allen, T. J. 1984. *Managing the Flow of Technology.* Cambridge: MIT Press.

Allen, T. J., and Cooney, S. 1973. "Institutional Roles in Technology Transfer: A Diagnosis of the Situation in One Small Country." *R&D Management* 4: 41–51.

Allen, T. J., and De Meyer. 1982. "Technical Communication Among Scientists and Engineers in Four Organizations in Sweden: Results of a Pilot Study." M.I.T. Sloan School Working Paper WP1318-82.

Battelle Memorial Institute. 1973. *Interactions of science and technology in the innovation process:*

Some case studies. Final report to the National Science Foundation NSF-C667, Columbus, Ohio.

Gibbons, M., and Johnston, R. D. 1974. The roles of science in technological innovation. *Research Policy* 3: 220–242.

IIT Research Institute. 1968. *Technology in retrospect and critical events in science.* Report to the National Science Foundation NSF C-235.

Krulee, G. K., and Nadler, E. B. 1960. Studies of education for science and engineering: Student values and curriculum choice. *IEEE Transactions on Engineering Management* 7: 146–158.

Kuhn, T. B. 1970. *Structure of Scientific Revolutions.* Rev. ed. Chicago: University of Chicago Press.

Langrish, J. 1971. Technology transfer: Some British data. *R&D Management* 1: 133–136.

Marquis, D. G., and Allen, T. J. 1966. Communication patterns in applied technology. *American Psychologist* 21: 1052–1060.

Morton, J. A. 1965. From physics to function. *IEEE Spectrum* 2: 62–64.

Pelz, D. C., and Andrews, F. M. 1966. *Scientists in Organizations.* New York: Wiley.

Price, D. J. DeSolla. 1965a. Networks of scientific papers. *Science* 149: 510–515.

———1965b. Is technology independent of science? *Technology and Culture* 6: 553–568.

———1970. In D. K. Pollock and Nelson, C. E. (eds.) *Communication Among Scientists and Technologists.* Lexington, Mass.: Heath.

Ritti, R. R. 1971. *The Engineer in the Industrial Corporation.* New York: Columbia University Press.

Roberts, E. B., and Wainer, H. A. 1971. Some characteristics of technical entrepreneurs. *IEEE Transactions on Engineering Management,* EM-18, 3.

Schein, E. H., and Bailyn, L. 1975. Work involvement in technically based careers: A study of M.I.T. alumni at mid-career. M.I.T. Sloan School of Management.

Shapero, A. 1967. Preliminary analysis of inter-specialty mobility of technical professional manpower resources. National Science Foundation.

Sherwin, E. W., and Isenson, R. S. 1967. Project Hindsight. *Science* 156: 1571–1577.

Motivating Your R&D Staff

George E. Manners, Jr.

Joseph A. Steger

Thomas W. Zimmerer

Ten basic tenets form a body of practical knowledge for generating the excitement that is the essence of motivation for technical people.

Over the years, we have found that research managers list "motivation" as the most perplexing requirement of the managerial role. This observation is true in many management situations. Motivation is one of the most critical ingredients in work performance as well as *the* most difficult to understand. There is a voluminous amount of literature on the topic, some of it quite valuable to the manager. However, this enormity of information lacks focus and, shall we say, a common body of practical knowledge.

We conceive of motivation simply as excitement—an energizer that is reflected as excitement or arousal. This definition makes the concept of motivation more understandable and applicable. Most managers tend to conceive of motivation as a complex set of dimensions that in fact are not encompassed in our definition. Thus, performance is not motivation. Satisfaction is not motivation. Behaviors are not motivation. Results are not motivation. Too often these are in some confusing and ambiguous fashion encompassed in the concept of motivation when discussed by managers.

Another point: Because people are excited about work and are exhibiting lots of activity does not mean they are productively active. That is, the group could be highly motivated and running amuck because they are not managed to optimize the motivational spirit.

While the presence of motivation does not guarantee performance, the absence of motivation guarantees long-term performance problems. Obviously, a lack of arousal begets no effort and the precursor to *effort* is excitement or arousal. Edison's famous quote about genius being 99 percent perspiration and 1 percent inspiration is the essence of what motivation in our conception yields.

Thus, as long as one does not over-define motivation, we think that a focus—or common body of knowledge—is available to the practicing manager. This focus is contained in ten basic tenets which yield useful insight into how to generate work-group excitement without requiring the vocabulary of a clinical psychologist.

Reprinted with permission from Manners, and Steger, and Zimmerer, "Motivating Your R&D Staff," *Research Management*, September–October 1983.

A tenet is an opinion which is held to be true—our opinion. These opinions, however, have been slowly articulated over a ten-year period by carefully observing successful motivational practices through our interactions with industrial and government R&D laboratories. We have come to view these tenets as fundamental truths of work excitement. We have found that the extent to which these tenets—and their prescriptions for managerial action—are understood by the practicing manager is the extent to which the capacity to motivate is understood. Some of these tenets may be viewed as simple platitudes, some not. Taken as a whole, however, they do form a common body of practical knowledge. The tenets are as follows.

DIFFICULTY

The first tenet of motivation is, quite simply, that generating incremental excitement about work is very difficult. On the other hand, most managers have observed that destroying excitement is relatively easy. Many young project managers find that the old excitement created by technical interactions while on the bench no longer works when they assume "power." Or, they agonize over how to rekindle work excitement in a bench scientist many years their elder.

It is interesting how many of these befuddled research managers blame "the corporation" for their motivational difficulties. Meanwhile, the effective motivators understand a fact of managerial existence: Do not expect much help from the larger organization. Many of the reasons why the larger organization (the laboratory *or* the corporation) will not necessarily aid the individual manager in his day-to-day motivations of researchers will become more clear once the other basic tenets are offered.

Difficult though this business is, the prize is worth the chase. We offer this advice, *Never give*

up. The motivated work group is too important an antecedent to research success to stop trying. One can feel its effects simply by walking in the door of research offices. As the sage football scout once said: "I don't know what it is, but I know it when I see it."

FAT HAPPY RATS

Since so much of the literature on motivation emanates from experimental psychology, we should offer the observation that fat, happy rats never run mazes. They sit there. Now, this tenet should not lead to the conclusion that research managers should keep researchers deprived. On the contrary, keep the rewards coming to those who perform. And as the Japanese have so effectively pointed out, one must maintain a "positive tension." That is, an excitement that is directed toward answering, "How do we do it better?" Thus, no resting on one's laurels is allowed.

The other facet of the "Fat Happy Rat" tenet is that most "positive tension" is generated within the individual. Thus, *selection* of talent that are generators of their own excitement is critical and yet often neglected by R&D managers who focus on credentials.

The literature on achievement motivation reinforces this fact by concluding that those possessing the motivation to achieve (which is terribly difficult to "train"—thus the focus selection) tend to maintain that motivation to the extent that the desire to excel is given a climate to operationalize the desire. Thus, hungry researchers tend to stay hungry—given the manager's understanding of the other basic tenets.

An anecdote may serve to make the point about achievers: We once asked a research manager what he looked for in a young scientist or engineer. His response was "I will tell you what *not* to look for—'Soft Suburbanites.' They are never hungry enough!" While we all can observe some exceptions to this manager's rule, the work excitement of the hungry researchers in his laboratory was truly exceptional.

The observation of the achiever during the employment interview takes no special skill on the part of the manager. Thus, we are amused at how many R&D labs have dropped the practice of having prospective researchers make a presentation on their dissertation or other current research because "we do not learn much." Technically, this is probably true. But if a young researcher has just spent several years on a scientific/engineering problem and cannot communicate some excitement about it, that really tells you something about that candidate. We would argue that you reinstitute the presentation if you do not have one and consider the motivation impact of the candidate as well as his/her technical content.

LOW INTELLECTUAL CONTENT

A very interesting facet of motivation is the fact that emotion has almost no intellectual content. This creates problems for the research community because it is staffed by people of high intellect who believe you can intellectualize all motivational problems away. Thus, you will hear the argument that if so-and-so only understood he would act differently. The research manager has missed the motivational point—intellectualizing doesn't handle emotion. And so-and-so acts the way he does not because of lack of understanding but in spite of understanding. The act makes him *feel good* regardless of the content.

The manager must understand that every managerial act has two principle components, namely, information and affect (or emotion). We observe that there is rarely much intellectual content in emotion but, where motivation is concerned, there is also very little intellectual content in information. A manager must be intellectually aware of his motivational objectives, but should not necessarily try to communicate it. Emotion gets in the way.

Even if a research manager possesses a Ph.D., he is rarely a clinical psychologist. Thus, *if it feels good, do not ask why, do it again.* We once had a manager say that you could not motivate adult researchers by sticking stars on poster paper the way they did in grade school. Meanwhile, his staff was falling all over themselves to get their names listed on the "patent award" plaque in the office foyer.

HEDONISM

As a fundamental determinant of motivation, we must observe that all individuals "seek pleasure and avoid pain." Although this may appear to be a worthless platitude, managers must first understand this to be absolutely true—because its implications for managerial thought and action are substantive.

First, hedonism implies *get to know your people.* What is pleasurable to person A may be quite unpleasant to person B. Especially where delegation is concerned, research managers tend to assume that a researcher will enjoy a task because the manager himself would enjoy it and yet it may threaten the researcher who is assigned to the task.

All individuals are different in what they like and what they fear. Thus, one of the most critical errors a manager can commit is to make broad generalizations about what people like—or what motivates them. This is extremely important if for no other reason than the fact that formal reward systems do imply such broad generalizations. Pay systems have become very standardized, even in the unlikely event that they are based only on performance. The individual manager in his day-to-day interactions has very little control over formal reward systems. He does, however, have considerable control over many informal rewards and these should be applied to specific individuals in terms of their specific likes and dislikes. Thus, for example, the manager can

21

use job assignments, travel, equipment, and his time as important elements in his system to motivate his employees.

The key to hedonism as a tenet of motivation begins with the recognition of individual differences.

Second, hedonism requires the manager to *maintain control over (informal) rewards.* We find it interesting how many managers give up control over obvious rewards because they are an administrative headache. If the manager loses control over what a researcher likes (or, may like), he may lose the capacity to excite that individual about work. He must then rely on the employee's "self motivation"—which may be fine in some cases but we do not suggest that one rely solely on it.

PROTECTION OF SELF

All individuals have a certain desire for protection of self. Particularly in research work, the basic tenet of protection typically means protection from the possibility and consequences of failure. People who have spent their lives building self-esteem based upon technical competence will go to great lengths to avoid losing that fragile base. It is surprising how many managers cannot see through apathy, defensiveness, and aggression as a manifestation of the fear of failure.

In order to keep work excitement and openness high, the manager must communicate that you *take some risks and I will protect you if you fail.* This is an imperative step in a good motivational program. We once worked with an R&D manager who gave great inspirational speeches, always ending with: "you people must take more risks. The future of the company and the country depends on it!" The people who then took risks and failed were handed their heads. Needless to say, risk taking and research performance in that company are very low.

Protection also implies a desire to "save face," a concept which American managers continuously ignore. This tenet simply requires that we *treat people with dignity.* Many researchers who tour an operating division—particularly blue-collar situations—have observed the pervasive attacks on simple human dignity and have commented, "no wonder the union is hostile." But some of the same researchers will return to the lab and exhibit the same attacks on the dignity of a technician. *Respect* and *dignity* are precursors to the generation of work excitement.

Given the contemporary economic climate, even well-educated employees work in a world of extreme uncertainty. This uncertainty is magnified by managers who feel that keeping subordinates "off-guard" keeps them "on their toes." These attacks can be quite subtle and when the desire for protection is aroused, the defenses can be very subtle. People find it difficult to respond openly to an injury to their self esteem although the damage, in fact, may be crippling to their capacity to perform.

ENHANCEMENT OF SELF

Managers must recognize the inherent conflict between the desire for protection and the desire for enhancement. By enhancement of self, we mean that all individuals seek some symbols of status. But in work, symbols of status should be associated with taking some risks—and succeeding. Thus, while a manager should communicate some protection from failure, he must also communicate that *incremental rewards should only be associated with success.* This is a difficult balancing act requiring a significant amount of self-discipline and consistency on the part of the manager. (It also assumes some control over rewards).

Aside from the distribution of rewards, an extremely simple corollary to this tenet is that *everybody wants to solo.* A researcher likes to be seen making an identifiable, perhaps singular, contribution to the group, however trivial this contribution may seem to an external observer. The emerging field of organization design seems to base its theory on this desire to solo.

We should also emphasize that soloing is not at all incompatible with teamwork. Our observation is that where effective team building has taken place, this tenet receives prime consideration. At one laboratory, a team-building exercise left us very impressed with the ability of each team to enhance its members—particularly the older professionals.

SOCIAL RELATIVITY

When a manager recognizes the first six tenets of motivation (i.e., he works hard at it, selects achievers, views excitement for excitement's sake, understands individual differences, provides a climate of dignity and protection, rewards incremental performance), he can still be perplexed at the level of dissatisfaction. Why? Because this tenet implies that all consequences in work are relative—relative to what other people are getting. This is one of the principal reasons why motivation, especially maintaining motivation, is so frustrating to many managers.

But satisfaction, as we have noted, is *not* motivation. Achievers are rarely satisfied. They want more. We have observed many managers who have gotten so tired of this "ingratitude" that they begin to believe that the only way to manage is to treat everybody absolutely equally. What the frustrated manager must realize is that *managing to motivate is incompatible with managing to minimize dissatisfaction.* The worst mistake a manager can make regarding motivation is to adopt a strategy to minimize dissatisfaction and yield a satisfied, complacent work group. Positive tension (by definition, lack of satisfaction) is a necessity.

Social relativity is also important as an input into how a manager allocates his time spent with those reporting to him. One must learn to distinguish between time spent on supervision and time spent on motivation. In general, low performers require disproportionate amounts of supervisory time. You have to give them that time. Their excuse of not understanding the role requirements just might be true. But do not spend motivational time on low performers, "invest" it on the higher performers. One moves the group's mean performance to a new plateau by further motivating the high performers, not by rescuing the low performers.

This tenet also requires that the manager *make the recognition of performance very visible* to as many people as possible. Many have heard and agree with the principle of not publically punishing a subordinate. But rewarding a high performer should be as public as possible. Not only does this prescription work on the show-off phenomenon (i.e., enhancement) but it also communicates what constitutes performance to other group members. Everybody likes to have their work displayed for others to see. How many artists create a piece of work and hide it? This tenet, more than any other, forces the manager to recognize both the information and emotion of a motivational act.

SATIATION VERSUS VARIABILITY

We earlier defined motivation as excitement—the managerial act being the proper mix of information and emotion. Nowhere is this act more perplexing than in the trade-off between constancy and variability in work. Research managers may understand this concept somewhat better than most, but it is nevertheless perplexing. Consider the following three conclusions from Pelz and Andrews' *Scientists in Organizations* (New York: John Wiley and Sons, Inc., 1966):

1. In both research and development, the more effective men undertook several specialties or technical functions (p. 54).

23

2. Effective scientists reported good opportunities for professional growth . . . (p. 112).
3. As age increased, performance was sustained with periodic change in project . . . (p. 200).

In work, satiation on the job has a pejorative effect on motivation. Change is exciting. Change is developmental. Change shapes expectations about the future. As one R&D director related: ''I reorganize my lab periodically whether it needs it or not.''

Thus, this tenet implies that a manager should *create change, but not too fast.* In this regard, the time-honored principle that there should not be change for change sake is simply incorrect. We might even suggest that managers should engage in a form of "limited Trotsky-ism," implying a small dose of permanent revolution (or evolution). Continuous small change sensitizes researchers to the fact of change, and this in itself is exciting. (But not too fast—the protection tenet—or too equally as regards specific individuals—the hedonism tenet).

Small continuous change prevents the necessity of huge change which is too threatening.

The satiation versus variability tenet also implies that a manager should *vary the delivery of rewards.* Meaning, of course, that (1) no manager should reward incremental performance every time, or (2) no manager should use the same reward every time. Even if managers had an infinite pool of resources, a 100 percent reinforcement schedule has little information (it's redundant) and little emotion (it's boring).

Finally, this tenet implies that *career planning is not just for the young.* The aging technical specialist has too often been allowed to become obsolete. In this regard, dual-track systems have been a dismal failure. (We will re-address this question shortly). Hard work at team building is extremely important in this area. The research manager who can provide a work climate where coworkers are willing to provide others with growth support will find that they have a valuable motivational tool. The *Zeitgeist* of

teamwork and mutual respect for the growth of others is what every manager, whatever their level in the organization, should seek to establish.

JUXTAPOSITION

One of the facts of organizational life that any manager must come to accept if he is to be an effective motivator is that most formal systems of rewards are inherently not motivational. We are not saying that money is not motivational, we are saying the *system* of delivering money is not motivational. This is because the basic tenet of the juxtaposition of act and consequence is invariably violated by pay systems. In essence the effectiveness of a reward is largely predicated upon the reward being tied to the act (to be rewarded) in time and space.

Rewards should be delivered in a timely manner. Although human beings have a greater capacity for memory than primates, it is surprising how short that memory span is where excitement about rewards and its association with appropriate behaviors is concerned. This is not an idle behavioral science concept, but too many managers treat it that way. One reason for this is that the juxtaposition concept requires a compulsion to observe the day-to-day performance of subordinates and provide something, anything, in the way of positive reinforcement to performers.

This returns us to an unavoidable conclusion: *a manager's motivational resources are rarely formal.* This is because the vast majority of managers have no control over the timely delivery of formal rewards. Ineffective managers translate this fact into the assumption that they have no power. Effective managers do not worry about it, and employ a continual stream of informal rewards to generate employee excitement. Moreover, we have observed how effective managers must keep coming up with new types of reward schemes; not only because their resources are not finite but because "higher" management will see a certain approach working, take control of it, routinize it, standardize it, and destroy it.

One of the more pleasing implications of this tenet is that performance *per se* is immediately exciting. In other words, if the manager can get the performance up, the excitement should go up. ("Eureka, I did it!"). Nevertheless, the rapid recognition must still be there. A beautiful golf shot may be exciting, but much less so if no one sees it.

EXPECTATIONS

As a final tenet of employee motivation, this is the most pervasive. Expectations are the essence of motivation. As such, this tenet is highly correlated with the other tenets.

First, this tenet implies that *the capacity to motivate is dependent upon managerial credibility.* If a manager has little credibility relative to his willingness or ability to deliver rewards, employees are not likely to be excited about the manager's requests for incremental effort. Credibility is hard to establish; easy to lose. If the subordinate does not believe in you, you cannot motivate him or her.

The demise of dual track systems in many research laboratories classically illustrates the role of expectations. In terms of the tenets of motivation, such systems are imperative. Over the years, however, the administration of the dual career path was such that the management track was perceived, usually correctly, as the only path to personal and professional growth. The director of research will say the system works, the researchers know better—they just saw an ineffective manager "moved" from the management track to high-up on the technical track to "save his face" because he was actually fired and ended up better than many on the technical track. The expectations are then changed and become very difficult to reverse.

Where expectations are concerned; establishing *an image of objectivity* requires a balance between information and emotion. A good research manager must draw a distinction between having a reputation for objectivity about research goals versus having a reputation for objectivity about people. Effective research managers are often viewed as somewhat lacking in objectivity in goal setting (they set very high goals, then orchestrate the motivation to achieve them), but are typically viewed as very objective (by high performers) in their evaluation of people.

In other words, the manager creates motivations about work goals by holding great expectations. He pushes for the three-minute mile and is seen as somewhat nonobjective in his expectations. Yet his target is motivation and the ventilation by the researchers about such targets is in fact a reflection of excitement, be it, a bit frightening.

The expectations tenet certainly implies that *rewards are vastly superior to punishments* as a motivational device. Obviously we are not saying that ineffective research managers run around punishing technical professionals. What they resort to, however, are threats, subtle attacks on self-esteem, and so forth. These approaches have plenty of emotion, but little information. They only tell you what not to do. They generate minimal compliance and a desire to escape. Effective motivators recognize that attention to rewards provides both information and emotion. In short, they tell you what to do—and make you feel great doing it.

In summary, effective research managers have long ago learned that the recipe for success in motivating in a technical environment requires the careful formulation or an approach tailored to each individual. Successful motivation of employees begins with an in-depth understanding of the person in question. Blending these ten tenets into a conscious managerial style requires thoughtful consideration of the needs and expectations of the persons involved and the circum-

25

stances of the specific situation. It is obvious that if the manager cannot offer what the individual wants he cannot motivate that individual. This is an axiom that managers should never forget. The manager should strive to control rewards or access to those rewards and not let the rewards get lost in a bureaucratic system.

Employees' trusts and confidence in you as their manager will go a long way in forgiving a lack of skill in delivery, but a perception by subordinates of deceit and false manipulation will emasculate any plan. Never forget the emotional component of motivation. Blend these tenets of motivation with an honest and straightforward managerial delivery and we feel you will reap the rewards of your time and efforts.

One More Time:
How to Motivate Your Engineers

Michael K. Badawy

Abstract. As a result of changes in economic, social, and technological conditions, engineering managers are increasingly facing problems in motivating engineers. This, coupled with engineers' orientations and expectations to be treated as "professionals," has caused considerable tensions and strains in the engineer-management relationship. This calls for changes in engineering management styles to maintain motivation and productivity.

I. PROBLEM AND BACKGROUND

Engineering productivity is largely determined not by the efficiency of the factory worker, but by the effectiveness of the knowledge worker.* As knowledge workers, engineers seem to be more productive when they are properly motivated. This poses significant challenges to engineering managers charged with the responsibility of effective utilization and motivation of these technical resources. Yet, while no single force will have a greater impact on the quality of life than engineers, there is substantial evidence derived from the author's own research studies and those of others that engineering resources are poorly managed and misutilized, and that understanding between management and these technical resources is lacking in industrial settings.[2-6, 25]

Research has demonstrated that engineers' dissatisfaction and alienation in industry are mounting. Management's failure to reward engineers with motivations beyond those appealing to nonprofessionals has resulted in a higher rate of turnover among the first than among the latter group on comparable organizational levels.[17, 19] Another reason relates to management's failure to recognize that engineering is intrinsically creative and cannot be managed like other labor, that engineers are professionals who demand special treatment, and that the engineering environment is characterized by unknowns and uncertainties which mitigate close control.[1] The net result is that engineers, as an expensive and scarce resource, very often are badly mismanaged. A third reason for engineers' dissatisfaction relates to the improper utilization of technical personnel, since as much as 30 percent of a professional's time is spent on work within the

---

*"Knowledge organizations" are defined here as those organizations (or units of) whose essential job is to sell the professional knowledge of its people. These include R&D laboratories, engineering firms, and advertising agencies. "Knowledge workers" refer to highly skilled types of labor where education, sophisticated training, and sharp talents are needed to perform these highly specialized activities in organizations.

reach of a high school graduate.[14] Furthermore, the increasing tendency of engineers (and other professionals) to unionize is glaring evidence as to the tremendous discontent and alienation altogether felt by these groups in industry.[24, 32]

It would appear that if management is serious about getting its "money's worth" and improving productivity and engineering performance, effective utilization of engineering resources is the key. Appropriate motivation and technical vitality of the engineering staff is, in turn, central to the question of utilization. The foregoing analysis, however, clearly suggests that engineers in industry generally are demotivated and largely dissatisfied. Changing the status quo calls for developing better styles for motivating engineers. This is the purpose of this paper. After developing a profile of engineers' job expectations and motivational styles, some of the myths and misconceptions in current motivational practices will then be discussed. Finally, some guidelines for better motivation and utilization of engineering manpower will also be presented.

II. MOTIVATIONAL STYLES OF ENGINEERS: A PROFILE

There are a number of theories that are relevant to engineers' motivation.[22, 26, 27] For space limitation, it will suffice for our purposes here to briefly identify the most basic form of motivational need theories commonly known as "Maslow's hierarchy of needs." Maslow's theory (1954) postulates five general classes of needs arranged in levels of prepotency, so that when one level is satisfied, the next level is activated. The five levels are: 1) physiological needs, 2) security or safety needs, 3) social needs, 4) self-esteem needs, and 5) self-actualization needs.

From the standpoint of motivating engineers, it is quite important for engineering managers to keep the following points in mind in applying Maslow's need model[8]: 1) The view that people inherit most of their performance capabilities and are motivated only by reward and punishment has been proved inadequate. 2) Every person has multiple needs. Though the specific forms those needs take are highly individualized, the basic needs themselves are shared by everyone. 3) The emergence of needs does follow a specific rigid pattern. 4) A satisfied need is not a motivator of behavior. As one need is fulfilled, another higher need emerges. 5) It is not necessary to satisfy a "lower" need fully before a "higher" need may emerge and operate as a motivator. 6) There is no universal motivator for all people nor is there a single motivating force for any one individual. Rather, the significance of each need varies from one individual to another and varies for the same individual from time to time. 7) There are individual differences in the most appropriate ways for satisfying the same need. Two hungry individuals, for example, might choose different types of food to satisfy the hunger drive. Thus management should develop different motivational patterns to fit different employees' needs at different levels of administration. 8) Motivation is internal to the individual. A person is not motivated by what people think he ought to have, but rather by what he himself wants. It follows that management cannot really force or push people to produce. The most that can be done is to create a motivational environment by providing opportunities for people to satisfy their own needs. And 9) there are factors other than human needs that influence motivation. Among these other factors are the individual's evaluation of himself and his interpretation of his environment.

To sum up—needs are the keys to motivation. They initiate and guide the individual's actions until the goals that generated them are reached, at which time the tensions created by those needs are dissipated. It follows that, in order to motivate engineers, the manager must either act to create the feelings of need within the individuals involved or offer means for satisfying already existing needs.

Based on the foregoing analysis, what does

current research tell us about engineers' motivation? The available research clearly demonstrates that there is a wide gap between what engineers want and what they actually get. This generally results in job dissatisfaction and alienation of engineers. Achievement, recognition, work assignments, and professional administration were found to be of overriding importance for professional personnel in general.[10] Freedom of action, increasing responsibility, and a high degree of autonomy and control over their own activities were reported to have significant value for knowledge workers.[18, 31] Furthermore, a number of recent studies have shown that the top three motivating factors among knowledge workers are 1) salary or wages, 2) recognition, and 3) opportunity for growth.

The importance of money as a motivational incentive for engineers is controversial in the literature. It was reported that the amount of money an employee receives is only tenuously related to his actual or potential output.[21] This argument states that salary influences tend to move the individual from job dissatisfaction to no job dissatisfaction, as contrasted to the motivational factors which would move a person from no job satisfaction to job satisfaction. Once an adequate salary is attained, greater motivational mileage is gained from such factors as the awarding of advanced positions or titles.

However, in a study comparing motivational styles of engineers and scientists, salary was found to have more motivating value for engineers.[6] Financial considerations, in fact, emerged as the front-running incentives. Engineers, more than people in other professions, were found to value concrete material rewards. Salary has come to mean a great deal more than just money to the engineer. It represents to him the tangible evidence of how he rates in the organization. It has become to him a key symbol of status and recognition. In short, one cannot deny that salary increases embrace a nonfinancial measure of achievement, and as such can be useful motivators for engineers in that light.[16, 19]

Another study shows that work itself has the greatest impact on engineers' motivation and, yet, it is one least used by management.[29] Advancement in the company was also found to be a high motivating factor. The most commonly used motivation technique by management, according to this study, is the recognition of achievement.

To sum up—the above discussion and the available research suggest the following propositions concerning motivational styles of engineers: 1) Getting ahead and advancement within his position within the company, pay, and working on challenging assignments are the basic features of the need system of the engineer.[6] 2) Engineers are particularly sensitive to what they regard as "unfairness," and they resent rewards based on any other basis but recognizable professional achievement. They also resent having their professional activities evaluated by those for whose professional judgment they have less than great respect[17, 32]. 3) Technical personnel are neither going to be motivated through films or memorandums demanding that everyone look motivated, nor through the hiring of an outside consultant to make the "one and lasting" inspirational speech on motivation[20]. Rather, motivation of engineers tends to be internally generated.

III. CURRENT MANAGERIAL PRACTICES IN MOTIVATING ENGINEERS: SOME MISCONCEPTIONS

In this section the author will identify some problem areas relating to current managerial practices in motivating engineers.

A. Management's Image of the Engineer
A major source of tension and misunderstanding between management and engineers is management's concept of the "professional employee."

Although engineers and scientists are professionals with extensive intellectual training and a high degree of specialization, there are important differences in work orientations, need systems, and career objectives between the two groups.[4, 5] While most scientists are committed to the creation of new knowledge, most engineers are committed to the application of present knowledge.[32] In addition, the typical scientist might have a primary professional orientation characterized by a basic interest in advancing science, contribution to knowledge, and enhancing his professional reputation in his field. The typical engineer, on the other hand, might have an organizational orientation that manifests itself in a lesser commitment to the profession, but with a greater concern for the goals and approval of the organization with a focus on an organizational career.

The point is that the use of "professionalism" as an organizing concept is serious and misleading. For management to lump the two groups together in a professional stereotype and use that image as a basis for developing motivational practices is entirely wrong, because a policy based on an erroneous assumption cannot satisfy either group.

Another related source of problems in the engineer-management relationship is management's failure to differentiate between knowledge and nonknowledge workers. Current methods of engineering management are old, outdated, and were developed basically to manage production employees where physical labor was important. Now, when these techniques are used in managing knowledge workers, they get frustrated, dissatisfied, and altogether alienated. Examples include the traditional techniques of work organization, bureaucratic controls and authority systems, and excessive focus on organizational efficiency.

In addition, the small salary differential between engineers as professionals and skilled workmen who are not professionals (as seen by engineers), lends further support to the inappropriateness or management methods and policies. A small salary differential violates the professional engineers' sense of self-esteem, distorts their self-images, and causes dissatisfaction, particularly among the younger engineers at the bottom of the engineering salary range.[24]

Thus management's distorted image of engineers seems to emanate partly from the inappropriate practice of not differentiating between engineers as knowledge workers and nonknowledge workers. Furthermore, management does not usually take a truly professional attitude in treating engineers as "professionals" even when this is appropriately done, engineers are usually lumped in a large group with other professionals. Both practices are dysfunctional and thus lead to demotivational consequences. They also reflect a lack of management understanding of the particular needs of engineers. This has eventually led to the erosion of the engineer's sense of professionalism, identity, and status.

B. Inadequate Training of Engineering Managers

Managerial competency has three interrelated components: knowledge, skills (technical, administrative, and interpersonal), and attitudes. However, there is accumulated evidence suggesting that engineers are generally ill-equipped for careers in management.[8] While the training of the engineer typically emphasizes the reduction of all problems to terms that can be dealt with by objective measurement and established formulas based on predictable regularities, success in management is entirely based on different criteria. The world of management is far less exact, less regular, fuzzier, and less predictable than the world of engineering.

It follows that, because of the inadequate preparation of engineers for careers in management, many competent engineers may not become competent managers. Consequently, this has caused great dissatisfaction for many engineers who demand that managers be as competent at managing as the professionals are in their technical fields.[32] The fact of the matter, however, is that many engineering managers are promoted technical professionals who, without any additional training, do not qualify as management professionals and are vastly less competent at managing than their subordinates are in technical work.

It would appear that the balance between technical and managerial competency is a delicate one, and those who are equally capable in both areas are "rare birds" indeed. I would also maintain that technical capability is hardly a sufficient prerequisite for success in management. Identification of managerial potential, it follows, is a must, as people should be appointed to management positions based on demonstrated or at least potential managerial skills.

In short, current practices of promoting good technologists to managerial positions are poor, inappropriate, and put engineering management in the hands of a group of engineers who were hardly trained for management in the first place. Therefore, they will not be able to manage or motivate others effectively.

C. Managerial Policies and Supervisory Practices

Management systems and policies in some areas do not reflect an adequate understanding of engineers' expectations as professionals. One example is the area of supervising engineers by administrative managers with engineering merely one of their functional responsibilities. Superior authority exercised by a nonprofessional engineer is resented by engineers, as it violates their professional pride. The working engineer feels himself downgraded by his company where this occurs, and the natural reaction is a disdain for company management.[24]

Another source of problems and tensions for engineers relates to criteria for promotion and professional advancement. These criteria are always vague and too general. Organizational policies regarding standards of performance, job descriptions, and professional recognition and promotions are not laid out clearly to career-minded engineers. This, combined with the minimum efforts made by superiors to develop subordinates' skills and potential, generates concern for professional advancement and dissatisfaction among engineers. Thus when subordinates' development becomes a key criterion for evaluating managerial performance, engineering managers will pay appropriate attention to this activity.

A third area of concern to engineers relates to management methods in measuring engineering productivity. Because the "mental component" of engineering is constantly increasing as more of the routine tasks are automated, new techniques and modified measures must be found to relate creative efforts to the traditional measures of productivity. It is noteworthy here that the difficulty to see or measure individual's achievement in most engineering activity, and the difficulty for the individual to relate himself to what happens, has "turned off" or demotivated some engineers. A much better way to increase the efficiency of the engineering department is to concentrate on improving its effectiveness.[11] This requires making the best use of creative abilities of engineering personnel.

D. Failure to Develop Task-Related Motivational Potential

The greatest motivational potential of engineers can be generated through the task itself where work must be considered as the prime challenge to the individual, and thus worthy of their effort. This means that through work designs containing strong elements of challenge, professional achievement, ingenuity, imagination, and flexibility, engineering managers can create significant opportunities with tremendous motivational potential for their subordinates. It is tragic, however, to note that one of the largest failings of American industry is the improper utilization of technical personnel.[16] There is also evidence, as mentioned earlier, that many engineers are handling assignments requiring many fewer skills and qualifications.[14]

Furthermore, the fact that many engineers are unable to see where their contribution fits into the total picture contributes significantly to their dissatisfaction, disappointed expectations, and consequent disillusionment. There is, in fact, a strong indication that engineers in general are underemployed, underutilized, and misutilized.[30]

E. Adoption of the Wrong Reward System

The value of a "dual ladder" as an advancement path for both technically and administratively oriented personnel has been frequently questioned in the literature. The problem, basically, is that the rewards for both careers have never been equally attractive[6], as will be discussed further below. In addition, scientists and engineers reported almost total reliance upon their supervisors for needed recognition rather than upon the organization itself, with very little faith in "so-called dual ladders" or other "structural gimmicks" designed to provide opportunity for financial and organizational advancement.[16] The major point here is that the major consideration in rewarding engineers is to reward achievement, not compliance or noncompliance with management's wishes.

Current reward systems for engineers are also inadequate for another reason. The higher compensation associated with administrative positions has caused a great many engineers and scientists to effectively abandon their profession.[31] In most organizations, the incentives are almost totally associated with hierarchical advancement (this, incidentally, is equally true in other functional areas).

F. Inadequate Motivational Systems for Older Engineers

The gap between the engineer's age and performance (the over-40 engineer) is a well-known problem in industry. Giving challenging assignments to younger persons creates obsolescence by depriving the senior person of chances to learn, change, and grow.[28] It also reflects a built-in bias for the youth. Furthermore, there is evidence attributing the growing trend toward earlier obsolescence to corporate management's establishment of rigid performance appraisal systems, inequitable job assignments, and insensitivity to the needs of older engineers.[12]

IV. TOWARD BETTER MOTIVATION OF ENGINEERS: SOME IMPLICATIONS FOR ENGINEERING MANAGEMENT

A. Treat Engineers as Professionals

As discussed above, the greatest source of tension and disappointment for engineers is that current management methods and policies do not reflect an adequate understanding of their need orientations and expectations as professionals. This needs to be changed. Responsibility, achievement, and contribution are very important ingredients of motivational systems for engineers. Engineering managers, in their quest for better productivity, should, therefore, stress these elements directing engineering efforts toward maximum contribution and judging them strictly on the basis of performance and quality of work.

Management methods and policies should also reflect an understanding and appreciation of the differences in work orientations and expectations between engineers, as knowledge workers, and nonknowledge workers. Engineers, for example, should be given the opportunity to review, appraise, and judge their own performance, and should be given the information and tools to do their job. Perhaps the most important rule, and the one to which few managements pay much attention, is to enable the knowledge workers to do what they are being paid for. Not to be able to do what one is being paid for infallibly quenches whatever motivation there is.[15]

**B. Enhancing Managerial Competency
of Engineering Managers**

The single most important factor in motivating engineers is the engineering manager, simply because he constitutes the linking pin between management, on the one hand, and engineers on the other hand. However, because of their inadequate preparation for careers in management, many competent engineers, as discussed above, may become incompetent managers. This suggests at least three possibilities to enhance managerial competency of engineering managers. First, the practice of promoting the most technically competent to an administrative position simply for their technical abilities should be abandoned, as strong evidence now suggests that these individuals make the poorest managers.[23] Supervisors should be technically competent, to command the respect of their subordinates, be desirous of a supervisory assignment, and be trained to bridge the gap from "technical orientation" to "management orientation".[16] In other words, management should look well beyond the candidate's technical ability, searching for possible ingredients and characteristics that would make him a successful manager.

Secondly, better selection methods must be employed to identify those promising candidates who are likely to have the psychological prerequisites for managerial competency: a strong will to manage, a strong need for power, and a strong capacity for empathy.[8]

In addition to proper identification of managerial potential and sound selection, the third mechanism to promote and develop engineers' managerial skills is via changing the current educational orientation of industrial engineers. The present system erroneously overdevelops their analytical skills (as model builders), while their managerial skills (as decision-makers) remain highly underdeveloped. While changes in the formal education of engineers is obviously beyond management's control, continuing management education is not.[3] In fact, it provides an excellent vehicle for engineers' personal development and career growth. "In-house" programs have been undertaken by several companies, offering training and coaching activities to smooth the transition from engineering to administration.

C. Establishing Positive Motivational Climates

A powerful motivational mechanism is through job redesign. The meaning of meaningful work for engineers is changing due to changes in cultural values and social expectations. Engineers are changing their specifications for work satisfaction.[28] Meaningful work is not solely solving a technical challenge, and scientific progress for its own sake is under serious question. It follows that jobs need to be redesigned containing elements of challenge, achievement, and conveying the feeling that work has meaning and would make a positive contribution causing no ecological damages or future problems. In short, the concept of job enrichment is quite relevant here and should be used by engineering managers to enhance the motivational potential and productivity of engineers.

Reward systems appropriate for engineers are those emphasizing such factors as status, advancement to managerial positions, and authority and influence within the organization hierarchy.[8] Opportunities for participation and involvement in managerial and technical planning and decision-making are expected to enhance the engineer's status, influence, satisfaction, and productivity.[8, 30]

In order to stimulate and reinforce creativity, appropriate organizational climates should be established. An organization with a more decentralized and less formal structure with variety of opportunities for communication, interaction, and participation should be designed.[3] More positive and enthusiastic responses to new ideas, less concern with personal "fitness" for an organizational pattern, and a reasonable degree of freedom and autonomy are some positive ingredients of a creative organizational climate.

Furthermore, a new set of criteria for evaluating engineering managers' performance is needed. These criteria should include not only performance goals (cost, product features, and efficiency), but also personal and subordinates' development efforts. This would encourage managers to help subordinates develop their skills and potential, and thus enhance subordinates' satisfaction and motivation. An excellent management system in this connection is management by objectives (MBO) which has been implemented by several organizations with impressive results.[7]

D. Better Personnel Management Policies

The human resource is certainly the only asset of significant worth in the engineering function. People are more productive when they feel they are a valuable part of the organization and that the organization cares about them as individuals. In addition, knowledge workers are a special kind of asset because they gain in value with time, especially when improvements and developments are made. This means that the future of the knowledge organization is dependent on recruiting good people, and personnel managers must, therefore, do a better job in this area.

Placement is another important area because placement of knowledge workers is the key to their productivity. Not only do opportunities have to be staffed with people capable of running with them and of turning them into results, but knowledge workers must also be placed where their strengths can be productive.[15] Designing appropriate placement policies for engineers is thus a vital concern for personnel managers.

In view of the importance to engineers of salary and economic incentives, as discussed above, a sound scheme is a necessity. Salary ranges for various engineering classifications should be specifically spelled out, with recognition for extra schooling, personal development efforts, and attendance of technical and professional seminars.

Pension is a fourth related area where changes are needed. Engineers should not be "tied" to a particular company. An engineer should stay with a company because he is interested and challenged by his work and feels adequately compensated, not because of his pension plan, extended vacation, or other such "captive" fringe benefits. Engineers retained under the former set of circumstances are usually highly productive and represent minimal personnel problems, while those retained under the latter circumstances could, in fact, be far more expensive and may even constitute a bad investment. This argument suggests that companies should consider participation in portable pension plans which will allow an engineer to move from employer to employer without losing benefits. Vesting could either be immediate or after a very short period of employment.

Another mechanism that has considerable effect on engineers' motivation is the powerful communication content of incentives. If there is conflict between formal verbal communications and the implications of an incentive, it will always be resolved in favor of the message carried by the incentive.[31] Management actions actually speak louder than words.[28] For example, the engineer listening to top management talk about the need for technical vitality finds it hard to reconcile what he is hearing with overtime work requirements which cause him to drop educational activity. The point is that, although overtime work might be necessary under the circumstances, management somehow must show that it recognizes the impact on vitality; otherwise, management intentions will be misunderstood. Engineering managers, therefore, should understand that the design of the task environment can affect learning, growth, and motivation. Open communications, integrity, and positive reinforcement of company and professional values are certainly vital ingredients of an effective motivational climate.

E. Better Strategies for Career Planning and Motivation of Older Engineers

There is a need for improved management understanding of the concept of career planning for professional enrichment and growth of engineers. Management must also learn how to manage and motivate older engineers. This is because technological obsolescence, as discussed above, is partly caused by a built-in bias for the youth and the way work is organized.[28] Research on career planning shows that diversity is a vital ingredient in maintaining a productive and satisfying career, especially for older professionals.[13] However, most organizations do not provide the necessary opportunities for and encouragement of diversity. In short, there is strong evidence suggesting that pushing technical personnel in their late thirties and early forties into new fields will broaden their interests on and off the job, and will have a significant effect on motivation and productivity.[12, 13]

From the standpoint of maintaining technical vitality and motivation of engineers, several strategies can be adopted. These include continuing education, retraining, sabbatical leaves, rotation programs, job transfers, and redesign. For these strategies to work, however, management must show its total commitment to the concept of continued learning throughout life as a powerful tool. That is, company policy and reward system must reinforce these learning behaviors and professional enrichment programs. It is noteworthy here that these mechanisms are particularly important for motivation and technical vitality of older engineers, as they can become bored with the same work after 5 or 10 years.

V. SUMMARY AND CONCLUSION

The purpose of this paper has been to develop a viable framework of motivational orientations of engineers, show some of the myths and misconceptions in current management practices in this area, and finally present some mechanisms and guidelines for better engineers' motivation and productivity. The theme of this paper is that motivation is intrinsic in nature, and that all the engineering manager can do is create the conditions and the appropriate environment conducive to engineers' motivation. While this is the responsibility of the engineering manager, the responsibility of the individual engineer is to whether or not to take advantage of this environment and respond in such a manner to promote his personal as well as organizational goals.

Throughout the discussion, the author has tried to stay away from the conflicting theories and the controversial issues so persistent in the literature, simply because none of the available motivational theories has completely satisfied the test of empirical data. He has also tried to stay away from a "cookbook" approach to such a complex subject, as motivational schemes will work with varying degrees of success at different organizations and under different sets of circumstances. While the challenge for engineering management is to create the conditions for motivation, the challenge for industry is the creation of an atmosphere where emphasis can be placed on the motivational needs of the individual.

REFERENCES

1. D. C. Aird, "Improving the performance of engineers," in *Effective Management of Engineering Resources (Proc. 23rd Annu. Conf. of Joint Engineering Management Conf.).* The American Society of Mechanical Engineers, 1975, pp. 75–86.
2. C. Argyris, "On the effectiveness of R&D organizations," *Amer. Sci.,* vol. 56, no. 4, pp. 344–355, Winter 1968.
3. M. K. Badawy, "Towards better management of research organizations." *Soc. Res. Admin. J.,* pp. 9–15, Fall 1976.
4. ———, "The myth of the professional employee," *Personnel J.,* pp. 449–455, Jan. 1973.

5. ——, "Organizational designs for scientists and engineers: Some research findings and their implications for managers," *IEEE Trans. Eng. Manag.,* vol. EM-22. pp. 134–138, Nov. 1975.

6. ——, "Industrial scientists and engineers: Motivational style differences," *Calif. Manag. Rev.,* vol. 14, no. 1, pp. 11–16, Fall 1971.

7. ——, "Applying management by objectives to R&D labs," *Res. Manag.,* pp. 35–40, Nov. 1976.

8. ——, "Motivating engineers: A little psychology goes a long way," *Machine Des.,* pp. 120–122, Oct. 16, 1975.

9. ——, "Easing the switch from engineer to manager," *Machine Des.,* May 15, 1975.

10. W. Campfield, "Motivating the professional employee." *Personnel J.,* Sept. 1965.

11. T. Comella, "Engineering productivity formulating a plan of attack," *Machine Des.,* pp. 118–119, Dec. 11, 1975.

12. G. W. Dalton and P. H. Thompson, "Accelerating obsolescence of older engineers." *Harvard Business Rev.,* Sept.–Oct. 1971.

13. H. Dewhirst and R. Arvey, "Range of interests vs. job performance and satisfaction," *Res. Manag.,* pp. 18–23, July, 1976.

14. P. F. Drucker, "Management and the professional employee." *Harvard Business Rev.,* May/June 1952.

15. ——, "Managing the knowledge worker," *The Wall Street Journal,* Nov. 7, 1975.

16. B. Evans and J. Whitten, "A critical reanalysis regarding the management of professionals," *Personnel Admin.,* pp. 35–40, Sept.–Oct. 1972.

17. W. Exton, "Optimizing professional performance with motivational leverage," in *Effective Management of Engineering Resources (Proc. 23rd Annu. Conf. of Joint Engineering Management Conf.).* The American Society of Mechanical Engineers, 1975, pp. 1–8.

18. S. Gellerman, *Motivation and Productivity.* New York: American Management Association, Inc., 1963.

19. A. Gerstenfeld and G. Rosica, "Why engineers transfer," *Business Horizons,* vol. 13, pp. 47–48, Apr. 1970.

20. E. Gomersall, "Current and future factors affecting the motivation of scientists, engineers and technicians," *Res. Manag.,* pp. 43–51, May 1971.

21. F. Herzberg, "Does money really motivate?" *Package Eng.,* May 1970.

22. ——, *Work and the Nature of Man.* Cleveland, OH: World Publishing, 1966.

23. E. Hughes, "Preserving individualism on the R&D team," *Harvard Business Rev.,* Jan./Feb. 1968.

24. W. Imberman, "As the engineer sees his problem." *The Conf. Board Rec.,* pp. 30–34, Apr. 1976.

25. S. Marcson, "Utilization of scientific and technical personnel in industry," *Calif. Manag. Rev.,* pp. 33–42, Summer 1970.

26. A. H. Maslow, *Motivation and Personality.* New York: Harper & Row, 1954.

27. D. McGregor, *The Human Side of Enterprise.* New York: McGraw-HIll, 1960.

28. D. Miller, "Managing for long term technical vitality," *Res. Manag.,* pp. 15–19, July 1975.

29. S. Myers, "Who are your motivated workers?" *Harvard Business Rev.,* vol. 43, pp. 74–83, Jan./Feb. 1964.

30. R. R. Myers, "Under-employment of engineers," *Ind. Relations,* vol. 9, no. 4, pp. 437–452, Oct. 1970.

31. G. A. Roberts, "An approach to the management of knowledge workers," Basic Fluid Power Research Conf., Oklahoma State University, Annu. Rep. 9, 1975, pp. 1–8.

32. G. Rosica, "Organized professionals: A management dilemma," *Business Horizons,* pp. 59–65, June 1972.

Creative Tensions in the Research and Development Climate

Donald C. Pelz

What kinds of climate in research and development organizations are conducive to technical accomplishment? What is the optimum degree of freedom versus coordination? of pure research versus practical development? of isolation versus communication? of specialization versus diversification?

To find some answers, my colleagues and I studied 1300 scientists and engineers in 11 research and development laboratories. Since the answers in different kinds of settings might vary, we included five industrial laboratories, five government laboratories, and seven departments in a major university. Their objectives ranged from basic research to product development.

Among the findings appeared a number of apparent inconsistencies. The optimum climate was not necessarily some compromise between extremes. Rather, achievement often flourished in the presence of factors that seemed antithetical.

Some examples are given below and summarized in Table 1.[1] As we pondered these findings, it seemed possible to fit many of them under two broad headings. On the one hand, technical men were effective when faced with some demand from the environment—when their associates held divergent viewpoints or the laboratory climate required disruption of established patterns. These might be called conditions of challenge.

On the other hand, technical men also performed well when they had some protection from environmental demands. Factors such as freedom, influence, or specialization offer the scientist stability and continuity in his work—conditions of security.

It seemed reasonable to say that the scientists and engineers of our study were more effective when they experienced a "creative tension" between sources of stability or security on the one hand and sources of disruption or challenge on the other. The term was suggested by T. S. Kuhn in a paper entitled "The essential tension: tradition and innovation in scientific research."[2]

Necessity is said to be the mother of invention, but our data suggest that invention (technical achievement) has more than one parent. Necessity might better be called the father—since necessity is one form of challenge, a masculine component. The role of mother is, rather, some source of security. When both are present, the creative tension between them can generate scientific achievement.

METHODS

The findings were not obtained by polling scientists concerning what climate they preferred. Rather, we obtained measures of each man's scientific performance, including his scientific or

Reprinted from *Science,* Vol. 157, No. 3785, July 1967, pp. 160–165 with permission of the publisher. Copyright 1967 by American Association for the Advancement of Science.

TABLE 1.   *Eight Creative Tensions*

Security	Challenge
Tension 1	
	Effective scientists and engineers in both research and development laboratories did not limit their activities either to pure science or to application but spent some time on several kinds of R&D activities, ranging from basic research to technical services
Tension 2	
Effective scientists were intellectually independent or self-reliant; they pursued their own ideas and valued freedom . . .	. . . But they did not avoid other people; they and their colleagues interacted vigorously
Tension 3	
a) In the first decade of work, young scientists and engineers did well if they spent a few years on one main project . . .	. . . But young non-Ph.D.'s also achieved if they had several skills, and young Ph.D's did better when they avoided narrow specialization
b) Among mature scientists, high performers had greater self-confidence and an interest in probing deeply . . .	. . . At the same time, effective older scientists wanted to pioneer in broad new areas
Tension 4	
a) In loosest departments with minimum coordination, the most autonomous individuals, with maximum security and minimum challenge, were ineffective . . .	. . . More effective were those persons who experienced stimulation from a variety of external or internal sources
b) In departments having moderate coordination, it seems likely that individual autonomy permitted a search for the best solution . . .	. . . to important problems faced by the organization
Tension 5	
Both Ph.D.'s and engineers contributed most when they strongly influenced key decision-makers . . .	. . . but also when persons in several other positions had a voice in selecting their goals
Tension 6	
High performers named colleagues with whom they shared similar sources of stimulation (personal support) . . .	. . . but they differed from colleagues in technical style and strategy (dither or intellectual conflict)
Tension 7	
R&D teams were of greatest use to their organization at that "group age" when interest in narrow specialization had increased to a medium level . . .	. . . but interest in broad pioneering had not yet disappeared
Tension 8	
In older groups which retained vitality the members preferred each other as collaborators . . .	. . . yet their technical strategies differed and they remained intellectually combative

technical contribution to his field of knowledge in the past 5 years, as judged by panels of his colleagues; his overall usefulness to the organization, through either research or administration, also as judged by his colleagues; the number of professional papers he had published in the past 5 years (or, in the case of an engineer, the number of his patents or patent applications); and the number of his unpublished reports in the same period.

The performance measures were modified in several ways. Since distributions of papers, patents, and reports were skewed, a logarithmic transformation was applied to normalize them. Systematic variations with level of education, length of working experience, time in the organization, and type of institution were removed by adding constants so as to equalize the means. Each scientist, that is, was scored relative to others with similar background.

Characteristics of the climate were obtained on a carefully tested questionnaire. The two sets of data (on performance and on climate) were analyzed to find those conditions under which scientists actually performed at a higher or lower level.

Since optimum conditions might differ in different settings, all analyses were replicated within five subcategories: Ph.D.'s in research-oriented laboratories; Ph.D.'s in development-oriented laboratories; non-Ph.D.'s in research-oriented and in development-oriented laboratories (for convenience the latter have been called "engineers"); and non-Ph.D.'s in laboratories where 40 percent or more of the staff members held a doctoral degree (because of the limited influence and promotional opportunity of these non-Ph.D.'s we have called them "assistant scientists").

SCIENCE VERSUS APPLICATION

For the first illustration, consider a tension not between factors of security and challenge but rather between science-oriented and product-oriented activity. The respondent estimated the proportion of his technical time (that is, time spent on research or development, as opposed to administration or teaching) that he allocated to each of the following five "R&D functions":

Research (discovery of new knowledge, either basic or applied):

- General knowledge relevant to a broad class of problems ___%
- Specific knowledge for solving particular problems ___%

Development and invention (translating knowledge into useful form):

- Improving existing products or processes ___%
- Inventing new products or processes ___%

Technical services (either analysis by standardized techniques or consultation and trouble-shooting) ___%

Some interesting trends appeared. For instance, Ph.D.'s in both research-oriented and development-oriented laboratories were judged most effective, on the basis of several criteria, when they devoted only half their technical time to research as such (first two categories above) and the rest to activities described as development or technical services. Similarly, Ph.D.'s in development-oriented laboratories were most effective when they spent only one-quarter or one-third of their time on activities labeled "development."

Another way to summarize the same data is illustrated in Figure 1, where technical contribution is plotted against the number of R&D functions to which the individual devoted at least a little time (6 percent or more). Similar curves (not shown) were obtained for other measures of

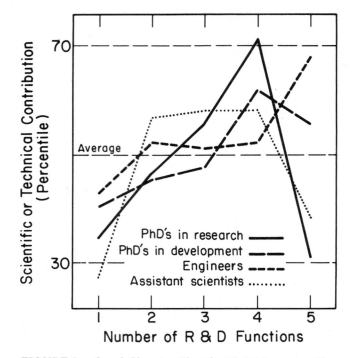

FIGURE 1.   *Graph Showing That the More Numerous Were the R&D Functions, up to Four, Performed by Ph.D.'s and Assistant Scientists in Development-oriented and Research-oriented Laboratories, the Higher Was Their Scientific or Technical Contribution as Judged by Colleagues; Engineers Did Best When They Had Five R&D Functions*

achievement usefulness, publications, patents, and unpublished reports. Even in laboratories devoted to pure research the best performers carried on four functions; they did not concentrate on research alone, but spent some time on development or service functions. Performance dropped if Ph.D.'s or assistant scientists tried to perform all five functions, although engineers flourished under this condition.

Effective scientists, in short, did not limit their efforts either to the world or pure science or to the world of application but were active in both (see Table 1, tension 1).

Is this involvement with both worlds a genuine tension? I am inclined to think so. As time invested in one increases, investment in the other must decrease. Demands for solution of practical problems can interfere with long-range research.

Why, then, should such a tension be creative? Several writers have proposed that a creative act occurs when a set of elements not previously associated is assembled in a new and useful combination. Diversity in technical activities may broaden the range of elements from which the scientists or engineer can draw in synthesizing new combinations.

Other findings reinforced the importance of diversity. Individuals performed better when they had two or three "areas of specialization" within their scientific discipline, rather than one.

The Ph.D.'s did their best work not when they devoted full time to technical activities but when they spent about one-quarter of their time in either teaching or administration.

In the framework of challenge versus security, diversity in the task may also be viewed as a source of disruption and hence a condition of challenge. For data on specialization versus diversity, see Table 1, tension 3.

INDEPENDENCE VERSUS INTERACTION

Scientists place high priority on freedom. To measure this need, an index of "motivation from own ideas" was constructed, from self-reported (i) stimulus by one's previous work, (ii) stimulus by one's own curiosity, and (iii) desire for freedom to follow one's own ideas. This score—the index might also be labeled intellectual independence—was analyzed in relation to the four performance measures within each category of scientific personnel. A series of positive correlations appeared. Among the 36 correlation coefficients, 25 were positive ($r = +.10$ or larger) and none were negative; this was one of the most stable trends in the analysis, and was consistent with other research. As stated by Anne Roe,[3] "almost all studies of scientists agree that the need for autonomy, for independence of action, is something that seems to be particularly strong in this group."

In what seemed an inconsistency, however, effective scientists did not avoid other people; they and their colleagues interacted vigorously. High performers conferred with their most important colleagues several times a week or daily; they regularly conferred with several colleagues in their own section and often with ten or more elsewhere in the organization.

In our speculative framework, independence or self-reliance is a source of security. Interaction with colleagues is a source of challenge, for they may criticize and prod. The high contributor experienced a creative tension between independence and interaction (Table 1, tension 2).

The skeptic may ask, Are the two conditions antithetical? In terms of their occurrence in our data, not necessarily. Yet in common experience it is often difficult to maintain one's independence under social pressure. As Ralph Waldo Emerson put it over a century ago in his essay "Self-Reliance": "It is easy in the world to live after the world's opinion; it is easy in solitude to live after our own; but the great man is he who in the midst of the crowd keeps with perfect sweetness the independence of solitude." The aphorism fits our effective scientists today. In the midst of the crowd they retained—with enough sweetness to be creative—the independence of solitude.

AGE, SPECIALIZATION, DIVERSITY

In one analytical study we considered the question, Under what conditions can younger or older scientists, respectively, do their best work? Andrews and I had speculated that younger scientists already face challenge because their work is new; mainly they need security. Older scientists, we thought, possess security and mainly need challenge. To test these ideas we correlated several measures of climate against performance within successive age brackets.

The findings were far from simple. The overall conclusion, however, was that, among younger and older scientists alike, *both* security and challenge were required for achievement.

In the youngest age categories (up to age 34), positive correlations appeared between technical performance and length of time the scientist or engineer had spent in his main project. Devoting 2 or 3 years to one undertaking is a source of security. It enables the young man to build contributions in which he can take pride. But, at the same time, young non-Ph.D.'s were effective when they had several areas of specialization, and young Ph.D.'s did better when they were *not* preoccupied with "digging deeply in a narrow area." A diversified task provides challenge (Table 1, tension 3*a*).

After age 40, a somewhat different set of measures accompanied high performance. Older individuals achieved only when self-confident—when motivated from their own ideas and willing to take risks. After age 50, achievement was also linked with an interest in probing deeply. These factors both suggest security. On the other hand, achievement after 50 was also linked strongly with interest mapping broad features of new areas (Table 1, tension 3*b*). Thus, among older scientists, positive correlations appeared between performance and *both* penetrating study and wide-ranging study. The tension in this case was genuine; self-ratings of the two interests were found to be negatively correlated.

One wonders whether, in the creative tensions discussed thus far, the opposing conditions occur simultaneously or successively. Does the effective scientist pursue one narrow specialization at the same time he is exploring several new frontiers, or does he alternate between these postures? Does he retreat one month to his own ideas and engage in dialogue the next, or does he do both at the same time?

Our data contain no means of distinguishing. My hunch is that many creative scientists are flexible; they are able to alternate between contrasting roles.

THE INDIVIDUAL AND THE ORGANIZATION

We saw previously the importance of desire for independence. But to desire independence does not mean that one *is* independent. We therefore measured the individual's freedom to choose his own research or development tasks by asking who exerted weight in deciding what his technical goals or assignments were to be. The more weight exerted by the technical man himself, relative to that exerted by his chief, his colleagues, or higher executives or clients, the greater his perceived autonomy. The measure appeared valid: it was highest for Ph.D.'s in research, and lowest for "assistant scientists."

Now the more autonomy an individual has (the more weight in selecting his own assignments), the greater should be the stability and continuity of his work—the greater his security. And we found that, as autonomy increased, so did performance—up to a point. We were puzzled, however, to observe that when Ph.D.'s in both research-oriented and development-oriented laboratories had more than half the weight in choosing their goals their performance dropped, whereas in the case of non-Ph.D.'s, as their autonomy increased their performance continued to rise. Why?

In one search for answers we examined an organizational variable: the tightness or looseness of coordination within the department, measured by nonsupervisory scientists' ratings of the coordination within their section and supervisors' ratings of coordination between sections. (Individual autonomy and departmental looseness are of course interrelated, but within a given department the freedom of individuals can vary.) A loose organization does not make demands on its members; it provides high security with little challenge.

We found first that, in the most loosely coordinated departments, highly autonomous individuals actually experienced *less* stimulation, from either external or internal sources. They withdrew from contact with colleagues; they specialized in narrow areas; they even became less interested in their work. In these settings, maximum autonomy was accompanied by minimum challenge

Yet in the most loosely coordinated settings, we also found, it was essential that the person be challenged if he were to achieve. It was here that the strongest correlations appeared between performance and various stimulating factors: diversity in the work, communication with colleagues, competition between groups, involvement in the job.

In these loosely coordinated settings, the most autonomous individuals were able to isolate themselves from challenge. A nondemanding organization permitted them to withdraw into an ivory tower of maximum security and minimum challenge. There they atrophied (Table 1, tension 4a).

What about the more demanding organizations—those of moderately tight coordination? Why was autonomy an asset here and not a handicap? We found that autonomous persons here had more diversity in their work, not less. One can speculate that in these departments the technical man had to face problems important to the organization; personal freedom enabled him to find the best solutions. Again a creative tension; the organization itself presented challenges; autonomy provided security for solving them (Table 1, tension 4b).

INFLUENCE GIVEN AND RECEIVED

The question used to measure autonomy also indicated the weight exerted by other persons in the choice of an individual's assignments. The "decision-making sources" were grouped into four categories: the individual, his immediate supervisor, his colleagues or subordinates, and higher executives or clients. We scored for each scientist how many of the four sources were said to have had at least some weight (10 percent or more) in selecting his technical goals.

Now, to discuss one's projects with persons in several positions is to run the risk of criticism and disruption. The more sources there are involved in decision, the greater is the likelihood of challenge.

For the scientist to allow other people some weight in his assignments does not, however, mean that he is powerless. He can *influence* the decision-shapers, and influence provides security.

We divided respondents into those who felt they exerted strong influence over key decision-makers and those who felt they exerted little. Responses on this item appeared valid; the highest influence was reported by Ph.D.'s in research laboratories, and the lowest by assistant scientists.

The results were clear: both Ph.D.'s and engineers performed well when all four sources had some voice in shaping their goals but when, at the same time, the individual could influence the main decision-makers. From this arose creative tension 5 (Table 1): influence received from several others (challenge) combined with influence exerted on others (security).

The reader may ask, To what extent are the receiving and giving of influence antithetical? In conventional views of bureaucracy, each is seen as restricting the other; the size of the "influence pie" is considered a constant, so that if superiors have more, subordinates have less. Likert[4] argues, however, in a fashion compatible with our results, that the total amount of influence is not fixed. When everyone exerts more—when total control rises—performance is likely to improve.

But why should participation enhance the scientist's performance? Mainly, I suspect, because it helps him to avoid the narrow or trivial, to select tasks of *significance,* either to the organization or to science. Diverse contacts may also turn up unrecognized problems, or suggest new approaches to old ones. Finally, the interest of others in the scientist's work will enhance his own involvement in it.

"DITHER"

Another way in which a man's colleagues can provide challenge is through questioning his ideas. An apt label was borrowed by Warren Weaver[5] from British colleagues who built into

43

antiaircraft computing devices a "small eccentric or vibrating member which kept the whole mechanism in a constant state of minor but rapid vibration. This they called the 'dither.'. . . We need a certain amount of dither in our mental mechanisms. We need to have our ideas jostled about a bit so that we do not become intellectually sluggish."

A scientist's colleagues may jostle his ideas if they and he approach a problem differently. To test this hypothesis, we measured similarity or dissimilarity between the scientist and his colleagues in several ways. One method was subjective—the respondent's perception of how his own technical strategy resembled that of his co-workers. Other measures were objective, in the sense that we examined the approaches reported by the respondent and by each of his colleagues and numerically scored the similarity among them.

How much dither or disagreement is healthy? In our data the answer depended on the kind of dither. One objective measure concerned the source of motivation—whether one's superior, the technical literature, or some other source. Scientists who responded to the same sources were somewhat more effective—perhaps because they had similar interests.

On three other measures we found the opposite to be true. Scientists and engineers did somewhat better when they saw themselves as different from colleagues in technical strategy, and when as scored objectively, they differed from colleagues in style of approach (when, for example, the individual stressed the abstract, his colleagues the concrete) or differed in career orientation.

How to reconcile this paradox? In some preliminary data obtained by Evan[6] for industrial R&D groups, the teams he found most effective reported personal harmony or liking among members, but intellectual conflict. Colleagues who report the same sources of motivation as the scientist's own probably provide personal harmony and support—a form of security. When they argue about technical strategy or approach, they provide dither or challenge (Table 1, tension 6).

GROUP AGE

Another portion of our analysis concerned the age of groups—the average tenure of membership in a given section or team. A resonable hunch is that, as a group gets "older," security is likely to rise and challenge is likely to diminish. If this is so, what conditions are needed to maintain vitality as the group ages?

To study this question, Wallace P. Wells identified 83 sections or teams in industrial or government laboratories (ranging in number of members from 2 to 25, with a median of 6). He averaged the measures for scientific contribution and usefulness of members in each group and adjusted the averages to rule out the effects of individual age, percentage of Ph.D.'s, and type of setting.

When he plotted the adjusted measures against group age, Wells found that group performance generally declined as group age increased, although usefulness was highest for groups with an average tenure of 4 to 5 years.

Why the decline after 5 years? In a search for clues, Wells examined several measures of the group's climate in relation to its age. Two of these measures are plotted in Figure 2. The average preference for "deep probing of narrow areas" (a source of security) rose steadily as group age increased, while the interest in "broad mapping of new areas" (a source of challenge) dropped. Note in Fig. 2 that usefulness was highest shortly beyond the point where the two curves cross, where both interests were present in some degree (Table 1, tension 7). The finding is similar to that for tension 3*b* and may partly overlap it, since older groups tend to contain older individuals.

Not all older sections declined in vitality;

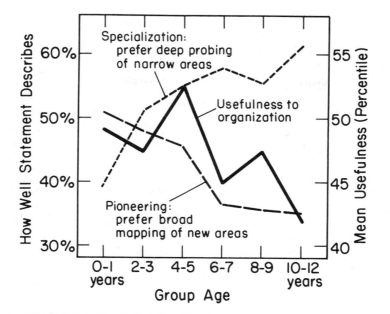

FIGURE 2. *Graph Showing That R&D Teams Were Most Useful at That Group Age When the Members Wanted Both to Specialize and to Pioneer*

some continued to be both useful and technically creative. Why? Wells examined other measures of group climate. One he called "cohesiveness"; a group scored high on this measure if its members listed other members of the team as their main colleagues. If group members prefer one another as collaborators, they are undoubtedly secure.

Wells found that in older groups (average group age, 4 years or more), cohesiveness was correlated strongly with usefulness and technical contribution. That is, if an older team continued to be cohesive, it stayed effective. Also, those older groups whose members communicated freely with one another performed better than younger ones did.

Yet the climate in effective older groups could hardly be called relaxed. On the measure of felt similarity to colleagues in technical strategies, Wells found that, in older groups, the more dissimilar the approach was, the higher was the performance.

One other measure proved surprising. Scientists rated the "hesitance to share ideas" within their section (for convenience we called it "secretiveness"). Usually such hesitance was absent or mild. When some of this feeling was present in new groups, it was a handicap; it hindered their work. But this feeling *enhanced* the performance of older groups.

On reflection, this contrast makes sense. A new, insecure group must suspend criticism while it searches for new ideas. An old, secure group, on the other hand, will profit from criticism. If it stays effective it is not a club where one can lower his intellectual guard. On the contrary, there is competition in ideas; members sharpen their wits and marshal their evidence before speaking. Such a climate indicates challenge rather than insecurity.

Creative tension 8 (Table 1)—intellectual combativeness among colleagues who value each other—resembles tension 6. To prefer one's section members as collaborators is a sign of personal support, while the atmosphere of combativeness indicates intellectual conflict.

PRACTICAL IMPLICATIONS

Before considering practical implications I should raise the question, What is cause and what is effect? Does a combination of security and challenge help to generate achievement? Or do scientists who achieve experience more security and sense of challenge?

My own speculation is that a feedback loop exists. Usually a high performer has not only ability but also personality traits of curiosity and confidence. He is attracted to diverse problems and to contact with colleagues (a source of challenge) and at the same time insists on freedom and a voice in decision (conditions of security.) He thus exposes himself to conditions which in turn stimulate him to achieve. If this is the case, might lower achievers surround themselves with a similar climate and so enhance their own performance? Can R&D managers help to create such environments? I believe they can, and offer the following suggestions.

CONDITIONS OF SECURITY

An important quality (see Table 1, tension 2) is self-reliance and pursuit of one's own ideas. But in development-oriented laboratory the manager cannot give each man a free hand: how then can he build an individual's pride in his own work? One way perhaps is to insure that once or twice a year each man produces a product which bears his own name—even if this requires that a jointly prepared document be broken into parts. It was disturbing to find in our sample that two out of five non-Ph.D.'s in research had not published a single paper in 5 years; among engineers the figure was four out of five. Half the engineers had not a single patent to their credit in the past 5 years, and one out of five had not authored even an unpublished report. How can a scientist feel confident of his own ideas if he has no output in which to take a fatherly pride?

Consider how the method of rewarding performance may affect self-reliance. Typically a single chief assigns tasks, judges results, evaluates performance, and recommends promotions. What better way to stamp out independent thought? To build self-reliance there must be multiple channels for recognizing achievement. Make sure that each subordinate has a chance once or twice a year to explain his work to colleagues *outside* his group. In review sessions with executives or clients, include the engineer who is doing the work and let him do some of the talking.

Another security factor is autonomy—substantial weight exerted by the individual in choice of assignment (see Table 1, tension 4). Such weight does not mean, however, that the individual should be completely on his own. From a further analysis (not reported above) it appeared that a technical worker in a development-oriented laboratory performed best when he and his supervisor *jointly* determined assignments. For Ph.D.'s in research laboratories, an effective condition was joint determination by the scientist and his colleagues. Assignment by the supervisor alone was the worst condition in all settings.

Security can be provided by the opportunity to influence others who decide one's assignments (Table 1, tension 5). Organizational structure plays a part here. Such influence is probably weaker in a many-leveled impersonal organization where each level has a veto. The individual's voice counts more in an organization of flat structure with fewer levels, where there is a chance for face-to-face contact with the people who shape his assignments.

Security increases with the length of time an individual spends on a given project (tension 3), particularly in the case of the younger man. Give him a year or two to dig into his main project, instead of shifting him every 3 months. He must have time to build a solid contribution.

One's colleagues can also be a source of security. In forming teams, managers can put together individuals who have similar sources of motivation—who are interested in the same kinds of problems (tension 6).

As R&D teams get older they can remain productive if they stay cohesive (tension 8). The supervisor can encourage cohesion by giving credit to the group rather than to himself. He can build mutual respect by publicizing the contribution of each member. He can strengthen teamwork through promoting competition with other groups in the solution of technical problems.

CONDITIONS OF CHALLENGE

Scientists and engineers performed well not only when they had continuity and stability but also when they were challenged by demands from their environment. Frequent contact with one's colleagues (tensions 2 and 5) can be an important source of challenge. Such contacts can stimulate the individual in many ways. They can point to significant problems, suggest new approaches, or correct errors in a present approach.

How can the R&D manager encourage fruitful interaction? Often simply by knowing who in the organization or the field is doing what; he can steer the scientist to others who can give or use help. He can invite the individual to talk to a seminar, set up study teams and evaluation groups, pose problems which require consultation for their solution.

To encourage friendly disagreement, the R&D manager can invite members of an older group to look for flaws in each other's presentations (tension 8). When forming a new project committee he can include individuals who like each other but who use different strategies (tension 6). Periodic regrouping of teams—always with the consent of the persons involved—may help in maintaining a vital atmosphere.

Specialization lends security but diminishes challenge; some degree of diversity is required (tensions 1, 3, and 4). The manager should be aware of letting some individuals focus exclusively on research, others exclusively on development. He should encourage his staff to tackle some jobs in both areas.

A younger scientist needs more than one area of specialization (tension 3*a*). In addition to a main continuing assignment, give him each year a second, shorter assignment which demands that he learn a new skill. Keep the older man's interest in broad areas strong by tempting him with problems on the pioneering edges of his field (tension 3*b*. Set up refresher courses; arrange sabbatical exchanges with a university.

Teams as well as individuals can become too specialized and lose interest in pioneering (tension 7). The R&D manager should not assume that one group has become *the* expert group in a specific area. As problems in this area arise, occasionally he will give one of them to a different team. He will challenge the expert group now and then with a task outside its specialty.

In the short run, a policy may not be the most efficient way to manage a laboratory. It may cost more and take more time. But in the long run it will make for breadth and flexibility, and these will continue to open doors for creative advances.

SUMMARY

As Andrews and I examined the conditions under which scientists and engineers did effective work, we observed a number of apparent paradoxes. Achievement was high under conditions that seemed inconsistent, including on the one hand sources of stability or confidence (what I have called "security") and on the other hand sources of disruption or intellectual conflict (that is, "challenge"). It appears that, if both are present, the creative tension between them can promote technical achievement.

NOTES

1. Data concerning the various tensions of Table 1 appear in the following chapters: tension 1, chap. 4; tension 2, chaps. 3 and 6; tension 3, chap. 11; tension 4, chap. 12; tension 5, chap. 2; tension 6, chap. 8; tensions 7 and 8, chap. 13; the performance measures are described in appendices A-C.

2. T. S. Kuhn, in *Scientific Creativity: Its Recognition and Development,* C.W. Taylor and F. Barron, Eds. (Wiley, New York, 1963), pp. 341–54.

3. A. Roe, *ibid.,* p. 135.

4. R. Likert, *New Patterns of Management* (McGraw-Hill, New York, 1961), especially chap. 4.

5. W. Weaver, *Science,* 130, 301 (1959).

6. W. Evan, *Ind. Management Rev.* 7, 37 (1965).

7. Collaborating in this research were W. P. Wells, S. S. West, A. M. Krebs, and G. R. Farris. The work has been supported by grants from the Carnegie Corporation of New York, the National Science Foundation, the U.S. Army Research Office (Durham), the Foundation for Research on Human Behavior, the U.S. Public Health Service, The National Aeronautics and Space Administration, and industrial laboratories. This article is based on a lecture presented in Miami in August 1966 before a meeting of the American Sociological Association.

2

ISSUES IN PRODUCTIVITY AND PERFORMANCE

Academic Achievement, Task Characteristics, and First Job Performance of Young Engineers

Denis M. S. Lee

Abstract. This study investigated the first industrial job performance of a group of engineering students. The dimensions of task characteristics and performance evaluation criteria were examined. It was found that a significant portion of total variance in overall performance rating could be accounted for by a mixed measure of the student's intellectual, motivational, and interpersonal qualities. No significant relationship, however, was found between academic achievement and job performance overall. Instead, the results suggested that academic achievement might be only one of several important factors that could affect job performance.

I. INTRODUCTION

Engineering has been regarded as a profession based on technical knowledge and academic training. A university degree is generally considered a requisite for a professional engineer. Moreover, academic achievement is used by many people as an indicator of a young engineer's potential for future success. Industrial

firms often compete fiercely with each other to hire the top university engineering graduates.

In spite of the implicit assumption that there is a direct relationship between academic achievement and subsequent professional performance, there has been little empirical evidence to support this assumption. In fact, studies by psychologists on methods for early identification of technical manpower talent have found no relationship between academic achievement and future accomplishments; psychological orientation of individuals, however, appeared to be useful in forecasting long-term professional performance.[17] The major limitation in these studies is that they have been approached from a predictive perspective. No attempts have been made to explain or show why certain types of psychological orientations might be important for performance of technical work.

On a broader scope, job performance of engineers has been a central interest of both engineering managers and researchers in technology management. Previous studies have shown that high-performance engineers differ significantly from low performers in their work activities[19] and communication patterns.[1] High performers also differ from low performers in their career patterns.[2] In addition, empirical studies revealed that the initial years of an engineer's career are often the most important years. For example, longitudinal studies by Thompson *et al.*[18] found that it was possible to predict an engineer's future performance as far as 10–20 years later based on the early part of the person's career. Similarly, Kaufman[8] found that engineers whose initial job experience involved challenging technical work tended to contribute to knowledge relatively early and to maintain professional competence and good job performance during their careers. And, another more recent study by Katz and Tushman[9] found that young engineers who worked for high performance, boundary-spanning supervisors had a higher retention rate as well as a higher chance of getting promoted five years later.

In spite of the large amount of empirical evidence which suggests the crucial importance of the initial stage of an engineer's career, research in this area has been largely lacking. In order to understand what accounts for differences in job performance of young engineers, and why some flourish while others fail to develop, we must first find out the pertinent dimensions of engineering activities and what is required for good performance. The objective of this paper is to present some empirical findings on the relationship between task characteristics, academic achievement, and first industrial job perform-

ance of a group of cooperative engineering students. In a cooperative educational program, the students alternate between academic study and industrial work. The cooperative education program thus provides an opportune natural experimental situation for field research, since a number of variables such as academic background (e.g., course preparation), work assignment comparisons, and work environment can be held constant. The results presented here are based on a larger study designed to investigate what factors might account for the differences in first industrial job performance of these engineering students.

II. DATA COLLECTION

The research project was initiated to track the work activities and job performance of a group of students who were enrolled in a cooperative education program. These coop students were employed by five organizations including three "Fortune 500" companies, a university affiliated R&D laboratory, and a government R&D laboratory. At each location, a company manager, typically the one in charge of hiring the students, served as the research coordinator and lent considerable help to the data collection effort.

Toward the end of each work assignment, two separate job evaluation questionnaires were sent to the students and their supervisors. The supervisor's questionnaire solicited information regarding the type of work the student was assigned to do, requisite skills and knowledge for the job, as well as performance evaluation. The students also were asked to fill out and return a questionnaire which included similar questions on the type of work assigned, requisite skills and knowledge for the job, job requirements, as well as certain background information such as major field of study, academic grade point average, and the number of extracurricular activities in which they participated.

Over a 24 month period, data were collected on 279 coop work assignments. Each work assignment was either three or six months in duration. A total of 224 students and 217 supervisors returned the questionnaires after one follow-up, yielding response rates of approximately 80 and 78 percent, respectively. Among the returns, there were 162 matched responses from both the students and the supervisors regarding the same job assignments.

The students in this sample majored in a variety of engineering disciplines including; electrical engineering 41 percent, mechanical engineering 31 percent, computer science 12 percent, civil engineering 4 percent, chemical engineering or chemistry 3.5 percent, industrial engineering 3 percent, mathematics or physics 5 percent. Their academic grade point averages (GPA's) were approximately normally distributed, with a mean of 2.73, and a range of 1.70 to perfect 4.0 (straight A's). The self-reported GPA's by the students were checked against official records and were found to be very accurate. These students worked on a variety of engineering activities for their industrial work assignments, ranging from research, design and development, testing and analysis, computer programming, production and quality control, to drafting.

III. MEASURES

A. Task Characteristics

One of the objectives of the present study is to identify the characteristics of activities carried out by new engineers. The goal is to measure intrinsic dimensions of engineering activities that are universal. While the organizational literature is replete with measures of job characteristics[3, 7, 13, 15], most of the items in the standard instruments of job characteristics were found to be inappropriate for the purpose of the present study since they typically involve such constructs as autonomy, task identity, friendship opportu-nities, feedback, and support. These constructs often involve perceived roles of the respondent which might be influenced by the respondent's work environment, e.g., relationship with supervisor, or organizational climate. Inclusion of these constructs would confound the results and render them difficult to interpret.[12]

Following the suggestions by Roberts and Glick[12], the measures of task characteristics for the young engineers are aimed to explore the situational attributes of engineering activities (as opposed to people-situation relations) by focusing on the specific job requirements. In addition, differences in incumbent cognitions about the job are explored by comparing the responses from the young engineers and their supervisors regarding the same assignments. The measures were developed by first reviewing the existing list of written job descriptions for the coop engineering assignments at the five organizations participating in the study. Two components of task characteristics were identified as a result of this process. The first component consisted of a set of four job requisite knowledge or skills including 1) academic knowledge and quantitative skills, 2) knowledge of machine shop and model building skills, 3) ability to work with specific instruments, and 4) computer programming (applications programming) knowledge. The second component consisted of a set of seven requirements for the work assignment including 1) requirement to think conceptually, 2) requirement to deal with unstructured tasks, 3) requirement to build a working model, 4) requirement to collect and analyze data carefully, 5) requirement to gather relevant information from different sources, 6) requirement to work with many people, and 7) requirement to work in a team. Respondents were asked to indicate on a five point scale the degree to which each item was an important prerequisite or requirement for the specific job assignment. Respondents were also allowed to add any other requisite knowledge or job requirements they thought relevant. However, no significant additional items were identi-

51

fied in the pretesting or from subsequent data collection.

B. Job Performance

Previous research studies on performance assessment of engineers have included both multiple criteria as well as overall performance ranking.[5, 11, 16] However, many important performance criteria for professional engineers, such as patents, papers published, contribution to professional knowledge or contribution to the organization, were obviously inappropriate for the population of student engineers in this study. The objective of the job performance measurement in the present study is to identify in which specific ways the performance of one student was better or worse than others. This instrument was developed through in-depth interviews with a select group of engineering managers who had considerable experience supervising coop students and other young engineers. Each manager was asked to recall certain outstanding young engineers or coop students whom he or she had supervised within the last five years, and to explain the qualities that made each person outstanding. This procedure produced 12 performance criteria including: 1) understanding of job objectives and what needs to be done to accomplish the assignment, 2) creativity and originality, 3) ability to deal with unstructured tasks, 4) ability to collect and analyze data carefully, 5) ability to gather relevant design information from different sources, 6) quality of machine shop and model building work, 7) quality of work with instruments and test machines, 8) ability to learn on the job, 9) ability to accomplish difficult assignments, 10) self-initiative, 11) delivering promises and meeting deadlines, 12) interpersonal relationships. These performance criteria were similar to those used by other researchers.[20] A review of performance measures for engineers in the literature also found three other criteria of performance which might be important for young engineers, but which were not identified explicitly by the managers in the interviews. These include decisionmaking abilities, written communication skills, and oral communication skills. These three evaluative criteria were then added to the supervisor's questionnaire. Each respondent was asked to rate job performance for each performance criterion on a five point scale, with one as poor, and five as outstanding. Respondents were also allowed to indicate if a particular performance criterion might be considered irrelevant or when there is no basis to evaluate that specific criterion. They also could add to the list of performance criteria, although no significant new items were found from the responses.

Besides the set of performance criteria, each supervisor also was asked to give an overall performance evaluation of the students based on a seven point percentile ranking. This scale was deliberately skewed to avoid some of the response biases[11], with one being bottom 20 percent; two, bottom 40 percent; three, average; four, top 40 percent; five, top 20 percent; six, top 10 percent; seven, top 5 percent. Distribution for the performance ratings followed an approximately normal distribution but skewed towards the higher ratings, with a mean of 4.84 and a range of two to seven.

IV. RESULTS

We will first explore the underlying dimensions of task characteristics for these young engineers' first work assignments. Next we will investigate the criteria of job performance. Finally, we will examine the relationship between job performance and academic achievement.

A. Characteristics

Table 1 shows a comparison between the students' and the supervisors' assessment of job requisite skills/knowledge and job requirements, based on match-paired responses regarding the

TABLE 1. *Comparison between Students' versus Supervisors' Assessment of Job Requisite Knowledge and Job Requirements*

	No. of Match-paired Respondents n	Mean for Students $\bar{R}_{i,t}$	Mean for Supervisors $\bar{R}_{i,s}$	$\bar{d}_i$ $(d_i = R_{i,t} - R_{i,s})$	t Statistic	Pearson Corr. r
Job Requisite Knowledge:						
R_1 = Academic engr. knowledge	159	3.44	3.77	−0.33	−3.96***	.26***
R_2 = Knowledge of machine shop & model building skills	154	2.44	2.48	−0.04	−0.41	.53***
R_3 = Ability to work with specific instruments or test machines	155	3.05	3.03	0.02	0.18	.49***
R_4 = Computer programming knowledge	158	2.63	3.02	−0.39	−3.96***	.60***
Job Requirements:						
R_5 = To think coonceptually & creatively	160	3.91	3.84	0.07	0.78	.18*
R_6 = To deal with unstructured tasks	160	3.77	3.73	0.04	0.49	.17*
R_7 = To collect and analyze data carefully	160	3.77	3.93	−0.16	−1.43	.32***
R_8 = To gather relevant design information from diff. sources	160	3.37	3.85	−0.48	−4.37***	.24***
R_9 = To build a working model	158	2.66	2.63	0.03	0.20	.11*
R_{10} = To interact with many people	160	3.52	3.49	0.03	0.21	.21**
R_{11} = To work with others in a team effort	161	3.75	4.11	−0.37	−3.87***	.29***

***p < .001
**p < .01
*p < .10

same work assignments. The supervisors' assessment of job characteristics are all correlated significantly with the students' assessment. In particular, the agreement is strongest for the three specific requisite knowledge or skills involving computer programming knowledge, machine shop and model building skills, and the requirement to work with instruments or test machines.

Among the subset of four job requisite skills and knowledge, both the students and the supervisors ascribed the most importance to academic engineering knowledge. Moreover, the supervisors placed even greater importance on academic knowledge than the students. Among the subset of job requirements, conceptual and creative thinking was rated as the most important by the students and second most important by the supervisors. In addition, supervisors placed significantly greater importance than students on the requirement to gather relevant design information from different sources ($t = 4.37$, $p < 0.001$), and the requirement to work with others in a team effort ($t = 3.87$, $p < 0.001$).

A factor analysis procedure was used next to examine the dimensionality of task characteristics, based on the supervisors' and the students' responses separately. The analysis employed principal factor extraction with R^2 communality estimates and varimax rotation.[10] Using the Scree[4] and discontinuity tests[14], four factors were extracted in each case for task characteristics assessed by the supervisors and the students, as shown in Tables 2 and 3.

Comparison of the factor loading patterns in the two cases revealed that two of the four factors, i.e., factors II and III, were identical for both groups of student and supervisor respondents. Factor II may be labeled as a measure of "requirements or requisite skills to work with hands" and included three items, i.e., knowledge of machine shop and model building skills, requirement to build a working model, and skills to work with specific instruments or test machines ($\alpha_{II} = 0.61$ for supervisors, and $\alpha_{II} = 0.67$ for students). Factor III may be labeled as a measure of "requirement for interpersonal skills." It included two items: requirement to interact with many people, and requirement to work with others in a team effort ($\alpha_{III} = 0.73$ for supervisors and $\alpha_{III} = 0.61$ for students).

TABLE 2.   *Factor Analysis of Task Characteristics as Perceived by Supervisors*

		Factor Loading			
	Item	I	II	III	IV
R_1:	Academic engr. knowledge	0.56[a]	0.13	0.11	0.18
R_7:	Reqm't to collect & analyze data carefully	0.39	0.17	0.05	0.49
R_8:	Reqm't to gather relevant design information	0.13	0.06	0.16	0.84
R_6:	Reqm't to deal with unstructured tasks	0.46	0.30	0.15	0.22
R_5:	Reqm't to think conceptually and creatively	0.61	0.13	0.09	−0.01
R_4:	Computer programming knowledge	0.52	−0.17	−0.18	0.16
R_2:	Knowledge of machine shop & model building skills	−0.26	0.50	0.26	0.08
R_9:	Reqm't to build a working model	0.20	0.76	−0.04	−0.04
R_3:	Ability to work with specific instruments or machines	0.23	0.60	−0.13	0.17
R_{10}:	Reqm't to interact with many people	0.03	−0.06	0.63	0.33
R_{11}:	Reqm't to work with others in a team	0.11	0.03	0.88	−0.02
Unrotated eigenvalue:		2.92	1.73	1.58	1.06
Percent of total variance:		27%	16%	14%	10%

[a]Solid underline indicates those items which load consistently on the factor in repeated analysis with different sample sizes.

TABLE 3. *Factor Analysis of Task Characteristics as Perceived by Students*

Item	Factor Loading			
	I	II	III	IV
R_1: Academic engr. knowledge	0.53[a]	0.20	0.12	0.23
R_7: Reqm't to collect & analyze data carefully	0.71	−0.09	−0.06	0.05
R_5: Reqm't to think conceptually and creatively	0.56	0.06	0.12	0.18
R_6: Reqm't to deal with unstructured task	0.52	0.19	0.10	−0.02
R_8: Reqm't to gather information from diff. sources	0.34	0.16	0.23	−0.21
R_4: Computer programming knowledge	0.21	−0.10	−0.07	0.84
R_2: Knowledge of machine shop and model building skills	−0.02	0.73	0.12	−0.36
R_9: Reqm't to build a working model	0.07	0.56	0.06	0.12
R_3: Ability to work with specific instruments or machines	0.22	0.62	0.06	−0.08
R_{10}: Reqm't to interact with many people	0.02	0.06	0.99	−0.07
R_{11}: Reqm't to work with others in a team	0.32	0.16	0.42	−0.01
Unrotated eigenvalue:	2.81	1.94	1.25	1.01
Percent of total variance:	26%	18%	11%	9%

[a]Solid underline indicates those items which load consistently on the factor in repeated analysis with different sample sizes.

Different items seemed to load on factors I and IV for the two groups of respondents. For the supervisors, factor I included i) academic engineering knowledge, ii) computer programming knowledge as well as iii) requirement to think conceptually, and iv) requirement to deal with unstructured tasks; while factor IV included i) information gathering and ii) data analysis. For the students, computer programming knowledge was the only item that loaded on factor IV, while the remaining items all loaded on factor I.

A question is raised whether the differences in loadings for factors I and IV for the students and supervisors were in fact due to differences in perceptions of task characteristics between the groups of respondents or whether they were due to peculiarities of the specific sample selected. To explore this question further, the factor analysis procedure was repeated using different sample sizes of respondents. Results of these analyses indicated that the underlying structure for perceived task characteristics remained stable for the student respondents, similar to the results shown in Table 3. However, for the supervisors, only the loading patterns for factors II and III remained stable. With the exception of item i) academic knowledge, which loaded consistently on factor I, the remaining items did not have a stable loading pattern on factors I and IV. Hence, different subgroups of supervisors appeared to have somewhat different perceived structures of task characteristics for items relating to information gathering, data collection and analysis, thinking conceptually, dealing with unstructured tasks and computer programming knowledge.

B. Performance Evaluation

Each supervisor was asked to assess the student's job performance with a set of fifteen criteria as well as to give an overall performance rating. As shown in Table 4, the overall correlation matrix indicated a large amount of halo effect in the performance evaluation, a finding consistent with results reported by other researchers.[5, 20] The overall performance rating was significantly correlated with each of the 15 performance criteria at the 0.1-percent significance level. Moreover, all but two of the 105 intercorrelations among

TABLE 4. Performance Correlation Matrix

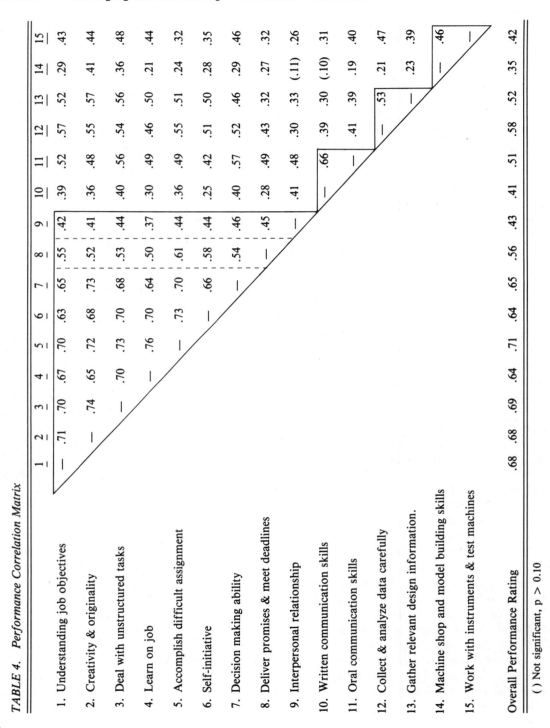

	1	2	3	4	5	6	7	8	9	10	11	12	13	14	15
1. Understanding job objectives	—	.71	.70	.67	.70	.63	.65	.55	.42	.39	.52	.57	.52	.29	.43
2. Creativity & originality		—	.74	.65	.72	.68	.73	.52	.41	.36	.48	.55	.57	.41	.44
3. Deal with unstructured tasks			—	.70	.73	.70	.68	.53	.44	.40	.56	.54	.56	.36	.48
4. Learn on job				—	.76	.70	.64	.50	.37	.30	.49	.46	.50	.21	.44
5. Accomplish difficult assignment					—	.73	.70	.61	.44	.36	.49	.55	.51	.24	.32
6. Self-initiative						—	.66	.58	.44	.25	.42	.51	.50	.28	.35
7. Decision making ability							—	.54	.46	.40	.57	.52	.46	.29	.46
8. Deliver promises & meet deadlines								—	.45	.28	.49	.43	.32	.27	.32
9. Interpersonal relationship									—	.41	.48	.30	.33	(.11)	.26
10. Written communication skills										—	.66	.39	.30	(.10)	.31
11. Oral communication skills											—	.41	.39	.19	.40
12. Collect & analyze data carefully												—	.53	.21	.47
13. Gather relevant design information.													—	.23	.39
14. Machine shop and model building skills														—	.46
15. Work with instruments & test machines															—
Overall Performance Rating	.68	.68	.69	.64	.71	.64	.65	.56	.43	.41	.51	.58	.52	.35	.42

( ) Not significant, p > 0.10

the performance criteria were significant at the 10-percent level.

The performance correlation matrix also showed three clusters of performance criteria, which were derived from a factor analysis procedure. The first cluster of nine variables appeared to measure a mixture of intellectual, motivational, and interpersonal qualities of the student ($\alpha = 0.93$). The second cluster included two variables which measured the written and oral communication abilities of the students ($\alpha = 0.79$). The third cluster included two variables which measured the ability to gather relevant information and the ability to collect and analyze data ($\alpha = 0.69$). The last cluster included two variables which measured the performance in model building and in working with instruments and test machines ($\alpha = 0.63$).

It might also be noted that within the first cluster, the first seven variables formed a particularly strong subcluster. Intercorrelations among the first seven variables were all above 0.6 with a median of close to 0.7, whereas the correlations for variables nine and 10 (deliver promises and meet deadlines, and interpersonal relationships) with the first seven variables dropped generally to the 0.5 and 0.4 range. However, since further data analysis did not find any advantage in separating variables 9 and 10 from the first cluster, they were hence included in the first group of variables.

A regression model was used to summarize the relationship between overall performance rating and the performance criteria. Based on the cluster analysis of the performance criteria discussed above, a new variable QUAL was defined by using the average of the first nine performance criteria as a summary measure for the overall intellectual, motivational, and interpersonal quality of the students. Similarly, a new variable COMM was defined as the average of oral and written communications scores, another variable INFO was defined as the average of the scores on gathering relevant information and collecting and analyzing data carefully. Finally, variable

HANDY was defined as the average of the scores on model building and working with instruments and test machines.

Table 5 shows the results of regression analysis using stepwise inclusion of the four variables: QUAL, COMM, INFO, and HANDY. With all four variables included, the overall R^2 is 0.63 ($p < 0.001$). However, one independent variable, QUAL, is the most important and can account for most of the variance in explaining overall performance rating. Inclusion of the other independent variables brought little improvements in R^2. While the regression coefficient for variable QUAL is significant at the 0.1-percent level, the regression coefficient for HANDY is barely significant at the 10-percent level, and the regression coefficients for the remaining two independent variables are not significant. The results of this analysis suggests that the overall intellectual, motivational, and interpersonal quality of the students accounted for the major factor in their performance evaluation by their supervisors.

C. Relation Between Job Performance and Academic Achievement

The above results indicate that academic engineering knowledge is considered an important job requisite, especially by the supervisors of the young engineers. On the other hand, a significant portion of the variance in overall performance could be accounted for by a mixed measure of the student's intellectual, motivational, and interpersonal quality. It is thus logical to examine next whether academic achievement might be predictive of first job performance.

Table 6 shows the correlation between job performance and various indicators of achievement in college, including grade point average, number of honors received, and the number of extracurricular activities in which the student participated. All the coefficients are close to zero and nonsignificant.

A closer examination of the scattergram plot of job performance with grade point average re-

TABLE 5.   *Multiple Regression of Performance Using Step-wise Inclusion*

Dependent Variable: PERF, Performance rating

Independent Variable Entered		R^2	ΔR^2	Regression Coef.	Std. Regress. Coef.
1. QUAL,	intellectual, motivational & interpersonal factor	0.63***	0.63	1.41***	0.68
2. HANDY,	model building and working instruments	0.64***	0.02	0.50*	0.30
3. COMM,	oral and written communication	0.65***	0.01	0.09	0.05
4. INFO,	gathering information, analyzing data	0.65***	0.00	0.05	0.02
Constant				−2.21	
	Adjusted R^2 at final step = 0.63				

*p < 0.10
***p < 0.001

vealed that among the students with grade point averages of 3.25 or better (i.e., top 17 percentile of the respondents), only one (representing 3.3 percent of this group) was considered as a low performer by his supervisor. For the rest of the students with grade point averages of less than 3.25, about 23 percent were considered as low performers, i.e., with performance ratings of two or three. However, except for this, grade point average appeared to have no relationship with job performance. Even students with perfect 4.0 (straight A) grade point averages might be rated as mediocre by their supervisors, while at the other end of the distribution some students with less than 2.0 (C −) grade averages were given outstanding job performance ratings by their supervisors. These results seem to suggest that outstanding academic records might be more indicative of a student's willingness to work hard and accept responsibility. They are hence unlikely to be regarded as total disappointments by their supervisors.

Examination of the other scattergrams revealed that the number of extracurricular activities in which the students participated in college might be a better predictor of job performance than academic record, although the relationship appeared to be nonlinear. Among the subgroup

TABLE 6.   *Correlation between Job Performance and Academic Achievement*

Correlation between:	Overall Grade Point Avg.	Grade Point Avg. in Major Field	No. of Honors Received	No. of Extracurricular Activities
Overall Job Performance Rating	.06 n = 146 n.s.	.03 n = 91 n.s.	.05 n = 152 n.s.	.10 n = 153 n.s.

n.s. not significant, p > 0.10

of students who did not participate in extracurricular activities, no relationship was found. But among the subgroup of students who participated in at least one extracurricular activity, there was a significant positive correlation ($r = 0.31$, $n = 79$, $p < 0.01$). At the same time, no significant difference in performance was found for students who held offices in school activities versus those who did not, or between the students who joined professional societies versus those who did not.

Since it is possible that academic achievement might be more important for certain types of engineering activities than others, the relation between job performance and academic grade point average, moderated by task characteristics, was explored (Table 7). The medium scores in the task characteristic distributions were used to define the high versus low task requirement groups.

We might expect that academic achievement would be related to job performance at least for the more analytical types of engineering activities, i.e., those tasks which require more academic knowledge or conceptual thinking. However, our results failed to support this. (Table 7 (a) (b)). Only in the case where the requirement to deal with unstructured tasks was rated as high do we find a significant positive relationship between job performance and GPA. (Table 7 (c)). However, it should be noted that this is the only significant correlation found out of eleven high task requirement groups.

Interestingly, significant positive correlations are found for tasks that have *low* requirements to work with people or collect information from others. (Table 7 (d)–(f)). The results seem to suggest that other factors might be more important than academic knowledge in affecting job performance for tasks that demand people interactions and information gathering. Finally, no significant relations were found between performance and GPA for tasks that were rated as either high or low in the remaining task characteristics involving specific machine shop or laboratory instrument skills, or computer knowledge. (Results not shown.)

TABLE 7. Correlation between Job Performance and Academic Grade Point Average Moderated by Task Characteristics

	A. Requisite Academic Knowledge	
	High	Low
Correlation between Job Performance & GPA	.12 (n=39)	.06 (n=63)
	B. Requirement to Think Conceptually	
	High	Low
Correlation between Job Performance & GPA	.19 (n=35)	−.02 (n=51)
	C. Requirement to Deal with Unstructured Tasks	
	High	Low
Correlation between Job Performance & GPA	.33** (n=28)	.09 (n=59)
	D. Requirement to Collect and Analyze Data	
	High	Low
Correlation between Job Performance & GPA	.14 (n=54)	.25** (n=44)
	E. Requirement to Gather Information	
	High	Low
Correlation between Job Performance & GPA	.11 (n=56)	.19* (n=55)
	F. Requirement to Interact with Many People	
	High	Low
Correlation between Job Performance & GPA	−.13 (n=29)	.30*** (n=69)
	G. Requirement to Work in a Team	
	High	Low
Correlation between Job Performance & GPA	−.13 (n=52)	.15 (n=29)

*p < 0.10   **p < 0.05   ***p < 0.01

V. SUMMARY AND CONCLUSION

This paper investigated the first industrial job performance of a group of engineering students. The results corroborate the findings by Taylor and Ellison[17] that there is no significant correlation between the student's academic achievement and job performance overall. For us to understand this puzzling result, we should examine more carefully the task characteristics of engineering activities.

Engineering work requires more than just knowledge of academic subjects. It also requires students to deal with unstructured tasks, to work with other people, or to work with their hands. Real world engineering problems are seldom as well defined as those found in engineering textbooks. In many cases, there are even no "best" solutions. Engineering design often involves more art than exact science. Gathering the relevant information, defining the problem properly, and interacting effectively with other people often constitute the most difficult part of accomplishing engineering task objectives.[1] This study has examined some of the important dimensions of task characteristics for young engineers. Moreover, results from this study also have indicated that academic knowledge is only one of several important factors that could affect job performance.

The purpose of the present study is exploratory and the data collection has been limited to engineering students and their first industrial job performance. Nonetheless, it focused on a critical stage in the professional development of young engineers. It is hoped that the results have contributed to an understanding of the dimensionality of engineering work and performance of young engineers. On the other hand, care also should be used in interpreting the results. One should not conclude that the lack of statistical association between academic record and first job performance would imply that academic preparation is not important for long-term career development of engineers. Simple logic would dictate otherwise. Rather the results indicate that traditional engineering education programs in universities are limited in the type of training they provide for engineers. A number of researchers and educators have advocated that the traditional training of engineers be modified to allow for more well-rounded professional training.[6] Results from the present study suggest some of the important factors to consider.

REFERENCES

1. T. J. Allen, *Managing the Flow of Technology.* Cambridge, MA: M.I.T. Press, 1977.
2. L. Bailyn, *Living With Technology: Issues at Mid Career.* Cambridge, MA: M.I.T. Press, 1980.
3. D. J. Brass, "Structural relationships, job characteristics, and worker satisfaction and performance," *Administrative Sci. Quart.,* vol. 26, pp. 331–348, 1981.
4. R. B. Cattell, "The scree test for the number of factors," *Multivariate Behavioral Res.,* vol. 1, pp. 245–276, 1966.
5. S. A. Edwards and M. W. McCarrey, "Measuring the performance of researchers," *Res. Manag.,* Jan. 1973.
6. W. R. Grogan, "Performance-based engineering education and what it reveals," *Eng. Education,* vol. 69, no. 5, Feb. 1979.
7. J. R. Hackman and C. R. Oldham, "Development of the job diagnostic survey," *J. Appl. Psych.,* vol. 60n, pp. 159–170, 1975.
8. H. G. Kaufman, "Relationship of early work challenge to job performance, professional contribution, and competence of engineers," *J. Appl. Psych.,* vol. 59, no. 3, pp. 377–379, June 1974.
9. R. Katz and M. L. Tushman, "A longitudinal study of the effects of boundary spanning supervision on turnover and promotion in research and development," *Acad. Manag. J.,* vol. 26, no. 3, pp. 437–456, 1983.
10. N. H. Nie, C. H. Hull, J. G. Jenkins, K. Steinbrenner, and D. H. Bent, *Statistical Package for the Social Sciences.* New York: McGraw-Hill, 1975.

11. D. C. Pelz and F. M. Andrews, *Scientists in Organizations,* revised edition, Institute for Social Research, The Univ. of Michigan, 1976.

12. K. H. Roberts and W. Glick, "The job characteristics approach to task design: A critical review," *J. Appl. Psych.,* vol. 66, no. 2, pp. 193–217, 1986.

13. J. P. Robinson, R. Athanasion, and K. B. Head, *Measures of Occupational Attitudes and Occupational Characteristics,* Inst. for Social Res., The Univ. of Michigan.

14. R. J. Rummel, *Applied Factor Analysis.* Evanston, IL: Northwestern Univ. Press, 1970.

15. H. R. Sims, A. D. Szilagyi, and R. T. Keller, "The measurement of job characteristics," *Acad. Manag. J.,* vol. 19, no. 2, 1976.

16. W. J. Smith, L. E. Albright, and J. R. Glennon, "The prediction of research competence and creativity from personal history," *J. Appl. Psych.,* vol. 45, no. 1, pp. 59–62, 1961.

17. C. W. Taylor and R. L. Ellison, "Biographical predictors of scientific performance," *Science,* vol. 155, pp. 10975–80, Mar. 1967.

18. P. Thompson, G. Dalton, and R. Kopelman, "But what have you done for me lately—the boss," *IEEE Spectrum,* Oct. 1974.

19. P. H. Thompson and G. W. Dalton, "Are R&D organizations obsolete?," *Harvard Bus. Rev.,* pp. 105–116, Nov.–Dec. 1976.

20. M. F. Tucker and V. B. Cline, "Prediction of creativity and other performance measures from biographical information among pharmaceutical scientists," *J. Appl. Psych.,* vol. 51, no. 2, pp. 131–138, 1967.

Managing the Career Plateau

Thomas P. Ference

James A. F. Stoner

E. Kirby Warren

Managerial careers are characterized by early rapid upward mobility followed by inevitable leveling-off or plateauing. Based on interviews with managers in nine major organizations, a general dynamic model of managerial careers is presented. Some key issues associated with the career plateau are isolated and suggestions for managing the plateau process are offered.

A plateau is defined as the point in a career where the likelihood of additional hierarchical promotion is very low. Career plateaus are a natural consequence of the way organizations are shaped. Since there are fewer positions than aspirants at each higher rung of the organizational ladder, virtually all managers reach positions from which further upward mobility is unlikely.

Unfortunately, the phrase "career plateau" has a negative tone, suggesting failure and defeat, which hinders understanding and management of this aspect of careers. Discussions of plateaued managers have focused largely on problem situations: "shelf sitters," "deadenders," "deadwood," and so on.[7, 18, 21] But there is nothing inherently negative about the notion of a career plateau. To say that a person has plateaued tells us nothing about that person's performance on the job, morale, ambition, or any

other personal or behavioral characteristic. It simply describes that individual's current career status within a particular organization.

During the past few years, the authors have discussed the career plateau phenomenon with experienced managers in a variety of organizations. The observations and conceptual model presented here are based on exploratory interviews conducted with 55 senior executives in nine major organizations. The interview sample was composed of senior personnel, management development executives, and division-level line and staff management. The organizations were drawn from the following industries: banking, insurance, entertainment, paper manufacturing, petroleum, pharmaceutical, technical products, steel, and electrical equipment. (For a full report of the total study, see Stoner et al.[27])

The interviews were intended to elicit the reactions of these executives to the conceptual model we were formulating and to obtain their insights into major issues associated with mana-

From the *Academy of Management Review,* October 1977, Vol. 2, 602–612. Reprinted by permission.

gerial career plateaus. This article describes a method of viewing the career plateau in the context of the entire organizational career and presents a series of issues associated with plateauing, as well as suggestions as to how organizations might manage this phenomenon more effectively.

A MODEL OF MANAGERIAL CAREERS

The first parameter in a model for classifying managerial career states is the likelihood of future promotion—the *organization's* estimate of the individual's chances for receiving a hierarchical promotion. The second characteristic is performance in present position—how well the individual is seen by the organization as doing his or her present job. By classifying individuals as "high" or "low" on these two parameters, we can produce a straightforward classification of managerial career states, as shown in Figure 1. Naturally, a more detailed model would allow for finer gradations of each characteristic or would introduce other dimensions. Some elaborations on the basic model are discussed below and in a subsequent paper[10].

The four principal career states in the model are:

"*Learners*" or "*comers*." These individuals have high potential for advancement but presently perform below standard. Obvious examples are trainees who are still learning their new jobs and are not yet integrated into the organization's culture. Also included are longer service managers who have recently been promoted to new positions which they have not yet mastered.

"*Stars*." These persons presently do outstanding work and are viewed as having high potential for continued advancement. They are on the "high potential", "fast track" career paths. They are a readily identifiable group in most organizations, and probably receive the most attention in development programs and managerial discussions.

"*Solid citizens*." Their present performance is rated satisfactory to outstanding, but they are seen as having little chance for future advancement. These individuals are probably the largest group in most organizations and perform the bulk of organizational work. Management effort and research seldom has focused on them.

"*Deadwood*." These individuals have little potential for advancement, and their performance has fallen to an unsatisfactory level. These people have become problems, whether for reasons of motivation, ability, or personal difficulty. Probably a small group in most organizations, they are often the recipients of considerable attention, either for rehabilitation or dismissal.

Current Performance	Likelihood of Future Promotion	
	Low	High
High	Solid Citizens (effective plateauees) Organizationally Plateaued Personally Plateaued	Stars
Low	Deadwood (ineffective plateauees)	Learners (comers)

FIGURE 1.   *A Model of Managerial Careers*

The individuals on the left-hand side of the model—the "solid citizens" and the "deadwood"—are the plateaued managers. The solid citizens are effective plateauees; the deadwood are ineffective. For most organizations, only individuals in the deadwood category are seen as current problems.

Formulation of the model in this manner suggests three major implications. First, an important challenge for management is to prevent solid citizens from slipping into the deadwood category. Second, different managerial approaches and styles are likely to be needed for effective management of individuals in each career state. Third, while there is considerable "technology" in place for dealing with managers in these three categories, few measures are available for dealing with the solid citizen. There are highly developed assessment and training programs for learners[4, 5], development programs for stars[24], and rehabilitation or outplacement programs for deadwood.[7, 17] Ironically, the largest group, the effective solid citizens, frequently must fend for themselves.

SOME ELABORATION OF THE CAREER MODEL

The basic model can be elaborated to analyze sources of plateauing and to consider different types of effective plateauees. It is also amenable to an analysis of the development of careers over time.

Types of Effective Plateauees

Respondents indicated more than one identifiable subgroup within the solid citizen (effective plateauee) category. Individuals may become plateaued for reasons that can be grouped into two broad categories:

1. Some are *organizationally plateaued*, although having the ability to perform well in higher level jobs, because of lack of openings.
2. Some are *personally plateaued*, because they are seen by the organization either as lacking in *ability* for higher level jobs, or as *not desiring* a higher level job.

The most important source of organizational plateauing is the narrowing pyramid (or cone) as diagrammed by Schein.[25] At each sequentially higher level, there are fewer positions above (the pool of opportunities shrinks) and more positions below (the pool of potential candidates increases). For a specific manager, jumping a major hurdle, such as obtaining a general management position by age 35, may indicate many opportunities ahead with few true competitors, an apparent broadening of the funnel. But for all managers as a group, the probability that each promotion will be the last increases with every step.

Other sources of organizational plateauing include:

1. *Competition*. For a given position, the individual may be seen as less qualified than other candidates, including some presently outside the organization.
2. *Age*. The individual may be seen as a less desirable candidate because of the need to utilize the position for training younger, high potential managers who might have longer useful lives with the organization.
3. *Organizational needs*. The individual may be seen as too valuable in his or her present position to be spared for other, albeit higher level, work.

These considerations may or may not be seen as equitable from the perspective of a given individual, but they are part of an individual organizational decision-making process.

For individuals who are *personally* plateaued, promotion to a higher level position is unlikely even if openings occur. The organization's judgment might be based on a number of personal factors and qualities, including:

1. *Lack of technical and managerial skills.* This includes absence of job *context* (interpersonal competence) or job *content* (technical proficiency) skills needed for effective work at the next level. Skill deficiencies could arise from lack of aptitude, lack of exposure to responsibility or development opportunities, or lack of ability to respond to changing job requirements.

2. *Lack of career skills.* Some individuals are organizationally naive and lack an adequate understanding of the complexity of organizational realities.[12] Others tend to stay within a limited definition of their present job, failing to take active steps to move along a viable career path; they may be sidetracked too long in a job that has been mastered.

3. *Lack of sufficient desire.* Some individuals explicitly make known their desires not to be promoted further; others send ambiguous signals or place constraints on proposed promotions and transfers. An individual classified as a star by the organization may not desire additional promotion; such a person may become increasingly frustrated by the organization's efforts at advancement and development.[2]

Cognizance of an individual's career state and how he or she got there is an essential input to management decisions about that individual. Different management styles and strategies should be adopted for different managers. Individuals who are organizationally plateaued because of lack of openings may thrive on managerial job enrichment efforts which distribute some of the boss's responsibility downwards. The same approach might overwhelm managers who are personally plateaued because their abilities are being fully utilized in their present job.

The "Elusive Learners"

In discussing the "learner" or "comer" category, several managers indicated difficulty identifying specific individuals currently in that category. Yet they recognized the category as logically consistent. They offered three major reasons for their difficulty in citing examples of learners. First, many managers above entry-level positions learn new jobs and achieve high performance quickly, and thus are learners only a short time. Second, some managers are prepared for a new job before being promoted into it, often doing the work before the promotion becomes official; an assistant vice president may become a high performing vice president from the first official day in the job because the work was mastered before the promotion. Finally, expectations of potential often influence formal evaluation of managers during that learning period. Such managers are likely to be rated as "doing very well for someone new at the job" or are given a "too early to evaluate" performance rating. Thus, for a specific promotion or movement into a new job, a given manager may skip the learner category, may remain in it for only a short period of time, or may be in the category without public acknowledgement by other organizational members. These possibilities were not seen by the interviewers as challenging the validity of the category, nor were they seen as mitigating the necessity of managing and supporting the development process during the learning period.

Careers over Time

This essentially static model classifies managers at a particular point in time. But the model also can be viewed as a description of how careers progress over time. Individuals typically enter an organization and embark upon their careers as learners. Mastery of the job brings movement into the star category and candidacy for promotion. Subsequent promotions and sustained performance produce passages between the learner and star categories. Individuals gradually or abruptly drop out of competition for the next promotion and move on to the inevitable career plateau—they become solid citizens and remain there as long as their performance holds up. As age, lack of challenge, lack of motivation, or lack of attention begin to undermine performance, they drift toward the deadwood category. This progression traces out a life cycle of growth-stability-decline (Figure 2a) which parallels descriptions of other aspects of human development.

This description of the progress of a managerial career resembles the Peter Principle, a pop-

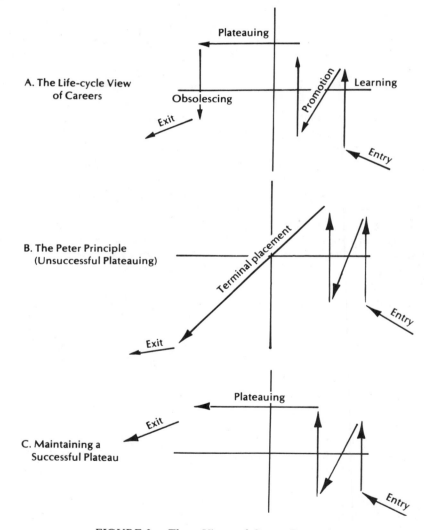

FIGURE 2.   *Three Views of Career Dynamics*

ular but pessimistic description of organizational life[21]. This principle suggests that the typical career is a series of promotions based upon effective performance in successively higher positions, culminating with promotion to the individual's "level of incompetence." If organizations were allowed to follow their preferred procedures, managers would not reach the solid citizen category but would recycle between learner and star until they are "terminally placed" as deadwood (Figure 2b).

Neglecting the "Solid Citizen"

The solid citizen—the effective plateauee—is performing well in her or his present job, not identified as a "star" nor as "deadwood." Much of an organization's management development efforts are focused on the extremes of the performance continuum. High-potential managers are most likely to have access to development programs, and poor performancers are likely to be targets for remedial programs or decisive action such as demotion or dismissal.

Comparable attention is not focused on maintaining the performance of the solid citizens who constitute the greater bulk of the management group. Organizations need solid citizens to maintain stability, provide continuity, and keep the level of competition for higher level jobs within manageable bounds. But interviewees reported a tendency to treat solid citizens passively. They may be denied access to development programs and challenging assignments. Such practices may starve solid citizens of exactly the types of stimulation and opportunity they require to remain effective.

WHAT TO DO: TENTATIVE SUGGESTIONS

Although understanding in this area is at an early stage, recent research offers suggestions about what senior executives and their organizations

should and should not do to manage the plateauing process more effectively. Three areas of action are: (a) preventing plateauees from becoming ineffective (preventing a problem from arising); (b) integrating the relevant career-related information systems (improving monitoring so emerging problems can be detected and treated early); and (c) managing ineffective plateauees and frustrated managers more effectively ("curing" the problem once it has arisen). These three areas of action focus specifically upon the career plateau. Hall[14] provides a more general yet thorough discussion of ways in which organizations can promote more effective careers on a continuing basis.

Preventing Deadwood

The ineffective plateauee's performance has declined, and he or she may have a negative impact on the performance of subordinates and co-workers. While dismissal is a possibility, it is a distasteful action for many managers. Consideration of obligations incurred through past service, age, and the limited availability of alternative work opportunities mitigate against severe action. Recognition that the organization has played a role in making some managers ineffective contributes to reluctance to use the dismissal route.

Rising concern among middle managers about their career situations and prospects is accompanied by increasing pressures for job security, education opportunities, and an improved bargaining position with upper management.[17] Potential for these trends to result in organized collective action by middle managers, including unionization[8], provides a further rationale for attention to organizational career management practices.

To the extent that management can avoid practices that lead to ineffective plateauing, painful decisions arising from dealing with "deadwood" can be reduced. Some potentially harmful practices include:

1. Failure to appraise accurately marginal or poor performance and to initiate corrective action. Long-run problems can be fostered by avoiding the short-run unpleasantness of negative appraisal, thus allowing possibly correctable behavior to become entrenched habit, which later becomes "someone else's problem."[14, 22]

2. Failure to provide training, skill upgrading, and development of solid citizens. This tends to assure that performance will slip as the requirements of a given position change, even if the incumbent's motivation remains high. Kaufman[17] and Kay[18] suggest ways to combat obsolescence.

3. Failure to appraise, counsel, and develop career paths in the context of an individual's total life situation, and the parallel tendency to promote individuals beyond current ability, leading to ineffectiveness and psychological stress.

4. Failure to monitor the attitudes and aspirations of individual managers. Many organizations depend upon informal observations and interpretations of superiors. Conditions maintaining individual performance vary across individuals as a function of particular goals and values.[13]

The authors of this article feel that it is unduly cynical to assume that all plateaued managers are incompetent. The Peter Principle is a special case of plateauing, which leaves little room for healthy, constructive solutions (although some suggested solutions for the individual to use in managing his or her own career do appear in *The Peter Prescription*[20]). A more reasonable assumption is that managers can plateau while still effective and are capable of performing well and adjusting constructively to their career situations. Plateauing indicates only arrival at a presumably permanent position in the organizational hierarchy; it does not necessarily imply cessation of personal growth and development. Many avenues for personal and career develop-

ment remain available to the plateaued individual[18, 25], and it is the task of senior management to assist individuals in adjusting effectively to their hierarchical situation—to remain in the solid citizen category until they leave the organization (Figure 2c).

TWO KEY ISSUES

The managers interviewed identified two ways in which their organizations made the inevitable plateauing phenomenon into a potential organizational problem.

Early Identification and Creation of Plateauees

The judgment that an individual has plateaued is becoming increasingly more explicit and, as a result, probably more permanent and consequential. Interviewers reported that their organizations are developing increasingly sophisticated performance appraisal and succession planning systems which bring the managerial workforce and particularly their promotability under continual scrutiny.

In addition to assessing current performance, managers are being asked to estimate: (a) extent of the appraisee's potential for promotion; (b) when the appraisee will be ready for promotion; and (c) the appraisee's training and development needs and plans. Performance appraisal, especially in the early years of an individual's career, frequently determines visibility to higher level managers and access to development opportunities. Thus it initiates organizational actions which subsequently confirm the appraisal.

Even more explicit decisions about an individual's long range career possibilities are made by succession planning processes that attempt to link individual potential to particular positions. The principal concerns of such systems are to: (a) identify specific candidates for specific positions; (b) determine when the candidate will be ready; (c) determine the candidate's need for additional skills and experiences; and (d) develop plans for filling these needs.

The succession plan becomes a definitive mechanism for identifying plateauees because it forces a distinction between abstract potential (common in the appraisal process) and potential for a specific position. To the extent that these formal systems become more widely adopted, definitive judgments increasingly will be made early in the individual's career. These judgments, whether accurate or not, affect training and development opportunities offered to individuals, and strongly influence eventual career experience. Studies show that early job experiences and events are powerful predictors of future work performance and career mobility.[3, 4, 9, 26] As early organizational judgments increasingly become formalized, these judgments will more nearly become self-fulfilling prophecies. Organizations will have to develop conscious strategies for managing the plateauees that the systems help to create.

Integrating Career Management Procedures

Performance appraisal and succession planning, which make the plateauing judgment explicit and self-confirming, are seldom integrated or cross referenced within an organization. In many organizations, the several personnel functions, such as development, internal placement, out-placement services, and counseling, are not only vested in different units or individuals but are frequently conducted as if the other activities did not exist. Poor coordination leads to confusion in signals transmitted to individuals and to failure to identify developing problem areas.

The systematic integration of appraisal systems and succession planning would sharpen the organization's manpower planning efforts, facilitating attention to career progress and increasing possibilities for intraorganizational transfer of individuals. It also would highlight discrepancies between assessment of potential on appraisal forms and designation for promotion in succession plans. Hall[14] suggested potential for improved organizational performance and individual satisfaction through a more explicit integration of the wealth of information buried within personnel systems.

Managing Ineffective or Frustrated Pleasures

There are no easy answers to the critical problem of how to bring the performance of ineffective plateauees to an effective level or how to motivate plateauees frustrated by the absence of advancement. For the ineffective plateauee, promising paths for restoring performance include:

1. Educational programs which upgrade technical skill, allowing the individual to keep pace with the changing job;
2. Development programs that allow for emotional and intellectual recharging, although care must be taken to avoid undeliverable promises of advancement or unintentional threats of being phased out[7];
3. Job rotation to provide a change of scene, through new duties, skill demands, or location. This can provide some of the stimulation normally associated with promotion although careful planning is needed to encourage managers to move from comfortable niches into new challenges. Ironically, the same effect can be obtained under certain circumstances through demotion as through lateral transfer.[11]

For the frustrated plateauee, the potential and need for job enrichment in place is considerable. Possibilities for growth through education and other special focus activities are limited only by the imagination of senior managers and their willingness to share the excitement and potential of their jobs with subordinates.

CRITICAL QUESTIONS FOR RESEARCH AND POLICY

These suggestions only begin to touch upon the intensity of the challenge to managerial ingenuity presented by plateaued managers. Remaining questions for research and managerial thought include:

1. To what degree is personal and professional stagnation the inevitable consequence of long tenure in a given position?
2. Is it better to tell a manager that he or she has plateaued or to allow the individual to maintain hope of eventual promotion?
3. Are plateaued individuals more effective when they accept their situation realistically or when they continue to aspire?
4. Which career management methods are likely to lead to continued satisfactory performance and a healthy adjustment to one's career situation?

Relationship to Other Career Models

Further directions for research are suggested by this model's potential to guide extensions of the career models of Schein[25], Hall[14, 15], and Hall and Schneider.[16] Schein has discussed the timing of innovative behavior of managers during their careers. He hypothesizes that managers will be more innovative in the later part of their careers, because they have achieved "organizational tenure," and between "boundary passages" (sometime after a promotion is received and before the next promotion is anticipated). While lacking empirical support, his reasoning is provocative. But conventional wisdom suggests that late career managers are not generally seen as particularly innovative. The distinction between effective and ineffective plateauees, as well as consideration of the timing and level of plateauing, should sharpen an understanding of the conditions under which the innovation hypothesis is likely to hold.

The predictive and explanatory power of Hall's "psychological success" model might be enhanced by contrasting trainees and stars with effective plateauees and ineffective plateauees. Based on the work of Lewin[19] and Argyris[1], its basic components are summarized by Hall and Schneider as follows:

> If (1) the individual sets a challenging goal for himself, . . . and (2) he determines his own means of attaining that goal, and (3) the goal is relevant to his self-concept, then he will experience *psychological success* upon attainment of that goal. This sense of personal success will lead to an increase in self-esteem, which in turn will lead to increased future levels of expectation[16] (p. 2).

The data used to test their more elaborate version of this basic model did not yield strong confirmation, and led to some revision of the model.

One elaboration that might sharpen the model would be inclusion of the individual's perception of organizational career state as a moderating variable. This would allow a distinction between individuals who direct their efforts towards enhanced organizational performance and those who channel increased motivation stemming from enhanced self-esteem in other directions.

The phenomenon of plateaus in managerial careers presents a challenging problem to organizations. The culture has increasingly emphasized the desirability of fully utilizing one's potential, and somewhere along the way self-actualization has come to be correlated with career success. Aspiring managers have grown up in a society which provides an official view—a conventional wisdom—of the world of work and the nature of proper ambition.

The rhetoric of management thought sustains this imagery. Ambition and desire for promotion are more than just acceptable; they are often essential to being judged as an effective contributor. One manager, in describing a subordinate who turned down an offer to join another company at a higher position and salary, said, "My estimate of his abilities and his work has gone down a lot. I have to question his motivation and ambition." Some respondents doubted that a subordinate who did not desire promotion could really do an outstanding job, and expected such a person to become a problem.

The official description of a managerial career fosters expectations of reasonably steady upward progression in the organization hierarchy and of achieving self-fulfillment through this progression. This expectation is often so pervasive that the termination of upward movement is seen as a sign of failure. Despite this "official" climate, increasing numbers of managers do reject promotions and transfers; solid citizens are necessary and valuable, and the proportion of plateauees in managerial ranks is likely to increase.

The emphasis on promotion has led many in the managerial and professional ranks to question the quality and value of managerial work. The experience of middle managers in implementing job enrichment programs for their subordinates has led some of them to ask, "What about job enrichment for me?" The need to find ways to enrich managerial jobs is receiving some attention. The challenge to top management is to develop climates that acknowledge the validity of plateauees, and accept and confirm commitments to quality work which do not involve desires or expectations of hierarchical advancement.

REFERENCES

1. Argyris, C. *Integrating the Individual and the Organization* (New York: Wiley, 1964).
2. Beckhard, R. "Mutiny in the Executive Ranks," *Innovation,* Vol. 31 (1972), 2–11.
3. Berlew, D. E., and D. T. Hall. "The Socialization of Managers: Effects of Expectations on Performance," *Administrative Science Quarterly,* Vol. 11, No. 2 (1966), 207–223.
4. Bray, D. W., R. J. Campbell, and D. L. Grant. *Formative Years in Business: A Long-Term A.T. & T. Study of Managerial Lives* (New York: Wiley, 1974).
5. Byham, W. C. "Assessment Centers for Spotting Future Managers," *Harvard Business Review,* Vol. 48, No. 4 (1970), 150–167.
6. Campbell, J. P., M. D. Dunnette, E. E. Lawler, and K. E. Weick. *Managerial Behavior, Performance, and Effectiveness* (New York: McGraw-Hill, 1970).
7. Connor, S.R., and J. S. Fielden. "Rx for Managerial 'Shelf Sitters,' " *Harvard Business Review* (November–December 1973), 113–120.
8. DeMaria, A. T., D. Tarnowieski, and R. Gurman. *Manager Unions?* (New York: American Management Association, 1972).
9. Dunnette, M. D., R. D. Arvey, and P. A. Banas. "Why Do They Leave?" *Personnel* (May–June 1973), 25–39.
10. Ference, T. P., J. A. F. Stoner, and E. K. Warren. "Managing the Career Plateau: Alternatives for the Individual," in process.
11. Goldner, F. H. "Demotion in Industrial Management," *American Sociological Review,* Vol. 30, No. 5 (1965).
12. Goldaner, F. H. "Success vs. Failure: Prior Managerial Perspectives," *Industrial Relations,* Vol. 9, No. 4 (1970), 453–74.
13. Goldner, F. H., and R. R. Ritti. "Professionalism as Career Immobility," *American Journal of Sociology,* Vol. 72 (March 1967), 489–502.
14. Hall, D. T. "A Theoretical Model of Career Subidentity Development in Organizational Settings," *Organizational Behavior and Human Performance,* Vol. 6 (1971), 50–76.
15. Hall, D. T. *Careers in Organizations* (Pacific Palisades, Calif.: Goodyear, 1976).
16. Hall, D. T., and B. Schneider. *Organizational Climates and Careers: The Work Lives of Priests* (New York: Seminar Press, 1973).
17. Kaufman, H. G. *Obsolescence and Professional Career Development* (New York: Amacom, 1974).
18. Kay, E. *The Crisis in Middle Management* (New York: Amacom, 1974).
19. Lewin, K. "The Psychology of Success and Failure," *Occupations,* Vol. 14 (1936), 926–930.
20. Peter, L. *The Peter Prescription* (New York: Morrow, 1972).

21. Peter, L., and R. Hull. *The Peter Principle* (New York: Morrow, 1969).

22. Porter, L. W., E. E. Lawler III, and J. R. Hackman. *Behavior in Organizations* (New York: McGraw-Hill, 1975).

23. Ritti, R. R., T. P. Ference, and F. H. Goldner. "Professions and their Plausibility," *Sociology of Work and Occupations,* Vol. 1 (1974), 24–51.

24. Revans, R. W. *Developing Effective Managers: A New Approach to Business Education* (New York: Praeger, 1971).

25. Schein, E. H. "The Individual, the Organization, and the Career: A Conceptual Scheme," *Journal of Applied Behavioral Science,* Vol. 7 (1971).

26. Stoner, J. A. F., J. D. Aram, and I. M. Rubin. "Factors Associated with Effective Performance in Overseas Work Assignments," *Personnel Psychology,* Vol. 25 (1973), 303–318.

27. Stoner, J. A. F., T. P. Ference, E. K. Warren, and H. K. Christensen. *Patterns and Plateaus in Managerial Careers, Report to the Ford Foundation* (May 1974).

28. Tarnowieski, D. *The Changing Success Ethic* (New York: American Management Association, 1973).

How Companies Measure the Productivity of Engineers and Scientists

Alfred H. Schainblatt

A state-of-the-practice review reveals no system of productivity measurement that is able to make meaningful comparisons over time in a given organization or among different organizations

There are no currently used systems for measuring the productivity of scientific and engineering groups without substantial flaws. Nor does the literature on productivity measurement offer encouragement that suitable systems will soon be available.

I draw this conclusion on the basis of a survey that was conducted to find out how industrial firms and government agencies *measure* the productivity of scientific and engineering groups

This work was supported by the U.S. Office of Personnel Management, Workforce Effectiveness and Development Group, Office of Productivity Programs, Measurement and Analysis Division. The author gratefully acknowledges the assistance of Allan Udler, Jeanne O'Leary, Michael Hoefer, Joseph Sennott, and Katherine Warren, all from the Measurement and Analysis Division. Assistance was also provided by the following OPM regional staff: David Caldwell, Director, Southeast Region; Steven Cohen, Acting Director, Great Lakes Region; Gerald Hinch, Director, Mid-Continent Region; Janet Rosselle, Agency Liaison Division, Western Region; and Edward Vela, Director, Southwest Region. However, the interpretations and conclusions expressed are those of the author and should not be attributed to OPM, the persons contacted, or to The Urban Institute, its trustees, or to other organizations that support its research.

Reprinted with permission from A. Schainblatt, "How Companies Measure the Productivity of Engineers and Scientists," *Research Management*, May 1982, 58–66.

engaged in R&D. In this study, "productivity" means a measure of the efficiency with which resources are used to achieve a desired product or attain some stated goal. The concept of "effectiveness" is thus also included in this definition.

We were primarily interested in systems for measuring the productivity of scientific and engineering *groups, programs* or other *organizational* units rather than the productivity of individual scientists or engineers. R&D is often shared work for which it is quite difficult to assign a meaningful output to any one individual. In particular, however, the findings do not cover individual performance appraisal approaches.

Because of the limited resources available for data collection (about one staff-person month), the survey was conducted by telephone. For the industrial portion, on which this article focuses, the author telephoned at least one official in each of 34 firms which were suggested by the executive director of the Industrial Research Institute as being firms whose productivity measurement activities probably reflect the state-of-the-art (see Table 1). The results follow:

Respondents from only seven of the firms (20 percent) indicated that R&D managers rou-

TABLE 1.   Firms Contacted

American Can
American Telephone & Telegraph
Bell Laboratories
Bendix
Borg-Warner
Detroit Edison
Dow Chemical
Dravo
E.I. DuPont
Eastman Kodak
Eaton
Exxon
General Electric
General Foods
Hewlett-Packard
Honeywell
Hughes Aircraft
International Business Machines
Lockheed
Monsanto Chemical
Motorola
Phillips Petroleum
Polaroid
Procter & Gamble
RCA
Rockwell-International
TRW
Texas Instruments
3M
U.S. Steel
Westinghouse
Weyerhaeuser
Whirlpool
Xerox

tinely collect some type of productivity index. None of the remaining firms use a formal system for regularly measuring R&D productivity as such, although managers in four firms (12 percent) use performance or output indicators as part of their regular review of R&D programs, and managers in three firms (9 percent) occasionally use a productivity or output indicator. No productivity-related measurement activities were indicated for 20 of the 34 firms. These results,

although somewhat disappointing, are perhaps not very surprising given the difficulty of measuring R&D productivity.

Several of the officials who indicated that there were no R&D productivity-related measurement activities in their firms made interesting comments by way of elaboration. The first type of comment expressed the idea that measuring R&D productivity is too difficult. For example, one official said, "The whole process tends to be subjective and dynamic in such a way that we would find it very difficult to quantify in any precise way or to define a measuring technique beyond a narrow sampling of a particular discipline." Another official commented that "Both our Research and Engineering Divisions are made up of groups working on such diverse projects, that the output of different groups within either Research or Engineering really cannot be compared one to another." Two other officials indicated that they were "hard pressed to measure productivity" and that "they did not know how to measure it."

A second group of officials noted that they had tried for several years to devise or find a method of measuring R&D productivity but were unsuccessful. In the words of one, "We made several attempts during the past five years to measure productivity and came to the conclusion that there is no good way to do it on a week-to-week or month-to-month-basis."

A third group was skeptical about the meaningfulness of R&D productivity measurements. One said he had no confidence in numbers used to measure productivity; another didn't think the idea was reasonable, calling it "bean counting". Another official felt that "attempts to quantify benefits of R&D have led to monstrosities that caused more harm than good." Finally, there was the official who described himself as a disbeliever and was very negative about quantifying R&D performance, saying that he really didn't like discussions of the idea because he had convinced his top management that it wasn't necessary.

The fourth group noted that while their firms did not explicitly measure the productivity or performance of R&D units, they did track how actual budgets and schedules compared to planned or expected budgets and schedules. In some cases, this type of tracking was part of an MBO system.

Despite the limitations of our survey, we felt fairly confident that we had not missed an ongoing system that measures R&D productivity in a way that is remarkably different from the ways we uncovered. This confidence stems in part from the results of an extensive study of R&D productivity undertaken by Hughes Aircraft Company (1978) during the period 1973–1977.[1,2] This study involved (1) the participation of 34 private firms (14 of which were also included by chance in our survey), 12 government agencies, and 13 universities; (2) a survey of 350 R&D managers regarding currently used techniques for measuring R&D productivity; (3) attendance at 23 productivity seminars; and (4) an extensive literature search. The director of the Hughes study told us he did not know of any currently used methods or procedures for measuring R&D productivity beyond those we have uncovered. In addition, our survey of industrial firms was supplemented by information supplied by over 50 knowledgeable individuals from relevant professional associations, university research programs, productivity centers, and government agencies.

MEASURING PRODUCTIVITY AT BORG WARNER

Among the productivity systems routinely used by the firms contacted, we only obtained sufficient information about a system used by Borg-Warner to allow a detailed description and discussion. For the remaining six firms that routinely measure productivity in some way, we can do little more than enumerate the productivity indexes they use.

Borg-Warner's research center divides productivity measurement into two parts: rating how well research projects have met their objectives, and calculating the potential value of business opportunities generated by research projects that have met their objectives to the extent that some other company unit has taken primary responsibility for their future development.

The process starts with an agreement between the research center and its customer (i.e., the other parts of the company that will use the research results) on the objectives of each project to be undertaken. Research in support of existing business might involve a statement of objectives such as, "To improve the overall efficiency of product A by 10 percent more than the best competitive unit." Objectives for exploratory research, on the other hand, will be more qualitative and flexible; for example, "to explore the chemical properties of such-and-such class of compounds." The agreement also covers the project budget and schedule.

At the end of the year, the people who set the objectives rate actual performance on a scale of 0 to 3. A "zero" rating is assigned to a project that badly missed its objectives either by not achieving its technical goals or badly overrunning the agreed-upon budget or schedule. A "one" rating is assigned to projects that made progress but which did not meet their technical goals within their budgets or time limits. A "two" rating is assigned to projects that fully met their objectives, and a "three" rating to projects that significantly exceeded their objectives or accomplished them well below the budget or significantly sooner than planned.

Departmental performance scores are calculated by multiplying each project rating by the money spent on it and dividing the sum of these products by the total cost of the projects. This gives for each department in the research center a weighted average of its project ratings, the weights being the size of each project expressed in terms of money spent on each individual project. These performance indexes have been rou-

RESEARCH ON MEASURING R&D PRODUCTIVITY

An important theme running through several general works on productivity measurement is the fact that productivity measurement can go wrong in serious, but perhaps subtle ways. Thor[8] warns against several common practices: expecting to use performance standards to measure the output of work (such as R&D) which is not repetitive; not adjusting productivity indexes for inflation (where dollars are used for weighting different kinds of either input or output units); and using as a productivity index any indicator that is affected by factors that do not have any direct effect on the basic efficiency with which the outputs were produced (such as an indicator of profitability).

Ruch[9] reflects this theme by discussing five basic categories of obstacles to measuring the productivity of "knowledge workers," which include scientists and engineers:

(1) The difficulty of defining the output or contribution that is made by the knowledge worker.
(2) Overcoming the tendency to measure activities (e.g., number of reports created, number of lines of computer programs written) rather than results.
(3) The matching of inputs within a time frame. The inputs consumed by scientists in one period may not show results until several periods later.
(4) Including a quality dimension in the measure.
(5) Including the concept of effectiveness as well as efficiency in the productivity measure.

Mundel[10], arguing that how we define productivity implies our definition of improvement, cautions against using an input-output relationship which does not measure the area needing improvement; e.g., use of labor, dollar resources, or foreign exchange. He also cautions against errors due to using overly simplistic output measures, counting outputs which are not final outputs, counting outputs in a manner not related to either goals or inputs, and suboptimizing; i.e., measuring the productivity of too small a part of an organization.

Terleckyj[11] formulates the suboptimization problem in terms of three types of measurement levels: managerial efficiency, program efficiency, and policy effectiveness. He illustrates these measurement levels in a network of government health units providing immunization against a communicable disease. Managerial efficiency is measured by the unit cost of immunizations performed. Program efficiency indicators would include incidence rates of the disease or perhaps percentages of the population reached—in other words, indicators that reflect the basic program objectives. Notice that improving managerial efficiency may run counter to the program objectives. For example, unit costs of immunizations may be driven down by not going after a hard-to-reach part of the population. Similarly, improving the effectiveness of a program dealing with a specific disease may be a suboptimization relative to the wider framework of public health policy. More destructive and prevalent diseases which could be controlled may be left uncontrolled. Policy effectiveness indicators should therefore reflect the general health status of the population, such as indicators of life expectancy or prevalence of disabilities.

One particularly misleading type of productivity measure that is sometimes suggested because of the difficulty of quantifying R&D outputs is based on measuring the "productive" time spent by scientists and engineers. For example, Newburn[12] suggests that

> the number of times the staff is engaged in productive work (as opposed to unproductive work, definitions of which are agreed upon prior to the study) provides an accurate measure of productivity which may be expressed as a percentage. This measurement may be used, for example, to question whether a group of scientists in one research department is more productive than a group in another department.

This type of measure has also been used in the aerospace industry.[13] However, as Thor[8] (p. 6) points out, "spending time on a project does not necessarily have a direct relation to successful completion of a project." It is also clear that knowing that two groups of scientists are 100 percent "productive" as measured by such an index tells us nothing in fact about their relative productivity. At best, "the percentage of time spent on productive work" may be useful as a variable for explaining differences in productivity measurements, and in identifying potential sources of poorly used time (e.g., excessive administrative paperwork).

Another approach commonly put forth as a method for measuring productivity is based on comparing actual to planned progress on a project. This management-by-milestone approach has many variations[14,15,16,17] and can be a useful management tool, but it does not measure productivity. Indeed, in some variations of this approach, what is measured is essentially the accuracy of resource estimates.[17]

Aynardi, Kustura, and Shauer[18] describe a technique for measuring engineering productivity in a large instrument and electrical department in a private firm. The productivity index they use assumes a constant flow of project work through the office, at overlapping stages of completion at any instant. The index measures changes in staff-hours per output between a base period and the current period. In effect, what is compared is the staff-hours per output in the base period to the staff-hours in the current period required to produce the base period output.

However, the assumption of constant output seems unrealistic for most true R&D activities.

Measuring R&D Outputs

A large portion of the literature concerned with measuring R&D output focuses on the use of counts of publications (see, for example, 19, 20, and 21, counts of citations to publications (see, e.g., 22), or combinations of both publications and citations (see, e.g., 23 and 24) These studies are usually not unmindful of the many obvious and not so obvious objections to these types of measures. (For a discussion of some of the major objections see 25 and 26. However, the countability of publications and citations, and the relative lack of alternative things to count, apparently makes them too hard to resist.

Lipetz[27], seeing the need for finding recurrent products of scientific research as a prerequisite to applying the productivity concept, is led to counting "novel" or "original" forms of descriptions, definitions, hypotheses, explanations, predictions, and experiments found in scientific publications. Although one must admire Lipetz' attempts to make such counts meaningful (e.g., the use of weights and scales to better relate the things counted to specific objectives and fields of interest), the approach seems little more than an academic exercise.

Another study that should be mentioned for its scope, if not for its contribution to R&D productivity measurement, is the UNESCO project to assess organizational factors and performance of research units.[28] This study involved 11,000 participants in about 1,200 research units located in Austria, Belgium, Finland, Hungary, Poland, and Sweden. Information was collected by means of questionnaires from five types of respondents: research unit heads, other professional members of the units, technical support personnel in the units, unit administrators, and external evaluators. Ten basic performance indicators were obtained from the questionnaire: Published written output; Patents and prototypes; Reports and algorithms; General contribution to science and technology; Recognition accorded to the unit; Social effectiveness of the unit; Training effectiveness of the unit; Administrative effectiveness of the unit; R&D effectiveness of the unit; and Applications effectiveness of the unit.

The source of the quantitative indicators (items 1–3) was the unit head, who was asked to supply the number of products of each type produced by his unit during the previous three years. Measures of the qualitative indicators (items 4–10) were developed from ratings on a five point scale by the unit head, a staff scientist from the unit, and one or more external evaluators (items 5 and 10 were not rated by the external evaluators). For purposes of analysis, the data were grouped by country, type of research unit, and scientific field. The authors of the study acknowledge that ideally, one would not use as sources of the output, members of the research unit being assessed. They felt, however, that unit members know how good their work is and, given strong pledges of confidentiality, would provide accurate ratings. They also found agreement between the ratings from the external judges and those from the unit members.

Byatt and Cohen[29] suggest an approach for quantifying the output of basic research that may appeal to those who are comfortable with the idea of expressing such outputs in economic terms. Their interest is in measuring the long-term benefits resulting from the applications in the economy of fundamental ideas resulting from basic research. Such research can be considered a type of investment which gives rise to major industries or to the complete reorientation of existing industries in several decades or less. Examples are the electricity, semiconductor, and nuclear power industries. Each industry provides or will provide some total economic benefit to the nation. This total benefit can be discounted to a present value at the beginning of the applied research directly relevant to the industry. The discounted value of the necessary applied research, development, and physical investment can be deducted to give a capitalized net benefit.

To estimate the value of a particular scientific discovery is to ask what the effect on the net benefit would have been if the discovery in question had been delayed (or accelerated) as a result of changes in research expenditure. Thus Byatt and Cohen's interest is in the economic consequences of marginal changes in government support for basic research, not in the consequences of a discovery not being made at all. Note that since the time lag between fundamental discoveries which eventually lead to whole new industries and the start of the new industry can be from 15 to 50 years, such changes in research expenditures may in some cases have little economic consequence. The calculations required for such an approach will, of course, be quite crude.

Perhaps the most meaningful way of dealing with the output measurement problem is the method used by Allen[30] in his evaluation of communication and information networks used by scientists and engineers and their organizations. Allen selected for study, sets of two or more groups or projects that had been established to solve the same collection of technical problems. He cleverly located such "twin projects" through RFP's announced in the Commerce Business Daily. Allen thus took advantage of situations which involved the replication of R&D activities. The quality of these common outputs of the twin projects was evaluated by the technical personnel in the government laboratories whose responsibility it was to monitor and evaluate the work.

tinely calculated since 1971 and have been used both to compare departments with each other and to monitor the progress of departments over time. The departmental ratings are also used as one of four equally weighted factors which determine the annual bonus each department head receives.

The project ratings are not applied mechanically. Extenuating circumstances are taken into account. For example, projects that would otherwise have been assigned a "zero," are assigned a "one" if failure to meet the objectives was due to factors outside the control of the project team. Because of this, employee response to the system, after an initial resistance and uneasiness, tends to be positive.

The second part of the system—evaluating the potential value of each research project that has been turned over to some other company unit for further development—is a much more complex procedure than the first. The calculations require estimating:

(1)   The entire market for which the new development is technically and economically suited;

(2)   The customer's total cost to accomplish the function the new development is intended to serve, assuming the customer uses the best present alternative to the new development;

(3)   The annual income resulting from sales to the entire market if the price of the new development were set so that the customer's total cost were equal to the value estimated in (2).

Step (3) gives the value of the business opportunity generated by the new development. The efficiency of a research unit in producing opportunity is obtained by summing the value of all business opportunities generated by research projects during the year and dividing by the total cost of operating the research unit being evaluated. This calculation yields a return-on-research index for the research unit. Both the total opportunity produced and the return-on-research index

are used to make cross-departmental and year-to-year comparisons. Different categories of research are also compared in these ways. An example of a business opportunity calculation is provided in a previous *Research Management* article.[3]

COLLECTING R&D PRODUCTIVITY INDEXES

The Corporate Engineering Department of the Phillips Petroleum Company has developed and currently uses numerical indicators to represent the productivity of those sections whose outputs were determined to be at least somewhat uniform and countable.[4] These include the Design, Cost Estimating, and Illustrated Drafting Sections. Examples of outputs that are counted from these sections are flow sheets, cost estimates, and drawings. Standard times to produce each type of output were developed over a two-year period. Complexity factors were also established to take into account different levels of complexity for outputs of a given type. Drawing density and the number of items in a cost estimate are examples of such factors. Productivity of individual sections is measured each quarter by indexes which compare actual hours per output for the quarter to standard hours per output. The output count is performed by the section supervisors.

The productivity indexes are used as aids in staffing and as barometric indicators of possible problem areas. However, they are primarily used to satisfy a blanket corporate requirement that all units of the company develop a system of productivity measures and incorporate them into the management system. The engineering staff covered by the productivity system, which includes chemical, civil, and electrical engineers, are not comfortable with the indexes. They question the meaningfulness of the output measures, which are basically counts of things. Also, as technical and professional employees, they resent and resist being measured in this way. As a result, Corporate Engineering plans to replace the current output collection method with one that is nonobtrusive. The output counts will be obtained from already existing data sources. However, the more passive collection method will not be able to include the complexity factors.

Detroit Edison uses "the number of drawings per engineering staff-hour" and "the number of engineering projects (adjusted by a complexity factor) per engineering staff-hour" to measure the productivity of engineering units.[5] Productivity improvement programs are regularly evaluated in terms of the estimated annual savings in engineering staff-years produced by the program. For example, replacing manual map records with computer-generated maps reduced the number of drafters required to maintain the maps from 50 to 10. This type of measurement is possible because the same service or output is provided both before and after the improvement.

Another area where we found an example of actual performance being regularly compared to established standards is software development for large, one-of-a-kind computer systems. The outputs in this company plant are defined in terms of "delivered source lines of code," which are all lines that a programmer writes except comments, and in terms of the amount of high-speed memory used. Judgmental weights reflecting the difficulty of the program are also assigned. The input side of the index is programmer-weeks.

A fourth company relies heavily on comparative analysis and trends because of the difficulty of quantifying the productivity of research and development. All units within the company attempt to measure or monitor productivity. However, each unit uses methods considered most appropriate for its function, and consequently, the methods vary from unit to unit. The executive vice president of the company briefly described the methods for basic research, development, and engineering units:

Our basic research management stresses technical evaluation methods to measure performance. These include science panels to judge the quality of their science resources and impact of discoveries, indices of literature citations to measure external impact and perceptions, analysis of patents, and value ratings for research projects, taking into account an estimate of the probability of a discovery and the potential value of such a discovery.

Our developmental research management uses resource allocation indices to monitor research efficiency. These indices measure such things as the number of analytical tests performed per professional, the number of reactors operated per professional, the number of laboratory technicians per professional, and the number of pilot plant non-professionals per professional. The trend of these indices, or more specifically changes in the trends, serve as a barometer to pay closer attention to productivity.

Techniques used by our engineering management include the use of special task forces to study and judge effectiveness, comparison of internal manpower and costs versus those of outside contractors for similar jobs, and trend analysis of internal costs and manpower requirements for engineering tasks. We also conduct before and after studies of a specified group to identify and study changes in productivity due to implementation or removal of a purported productivity improvement device (various uses of computers, for example).

A fifth company evaluates its divisions by means of a "figure of merit" which is essentially a measure of the return on R&D investment. The index is defined as the pre-tax profit earned during a five-year period divided by the relevant R&D expenditures. The company assumes that changes in sales and profits are due to changes in R&D expenditures, and that the impact of other functions, such as production and marketing, is relatively constant. The index is computed for each division, and is used to help determine salary increases and promotions of division managers. The company also occasionally prepares "vintage charts" which depict sales in a given year of products developed in previous years. From these charts, the company determines its "vintage years."

The director of an R&D division in another company estimates the following quantities before the development of a product and compares them to actuals after the commercialization of the product: the three-year pre-tax earnings expected if the product is developed; the cost of developing the product; the ratio of these two estimates; the time required to develop the product; and the staff-months required. The before estimates are made in conjunction with the marketing department and are based on its best judgment of the size and penetration of the market. The before and after estimates are prepared in tabular form for each program or product.

The director feels that the method is relatively simple, easy to apply, and does not require much time to operate. Since the method was begun in 1970-71, they have constantly challenged themselves, with help from the literature and other divisions in the company, to come up with a better method, but have not found one. Performance, as measured by the method, is not directly tied to individual salaries, although at the program level a poor performance could affect the bonuses distributed to the program. The director views the method primarily as a self-educational process, and as a vehicle for communication with and among his managers. Also, it serves as an internal control device.

A QUANTITATIVE ALGORITHM

Over the last decade, one company has experimented with various forms of a quantitative algorithm which is used annually for ranking the outputs of its R&D programs. The algorithm, which provides a "program value," currently includes four factors: potential annual benefit, probability of commercialization, competitive technical status, and comprehensiveness of the

R&D program. These are evaluated on a series of judgmental rating scales. The company's manager of R&D planning provided the following guidelines for calculating a "program value":

The starting point in the calculation of a "program value" is the evaluation of potential annual benefit. Potential annual benefit is defined as annual pretax income which will result from successful commercialization of the research or development program output. Financial benefits can come in three principal ways:

1. A totally new product and business may result from a R&D program, generating income through new sales.
2. R&D programs may allow new features to be added to existing products and so protect, and possibly extend, existing sales.
3. R&D programs may also be effective in producing cost improvements.

The output of a given R&D program may impact several areas and possibly several businesses, and more than one can be included in the potential benefit, provided separate benefits are shown for each.

The next factor to be considered is the "probability of commercialization." This attempts to assess the overall fit of the R&D program with strategic plans, long term goals, and aspirations of present or future businesses. As a rough guide the following quantitative values might be used, with intermediate or extrapolated values if necessary.

Factor	Probability of Commercialization
1.0	Transfer of technology is underway or covered in strategic plans of the businesses.
.7	Technology is closely related to business interests and the businesses have some investment in the technology.

.4   Low interest level or negative view in existing businesses.

.1   No business home yet identified for program output.

The third factor is "competitive technical status." This factor attempts to recognize the intrinsic competitive status of the R&D effort, historical strengths, caliber of resources and position, and momentum with respect to competitive efforts. Again as a guide:

Factor	Competitive Technical Status
1.0	The program has had continued historic scientific and technical leadership and is ahead of competitive activities.
.8	The scientific and technical approach is believed to be superior.
.5	The approach is equally effective as parallel competitive R&D.
.3	Other approaches are receiving heavy support but the approach in question has specific advantages.
.1	The work is a backup or alternative solution where competitive approaches being pursued elsewhere are likely to succeed.

The final factor is "comprehensiveness." As pointed out in the discussion on potential benefit, some latitude is allowed in the choice of product when determining future sales. Some R&D programs comprehensively address the complete product. These programs are clearly central to the achievement of sales and the potential benefit should not be discounted. Benefits which are calculated from direct cost improvements should not be discounted by the comprehensiveness factor either. Other R&D programs may have a specific target which is only part of the complete product for which sales were identified. In still other areas, programs may be only vaguely addressing the potential annual benefit as the work is still in an early stage of definition. Again as a guide:

Factor	Comprehensiveness of R&D Program
1.0	All cost reductions result directly from the R&D program, or the R&D program comprehensively addresses the product used for calculation of potential annual benefit.
.3	The program comprehensively addresses the principal component or major technical area of the product used to calculate potential annual benefit.
.1	The program addresses one of several major components or key technical areas critical to the product used to calculate potential annual benefit.
.01	The program is targeted to a general area of opportunity. Vague connection between the R&D program and total benefits claimed as potential annual benefit.

The calculation of "program value" now proceeds as follows:

1. Estimated annual new or protected sales for complete product
2. OR—annual cost improvements
3. Potential annual benefit = (assumed percentage of line 1 that represents average incremental pretax income plus 100% of line 2)
4. Probability of commercialization
5. Competitive technical status
6. Comprehensiveness
7. Program value = line 3 × 4 × 5 × 6
8. Total program value is sum over all businesses or products
9. A discount factor can be added depending on the number of years to potential annual benefit.

As mentioned earlier, the details of the "program value" calculation change from time to time. Although each program manager can compute his own program's value by means of the algorithm, the company does not attach much significance to the exact values of the program value parameters. On the other hand, large differences between program values, like two orders of magnitude, do give a good indication of priority and are considered an excellent starting point for questioning the relative effort. Thus the algorithm does not constitute a decision-making mechanism, but rather is an instrument used in making decisions regarding how to change the R&D program mix. Judgments regarding the productivity of the programs are a factor in these decisions. However, the "program value" is not explicitly related to a measure of input in order to systematically measure productivity.

OTHER INDICATORS

Two other companies regularly monitor the technical excellence of their R&D programs by keeping track of such indicators as the number of patent disclosures and publications produced, honors and awards received by R&D staff, staff elected to national academies, and government committees staff are asked to serve on. While records are kept of these indicators, no attempt is made to systematically relate them to input indicators. Rather, managers use them along with other information (actual versus expected products, costs, and schedules) to make an integrated judgment regarding the performance of their R&D programs.

Officials of the central research laboratory in another company view such things as patents, publications, and meetings attended as "image enhancements," but not as outputs to be related to inputs. They do try to measure the productivity increase due to investment in labor-saving equipment. For example, they estimate that in 1979, certain types of experiments were accomplished with 10 less people than were used in previous years as a result of investment in equipment to help facilitate the conduct of the experiments. Since the laboratory staff numbers about 500, this translates into a 2 percent increase in productivity.

Officials from two other companies each mentioned a productivity indicator that they collect from time to time in order to track trends.

- Number of patent applications per professional (and per employee). A patent attorney appraises each patent on a scale from one to five, and the company vice-president in charge of the laboratory (or someone on his staff) grades the relevance of each patent to the company's business, also on a scale from one to five.
- Costs to support R&D staff per number of cases of goods produced. (Ranftl[2] (pp. 44–47) lists a number of quantitative and qualitative productivity indicators used off and on by Hughes managers. Several on his list have been mentioned above; others, such as, "sales per employee," "profit per payroll dollar," "absentee rate," do not seem particularly germane to our concerns. And Bell Labs, in one "attempt to encompass the immeasurable," compiled a list of 683 Bell system innovations for the period 1927 through 1977 which their technical experts felt represented significant discoveries).[6]

OBSTACLES TO MEASURING PRODUCTIVITY

It is generally felt that the major obstacle to measuring R&D productivity is the difficulty of measuring the output of R&D. As we saw, some go so far as to say there is *no* way to measure R&D outputs, and some even say the idea of measuring R&D outputs, and hence R&D productivity, makes no sense. We conclude that this is a half truth. Without wanting to minimize the problem of measuring outputs, we believe that the major problem in measuring R&D productivity comes after an output is measured: it is the problem of finding another output to compare with it. Systems which are based on comparing actual with planned performance, such as the first part of the Borg-Warner system, will provide comparable productivity data only if the projects themselves are comparable, and only if common rather than relative targets are compared to actual performance.

Our belief that the essence of R&D productivity measurement is finding meaningful comparisons, whether over time in a given organization or across organizations, is a recognition of the fact that a productivity measurement of an organization at one point in time is of no value if it cannot be compared to another measurement. This, of course, is not unique to R&D organizations—it applies to any type of organization. ("It is hard to imagine any use for a single measure of productivity. . . . Productivity measures exist largely to be compared—we are interested almost exclusively in productivity differences or productivity changes."[7]) In short, then, the idea of measuring R&D productivity makes sense only if there are reasonable comparisons.

REFERENCES

1. Ranftl, R. M., "Improving R&D Productivity—A Study Program and Its Application," *Research Management:* Jan. 1977, pp. 25-29.
2. Ranftl, R. M., *R&D Productivity,* Culver City, CA: Hughes Aircraft Company 1978 (second edition).
3. Collier, D. W. "Measuring the Performance of R&D Departments," *Research Management:* Vol. 20, No. 2, March 1977, pp. 30-34
4. Millis, W. B., "Productivity Improvement Programs: What One Engineering Organization Is Doing," *Proceedings of the Conference Improving the Productivity of Technical Resources:* Chicago: IIT Manufacturing Productivity Center, 1980.
5. Coombe, L. W., "Engineering Productivity Improvement at Detroit Edison Company," *Proceedings of the Conference, Improving the Productivity of Technical Resources;* Chicago: IIT Manufacturing Productivity Center, 1980.
6. McKay, K. G., "The Measure of Innovation," *Bell Laboratories Record;* July/August 1980.
7. National Research Council, *Measurement and Interpretation of Productivity;* Washington, D.C.: National Academy of Sciences, 1979, pp. 21-22.
8. Thor, C. G., "Productivity Program Development and Measurement in a Technical Group," *Proceedings of the Conference, Improving the Productivity of Technical Resources.* Chicago: IIT Manufacturing Productivity Center, 1980.
9. Ruch, W. A., "Measuring Knowledge Worker Productivity," paper presented at Conference on Productivity Research: American Productivity Center, April 20-24, 1980.
10. Mundel, M. E., "Measures of Productivity," *Industrial Engineering;* Vol. 8, No. 5, 1976
11. Terleckyj, N. E., "Productivity Analysis Tempered with Judgment Improves Efficiency," *Defense Management Journal:* Vol. 8, No. 3, Oct. 1972, pp. 25-28.
12. Newburn, R. M. Measuring Productivity in Organizations with Unquantifiable End-Products. *Personnel Journal.* Vol. 51, No. 9, September 1972, pp. 655-657.
13. "Measuring Engineering Efficiency," *Chemical Engineering,* December 24, 1962. pp. 91-92.
14. Baumgartel, G. P. and Johnson, T. D., *Productivity Measurement in a Base Level USAF Civil Engineering Organization,* Master's thesis presented to Air Force Institute of Technology, Air University, School of Systems and Logistics. Wright-Patterson AFB, OH, June 1979.
15. Erickson, J. M., *A Firm Model for Productivity Assessment and White-Collar Productivity Measurement.,* Masters Thesis, University of Minnesota, October 1980.
16. Tauss, K. H., "A Pragmatic Approach to Evaluating R&D Programs," *Research Management;* September 1975, pp. 13-15.
17. Zink, D. A., "Monitoring the Adequacy of the

Amount and Productivity of Engineering and Construction Manpower," *1980 Transactions of the American Association of Cost Engineers;* Morgantown, W.V.: American Association of Cost Engineers, 1980.

18. Aynardi, L., Kustuna, J. J., and Shauer, H. L., Measuring Engineering Productivity in a Large Instrument and Electrical Department; ISA AC 1976.

19. Hodge, M. H., "Rate Your Company's Research Productivity," *Harvard Business Review,* Vol. 41, No. 6, Nov–Dec. 1963, pp. 109–122.

20. Koser, M. C., *Quantitative Scientist/Engineer Productivity and Some Associated Individual and Organizational Variables,* Thesis; Air Force Institute of Technology. Wright-Patterson AFB, Ohio, December 1976.

21. Stahl, M. J. and Steger, J. A., "Measuring Innovation and Productivity A Peer Rating Approach," *Research Management;* Vol. 20, No. 1, Jan. 1977, pp. 35–38.

22. Sher, I. H. and Garfield, E., "New Tools for Improving and Evaluating the Effectiveness of Research," in *Research Program Effectiveness,* ed. by M. C. Yovits, D. M. Gilford, R. H. Wilcox, E. Staveley, and H.D. Lerner; New York, Gordon and Breach, 1966, pp. 137–146.

23. Edwards, S. A. and McCarrey, M. W., "Measuring the Performance of Researchers," *Research Management;* Vol. 16, No. 1, Jan. 1973, pp. 34–41.

24. Vollmer, H. N., "Evaluating Two Aspects of Quality in Research Program Effectiveness," In *Research Program Effectiveness;* ed. by M. C. Yovits, D. M. Gilford, R. H. Wilcox, E. Staveley, and H. D. Lerner, New York: Gordon and Breach, 1966, pp. 149–167.

25. Hall, J. T. and Dixon, R. A., *Productivity Measurement in R&D: Productivity Measurement Experiment (PROMEX) in Selected Research and Development Programs at the National Bureau of Standards,* NBS Technical Note 890; Washington D.C.: U.S. Government Printing Office, 1975.

26. U.S. Committee on Federal Laboratories, Federal Council for Science and Technology. *Performance Measures for Research and Development,* Vol. 1., Executive Summary and Report, May 1973.

27. Lipetz, B., *The Measurement of Efficiency of Scientific Research;* Carlisle, MA: Intermedia, Inc., 1965.

28. Andrews, F. M. (Ed.), *Scientific Productivity;* London: Cambridge U. Press and Unesco, 1979.

29. Byatt, I. R. C. and Cohen, A. V., *An Attempt to Quantify the Economic Benefits of Scientific Research;* Science Policy Series 4, London: H.M.S.O. 1969.

30. Allen, T. J., *Managing the Flow of Technology;* Cambridge, Mass: The MIT Press 1978.

Project Hindsight: A Defense Department Study of the Utility of Research

Chalmers W. Sherwin

Raymond S. Isenson

No matter how much science and technology may add to the quality of life, no matter how brilliant and meritorious are its practitioners, and no matter how many individual results that have been of social and economic significance are pointed to with pride, the fact remains that public support of the overall enterprise on the present scale eventually demands satisfactory economic measures of benefit. The question is not whether such measures should be made, it is only how to make them.

We wish to report here on an attempt by the Department of Defense to make such measures. This effort, known as Project Hindsight, is a study of the role that research played in the development of weapon systems between the end of World War II and about 1962.

To appreciate the need for Project Hindsight one has merely to examine the budget of the Defense Department. In recent years, the Department has been spending $300 to $400 million a year for "research." Of this sum, we estimate that about 25 percent is committed to basic or undirected science, although concentrated in areas generally relevant to the DOD missions,

and about 75 percent to applied science more directly related to defined DOD needs. The Department has been spending an additional billion dollars a year for "exploratory development," which includes the more sharply defined applied research, small-component development, and other activities of the sort generally characterized as "technology." (This $1.4-billion expenditure does not include the system development programs which are its main reason for existence.) Questions were constantly being asked, both in the Executive Branch of Government and in Congress: Was this large a sum really needed? What has been the return for the expenditure? Can the Defense Department not depend for more of its science and technology on the private sector of on other Government agencies? These are reasonable questions, but there seemed to be no systematic, quantitative answers. One of the objects of Project Hindsight was to try to provide such answers; that is, to try to measure the payoff to Defense of its own investments in science and technology. A second object was to see whether there were some patterns of management that led more frequently than others to usable results and that might therefore suggest ways in which the management of research could be improved. In particular, we wanted to deter-

Reprinted from *Science,* June 1967, pp. 1571–1577 with permission of the publisher. Copyright 1967 by AAAS.

mine the relative contributions of the defense and non-defense sectors, and, within the defense sector, the relative contributions of in-house laboratories and those of contractors.

ASSUMPTIONS AND METHODS

Given these objects, how does one start? Since the challenge was essentially an economic one, the answers would have to be based upon economic benefits. The economic return of a scientific or technical innovation is through its utilization in an end-item—a piece of equipment, a process, or an operational procedure. Therefore in order to assess return one has to measure the value of the end-item made possible by the innovation. As a practical matter, for military hardware the easiest way of measuring economic benefit is by comparing the value of an end-item with that of some predecessor end-item which it partly or wholly replaces.

Our method of analysis was as follows: One begins by comparing a successor item with a predecessor, identifying all the contributions from science and technology which were significant in the improvement in performance or the reduction in cost of the item. One then estimates the portion of the increase in the cost-benefit of the end-item which is attributable to the scientific and technical innovations utilized. (This portion is, of course, very large for defense equipment.) One then calculates what it would cost to obtain enough predecessor equipment to do the job that the successor equipment is now doing, assuming that the same capital resources and management skills were available for the predecessor as for the successor. The difference between this cost and the actual cost of the successor is a measure of the economic benefit assignable to the set of significant contributions from science and technology which were utilized in the successor and not in the predecessor. Although this method makes it possible to attach an economic value to the set

of identified technical contributions, it has the effect of focusing on recent contributions from science and technology, for, as might be expected, the difference in technological content between the successor and predecessor is found to be predominantly of recent origin. (The time between predecessor and successor in defense equipment is typically 10 to 20 years.) Since the common base extant at the time of the predecessor is largely ignored, the method has built into it a bias against the identification and evaluation of longer-range research. We were aware of this bias from the beginning of the study, but since what we were interested in was the utilization of knowledge generated in the past 15 to 20 years, it seemed not to cast doubt on the soundness of the method.

THE PROCESS OF ANALYSIS

The most critical step in the analysis was the identification of the key contributions, those which significantly improved the performance or reduced the cost of the successor. The insight of a team of scientists and engineers, working together, and experienced in the system being analyzed, was essential. Each contribution then had to be traced back (again, by scientists and engineers) to a time and place of origin or, as it often turned out, to two or three (usually related) sources. Although we were not sure when we started that a key contribution could be traced back to identifiable people at a definite time, or to an "Event" as it came to be called, we found that almost invariably it could. We shall give some examples shortly.

Research Events are distinguished on the on hand from routine engineering design, and on the other from the broad base of knowledge generally available, or "in the textbooks." An Event is defined as a period of creative effort ending with new, significant knowledge or with the demonstration of the applicability of a new engineering concept. Each Event was written up in a standard format giving considerable detail regarding its significance to the system, its relation to contemporary science and technology, key personnel, and so on.

Having selected the retrospective approach for the reasons described above, we found that it had additional advantages. First, tracing backwards in time from utilization to the originating Event is much easier than the reverse process, for the user of technical information almost invariably knows his sources, whereas the source frequently does not know the ultimate user. A second advantage is that, when one starts with and end-item and tabulates all the significant contributions that have made its improved performance possible, one gets a good perspective on the relative numbers and the importance of the contributions from different sources. Typically, scientists and engineers use the "example argument"; that is, they trace one idea at a time from a source to an application, begging the questions What *other* ideas were important in making the end-item practical? Where did they come from? (For this reason, forward-tracing of ideas does not lead easily to quantitative, economic analysis unless one makes a complete detailed technical analysis of the end-item which brings us right back to the Hindsight approach.) Or even more frequently, enthusiasts point to *anticipated* applications, which are even harder to evaluate since many of the supporting innovations have yet to be created, and whose economic value is almost completely a matter of speculation.

THE SYSTEMS STUDIED

The first study in the project, begun in 1964, was an analysis, made by a small group of scientists and engineers working in the Defense Department, of the "Bullpup" air-to-ground tactical guided missile system. The effort was augmented by a contract study performed by Arthur D. Lit-

tle, Inc. on six additional systems. These early studies developed the techniques and demonstrated the feasibility of the method of analysis. Then in the summer of 1965, with the support of Harold Brown, then Director of Defense Research and Engineering, a much larger effort was undertaken by teams of Defense Department scientists and engineers working closely with the principal contractors. All told, 20 systems of diverse character were studied, and we estimate that some 40 professional man-years were expended. Counting the initial study group and the Arthur D. Little team, there have been 13 different teams independently analyzing systems for key contributions and tracing them back to their origins. There are now 710 documented Events in the data file. We think it is significant that, in spite of the diversity of end-items studied (for a list see Table 1), and in spite of the fact that 13 different teams made the analyses, the conclusions are of a piece. Indeed, the properties of our sample have not changed substantially since the data base included fewer than 100 Events.

TABLE 1.   *Systems Studied in Project Hindsight*

Hound Dog, air-to-surface missile
Bullpup, air-to-surface missile
Polaris, submarine-launched ballistic missile
Minuteman I, intercontinental ballistic missile
Minuteman II, intercontinental ballistic missile
Sergeant, tactical ballistic missile
Lance, tactical ballistic missile
Mark 46 Mod 0, acoustical torpedo
Mark 46 Mod 1, acoustical torpedo
M-102, 105-mm howitzer
AN/SPS-48, frequency scan search radar
Mark 56, sea mine
Mark 57, sea mine
Starlight Scope, night vision instrument
C-141, transport aircraft
Navigation Satellite
M-61, nuclear warhead
M-63, nuclear warhead
XM-409, 152-mm artillery round
FADAC, digital computer for field operations

TYPES OF EVENTS
AND SOME EXAMPLES

The identified Events are classified according to the intention with which the work that led to them was carried out. *Science Events* are defined as theoretical or experimental studies of new or unexplored natural phenomena. Science Events are divided into two categories: *Undirected Science,* in which the object of the work is the advancement of knowledge, without regard to possible application, and *Applied* or *Directed Science,* in which the object of the work is to produce specific knowledge or an understanding of phenomena which is needed for some particular use or uses. *Technology Events* include the conception or demonstration of the possibility of performing a specific elementary function with the use of new or untried concepts, principles, techniques, or materials; the first demonstration of the possibility of performing a specific elementary function with the use of established concepts, principles, or materials; the measurement of the behavior of materials and equipment as required for design; or the development of new manufacturing techniques.

An example of a series of related technology Events involved the development, starting in 1949, of the titanium-aluminum-vanadium alloy used in the compressor blades of the turbo-fan engine in the C-141 transport aircraft. The high and uniform strength-to-weight ratio, the corrosion and erosion resistance, and the notch-toughness and creep resistance of this material substantially increased the efficiency and reliability and reduced the weight and extended the life of the engine compared to what they would have been had one used the steel blades employed in the turbine engine that drives the propellers on the C-130A aircraft (the predecessor system). The early development of this alloy was the result of the efforts of individuals in two organizations. Some of the basic work was done in 1949 and 1950 at the Armour Research Foundation, supported by the Army and the Air Force, for military applications. At about the same time, further work was performed at the Battelle Memorial Institute funded partly by the Air Force and partly by industry (the Remcru Titanium Corporation). Over the next 10 years, Remcru and others carried the alloy developed for them at Battelle into production, and thus it was available for use in the Pratt and Whitney turbo-fan engine used in the C-141, where the team identified it. This material is known to have many other military and commercial applications as well.

Another example, also a series of related Events, is the development of the anti-jam radio link that controlled the Bullpup missile, designed (in 1954) and built by the Martin Company. This radio control link was critically dependent upon the principle of correlation detection which emerged in 1942 at the Massachusetts Institute of Technology from Norbert Wiener's theory of correlation, statistical filtering, and prediction. (An applied science Event, since at the time Wiener was working on the problem of anti-aircraft fire control.) Then (1947–1950) Lee, Cheatham, Singleton, and Wiesner of the Research Laboratory for Electronics at M.I.T. applied Wiener's general correlation techniques to the specific case of radar modulation and detection and demonstrated that very large improvements in signal-to-noise ratios were possible. (An applied science Event.) In 1952, J. Alpert of the Martin Corporation picked up the M.I.T. results at a technical meeting and, using them as a starting point, developed a practical jam-resistant radio link as a proposed alternative to the guidance system of the Matador missile. (A technology Event). The link was never used for the Matador system, but the concept was available for use in the engineering design of Bullpup in 1954.

Our third example is a series of six related Events. The performance of the SPS-48 radar depends critically upon a high-power hydrogen thyratron not available for the predecessor system, the SP radar of design date 1944. The historical analysis made by the team (mostly from the Naval Research Laboratory) revealed the following sequence. In 1942, K. Germeshausen, working alone, but starting with a knowledge of the work on hydrogen-filled triodes for electronic sweep circuits reported in 1936 by P. Drewell, in Germany, developed the boxed anode structure which made the high voltage thyratron possible. (A technology Event.) Drewell's work was not included as an Event, for it substantially antedated the period of interest. In 1943, to prevent gas "clean-up" due to impurities in the electrodes, the International Nickel Company, working with Germeshausen, developed an electrolytic refining process. (A technology Event.) In 1944 Marsh and Rothstein, of the Army Signal Corps Laboratories, by theoretical calculation of the internal electric field identified the source of the "long path breakdown problem," pointing the direction for the new electrode designs. (An applied science Event.) In 1945, Germeshausen at the M.I.T. Radiation Laboratory, in collaboration with Marsh and Rothstein, conceived and demonstrated the practicality of the titanium hydride reservoir needed to compensate for the residual hydrogen clean-up accompanying very-high-voltage operation. (A technology Event.) In 1951–1955, Martin, Goldberg, and Riley, all of Edgerton, Germeshausen & Grier Company, as a result of a detailed theoretical and experimental study of the hydrogen gas discharge and its effect on tube life, were able to develop a much smaller, more rugged, longer-lived tube. (A technology Event.) Finally, in 1957, the same group developed the high-temperature, metal and ceramic long-life tubes (A technology Event) which were actually used in the SPS-48 radar and which so significantly contributed to its performance and reliability.

The six technology and three applied science Events described above are representative of the type of work identified in the study as the basis of improved system performance, except that if anything these Events have more science content and less practical engineering content than the population of Events as a whole. We hope we can explain below why it is that such practical, even "pedestrian" technical efforts are credited with so big a role in improving weapon systems.

MANY INNOVATIONS ARE NEEDED

When a weapon system is compared with its predecessor of 10 to 20 years earlier, its ratio of performance to cost and its mean time to failure typically are greater by factors of 2 to 10. Moreover, the operating manpower needed to obtain the same calculated military effectiveness usually drops by a factor of 2 or more. That is, the increase in effectiveness/cost is often 100 percent or more. Yet when one examines the equipment design in detail and tries to determine why this large change has occurred, no one item seems capable of accounting for more than a small fraction of the net change. Thus, for example, if one were forced to use the older steel compressor blades in the C-141 turbo-fan engines, rather than the titanium-aluminum-vanadium alloy mentioned above, the performance of the aircraft would be reduced only slightly, perhaps a percent or so. Still, the C-141 designed in 1964 has a ton-mile cost of only 60 percent that of the turboprop C-130 designed in 1954, which did use steel compressor blades. A careful examination of the C-141 design shows, however, that there are a large number of identifiable significant technical contributions which together explain the improved performance.

In the case of the C-141, the team from Wright Air Development Center, working with the help of engineers from the Pratt and Whitney Division of United Aircraft and from Lockheed Corporation, analyzed over 80 Events that they judged to be the most significant in accounting for the improved performance of the C-141. Some two or three times as many additional Events were tentatively identified but were not subjected to a detailed historical tracing because the study was terminated when the analysis showed that the Events tended to conform to a uniform pattern with respect to motivation, time to utilization, and so forth.

Our finding in the case of the C-141 was repeated in all the systems we studied—that is, it is the interactions of many mutually reinforcing innovations that appear to account for most of the increase in performance/cost of weapon systems compared to their predecessors.

In the larger systems, 50 to 100 Events were common. Even for small pieces of equipment a number of Events—18 in the case of the night-vision device, for example—were readily identified.

We should, perhaps, note here that an appreciation of the significance of the finding which we have just described is crucial to an understanding of the whole study. All 13 teams arrived at the same conclusion. They simply could not find a dominant invention or discovery which by itself seemed to account for most of the performance/cost increase. Even the invention of the transistor, brilliant though it was, was followed by a long series of other Events in both transistors and components which were necessary before its full benefits could be realized. Incidentally, we classified the series of eight transistor Events occurring at the Bell Telephone Laboratories as applied science since they occurred in a mission-oriented environment and were clearly in support of the mission. Together, the transistor-associated Events did play a dominant role in the FADAC computer and in certain parts of other systems such as the on-board electronics in the Minuteman, the torpedo, and the satellite.

AN IMPORTANT APPROXIMATION

At this point we make a zero-order approximation: we will treat all Events as if they were of equal value. Even in a given system, this cannot be true in detail, and it certainly cannot be true when one considers uses in more than one system, such as the sequences of transistor and aluminum-weldment Events, which contributed more frequently and more importantly than others of a much more specialized nature. We are not satisfied with this assumption but see no easy way to avoid it, for much of the value of an Event is derived from its association with other Events and even some of the most elegant contributions that we have identified would have remained unutilized in the absence of a complementary display of creativity in related areas. Within this study, therefore, we have been limited to the mere number of identified Events, and this means that any inferences based upon such counts are reasonably dependable only when they are based upon large numerical ratios.

A SUMMARY OF THE DATA

Let us then look at the total data base of 710 Events.

First, we find that 9 percent of the Events are classified as science Events and 91 percent as technology Events. The science Events are distributed as follows: 6.7 percent of all Events were motivated by a DOD need and are therefore classified as applied science: 2 percent were motivated by a commercial or non-defense need and are also applied science. Only 0.3 percent of all Events were classified as undirected science. Of all science Events 76 percent were motivated by a DOD need. If we look at the technology Events, we find that, of all Events, 27 percent were directed at what we call a "generic, DOD-oriented technology," that is, a broad class of defense needs not related to a particular system of system concept—for example, high-power radar components, improved solid propellants, or titanium alloys. Forty-one percent of all Events were motivated by a system or system concept in the early or "advanced development" stage, and 20 percent by systems in the later, or "engineering development," stage. Finally, 3 percent of all Events were motivated by non-DOD end-item need. Of the technology Events 97 percent were motivated by a DOD need. Overall, nearly 95 percent of all Events were directed toward filling a DOD need.

We found that in the great majority of cases the initial recognition of need came from an external group associated with systems design, but that the technical initiative for the solution came primarily from the research-performing group. That is, the need-recognizers made the researchers aware of the nature of the problems but did not dictate the nature of the solutions.

We find that 86 percent of the Events were funded directly by the Department of Defense and an additional 9 percent by defense-oriented

industry. Only 3 percent were funded by commercially oriented industry, and only 1 percent by other government agencies. One percent were funded by other sources. It is interesting that, although the non-defense sector had available an estimated 40 percent of all science and technology funds expended in the U.S. during the period covered by the study, only 5 percent of the Events identified by Project Hindsight were funded there. Per dollar of input effort, the non-defense sector produced less than one-tenth as many defense-utilized innovations as did the defense sector.

We tabulated the time distribution of the occurrence of Events for all systems with respect to the engineering design date. The results are shown in Figure 1. Several significant features

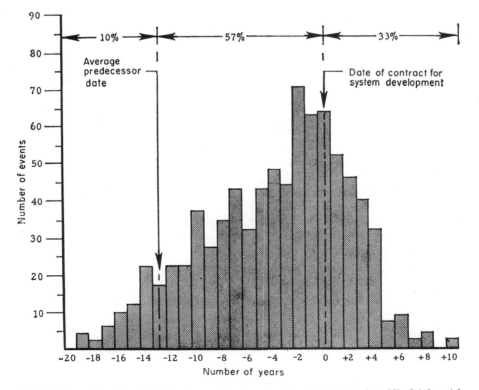

FIGURE 1. The Time Distribution of the Events Identified in Project Hindsight with Respect to the Development-Contract Dates of the Systems in which the Events Appear

can be seen from this figure. The average time interval between predecessor and successor is 13 years, and only 10 percent of the Events utilized in the successor had occurred by the time the predecessor was designed. This demonstrates that it is indeed recent technical activity that accounts for the specific advances to which the improved performance is ascribed. It is significant that many innovations generated after the engineering design date, or contract date, were utilized, some during the system-engineering processes and some even later in the stage called "operational systems development." Despite the very applied nature of the work leading to the innovations, 5 or 10 years often elapsed before an Event was used (see Figure 1). The median delay for science Events was 9 years, and for technology Events 5 years. One should not, then, be surprised that in a study covering as little as 20 years undirected work should not be found to play a significant role.

Of the research-performing organizations, we found that industry accounted for 47 percent of the Events, DOD in-house laboratories for 39 percent, universities (including contract research centers) for 12 percent, non-DOD federal for 2 percent, and foreign for less than 2 percent. This suggests that, considering their relative funding and size, the in-house laboratories contribute their share of Events.

IMPLICATIONS OF THE FINDINGS

These then are the principal findings of the study thus far obtained. What inferences can be drawn with respect to the R&D enterprise as a whole and with respect to the science or research components of this enterprise?

The most significant finding is that in the weapon systems we studied, large changes in performance/cost are the synergistic effect of many innovations, most of them quite modest. This finding provides a rationale for most of the other

findings. Thus, for example, if many innovations must be skillfully fitted together to produce a large net improvement, it is likely that they are not the result of random efforts directed toward diverse and unrelated goals, but are due to a conscious plan. This at once suggests that the great majority of Events will be technology or applied science Events. It suggests to us that the isolated invention or the random scientific fact is not likely to "fit in" or, therefore, to be utilized. In other words, it tells us once again that recognized need is the key to efficient utilization. But to recognize need one has to have very detailed knowledge of either a class of systems or a specific system so that the critical problems can be addressed. Thus one predicts that actual systems—particularly those in the early stages of design—will be the most frequent sources of the recognized need. One also predicts that, because they are so intimately exposed to system development problems, the in-house laboratories and defense industry will have a very favored position from which to make useful contributions and that non-defense industry will play a small role. In some cases, of course, such as the early transistor developments and aluminum weldment, when its needs happened to coincide almost exactly with defense needs, non-defense industry has been the source of important contributions. For example, the properties needed in solid-state devices for the commercial electronics and communications were just those needed for military electronics and communications, and reliable, tight aluminum welds were as important for beer barrels as they were for missile fuel tanks. In general, however, because of the high performance and reliability requirements and higher allowable cost of defense equipment, one would expect such cases to be rare.

The "many-innovations-are-needed" concept even gives us insight into the time-distribution curve of Figure 1. As several of our examples illustrate, later innovations may depend on ones that preceded them. Since one innovation may engender several others, it is reasonable to expect that the rate of accumulation of potentially useful innovations will increase over time (assuming that the level of effort is not reduced).

Because these expectations are in fact borne out by the detailed studies, both individually and in sum, we believe that the picture we present is consistent.

THE CASE FOR DIRECTED EFFORT

We made a crude estimate of the military effectiveness of the successor system in a defined role, divided by its total procurement and operating cost, and made a similar estimate for the predecessor system in the same role. We obtained improvement factors of 1.6:1 for the transport aircraft, 10:1 for the sea mine, and, for the search radar, 40:1 when we require current performance from the old technology and 5:1 when we require the old performance with current technology. We believe that an average improvement factor of 2:1 would be a conservative estimate for the systems we studied. If this same improvement factor were to apply to all the equipment in the total inventory of some $80 billion, we can see that the approximately $10 billion of DOD funds expended in the support of science and technology over the period 1946 to 1962, when most of our Events occurred and which, in fact, financed most of these Events, has been paid back many times over. We believe our study shows, also, that, had the Defense Department merely waited passively for the non-defense sectors of the economy or government to produce the science and technology it needed, our military equipment would be far inferior to what it is today. We believe that the traditional DOD management policy of keeping applied science and technology closely related to the needs of systems and equipment in development (a policy which, of course, is also characteristic of industry) is basically sound if one wants an economic payoff on the 10-year (or shorter) time scale.

What the Hindsight study has done, therefore, on a scale previously not attempted, is to develop a strong, factual demonstration that recent, mission-oriented science and technology are a good investment in the short term—the 10- to 20-year period. What we have not been able to do is to demonstrate value for recent undirected science. Our observations on why we failed to make this case are discussed in the next section.

THE CASE FOR RECENT UNDIRECTED SCIENCE

It is clear that, on the 50-year or more time scale, undirected science has been of immense value. Without basic physical science we could scarcely have had nuclear energy or the electrical industry or modern communications or the modern chemical industry. None of our science Events could have occurred without the use of one or more of the great systematic theories—classical mechanics, thermodynamics, electricity and magnetism, relativity and quantum mechanics. These theories also played an important role in many of the technology Events. If, for example, we were to count the number of times that Newton's laws, Maxwell's equations, or Ohm's law were used in the systems we studied the frequencies of occurrence would be so high that they would completely overshadow any of the recent Events we identified. But, however important science may be, we suspect its primary impact may be brought to bear not so much through the recent, random scraps of new knowledge, as it is through the organized, "packed-down," thoroughly understood and carefully taught *old* science. Similar conclusions have been reached by others who have considered the question. Thus when one debates the utility of science the real issue is not the value, but rather the time to utilization. We believe that the Hindsight study has merely re-emphasized an old mystery: What *is* the process by which science moves into technology and utilization? It is clearly not the simple, direct sequence taught by the folklore of science.

We feel, however, that entirely aside from the research results themselves—which, of course, go primarily into the "eternal archive," from which they may ultimately contribute to the next great consolidation of science—a laboratory carrying on undirected research, co-located with and skillfully related to an applied research and development organization, more than pays its way.

A mission-oriented organization needs highly trained scientists and engineers to help supply what Marquis and Allen call "technology-pull science"—the additional knowledge needed to make older, organized knowledge usable—and a very large part of the estimated $100 million a year spent in support of fundamental scientific investigations by Defense goes into research that supports graduate education. Table 2 shows the percentages of individuals with advanced degrees who were identified as contributors to the Events in the Hindsight study, as well as several sets of comparable figures for larger research communities. Advanced degrees are several times more frequent among the Hindsight

contributors than among the less select groups. About one-third of the contributions to Project Hindsight Events appear to have depended upon graduate education.

There is, moreover, an important practical need, related to the sociology of science, to carry on some undirected, although generally relevant, research in the mission-oriented research and development organizations themselves. Undirected research serves as a form of postdoctoral training; it provides initial jobs for new Ph.D.'s who are inclined toward basic research but who want a closer look at mission-oriented research before making a career commitment; it provides intellectual stimulation and a link between the research frontier and the applied activities and it provides a body of in-house expert consultants to help on unusually difficult applied technical problems.

In the strongest and most productive mission-oriented laboratories undirected research generally amounts to about 15 percent of the total research effort. If 15 percent of the 30,000 scientists and engineers, military and civilian, who are directly involved in the Defense Department's R&D enterprise were active in undirected

TABLE 2.   *Educational Level of Contributors to Project Hindsight Events and of Research Performers in General*

Highest Degree Held	Hindsight Contributors* (%)	All S&T[†] (%)	All R&D[‡] (%)	All S&T[§] (%)	All Engineers[‖] (%)
Ph.D.	10.5	3.1	1.2	3.8	
M.S.	22.5	8.6	7.2		} 63
B.S.	57.0	34.6	47.0		
Some college	6.8	39.5			
No college	3.2	14.2	44.6		} 37

*Base number, 1725.

[†]S. Warkov and J. Marsh, "The Education and Training of America's Scientists and Engineers: 1962," National Opinion Research Center, University of Chicago, Chicago, Ill., 1965, p. 17.

[‡]A. Shapero, R. P. Howell, J. R. Tombaugh, "An Exploratory Study of the Structure and Dynamics of the R&D Industry," Stanford Research Institute, Stanford, Calif., June 1964, p. 31.

[§]"Profiles of Manpower in Science and Technology," NSF 63–23, National Science Foundation, Washington, D.C., 1963, p. 17ff.

[‖]"How Many Engineers?" *Engr. Manpower Bull.* No. 5, Engineers' Joint Council, New York, July 1966.

but generally relevant science, the cost would be about $150 million a year. This is not a large figure considering the size of the science and technology budget alone of about $1.4 billion a year, and a development, test, and evaluation budget some four times greater still.

WHAT NEEDS TO BE DONE NEXT?

In the original design of Project Hindsight, we recognized that the physical scientists and engineers tracing the historical record might not be sensitive to psychological and other behavioral factors affecting the generation and utilization of scientific and technical knowledge. In order to assure that proper attention would be given to these aspects, Task II of the project was established concurrently with the task that led to the results we have been describing. The second task is directed at understanding the actual processes going on today in the organizations (and in many cases with the same people) involved in the Events identified in Task I.

Within 6 months after the onset of Task I, ten organizations had been identified as being prolific contributors of the science and technology upon which the examined weapon systems were based. Among these organizations were represented industry, the DOD, in-house laboratories, and the Atomic Energy Commission. Management scientists from each of the organizations were formed into a team to conduct field studies, each within his own organization, looking into information sources, idea flow, skill development, project selection, relations between research groups, and other such aspects of the R&D process. The field studies were designed by management scientists of Northwestern University and the Sloan School of the Massachusetts Institute of Technology. Participating organizations include Raytheon, Ling-Temco, North American Aviation, Lockheed, United Aircraft, the Army's Picatinny and Redstone arsenals, the Air Force's Wright Air Development Center, the Naval Ordnance Laboratory at White Oak, and the Naval Ordnance Test Station at China Lake. Data are now being collected, and analysis will be initiated in the near future. The findings will be reported by the university groups conducting the research.

It is possible that if systematic retrospective analyses were to be applied to scientific, rather than to engineering accomplishments a great deal more could be learned about the scientific process. Have the randomly directed research efforts so characteristic of much of science in the past played as big a role as they are often thought to do? Or, is it sharply focused effort directed at well-defined, limited goals, which are more frequently the key events in the scientific advance?

Finally, if Project Hindsight tells us anything about science, it is that it is unusual for random, disconnected fragments of scientific knowledge to find application rapidly. It is, rather, the evaluated, compressed, organized, interpreted, and simplified scientific knowledge that we find to be the most effective connection between the undirected research laboratory and the world of practical affairs. If scientists would see their efforts in undirected science used on a more substantial scale in a time period shorter than 20 years, they must put a bigger fraction of their collective, creative efforts into organizing scientific knowledge expressly for use by society.

SUMMARY

Recently developed weapon systems were compared with systems of similar function in use 10 to 20 years earlier. The most significant finding was that the improvement in performance or reduction in cost is largely the synergistic effect of a large number of scientific and technological innovations, of which only about 10 percent had been made at the time the earlier system was designed. The common scientific and technological base of the systems was not analyzed. Of the innovations, or Events, 9 percent were classified as science and 91 percent as technology. Ninety-five percent of all Events were funded by the defense sector. Nearly 95 percent were motivated by a recognized defense need. Only 0.3 percent came from undirected science. The results of the study do not call in question the value of undirected science on the 50-year-or-more time scale. In light of our finding that 5 to 10 years are often required before even a piece of highly applied research is "fitted in" as an effective contributing member of a large assembly of other Events, it is not surprising that "fragments" of undirected science are infrequently utilized on even a 20-year time scale. The most obvious way in which undirected science appears to enter into technology and utilization on a substantial scale seems to be in the compressed, highly organized form of a well-established, clearly expressed general theory, or in the evaluated, ordered knowledge of handbooks, textbooks, and university courses.

SECTION II

Managing Innovation and Leadership Activity

3

STAFFING THE INNOVATION PROCESS

Critical Functions: Needed Roles in the Innovation Process

Edward B. Roberts

Alan R. Fusfeld

This article examines the main elements of the technology-based innovation process in terms of certain usually informal but critical "people" functions that can be the key to an effective organizational base for innovation. This approach to the innovation process is similar to that taken by early industrial theorists who focused on the production process. Led by such individuals as Frederick W. Taylor, their efforts resulted in basic principles for increasing the efficiency of producing goods and services. These principles of specialization, chain of command, division of labor, and span of control continue to govern the operation of the modern organization (despite their shift from popularity in many modern business schools). Hence, routine tasks in most organizations are arranged to facilitate work standardization with expectations that efficient production will result. However, examination of

how industry has organized its innovation tasks—that is, those tasks needed for product/process development and for responses to nonroutine demands—indicates an absence of comparable theory. And many corporations' attempts to innovate consequently suffer from ineffective management and inadequately staffed organizations. Yet, through tens of studies about the innovation process, conducted largely in the last fifteen years, we now know much about the activities that are requisite to innovation as well as the characteristics of the people who perform these activities most effectively.

The following section characterizes the technology-based innovation process via a detailed description of a typical research and development project life cycle. The types of work activities arising in each project phase are enumerated. These lead in the third section to the identification of the five basic critical roles that are needed for effective execution of an innovative effort. Problems associated with gaps in the fulfillment of the needed roles are discussed. Detailed characteristics and specific activities that are associated with each role filler are elaborated upon in

From E. Roberts and A. Fusfeld, "Critical Functions: Needed Roles in the Innovation Process," in *Career Issues in Human Resource Management,* R. Katz (ed.), © 1982, pp. 182–207. Reprinted by permission of Prentice-Hall, Inc., Englewood Cliffs, NJ.

the fourth section. The multiple roles that are sometimes performed by certain individuals are observed, as are the dynamics of role changes that tend to take place over the life span of a productive career. The fifth section presents several areas of managerial implications of the critical functions concepts, beginning first with issues of manpower planning, then moving to considerations of job design and objective setting and to the determination of appropriate performance measures and rewards. How an organizational assessment can be carried out in terms of these critical functions dimensions is discussed in the sixth section, with the illustrative description of one such assessment in a medium-sized research and development organization. The final paragraphs summarize the chapter and indicate the transferability of critical functions to other kinds of organizations.

THE INNOVATION PROCESS

The major steps involved in the technology-based process are shown in Figure 1. Although the project activities do not necessarily follow each other in a linear fashion, there is more or less clear demarcation between them. Moreover, each stage, and its activities, require a different mix of people skills and behaviors to be carried out effectively.

This figure portrays six stages as occurring in the typical technical innovation project, and sixteen representative activities that are associated with innovative efforts. The six stages are here identified as:

1. Pre-project
2. Project possibilities
3. Project initiation
4. Project execution
5. Project outcome evaluation
6. Project transfer

These stages often overlap and frequently recycle.[1] For example, problems or findings that are generated during project execution may cause a return to project initiation activities. Outcome evaluation can restart additional project execu-

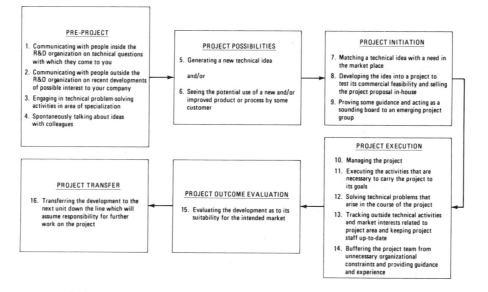

FIGURE 1.   *A Multistage View of a Technical Innovation Project*

tion efforts. And, of course, project cancellation can occur during any of these stages, redirecting technical endeavors back into the pre-project phase.

A variety of different activities are undertaken during each of the six stages. Some of the activities, such as generating new technical ideas, arise in all innovation project stages from pre-project to project transfer. But our research studies and consulting efforts in dozens of companies and government labs have shown other activities to be concentrated mainly in specific stages, as discussed below.

(1) Pre-Project. Prior to formal project activities being undertaken in a technical organization, considerable technical work is done that provides a basis for later innovation efforts. Scientists, engineers, and marketing people find themselves involved in discussions internal and external to the organization. Ideas get discussed in rough-cut ways and broad parameters of innovative interests get established. Technical personnel work on problem-solving efforts to advance their own areas of specialization. Discussions with numerous industrial firms in the United States and Europe suggest that from 30 to 60% of all technical effort is devoted to work outside of or prior to formal project initiation.

(2) Project Possibilities. Arising from the pre-project activities, specific ideas are generated for possible projects. They may be technical concepts for assumed-to-be-feasible developments. Or they may be perceptions of possible customer interest in product or process changes. Customer-oriented perspectives may be originated by technical or marketing or managerial personnel out of their imagination or from direct contact with customers or competitors. Recent evidence indicates that many of these ideas enter as "proven" possibilities, having already been developed by the customers themselves.[2]

(3) Project Initiation. As ideas evolve and get massaged through technical and marketing dis-cussions and exploratory technical efforts, the innovation process moves into a more formal project initiation stage. Activities occurring during this phase include attempts to match the directions of technical work with perceived customer needs. (Of course, such customer needs may exist either in the production organization or in the produce marketplace.) Inevitably, a specific project proposal has to be written up, proposed budgets and schedules have to get produced, and informal pushing as well as formal presentations have to be undertaken in order to sell the project. A key input during this stage is the counseling and encouragement that senior technical professionals or laboratory and marketing management may provide to the emerging project team.

(4) Project Execution. With formal approval of a project aimed at an innovative output, activities increase in intensity and focus. In parallel, someone usually undertakes planning, leadership, and coordination efforts related to the many continuing technical idea-generating and problem-solving activities being done by the engineers and scientists assigned to the project. Technical people often make special attempts to monitor (and transfer in) what had been done previously as well as what is then going on outside the project that is relevant to the project's goals. Management or marketing people frequently take a closer look at competitors and customers to be sure the project is appropriately targeted.[3] Senior people try to protect the project from overly tight control or from getting cut off prematurely, and the project manager and other enthusiasts keep fighting to defend their project's virtues (and budget). Unless canceled, the project work continues toward completion of its objectives.

(5) Project Outcome Evaluation. When the technical effort seems complete, most projects undergo another often intense evaluation to see how the results stack up against prior expecta-

tions and current market perceptions. If a successful innovation is to occur, some further implementation must take place, either by transfer of the interim results to manufacturing for embodiment in its process or for volume production activities, or by transfer to later stages of further development. All such later stages involve heavier expenditures and the post-project evaluation can be viewed as a pre-transfer screening activity.

(6) Project Transfer.   If the project results survive this evaluation, transfer efforts take place (e.g., from central research to product department R&D, or development to manufacturing engineering).[4] The project's details may require further technical documentation to facilitate the transfer. Key technical people may be shifted to the downstream unit to transfer their expertise and enthusiasm, since downstream staff members, technical or marketing, often need instruction to assure effective continuity. Within the downstream organizational unit, the cycle of stages may begin again, perhaps bypassing the earliest two stages and starting with project initiation or even project execution. This "passdown" continues until successful innovation is achieved, unless project termination occurs first.

NEEDED ROLES

Assessment of activities involved in the several-stage innovation process, as just described, points out that the repeated direct inputs of five different work roles are critical to innovation. The five arise in differing degrees in each of the several steps. Furthermore, different innovation projects obviously call for variations in the required role mix at each stage. Nevertheless, all five work roles must be carried out by one or more individuals if the innovation is to pass effectively through all six steps.

The five critical work functions are:

- *Idea generating:* Analyzing and/or synthesizing (implicit and explicit) information

(formal and informal) about markets, technologies, approaches, and procedures, from which an idea is generated for a new or improved product or service, a new technical approach or procedure, or a solution to a challenging technical problem.[5]

- *Entrepreneuring or championing:* Recognizing, proposing, pushing, and demonstrating a new (his or her own or someone else's) technical idea, approach or procedure for formal management approval.[6]

- *Project leading:* Planning and coordinating the diverse sets of activities and people involved in moving a demonstrated idea into practice.[7]

- *Gatekeeping:* Collecting and channeling information about important changes in the internal and external environments; information gatekeeping can be focused on developments in the market, in manufacturing, or in the world of technology.[8]

- *Sponsoring or coaching:* "Behind-the-scene" support-generating function of the protector and advocate, and sometimes of the "bootlegger" of funds; the guiding and developing of less-experienced personnel in their critical roles (a "Big Brother" role).[9]

Lest the reader confuse these roles as mapping one-for-one with different people, three points need emphasis: (1) some roles (e.g., idea generating) frequently need to be fulfilled by more than one person in a project team in order for the project to be successful; (2) some individuals occasionally fulfill more than one of the critical functions; and (3) the roles that people play periodically change over a person's career with an organization.

Critical Functions

These five critical functions represent the various roles in an organization that must be carried out for successful innovation to occur. They are critical from two points of view. First, each role is different or unique, demanding different skills. A deficiency in any one of the roles contributes to serious problems in the innovation effort, as we illustrate below. Second, each role tends to be carried out primarily by relatively few individuals, thereby making even more unique the critical role players. If any one critical function-filler leaves, the problem of recruiting a replacement is very difficult—the specifics of exactly who is needed is dependent on usually unstated role requirements.

We must add at this point that another role clearly exists in all innovative organizations, but it is not an *innovative* role! "Routine" technical problem-solving must be carried out in the process of advancing innovative efforts. Indeed the vast bulk of technical work is probably routine, requiring professional training and competence to be sure, but nonetheless routine in character for an appropriately prepared individual. A large number of people in innovative organizations do very little "critical functions" work; others who are important performers of the critical functions also spend a good part of their time in routine problem-solving activity. Our estimate, supported now by data from numerous organizations, is that 70 to 80% of technical effort falls into this routine problem-solving category. But the 20 to 30% that is unique and critical is the part we emphasize.

Generally, the critical functions are not specified within job descriptions since they tend to fit neither administrative nor technical hierarchies; but they do represent necessary activities for R&D, such as problem definition, idea nurturing, information transfer, information integration, and program pushing. Consequently, these role behaviors are the underlying informal functions that an organization carries out as part of the innovation process. Beyond the five above, different business environments may also demand that additional roles be performed to assure innovation.[10]

It is desirable for every organization to have a balanced set of abilities for carrying out these roles as needed, but unfortunately few organizations do. Some organizations overemphasize one role (e.g., idea generating) and underplay another role (e.g., entrepreneuring). Another organization might do just the reverse. Nonetheless, technical organizations tend to assume that the necessary set of activities will somehow be performed. As a consequence, R&D labs often lack sensitivity to the existence and importance of these roles, which, for the most part, are not defined within the formal job structure. How the critical functions are encouraged and made a conscious part of technology management is probably an organization's single most important area of leverage for maintaining and improving effective innovation. The managerial capabilities required for describing, planning, diagnosing problems, and developing the necessary teamwork in terms of the people functions demanded by an innovative program are almost entirely distinct from the skills needed for managing the technical requirements of the tasks.

Impact of Role Deficiencies

Such an analytic approach to developing an innovative team has been lacking in the past and, consequently, many organizations suffer because one or more of the critical functions is not being performed adequately. Certain characteristic signs can provide evidence that a critical function is missing.

Idea generating is deficient if the organization is not thinking of new and different ways of doing things. However, more often than not when a manager complains of insufficient ideas, we find the real deficiency to be that people are not aggressively entrepreneuring or championing ideas, either their own or others'. Evidences of entrepreneuring shortages are pools of unexploited ideas that seldom come to a manager's attention.[11]

Project leading is suspect if schedules are not met, activities fall through cracks (e.g., coordinating with a supplier), people do not have a sense for the overall goal of their work, or units that are needed to support the work back out of their commitments. This is the role most commonly recognized formally by the appointment of a project manager. In research, as distinct from development, the formal role is often omitted.

Gatekeeping is inadequate if news of changes in the market, technology, or government legislation comes without warning, or if people within the organization are not getting the information that they need because it has not been passed on to them. When, six months after the project is completed, you suddenly realize that you have just succeeded in reinventing a competitor's wheel, your organization is deficient in needed gatekeeping! Gatekeeping is further lacking when the wheel is invented just as a regulatory agency outlaws its use.

Inadequate or inappropriate sponsoring or coaching often explains projects that get pushed into application too soon, or project managers who have to spend too much time defending their work, or personnel who complain that they do not know how to "navigate the bureaucracy" of their organizations.

The importance of each critical function varies with the development stage of the project. Initially, idea generation is crucial; later, entrepreneurial skill and commitment are needed to develop the concept into a viable activity. Once the project is established, good project leading/managing is needed to guide its progress. Of course, the need for each critical function does not abruptly appear and disappear. Instead, the need grows and diminishes, being a focus at some point, but of lesser importance at others. Thus, the absence of a function when it is potentially very important is a serious weakness regardless of whether or not the role had been filled at an earlier, less crucial time. As a corollary, assignment of an individual to a project, at a time when the critical role that he or she provides is not needed, leads to frustration for the individual and to a less effective project team.

Frequently, we have observed that personnel changes that occur because of career development programs often remove critical functions from a project at a crucial time. Since these roles are usually performed informally, job descriptions are made in terms of technical specialties, and personnel replacements are chosen to fill those job vacancies, rather than on their ability to fill the needs of the vacated critical roles. Consequently, the project team's innovative effectiveness is reduced, sometimes to the point of affecting the project's success. Awareness of which roles are likely to be required at what time will help to avoid this problem, as well as to allow people performing functions no longer needed to be moved to other projects where their talents can be better utilized.

CHARACTERISTICS OF THE ROLE PLAYERS

Compilation of several thousand individual profiles of staff in R&D and engineering organizations has demonstrated patterns in the characteristics of the people who perform each innovation function.[12] These patterns are shown in Table 1, indicating which persons are predisposed to be interested in one type of activity more than another and to perform certain types of activity well. For example, a person who is theoretically inclined and comfortable with abstractions feels better suited to the idea-generating function than does someone who is very practical and uncomfortable with seemingly discrepant data. In any unit of an organization, people with different characteristics can work to complement each other. Someone good at idea generating might be teamed with a colleague good at gatekeeping and another colleague good at entrepreneuring to provide necessary supporting roles. Of course, each person must understand his or her own expected role in a project and appreciate the roles of others for the teaming process to be success-

TABLE 1. Critical Functions in the Innovation Process

Personal Characteristics	Organizational Activities

Idea Generating

Is expert in one or two fields	Generates new ideas and tests their feasibility
Enjoys conceptualization, comfortable with abstractions	Good at problem solving
Enjoys doing innovative work	Sees new and different ways of viewing things
Usually is an individual contributor, often will work alone	Searches for the break-throughs

Entrepreneuring or Championing

Strong application interests	Sells new ideas to others in the organization
Possesses a wide range of interests	Gets resources
Less propensity to contribute to the basic knowledge of a field	Aggressive in championing his or her "cause"
Energetic and determined; puts himself or herself on the line	Takes risks

Project Leading

Focus for the decision making, information, and questions	Provides the team leadership and motivation
Sensitive to accommodating to the needs of others	Plans and organizes the project
Recognizes how to use the organizational structure to get things done	Ensures that administrative requirements are met
Interested in a broad range of disciplines and how they fit together (e.g., marketing, finance)	Provides necessary coordination among team members
	Sees that the project moves forward effectively
	Balances the project goals with organizational needs

Gatekeeping[a]

Possesses a high level of technical competence	Keeps informed of related developments that occur outside the organization through journals, conferences, colleagues, other companies
Is approachable and personable	Passes information on to others; finds it easy to talk to colleagues
Enjoys the face-to-face contact of helping others	Serves as an information resource for others in the organization (i.e., authority on whom to see and/or what has been done)
	Provides informal coordination among personnel

Sponsoring or Coaching

Possesses experience in developing new ideas	Helps develop people's talents
Is a good listener and helper	Provides encouragement and guidance and acts as a sounding board to the project leader and others
Can be relatively more objective	Provides access to a power base within the organization—a senior person
Often a more senior person who knows the organizational ropes	Buffers the project team from unnecessary organizational constraints
	Helps the project team to get what it needs from the other parts of the organization
	Provides legitimacy and organizational confidence in the project

[a]Our empirical studies have pointed out three different types of gatekeepers: (1) technical, who relates well to advancing world of science and technology; (2) market, who senses and communicates information relating to customers, competitors, and environmental and regulatory changes affecting the marketplace; and (3) manufacturing, who bridges the technical work to the special needs and conditions of the production organization. See Rhoades et al., "A Correlation of R&D Laboratory Performance with Critical Functions Analysis," *R&D Management*, 1978.

ful. Obviously, as will be discussed later, some people have sufficient breadth to perform well in multiple roles.

Table 1 underlies our conclusion that each of the several roles required for effective technical innovation presents unique challenges and must be filled with essentially different types of people, each type to be recruited, managed, and supported differently, offered different sets of incentives, and supervised with different types of measures and controls. Most technical organizations seem not to have grasped this concept, with the result that all technical people tend to be recruited, hired, supervised, monitored, evaluated, and encouraged as if their principal roles were those of creative scientists or, worse yet, routine technical problem-solvers. But only a few of these people in fact have the personal and technical qualifications for scientific inventiveness and prolific idea generating. A creative idea-generating scientist or engineer is a special kind of professional who needs to be singled out, cultivated, and managed in a special way. He or she is probably an innovative technically well-educated individual who enjoys working on advanced problems, often as a "loner."

The technical champion or entrepreneur is a special person, too—creative in his own way, but his is an aggressive form of creativity appropriate for selling an idea or product. The entrepreneur's drives may be less rational, more emotional than those of the creative scientist; he is committed to achieve, and less concerned about how to do so. He is as likely to pick up and successfully champion someone else's original idea as to push something of his own creation. Such an entrepreneur may well have a broad range of interests and activities; and he must be recruited, hired, managed, and stimulated very differently from the way an idea-generating scientist is treated in the organization.

The person who effectively performs project leading or project managing activities is a still different kind of person—an organized individual, sensitive to the needs of the several different people she is trying to coordinate, and an effective planner; the latter is especially important if long lead time, expensive materials, and major support are involved in the development of the ideas that she is moving forward in the organization.

The information gatekeeper is the communicative individual who in fact, is the exception to the truism that engineers do not read—especially that they do not read technical journals. Gatekeepers link to the sources of flow of technical information into and within a research and development organization that might enhance new product development or process improvement. But those who do research and development need market information as well as technical information. What do customers seem to want? What are competitors providing? How might regulatory shifts affect the firm's present or contemplated products or processes? For answers to questions such as these, research and development organizations need people we call the "market gatekeepers"—engineers or scientists, or possibly marketing people with technical background, who focus on market-related information sources and communicate effectively with their technical colleagues. Such a person reads journals, talks to vendors, goes to trade shows, and is sensitive to competitive information. Without him, many research and development projects and laboratories become misdirected with respect to market trends and needs.

Finally, the sponsor or coach may in fact be a more experienced, older project leader or former entrepreneur who now has matured to have a softer touch than when he was first in the organization. As a senior person he can coach and help subordinates in the organization and speak on their behalf to top management, enabling ideas or programs to move forward in an effective, organized fashion. Many organizations totally ignore the sponsor role, yet our studies of industrial research and development suggest that many projects would not have been successful were it not for the subtle and often unrecognized assistance of such senior people acting in the role of sponsors. Indeed, organizations are more successful when chief engineers or laboratory directors naturally behave in a manner consistent with this sponsor role.

The significant point here is that the staffing needed to cause effective innovation in a technical organization is far broader than the typical research and development director has usually assumed. Our studies indicate that many ineffective technical organizations have failed to be innovative solely because one or more of these five quite different critical functions has been absent.

Multiple Roles

As indicated earlier, some individuals have the skills, breadth, inclination, and job opportunity to fulfill more than one critical function in an organization. Our data collection efforts with R&D staffs show that a few clusters explain most of these cases of multiple role-playing. One common combination of roles is the pairing of gatekeeping and idea generating. Idea-generating activity correlates in general with the frequency of person-to-person communication, especially external to the organization.[13] The gatekeeper, moreover, in contact with many sources of information, can often synergistically connect these bits into a new idea. This seems especially true of market gatekeepers, who can relate market relevance to technical opportunities.

Another role couplet is between entrepreneuring and idea generating. In studies of formation of new technical companies the entrepreneur who pushed company formation and growth was found in half the cases also to have been the source of the new technical idea underlying the company.[14] Furthermore, in studies of M.I.T. faculty, 38% of those who had ideas they perceived to have commercial value also took strong entrepreneurial steps to exploit their ideas.[15] The idea-generating entrepreneuring pair accounts for less than one half of the entrepreneurs, but not the other half.

Entrepreneuring individuals often become project leaders, usually in what is thought to be a logical organizational extension of the effective selling of the idea for the project. And some people strong at entrepreneuring indeed also have the interpersonal and plan-oriented qualities needed for project leading. But on numerous occasions the responsibility for managing a project is mistakenly seen as a necessary reward for successful idea championing. This arises from lack of focus upon the functional differences. What evidence indicates that a good salesperson is going to be a good manager? If an entrepreneur can be rewarded appropriately and more directly for his or her own function, many project failures caused by ineffective project managers might be avoided. Perhaps giving the entrepreneur a prominent project role, together with a clearly designated but different project manager, might be an acceptable compromise.

Finally, sponsoring, although it should be a unique role, occasionally gives way to a takeover of any or all of the other roles. Senior coaching can degenerate into idea domination, project ownership, and direction from the top. This confusion of roles can become extremely harmful to the entire organization. Who will bring another idea to the boss, once he steals some junior's earlier concept? Even worse, who can intervene to stop the project once the boss is running amok with his new pet?

All of the critical innovative roles, whether played singly or in multiples, can be fulfilled by people from multiple disciplines and departments. Obviously, technical people—scientists and engineers—might carry out any of the roles. But marketing people also generate ideas for new and improved products, "gatekeep" information of key importance to a project—especially about use, competition and regulatory activities—champion the idea, sometimes sponsor projects, and in some organizations even manage innovation projects. Manufacturing people periodically fill similar critical roles, as do general management personnel.

The fact of multiple role filling can affect the minimum-size group needed for attaining "critical mass" in an innovative effort. To achieve continuity of a project, from initial idea all the way through to successful commercialization, a project group must have all five critical roles effectively filled while satisfying the specific technical skills required for project problem-solving. In a new high-technology company this critical mass may sometimes be ensured by as few as one or two co-founders. Similarly, an "elite" team, such as Cray's famed Control Data computer design group, or Kelly Johnson's "Skunk Works" at Lockheed, or McLean's Sidewinder missile organization in the Navy's China Lake R&D center, may concentrate in a small number of select multiple-role players the staff needed to accomplish major objectives. But the more typical medium-to-large company organization had better not plan on finding "Renaissance persons" or superstars to fill its job requirements. Staffing assumptions should more likely rest on estimates that 70% of scientists and engineers will turn out to be routine problem-solvers only, and that most critical role-players will be single dimensional in their unique contributions.

Career-Spanning Role Changes

We showed above how some individuals fulfill multiple critical roles concurrently or in different stages of the same project. But even more people are likely to contribute critically but differently at different stages of their careers. This does not reflect change of personality, although such changes do seem partly due to the dynamics of personal growth and development. But the phenomenon also clearly reflects individual responses to differing organizational needs, constraints, and incentives.

For example, let us consider the hypothetical case of a bright, aggressive, potentially multiple-role contributor, newly joining a company fresh from engineering school. What roles can he play? Certainly, he can quickly become an effective routine technical problem-solver and, hope-fully, a productive novel idea generator. But even though he may know many university contacts and also be familiar with the outside literature, he cannot be an effective information gatekeeper, for he does not yet know the people inside the company with whom he might communicate. He also cannot lead project activities. No one would trust him in that role. He cannot effectively act as an entrepreneur, as he has no credibility as champion for change. And, of course, sponsoring is out of the question. During this stage of his career, the limited legitimate role options may channel the young engineer's productive energies and reinforce his tendencies toward creative idea output. Alternatively, wanting to offer more and do more than the organization will "allow," this high-potential young performer may feel rebuffed and frustrated. His perception of what he can expect from the job and, perhaps more important, what the job will expect from him, may become set in these first few months on the job. Some disappointeds may remain in the company, but "turn off" their previously enthusiastic desire for multidimensional contributions. More likely, the frustrated high-potential will "spin-off" and leave the company in search of a more rewarding job, perhaps destined to find continuing frustration in his next one or two encounters. For many young professionals the job environment moves too slowly from encouraging idea generating to even permitting entrepreneurial activities.

With two or three years on the job, however, the engineer's role options may broaden. Of course, routine problem solving and idea generating are still appropriate. But some information gatekeeping may now also be possible, as communication ties increase within the organization. Project leading may start to be seen as legitimate behavior, particularly on small efforts.[16] And the young engineer's world behavior may begin to reflect these new possibilities. But perhaps his attempts at entrepreneurial behavior would still be seen as premature. And sponsoring is not yet a relevant consideration.

With another few years at work, the role opinions are still wider. Routine problem-solving, continued idea generating, broad-based gatekeeping (even bridging to the market or to manufacturing), responsible project managing, as well as project championing may become reasonable alternatives. Even coaching a new employee becomes a possibility. The next several years can strengthen all these role options, a given individual tending usually to focus on one of these roles (or on a specific multiple-role combination) for this midcareer period.

Getting out of touch with a rapidly changing technology may later narrow the role alternatives available as the person continues to age on the job. Technical problem-solving effectiveness may diminish in some cases, idea generating may slow down or stop, technical information gatekeeping may be reduced. But market and/or manufacturing gatekeeping may continue to improve with increased experience and outside contacts, project managing capabilities may continue to grow as more past projects are tucked under the belt, entrepreneuring may be more important and for higher stakes, and sponsoring of juniors in the company may be more generally sought and practiced. This career phase is too often seen as characterized by the problem of technical obsolescence, especially if the organization has a fixation on assessing engineer performance in terms of the narrow but traditional stereotypes of technical problem solving and idea generating. "Retooling" the engineer for an earlier role, usually of little current interest and satisfaction to the more mature, broader, and differently directed person, becomes a source of mutual grief and anxiety to the organization and the individual. An aware organization, thinking in terms of critical role differences, can instead recognize the self-selected branching in career paths that has occurred for the individual. Productive technically trained people can be carrying out critical functions for their employers up to retirement, if employers encourage the full diversity of vital roles.

At each stage of his evolving career an individual can encounter severe conflicts between his organization's expectations and his personal work preferences. This is especially true if the organization is inflexible in its perception of appropriate technical roles. In contrast, with both organizational and individual adaptability in seeking mutually satisfying job roles, the scientist or engineer can contribute continuously and importantly to accomplishing innovation. As suggested in this illustrative case, during his productive career in industry the technical professional may begin as a technical problem solver, spend several years primarily as a creative idea generator, add technical gatekeeping to his performance while maintaining his earlier roles, shift toward entrepreneuring projects and leading them forward, gradually grow in his market-linking and project managing behavior, and eventually accrue a senior sponsoring role while maintaining senior project-program-organizational leadership until retirement. But this productive full life is not possible if the engineer is pushed to the side early as a technically obsolete contributor. The perspective taken here can lead to a very different approach to career development for professionals than is usually taken by industry or government.

MANAGING THE CRITICAL FUNCTIONS FOR ENHANCED INNOVATION

To increase organizational innovation, a number of steps can be taken that will facilitate implementation of a balance among the critical functions. These steps must be addressed explicitly or organizational focus will remain on the traditionally visible functions that produce primarily near-term incremental results, such as problem solving. Indeed, the "results-oriented" reward systems of most organizations reinforce this short-run focus, causing other activities to go unrecognized and unrewarded.

We are not suggesting that employees should ignore the problem-solving function for the sake of the other functions. Rather, we are emphasizing the need for a balance of time and energy distributed among all functions. As indicated earlier, our impressions and data suggest that 70 to 80% of the work of most organizations is routine problem-solving. However, the other 20 to 30% and the degree of teamwork among the critical functions make the difference between an innovative and a noninnovative organization.

Implementing of the results, language, and concepts of a critical functions perspective is described below for the selected organizational tasks of manpower planning, job design, measurement, and rewards. If critical functions awareness dominated managerial thinking, other tasks, not dealt with here, would also be done differently, including R&D strategy, organizational development, and program management.

Manpower Planning

The critical functions concept can be applied usefully to the recruiting, job assignment, and development or training activities within an organization. In recruiting, an organization needs to identify not only the specific technical or managerial requirements of a job, but also the critical function activities that the job requires. That is, does the job require consulting with colleagues as an important part of facilitating teamwork? Or does it require the coaching and development of less experienced personnel to ensure the longer-run productivity of that area? To match a candidate with the job, recruiting should also include identification of the innovation skills of the applicant. If the job requires championing, the applicant who is more aggressive and has shown evidence of championing new ideas in the past should be preferred over the less-aggressive applicant who has shown much more technically oriented interests in the past.

As indicated above, there is room for growth from one function to another, as people are exposed to different managers, different environments, and jobs that require different activities. Although this growth occurs naturally in most organizations, it can be explicitly planned and managed. In this way, the individual has the opportunity to influence his growth along the lines that are of most interest to him, and the organization has the opportunity to oversee the development of personnel and to ensure that effective people are performing the essential critical functions.

Industry has at best taken a narrow view of manpower development alternatives for technical professionals. The "dual ladder" concept envisions an individual as rising along either "scientific" or "managerial" steps. Attempted by many but with only limited success ever attained, the dual ladder reflects an oversimplification and distortion of the key roles needed in an R&D organization.[17] As a minimum, the critical function concept presents "multiladders" of possible organizational contribution; individuals can grow in any and all of the critical roles while benefiting the organization. And depending on an organization's strategy and manpower needs, manpower development along each of the paths can and should be encouraged. Most job descriptions and statements of objectives emphasize problem-solving, and sometimes project leading. Rarely do job descriptions and objectives take into account the dimensions of a job that are essential for the performance of the other critical functions. Yet availability of unstructured time in a job can influence the performance of several of the innovation functions. For example, to stimulate idea generating, some slack time is necessary so that employees can pursue their own ideas and explore new and interesting ways of doing things. For gatekeeping to occur, slack time also needs to be available for employees to communicate with colleagues and pass along information learned, both internal to and external to the organization. The coaching role also requires slack time, during which the "coach" can guide less experienced personnel. Table 2 elabo-

TABLE 2. *Job Design Dimensions*

Dimension of Job	Critical Function				
	Idea Generating	Entrepreneuring or Championing	Project Leading	Gatekeeping	Sponsoring or Coaching
Emphasis on deadlines	Little emphasis; exploring encouraged	Jointly set deadlines emphasized by management	Management identifies; needs strong emphasis	Set by the job (i.e., the person needing the information)	Little emphasis
Emphasis on specifically assigned tasks	Low; freedom to pursue new ideas	High; assignments mutually planned and agreed by management and champion	High with respect to overall project goals	Medium; freedom to consult with others	Low

rates our views on the different emphasis on deadlines (i.e., the alternative to slack time) for each of the critical functions and the degree of specificity of task assignments (i.e., another alternative to slack) for each function.

These essential activities also need to be included explicitly in the objective of a job. A gatekeeper would, for example, see his goals as including provision of useful information to colleagues. A person who has the attitudes and skill to be an effective champion or entrepreneur could also be made responsible for recognizing good new ideas. This person might have the charter to roam around the organization, talk with people about their ideas, encourage their pursuit, or pursue the ideas himself.

This raises a very sticky question in most organizations: Who gets the credit? If the champion gets the credit for recognizing the idea, not very many idea generators will be eager to let the champion carry out his job. This brings us to the next item, measures and rewards.

Performance Measures and Rewards

We all tend to do those activities that get rewarded. If personnel perceive that idea generating does not get recognized but that idea exploitation does, they may not pass their ideas on to somebody who can exploit them. They may try to exploit them themselves, no matter how unequipped or uninterested they are in carrying out the exploitation activity.

For this reason, it is important to recognize the distinct contributions of each of the separate critical functions. Table 3 identifies some measures relevant to each function. Each measure has both a quantity and quality dimension. For example, the objective for a person who has the skills and information to be effective at gatekeeping could be to help a number of people during the next twelve months. At the end of that time, his manager could survey the people whom the gatekeeper feels he helped to assess the gatekeeper's effectiveness in communicating key information. In each organization specific measures chosen will necessarily be different.

Rewarding an individual for the performance of a critical function makes the function both more discussable and manageable. However, what is seen as rewarding for one function may be seen as less rewarding, neutral, or even negative for another function because of the different personalities and needs of the role fillers.

TABLE 3. *Measuring and Rewarding Critical Function Performance*

Dimension of Management	Critical Function				
	Idea Generating	Entrepreneuring or Championing	Project Leading	Gatekeeping	Sponsoring or Coaching
Primary contribution of each function for appraisal of performance	Quantity and quality of ideas generated	Ideas picked up; percent carried through	Project technical milestones accomplished; cost/schedule constraints met	People helped; degree of help	Staff developed; extent of assistance provided
Rewards appropriate	Opportunities to publish; recognition from professional peers through symposia, etc.	Visibility; publicity; further resources for project	Bigger projects; material signs of organizational status	Travel budget; key "assists" acknowledged; increased freedom and use for advice	Increased freedom; discretionary resources for support of others

Table 3 presents some rewards seen as appropriate for each function. Again, organizational and individual differences will generate variations in rewards selected. Of course, the informal positive feedback of managers to their day-to-day contacts is a major source of motivation and recognition for any individual performing a critical innovation function, or any job for that matter.

Salary and bonus compensation are not included here, but not because they are unimportant to any of these people. Of course, financial rewards should also be employed as appropriate, but they do not seem to be explicitly linked to any one innovative function more than another. Table 3 identifies the rewards that are related to critical roles.

PERFORMING A CRITICAL FUNCTIONS ASSESSMENT

The preceding sections demonstrate that the critical functions concept provides an important way of describing an organization's resources for effective innovation activity. To translate this concept into an applied tool, one would need the capability for assessing the status of an R&D unit in terms of critical functions. Such an assessment could potentially provide two important types of information. The first is input for management decisions about ability to achieve organizational goals and strategy. The second is information that can assist management and R&D professionals in performance evaluation, career development, and more effective project performance.

Methods of Approach

The methodology for a critical functions assessment can vary depending on the situation—size of organization, organization structure, scope of responsibilities, and industry and technology characteristics. From experience gained with a dozen companies and government agencies in North America, the authors have found the most flexible approach to be a series of common questionnaires, developed from the replicated academic research techniques on innovative contributors, modified as needed for the situation. Questionnaires are supplemented by a number of structured interviews or workshops. Data are collected and organized in a framework that represents (1) the critical functions, (2) special characteristics of an organization's situation, (3) additional critical functions required in the specific organization, and (4) the climate for innovation provided by management. (See Table 4 for a sample of the approach used in one of the questionnaires.) The result is a measure of an organization's current and potential strengths in each critical function, an evaluation of the compatibility of the organization's R&D strategy with these strengths, and a set of personnel development plans for both management and staff that support the organization's goals.

This information is valuable for the organization and the individual. The organization first gains a complete and meaningful set of information on its own balance among the critical innovation skills. The match between the strengths and mix of these skills and the staffing requirements of present goals and strategy can then be evaluated. The assessment process also reinforces the explicit recognition of the need for performance of different types of innovation-enhancing skills in an effective R&D organization. For management this underlines the need for developing different expectations of a person's job and different ways of managing, motivating, and rewarding individuals in order to support the overall strategy. Finally, it gives the organization a framework for considering how the strengths of different individuals should be combined to be consistent with a productive long-range R&D strategy.

For the individual, the results provide a broader view of the role of a professional in an R&D organization, increased sensitivity to his own functioning and to his and his colleagues'

TABLE 4. Sample of the Critical Functions Questionnaire

Each respondent is asked to rate statements such as those below according to three separate criteria: (1) the respondent's personal preference, (2) his or her perceived skills for performing each activity, and (3) each activity's importance in the person's present job. In the usual instrument three or four item sentences scattered throughout the questionnaire provide multiple indications for each critical role, thus assuring reliability of the assessment.

Working as an effective, contributing member of a team in carrying out a task with one or more colleagues. (A)

Creating or developing ideas that result in new programs or services. (B)

Being a "one-stop" question-answering service for others by maintaining an in-depth competence in a few areas. (C)

Acting as a link between my unit and users to ensure that users' needs are being met. (D)

Searching out or identifying unexploited ideas that can be developed into a new program or service. (E)

Bringing people together and developing them into a smoothly working team. (F)

Lending credibility or power to less experienced or less visible personnel so that they may be more effective in the organization. (G)

The letters shown in the examples above for the reader's guidance indicate perceived ties to the several critical functions:

A—Problem solving   E—Entrepreneuring or championing
B—Idea generating   F—Project leading
C—Technical gatekeeping   G—Sponsoring or coaching
D—Market gatekeeping

Source: This sample is reprinted here with the permission of Pugh-Roberts Associates, Inc., which holds the copyright on the questionnaire.

relative strengths, and a very persuasive rationale for teamwork—the use of multiple functions to move an idea forward. In addition, the assessment can assist the individual in eliminating or reducing a mismatch between his perceived skills and talents and the requirements of the job. (These mismatches are probably the single greatest factor lowering motivation of technical professionals.) The critical functions assessment helps by providing both managers and professionals working for them a clarified set of job dimensions appropriate to the innovation activity that can be used as a better base for performance evaluation, career planning, and the development of job expectations. It is then easier to recognize and work with individual differences

and strengths that they may have already known existed, as well as being able to use new approaches and specific vocabulary to identify new strengths or personal goals.

One result of the assessment is a profile for the organization based upon the aggregate self-perceptions of the individual members. For validity, each of the self-reports is checked with the person's manager and with a set of colleague responses. Where differences exist they can then be reconciled.

Application of the Critical Functions Approach
To illustrate the kinds of empirical and managerial results deriving from a critical functions

assessment, we present here some outcomes developed from one moderate-sized R&D organization. The analysis in this company included three main lines of inquiry:

1. Identification of the balance the company desired to have among the critical functions.
2. Identification of existing strengths in each function.
3. Identification of the factors supporting and inhibiting the performance of each function in the R&D organization.

Balance among the Functions. Based upon careful examination of the organization's goals and requirements as discussed earlier, the management team determined what would be an "ideal" number of staff highly skilled at performing each function. This was accomplished by looking at each group and subjectively assessing the number required for each function, given the goals and human and physical resources of that unit. Table 5 presents the management group's assessment of the ideal number performing each function. Table 5 also shows questionnaire results on the number of people appearing to have the skills and strengths needed to perform each function well in addition to those actually carrying out the critical roles.

Factors Affecting the Balance. In addition, the R&D staff was asked to assess a number of fac-

tors affecting the performance of the critical functions. The data collection instrument designed for this purpose was called the "Innovation Climate Questionnaire." The results of these data provided substantial insights into the causes of discrepancies between the ideal and actual balance among the functions. For example, the staff's perception that they did not have management skills, (i.e., familiarity with management concepts and techniques) helps to explain why the "actual" number who are project leading is lower than the "ideal" number and the relatively few who report strengths in project leading. Another factor was the R&D staff's lack of understanding of what project leading/managing was expected in its new matrix organization. Market gatekeeping, on the other hand, was blessed with sufficient staff performing the function, but they seemed to be performing far in excess of their abilities. This was explained by the perception that this function was well recognized and well rewarded by upper management, who continually stressed the importance of being market-oriented.

Table 6 lists some of the factors serving to support and inhibit each of the critical functions in the organization studied.

Actions Taken. As a result of the analysis, multiple actions were taken and it is useful to consider some of them. The first action was that

TABLE 5. *"Ideal" versus Actual Distribution of Staff Performing Each Critical Function and Principal Strengths of the Staff*[a]

	Idea Generating	Entrepreneuring/ Championing	Project Leading	Technical Gatekeeping	Market Gatekeeping	Sponsoring/ Coaching
"Ideal"	6	11	17	5	14	4
Actual	5	5	11	9	12	3
Strength	10	9	6	12	4	11

[a]Total population = 90 professionals.

Source: These data are drawn from Alan R. Fusfeld, "Critical Functions: The Key to Managing Teamwork in the Innovation Process," presented at Innovation Canada, 1976. Numbers of "actuals" and "strengths" are not additive because many of the individuals sampled performed or were strong in more than one critical function. Most of the professionals performed no critical functions.

TABLE 6.   *Organizational "Climate" Factors Affecting the Critical Functions in One Company*

Function	Factors Supporting the Performance of the Function	Factors Inhibiting the Performance of the Function
Idea generating	Well-recognized function Reasonable freedom Good linkages with the market	Tight resources Focus on the short term
Entrepreneuring/championing	Freedom to act Recognition of function	High cost of failure Limited reward for risk taking Receives poor coaching
Project leading/managing	Strong management support Freedom to act Clear goals	Low acceptance by outside units Lack of management skills High cost of failure
Technical gatekeeping	Well known by peers Freedom to travel	Emphasis on measurable performance Emphasis on creating new ideas Physical design—distances Poorly recognized function
Market gatekeeping	Well-recognized function Ready market access	Poor customer credibility due to premature introduction of products
Sponsoring/coaching	Clear business goals	Function not recognized Lack of company growth strategy "Firefighting" orientation

every first-line supervisor and above, after some training, discussed with each employee the results of the employee's critical functions survey. (In other companies employee anonymity has been preserved, data being returned only to the individual. In these companies employees have frequently used the results to initiate discussions with their immediate supervisors regarding job "fit" and career development.) The purpose of the discussion was to look for differences in how the employee and his boss each perceived the employee's job skills and to engage in developmental career planning. The vocabulary of the critical functions plus the tangible feedback gave the manager and the employee a meaningful, commonly shared basis for the discussion.

Several significant changes resulted from these discussions. A handful of the staff recognized the mismatch between their present jobs and skills. With the support of their managers, job modifications were made. Another type of mismatch that this process revealed was between the manager's perception of the employee's skills and the employee's own perception. Most of the time the manager was underutilizing his human resources.

The data also prompted action to improve the performance of the project leading function. The insufficient number who saw themselves performing the function and the perceived lack of skills resulted in several "coaching" sessions by upper management, further role clarification, and increased upper management sensitivity to the support needed for project leading. These activities also involved personnel from outside units to develop broader support outside the technical organization for the project leading role.

Important changes were made in how the technical organization recruited. To begin with, the characteristic strengths behind each critical function were explicitly employed in identifying the skills necessary to do a particular job. This led to a framework useful for interviewing candidates to determine how they might fit into the present organization and how they saw themselves growing. Also, upper management became conscious of the unintended bias in the recruiting procedure that was introduced by the universities at which they recruited and by those who did the company's recruiting. Personnel primarily interested in idea generating (i.e., senior researchers) did most of the university interviewing. They tended to try to identify and favored hiring other people interested in idea generating, and described the organization in terms of interest to those people. As a result of the analyses, upper management was careful to have a mix of the critical functions represented by the people interviewing job candidates.

Other values resulted from the analyses which were less tangible than those listed above but equally important. Jobs were no longer defined solely in technical terms (i.e., the educational background and/or work experience necessary). For example, whether or not a job involved idea generation or exploitation was defined, and these typical activities were included in the description of the job and the skills needed to perform it well. The objectives of the job, in the company's management-by-objectives (MBO) procedure, were then expanded to include the critical functions. However, since all five functions are essential to innovation and it is the very rare person who can do all five equally well, the clear need for a new kind of teamwork was also developed. Finally, the critical functions concept provided the framework for the selection of people and the division of labor on the "innovation team" that became the nucleus for all new R&D programs.

SYNOPSIS

This chapter has examined the main elements of the technology-based innovation process in terms of certain usually informal but critical behavioral functions. The life cycle of activities encountered in an R&D project served to identify five critical roles as reoccurring: idea generating, entrepreneuring or championing, project leading, gatekeeping, and sponsoring or coaching. Organizational problems associated with weaknesses in the playing of each of these roles were described.

Each critical role was detailed in terms of representative activities during a project, and dominant characteristics of typical role players were presented from surveys conducted among many North American R&D/engineering organizations. Two key observations were that some unique individuals concurrently perform more than one of the critical roles, and that patterns of roles for an individual often change during a productive work career.

Managerial implications of the critical functions concepts were developed in regard to manpower planning, job design and objective setting, and performance measurement and rewards. These discussions provide a basis for design of a more effective "multiladder" system to replace many R&D organizations' ineffectual "dual-ladder" systems.

Techniques employed in carrying out a critical functions assessment were those described, together with the results obtained at one medium-sized R&D organization. A combination of survey questionnaires and management workshops were used to develop, interpret, and apply the critical functions data to organization improvement.

The critical functions approach was conceived as embodying the essence of innovative work in a research and development process. But several years of development, testing, and discussion of this perspective have led to broadened views and applications. Computer software development was an early area of extension of the methods, as was their use in an architectural firm. Recent discussions with colleagues suggest an obvious appropriateness for marketing organizations, with more difficult translation expected in the areas of finance and/or manufacturing. To the extent that innovative outcome, rather than routine production, is the output sought, we have confidence that the critical functions approach will afford useful insights for organizational analysis and management.

NOTES

1. For a different and more intensive quantitative view of project life cycles, see Edward B. Roberts, *The Dynamics of Research and Development* (New York: Harper & Row, 1964).
2. Eric von Hippel, "Users as Innovators," *Technology Review, 80,* No. 3 (January 1978), 30–39.
3. See Alan R. Fusfeld, "How to Put Technology into Corporate Planning," *Technology Review, 80,* No. 6, for issues that need to be highlighted in a comparative technical review.
4. For further perspectives on project transfer, see Edward B. Roberts, "Stimulating Technological Innovation: Organizational Approaches," *Research Management, 22,* No. 6 (November 1979), 26–30.
5. D. C. Pelz and F. M. Andrews, *Scientists in Organizations* (New York: Wiley, 1966).
6. E. B. Roberts, "Entrepreneurship and Technology," *Research Management, 11,* No. 4 (July 1968), 249–66.
7. D. G. Marquis and I. M. Rubin, "Management Factors in Project Performance," M.I.T. Sloan School of Management, Working Paper, Cambridge, Mass., 1966.
8. T. J. Allen, *Managing the Flow of Technology* (Cambridge, Mass.: MIT Press, 1977); and R. G. Rhoades, et al., "A Correlation of R&D Laboratory Performance with Critical Functions Analysis," *R&D Management, 9,* No. 1 (October 1978), 13–17.
9. Roberts, "Entrepreneurship and Technology," p. 252.
10. One role we have frequently observed is the "quality controller," who stresses high work standards in projects. Other critical roles relate more to organizational growth than to innovation. The "effective trainer" who could absorb new engineers productively into the company was seen as critical to one firm that was growing 30% per year. The "technical statesman" was a role label developed by an electronic components manufacturer which valued the ability of some engineers to generate a leadership technical reputation through authorship and presentation of advanced concepts.
11. One study that demonstrated this phenomenon is N. R. Baker, et al., "The Effects of Perceived Needs and Means on the Generation of Ideas for Industrial Research and Development Projects," *IEEE Transactions on Engineering Management, EM-14* (1967), 156–65.
12. The later section "Performing a Critical Functions Assessment" describes a methodology for collecting these data.
13. Allen, *Managing the Flow of Technology.*
14. Roberts, "Entrepreneurship and Technology."
15. E. B. Roberts and D. H. Peters, "Commercial Innovations from University Faculty," *Research Policy, 10,* No. 2 (April 1981), 108–26.
16. One study showed that engineers who eventually became managers of large projects began supervisory experiences within an average of 4.5 years after receiving their B.S. degrees. I. M. Rubin and W. Seelig, "Experience as a Factor in the Selection and Performance of Project Managers," *IEEE Transactions on Engineering Management, EM-14,* No. 3 (September 1967), 131–35.
17. For a variety of industrial approaches to the dual ladder, see the special July 1977 issue of *Research Management* or, more recently, *Research Management,* November 1979, 8–11.

Innovation through Intrapreneuring

Gifford Pinchot III

In-house entrepreneurs—those "dreamers who do"—can increase the speed and cost-effectiveness of technology transfer from R&D to the marketplace.

The economy of the United States is on an innovation treadmill. Our competitors enjoy cheaper labor, cheaper capital, and more government support than we. To maintain our competitive position, we need superior technology, more proprietary products and services, and better processes. As our competitors become more scientifically and managerially sophisticated, it takes them less and less time to understand and copy our innovations. We have to increase our speed and cost-effectiveness of innovation in our country to match our competitors' increasing sophistication in copying and capitalizing on our technology.

Most large companies operate stable businesses well. However, they are not as adept at starting new ones. Most are good at developing a new business from the idea stage on through research and prototype development. But they falter at the start-up stage—the stage of commercialization. Inefficient commercialization by big business has created opportunity for venture capitalists. The venture capital industry is producing 35 percent return on investment by taking frustrated R&D people and their rejected ideas out

of large companies, and financing the commercialization of those ideas. That the venture capital community can make 35 percent ROI on rejected ideas and people should be a constant rebuke to everyone in the R&D community. Venture capitalists have found a different way of managing innovation that gets returns which few of us can equal inside large organizations.

A MISSING FACTOR IN CORPORATE INNOVATION

The primary secret of the venture capitalists' success is revealed in the way they select ventures for investment. They say: "I would rather have a class A entrepreneur with a class B idea than a class A idea with a class B entrepreneur." They put their faith in choosing the right people and then sticking with them, while many corporate managers would feel uncomfortable with a strategy dependent on trusting the talent, experience, and commitment of those implementing it. I believe the primary cause for the lower returns of corporate managers of innovation is their failure to understand the importance of backing the right people—this is their failure to identify, support, and exploit the "intrapreneurs" who drive innovation to successful conclusions.

Reprinted with permission from Gifford Pinchot III, "Innovation through Intrapreneuring," *Research Management,* March-April 1987.

121

Imagine the organization as a cell, with R&D producing new genes. In the cell, there are also the productive capacity of the ribosomes, which are like factories ready to use the information in those new genes to produce new products. What's missing in most large organizations is linkage from idea to operation—by analogy the RNA. In most large organizations there are exciting new genes—new technologies but no broadly effective system of technology transfer. What is absent are large numbers of intrapreneurs devoted to turning new technologies into profitable new businesses, cost reductions, new features, and competitive advantages. Because we have tended to have scientific standards of excellence in R&D, we have tended to honor the inventor more than the implementor, more than the intrapreneur. The result is that we not only reward inventing more than intrapreneuring, but our management systems are far more supportive of invention than of commercialization.

The future role of R&D, the size of its budgets and its degree of autonomy all depend on efficient technology transfer. Older "hand-off systems" of development which ignore the role of the intrapreneur don't work, or at best are so slow and expensive they make R&D appear ineffective. Cost-effective innovation happens when someone becomes the passionate champion of a new idea and acts with great courage to push it through the system despite the "Not Invented Here" syndrome, and all the other forms of resistance which large organizations supply. It is therefore important for R&D managers to understand and recognize intrapreneurs who can, when properly managed, greatly increase the speed and cost effectiveness of technology transfer.

DREAMERS WHO DO

Intrapreneurs are the "dreamers who do." In most organizations people are thought to be either dreamers or doers. Both talents are not generally required in one job. But the trouble with telling the doers not to bother about their dreams is that they dream anyway. When they are blocked from implementing dreams of how to help your company, they're dreaming dreams of revenge. A mind is meant to imagine and then act. It is a terrible thing to split apart the dreamer and the doer.

What we need, then, is to restore the place for vision in everyone's job. One of my favorite stories is the story of Nikola Tesla who invented the three-phase electric motor and a host of other things. It is said that he would build a model in his mind of a machine, such as a new generator, and then push it into the background of his consciousness, set it running, and leave it going for weeks while he went about his other business. At the end of that time he'd pull it back into the foreground of his mind, tear it down and check the bearings for wear. With such detailed imagination, what need is there for computer-aided design and finite element analysis?

While few of us can match Tesla's talent, imagination is the most concrete mental skill that people have. It is more concrete than all the tools we have for analyzing businesses and all the formulas we have for analyzing stresses. Imagination is simply the ability to see something that doesn't yet exist as it might be. Unless we have Tesla's clarity of imagination, what we see may not be as precise as the results we can reach from doing calculations, but our vision is more concrete and more whole than any formula describing some aspect of a new design. And without this concrete skill, we do not have innovation.

An intrapreneur's imagination is very different from an inventor's. Inventors look five or ten years ahead and say, "wouldn't it be wonderful if such and such." They imagine how a customer would respond to their new product, what the technology would be, how the technology could produce desired features, and all those sorts of things. Good inventors have the customer in mind, but their vision is usually incomplete unless they are also intrapreneurs. They don't imagine in detail how to get from the here and now to that desired future. An intrapreneur, on the other hand, having seen the Promised Land, moves back to the present and takes on the rather mundane and practical task of turning the prototype into a marketplace success. This too requires enormous imagination.

Intrapreneurs ask questions such as, "Who would I need to help me with this? How much would it cost? What things have to happen first?" and so forth. They may ask, "Could we release this technology onto the marketplace in product form aimed at such-and-such a customer need? No. If we did that it would immediately bite into a very important market of one of our competitors who has the ability to respond, and before we produced our second generation products there would be a tremendous competitive response. Let's back up a little bit. What if we put it out in this way instead? Well it wouldn't do quite as well on the first round, but I begin to see it would give us a little more time to develop unbeatable second generation products."

Intrapreneurs have to constantly juggle potential implementation plans. They do this in their imaginations initially. Of course, intrapreneurs also juggle implementation plans on paper as business plans and drawings, but much of the initial work is done in the shower, or when driving the car, or any situation in which one neither fells guilty about not doing something useful nor can one get to pencil and paper. At such times, we are forced to use our imaginations, and thus often do our most creative work.

DISTINGUISH INTRAPRENEURS FROM PROMOTERS

One of the keys to managing innovation cost-effectively is to choose the right people to trust. Too often when managers look for intrapreneurs they choose promoters instead. Promoters are very good at convincing people to back their ideas, but they lack the ability to follow through.

Thus, one of the keys to managing innovation is to be able to distinguish between intrapreneurs and promoters.

One of the best ways to separate the intrapreneurs from the promoters is to see how they handle, and even how they think about, barriers to their ideas. When analyzing a potential intrapreneur, think of some of the ways their project might go wrong. Ask them how they might handle such a problem. Real intrapreneurs will have explored these problems in their imagination. They will have considered them while driving to work or taking a shower. The real intrapreneur has thought of three, five, or even ten possible solutions. They may pause for a moment trying to figure out which of those answers would appeal most to you because intrapreneurs do have a certain ability to sell, but they are not hearing the question for the first time. It will be very hard for you to think of a problem which they haven't considered.

Promoters, on the other hand, respond by saying the problem you bring up will never occur. They remind you again of how wonderful things will be ten years from now, of the hundreds of millions of dollars their product will be making. They will not even talk about the problem because they have no interest in the barriers along the way to implementation. They are counting on you to solve all problems by giving them enough funding. They just want to tell you why their idea is so much better than anyone else's. They are, in fact, so focused on getting approvals and funding, that they haven't planned how to get the job done. If you give them money in the name of intrapreneurship, you will not only give intrapreneurship a bad name, but you will waste everything you invested. The most important thing a manager can do when managing innovation is to separate out the promoters, and invest only in intrapreneurs.

Many people doubt that they want entrepreneurial people in their organizations. Entrepreneurs, they believe, are driven by greed. They are high risk-takers, they shoot from the hip, and furthermore, they are dishonest. Fortunately every one of these myths is false. In fact, entrepreneurs seem to be driven by a vision which they believe is so important that they are willing to dedicate their lives to it even when it starts to have trouble. Every new idea runs into terrible obstacles. People who are driven only by a desire for money, or promotion, or status, simply do not have the persistence to move a new idea forward. It is the person with the commitment to carry through who will move an idea into a practical reality.

Intrapreneurs and entrepreneurs are not high risk-takers, as many studies have shown. They like a 50–50 set of odds—not too easy, not too hard. Having chosen a challenging objective, they do everything they can to reduce the risk.

Intrapreneurs seem to be equally right brain and left brain, equally intuitive and analytic. They make decisions based on intuition when data or time don't permit analytical solutions. When analysis will work, they use it.

Intrapreneurs may operate a little differently than other people. They often have personalities which make them difficult to live with, but their difficulties stem less from dishonesty than excessive directness. They often get themselves in trouble by saying exactly what they think because they don't seem to be good at compromising—strong politics are inherent in the cultures of very large organizations.

A NEW MONITOR FOR THE FAA

Vision and imagination make up half of "the dreamers that do." Action is the other half.

Intrapreneurs are often in trouble because they act when they are supposed to wait. They tend to act beyond the territory of their own job description and function. This boundary crossing is important. Charles House at Hewlett-Packard is a perfect example. House developed a new monitor for the Federal Aviation Administration that turned out to not quite meet the specs. (Failure is a typical way for stories of innovation to begin.) He responded to the disappointment by observing that despite not meeting the spot size criteria for this particular application, the fact that he had a monitor which was half as heavy, used half the power, and cost half as much meant he should find out what else it could be used for. He took the idea to the marketing people who asked the division's traditional customers if they would like a monitor that was cheaper, but which had a slightly blurry display.

Nobody seemed to want it. Being an intrapreneur, as opposed to just a researcher, House wasn't satisfied with talk. He took out the front seat of his Volkswagen Bug, put the monitor in its place, and visited 40 customers in three weeks. At each stop he moved the monitor into the prospective customer's shop, hooked it up to their equipment, and asked whether this thing would do anything that's useful. By the end of the trip, he had found several new markets. House succeeded because he took the actions which were necessary for his prototype to go from technology to business reality.

There are two important points in this story. One is that intrapreneurs perform their own market research. If your scientists and engineers are not allowed to do their own market research, then you have a major barrier to innovation.

The second point is that generally a new idea is so ugly only its mother could love it. Consequently, it is unrealistic to think that people in marketing will understand a research idea in its early stages well enough to do valid marketing research. In general, they ask the wrong questions. They are trying to find out if it is a good idea, which in the early stages is the wrong question. The right question is: "I know this is a good idea; how am I going to present it in a way that some class of customers will agree? What are the ways in which this is a good idea? Who really needs it? How do I have to say this so that they will understand?"

The early stage of market research is searching for the market, not testing whether or not it is there. It is only after we have found a group of customers and learned how to talk to them, redesigned the product to meet their needs, and figured out how to position the product, that we can do the traditional form of market research which asks, "Will they buy it—is this a good idea?"

The idea of technically-driven research is drifting into disrepute. We are told that we must first carefully identify market needs and then invent what customers already know they want. This is rarely the way fundamental innovation works because we are not smart enough to invent to order. We are lucky to invent anything with fundamentally new and protectable properties, and when we do so, we must then hunt for the most applicable markets.

To be sure, researchers do pursue what they perceive to be marketplace needs, but the final applications often turn out to be in some entirely different market. Scotch Tape was invented to better insulate refrigerated railroad cars. Radio was invented for point-to-point communication—missing the broadcast market entirely. Riston circuit board systems began with a failure to produce a new photopolymer-based photographic film.

It is important for researchers to know about the marketplace, but important also to realize that for all of the thousands of unfilled or poorly filled marketplace needs each of us wishes to invent a proprietary solution for, we have the ability to invent a few. We know an anti-gravity device would be useful and probably well-received by customers. We don't work on it because we don't know how to begin.

We know that television sets with better reception are desirable. Most of us don't work on them because we believe others have a competitive advantage in making them inexpensively.

We left Hewlett-Packard's Charles House doing his own market research and thus doing somebody else's job, as intrapreneurs often do. He came home enthusiastic and his boss's boss,

Dar Howard, believed in him and told him to go ahead for another year. Unfortunately, a few months later the chairman visited the laboratory in Colorado. David Packard listened to the marketing people say that the idea was no good, even after House's research. He also heard a negative vote from the corporate chief of technology, who was backing a different technology.

At the time, Tektronix was giving Hewlett-Packard a hard time in the division's core business, and Packard said that when he came back to this laboratory next year, he did not want to see this product in the lab. Dar Howard went back to House and told him he just didn't know what excuse he could give for going on now. With that remark he left the door open just wide enough for Chuck to get his foot in. He showed that he felt for Chuck, but . . .

House said, "What exactly did Packard say?" "When I come back to this laboratory next year, I don't want to see this product in the lab." "Good," said Chuck, "we'll have it out of the lab and into manufacturing." And so it was. The monitor was used in the first manned moon landing and turned out to be a great success.

A few years later, Packard awarded House the Hewlett-Packard Award for Meritorious Defiance. "For contempt and defiance above and beyond the call of engineering duty," the certificate read. He made it clear that at Hewlett-Packard, courage counts more than obedience. Innovation requires this attitude.

SUCCEEDING AT INTRAPRENEURSHIP

Every new idea will have more than its share of detractors. There is no doubt that being an intrapreneur is difficult, even in the most tolerant of companies. So how can people succeed at it?

1. *Do anything needed to move your idea forward*. If you're supposed to be in research but the problem is in a manufacturing process, sneak into the pilot plant and build a new process. If it

REWARDS ARE THE LITMUS TEST

For many intrapreneurs who have given up and are hiding in the wood-work, rewards for innovation are the litmus test of a company's sincerity. If a company isn't willing to reward intrapreneurship, it does not really want it. I underestimated the importance of rewards when I wrote *Intrapreneuring* four years ago. It requires care since you can make a lot of mistakes designing a reward system. If you reward just the leader and not the whole team, for instance, you will have a disaster on your hands. But if you don't reward, then people will say you don't really want innovation.

Several kinds of rewards are useful. First is recognition programs which, though obvious, are generally underused. We advise our clients to create many award programs—awards for process innovation and various awards for different kinds of new product innovation. Each recipient will be one of a few who received that award even though in total large numbers are recognized. But recognition, no matter how well done, is not enough.

Financial rewards are also important and must be arranged so as not to arouse excessive jealousy in the managers of stable and mature businesses. One technique that works well in designing predetermined (prospective) rewards is to ask those who are signing up for a program that promises unusual rewards in the event of success to take personal risk. We often advise putting 10–20 percent of salary at risk or freezing salary until the rewards are due.

Compensation alone or even combined with recognition still does not make an adequate reward. In fact, if it is not combined with increasing freedom to try new things, bonuses may simply provide seed money for successful intrapreneurs to start their own businesses. The essential reward is freedom.

Entrepreneurs, in fact, find freedom to try their new ideas their most important reward. Their wealth is not mainly used for personal consumption: the bulk is used to find the next idea. The most tangible form of freedom in a large organization is a budget. We have developed a reward system called intracapital—a one-time earned discretionary budget to be used on behalf of the corporation to try out new ideas.

We know we must give intrapreneurs, inventors, and their collaborators an unusual degree of freedom. We all do this instinctively. As organizations grow and develop levels of bureaucracy, we must do it systematically.

is a marketing problem, do your own marketing research. If it means sweeping the floor, sweep the floor. Do whatever has to be done to move the idea forward. Needless to say, this isn't always appreciated, and so you have to remember that:

2. *It is easier to ask for forgiveness than for permission.* If you go around asking, you are going to get answers you don't want, so just do the things that need to be done and ask later. Managers have to encourage their people to do this. It may be necessary to remove some layers of management that complicate and slow down the approval process.

3. *Come to work each day willing to be fired.* I began to understand this more from talking to an old sergeant who had seen a lot of battle duty. He said, "You know, there is a simple secret to surviving in battle; you have to go into battle each day knowing you're already dead. If you are already dead, then you can think clearly and you have a good chance of surviving the battle."

Intrapreneurs, like soldiers, have to have the courage to do what's right instead of doing what they know will please the myriad of people in the hierarchy who are trying to stop them. If they are too cautious, they are lost. If they are fearful, the smell of fear is a chemical signal to the corporate immune system, which will move in quickly to smother the "different" idea.

I find that necessary courage comes from a sure knowledge that intrapreneurs have—that if their employer were ever foolish enough to fire them, they could rapidly get a better job. There is no way to have innovation without courage, and no real courage without self-esteem.

4. *Work underground as long as you can.* Every organization has a corporate immune system. As soon as a new idea comes up the white blood cells come in to smother it. I'm not blaming the organization for this. If it did not have an immune system it would die. But we have to find ways to hide the right new ideas in order to keep them alive. It is part of every manager's job to recognize which new ideas should be hidden and which new ideas should be exposed to the corporate immune system and allowed to die a natural death. Too often it is the best ideas that are prematurely exposed.

THE INTRAPRENEURIAL SHORTAGE

I've made an interesting discovery since I wrote *Intrapreneuring*. I used to think potential intrapreneurs were commonplace, that they were hard to find because they were in hiding. But I have found they are more rare in most large organizations than the 10 percent who are entrepreneurial in the population at large. There is a scarcity of people who are brave enough to take on the intrapreneurial role; therefore, we have to lower the barriers and increase the rewards.

If there are not enough intrapreneurs in your company, you can hire more. There are two ways to go about it: raiding successful intrapreneurs from other companies, and hiring more intrapreneurial people in entry positions.

Were I running an R&D organization, I would even take ads saying, "Wanted: Intrapreneurs." One could capitalize on widespread intrapreneurial frustration and selectively hire a fair number of courageous people who would move innovation forward. Second, I would focus on hiring potential intrapreneurs out of school. Here are two hints: One is that candidates' transcripts should contain both A's and D's. When intrapreneurial people are interested they get A's. When they are not interested, they don't pretend. They are self-driven.

The second hint is that any history of self-employment predicts intrapreneurial success. The strongest demographic predictor of intrapreneurial success is having one or more self-employed parents. It is more important than birth order or any of the other commonly cited predictors. I guess it is a matter of having an entrepreneurial role model.

It is a particularly good idea to hire farm

kids. They seem to make good intrapreneurs. I guess farm kids grow up with a kind of a can-do attitude and it never occurs to them that there is anything they aren't supposed to do. If the hay is on the ground, the bailer is broken and it is going to rain in six hours, you don't worry that you don't have a degree in bailer mechanics. Somehow farmers learn to get the job done.

TRAINING INTRAPRENEURS

Training your people in acquiring intrapreneuring skills is as important as knowing whom to hire. Though most people imagine that intrapreneurs are born and not made, we have had good results training intrapreneurs. In our Intrapreneur Schools we ask for volunteers. This way we are training a select group of people who are courageous enough to volunteer for an intrapreneurial role. Training succeeds partly because it gives people permission to use a part of themselves that their supervisors have been trying to beat out of them for quite some time. They look around the room and say, "My goodness, there are other people like me in this world and it seems that the corporation is really serious now about wanting this aspect of me employed." They get a tremendous rejuvenation and rebirth of vision and drive.

In addition, most intrapreneurs are missing skills for which training can help. They have some functional abilities which are often technical, and they've been convinced that they really cannot understand some things like accounting or marketing. They believe that those blind spots keep them from being the general manager of a new idea. They do not have to become excellent at all functions; they just have to understand enough to work easily with others in those fields. In fact, if the idea is good, success does not require great sophistication in many disciplines, just a journeyman-like job that doesn't overlook the obvious. Training should be structured to

build teams and so the whole team should work together while training.

MANAGING INTRAPRENEURS

Managers must choose intrapreneurs who are persistent, impatient, who laugh, and who face the barriers. Then they have to be willing to trust that the intrapreneurs know how to do their jobs and must give them what they are asking for— resources and people to help carry forward their ideas. Since resources are not infinite, they may have to take these things away from other people who are not intrapreneurs.

I know we are living in an age of head-count restrictions. Too often this means that everything stays the same. Whoever has three people gets three people next year. Anything new and growing will have too few people resources, and anything old and over the hill is going to have too many. We have to be courageous in sweeping out the old and giving the right people the resources they need to get the job done. The most effective use of a manager's time is in choosing whom to trust.

One very effective approach is to create heroes so intrapreneurs have role models within the company. Select a few of the most courageous intrapreneurs and publish their stories for everyone in the company to read. These stories should be written honestly, so that all the difficulties and problems faced by the intrapreneurs are presented so that people can see how barriers were overcome.

KEEP R&D CLOSE TO THE ACTION

It is important to bring your researchers close to model shops and pilot plants that allow dirty-finger research. R&D people need to be able to test their ideas themselves—if they can't, they will fall back on more intellectual forms of research. Obviously, we'll hear more about discretionary time, the so-called 15 percent rules that many companies have. Other useful reward tools are seed money programs, the creation of cross-functional teams, and other ways to reduce the bureaucracy.

In conclusion, I issue a challenge to get your people to display courage, to display integrity and honesty, to have a sense of proprietorship— as if the business belonged to them. Help them to make the kind of decisions that would have to be made if that were true, rather than the kinds they have to make in order to negotiate the turfs of a hostile bureaucracy. Encourage them to go into action and not wait for permission. Talking about these ideas is not enough. Between the words of top management and the intrapreneurs who can carry them out there are layers of management which punish independent thought, courage, impatience, and blunt honesty. This is not something that you can devote a few hours to and fix. It is probably the most important aspect of your job, more important than getting the strategy right, because enough attention is being paid to strategy already.

You cannot have cost-effective innovation unless you hire, train and encourage intrapreneurs. The future legitimacy of R&D, the success of America's companies and of her economy depends on you, the R&D community, to do it right.

Lessons from a New Ventures Program

Hollister B. Sykes

As Exxon's experience shows, if internal venturing is to work, it must be an important mainstream operation.

In 1970, Exxon Enterprises launched a major new ventures program. I was responsible for initiating that program and for managing it until 1981, when the program's focus shifted to the tasks of consolidation and divestment. At the time I left the program, things had not worked out as I had hoped. In retrospect, I think I have a clear understanding of what went wrong—and of what was needed for success.

Our plan was to make exploratory investments in new ventures operating in emerging markets. We would then accelerate investments that proved to have high potential, spin off the rest, and eventually consolidate ventures with related product lines in promising growth areas. We followed two strategies: the creation of internal ventures and direct investment in venture capital situations.

From 1970 through 1980, we made a total of 37 investments, 19 of which were internal ventures (see Table 1). Of the 18 venture-capital-funded companies, Exxon later acquired the 6 most promising.

Mr. Sykes was senior vice president of Exxon Enterprises, where from 1970 to 1981 he headed up the new ventures program. Reprinted with permission of *Harvard Business Review,* May–June 1986. Copyright © 1986 by the President and Fellows of Harvard College; all rights reserved.

TABLE 1. *37 Venture Investments*

19 Internal Ventures	
Advanced materials, components, and systems	7
Energy conversion and storage systems	5
Information systems and system components	7
18 Venture Capital Investments	
Air pollution control	1
Health care	1
Advanced materials	2
Energy conversion and storage systems	3
Information systems	11

Financially, the venture capital program was very successful. Total investment in the 12 companies that Exxon Enterprises did not ultimately acquire was $12 million. By the end of 1982, they had returned—in cash and the value of securities—$218 million. By contrast, the internal ventures, including those acquired from the venture capital portfolio, though strategically important, did not provide Exxon with a profitable major new business diversification.

My reflections on this experience have taught me some lessons that may be of use to other corporations undertaking an internal ventures program.

CHALLENGES TO MANAGEMENT

Our internal ventures program was not profitable—in part, because of a heavy R&D orientation and, in part, because of an inability to manage growth. Present and projected R&D expenditures for these ventures were quite heavy, and that meant an open-ended drag on future profits. Even where the R&D was successful, we often had to make large additional investments before we could bring products to market. When we sold an optical disk memory venture to Storage Technology Corporation, it was still in the R&D stage. STC then spent more than $100 million on the program without completing the development work needed for commercialization.

Of our 19 internal ventures, 13 involved entirely new technologies. Inevitably, then, our search for emerging technologies and early entry opportunities meant facing unproven markets—and greater risk. At best, some ventures would not make sales until four or five years down the road. We had to educate potential customers on how to use the products, and we had to try out applications before we could assess their cost-effectiveness.

Where both technology and market were new, as in computerized speech recognition, the risk was doubled. We made our initial investment in Verbex in 1972 and introduced commercial products several years later. Market development costs exceeded revenues, however, and experience showed us that we needed a lower cost, higher performance technology.

Delphi was a venture we began in 1974 to develop a computer with a parallel processor architecture for use in electronic voice mail. It made ground-breaking technical progress. We killed it, though, because the definable market did not justify the huge added costs we faced to complete development. We were there too soon.

Looking back, I compared the relative financial success of all 37 ventures and found an inverse relationship between venture success and the level of market and technical risk at the time of our investment (see Figure 1). As a statistical analysis indicates, market risk (RM) plus technical risk (RT) account for roughly 45% of the variability in venture success.

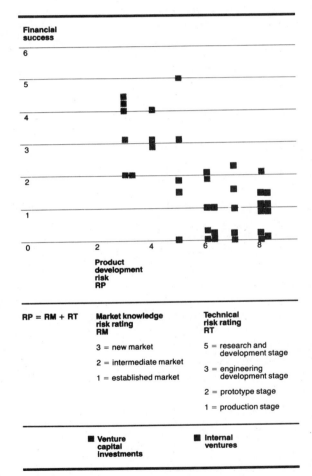

FIGURE 1. *Product Development Risk and Venture Success*

The real issue, though, was management. The managers of our internal ventures were usually technical people with limited supervisory experience and little or no marketing or sales experience. Those responsible for venture-capital-funded companies were usually more experienced and knew more about their industries and technologies. For example, the six key managers of Intecom Corporation, our successful digital PBX venture, had all held executive positions in their former companies and averaged 15 years of experience apiece.

As shown in Figure 2, which plots relative financial success against the managerial (XM) and the relevant sales and marketing (XS) experience of venture management, differences in experience affected venture success. Surprisingly, the level of technical experience (XT) showed no meaningful correlation with venture success. The correlation here is higher than in Figure 1: levels of sales and managerial experience account for some 65% of the variability in venture success. Taken together with product risk, differences in experience explain a total of 68% of such variance.

Even when initially successful, however, ventures often succumb to the "second-product syndrome." Its primary symptoms are a poor coordination of marketing and R&D and a belief that the first success proves the wisdom of management and ensures success the next time around.

The first product is usually created by a small, closely knit team that communicates well, has a single goal, faces none of the distractions of maintaining an ongoing business, and does not have to worry about making a prior product obsolete or a new product compatible. By the time of the second product, the original team members are usually managing functional departments and spending most of their time supervising others or solving problems on the existing product line. Communications about the new product grow cumbersome, and committees inevitably spring up.

Moreover, the greater the first product's suc-

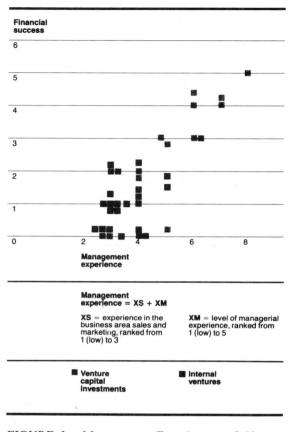

FIGURE 2. *Management Experience and Venture Success*

cess, the more convinced managers are of their ability to introduce another winner. Often forgetting why that product did so well, they set out to conquer new markets without doing adequate analysis or getting the required capabilities in place. The corollary, of course, is that they fail to build on the success of their initial product by enhancing it or lowering its cost. Apple Computer, with its follow-on products to the Apple II, is a good example here, as is the IBM entry systems division with its PC Jr.

Two of Exxon's most successful initial products were the Vydec word processor and the Zilog Z-80 microprocessor. Vydec led its industry by designing the first CRT text editor with floppy disk memory and daisy wheel printer—features that are still industry standards. Later upgrades did offer more features, but the next major new product introductions aimed at new market niches and fell many months behind the promised dates.

The base product, which had a broad market, was slow to apply new microprocessor technology that would have significantly reduced costs. Competitors entered the market and pushed Vydec out of its leadership position. Indeed, Vydec fell so far behind in the product development race that it had to resort to the purchase of a third-party design to try to catch up.

The Zilog Z-80, still the leading 8-bit microprocessor, was compatible with its competitive forerunner, the Intel 8080, but more powerful. Thus it enjoyed a ready-made market base, without having to make the investment normally required to support a new processor with software and peripheral chips. Riding this success, Zilog tackled the RAM market and then the design of a 16-bit microprocessor (the Z-8000) to compete with the Intel 8086.

Chip yields on the RAMs were too low to provide acceptable margins. The ensuing management turmoil, combined with efforts to achieve profitability, was partly responsible for inadequate allocation of resources to the development and marketing of the 16-bit microprocessor. Consequently, the Z-8000 never reached a significant commercial market share. Meanwhile, the market potential for an upwardly compatible extension of the Z-80 line went unrecognized. When at last development of the Z-800 began, it received inadequate support and so lost the large market opportunity now partly filled by the Intel 8088, which is used in the IBM PC.

CHANGES IN THE ENVIRONMENT

As our ventures grew and required new levels of investment, corporate involvement expanded.

Exxon's management procedures and strategic objectives conflicted with the independent start-up environment of the ventures and pushed them toward a more structured, controls-oriented mode of operation. This was perhaps inevitable, but the way it happened hurt the motivation of key people, slowed decision making, and added to venture managers' work loads.

To Exxon's management, multiple ventures with overlapping sales, manufacturing, and engineering organizations appeared inefficient. To the venture managers, especially in the office systems area, requests to coordinate their product design and sales strategies proved unwelcome and easy to resist. The entrepreneurial factors that had originally made the ventures successful began to hinder their operation as an integrated multiproduct organization. In 1981, we joined six of the ventures to form Exxon Office Systems.

My original venture plan had been to grow successful businesses by allowing only the fittest to survive. This approach would test both venture management capability and the commercial viability of the products. We would then either weed out the weak or merge them into the strongest company, where a single management team that had survived the growth phase would carry out needed integration.

Instead, I bowed to pressures for an early consolidation of the office systems ventures in order to achieve efficiencies in product development, manufacturing, and sales. Since no single venture was strong enough to command the respect of the others, we created a new superstructure to which all six ventures were subordinated.

The new management team members had no history of working together. Commitments to goals set by the previous venture managers were put aside because most of the managers no longer had responsibility for the same activities in the new organization. A number eventually resigned, as did talented product development people, who left for greener pastures when development budgets were cut and programs consoli-

133

dated. The result: overhead increased, sales fell off, and losses widened.

Failure to meet expectations about profitability is bad enough. Coupled with a high profile in the media, it can quickly undermine chances for recovery. Negative publicity turned potential customers away and made it harder for us to recruit the managers we needed. Also, R&D-based ventures are sufficiently risky without throwing a spotlight on them too soon, as happened with a number of ours.

Increased corporate involvement led, in turn, to more complex management procedures and to a shift in the way managers were held accountable—as well as rewarded—for the results they had forecast. Corporate review procedures removed decision-making authority from the ventures' boards and moved it up to Exxon staff and committees. Venture managers had to spend extra time and effort bringing Exxon's management up to speed. Although justified by the inexperience of some venture managers, these additional reviews slowed the response to a rapidly changing business environment and distracted attention from venture operations.

Corporate concerns about publicity, image, ethics, legal liabilities, and personnel policies required frequent reports to, and reviews by, corporate staff. Exxon's high profile opened it to spurious lawsuits and complaints that would not have come up in connection with a small, independent company. Because of Exxon's high ethical and legal standards, considerable staff effort went to educate venture personnel on these issues and to review venture contracts and agreements. Worries that a venture's advertising might be misleading or affect another venture or an Exxon affiliate led corporate staff to approve all venture advertising.

The proliferation of new ventures led as well to a variety of financial reporting formats and MIS systems. In several cases, a venture's sales outgrew its accounting systems and caused serious control problems. To promote overall efficiency and improved control, the ventures were eventually asked to change over to compatible systems and to install additional procedures and personnel. Corporate financial staffs expanded to assist and monitor these activities.

Ensuring and documenting fairness and consistency in rating systems, termination policies, and salary administration proved a time-consuming challenge. Above certain levels, Exxon management approved all starting salaries, salary increases, and performance bonus plans. At the ventures and at headquarters, staffs grew larger.

Considered separately, each of these procedures made good sense. Taken together, however, they imposed on each venture the superstructure of a larger corporation and the burden of frequent reporting to the parent corporation. The whole amounted to less than the sum of its parts. As Don Valentine, a long-time venture capitalist, describes it, this corporate bear hug amounts to "death by a thousand cuts. A little nick here, a little cut there, a little change here—nothing significant. But at the end of a short period of time the people are so driven by controlling and accounting that the environment of nonconventional solutions is lost."

Exxon's ability to fund rapid growth might seem from the outside to be an enviable advantage. In practice, however, it tended to cushion venture managers from concern about profitability, cost control, focused product development, and competitive realities. Although we stressed that a successful venture has to run "lean and mean"—and most started out that way—our internal ventures lost touch with the harsh realities of a cash-thin existence.

Sometimes it took traumatic circumstances to convince managers that their ventures could operate in a leaner fashion. When they grossly missed development schedules or marketing forecasts, they had to justify continuing expenses to a skeptical Exxon management. In marginal cases, when expenses had been cut half-heartedly, the top group often concluded that the venture should be sold or shut down. Only when that threat began to sink in did some venture managers come up with tough-minded proposals to get costs under control. As a former manager of Zilog later learned when managing his own independent venture, "Cash is more important than your mother."

Since most of the new businesses required skills not available within Exxon, we had to look outside for qualified personnel. At lower levels, this was not a problem at first, but we had trouble recruiting key people at the managerial level. Candidates wondered about Exxon's long-term commitment to such small and unfamiliar businesses. Would the company really stay with it?

We could not offer equity participation. Although an equity-like incentive compensation plan did come on stream in 1979 for selected ventures, it was too late and too little. Debate over the valuation of equity when ventures were sold or merged hampered the plan's effectiveness. Any formula that does not rely on a public market to determine value is likely to be controversial.

Further, because we pegged managers' salaries to the size of the activity they ran—and not to future business potential—we could not put experienced senior executives in charge of new internal ventures. If the ventures proved successful, they often outgrew the capabilities of the technical people who started them up.

As the ventures grew, it became apparent that the most important environmental issue was Exxon's inability to provide functional support in the new business areas. For example, the company had no computer-industry-experienced manufacturing or sales executives to fill the holes left when the entrepreneurs departed or proved incapable of managing growth. By contrast, Philip Estridge needed only one month to recruit 150 people from with IBM to staff its new PC small business unit. The first day notices went up about the new unit, 500 IBM employees inquired.

Our Vydec word processor was a preemptive product when it came on the market. During the three years it took us to build a na-

tionwide direct marketing organization, Wang, Lanier, IBM, and others moved in with competitive products.

LESSONS LEARNED

Knowing what I know now, here's what I think I would do differently:

1. Acquire an established company in a new business area. Our original "probe and assess" strategy was sound. We made exploratory investments in new areas to determine their potential and to learn about market opportunities. Once we identified these opportunities, however, we should have acquired an established company. Doing so would have given us profits to offset the losses of our R&D ventures, a source of knowledgeable executives, a more attractive career path for new recruits, and a stronger competitive base from which to launch innovative products. We did not follow this course because we were concerned about antitrust objections.

Had we followed this course, we still would have had management problems. In the information systems area, for example, we would have had to give acquired management real autonomy. Even then, we might have lost those key people who valued their complete independence or those for whom we could not work out acceptable compensation and incentive plans.

There is a larger issue here. If a parent company does not provide some added value, then the purchase is no more than a portfolio investment. The alternative is to return the cash to shareholders to invest. The current wave of corporate "restructurings" has the same effect—returning underutilized asset value to the shareholder. We would have to have shown a better return on dollars used to make an acquisition than used to buy back stock. Management is more likely to add value if an acquired company is functionally close to the parent's base business.

2. Start fewer R&D-oriented ventures. The high proportion of R&D ventures in our portfolio greatly increased our risk of failure and stretched out the time from start-up to projected sales. Because most corporations go through cycles in their base businesses, unprofitable operations not in the mainstream are especially vulnerable. Exxon was no exception. The steep slump in the consumption of oil products and natural gas from 1979 to 1982 caused concern. Along with the cutback in Exxon's base business operations, we either sold or liquidated most of our smaller ventures.

The corollary, of course, is to choose new ventures with a short time span between initial investment and profitability. This will cut out most research-based ventures and eliminate the chance of developing another Xerox or Polaroid. But those are pretty long odds anyway.

Because the initial focus of many of our ventures was on developing new technology, we did not bring experienced, high-level marketing managers on board soon enough to shed light on our assumptions about product features and pricing. It is, however, hard to justify full-time marketing executives during a long R&D phase.

3. Use venture capital investments as the primary "probe" strategy. Venture-capital-funded companies are truly independent operations that can attract and hold experienced managers. The incentive for such people to leave solid careers is that they can make a lot of money through capital gains. The drawback, of course, is that successful independent companies usually do not want to be acquired, at least not before the founders and early investors have taken them public. Still, a minority position in a leading growth company can benefit an established corporation—if there is a real fit like that between IBM and Intel in microcomputers.

What are the lessons I have learned?

- As Exxon's experience shows, if internal venturing is to work, it must be an important mainstream operation. The corporation should focus new venture activities on those areas where it has (or intends to commit the necessary long-term resources to build) relevant operating capabilities and management experience. The internal venture approach can be a quick and effective way to develop new products and markets. At that point, however, the parent's resources in manufacturing, marketing, and sales are needed to capitalize fully on the venture's promise.

- It is impossible to preserve completely an independent entrepreneurial environment within a large, multiproduct corporate setting. The principal problems involve equity compensation, product compatibility and coordination, and corporate liability for what ventures do. Venture personnel should understand from the start that they will eventually have to be integrated back into the larger organization if their venture proves successful.

- Politically and strategically, longer term R&D projects are more appropriate to support an established business than to initiate a portfolio of diversified businesses. Unless managers of the base business view the new endeavor as critical to the whole company's future, they are not likely to be tolerant of the high risk of failure and the long period of unprofitability that may precede commercialization.

- Successful new ventures usually focus on a single product. Successful mature companies must learn to manage the complexities of multiple products, new product introductions that make older products obsolete, and product compatibility.

- Management experience in the relevant industry is a significant factor in determining venture success.

- A venture environment that encourages resourcefulness is more important than ample financing.

4

TECHNICAL MANAGEMENT AND LEADERSHIP

Planning on the Left Side and Managing on the Right

Henry Mintzberg

In the folklore of the Middle East, the story is told about a man named Nasrudin, who was searching for something on the ground. A friend came by and asked: "What have you lost, Nasrudin?"

"My key," said Nasrudin.

So, the friend went down on his knees, too, and they both looked for it. After a time, the friend asked: "Where exactly did you drop it?"

"In my house," answered Nasrudin.

"Then why are you looking here, Nasrudin?"

"There is more light here than inside my own house."

This "light" little story is old and worn, yet is has some timeless, mysterious appeal, one which has much to do with the article that follows. But let me leave the story momentarily while I pose some questions—also simple yet mysterious—that have always puzzled me.

First: Why are some people so smart and so dull at the same time, so capable of mastering certain mental activities and so incapable of mastering others? Why is it that some of the most creative thinkers cannot comprehend a balance sheet, and that some accountants have no sense of product design? Why do some brilliant management scientists have no ability to handle organizational politics, while some of the most politically adept individuals cannot seem to understand the simplest elements of management science?

Second: Why do people sometimes express such surprise when they read or learn the obvious, something they already must have known? Why is a manager so delighted, for example, when he reads a new article on decision making, every part of which must be patently obvious to him even though he has never before seen it in print?

Third: Why is there such a discrepancy in organizations, at least at the policy level, between the science and planning of management on the one hand, and managing on the other? Why have none of the techniques of planning and analysis really had much effect on how top managers function?

Reprinted with permission of *Harvard Business Review,* July–August 1976. Copyright © 1976 by the President and Fellows of Harvard College; all rights reserved.

What I plan to do in this article is weave together some tentative answers to these three questions with the story of Nasrudin around a central theme, namely, that of the specialization of the hemispheres of the human brain and what that specialization means for management.

THE TWO HEMISPHERES
OF THE HUMAN BRAIN

Let us first try to answer the three questions by looking at what is known about the hemispheres of the brain.

Question One

Scientists—in particular, neurologists, neurosurgeons, and psychologists—have known for a long time that the brain has two distinct hemispheres. They have known, further, that the left hemisphere controls movements on the body's right side and that the right hemisphere controls movements on the left. What they have discovered more recently, however, is that these two hemispheres are specialized in more fundamental ways.

In the left hemisphere of most people's brains (left-handers largely excepted) the logical thinking processes are found. It seems that the mode of operation of the brain's left hemisphere is linear; it processes information sequentially, one bit after another, in an ordered way. Perhaps the most obvious linear faculty is language. In sharp contrast, the right hemisphere is specialized for simultaneous processing; that is, it operates in a more holistic, relational way. Perhaps its most obvious faculty is comprehension of visual images.

Although relatively few specific mental activities have yet been associated with one hemisphere or the other, research is proceeding very quickly. For example, a recent article in *The New York Times* cites research which suggests that

emotion may be a right-hemispheric function.[1] This notion is based on the finding that victims of right-hemispheric strokes are often comparatively untroubled about their incapacity, while those with strokes of the left hemisphere often suffer profound mental anguish.

What does this specialization of the brain mean for the way people function? Speech, being linear, is a left-hemispheric activity, but other forms of human communication, such as gesturing, are relational rather than sequential and tend to be associated with the right hemisphere. Imagine what would happen if the two sides of a human brain were detached so that, for example, in reacting to a stimulus, a person's words would be separate from his gestures. In other words, the person would have two separate brains—one specialized for verbal communication, and the other for gestures—that would react to the same stimulus.

This "imagining," in fact, describes how the main breakthrough in the recent research on the human brain took place. In trying to treat certain cases of epilepsy, neurosurgeons found that by severing the corpus callosum, which joins the two hemispheres of the brain, they could "split the brain," isolating the epilepsy. A number of experiments run on these "split-brain" patients produced some fascinating results.

In one experiment doctors showed a woman epileptic's right hemisphere a photograph of a nude woman. (This is done by showing it to the left half of each eye.) The patient said she saw nothing, but almost simultaneously blushed and seemed confused and uncomfortable. Her "conscious" left hemisphere, including her verbal apparatus, was aware only that something had happened to her body, but not of what had caused the emotional turmoil. Only her "unconscious" right hemisphere knew. Here neurosurgeons observed a clear split between the two independent consciousnesses that are normally in communication and collaboration.[2]

Now, scientists have further found that some common human tasks activate one side of the brain while leaving the other largely at rest. For example, a person's learning a mathematical proof might evoke activity in the left hemisphere of his brain, while his conceiving a piece of sculpture or assessing a political opponent might evoke activity in his right.

So now we seem to have the answer to the first question. An individual can be smart and dull at the same time simply because one side of his or her brain is more developed than the other. Some people—probably most lawyers, accountants, and planners—have better developed left-hemispheric thinking processes, while others—artists, sculptors, and perhaps politicians—have better developed right-hemispheric processes. Thus an artist may be incapable of expressing his feelings in words, while a lawyer may have no facility for painting. Or a politician may not be able to learn mathematics, while a management scientist may constantly be manipulated in political situations.

Eye movement is apparently a convenient indicator of hemispheric development. When asked to count the letters in a complex word such as *Mississippi* in their heads, most people will gaze off to the side opposite their most developed hemisphere. (Be careful of lefties, however.) But if the question is a specialized one—for example, if it is emotionally laden, spatial, or purely mathematical—the number of people gazing one way or another will change substantially.

Question Two

A number of word opposites have been proposed to distinguish the two hemispheric modes of "consciousness," for example: explicit versus implicit; verbal versus intuitive; and analytic versus gestalt.

I should interject at this point that these words, as well as much of the evidence for these conclusions, can be found in the remarkable book entitled *The Psychology of Consciousness* by Robert Ornstein, a research psychologist in California. Ornstein uses the story of Nasrudin

to further the points he is making. Specifically, he refers to the linear left hemisphere as synonymous with lightness, with thought processes that we know in an explicit sense. We can *articulate* them. He associates the right hemisphere with darkness, with thought processes that are mysterious to us, at least "us" in the Western world.

Ornstein also points out how the "esoteric psychologies" of the East (Zen, Yoga, Sufism, and so on) have focused on right-hemispheric consciousness (for example, altering pulse rate through meditation). In sharp contrast, Western psychology has been concerned almost exclusively with left-hemispheric consciousness, with logical thought. Ornstein suggests that we might find an important key to human consciousness in the right hemisphere, in what to us in the West is the darkness. To quote him:

> Since these experiences (transcendence of time, control of the nervous system, paranormal communication, and so on) are, by their very mode of operation, not readily accessible to causal explanation or even to linguistic exploration, many have been tempted to ignore them or even to deny their existence. These traditional psychologies have been relegated to the "esoteric" or the "occult," the realm of the mysterious—the word most often employed is "mysticism." It is a taboo area of inquiry, which has been symbolized by the Dark, the Left side (the right hemisphere) of ourselves, the Night.[3]

Now, reflect on this for a moment. (Should I say meditate?) There is a set of thought processes—linear, sequential, analytical—that scientists as well as the rest of us know a lot about. And there is another set—simultaneous, relational, holistic—that we know little about. More importantly, here we do not "know" what we "know" or, more exactly, our left hemispheres cannot articulate explicitly what our right hemispheres know implicitly.

So here is, seemingly, the answer to the second question as well. The feeling of revelation about learning the obvious can be explained with the suggestion that the "obvious" knowledge was implicit, apparently restricted to the right hemisphere. The left hemisphere never "knew." Thus it seems to be a revelation to the left hemisphere when it learns explicitly what the right hemisphere knew all along implicitly.

Now only the third question—the discrepancy between planning and managing—remains.

Question Three

By now, it should be obvious where my discussion is leading (obvious, at least, to the reader's right hemisphere and, now that I write it, to the reader's left hemisphere as well). It may be that management researchers have been looking for the key to management in the lightness of logical analysis whereas perhaps it has always been lost in the darkness of intuition.

Specifically, I propose that there may be a fundamental difference between formal planning and informal managing, a difference akin to that between the two hemispheres of the human brain. The techniques of planning and management science are sequential and systematic; above all, articulated. Planners and management scientists are expected to proceed in their work through a series of logical, ordered steps, each one involving explicit analysis. (The argument that the successful application of these techniques requires considerable intuition does not really change my point. The occurrence of intuition simply means that the analyst is departing from his science, as it is articulated, and is behaving more like a manager.)

Formal planning, then, seems to use processes akin to those identified with the brain's left hemisphere. Furthermore, planners and management scientists seem to revel in a systematic, well-ordered world, and many show little appreciation for the more relational, holistic processes.

What about managing? More exactly, what about the processes used by top managers? (Let me emphasize here that I am focusing this discussion at the policy level of organizations, where I

believe the dichotomy between planning and managing is most sharp.) Managers plan in some ways, too, (that is, they think ahead) and they engage in their share of logical analysis. But I believe there is more than that to the effective managing of an organization. I hypothesize, therefore, that *the important policy processes of managing an organization rely to a considerable extent on the faculties identified with the brain's right hemisphere.* Effective managers seem to revel in ambiguity; in complex, mysterious systems with relatively little order.

If true, this hypothesis would answer the third question about the discrepancy between planning and managing. It would help to explain why each of the new analytic techniques of planning and analysis has, one after the other, had so little success at the policy level. PPBS, strategic planning, "management" (or "total") information systems, and models of the company—all have been greeted with great enthusiasm; then, in many instances, a few years later have been quietly ushered out the corporate back door. Apparently none served the needs of decision making at the policy level in organizations; at that level other processes may function better.

Managing from the Right Hemisphere

Because research has so far told us little about the right hemisphere, I cannot support with evidence my claim that a key to managing lies there. I can only present to the reader a "feel" for the situation, not a reading of concrete data. A number of findings from my own research on policy-level processes do, however, suggest that they possess characteristics of right-hemispheric thinking.[4]

One fact recurs repeatedly in all of this research: the key managerial processes are enormously complex and mysterious (to me as a researcher, as well as to the managers who carry them out), drawing on the vaguest of information and using the least articulated of mental processes. These processes seem to be more relational and holistic than ordered and sequential, and more intuitive than intellectual; they seem to be most characteristic of right-hemispheric activity.

Here are ten general findings:

1. The five chief executives I observed strongly favored the verbal media of communication, especially meetings, over the written forms, namely ready and writing. (The same result has been found in virtually every study of managers, no matter what their level in the organization or the function they supervised.) Of course verbal communication is linear, too, but it is more than that. Managers seem to favor it for two fundamental reasons that suggest a relational mode of operation.

First, verbal communication enables the manager to "read" facial expressions, tones of voice, and gestures. As I mentioned earlier, these stimuli seem to be processed in the right hemisphere of the brain. Second, and perhaps more important, verbal communication enables the manager to engage in the "real-time" exchange of information. Managers' concentration on the verbal media, therefore, suggests that they desire relational, simultaneous methods of acquiring information, rather than the ordered and sequential ones.

2. In addition to noting the media managers use, it is interesting to look at the content of managers' information, and at what they do with it. The evidence here is that a great deal of the manager's inputs are soft and speculative—impressions and feelings about other people, hearsay, gossip, and so on. Furthermore, the very analytical inputs—reports, documents, and hard data in general—seem to be of relatively little importance to many managers. (After a steady diet of soft information, one chief executive came across the first piece of hard data he had seen all week—an accounting report—and put it aside with the comment, "I never look at this.")

What can managers do with this soft, speculative information? They "synthesize" rather than "analyze" it, I should think. (How do you analyze the mood of a friend or the grimace someone makes in response to a suggestion?) A great deal of this information helps the manager understand implicitly his organization and its environment, to "see the big picture." This very expression, so common in management, implies a relational, holistic use of information. In effect, managers (like everyone else) use their information to build mental "models" of their world, which are implicit synthesized apprehensions of how their organizations and environments function. Then, whenever an action is contemplated, the manager can simulate the outcome using his implicit models.

There can be little doubt that this kind of activity goes on all the time in the world of management. A number of words managers commonly use suggest this kind of mental process. For example, the word "hunch" seems to refer to the thought that results from such an implicit simulation. "I don't know why, but I have a hunch that if we do x, then they will respond with y." Managers also use the word *judgment* to refer to thought processes that work but are unknown to them. *Judgment* seems to be the word that the verbal intellect has given to the thought processes that it cannot articulate. Maybe "he has good judgment" simply means "he has good right-hemispheric models."

3. Another consequence of the verbal nature of the manager's information is of interest here. The manager tends to be the best informed member of his organization, but he has difficulty disseminating his information to his employees. Therefore, when a manager overloaded with work finds a new task that needs doing, he faces a dilemma: he must either delegate the task without the background information or simply do the task himself, neither of which is satisfactory.

When I first encountered this dilemma of delegation, I described it in terms of time and of the nature of the manager's information; because so much of a manager's information is verbal (and stored in his head), the dissemination of it consumes much of his time. But now the split-brain research suggests that a second, perhaps more significant, reason for the dilemma of delegation exists. The manager may simply be incapable of disseminating some relevant information because it is removed from his verbal consciousness. (This suggests that we might need a kind of managerial psychoanalyst to coax it out of him!)

4. Earlier in this article I wrote that managers revel in ambiguity, in complex, mysterious systems without much order. Let us look at evidence of this. What I have discussed so far about the manager's use of information suggests that their work is geared to action, not reflection. We see further evidence for this in the pace of their work ("Breaks are rare. It's one damn thing after another"); the brevity of their activities (half of the chief executives' activities I observed were completed in less than 9 minutes); the variety of their activities (the chief executives had no evident patterns in their workdays); the fact that they actively exhibit a preference for interruption in their work (stopping meetings, leaving their doors open); and the lack of routine in their work (only 7% of 368 verbal contacts I observed were regularly scheduled, only 1% dealt with a general issue that was in any way related to general planning).

Clearly, the manager does not operate in a systematic, orderly, and intellectual way, puffing his pipe up in a mountain retreat, as he analyzes his problems. Rather, he deals with issues in the context of daily activities—the cigarette in his mouth, one hand on the telephone, and the other shaking hands with a departing guest. The manager is involved, plugged in; his mode of operating is relational, simultaneous, experiential, that is, encompassing all the characteristics of the right hemisphere.

5. If the most important managerial roles of the ten described in the research were to be isolated, *leader, liaison,* and *disturbance handler* would certainly be among them. (The other seven are *figurehead, monitor, disseminator, spokesman, negotiator, entrepreneur,* and *resource allo-*cator, and the last two are also among the most important roles.) Yet these three are the roles least "known" about. *Leader* describes how the manager deals with his own employees. It is ironic that despite an immense amount of research, managers and researchers still know virtually nothing about the essence of leadership, about why some people follow and others lead. Leadership remains a mysterious chemistry; catchall words such as *charisma* proclaim our ignorance.

In the *liaison* role, the manager builds up a network of outside contacts, which serve as his or her personal information system. Again, the activities of this role remain almost completely outside the realm of articulated knowledge. And as a *disturbance handler* the manager handles problems and crisis in his organization. Here again, despite an extensive literature on analytical decision making, virtually nothing is written about decision making under pressure. These activities remain outside the realm of management science, inside the realm of intuition and experience.

6. Let us turn now to strategic decision-making processes. There are 7 "routines" that seem to describe the steps involved in such decision making. These are *recognition, diagnosis, search, design, screening, evaluation/choice,* and *authorization.* Two of these routines stand out above the rest—the *diagnosis* of decision situations and the design of custom-made solutions—in that almost nothing is known of them. Yet these two stand out for another reason as well: they are probably the most important of the seven. In particular, diagnosis seems to be *the* crucial step in strategic decision making, for it is in that routine that the whole course of decision making is set.

It is a surprising fact, therefore, that diagnosis goes virtually without mention in the literature of planning or management science. (Almost all of the later literature deals with the formal evaluation of given alternatives, yet this is often a kind of trimming on the process, insig-

nificant in terms of determining actual outcomes.) In the study of the decision processes
themselves, the managers making the decisions
mentioned taking an explicit diagnostic step in
only 14 of the 25 decision processes. But all the
managers must have made some diagnosis; it is
difficult to imagine a decision-making process
with no diagnosis at all, no assessment of the situation. The question is, therefore, *where* did diagnosis take place?

7. Another point that emerges from studying
strategic decision-making processes is the existence and profound influence of what can be
called the *dynamic factors*. Strategic decision-
making processes are stopped by interruptions,
delayed and speeded up by timing factors, and
forced repeatedly to branch and cycle. The processes are, therefore, dynamic ones of importance. Yet it is the dynamic factors that the ordered, sequential techniques of analysis are least
able to handle. Thus, despite their importance,
the dynamic factors go virtually without mention
in the literature of management science.

Let's look at timing, for example. It is evident that timing is crucial in virtually everything
the manager does. No manager takes action
without considering the effect of moving more or
less quickly, of seizing the initiative, or of delay-
ing to avoid complications. Yet in one review of
the literature of management, the authors found
fewer than 10 books in 183 that refer directly to
the subject of timing.[5] Essentially, managers are
left on their own to deal with the dynamic factors, which involve simultaneous, relational
modes of thinking.

8. When managers do have to make serious
choices from among options, how do they in fact
make them? Three fundamental modes of selection can be distinguished—analysis, judgment,
and bargaining. The first involves the systematic
evaluation of options in terms of their consequences on stated organizational goals; the second is a process in the mind of a single decision
maker; and the third involves negotiations between different decision makers.

One of the most surprising facts about how
managers made the 25 strategic decisions studied
is that so few reported using explicit analysis;
only in 18 out of 83 choices made did managers
mention using it. There was considerable bargaining, but in general the selection mode most
commonly used was judgment. Typically, the options and all kinds of data associated with them
were pumped into the mind of a manager, and
somehow a choice later came out. *How* was
never explained. *How* is never explained in any
of the literature either. Yehezkel Dror, a leading
figure in the study of public policy making, is
one of the few thinkers to face the issue squarely.
He writes:

> Experienced policy makers, who usually explain
> their own decisions largely in terms of subcon-
> scious processes such as "intuition" and "judg-
> ment," unanimously agree, and even emphasize,
> that extrarational processes play a positive and es-
> sential role in policymaking. Observations of
> policymaking behavior in both small and large
> systems, indeed, all available description of
> decisional behavior, especially that of leaders
> such as Bismarck, Churchill, DeGaulle, and
> Kennedy, seem to confirm this opinion about
> policymaking.[6]

9. Finally, in the area of strategy formulation, I can offer only a "feel" for the results
since my research is still in progress. However,
some ideas have emerged. Strategy formulation
does not turn out to be the regular, continuous,
systematic process depicted in so much of the
planning literature. It is most often an irregular,
discontinuous process, proceeding in fits and
starts. There are periods of stability in strategy
development, but also there are periods of flux,
of groping, of piecemeal change, and of global
change. To my mind, a "strategy" represents the
mediating force between a dynamic environment
and a stable operating system. Strategy is the organization's "conception" of how to deal with
its environment for a while.

Now, the environment does not change in

any set pattern. For example, the environment does not run on planners' five-year schedules; it may be stable for thirteen years, and then suddenly blow all to hell in the fourteenth. And even if change were steady, the human brain does not generally perceive it that way. People tend to underreact to mild stimuli and overreact to strong ones. It stands to reason, therefore, that strategies that mediate between environments and organizational operations do not change in regular patterns, but rather, as I observed earlier, in fits and starts.

How does strategic planning account for fits and starts? The fact is that it does not (as planners were made so painfully aware of during the energy crisis). So again, the burden to cope falls on the manager, specifically on his mental processes—intuitional and experiential—that can deal with the irregular inputs from the environment.

10. Let me probe more deeply into the concept of strategy. Consider the organization that has no strategy, no way to deal consistently with its environment; it simply reacts to each new pressure as it comes along. This is typical behavior for an organization in a very difficult situation, where the old strategy has broken down beyond repair, but where no new strategy has yet emerged. Now, if the organization wishes to formulate a new strategy, how does it do so (assuming that the environment has stabilized sufficiently to allow a new strategy to be formulated)?

Let me suggest two ways (based on still tentative results). If the organization goes the route of systematic planning, I suggest that it will probably come up with what can be called a "main-line" strategy. In effect, it will do what is generally expected of organizations in its situation; where possible, for example, it will copy the established strategies of other organizations. If it is in the automobile business, for instance, it might use the basic General Motors strategy, as Chrysler and Ford have so repeatedly done.

Alternatively, if the organization wishes to have a creative, integrated strategy which can be called a "gestalt strategy," such as Volkswagen's one in the 1950s, then I suggest the organization will rely largely on one individual to conceptualize its strategy, to synthesize a "vision" of how the organization will respond to its environment. In other words, scratch an interesting strategy, and you will probably find a single strategy formulator beneath it. Creative, integrated strategies seem to be the products of single areas, perhaps of single right hemispheres.

A strategy can be made explicit, can be announced as what the organization intends to do in the future, only when the vision is fully worked out, if it ever is. Often, of course, it is never felt to be fully worked out hence the strategy is never made explicit and remains the private vision of the chief executive. (Of course, in some situations the formulator need not be the manager. There is no reason why a manager cannot have a creative right-hand man—really a left-hand man—who works out his gestalt strategy for him, and then articulates it to him.) No management process is more demanding of holistic, relational, gestalt thinking than the formulation of a creative, integrated strategy to deal with a complex, intertwined environment.

How can sequential analysis (under the label *strategic planning*) possibly lead to a gestalt strategy?

Another "famous old story" has relevance here. It is the one about the blind men trying to identify an elephant by touch. One grabs the trunk and says the elephant is long and soft; another holds the leg and says it is massive and cylindrical; a third touches the skin and says it is rough and scaly. What the story points out is that—

> Each person standing at one part of the elephant can make his own limited, analytic assessment of the situation, but we do not obtain an elephant by adding "scaly," "long and soft," "massive and cylindrical" together in any conceivable proportion. Without the development of an overall perspective, we remain lost in our individual investi-

gations. Such a perspective is a province of another mode of knowledge, and cannot be achieved in the same way that individual parts are explored. It does not arise out of a linear sum of independent observations.[7]

What can we conclude from these ten findings? I must first reemphasize that everything I write about the two hemispheres of the brain falls into the realm of speculation. Researchers have yet to formally relate any management process to the functioning of the human brain. Nevertheless, the ten points do seem to support the hypothesis stated earlier: *the important policy-level processes required to manage an organization rely to a considerable extent on the faculties identified with the brain's right hemisphere.*

This conclusion does not imply that the left hemisphere is unimportant for policy makers. I have overstated my case here to emphasize the importance of the right. The faculties identified with the left hemisphere are obviously important as well for effective management. Every manager engages in considerable explicit calculation when he or she acts, and all intuitive thinking must be translated into the linear order of the left if it is to be articulated and eventually put to use. The great powers that appear to be associated with the right hemisphere are obviously useless without the faculties of the left. The artist can create without verbalizing; the manager cannot.

Truly outstanding managers are no doubt the ones who can couple effective right-hemispheric processes (hunch, judgment, synthesis, and so on) with effective processes of the left (articulateness, logic, analysis, and so on). But there will be little headway in the field of management if managers and researchers continue to search for the key to managing in the lightness of ordered analysis. Too much will stay unexplained in the darkness of intuition.

Before I go on to discuss the implications for management science and planning, I want to stress again that throughout this article I have

been focusing on processes that managers employ at the policy level of the organization. It seems that the faculties identified with the right-hemispheric activities are most important in the higher levels of an organization, at least in those with "top-down" policy-making systems.

In a sense, the coupling of the holistic and the sequential reflects how bureaucratic organizations themselves work. The policy maker conceives the strategy in holistic terms, and the rest of the hierarchy—the functional departments, branches, and shops—implement it in sequence. Whereas the right-hemispheric faculties may be more important at the top of an organization, the left-hemispheric ones may dominate lower down.

IMPLICATIONS FOR THE LEFT HEMISPHERE

Let us return to practical reality for a final word. What does all I've discussed mean for those associated with management?

For Planners and Management Scientists

No, I do not suggest that planners and management scientists pack up their bags of techniques and leave the field of management, or that they take up basket-weaving or meditation in their spare time. (I haven't—at least not yet!) It seems to me that the left hemisphere is alive and well; the analytic community is firmly established, and indispensable, at the operating and middle levels of most organizations. Its real problems occur at the policy level. Here analysis must co-exist with—perhaps even take its lead from—intuition, a fact that many analysts and planners have been slow to accept. To my mind, organizational effectiveness does not lie in that narrow-minded concept called "rationality"; it lies in a blend of clear-headed logic *and* powerful intuition. Let me illustrate this with two points.

1. *First, only under special circumstances should planners try to plan.* When an organization is in a stable environment and has no use for a very creative strategy—the telephone industry may be the best example—then the development of formal, systematic strategic plans (and mainline strategies) may be in order. But when the environment is unstable or the organization needs a creative strategy, then strategic planning may not be the best approach to strategy formulation, and planners have no business pushing the organization to use it.

2. *Second, effective decision making at the policy level requires good analytical input; it is the job of the planner and management scientist to ensure that top management gets it.* Managers are very effective at securing soft information; but they tend to underemphasize analytical input that is often important as well. The planners and management scientists can serve their organizations effectively by carrying out ad hoc analyses and feeding the results to top management (need I say verbally?), ensuring that the very best of analysis is brought to bear on policy making. But at the same time, planners need to recognize that these inputs cannot be the only ones used in policy making, that soft information is crucial as well.

For the Teacher of Managers

If the suggestions in this article turn out to be valid, then educators had better revise drastically some of their notions about management education, because the revolution in that sphere over the last fifteen years—while it has brought so much of use—has virtually consecrated the modern management school to the worship of the left hemisphere.

Should educators be surprised that so many of their graduates end up in staff positions, with no intention of ever managing anything? Some of the best-known management schools have become virtual closed systems in which professors with little interest in the reality of organizational life teach inexperienced students the theories of mathematics, economics, and psychology as ends in themselves. In these management schools, management is accorded little place.

I am not preaching a return to the management school of the 1950s. That age of fuzzy thinking has passed, thankfully. Rather, I am calling for a new balance in our schools, the balance that the best of human brains can achieve, between the analytic and the intuitive. In particular, greater use should be made of the powerful new skill-development techniques which are experiential and creative in nature, such as role playing, the use of video-tape, behavior laboratories, and so on. Educators need to put students into situations, whether in the field or in the simulated experience of the laboratory, where they can practice managerial skills, not only interpersonal but also informational and decisional. Then specialists would follow up with feedback on the students' behavior and performance.

For Managers

The first conclusion for managers should be a call for caution. The findings of the cognitive psychologists should not be taken as license to shroud activities in darkness. The mystification of conscious behavior is a favorite ploy of those seeking to protect a power base (or to hide their intentions of creating one), this behavior helps no organization, and neither does forcing to the realm of intuition activities that can be handled effectively by analysis.

A major thrust of development in our organizations, ever since Frederick Taylor began experimenting in factories late in the last century, has been to shift activities out of the realm of intuition, toward conscious analysis. That trend will continue. But managers, and those who work with them, need to be careful to distinguish that which is best handled analytically from that which must remain in the realm of intuition, where, in the meantime, we should be looking for the lost keys to management.

NOTES

1. Richard Restak, "The Hemispheres of the Brain Have Minds of Their Own." *New York Times,* 25 January 1976.
2. Robert Ornstein, *The Psychology of Consciousness* (San Francisco: W. H. Freeman, 1975), p. 60.
3. Ibid., p. 97.
4. These findings are based on (a) my observational study of the work of five chief executives reported in *The Nature of Managerial Work* (New York: Harper and Row, 1973) and in "The Manager's Job: Folklore and Fact" (HBR July–August 1975, p. 49); (b) a study of twenty-five strategic decision processes reported in "The Structure of 'Unstructured' Decision Processes," coauthored with Duru Raisinghani and Andre Theoret, to appear in a forthcoming issue of *Administrative Science Quarterly;* and (c) a series of studies carried out under my supervision at McGill University on the formation of organizational strategies over periods of decades, reported in "Patterns in Strategy Formation," Working Paper I.A.E., Aix-en-Provence, France, submitted for publication.
5. Clyde T. Hardwick, and Bernard R. Landuyt, *Administrative Strategy and Decision Making,* 2nd ed. (Cincinnati: South-Western, 1966).
6. Yehezkel Dror, *Public Policymaking Re-Examined* (Scranton: Chandler, 1968), p. 149.

Leadership and the Professional

Morgan W. McCall, Jr.

A scientist usually conceives of managing as alien to his interests. Managers are usually looked down upon by scientists because they do not measure up to the high standards of technical competency that scientists see themselves as holding.
—A chemist reflecting on his work experience

At work. I'm a very difficult SOB, and that's not a character recommendation I'm particularly proud of. I feel guilty very often, but I'm so difficult that no one works for me unless they're good enough and tough enough. I explode all the time. I'm like the office plague; I snoop into everything and everyone wishes I'd stay out so I don't screw it up. But that lab is my baby.
—L. Janos, 1980

The explosion of technology has caused a dramatic increase in the number of professionals in the work force (1.7 million in 1970—about one in every fifty workers), and all indications are that knowledge industries will continue to grow (Kaufman, 1974). This is sufficient reason for interest in how to manage professionals, but their critical role in the invention and development of technology (often held out as the answer to society's many problems) creates a sense of urgency to use this talent effectively. Are professionals so different from other workers that leading them is a special challenge? Certainly the quotations above suggest some eccentricity in professionals, as workers and as managers, as do the new organizational structures emerging to accommodate professionals at work, including matrix designs and innovation-focused adhocracy.

We will address four topics here. The first order of business is to look at who is being led. Who are these "professionals"? What are they like and how are they different from the rest of us? Where is this "leading" taking place and how important is the setting?

The second topic is supervision, or the leadership of small groups of professionals. What can the "chief" or supervisor do that might make some difference in the productivity of his or her professional subordinates?

Third, what are the broader aspects of leadership? How do groups of professionals come to affect the organization and what does leadership at the interface look like?

Finally, we examine the tough choice faced by many professionals: to accept an opportunity to become a manager or to stay in a specialty area. Is it true that managerial work is the antithesis of scientific work?

From T. Connolly (ed.), *Scientists, Engineers, and Organizations,* PWS-Kent Publishing Co., copyright © 1983 by Wadsworth, Inc. Reprinted with permission.

WHO IS BEING LED?

They are about like other people, as assorted as
cobblers, labor leaders, Javanese dancers,
throat specialists, whalers, minor canons, or
asparagus growers.
　　　—Sinclair Lewis, quoted by S. James, 1980

The term "professional" is ambiguous. Doctors, lawyers, CPAs, engineers, scientists, and many others are called professionals, and battles for legitimacy occur as excluded groups, such as managers, seek recognition as professionals. Given the diversity of occupations typically considered professional, there is no reason to believe that professionals constitute a homogeneous class. As will be shown, scientists and engineers differ from each other in many ways, in spite of their professional status. Recognizing this ambiguity does not prevent a discussion of leadership and professionals, but it does dictate certain limitations. This chapter is based on research findings, and most of the research on professionals has been done with scientists and/or engineers. Furthermore, there are different kinds of scientists and engineers who vary dramatically in terms of education and training—in short, some are more "professional" than others. To accommodate these differences, we will define professionals by the degree to which they fit characteristics identified by Kerr, Von Glinow, and Schriesheim (1977):

1. **Expertise.** They have prolonged, specialized training.
2. **Autonomy.** They have the right to decide on the means and ends in their work.
3. **Commitment.** They are devoted to their work and to their profession.
4. **Identification.** Their lot is cast with their profession and their fellow professionals.
5. **Ethics.** They aspire to be unemotional and unselfish in the conduct of their professional activities.

6. **Collegial maintenance of standards.** They take responsibility for setting and enforcing standards for their profession.

For our purposes, then, leaders of professionals are managers of people who value expertise, autonomy, etc. (primarily scientists and engineers). These people can be found in all kinds of organizations, from small private firms to universities, the space agency, and high technology industries. For the most part, the research reported here was done in large, complex organizations.

As noted earlier, most of the research on this type of leadership deals with scientists and/or engineers. In general, scientists are more "professional" against the stereotype because they are generally more committed to professional goals than engineers (who tend to identify more with business goals) (Rotondi, 1975; Barth and Vertinsky, 1975). Furthermore, over 90 percent of engineers do not have doctoral degrees and fully one-third do not belong to a professional society (Kerr et al., 1977). In fact, scientists and engineers typically have an uneasy peace with one another, and getting them to work together can be a key managerial challenge (Sayles and Chandler, 1971). Scientists and engineers also differ in vocational interest patterns (see Table 1) (Holland, 1973).

These differences have two important implications. First, all professionals, even scientists and engineers, are not alike. There are immense differences among occupations and among individuals within occupations (see, for example, Gough and Woodworth, 1960). To speak of leadership of professionals is to speak in simplified terms about complex realities.

Second, the available research does not always distinguish among the types of professionals studied. Generalizations drawn from that research can be misleading to the extent that the variation among occupations comprising professional samples is as great as the variation between professionals and nonprofessionals.

TABLE 1.   *Differences in Vocational Interests*

Scientists: Investigative Type	Engineers: Realistic Type
• Prefer symbolic, creative investigation	• Prefer to manipulate objects
• Value science, scholarship in problem solving	• Solve problems with realistic competence
• Adverse to persuasive, social, repetitive activities	• Avoid activities of social occupations
• Deficient in persuasive competence	• Deficient in social competencies
• Avoid enterprising occupations	• Recognize their own low human relations skills
• See themselves lacking in leadership ability	

Source: Adapted from Holland, 1973, and Campbell, 1974.

With these reservations, we can proceed to describe professionals in general, relative to nonprofessionals. A summary of the research (Filley, House, and Kerr, 1976) suggests that professional workers are more likely than their nonprofessional counterparts to

- Be seen by the organization as esoteric and more interested in their narrow specialties than in solving organizational problems
- See the organization as too pragmatic, solving problems by the seat-of-the-pants approach
- Be less loyal to the employing organization and more critical of it
- Place less importance on money and more importance on the freedom to pursue projects of interest to them and on the quality of facilities and support services
- Accept authority based on expertise rather than hierarchy
- Emphasize professional values over organizational goals.

Obviously, the potential for conflict between professionals and the bureaucratic organizations employing them is high (Schriesheim, Von Glinow, and Kerr, 1977), but conflict is not inevitable. Professionals' commitment to the organization will be stronger when job opportunities outside the firm are absent or inferior to those within, when the organization bestows high prestige on its professional groups, as the profession-

als grow older, and as they move into management (Filley, House, and Kerr, 1976). The challenge of leading a less organizationally committed professional group is clearly different from, if not greater than, leading a committed one.

We have defined professionalism as a function of expertise, autonomy, commitment, identification, ethics, and collegial maintenance of standards. Although professionals differ among themselves in many ways, professionally oriented people differ even more from the less professionally oriented on many dimensions, including commitment to the organization, problem-solving approach, feelings about authority, and value of organizational rewards. These differences can amount to what has been called a "cosmopolitan" value system (see, e.g., Goldberg, 1976), which is, essentially, devotion to the profession and its standards that supersedes commitment to the organization and its goals.

Understanding these general differences about professionals is part of the foundation for looking at the leadership of professionals. Unfortunately the other parts are not well researched, and so can only be mentioned.

First, professionals often have some choice about the type of organization they will work in. Universities may be more consonant with the general professional value system described by Kerr, Von Glinow, and Schriesheim (1977) than are commercial enterprises. It is likely, therefore, that professionals who choose careers in industry are to some degree sympathetic to the exigencies of private enterprise.

Second, the structure of the organization is likely to affect at least some of the leadership problems faced. We know, for example, that the problems in project management differ from those in functional management (Reeser, 1969). Project organization generates more job insecurity beause projects end and people must be re-assigned; and leaders may have to create "makework" to keep people occupied between projects. Other structural factors are obviously important, such as the differences between an R&D lab isolated from ongoing operations and an organization with a high percentage of professionals on-line.

A third factor is the mission of the professionals. Leadership of a mission to produce new ideas or technological innovation would seem fundamentally different from leadership to use, develop, or improve that which already exists, even though both activities involve professional workers.

This is not to say that general conclusions about the leadership of professionals cannot be drawn. Rather, it emphasizes that generalities are not a substitute for thoughtful consideration of the situation at hand. Among the considerations are the degree of conflict between professional and organizational values; the structural relationships between professionals and the rest of the organization, and the structure of the professional groups themselves; and the kind of mission or goal they are pursuing.

SUPERVISION: LEADERSHIP OF PROFESSIONAL GROUPS

Leadership, then, is the ability to tie men and women to one's person and cause. But how is that done? Leadership is obviously a combination of many things. . . . When pressures increase, we turn to those we trust to act in the general interest. . . . Some people simply seem to have an aura around them that inspires trust and confidence. We have faith in them and in their ability to deal with matters in a way that will be satisfactory to us. They inspire our confidence and we grant them our loyalty. These are the qualities that unite followers and that leaders, somehow, in some mysterious way, are able to call forth. Quite simply, we know leadership when we experience it.

—L. P. Williams, 1980

For our purposes, leadership is defined as a relationship between a formal leader and a follower group consisting of professionals. For the most part, the research has not considered the context in which the group is embedded, thereby assuming that groups of professionals (generally in R&D settings) are similar. The "test" of leadership is some measure of group output, such as peer performance ratings, or the number of patents or papers.

We have already shown that professionals seek autonomy and have high levels of expertise. This suggests that leadership might not have as much impact on group performance for professionals as it does for nonprofessionals. Our first question, then, is how much difference does leadership make?

Kerr (1977) has argued that certain individual, task, and organizational characteristics can "neutralize or substitute for the formal leader's ability to influence work group satisfaction and performance for either better or worse." These "substitutes for leadership," Kerr argues, are particularly prevalent in professional settings:

There are several reasons why the working environment of professionals employed in organizations presents special opportunities for leadership substitutes to flourish and hierarchical leadership to be consequently less important. The professional's expertise, normally acquired as a result of specialized training in a body of abstract knowledge, often serves to reduce the need for structuring information; furthermore, a belief in peer review and collegial maintenance of standards often causes the professional to look to fellow professionals rather than to the hierarchical leader for what informational needs remain.

In an empirical study of leadership effects on eighty-one subunits of a research organization, Barnowe (1975) concluded that "clearly, the better part of variation in research outcomes was attributable to factors other than leadership." He went on to suggest that the behavior of leaders was more important when scientists were disadvantaged in some way, as when they are inexperienced or when they cannot easily consult with colleagues.

In another study of twenty-one research teams at NASA, Andrews and Farris (1967) tried to determine how much scientific performance varied from team to team. In short, if there is no variation in performance, differences in supervisory practices couldn't be having much effect. Looking at innovation (generation of *new* knowledge), productiveness (extending knowledge from previous lines of research), contribution (general contribution of knowledge to the field), and usefulness (degree to which the work was valuable to the organization), Andrews and Farris found that only innovation was significantly related to the particular team a scientist belonged to.

A lot of professional performance, then, seems to be independent of supervisory behavior. This does not mean that leadership is irrelevant (although it may be at times), but it does suggest clear limits on how much impact an individual leader can hope to have on a professional group. Even limited impact, if in the right place, can be enough to make a big difference, and leader behavior may have additional subtle or indirect effects on professionals.

If leadership does not fully explain professional performance, what does seem to matter? If we knew that, we might gain insight into how

leaders can affect performance. Pelz and Andrews (1976) looked at 1,311 scientists and engineers in industrial, university, and government settings. They found that technical achievement flourished when antithetical forces existed, for instance when there were *both* environmental demands (conditions of challenge) and protection from the environment (conditions of security), creating a tension between security and challenge. Pelz and Andrews suggest that the more productive groups:

- Did not focus exclusively on either basic or applied science, but rather did some of each
- Had individuals who pursued their own ideas independently but who also interacted vigorously with their colleagues
- Managed to pursue one main project while avoiding overspecialization in one area
- Were neither loosely nor rigidly structured
- Gave members strong influence on decision makers, although that influence was shared with supervisor, colleagues, and clients
- Consisted of scientists who argued about ideas while supporting each other personally.

If these characteristics do in fact differentiate productive from less productive groups, effective supervisory leadership is more orchestration than direct application of authority. It seems a matter of creating and/or maintaining (or at least not destroying) conditions that foster scientific productivity. Clearly, the supervisor is not the only factor determining those conditions, but what does it take for the leader to make some difference? The research suggests many possibilities, which can be clustered into four general areas: technical competence, controlled freedom, acting as a metronome, and work challenge.

Technical Competence

The supervisor's technical competence is related both to scientific productivity and to the scientists' willingness to comply with management directives (Kaufman, 1974; Andrews and Farris, 1967; Thamhain and Gemmill, 1974; Schriesheim et al., 1977). We saw earlier that professionals accept expertise based rather than hierarchically based authority, but far more is involved. Leaders of productive groups serve many roles that depend on technical expertise, including:

- Recognizing good ideas emerging inside and outside the group (Clagett, 1966; Farris, 1972; Andrews and Farris, 1967)
- Defining the significant problems (Clagett, 1966)
- Influencing work goals on the basis of expertise (rather than authority) (Baker and Wilemon, 1977)
- Providing technical stimulation (Clagett, 1966).

This constellation of activities shows that leaders arbitrate among points of view by suggesting, pushing, prodding, and choosing alternatives on the basis of technical knowledge. A leader without technical competence must find ways to do this through others, while establishing his or her expertise in another area (e.g., management control and cost systems) and while providing freedom to the professionals without creating chaos (Kaufman, 1974; Andrews and Farris, 1967).

Controlled Freedom

How the supervisor makes decisions, both technical and administrative, is related to productivity. Unfortunately, the relationships are complex, so there are no simple rules of thumb available (Clagett, 1966). In general, leaders of productive groups create controlled freedom, a condition under which decision making is shared but not given away, and autonomy is partially preserved. A critical element of this seems to be collegial give-and-take in decision making, a kind of consultation with group members that produces a high level of discourse and intellectual stimulation (Clagett, 1966), especially

around critical decisions on goals and resources. Apparently scientists will accept a decision if they understand the logic behind it and have had the chance to critically evaluate various alternatives.

Controlled freedom does not imply that decisions are totally in the hands of the group; in fact, laissez faire management is negatively related to productivity (Andrews and Farris, 1972; Cummings, Hinton, and Gobdel, 1975). Leaders of effective groups emphasize explicit goals but not the means of reaching them. They know the technical details of their people's work without overemphasizing control and monitoring (Cummings, Hinton, and Gobdel, 1975). Furthermore, effective leaders apply, and high-performing scientists want, relatively high pressure (Andrews and Farris, 1972). Scientists and engineers simply do not perform best in a completely relaxed environment.

It is often suggested that effective leaders of professionals buffer their people completely from administrative matters. Apparently this is not entirely true. Members of higher performing groups were involved to some extent in the solution of day-to-day operating problems, ranging from mundane matters to budgetary and policy issues (Clagett, 1966).

Controlled freedom, then, might be seen as a tough-minded form of participative decision making. Decisions must be made and the leaders must see to it that they are. When there is no consensus, the leader can (and should) decide, but only after give-and-take on the alternatives. Failure to take such responsibility—essentially, giving total freedom to subordinates—can result in professionals continually arguing about what they should work on (Kaufman, 1974). One of the most difficult leadership challenges may be staying loose while getting on with it.

Leader as Metronome

This image comes from Sayles and Chandler's (1971) intensive study of NASA, and is perhaps the best statement of the subtlety of leadership in professional groups. Looking at how project managers attempted to control the technical activities of others (including, incidentally, people outside their own groups), Sayles and Chandler described the project manager's job as one that "widens or narrows limits, adds or subtracts weights where trade-offs are to be made, speeds up or slows down actions, increases emphasis on some activities and decreases emphasis on others." These activities reflect leadership as rearranging priorities, changing sequences, responding to the ebb and flow of events: letting self-directed people do what they are good at while influencing them through the pace, the timing, the order.

Work Challenge

One of the most important things to a professional, if not the most, is to do challenging work (Kaufman, 1974). In a study at Bell, for example, 55 percent of professionals leaving the company early in their careers did so because of unchallenging work (cited in Kaufman, 1974). Supervisors seen as emphasizing work challenge are rated higher on overall performance, and tend to create a climate of involvement and willingness to disagree (Thamhain and Gemmill, 1974).

The importance of challenging work is not, of course, unique to professionals. Most people would like to use their skills to make a contribution and accomplish something challenging. With professionals, who are independent and inclined to define "important" in relation to the profession rather than the organization, the leader again has a problem. The individual professional's definition of what is challenging must be reconciled with organizational goals and with needs for teamwork and coordination. What is the leadership skill required? Weick (1980) might describe it as the management of eloquence, that is, using language to influence how people think about themselves:

Leaders who manage eloquence worry less about getting their subordinates to do something and more about supplying their subordinates with interesting versions of what they are doing.

In short, the leader must not only find interesting things to do, he or she must also help others stay interested and see the point. In at least one study (cited in Hellriegel and Slocum, 1974), high performing labs were seen as dominant, active, competitive, a clear reflection that something was challenging in them.

In summary, leaders of productive professional groups use their technical competence to evaluate and select among ideas, walk a tightrope between overcontrol and too much autonomy, make subtle changes in priorities and sequences, and ensure and channel professional challenge in the work. Human relations skills, which figure so prominently in most leadership theories, do not seem related to the productivity of scientific groups. As Kaufman (1974) put it:

It is the recognized competence of the manager, rather than his human relations skills, that is most important in encouraging professionals to keep up to date. Respect for their superior's competence and judgment is the most important reason professionals comply with his directives.

One study measured leaders' effectiveness at motivating others, letting people know where they stand, and sensitivity to differences among people (all human relations skills). The researchers found no relationships between these skills and the rated innovation of the groups. They concluded that, compared to nonprofessionals, scientists are more interested in the work itself than in the social conditions surrounding it (Andrews and Farris, 1967). Other research has indicated that professionals tend to draw support from colleagues rather than from superiors (Clagett, 1966), a finding compatible with Kerr's notions, mentioned earlier, of substitutes for leadership.

Andrews and Farris also found that the highest innovation occurred when the supervisor was seen as a poor administrator (administrative skills were defined as carrying out scheduling and planning, and handling intergroup relations). The lowest innovation occurred when supervisors were seen as effective at both administrative and human relations functions.

In spite of these findings, it is premature to conclude that human relations and administrative skills are irrelevant or undesirable for supervisors of professionals. First, the long-term effects of sloppy administration and insensitivity to people may be severe, even though short-term consequences are not as apparent. Second, a supervisor's preoccupation with administrative and human relations activities may be at the expense of other activities more directly related to performance of the group. Thus, what is not done may be the key element.

All this may mean that the primary skill for leaders of professionals is knowing how to use their technical competence. People apparently will follow and accept (at least in the short run) the decisions of a supervisor who is technically competent, in spite of deficiencies in human relations or administrative skills. Other eccentricities may also be accepted, as Janos's description of a lab director shows:

> Wasserburg neither appears nor acts like a casting office concept of someone who is director of the world's most prestigious rock-dating laboratory. "He looks like he's coming apart," says his friend William Fowler. "Here's this rumpled, prickly cactus, wearing a western string tie, smoking with an FDR cigarette holder, cussing like a drill sergeant, ogling pretty women, exploding like a string of Chinese firecrackers, who also happens to be the most precise measurement-maker in the world." All who know him well acknowledge the depth of Wasserburg's warm and emotional nature.

In conclusion, the effectiveness of professional groups is determined by many things other than the supervisor. The supervisor, however, is not irrelevant and has a part to play in orchestrating the work of others. One aspect of this is direct and based on competence: the leader must take an active role in stimulating the group, in calling attention to ideas and sorting them out, in evaluating proposals and ideas, in seeing to it that necessary decisions get made, and in keeping the objectives reasonably clear.

The second aspect is indirect, subtle: the leader needs to nurture, protect, and preserve the creative tensions that seem to spawn high levels of professional productivity. These include controlled freedom, metronomic changes in pace and emphasis, and work challenge balanced between personal and organizational values, as well as the tensions suggested by Pelz and Andrews (1976).

Breakpoint Leadership: Action at the Interface

[Erasmus] apparently felt that reform should be left to men of action, the princes and cardinals who could bring power to bear if they could be persuaded of the need to act. . . . So when the storm of the Reformation broke, he retired to his scholarly nook, and tried his best to avoid taking sides. . . .

Luther was not a cool, rational scholar. He was, instead, a volcano of emotions. . . .

Luther was a totally committed religious zealot; Erasmus was a pious scholar. Therein lay the difference.

—L. P. Williams, 1980

The leaders of superb performers tend to live by the dicta, "Try something. Fix it. Don't analyze it to death."

—T. J. Peters, 1980

To this point we have looked at leadership in terms of a supervisor and a small group of professional subordinates. Much of that job revolves around the effective use of technical competence. As Sayles and Chandler (1971) have described it, the leader is raising questions, confronting, challenging, playing devil's advocate, and making decisions in the face of conflicting technical judgments. For many managers of professionals, especially at lower levels, this is the primary challenge. But at some point on the way up the managerial ladder, a different kind of leadership demand emerges. When influencing other parts of the organization is as important, or more important, than influencing a subordinate group, leadership is at a breakpoint. Effectiveness is no longer measured simply as group productivity, but involves such things as impact on organizational direction, influence across organizational and even hierarchical boundaries, and securing and protecting organizational (and external) resources and support. If supervision's call for action through others puts a modest strain on professional values, breakpoint leadership represents an earnest move into management.

For many professionals the first breakpoint leadership role is that of project manager. In any case, project managers have received research attention while other breakpoint jobs have not, so by necessity we will deal primarily with them. There is no obvious reason to assume that the skills required of project managers are irrelevant at higher levels, although project management has unique characteristics.

The project manager has been described as a hybrid of a scientist, an engineer, and an administrator; he or she can seldom use formal authority to get things done and must reconcile the conflicting goals of professionals, clients, and functional managers (Organ and Greene, 1972). In addition to the vicissitudes of a group of subordinate professionals (or perhaps several groups), the project manager must cope with all manner of other groups and people in and out of the organization, over whom he or she has little formal control. The manager must be an adroit bargainer, able to negotiate, sell, cajole, and convince in a "ceaseless round of 'political' give-

and-take'' (Sayles and Chandler, 1971). He or she must be able to bypass the formal hierarchy when necessary and engage in improvised, off-the-record discussions. To maintain linkages among groups, the project manager may have to form (or fracture) coalitions, generate rapport among warlords, and serve as translator for the various technical languages involved. As Sayles and Chandler put it:

> The heart of project management is the influencing of outside organizational units to conduct their necessary (for you) activities in such a way that they integrate technically, financially, and timewise with other components of the project. It is particularly difficult to control at a distance the coordination of scientific experiments which are under the control of scientific investigators. Such men tend to consider independence from external authorities one of the canons of professionalism and modern scientific method.

Ironically, leaders of professionals may have their greatest problem leading professionals not directly subordinate to them.

Organizations that contain significant project structure (matrix or frequent ad hoc project teams, for example) have been described by Mintzberg (1979) as the most political of all structures, "un panier de crabes." In such an environment, the most intense conflict occurs between project teams and the supporting functional departments; the least intense between the project manager and his or her subordinates (Baker and Wilemon, 1977).

In many organizations, of course, professionals (particularly scientists) may be separated from the rest of the organization in an R&D location. There, organizational rules may be relaxed (for example, dress codes or nine-to-five hours) to accommodate professional "eccentricities" without affecting other parts of the organization. In such a structure, breakpoint leadership occurs where the lab interfaces with the line organization. The manager must keep the rest of the organization excited about the scientists' work (Pelz and Andrews, 1976) to ensure continued support and to have impact on organizational direction.

It is also at the breakpoint that the manager of professionals is less likely to have a professional boss. This adds a new level of complexity, because professionals and nonprofessionals tend to have different orientations. Unfortunately, how to manage a nonprofessional boss has not received much research attention. Research on the relationships between project managers and their bosses suggests that project managers may not want to be too visible to their bosses: the boss is only one of several clients to be served (Organ and Greene, 1972). Too much time with the boss, and thus overexposure to one viewpoint, may reduce the dynamic tension that multiple clients create.

In summary, leadership at the breakpoint is dramatically different from supervision. Where supervision of a group of professionals draws heavily on technical competence and its constructive use, breakpoint leadership requires political and diplomatic skills. Supervision requires knowing how professionals think and how to stimulate them to use their talents; breakpoint leadership requires knowing how the organization works and how to use power and influence to get things done. One type of leadership produces technical innovation; the other makes that innovation an organizational reality. Although technical competence may (it doesn't always) herald success at lower levels of management, it will not by itself sustain leadership at a breakpoint.

THE CHOICE TO LEAD

Thus managerial work is hectic and fragmented, requiring the ability to shift continually from person to person and from one problem to the next. It is almost the opposite of the studied, analytical, persisting work pattern of the professional, who expects

and demands closure: the time to do a careful and complete job that will provide pride of authorship.

—L. R. Sayles, 1980

The professional faces a fundamental dilemma. Frequently, he abhors administration, desiring only to be left alone to practice his profession. But that freedom is gained only at the price of administrative effort—raising funds, resolving conflicts, buffering the demands of outsiders. That leaves the professional two choices: to do the administrative work himself, in which case he has less time to practice his profession, or to leave it to administrators, in which case he must surrender some of his power over decision making. And that power must be surrendered, it should further be noted, to administrators who, by virtue of the fact that they no longer wish to practice the profession, probably favor a different set of goals.

—H. Mintzberg, 1979

At some point many professionals will have to decide whether or not to embark on the managerial ladder. Although some may naturally gravitate toward either the technical or the supervisory path, many young professionals may not be sure which path to take when the opportunity is presented (Klimoski, 1973). The choice is important, for two reasons. First, managerial jobs are quite different from technical jobs. The differences increase as one moves up the hierarchy, and the longer one stays in management the less likely one is to return to research (Kaufman, 1974). Second, there will be strong pressures to accept management responsibility, even in organizations that offer a dual ladder for professionals.

Managers Are Different

Researchers describe research as primarily an individual activity requiring long stretches of uninterrupted time. The important thing about it is

157

the influence a discovery has on one's colleagues (Roe, 1965). Managerial work is almost the exact opposite: it requires extensive contact with other people, and is highly fragmented with little reflective time (Mintzberg, 1973). One's contributions are weighed in organizational terms. These work differences are reflected in vocational interest patterns, which show managers to be oriented toward enterprising activities and political and economic achievement, averse to scientific activities, and inclined to work with people rather than with symbols or objects; they see themselves as being aggressive and sociable (Holland, 1973; Campbell, 1974). The contrast with both scientists and engineers (see Table 1) is stark.

Furthermore, studies of how managers and professionals spend their time show dramatic differences; managers spend much more time talking and attending meetings, and the differences increase as one moves up the hierarchy (Hinrichs, 1964).

Many professionals enter the managerial world expecting to continue their research. But in her interviews with scientists, Roe found that any managerial job takes significant time away from research and that higher level jobs stop it altogether. Comments from scientists who accepted managerial roles are most telling:

> I tried for a while to carry on with my research program, but this didn't work out very well, and I presently gave it up. . . .

> It soon became obvious that I couldn't do personal research and be a chairman. . . . I can't do research by delegation.

In summary, the move to management is a change of careers for most professionals, especially if they stay in management beyond the first level.

Pressures to Go into Management

There are many reasons for professionals to choose the managerial track, even in dual-ladder

organizations. A prominent reason, as Mintzberg (1979) has observed, is that power in professional bureaucracies flows to administrators, not professionals. Because managers make the important decisions about organizational direction and resources, to climb the professional ladder is to move away from power (Kaufman, 1974). A quote from Lebell (1980) illustrates that, for many professionals, management is the way to get things done:

> My managers are mostly engineers or scientists who accept management roles as the only way to get the job done. . . . Their subordinates know they'd rather be doing honest work than managing.

So a major reason for professionals to enter management is to control resources and direction (Goldberg, 1976).

A second reason for choosing management is the belief of many professionals that success, as defined by the organization, lies in management, even where a professional ladder is offered (Klimoski, 1973; Goldberg, 1976). To be passed up for a management position, or to pass one up, might be seen as a sign of inability, rather than unwillingness, to fill a managerial role (Schriesheim, Von Glinow, and Kerr, 1977).

A third factor leading to a career in management is professional obsolescence. Chemists, for example, can read only about .5 percent of the articles in chemistry (Kaufman, 1974). Management can become an escape from the pressure to keep up, although, ironically, "the immediate supervisors of specialists have been found to be somewhat more knowledgeable about newly emerging fields than their subordinates" (Kaufman, 1974).

Different factors seem to determine whether one is promoted than determine which path one will take. One large study found the best predictor of promotion into either the professional or managerial ladder was technical competence (Rosen, Billings, and Turney, 1976). This finding is consistent with our earlier discussion of supervision and with other research, for example, Gantz, Erickson, and Stephenson (1972), who found perceived creativity to be highly related to promotion rate.

Those professionals choosing the managerial ladder tend to be more like managers to begin with than their fellow professionals are (Klimoski, 1973; Rosen, Billings, and Turney, 1976). They are more likely to see themselves as being aggressive, gregarious, and self-confident. They are likely to feel more comfortable in a leadership role, and to see challenges and rewards in the job. In her 1965 study of eminent scientists, Roe concluded that, whether they ended up in research or administration, none of them regretted their choice and all were happy in their work. Perhaps the most telling evidence of this comes from the statements of two scientists, the first from one who opted out of management, the second from one who stayed in:

> I did that for about a year and a half and I found out I didn't want to be chairman of anything. The thing that really made me stop and realize how horrible it was is that I found myself liking it. It was all this trivia. It's so wonderful being an administrator because you're busy all the time, and you don't have to think. One day I was going around the laboratory deciding where to put new stuff. . . . I found myself liking it, so I quit.

> If you go into administration you must believe that this is a creative activity in itself and that your purpose is something more than keeping your desk clean. You are a moderator and an arbiter and you try to deal equitably with a lot of different people, but you've also got to have ideas and you've got to persuade people that your ideas are important, and see them into reality. The problems in a position like mine are almost unbelievable in their diversity and importance. This is part of the excitement of it. In both research and administration the excitement and the elation is in the creative power. It's bringing things to pass.

A career as a manager and a career as a professional are quite different. Each can be challenging and immensely rewarding. The failure to recognize the differences is a major reason some professionals are unsuccessful or unhappy as managers.

CONCLUSION

Professionals, scientists and engineers in particular, are not alike. The more they hold in common such values as autonomy in doing work and commitment to the profession and professional colleagues, the more they represent a special leadership situation. This is because the professional values described by Kerr, Von Glinow, and Schriesheim (1977) are likely to run counter to organizational values: pay, seniority, and benefits; authority based on hierarchical influence; allegiance to organizational goals; a proprietary view of science; and others. These conflicts not only reduce the leader's potential influence (especially as it flows from formal authority and control over rewards), but also limit the organization's hold over successful professionals, who are likely to have other opportunities.

Given the special characteristics of this leadership situation, it is not surprising that effective supervision of professional groups seems to be rooted in technical competence rather than in organizationally endowed authority. It is clear, however, that competence is not enough. It must be used wisely to stimulate the professionals to recognize and define interesting problems and to provide critical evaluation of ideas. Effective supervision also requires more subtle skills in making decisions (staying loose while getting on with it), in orchestrating work flow (through timing, pace, ordering, and nudges) and in creating and defining work challenge.

Supervision of professional groups requires one set of skills, but leadership at a breakpoint demands quite another. Where professional units interface with the larger organization, effective leadership takes on a decidedly managerial tone.

It becomes, essentially, knowing how to use power and influence to get things done in the organization. It also requires considerable ability to translate technicalities into exciting and comprehensible language for the rest of the organization. To other professionals, effective breakpoint leaders are likely to appear to have sold out their professional values.

It is not an easy choice for a good professional to leave a technical specialty to enter management. And it *is* leaving the specialty, since few people can do effective managerial and technical work at the same time. The key is to recognize that managerial work and professional work are both challenging, but in different ways. Managers typically work in a fragmented way and at a nonreflective pace, talk with many different kinds of people, and specialize in getting others to accomplish organizationally relevant goals. Professionals tend to work at a less hectic pace with longer periods of time to concentrate on a single or a few projects. They tend to work alone or in small teams and take pride in ownership of an idea or innovation. For some professionals, the lure of added clout—increased opportunity to get things done—leads to a managerial career. To create conditions that help other professionals get important things done is no small accomplishment and carries with it substantial gratification. To see the work that professionals have done through to reality is equally demanding and rewarding. These are the acts of leadership on which both individual professionals and organizations—and ultimately society itself—depend.

REFERENCES

Andrews, F. M., and Farris, G. F. "Supervisory Practices and Innovation in Scientific Teams." *Personnel Psychology* 20 (1967):497–515.

———."Time Pressure and Performance of Scientists and Engineers: A Five-year Panel Study." *Organizational Behavior and Human Performance* 8 (1972):185–200.

Baker, B. N., and Wilemon, D. L. "Managing Complex Programs: A Review of Major Research Findings." *R&D Management* 8 (1977):23–28.

Barnowe, J. T. "Leadership and Performance Outcomes in Research Organizations: The Supervisor of Scientists as a Source of Assistance." *Organizational Behavior and Human Performance* 14 (1975):264–80.

Barth, R. T., and Vertinsky, I. "The Effect of Goal Orientation and Information Environment on Research Performance: A Field Study." *Organizational Behavior and Human Performance* 13 (1975):110–32.

Campbell, D. P. *Strong Vocational Interest Blank: Manual for the Strong-Campbell Interest Inventory.* Palo Alto, Calif.: Stanford University Press, 1974.

Clagett, G. S. *Organizational Factors in Scientific Performance in an Industrial Research Laboratory.* Final Technical Report. Milwaukee: University of Wisconsin, 1966.

Cummings, L. L.; Hinton, B. L.; and Gobdel, B. C. "Creative Behavior as a Function of Task Environment: Impact of Objectives, Procedures, and Controls." *Academy of Management Journal* 18 (1975):489–99.

Farris, G. F. "The Effect of Individual Roles on Performance in Innovative Groups." *Research and Development Management* 3 (1972):23–28.

Filley, A. C.; House, R. J.; and Kerr, S. *Managerial Process and Organizational Behavior,* 2nd ed. Glenview, Ill.: Scott, Foresman, 1976.

Gantz, B. S.; Erickson, C. O.; and Stephenson, R. W. "Some Determinants of Promotion in a Research and Development Population." *Proceedings of the 80th Annual Convention of the American Psychological Association,* 1972.

Goldberg, A. I. "The Relevance of Cosmopolitan/Local Orientations to Professional Values and Behavior." *Sociology of Work and Occupations* 3 (1976):331–356.

Gough, H. G., and Woodworth, D. G. "Stylistic Variations Among Professional Research Scientists." *Journal of Psychology* 49 (1960):87–98.

Hellriegel, D., and Slocum, J. W., Jr. "Organizational Climate: Measures, Research and Contingencies." *Academy of Management Journal* 17 (1974):255–77.

Hinrichs, J. R. "Communications Activity of Industrial Research Personnel." *Personnel Psychology* 17 (1964):193–204.

Holland, J. L. *Making Vocational Choices.* Englewood Cliffs, N.J.: Prentice-Hall, 1973.

James, S. "Just Plain Folk." *Executive* 6 (1980):40–44.

Janos, L. "Timekeepers of the Solar System." *Science 80,* May/June 1980, pp.44–55.

Kaufman, H. G. *Obsolescence and Professional Career Development.* New York: AMACOM, 1974.

Kerr, S. "Substitutes for Leadership: Some Implications for Organizational Design." *Organizational and Administrative Sciences* 2 (1977):135–46.

———; Von Glinow, M. A.; and Schriesheim, J. "Issues in the Study of 'Professionals' in Organizations: The Case of Scientists and Engineers." *Organizational Behavior and Human Performance* 18 (1977):329–45.

Klimoski, R. J. "A Biographical Data Analysis of Career Patterns in Engineering." *Journal of Vocational Behavior* 3 (1973):103–113.

Lebell, D. "Managing Professionals: The Quiet Conflict." *Personnel Journal* 59 (1980):566–72.

Mintzberg, H. *The Nature of Managerial Work.* New York: Harper and Row, 1973.

———. *The Structuring of Organizations.* Englewood Cliffs, N.J.: Prentice-Hall, 1979.

Organ, D. W., and Greene, C. N. "The Boundary Relevance of the Project Manager's Job: Findings and Implications for R&D Management." *R&D Management* 3 (1972):7–11.

Pelz, D. C., and Andrews, F. M. *Scientists in Organizations.* Ann Arbor: University of Michigan, 1976.

Peters, T. J. "A Style for All Seasons." *Executive* 6 (1980):12–16.

Reeser, C. "Some Potential Human Problems of the Project Form of Organization." *Academy of Management Journal* (1969):459–67.

Roe, A. "Changes in Scientific Activities with Age." *Science* 150 (1965):313–18.

Rosen, N.; Billings, R.; and Turney, J. "The Emergence and Allocation of Leadership Resources Over Time in a Technical Organization." *Academy of Management Journal* 19 (1976):165–83.

Rotondi, T., Jr. "Organizational Identification: Issues and Implications." *Organizational Behavior and Human Performance* 13 (1975):95–109.

Sayles, L. R. "Managing on the Run." *Executive* 6 (1980):25–26.

———, and Chandler, M. K. *Managing Large Systems,* New York: Harper and Row, 1971.

Schriesheim, J.; Von Glinow, M. A.; and Kerr, S. "Professionals in Bureaucracies: A Structural Alternative." *North-Holland/TIMS Studies in the Management Sciences* 5 (1977):55–69.

Thamhain, H. J., and Gemmill, G. R. "Influence Styles of Project Managers: Some Project Performance Correlates." *Academy of Management Journal* 17 (1974):216–24.

Weick, K. "The Management of Eloquence." *Executive* 6 (1980):18–21.

Williams, L. P. "Parallel Lives." *Executive* 6 (1980):8–12.

Why Managers Fail

Michael K. Badawy

Generally ill-equipped for a management career, engineers and scientists will fail as managers unless they understand the reasons for such failure and take steps to prevent it.

Many engineers and scientists have made, or will make, the transition to management smoothly and successfully. However, the record is less than promising. While there is no law of nature that says good technical practitioners cannot be good managers, it is unlikely that they will be. Although they are well qualified for management by virtue of their analytical skills and backgrounds, many technologists switch to management for the wrong reasons and to satisfy the wrong needs. Hence, they do not make competent managers. There is substantial evidence derived from my own research studies and those of others that the transition to management has been troublesome for many technologists, and that many of them have failed because they were generally ill-equipped for such a career.

In order to understand why managers fail, one must first recognize that managerial competency has three interrelated components; knowledge, skills and attitudes. Although sophisticated knowledge in the principles and elements of administration is a prerequisite for managerial success, such knowledge by itself is not enough for managerial competency. While management

theory is a science, management practice is an art. Therefore, to be effective, the manager must develop a set of professional skills. These skills are:

- *Technical:* Technical skills include the ability of the manager to develop and apply certain methods and techniques related to his tasks. The manager's technical skills also encompass a general familiarity with, and understanding of, the technical activities undertaken in his department and their relation to other company divisions. The manager's technical specialization, formal education, experience, and background form a strong foundation for the development of technical skills.

- *Administrative:* Administrative skills relate primarily to the manager's ability to manage. Effective management, of course, reflects the ability to organize, plan, direct, and control. It is the capacity to build a workable group or unit, to plan, to make decisions, to control and evaluate performance, and finally to direct subordinates by motivating, communicating, and leading them into a certain direction that would help the organization achieve its objectives most effectively. The core elements of administrative skills are the ability to search out concepts and catalog events; the capacity to collect, evaluate, and process pertinent information; the ability to distinguish alternatives and make a decision; and resourcefulness in directing others and communicating to them the reasons behind the decisions and actions. Superior administrative skill is, of course, related to and based on other skills such as cognitive and conceptual skills.

- *Interpersonal:* Interpersonal skills are probably the most important of all. Since managing is a group effort, managerial competency requires a superior ability to work with people. The manager, to be effective, must interact with, motivate, influence, and communicate with people. People make an organization, and through their activities, organizations either prosper or fail. Managing people effectively is the most critical and most intricate problem for the manager of today.

ATTITUDES AND MANAGERIAL COMPETENCY

Attitudes, the third ingredient of managerial competency, are essentially the manager's value system and beliefs toward self, task, and others in the organization. Attitudes include those patterns of thought that enable one to characterize the manager and predict how well he will handle a problem. Attitudes are partly emotional in origin, but they are necessary because they determine two things. First, the acquisition of knowledge and skills is, in part, a function of attitudes, and second, attitudes determine how the manager applies his knowledge and techniques.

Attitudes are also important in determining managerial competency for another reason: They tell us what needs are dominant in an individual at a certain time, and thus we can predict and identify the individual's managerial potential.

This identification is crucial for enhancing future managerial effectiveness.

Modern psychological research tells us that effective managers share at least three major attitudinal characteristics: a high need to manage, a high need for power, and a high capacity for empathy.

The need or will to manage has to do with the fact that no individual is likely to learn how to manage unless he really wants to take responsibility for the productivity of others, and enjoys stimulating them to achieve better results. The "way to manage" can usually be found if there is the "will to manage." Many individuals who aspire to high-level managerial positions—including engineers and scientists—are not motivated to manage. They are motivated to earn high salaries and to attain high status, but they are not motivated to get effective results through others. Thus, they will not make competent managers.

The need to manage is a crucial factor, therefore, in determining whether a person will learn and apply what is necessary to get effective results on the job. The key point here is that an outstanding record as an individual performer does not indicate the ability or willingness to get other people to excel at the same tasks. This partly explains, for example, why outstanding scholars often make poor teachers, excellent engineers are often unable to supervise the work of other engineers, and successful salesmen are often ineffective sales managers.

Second, effective managers are characterized by a strong need for the power derived from such sources as job titles, status symbols, and high income. The point is that power seekers can be counted on to strive to reach positions where they can exercise authority over large numbers of people. Modern behavioral science research suggests that individuals who lack this drive are not likely to act in ways that will enable them to advance far up the managerial ladder.[1] Instead, they usually scorn company politics and devote their energies to other types of activities that are

163

more satisfying to them. For many engineers and scientists, power emanates from "professional" sources other than sources of managerial power. While managerial power is based on politics, titles, and organizational status, professional power is based on knowledge and excellence in one's discipline and profession. In short, the power game is part of management, and it is played best by those who enjoy it most.

The third characteristic of effective managers is the capacity for empathy—being able to cope with the emotional reactions that inevitably occur when people work together in an organization. Effective managers cannot be mired in the code of rationality, which explains, in part, the troublesome transition of some engineers and scientists to management. Individuals who are reluctant to accept emotions as part of being human will not make "human" managers, and, in turn, they will not be managerially competent.

THE MANAGERIAL SKILL MIX

The technical, administrative, and interpersonal skills are all closely interrelated and can be significant in determining your success in management. However, experience shows that the relative importance of these skills varies with the management level you are on and the type of responsibility you have.

As shown in Figure 1, technical skills are inversely related to your management level: They are most important at lower management levels but that importance tends to decrease as you advance to higher levels in the organization.

Managerial success on upper management levels is determined by your vision and ability to understand how the entire system works (the conceptual skill), as well as your capacity for organization and coordination between various divisions (the administrative skill). How much you know about the technical details of the operation becomes considerably less important. In fact, be-

yond middle management, "special knowledge" can actually be a detriment to the individual.

Handling people effectively is the most important skill at all levels of management. Knowing how to handle people effectively, I believe, is the art of the arts. If a manager has considerable technical and administrative skills, but his interpersonal skills are wanting, he is a likely candidate for managerial failure. Conversely, problems that occur because technical or administrative skills are not up to par will be more easily surmounted.

It is important to remember that success in management is largely determined by the manager's ability to understand, interact with, communicate with, coach, and direct subordinates. This statement should not be taken to undermine the importance of technical and administrative skills in managerial effectiveness, but rather to underscore the ability to get along with people as a prerequisite for success in management.

While interpersonal skills are presumably important at all levels of management, they are perhaps most important at the lower and middle levels, where managers interact with subordinates, supervisors, and associates. At upper management levels, where the frequency of these interactions tends to decrease, the importance of interpersonal skills decreases as conceptual and administrative skills become more important. It is also possible that with the increased degree of power and influence upper-level managers typically have, they can afford to pay less attention to interpersonal relations, and hence they become less sensitive to human needs and individual satisfaction.

Some technical managers and supervisors find it difficult to get away from "the bench" and do what they are paid for—namely managing. But everything in life has a price. Perhaps this is one of the prices managers must pay—the price of management! I have seen quite a few technologists in management who were not willing to pay this price, so they tried to do technical and managerial tasks simultaneously—with the

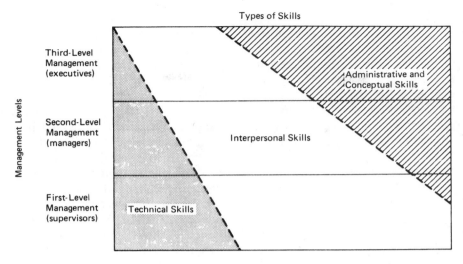

FIGURE 1. *The Managerial Skill Mix*

incompatible requirements of two different roles. I have seen others enter management without realizing what they were getting into. The paths taken by both groups turned out to be very costly—they failed! The lesson is quite clear: The "right" mix of the three skill types at different management levels must be properly maintained.

MANAGERIAL FAILURE

Organizations fail because managers fail. Managers fail because they perform poorly. Performance is one of the prime criteria that an organization uses in evaluating employee contributions. While many managers deny it in public, performance is hardly the sole basis for appraising employees. Managerial jobs are no exception. Given the difficulty of measuring managerial performance accurately and objectively, organizations consider the manager's contributions to the accomplishment of the company's goal to be the most concrete basis for distributing rewards and making salary adjustments and promotion decisions. Thus, managerial failure can be defined as

the inability of the manager to meet certain performance standards imposed by his superiors. It can also be defined in terms of organizational policies. A manager has failed if his performance is considered unsatisfactory or unacceptable by virtue of some preestablished criteria. Managerial success, on the other hand, is reflected in added responsibility, promotion, title change, and increased salary. Managerial "failure" is not intended to imply that the manager is demoted because he totally failed to get the job done but rather that he failed to accomplish results that he is capable of achieving.

Why do managers fail? Causes of managerial failure can be numerous. Since managerial performance is a product of the interaction of many factors inside the individual and in the surrounding environment, managerial success or failure will be determined by factors in both areas. Bear in mind that failures in management are rarely due to a single cause. Typically, aspects of the individual interact with aspects of the environment to create the problem.

Research has shown as many as 35 types of factors as potential causes of unsatisfactory managerial performance.[2] Any one of these factors can contribute to the failure of a manager. Some of these factors are more likely to operate than others because of the nature of managerial work. As shown in Table 1, there are three groups of factors containing nine categories representing possible causes of performance failures. The first four categories refer to aspects of the individual. The remaining five categories refer to different aspects of the environment: categories five to eight refer to the various groups of which the individual is a member, while the ninth category is contextual, referring to nonhuman aspects of the environment and the work itself which may be strategic to performance failure.

Note the relative importance of the different factors. As shown in the table, the most dominant causes of performance failure are deficiencies of an intellectual nature, frustrated motivations, membership in and relations with different groups, and economic and geographic factors.

Discussing all possible causes of managerial failure in detail would be impractical. Thus, for our purposes here, I shall focus on the forces relating to the individual manager himself or to his job.

The development of management skills and the ability to convert them into effective actions are crucial to managerial competency. The lack of ingredients necessary for effective managerial performance will lead to poor results. Lack of knowledge of management principles and concepts, for example, will hamper a manager's performance. In addition, developing managerial skills is difficult when management knowledge is insufficient or lacking.

Many technical managers get fired, not because they lack technical competence, but because they lack managerial competence (another common practice, sadly, is to transfer incompetent managers back into a heavy technical role!) Managerial failure can thus result from inadequate management and administrative skills. Establishing a well-functioning unit or division with a sound structure and clear authority and responsibility relationships is crucial for achieving divisional objectives. In addition, developing policies and procedures consistent with objectives and goals, allocating resources, and monitoring progress toward goal achievement are key managerial tasks. These activities call for considerable administrative skill on the manager's part.

The major cause of managerial failure among engineers and scientists is poor interpersonal skills. Many technologists are more comfortable dealing with matters in the laboratory than they are dealing with people. Because most of them are loners, they are used to doing things for themselves. Once promoted to management, however, they have to delegate responsibility to others. They often find this extremely difficult, especially if they have less than complete confidence in their subordinates' abilities. As a result, many technologists find that their advancement—and their managerial careers—are limited more by human factors than by technical ability.

Managerial failure also occurs when an individual becomes a manager for the wrong reasons. This happens when a person seeks the attractive rewards (e.g., economic) associated with a managerial position, yet has no strong will to manage. Such managers do so poorly that they become "retired on the job."

JOB-RELATED FACTORS

A brief account of some of the job-related factors causing managerial failure follows.

Some managers, especially new managers, are unwilling to pay the price of being a manager, i.e., loneliness. They seem to be unaware that the higher one climbs on the managerial ladder, the more lonesome it becomes, the fewer peers one has to talk to, and the more restraint one must exercise over what one says. As a result, while they may enjoy the new challenges and the greater opportunity to make unilateral decisions, they find themselves nostalgic for the "good old days" when it was not so lonely. They therefore

TABLE 1. *Causes of Managerial Failure**

Category	High	Low	Rare
A. Individual Factors			
I. *Problems of Intelligence and Job Knowledge*	X		
1. Insufficient verbal ability			
2. Insufficient special ability			
3. Insufficient job knowledge			
4. Defect of judgment or memory			
II. *Emotional Problems*		X	
5. Frequent disruptive emotion (anxiety, depression, guilt, etc.)			
6. Neurosis (anger, jealousy, and so on, predominating)			
7. Psychosis			
8. Alcohol and drug problems			
III. *Motivational Problems*			
9. Strong motives frustrated at work (fear of failure, dominance, need for attention, and so on)	X		
10. Unintegrated means used to satisfy strong motives	X		
11. Excessively low personal work standards			X
12. Generalized low work motivation			X
IV. *Physical Problems*		X	
13. Physical illness or handicap including brain disorders			
14. Physical disorders of emotional origin			
15. Inappropriate physical characteristics			
16. Insufficient muscular or sensory ability or skill			
B. Group Factors			
V. *Family-Related Factors*	X		
17. Family crises			
18. Separation from the family and isolation			
19. Predominance of family considerations over work demands			
VI. *Problems Caused in the Work Group*	X		
20. Negative consequences associated with group cohesion			
21. Ineffective management			
22. Inappropriate managerial standards or criteria			
VII. *Problems Originating in Company Policies*	X		
23. Insufficient organizational action			
24. Placement error			
25. Organizational overpermissiveness			
26. Excessive spans of control			
27. Inappropriate organizational standards and criteria			
VIII. *Problems Stemming from Society and Its Values*			X
28. Application of legal sanctions			
29. Enforcement of societal values by means other than the law			
30. Conflict between job demands and cultural values (equity, freedom, religious values, and so on)			
IX. *Contextual Factors*			
C. Factors in the Work Context and the Job Itself			
31. Negative consequences of economic forces	X		
32. Negative consequences of geographic location	X		
33. Detrimental conditions in the work setting			
34. Excessive danger			
35. Problems in the work itself			

From Miner, John B., "The Challenge of Managing." Philadelphia: Saunders, 1975, pp. 330–331.

try to act like "one of the boys."[3] In doing so, they often lose the respect of the people they manage. Employees want to look up to the boss. They want to feel that they can turn to him for necessary decisions. The genesis of this managerial failure is the desire to be liked rather than respected! It is interesting that managers who are found to be most effective are usually categorized by their subordinates as "fair but firm."

In addition, new managers sometimes fail to adjust to the demands of their role. Managerial positions are usually characterized by a high degree of power over other people, some standards for controlling human behavior in work settings, large amounts of visibility and influence, and a keen understanding of how corporate power and politics work. These characteristics require that managers play multiple roles. If managers are uncomfortable with these factors, they could develop a strong fear of failure. This situation might very well lead to poor managerial performance.

Other causes of managerial failure include the following:

Bias toward Objective Measurement. Having been trained in "hard" sciences, where exact measurement is one of the natural beauties of the scientific method, engineers and scientists are more comfortable working with things that they can objectively control and measure. Managers, on the other hand, must rely on intuition and judgment in dealing with attitudes, biases, perceptions, emotions and feelings. The fact that these intangible variables are hardly measurable—let alone controllable—makes the technical manager's job thoroughly frustrating. To be sure, one of the things that technologists must learn in order to succeed in management is to stop insisting on using a yardstick to measure everything. The nature of management—contrary to engineering and science—defies objective and tangible measurement.

Paralysis by Analysis. Engineers and scientists, more than others, suffer from this disease: the

tendency to wait for all information to be in before they make a decision. I can think of no worse cause of managerial failure—it is a clear case of how the professional's technical training can hamper rather than enhance his chances for success. In management, you will never have all the facts, nor will there ever be riskless decisions. All decision-making involves risk taking. An adaptation of Pareto's principle would be that 20 percent of the facts are critical to 80 percent of the outcome. Being slow to decide, waiting for more facts, is known as "paralysis by analysis."

The inability of engineering or R&D supervisors to adjust to making managerial decisions on the basis of incomplete data and in areas where they lack first-hand experience (since the information is usually provided by other people and divisions) results in managerial anxiety.[4] The fact that they must function within a highly ambiguous and unpredictable environment makes them unsure about the data available, thereby reinforcing a neurotic demand for more data in an attempt to make riskless decisions. If this cycle is not somehow broken and appropriate adjustments made, it can be a deadly time waster and a complicating factor in the transition to management.

Fear of Loss of Intimate Contact with Their Fields. Effective managers always focus on what needs to be done, when it should be done, and how much it should cost, rather than on how to do it. Since managers must get things done through other people, the question of "how" should always be left to them. Technologists usually find this difficult to understand, and in their zeal to stay professionally competent, they try to keep intimate contact with their specialties. As a result, they fail to delegate and they tend to handle the technical details as well—they try to do two jobs in the time of one! The manager, to be sure, is paid to get things done—not to do them himself; this is the job of his subordinates. Sacrificing some of their technical competence—in a relative sense—is the price technical managers must pay for staying managerially competent.

Technologists as Introverts. Many engineers and scientists are "introverts" rather than "extroverts." Research shows that introversion is usually associated with creativity. The problem is that while creating is an individual (introvert) activity, managing is a team (extrovert) activity. The ability to work with others and to be a good team player is one of the distinctive skills of successful and competent managers. The "lone wolf" nature of many technologists could, therefore, make it doubly difficult for them to function effectively as technical managers.

Poor Delegators. One of the most valuable skills a manager can possess is the ability to delegate. You should never undertake what you can delegate. You cannot grow as a technical manager unless you delegate, and your subordinates expect you to. However, technical managers have been found to be very poor in learning to achieve things through others: They are poor delegators. Technologists are doers rather than delegators because they believe, rightly or wrongly, that they perform a task better than anyone on their staff can. Developing the will to delegate requires a change in the technologist's attitudes, behavior, and assumptions about people working for him. He might even have to force himself to delegate tasks to his subordinates. At any rate, whatever it takes, delegation is one of the prime skills technical supervisors must acquire to enhance their managerial competence.

Farming Out Responsibilities. Some managers do not recognize their responsibility for on-the-job training and coaching. They are all too eager to send their subordinates to courses conducted by staff agencies and outside trainers and consultants. While there are many occasions when it is wise to use these outside resources, the manager must make certain that such training is utilized by the subordinates when they return to the job. Without a standing policy of what training should cover and who should be trained and by

whom, the manager runs the risk of abdicating coaching and training responsibilities. Poor development of subordinates hinders their professional growth, and the manager becomes indispensable. When a manager's responsibilities and salary remain the same over a long period of time, this stagnation is sometimes an indication of managerial failure. Upward movement on the managerial ladder, if based on one's managerial capability, is the ultimate reward of success.

In the absence of concrete figures on managerial "malpractice," it is difficult to estimate the number of ineffective or unsuccessful managers in organizations. However, experience shows that there are a lot of incompetent managers around. The best way to deal with performance failure, I believe, is to prevent it. Unfortunately, managers are willing enough to put out the fires but they take little interest in fire prevention. Dealing with ineffective performance requires diagnosing the causes and then coming up with appropriate remedies. The possible causes of managerial failure have been analyzed in this article. However, the scrutiny of your own performance and the development of a personal plan of action must remain your responsibility.

REFERENCES

1. McClelland, David C., and Burnham, David H. "Power-Driven Managers: Good Guys Make Bum Bosses." *Psychology Today* (December, 1975): pp. 69–70.
2. Miner, John. "The Challenge of Managing." Philadelphia: Saunders, 1975, pp. 215–216.
3. This discussion is partly based on McCarthy, John F. "Why Managers Fail." Second Edition. New York: McGraw-Hill, 1978, pp. 3–34.
4. For more on this point see Steele, Lowell W. "Innovation in Big Business." New York: Elsevier, 1975, p. 186; and Thompson, Paul and Dalton, Gene. "Are R&D Organizations Obsolete?" *Harvard Business Review* (November–December 1976).

Managers and Leaders: Are They Different?

Abraham Zaleznik

A bureaucratic society which breeds managers may stifle young leaders who need mentors and emotional interchange to develop

What is the ideal way to develop leadership? Every society provides its own answer to this question, and each, in groping for answers, defines its deepest concerns about the purposes, distributions, and uses of power. Business has contributed its answer to the leadership question by evolving a new breed called the manager. Simultaneously, business has established a new power ethic that favors collective over individual leadership, the cult of the group over that of personality. While ensuring the competence, control, and the balance of power relations among groups with the potential for rivalry, managerial leadership unfortunately does not necessarily ensure imagination, creativity, or ethical behavior in guiding the destinies of corporate enterprises.

Leadership inevitably requires using power to influence the thoughts and actions of other people. Power in the hands of an individual entails human risks: first, the risk of equating power with the ability to get immediate results; second, the risk of ignoring the many different ways people can legitimately accumulate power;

and third, the risk of losing self-control in the desire for power. The need to hedge these risks accounts in part for the development of collective leadership and the managerial ethic. Consequently, an inherent conservatism dominates the culture of large organizations. In *The Second American Revolution,* John D. Rockefeller, III describes the conservatism of organizations:

> An organization is a system, with a logic of its own, and all the weight of tradition and inertia. The deck is stacked in favor of the tried and proven way of doing things and against the taking of risks and striking out in new directions.[1]

Out of this conservatism and inertia organizations provide succession to power through the development of managers rather than individual leaders. And the irony of the managerial ethic is that it fosters a bureaucratic culture in business, supposedly the last bastion protecting us from the encroachments and controls of bureaucracy in government and education. Perhaps the risks associated with power in the hands of an individual may be necessary ones for business to take if organizations are to break free of their inertia and bureaucratic conservatism.

MANAGER VS. LEADER PERSONALITY

Theodore Levitt has described the essential features of a managerial culture with its emphasis on rationality and control:

> Management consists of the rational assessment of a situation and the systematic selection of goals and purposes (what is to be done?); the systematic development of strategies to achieve these goals; the marshalling of the required resources; the rational design, organization, direction, and control of the activities required to attain the selected purposes; and, finally, the motivating and rewarding of people to do the work.[2]

In other words, whether his or her energies are directed toward goals, resources, organization structures, or people, a manager is a problem solver. The manager asks himself, "What problems have to be solved, and what are the best ways to achieve results so that people will continue to contribute to this organization?" In this conception, leadership is a practical effort to direct affairs; and to fulfill his task, a manager requires that many people operate at different levels of status and responsibility. Our democratic society is, in fact, unique in having solved the problem of providing well-trained managers for business. The same solution stands ready to be applied to government, education, health care, and other institutions. It takes neither genius nor heroism to be a manager, but rather persistence, tough-mindedness, hard work, intelligence, analytical ability and, perhaps most important, tolerance and good will.

Another conception, however, attaches almost mystical beliefs to what leadership is and assumes that only great people are worthy of the drama of power and politics. Here, leadership is a psychodrama in which, as a precondition for control of a political structure, a lonely person must gain control of him or herself. Such an expectation of leadership contrasts sharply with the mundane, practical, and yet important conception that leadership is really managing work that other people do.

Two questions come to mind. Is this mystique of leadership merely a holdover from our collective childhood of dependency and our longing for good and heroic parents? Or, is there a basic truth lurking behind the need for leaders that no matter how competent managers are, their leadership stagnates because of their limitations in visualizing purposes and generating value in work? Without this imaginative capacity and the ability to communicate, managers, driven by their narrow purposes, perpetuate group conflicts instead of reforming them into broader desires and goals.

If indeed problems demand greatness, then, judging by past performance, the selection and development of leaders leave a great deal to chance. There are no known ways to train "great" leaders. Furthermore, beyond what we leave to chance, there is a deeper issue in the relationship between the need for competent managers and the longing for great leaders.

What is takes to ensure the supply of people who will assume practical responsibility may inhibit the development of great leaders. Conversely, the presence of great leaders may undermine the development of managers who become very anxious in the relative disorder that leaders seem to generate. The antagonism in aim (to have many competent managers as well as great leaders) often remains obscure in stable and well-developed societies. But the antagonism surfaces during periods of stress and change, as it did in the Western countries during both the Great Depression and World War II. The tension also appears in the struggle for power between theorists and professional managers in revolutionary societies.

It is easy enough to dismiss the dilemma I pose (of training managers while we may need new leaders, or leaders at the expense of managers) by saying that the need is for people who can be *both* managers and leaders. The truth of the matter as I see it, however, is that just as a managerial culture is different from the entrepreneurial culture that develops when leaders appear in organizations, managers and leaders are very different kinds of people. They differ in motivation, personal history, and in how they think and act.

A technologically oriented and economically successful society tends to depreciate the need for great leaders. Such societies hold a deep and abiding faith in rational methods of solving problems, including problems of value, economics, and justice. Once rational methods of solving problems are broken down into elements, organized, and taught as skills, then society's faith in technique over personal qualities in leadership remains the guiding conception for a democratic society contemplating its leadership requirements. But there are times when tinkering and trial and error prove inadequate to the emerging problems of selecting goals, allocating resources, and distributing wealth and opportunity. During such times, the democratic society needs to find leaders who use themselves as the instruments of learning and acting, instead of managers who use their accumulation of collective experience to get where they are going.

The most impressive spokesman, as well as exemplar of the managerial viewpoint, was Alfred P. Sloan, Jr. who, along with Pierre du Pont, designed the modern corporate structure. Reflecting on what makes one management successful while another fails, Sloan suggested that "good management rests on a reconciliation of centralization and decentralization, or 'decentralization with coordinated control'."[3]

Sloan's conception of management, as well as his practice, developed by trial and error, and by the accumulation of experience. Sloan wrote:

> There is no hard and fast rule for sorting out the various responsibilities and the best way to assign them. The balance which is struck . . . varies according to what is being decided, the circumstances of the time, past experience, and the temperaments and skills of the executive involved.[4]

In other words, in much the same way that the inventors of the late nineteenth century tried, failed, and fitted until they hit on a product or method, managers who innovate in developing organizations are "tinkerers." They do not have a grand design or experience the intuitive flash of insight that, borrowing from modern science, we have come to call the "breakthrough."

Managers and leaders differ fundamentally in their world views. The dimensions for assessing these differences include managers' and leaders' orientations toward their goals, their work, their human relations, and their selves.

Attitudes toward Goals

Managers tend to adopt impersonal, if not passive, attitudes toward goals. Managerial goals arise out of necessities rather than desires, and, therefore, are deeply embedded in the history and culture of the organization.

Frederic G. Donner, chairman and chief executive officer of General Motors from 1958 to 1967, expressed this impersonal and passive attitude toward goals in defining GM's position on product development:

> . . . To meet the challenge of the marketplace, we must recognize changes in customer needs and desires far enough ahead to have the right products in the right places at the right time and in the right quantity.
>
> We must balance trends in preference against the many compromises that are necessary to make a final product that is both reliable and good looking, that performs well and that sells at a competitive price in the necessary volume. We must design, not just the cars we would like to build, but more importantly, the cars that our customers want to buy.[5]

Nowhere in this formulation of how a product comes into being is there a notion that consumer tastes and preferences arise in part as a result of what manufacturers do. In reality, through product design, advertising, and promotion, consumers learn to like what they then say they need. Few would argue that people who enjoy taking snapshots need a camera that also develops pictures. But in response to novelty, convenience, a shorter interval between acting (taking the snap) and gaining pleasure (seeing the shot), the Polaroid camera succeeded in the marketplace. But it is inconceivable that Edwin Land responded to impressions of consumer need. Instead, he translated a technology (polarization of light) into a product, which proliferated and stimulated consumers' desires.

The example of Polaroid and Land suggests how leaders think about goals. They are active instead of reactive, shaping ideas instead of responding to them. Leaders adopt a personal and active attitude toward goals. The influence a leader exerts in altering moods, evoking images and expectations, and in establishing specific desires and objectives determines the direction a business takes. The net result of this influence is to change the way people think about what is desirable, possible, and necessary.

Conceptions of Work

What do managers and leaders do? What is the nature of their respective work?

Leaders and managers differ in their conceptions. Managers tend to view work as an enabling process involving some combination of people and ideas interacting to establish strategies and make decisions. Managers help the process along by a range of skills, including calculating the interests in opposition, staging and timing the surfacing of controversial issues, and reducing tensions. In this enabling process, managers appear flexible in the use of tactics: they negotiate and bargain, on the one hand, and use rewards and punishments, and other forms of coercion, on the other. Machiavelli wrote for managers and not necessarily for leaders.

Alfred Sloan illustrated how this enabling process works in situations of conflict. The time was the early 1920s when the Ford Motor Co.,

still dominated the automobile industry using, as did General Motors, the conventional water-cooled engine. With the full backing of Pierre du Pont, Charles Kettering dedicated himself to the design of an air-cooled engine, which, if successful, would have been a great technical and market coup for GM. Kettering believed in his product, but the manufacturing division heads at GM remained skeptical and later opposed the new design on two grounds: first, that it was technically unreliable, and second, that the corporation was putting all its eggs in one basket by investing in a new product instead of attending to the current marketing situation.

In the summer of 1923 after a series of false starts and after its decision to recall the copper-cooled Chevrolets from dealers and customers, GM management reorganized and finally scrapped the project. When it dawned on Kettering that the company had rejected the engine, he was deeply discouraged and wrote to Sloan that without the "organized resistance" against the project it would succeed and that unless the project were saved, he would leave the company.

Alfred Sloan was all too aware of the fact that Kettering was unhappy and indeed intended to leave General Motors. Sloan was also aware of the fact that, while the manufacturing divisions strongly opposed the new engine, Pierre du Pont supported Kettering. Furthermore, Sloan had himself gone on record in a letter to Kettering less than two years earlier expressing full confidence in him. The problem Sloan now had was to make his decision stick, keep Kettering in the organization (he was much too valuable to lose), avoid alienating du Pont, and encourage the division heads to move speedily in developing product lines using conventional water-cooled engines.

The actions that Sloan took in the face of this conflict reveal much about how managers work. First, he tried to reassure Kettering by presenting the problem in a very ambiguous fashion, suggesting that he and the Executive Committee sided with Kettering, but that it would not be practical to force the divisions to do what they were opposed to. He presented the problem as being a question of the people, not the product. Second, he proposed to reorganize around the problem by consolidating all functions in a new division that would be responsible for the design, production, and marketing of the new car. This solution, however, appeared as ambiguous as his efforts to placate and keep Kettering in General Motors. Sloan wrote: "My plan was to create an independent pilot operation under the sole jurisdiction of Mr. Kettering, a kind of copper-cooled-car division. Mr. Kettering would designate his own chief engineer and his production staff to solve the technical problems of manufacture."[6]

While Sloan did not discuss the practical value of this solution, which included saddling an inventor with management responsibility, he in effect used this plan to limit his conflict with Pierre du Pont.

In effect, the managerial solution that Sloan arranged and pressed for adoption limited the options available to others. The structural solution narrowed choices, even limiting emotional reactions to the point where the key people could do nothing but go along, and even allowed Sloan to say in his memorandum to du Pont, "We have discussed the matter with Mr. Kettering at some length this morning and he agrees with us absolutely on every point we made. He appears to receive the suggestion enthusiastically and has every confidence that it can be put across along these lines."[7]

Having placated people who opposed his views by developing a structural solution that appeared to give something but in reality only limited options, Sloan could then authorize the car division's general manager, with whom he basically agreed, to move quickly in designing water-cooled cars for the immediate market demand.

Years later Sloan wrote, evidently with tongue in cheek, "The copper-cooled car never came up again in a big way. It just died out, I don't know why."[8]

In order to get people to accept solutions to problems, managers need to coordinate and balance continually. Interestingly enough, this managerial work has much in common with what diplomats and mediators do, with Henry Kissinger apparently an outstanding practitioner. The manager aims at shifting balances of power toward solutions acceptable as a compromise among conflicting values.

What about leaders, what do they do? Where managers act to limit choices, leaders work in the opposite direction, to develop fresh approaches to longstanding problems and to open issues for new options. Stanley and Inge Hoffmann, the political scientists, liken the leader's work to that of the artist. But unlike most artists, the leader himself is an integral part of the aesthetic product. One cannot look at a leader's art without looking at the artist. On Charles de Gaulle as a political artist, they wrote: "And each of his major political acts, however tortuous the means or the details, has been whole, indivisible and unmistakably his own, like an artistic act."[9]

The closest one can get to a product apart from the artist is the ideas that occupy, indeed at times obsess, the leader's mental life. To be effective, however, the leader needs to project his ideas into images that excite people, and only then develop choices that give the projected images substance. Consequently, leaders create excitement in work.

John F. Kennedy's brief presidency shows both the strengths and weaknesses connected with the excitement leaders generate in their work. In his inaugural address he said, "Let every nation know, whether it wishes us well or ill, that we shall pay any price, bear any burden, meet any hardship, support any friend, oppose any foe, in order to assure the survival and the success of liberty."

This much-quoted statement forced people to react beyond immediate concerns and to identify with Kennedy and with important shared ideals. But upon closer scrutiny the statement must be seen as absurd because it promises a position which if in fact adopted, as in the Viet Nam War, could produce disastrous results. Yet unless expectations are aroused and mobilized, with all the dangers of frustration inherent in heightened desire, new thinking and new choice can never come to light.

Leaders work from high-risk positions, indeed often are temperamentally disposed to seek out risk and danger, especially where opportunity and reward appear high. From my observations, why one individual seeks risks while another approaches problems conservatively depends more on his or her personality and less on conscious choice. For some, especially those who become managers, the instinct for survival dominates their need for risk, and their ability to tolerate mundane, practical work assists their survival. The same cannot be said for leaders who sometimes react to mundane work as to an affliction.

Relations with Others

Managers prefer to work with people; they avoid solitary activity because it makes them anxious. Several years ago, I directed studies on the psychological aspects of career. The need to seek out others with whom to work and collaborate seemed to stand out as important characteristics of managers. When asked, for example, to write imaginative stories in response to a picture showing a single figure (a boy contemplating a violin, or a man silhouetted in a state of reflection), managers populated their stories with people. The following is an example of a manager's imaginative story about the young boy contemplating a violin:

> Mom and Dad insisted that junior take music lessons so that someday he can become a concert musician. His instrument was ordered and had just arrived. Junior is weighing the alternatives of playing football with the other kids or playing with the squeak box. He can't understand how his parents could think a violin is better than a touchdown.
>
> After four months of practicing the violin, junior has had more than enough, Daddy is going out of his mind, and Mommy is willing to give in reluctantly to the men's wishes. Football season is now over, but a good third baseman will take the field next spring.[10]

This story illustrates two themes that clarify managerial attitudes toward human relations. The first, as I have suggested, is to seek out activity with other people (i.e. the football team), and the second is to maintain a low level of emotional involvement in these relationships. The low emotional involvement appears in the writer's use of conventional metaphors, even clichés, and in the depiction of the ready transformation of potential conflict into harmonious decisions. In this case, Junior, Mommy, and Daddy agree to give up the violin for manly sports.

These two themes may seem paradoxical, but their coexistence supports what a manager does, including reconciling differences, seeking compromises, and establishing a balance of power. A further idea demonstrated by how the manager wrote the story is that managers may lack empathy, or the capacity to sense intuitively the thoughts and feelings of others. To illustrate attempts to be emphathic, here is another story written to the same stimulus picture by someone considered by his peers to be a leader:

> This little boy has the appearance of being a sincere artist, one who is deeply affected by the violin, and has an intense desire to master the instrument.
>
> He seems to have just completed his normal practice session and appears to be somewhat crestfallen at his inability to produce the sounds which he is sure lie within the violin.
>
> He appears to be in the process of making a vow to himself to expend the necessary time and effort to play this instrument until he satisfies himself that he is able to bring forth the qualities of music which he feels within himself.

With this type of determination and carry through, this boy became one of the great violinists of his day.[11]

Empathy is not simply a matter of paying attention to other people. It is also the capacity to take in emotional signals and to make them mean something in a relationship with an individual. People who describe another person as "deeply affected" with "intense desire," as capable of feeling "crest-fallen" and as one who can "vow to himself," would seem to have an inner perceptiveness that they can use in their relationships with others.

Managers relate to people according to the role they play in a sequence of events or in a decision-making *process,* while leaders, who are concerned with ideas, relate in more intuitive and empathetic ways. The manager's orientation to people, as actors in a sequence of events, deflects his or her attention away from the substance of people's concerns and toward their roles in a process. The distinction is simply between a manager's attention to *how* things get done and a leader's to *what* the events and decisions mean to participants.

In recent years, managers have taken over from game theory the notion that decision-making events can be one of two types: the win-lose situation (or zero-sum game) or the win-win situation in which everybody in the action comes out ahead. As part of the process of reconciling differences among people and maintaining balances of power, managers strive to convert win-lose into win-win situations.

As an illustration, take the decision of how to allocate capital resources among operating divisions in a large, decentralized organization. On the face of it, the dollars available for distribution are limited at any given time. Presumably, therefore, the more one division gets, the less is available for other divisions.

Managers tend to view this situation (as it affects human relations) as a conversion issue: how to make what seems like a win-lose problem into a win-win problem. Several solutions to this situation come to mind. First, the manager focuses others' attention on procedure and not on substance. Here the actors become engrossed in the bigger problem of *how* to make decisions, not *what* decisions to make. Once committed to the bigger problem, the actors have to support the outcome since they were involved in formulating decision rules. Because the actors believe in the rules they formulated, they will accept present losses in the expectation that next time they will win.

Second, the manager communicates to his subordinates indirectly, using "signals" instead of "messages." A signal has a number of possible implicit positions in it while a message clearly states a position. Signals are inconclusive and subject to reinterpretation should people become upset and angry, while messages involve the direct consequence that some people will indeed not like what they hear. The nature of messages heightens emotional response, and, as I have indicated, emotionally makes managers anxious. With signals, the question of who wins and who loses often becomes obscured.

Third, the manager plays for time. Managers seem to recognize that with the passage of time and the delay of major decisions, compromises emerge that take the sting out of win-lose situations; and the original "game" will be superseded by additional ones. Therefore, compromises may mean that one wins and loses simultaneously, depending on which of the games one evaluates.

There are undoubtedly many other tactical moves managers use to change human situations from win-lose to win-win. But the point to be made is that such tactics focus on the decision-making process itself and interest managers rather than leaders. The interest in tactics involves costs as well as benefits, including making organizations fatter in bureaucratic and political intrigue and leaner in direct, hard activity and warm human relationships. Consequently, one often hears subordinates characterize managers as inscrutable, detached, and manipulative. These adjectives arise from the subordinates' perception that they are linked together in a process whose purpose, beyond simply making decisions, is to maintain a controlled as well as rational and equitable structure. These adjectives suggest that managers need order in the face of the potential chaos that many fear in human relationships.

In contrast, one often hears leaders referred to in adjectives rich in emotional content. Leaders attract strong feelings of identity and difference, or of love and hate. Human relations in leader-dominated structures often appear turbulent, intense, and at times even disorganized. Such an atmosphere intensifies individual motivation and often produces unanticipated outcomes. Does this intense motivation lead to innovation and high performance, or does it represent wasted energy?

Senses of Self

In *The Varieties of Religious Experience,* William James describes two basic personality types, "once-born" and "twice-born."[12] People of the former personality type are those for whom adjustments to life have been straightforward and whose lives have been more or less a peaceful flow from the moment of their births. The twice-borns, on the other hand, have not had an easy time of it. Their lives are marked by a continual struggle to attain some sense of order. Unlike the once-borns they cannot take things for granted. According to James, these personalities have equally different world views. For a once-born personality, the sense of self, as a guide to conduct and attitude, derives from a feeling of being at home and in harmony with one's environment. For a twice-born, the sense of self derives from a feeling of profound separateness.

A sense of belonging or of being separate has a practical significance for the kinds of investments managers and leaders make in their careers. Managers see themselves as conservators

and regulators of an existing order of affairs with which they personally identify and from which they gain rewards. Perpetuating and strengthening existing institutions enhances a manager's sense of self-worth: he or she is performing in a role that harmonizes with the ideals of duty and responsibility. William James had this harmony in mind—this sense of self as flowing easily to and from the outer world—in defining a once-born personality. If one feels oneself as a member of institutions, contributing to their well-being, then one fulfills a mission in life and feels rewarded for having measured up to ideals. This reward transcends material gains and answers the more fundamental desire for personal integrity which is achieved by identifying with existing institutions.

Leaders tend to be twice-born personalities, people who feel separate from their environment, including other people. They may work in organizations, but they never belong to them. Their sense of who they are does not depend upon memberships, work roles, or other social indicators of identity. What seems to follow from this idea about separateness is some theoretical basis for explaining why certain individuals search out opportunities for change. The methods to bring about change may be technological, political, or ideological, but the object is the same: to profoundly alter human, economic, and political relationships.

Sociologists refer to the preparation individuals undergo to perform in roles as the socialization process. Where individuals experience themselves as an integral part of the social structure (their self-esteem gains strength through participation and conformity), social standards exert powerful effects in maintaining the individual's personal sense of continuity, even beyond the early years in the family. The line of development from the family to schools, then to career is cumulative and reinforcing. When the line of development is not reinforcing because of significant disruptions in relationships or other problems experienced in the family or other social institutions, the individual turns inward and struggles to establish self-esteem, identity, and order. Here the psychological dynamics center on the experience with loss and the efforts at recovery.

In considering the development of leadership, we have to examine two different courses of life history: (1) development through socialization, which prepares the individual to guide institutions and to maintain the existing balance of social relations; and (2) development through personal mastery, which impels an individual to struggle for psychological and social change. Society produces its managerial talent through the first line of development, while through the second leaders emerge.

DEVELOPMENT OF LEADERSHIP

The development of every person begins in the family. Each person experiences the traumas associated with separating from his or her parents, as well as the pain that follows such frustration. In the same vein, all individuals face the difficulties of achieving self-regulation and self-control. But for some, perhaps a majority, the fortunes of childhood provide adequate gratifications and sufficient opportunities to find substitutes for rewards no longer available. Such individuals, the "once-borns," make moderate identifications with parents and find a harmony between what they expect and what they are able to realize from life.

But suppose the pains of separation are amplified by a combination of parental demands and the individual's needs to the degree that a sense of isolation, of being special, and of wariness disrupts the bonds that attach children to parents and other authority figures? Under such conditions, and given a special aptitude, the origins of which remain mysterious, the person becomes deeply involved in his or her inner world at the expense of interest in the outer world. For

such a person, self-esteem no longer depends solely upon positive attachments and real rewards. A form a self-reliance takes hold along with expectations of performance and achievement, and perhaps even the desire to do great works.

Such self-perceptions can come to nothing if the individual's talents are negligible. Even with strong talents, there are no guarantees that achievement will follow, let alone that the end result will be for good rather than evil. Other factors enter into development. For one thing, leaders are like artists and other gifted people who often struggle with neuroses; their ability to function varies considerably even over the short run, and some potential leaders may lose the struggle altogether. Also, beyond early childhood, the patterns of development that affect managers and leaders involve the selective influence of particular people. Just as they appear flexible and evenly distributed in the types of talents available for development, managers form moderate and widely distributed attachments. Leaders, on the other hand, establish, and also break off, intensive one-to-one relationships.

It is a common observation that people with great talents are often only indifferent students. No one, for example, could have predicted Einstein's great achievements on the basis of his mediocre record in school. The reason for mediocrity is obviously not the absence of ability. It may result, instead, from self-absorption and the inability to pay attention to the ordinary tasks at hand. The only sure way an individual can interrupt reverie-like preoccupation and self-absorption is to form a deep attachment to a great teacher or other benevolent person who understands and has the ability to communicate with the gifted individual.

Whether gifted individuals find what they need in one-to-one relationships depends on the availability of sensitive and intuitive mentors who have a vocation in cultivating talent. Fortunately, when the generations do meet and the self-selections occur, we learn more about how to develop leaders and how talented people of different generations influence each other.

While apparently destined for a mediocre career, people who form important one-to-one relationships are able to accelerate and intensify their development through and apprenticeship. The background for such apprenticeships, or the psychological readiness of an individual to benefit from an intensive relationship, depends upon some experience in life that forces the individual to turn inward. A case example will make this point clearer. This example comes from the life of Dwight David Eisenhower, and illustrates the transformation of a career from competent to outstanding.[13]

Dwight Eisenhower's early career in the Army foreshadowed very little about his future development. During World War I, while some of his West Point classmates were already experiencing the war first-hand in France, Eisenhower felt "embedded in the monotony and unsought safety of the Zone of the Interior . . . that was intolerable punishment."[14]

Shortly after World War I, Eisenhower, then a young officer somewhat pessimistic about his career chances, asked for a transfer to Panama to work under General Fox Connor, a senior officer whom Eisenhower admired. The army turned down Eisenhower's request. This setback was very much on Eisenhower's mind when Ikey, his first-born son, succumbed to influenza. By some sense of responsibility for its own, the army transferred Eisenhower to Panama, where he took up his duties under General Connor with the shadow of his lost son very much upon him.

In a relationship with the kind of father he would have wanted to be, Eisenhower reverted to being the son he lost. In this highly charged situation, Eisenhower began to learn from his mentor. General Connor offered, and Eisenhower gladly took, a magnificent tutorial on the military. The effects of this relationship on Eisenhower cannot be measured quantitatively,

but, in Eisenhower's own reflections and the unfolding of his career, one cannot overestimate its significance in the reintegration of a person shattered by grief.

As Eisenhower wrote later about Connor, "Life with General Connor was a sort of graduate school in military affairs and the humanities, leavened by a man who was experienced in his knowledge of men and their conduct. I can never adequately express my gratitude to this one gentleman. . . . In a lifetime of association with great and good men, he is the one more or less invisible figure to whom I owe an incalculable debt."[15]

Some time after his tour of duty with General Connor, Eisenhower's breakthrough occurred. He received orders to attend the Command and General Staff School at Fort Leavenworth, one of the most competitive schools in the army. It was a coveted appointment, and Eisenhower took advantage of the opportunity. Unlike his performance in high school and West Point, his work at the Command School was excellent; he was graduated first in his class.

Psychological biographies of gifted people repeatedly demonstrate the important part a mentor plays in developing an individual. Andrew Carnegie owed much to his senior, Thomas A. Scott. As head of the Western Division of the Pennsylvania Railroad, Scott recognized talent and the desire to learn in the young telegrapher assigned to him. By giving Carnegie increasing responsibility and by providing him with the opportunity to learn through close personal observation, Scott added to Carnegie's self-confidence and sense of achievement. Because of his own personal strength and achievement, Scott did not fear Carnegie's aggressiveness. Rather, he gave it full play in encouraging Carnegie's initiative.

Mentors take risks with people. They bet initially on talent they perceive in younger people. Mentors also risk emotional involvement in working closely with their juniors. The risks do not always pay off, but the willingness to take them appears crucial in developing leaders.

CAN ORGANIZATIONS DEVELOP LEADERS?

The examples I have given of how leaders develop suggest the importance of personal influence and the one-to-one relationship. For organizations to encourage consciously the development of leaders as compared with managers would mean developing one-to-one relationships between junior and senior executives and, more important, fostering a culture of individualism and possibly elitism. The elitism arises out of the desire to identify talent and other qualities suggestive of the ability to lead and not simply to manage.

The Jewel Companies Inc. enjoy a reputation for developing talented people. The chairman and chief executive officer, Donald S. Perkins, is perhaps a good example of a person brought along through the mentor approach. Franklin J. Lunding, who was Perkins's mentor, expressed the philosophy of taking risks with young people this way: "Young people today want in on the action. They don't want to sit around for six months trimming lettuce."[16]

This statement runs counter to the culture that attaches primary importance to slow progression based on experience and proved competence. It is a high-risk philosophy, one that requires time for the attachment between senior and junior people to grow and be meaningful, and one that is bound to produce more failures than successes.

The elitism is an especially sensitive issue. At Jewel the MBA degree symbolized the elite. Lunding attracted Perkins to Jewel at a time when business school graduates had little interest in retailing in general, and food distribution in particular. Yet the elitism seemed to pay off: not only did Perkins become the president at age 37,

but also under the leadership of young executives recruited into Jewel with the promise of opportunity for growth and advancement, Jewel managed to diversify into discount and drug chains and still remain strong in food retailing. By assigning each recruit to a vice president who acted as sponsor, Jewel evidently tried to build a structure around the mentor approach to developing leaders. To counteract the elitism implied in such an approach, the company also introduced an "equalizer" in what Perkins described as "the first assistant philosophy." Perkins stated:

> Being a good first assistant means that each management person thinks of himself not as the order-giving, domineering boss, but as the first assistant to those who "report" to him in a more typical organizational sense. Thus we mentally turn our organizational charts upside-down and challenge ourselves to seek ways in which we can lead . . . by helping . . . by teaching . . . by listening . . . and by managing in the true democratic sense . . . that is, with the consent of the managed. Thus the satisfactions of leadership come from helping others to get things done and changed—and not from getting credit for doing and changing things ourselves.[17]

While this statement would seem to be more egalitarian than elitist, it does reinforce a youth-oriented culture since it defines the senior officer's job as primarily helping the junior person.

A myth about how people learn and develop that seems to have taken hold in the American culture also dominates thinking in business. The myth is that people learn best from their peers. Supposedly, the threat of evaluation and even humiliation recedes in peer relations because of the tendency for mutual identification and the social restraints on authoritarian behavior among equals. Peer training in organizations occurs in various forms. The use, for example, of task forces made up of peers from several interested occupational groups (sales, production, research, and finance) supposedly removes the restraints of authority on the individual's willingness to assert and exchange ideas. As a result, so the theory goes, people interact more freely, listen more objectively to criticism and other points of view and, finally, learn from this healthy interchange.

Another application of peer training exists in some large corporations, such as Philips, N.V. in Holland, where organization structure is built on the principle of joint responsibility of two peers, one representing the commercial end of the business and the other the technical. Formally, both hold equal responsibility for geographic operations or product groups, as the case may be. As a practical matter, it may turn out that one or the other of the peers dominates the management. Nevertheless, the main interaction is between two or more equals.

The principal question I would raise about such arrangements is whether they perpetuate the managerial orientation, and preclude the formation of one-to-one relationships between senior people and potential leaders.

Aware of the possible stifling effects of peer relationships on aggressiveness and individual initiative, another company, much smaller than Philips, utilizes joint responsibility of peers for operating units, with one important difference. The chief executive of this company encourages competition and rivalry among peers, ultimately appointing the one who comes out on top for increased responsibility. These hybrid arrangements produce some unintended consequences that can be disastrous. There is no easy way to limit rivalry. Instead, it permeates all levels of the operation and opens the way for the formation of cliques in an atmosphere of intrigue.

A large, integrated oil company has accepted the importance of developing leaders through the direct influence of senior on junior executives. One chairman and chief executive officer regularly selected one talented university graduate whom he appointed his special assistant, and with whom he would work closely for a year. At the end of the year, the junior executive would become available for assignment to one of the operating divisions, where he would be assigned to a responsible post rather than a training position. The mentor relationship had acquainted the junior executive firsthand with the use of power, and with the important antidotes to the power disease called *hubris*—performance and integrity.

Working in one-to-one relationships, where there is a formal and recognized difference in the power of the actors, takes a great deal of tolerance for emotional interchange. This interchange, inevitable in close working arrangements, probably accounts for the reluctance of many executives to become involved in such relationships. *Fortune* carried an interesting story on the departure of a key executive, John W. Hanley, from the top management of Procter & Gamble, for the chief executive officer position at Monsanto.[18] According to this account, the chief executive and chairman of P&G passed over Hanley for appointment to the presidency and named another executive vice president to this post instead.

The chairman evidently felt he could not work well with Hanley who, by his own acknowledgement, was aggressive, eager to experiment and change practices, and constantly challenged his superior. A chief executive officer naturally has the right to select people with whom he feels congenial. But I wonder whether a greater capacity on the part of senior officers to tolerate the competitive impulses and behavior of their subordinates might not be healthy for corporations. At least a greater tolerance for interchange would not favor the managerial team player at the expense of the individual who might become a leader.

I am constantly surprised at the frequency with which chief executives feel threatened by open challenges to their ideas, as though the source of their authority, rather than their specific ideas, were at issue. In one case a chief executive officer, who was troubled by the aggressiveness and sometimes outright rudeness of one of his talented vice presidents, used various indirect methods such as group meetings and hints from outside directors to avoid dealing with his subordinate. I advised the executive to deal head-on with what irritated him. I suggested that by direct, face-to-face confrontation, both he and his subordinate would learn to validate the distinction between the authority to be preserved and the issues to be debated.

To confront is also to tolerate aggressive interchange, and has the net effect of stripping away the veils of ambiguity and signaling so characteristic of managerial cultures, as well as encouraging the emotional relationship leaders need if they are to survive.

NOTES

1. John D. Rockefeller, 3rd., *The Second American Revolution* (New York: Harper-Row, 1973), p. 72.
2. Theodore Levitt, "Management and the Post Industrial Society," *The Public Interest,* Summer 1976, p. 73.
3. Alfred P. Sloan, Jr., *My Years with General Motors* (New York: Doubleday & Co. 1964), p. 429.
4. Ibid., p. 429.
5. Ibid. p. 440.
6. Ibid. p. 91.
7. Ibid. p. 91.
8. Ibid. p. 93.
9. Stanley and Inge Hoffmann, "The Will for Grandeur: de Gaulle as Political Artist," *Daedalus,* Summer 1968, p. 849.
10. Abraham Zaleznik, Gene W. Dalton, and Louis B. Barnes, *Orientation and Conflict in Career,* (Boston: Division of Research, Harvard Business School, 1970), p. 316.
11. Ibid. p. 294.
12. William James, *Varieties of Religious Experience* (New York: Mentor Books, 1958).
13. This example is included in Abraham Zaleznik and Manfred F. R. Kets de Vries, *Power and the Corporate Mind* (Boston: Houghton Mifflin, 1975).
14. Dwight D. Eisenhower, *At Ease: Stories I Tell to Friends* (New York: Doubleday, 1967), p. 136.
15. Ibid. p. 187.
16. "Jewel Lets Young Men Make Mistakes," *Business Week,* January 17, 1970, p. 90.
17. "What Makes Jewel Shine so Bright," *Progressive Grocer,* September, 1973, p. 76.
18. "Jack Hanley Got There by Selling Harder," *Fortune,* November, 1976.

The Middle Manager as Innovator

Rosabeth Moss Kanter

• When Steve Talbot, an operations manager, began a staff job reporting to the general manager of a product group, he had no line responsibility, no subordinates or budget of his own, and only a vague mandate to "explore options to improve performance."

To do this, Talbot set about collecting resources by bargaining with product-line managers and sales managers. By promising the product-line managers that he would save them having to negotiate with sales to get top priority for their products, he got a budget from them. Then, because he had the money in hand, Talbot got the sales managers to agree to hire one salesperson per product line, with Talbot permitted to do the hiring.

The next area he tackled was field services. Because the people in this area were conservative and tightfisted, Talbot went to his boss to get support for his recommendations about this area.

With the sales and service functions increasing their market share, it was easy for Talbot to get the product-line managers' backing when he pushed for selling a major new product that he had devised. And, to keep his action team functioning and behind him, Talbot made sure that "everyone became a hero" when the senior vice president of engineering asked him to explain his success to corporate officers.

• Arthur Drumm, a technical department head

of two sections, wanted to develop a new measuring instrument that could dramatically improve the company's product quality. But only Drumm thought this approach would work; those around him were not convinced it was needed or would pay off. After spending months developing data to show that the company needed the instrument, Drumm convinced several of his bosses two levels up to contribute $300,000 to its development. He put together a task force made up of representatives from all the manufacturing sites to advise on the development process and to ensure that the instrument would fit in with operations.

When, early on, one high-level manager opposed the project, Drumm coached two others in preparation for an officer-level meeting at which they were going to present his proposal. And when executives argued about which budget line the money would come from, R&D or engineering, Drumm tried to ease the tension. His persistence netted the company an extremely valuable new technique.

• When Doris Randall became the head of a backwater purchasing department, one of three departments in her area, she expected the assignment to advance her career. Understandably, she was disappointed at the poor state of the function she had inherited and looked around for ways to make improvements. She first sought information from users of the department's services and, with this information, got her boss to agree to a first wave of changes. No one in her position had ever had such close contacts with users before, and Randall employed her knowl-

Reprinted with permission of *Harvard Business Review,* July–August 1982, vol. 60, no. 4. Copyright © 1982 by the President and Fellows of Harvard College; all rights reserved.

edge to reorganize the unit into a cluster of user-oriented specialties (with each staff member concentrating on a particular need).

Once she had the reorganization in place and her function acknowledged as the best purchasing department in the region, Randall wanted to reorganize the other two purchasing departments. Her boss, perhaps out of concern that he would lose his position to Randall if the proposed changes took place, discouraged her. But her credibility was so strong that her boss's boss—who viewed her changes as a model for improvements in other areas—gave Randall the go-ahead to merge the three purchasing departments into one. Greater efficiency, cost savings, and increased user satisfaction resulted.

These three managers are enterprising, innovative, and entrepreneurial middle managers who are part of a group that can play a key role in the United States' return to economic leadership.

If that seems like an overly grand statement, consider the basis for U.S. companies' success in the past: innovation in products and advances in management techniques. Then consider the pivotal contribution middle managers make to innovation and change in large organizations. Top leaders' general directives to open a new market, improve quality, or cut costs mean nothing without efficient middle managers just below officer level able to design the systems, carry them out, and redirect their staffs' activities accordingly. Furthermore, because middle managers have their fingers on the pulse of operations, they can also conceive, suggest, and set in motion new ideas that top managers may not have thought of.

The middle managers described here are not extraordinary individuals. They do, however, share a number of characteristics:

Comfort with change. They are confident that uncertainties will be clarified. They also have foresight and see unmet needs as opportunities.

Clarity of direction. They select projects carefully and, with their long time horizons, view setbacks as temporary blips in an otherwise straight path to a goal.

Thoroughness. They prepare well for meetings and are professional in making their presentations. They have insight into organizational politics and a sense of whose support can help them at various junctures.

Participative management style. They encourage subordinates to put in maximum effort and to be part of the team, promise them a share of the rewards, and deliver on their promises.

Persuasiveness, persistence, and discretion. They understand that they cannot achieve their ends overnight, so they persevere—using tact—until they do.

What makes it possible for managers to use such skills for the company's benefit? They work in organizations where the culture fosters collaboration and teamwork and where structures encourage people to "do what needs to be done." Moreover, they usually work under top managers who consciously incorporate conditions facilitating innovation and achievement into their companies' structures and operations.

These conclusions come from a study of the major accomplishments of 165 effective middle managers in five leading American corporations. I undertook this study to determine managers' contributions to a company's overall success as well as the conditions that stimulate innovation and thus push a business beyond a short-term emphasis and allow it to secure a successful future.

Each of the 165 managers studied—all of whom were deemed "effective" by their companies—told the research team about a particular accomplishment; these covered a wide range. Some of the successes, though impressive, clearly were achieved within the boundaries of established company practice. Others, however, in-

THE RESEARCH PROJECT

After a pilot study in which it interviewed 26 effective middle managers from 18 companies, the research team interviewed, in depth, 165 middle managers from five major corporations located across the United States. The 165 were chosen by their companies to participate because of their reputations for effectiveness. We did not want a random sample: we were looking for "the best and the brightest" who could serve as models for others. It turned out, however, that every major function was represented, and roughly in proportion to its importance in the company's success. (For example, there were more innovative sales and marketing managers representing the "market-driven" company and more technical, R&D, and manufacturing managers from the "product-driven" companies.)

During the two-hour interviews, the managers talked about all aspects of a single significant accomplishment, from the glimmering of an idea to the results. We asked the managers to focus on the most significant of a set of four or five of their accomplishments over the previous two years. We also elicited a chronology of the project as well as responses to a set of open-ended questions about the acquisition of power, the handling of roadblocks, and the doling out of rewards. We supplemented the interviews with discussions about current issues in the five companies with our contacts in each company.

The five companies represent a range of types and industries: from rather traditional, slow-moving, mature companies to fast-changing, newer, high-technology companies. We included both service and manufacturing companies that are from different parts of the country and are at different stages in their development. The one thing that all five have in common is an intense interest in the topic of the study. Facing highly competitive markets (for the manufacturing companies a constant since their founding; for the service companies a newer phenomenon), all of these corporations wanted to encourage their middle managers to be more enterprising and innovative.

Our pseudonyms for the companies emphasize a central feature of each:

CHIPCO: manufacturer of computer products
FINCO: insurance and related financial services
MEDCO: manufacturer of large medical equipment
RADCO (for "R&D"): manufacturer of optical products
UTICO: communications utility

volved innovation: introduction of new methods, structures, or products that increased the company's capacity. All in all, 99 of the 165 accomplishments fall within the definition of an innovative effort.

Basic accomplishments differ from innovative ones not only in scope and long-run impact but also in what it takes to achieve them. They are part of the assigned job and require only routine and readily available means to carry them out. Managers reporting this kind of accomplishment said they were just doing their jobs. Little was problematic—they had an assignment to tackle; they were told, or they already knew, how to go about it; they used existing budget or staff; they didn't need to gather or share much information outside of their units; and they encountered little or no opposition. Managers performing such activities don't generate innovations for their companies; they merely accomplish things faster or better than they already know how to do.

In contrast, innovative accomplishments are strikingly entrepreneurial. Moreover, they are sometimes highly problematic and generally involve acquiring and using power and influence. (See the boxed insert on previous page for more details on the study's definitions of *basic* and *innovative* accomplishments.)

In this article, I first explore how managers influence their organizations to achieve goals throughout the various stages of a project's life. Next I discuss the managerial styles of the persons studied and the kinds of innovation they brought about. I look finally at the types of companies these entrepreneurial managers worked in and explore what top officers can do to foster a creative environment.

THE ROLE OF POWER IN ENTERPRISE

Because most innovative achievements cut across organizational lines and threaten to disrupt exist-ing arrangements, enterprising managers need tools beyond those that come with the job. Innovations have implications for other functions and areas, and they require data, agreements, and resources of wider scope than routine operations demand. Even R&D managers, who are expected to produce innovations, need more information, support, and resources for major projects than those built into regular R&D functions. They too may need additional data, more money, or agreement from extrafunctional officials that the project is necessary. Only hindsight shows that an innovative project was bound to be successful.

Because of the extra resources they require, entrepreneurial managers need to go beyond the limits of their formal positions. For this, they need power. In large organizations at least, I have observed that powerlessness "corrupts."[1] That is, lack of power (the capacity to mobilize resources and people to get things done) tends to create managers who are more concerned about guarding their territories than about collaborating with others to benefit the organization. At the same time, when managers hoard potential power and don't invest it in productive action, it atrophies and eventually blocks achievements.

Furthermore, when some people have too much unused power and others too little, problems occur. To produce results, power—like money—needs to circulate. To come up with innovations, managers have to be in areas where power circulates, where it can be grabbed and invested. In this sense, organizational power is transactional: it exists as potential until someone makes a bid for it, invests it, and produces results with it.

The overarching condition required for managers to produce innovative achievements is this: they must envision an accomplishment beyond the scope of the job. They cannot alone possess the power to carry their idea out but they must be able to acquire the power they need easily. Thus, creative managers are not empowered simply by a boss or their job; on their own they seek and find the additional strength it takes to carry out major new initiatives. They are the corporate entrepreneurs.

Three commodities are necessary for accumulating productive power—information, resources, and support. Managers might find a portion of these within their purview and pour them into a project; managers with something they believe in will eagerly leverage their own staff and budget and even bootleg resources from their subordinates' budgets. But innovations usually require a manager to search for additional supplies elsewhere in the organization. Depending on how easy the organization makes it to tap sources of power and on how technical the project is, acquiring power can be the most time-consuming and difficult part of the process.

Phases of the Accomplishment

A prototypical innovation goes through three phases: project definition (acquisition and application of information to shape a manageable, salable project), coalition building (development of a network of backers who agree to provide resources and support), and action (application of the resources, information, and support to the project and mobilization of an action team). Let us examine each of these steps in more detail.

Defining the Project. Before defining a project, managers need to identify the problem. People in an organization may hold many conflicting views about the best method of reaching a goal, and discovering the basis of these conflicting perspectives (while gathering hard data) is critical to a manager's success.

In one case, information circulating freely about the original design of a part was inaccurate. The manager needed to acquire new data to prove that the problem he was about to tackle was not a manufacturing shortcoming but a design flaw. But, as often happens, some people had a stake in the popular view. Even hard-nosed engineers in our study acknowledged that, in the early stages of an entrepreneurial project, man-

agers need political information as much as they do technical data. Without political savvy, say these engineers, no one can get a project beyond the proposal stage.

The culmination of the project definition phase comes when managers sift through the fragments of information from each source and focus on a particular target. Then, despite the fact that managers may initially have been handed a certain area as an assignment, they still have to "sell" the project that evolves. In the innovative efforts I observed, the managers' assignments involved no promises of resources or support required to do anything more than routine activities.

Furthermore, to implement the innovation, a manager has to call on the cooperation of many others besides the boss who assigned the task. Many of these others may be independent actors who are not compelled to cooperate simply because the manager has carved a project out of a general assignment. Even subordinates may not be automatically on board. If they are professionals or managers, they have a number of other tasks and the right to set some of their own priorities; and if they are in a matrix, they may be responsible to other bosses as well.

For example, in her new job as head of a manufacturing planning unit, Heidi Wilson's assignment was to improve the cost efficiency of operations and thereby boost the company's price competitiveness. Her boss told her she could spend six months "saying nothing and just observing, getting to know what's really going on." One of the first things she noticed was that the flow of goods through the company was organized in an overly complicated, time-consuming, and expensive fashion.

The assignment gave Wilson the mandate to seek information but not to carry out any particular activities. Wilson set about to gather organizational, technical, and political information in order to translate her ambiguous task into a concrete project. She followed goods through the company to determine what the process was and

187

how it could be changed. She sought ideas and impressions from manufacturing line managers, at the same time learning the location of vested interests and where other patches of organizational quicksand lurked. She compiled data, refined her approach, and packaged and repackaged her ideas until she believed she could "prove to people that I knew more about the company than they did."

Wilson's next step was "to do a number of punchy presentations with pictures and graphs and charts." At the presentations, she got two kinds of response: "Gee, we thought there was a problem but we never saw it outlined like this before" and "Aren't there better things to worry about?" To handle the critics, she "simply came back over and over again with information, more information than anyone else had." When she had gathered the data and received the feedback, Wilson was ready to formulate a project and sell it to her boss. Ultimately, her project was approved, and it netted impressive cost savings.

Thus, although innovation may begin with an assignment, it is usually one—like Wilson's—that is couched in general statements of results with the means largely unspecified. Occasionally, managers initiate projects themselves; however, initiation seldom occurs in a vacuum. Creative managers listen to a stream of information from superiors and peers and then identify a perceived need. In the early stages of defining a project, managers may spend more time talking with people outside their own functions than with subordinates or bosses inside.

One R&D manager said he had "hung out" with product designers while trying to get a handle on the best way to formulate a new process-development project. Another R&D manager in our survey got the idea for a new production method from a conversation about problems he had with the head of production. He then convinced his boss to let him determine whether a corrective project could be developed.

Building a Coalition. Next, entrepreneurial managers need to pull in the resources and support to make the project work. For creative accomplishments, these power-related tools do not come through the vertical chain of command but rather from many areas of the organization.

George Putnam's innovation is typical. Putnam was an assistant department manager for product testing in a company that was about to demonstrate a product at a site that attracted a large number of potential buyers. Putnam heard through the grapevine that a decision was imminent about which model to display. The product managers were each lobbying for their own, and

---

WHAT IS AN INNOVATIVE ACCOMPLISHMENT?

We categorized the 165 managers' accomplishments according to their primary impact on the company. Many accomplishments had multiple results or multiple components, but it was the breadth of scope of the accomplishment and its future utility for the company that defined its category. Immediate dollar results were *not* the central issue; rather, organizational "learning" or increased future capacity was the key. Thus, improving revenues by cutting costs while changing nothing else would be categorized differently from improving revenues by designing a new production method; only the latter leaves a lasting trace.

188

The Accomplishments Fall into Two Clusters:

Basic.   Done solely within the existing framework and not affecting the company's longer term capacity; 66 of the 165 fall into this category.

Innovative.   A new way for the company to use or expand its resources that raises long-term capacity; 99 of the 165 are such achievements.

Basic Accomplishments Include:
Doing the basic job—simply carrying out adequately a defined assignment within the bounds of one's job (e.g., "fulfilled sales objectives during a reorganization").

Affecting individuals' performance—having an impact on individuals (e.g., "found employee a job in original department after failing to retrain him").

Advancing incrementally—achieving a higher level of performance within the basic job (e.g., "met more production schedules in plant than in past").

Innovative Accomplishments Include:
Effecting a new policy—creating a change of orientation or direction (e.g., "changed price-setting policy in product line with new model showing cost-quality trade-offs").

Finding a new opportunity—developing an entirely new product or opening a new market (e.g., "sold new product program to higher management and developed staffing for it").

Devising a fresh method—introducing a new process, procedure, or technology for continued use (e.g., "designed and implemented new information system for financial results by business sectors").

Designing a new structure—changing the formal structure, reorganizing or introducing a new structure, or forging a different link among units (e.g., "consolidated three offices into one").

While members of the research team occasionally argued about the placement of accomplishments in the subcategories, we were almost unanimous as to whether an accomplishment rated as basic or innovative. Even bringing off a financially significant or flashy increase in performance was considered basic if the accomplishment was well within the manager's assignment and territory; involved no new methods that could be used to repeat the feat elsewhere, opened no opportunities, or had no impact on corporate structure—in other words, reflected little inventiveness. The manager who achieved such a result might have been an excellent manager, but he or she was not an innovative one.

the marketing people also had a favorite. Putnam, who was close to the products, thought that the first-choice model had grave defects and so decided to demonstrate to the marketing staff both what the problems with the first one were and the superiority of another model.

Building on a long-term relationship with the people in corporate quality control and a good alliance with his boss, Putnam sought the tools he needed: the blessing of the vice president of engineering (his boss's boss), special materials for testing from the materials division, a budget from corporate quality control, and staff from his own units to carry out the tests. As Putnam put it, this was all done through one-on-one "horse trading"—showing each manager how much the others were chipping in. Then Putnam met informally with the key marketing staffer to learn what it would take to convince him.

As the test results emerged, Putnam took them to his peers in marketing, engineering, and quality control so they could feed them to their superiors. The accumulated support persuaded the decision makers to adopt Putnam's choice of a model; it later became a strong money-maker. In sum, Putnam had completely stepped out of his usual role to build a consensus that shaped a major policy decision.

Thus, the most successful innovations derive from situations where a number of people from a number of areas make contributions. They provide a kind of checks-and-balances system to an activity that is otherwise nonroutine and, therefore, is not subject to the usual controls. By building a coalition before extensive project activity gets under way, the manager also ensures the availability of enough support to keep momentum going and to guarantee implementation.

In one company, the process of lining up peers and stakeholders as early supporters is called "making cheerleaders"; in another, "pre-selling." Sometimes managers ask peers for "pledges" of money or staff to be collected later if higher management approves the project and provides overall resources.

After garnering peer support, usually managers next seek support at much higher levels. While we found surprisingly few instances of top management directly sponsoring or championing a project, we did find that a general blessing from the top is clearly necessary to convert potential supporters into a solid team. In one case, top officers simply showed up at a meeting where the proposal was being discussed; their presence ensured that other people couldn't use the "pocket veto" power of headquarters as an excuse to table the issue. Also, the very presence of a key executive at such a meeting is often a signal of the proposal's importance to the rest of the organization.

Enterprising managers learn who at the top-executive level has the power to affect their projects (including material resources or vital initial approval power). Then they negotiate for these executives' support, using polished formal presentations. Whereas managers can often sell the project to peers and stakeholders by appealing to these people's self-interests and assuring them they know what they're talking about, managers need to offer top executives more guarantees about both the technical and the political adequacies of projects.

Key executives tend to evaluate a proposal in terms of its salability to *their* constituencies. Sometimes entrepreneurial managers arm top executives with materials or rehearse them for their own presentations to other people (such as members of an executive committee or the board) who have to approve the project.

Most often, since many of the projects that originate at the middle of a company can be supported at that level and will not tap corporate funds, those at high levels in the organization simply provide a general expression of support. However, the attention top management confers on this activity, many of our interviewees told us, makes it possible to sell their own staffs as well as others.

But once in a while, a presentation to top-level officers results in help in obtaining supplies.

Sometimes enterprising managers walk away with the promise of a large capital expenditure or assistance getting staff or space. Sometimes a promise of resources is contingent on getting others on board. "If you can raise the money, go ahead with this," is a frequent directive to an enterprising manager.

In one situation, a service manager approached his boss and his boss's boss for a budget for a college recruitment and training program that he had been supporting on his own with funds bootlegged from his staff. The top executives told him they would grant a large budget if he could get his four peers to support the project. Somewhat to their surprise, he came back with this support. He had taken his peers away from the office for three days for a round of negotiation and planning. In cases like this, top management is not so much hedging its bets as using its ability to secure peer support for what might otherwise be risky projects.

With promises of resources and support in hand, enterprising managers can go back to the immediate boss or bosses to make plans for moving ahead. Usually the bosses are simply waiting for this tangible sign of power to continue authorizing the project. But in other cases, the bosses are not fully involved and won't be sold until the manager has higher level support.

Of course, during the coalition-building phase, the network of supporters does not play a passive role; their comments, criticisms, and objectives help shape the project into one that is more likely to succeed. Another result of the coalition-building phase is, then, a set of reality checks that ensures that projects unlikely to succeed will go no farther.

Moving into Action. The innovating manager's next step is to mobilize key players to carry out the project. Whether the players are nominal subordinates or a special project group such as a task force, managers forge them into a team. Enterprising managers bring the people involved in the project together, give them briefings and assignments, pump them up for the extra effort needed, seek their ideas and suggestions (both as a way to involve them and to further refine the project), and promise them a share of the rewards. As one manager put it, "It takes more selling than telling." In most of the innovations we observed, the manager couldn't just order subordinates to get involved. Doing something beyond routine work that involves creativity and cooperation requires the full commitment of subordinates; otherwise the project will not succeed.

During the action phase, managers have four central organizational tasks. The technical details of the project and the actual work directed toward project goals are now in the hands of the action team. Managers may contribute ideas or even get involved in hands-on experimentation, but their primary functions are still largely external and organizational, centered around maintaining the boundaries and integrity of the project.

The manager's first task is to **handle interference** or opposition that may jeopardize the project. Entrepreneurial managers encounter strikingly little overt opposition—perhaps because their success at coalition-building determines whether a project gets started in the first place. Resistance takes a more passive form: criticism of the plan's details, foot-dragging, late responses to requests, or arguments over allocation of time and resources among projects.

Managers are sometimes surprised that critics keep so quiet up to this point. One manufacturing manager who was gearing up for production of a new item had approached many executives in other areas while making cost estimates, and these executives had appeared positive about his efforts. But later, when he began organizing the manufacturing process itself, he heard objections from these very people.

During this phase, therefore, innovative managers may have to spend as much time in meetings, both formal and one-to-one, as they did to get the project launched. Managers need to prepare thoroughly for these meetings so they

191

can counter skepticism and objections with clear facts, persuasion, and reminders of the benefits that can accrue to managers meeting the project's objectives. In most cases, a clear presentation of facts is enough. But not always: one of our respondents, a high-level champion, had to tell an opponent to back down, that the project was going ahead anyway, and that his carping was annoying.

Whereas managers need to directly counter open challenges and criticism that might result in the flow of power or supplies being cut off, they simply keep other interference outside the boundaries of the project. In effect, the manager defines a protected area for the group's work. He or she goes outside this area to head off critics and to keep people or rules imposed by higher management from disrupting project tasks.

While the team itself is sometimes unaware of the manager's contribution, the manager—like Tom West (head of the now-famous computer-design group at Data General)—patrols the boundaries.[2] Acting as interference filters, managers in my study protected innovative projects by bending rules, transferring funds "illicitly" from one budget line to another, developing special reward or incentive systems that offered bonuses above company pay rates, and ensuring that superiors stayed away unless needed.

The second action-phase task is **maintaining momentum** and continuity. Here interference comes from internal rather than external sources. Foot-dragging or inactivity is a constant danger, especially if the creative effort adds to work loads. In our study, enterprising managers as well as team members complained continually about the tendency for routine activities to take precedence over special projects and to consume limited time.

In addition, it is easier for managers to whip up excitement over a vision at start-up than to keep the goal in people's minds when they face the tedium of the work. Thus, managers' team-building skills are essential. So the project

doesn't lose momentum, managers must sustain the enthusiasm of all—from supporters to suppliers—by being persistent and keeping the team aware of supportive authorities who are clearly waiting for results.

One manager, who was involved in a full-time project to develop new and more efficient methods of producing a certain ingredient, maintained momentum by holding daily meetings with the core team, getting together often with operations managers and members of a task force he had formed, putting on weekly status reports, and making frequent presentations to top management. When foot-dragging occurs, many entrepreneurial managers pull in high-level supporters—without compromising the autonomy of the project—to get the team back on board. A letter or a visit from the big boss can remind everyone just how important the project is.

A third task of middle managers in the action phase is to engage in whatever **secondary redesign**—other changes made to support the key change—is necessary to keep the project going. For example, a manager whose team was setting up a computerized information bank held weekly team meetings to define tactics. A fallout of these meetings was a set of new awards and a fresh performance appraisal system for team members and their subordinates.

As necessary, managers introduce new arrangements to conjoin with the core tasks. When it seems that a project is bogging down—that is, when everything possible has been done and no more results are on the horizon—managers often change the structure or approach. Such alterations can cause a redoubling of effort and a renewed attack on the problem. They can also bring the company additional unplanned innovations as a side benefit from the main project.

The fourth task of the action phase, **external communication,** brings the accomplishment full circle. The project begins with gathering information; now it is important to send information out. It is vital to (as several managers put it)

192

"manage the press" so that peers and key supporters have an up-to-date impression of the project and its success. Delivering on promises is also important. As much as possible, innovative managers meet deadlines, deliver early benefits to others, and keep supporters supplied with information. Doing so establishes the credibility of both the project and the manager, even before concrete results can be shown.

Information must be shared with the team and the coalition as well. Good managers periodically remind the team of what they stand to gain from the accomplishment, hold meetings to give feedback and to stimulate pride in the project, and make a point of congratulating each staff member individually. After all, as Steve Talbot (of my first example) said, many people gave this middle manager power because of a promise that everyone would be a hero.

A MANAGEMENT STYLE
FOR INNOVATION . . .

Clearly there is a strong association between carrying out an innovative accomplishment and employing a participative-collaborative management style. The managers observed reached success by:

Persuading more than ordering, though managers sometimes use pressure as a last resort.

Building a team, which entails among other things frequent staff meetings and considerable sharing of information.

Seeking inputs from others—that is, asking for ideas about users' needs, soliciting suggestions from subordinates, welcoming peer review, and so forth.

Acknowledging others' stake or potential stake in the project—in other words, being politically sensitive.

Sharing rewards and recognition willingly.

A collaborative style is also useful when carrying out basic accomplishments; however, in such endeavors it is not required. Managers can bring off many basic accomplishments using a traditional, more autocratic style. Because they're doing what is assigned, they don't need external support; because they have all the tools to do it, they don't need to get anyone else involved (they simply direct subordinates to do what is required). But for innovative accomplishments—seeking funds, staff, or information (political as well as technical) from outside the work unit; attending long meetings and presentations; and requiring "above and beyond" effort from staff—a style that revolves around participation, collaboration, and persuasion is essential.

The participative-collaborative style also helps creative managers reduce risk because it encourages completion of the assignment. Furthermore, others' involvement serves as a check-and-balance on the project, reshaping it to make it more of a sure thing and putting pressure on people to follow through. The few projects in my study that disintegrated did so because the manager failed to build a coalition of supporters and collaborators.

. . . AND CORPORATE CONDITIONS
THAT ENCOURAGE ENTERPRISE

Just as the manager's strategies to develop and implement innovations followed many different patterns, so also the level of enterprise managers achieved varied strongly across the five companies we studied (see Table 1). Managers in newer, high-technology companies have a much higher proportion of innovative accomplishments than managers in other industries. At "CHIPCO," a computer parts manufacturer, 71 percent of all the things effective managers did were innovative; for "UTICO," a communications utility, the number is 33 percent; for "FINCO," an insurance company, it is 47 percent.

TABLE 1.   *Characteristics of the Five Companies in Order of Most to Least "Entrepreneurial"*

	CHIPCO	RADCO	MEDCO	FINCO	UTICO
Percent of effective managers with entrepreneurial accomplishments	71%	69%	67%	47%	33%
Current economic trend	Steadily up	Trend up but currently down	Up	Mixed	Down
Current "change issues"	Change "normal"; constant change in product generations; proliferating staff and units	Change "normal" in products, technologies; recent changeover to second management generation with new focus	Reorganized about 3–4 years ago to install matrix; "normal" product technology changes	Change a "shock"; new top management group from outside reorganizing and trying to add competitive market posture	Change a "shock"; undergoing reorganization to install matrix and add competitive market posture while reducing staff
Organization structure	Matrix	Matrix in some areas; product lines act as quasi-divisions	Matrix in some areas	Divisional; unitary hierarchy within divisions, some central services	Functional organization; currently overlaying a matrix of regions and markets
Decision-Making	Decentralized	Mixed	Mixed	Centralized	Centralized

Information flow	Free	Free	Moderately free	Constricted	Constricted
Communication emphasis	Horizontal	Horizontal	Horizontal	Vertical	Vertical
Culture	Clear, consistent; favors individual initiative	Clear, though in transition from emphasis on invention to emphasis on routinization and systems	Clear; pride in company, belief that talent will be rewarded	Idiosyncratic; depends on boss and area	Clear, but top management would like to change it; favors security, maintenance, protection
Current "emotional" climate	Pride in company, team feeling, some "burn-out"	Uncertainty about changes	Pride in company, team feeling	Low trust, high uncertainty	High certainty, confusion
Rewards	Abundant. Include visibility, chance to do more challenging work in the future and get bigger budget for projects	Abundant. Include visibility, chance to do more challenging work in future and get bigger budget for projects	Moderately abundant; conventional	Scarce; primarily monetary	Scarce; promotion, salary freeze; recognition by peers grudging

195

This difference in levels of innovative achievement correlates with the extent to which these companies' structures and cultures support middle managers' creativity. Companies producing the most entrepreneurs have cultures that encourage collaboration and teamwork. Moreover, they have complex structures that link people in multiple ways and help them go beyond the confines of their defined jobs to do "what needs to be done."

CHIPCO, which showed the most entrepreneurial activity of any company in our study, is a rapidly growing electronics company with abundant resources. That its culture favors independent action and team effort is communicated quickly and clearly to the newcomer. Sources of support and money are constantly shifting and, as growth occurs, managers rapidly move on to other positions. But even though people frequently express frustration about the shifting approval process, slippage of schedules, and continual entry of new players onto the stage, they don't complain about lost opportunities. For one thing, because coalitions support the various projects, new project managers feel bound to honor their predecessors' financial commitments.

CHIPCO managers have broad job charters to "do the right thing" in a manner of their own choosing. Lateral relationships are more important than vertical ones. Most functions are in a matrix, and some managers have up to four "bosses." Top management expects ideas to bubble up from lower levels. Senior executives then select solutions rather than issue confining directives. In fact, people generally rely on informal face-to-face communication across units to build a consensus. Managers spend a lot of time in meetings; information flows freely, and reputation among peers—instead of formal authority or title—conveys credibility and garners support. Career mobility at CHIPCO is rapid, and people have pride in the company's success.

RADCO, the company with the strongest R&D orientation in the study, has many of CHIPCO's qualities but bears the burden of recent changes. RADCO's once-strong culture and its image as a research institute are in flux and may be eroding. A new top management with new ways of thinking is shifting the orientation of the company, and some people express concern about the lack of clear direction and long-range planning. People's faith in RADCO's strategy of technical superiority has weakened and its traditional orientation toward innovation is giving way to a concern for routinization and production efficiency. This shift is resulting in conflict and uncertainty. Where once access to the top was easy, now the decentralized matrix structure—with fewer central services—makes it difficult.

As at CHIPCO, lateral relationships are important, though top management's presence is felt more. In the partial matrix, some managers have as many as four "bosses." A middle manager's boss or someone in higher management is likely to give general support to projects as long as peers within and across functions get on board. And peers often work decisions up the organization through their own hierarchies.

Procedures at RADCO are both informal and formal: much happens at meetings and presentations and through persuasion, plus the company's long-term employment and well-established working relationships encourage lateral communication. But managers also use task forces and steering committees. Projects often last for years, sustained by the company's image as a leader in treating employees well.

MEDCO manufactures and sells advanced medical equipment, often applying ideas developed elsewhere. Although MEDCO produces a high proportion of innovative accomplishments, it has a greater degree of central planning and routinization than either CHIPCO or RADCO. Despite headquarters' strong role, heads of functions and product managers can vary their approaches. Employers believe that MEDCO's complex matrix system allows autonomy and creates opportunities but is also time wasting because clear accountability is lacking.

Teamwork and competition coexist at

196

MEDCO. Although top management officially encourages teamwork and the matrix produces a tendency for trades and selling to go on within the organization, interdepartmental and interproduct rivalries sometimes get in the way. Rewards, especially promotions, are available, but they often come late and even then are not always clear or consistent. Because many employees have been with MEDCO for a long time, both job mobility and job security are high. Finally, managers see the company as a leader in its approach to management and as a technological follower in all areas but one.

The last two companies in the study, FINCO (insurance) and UTICO (communications), show the lowest proportion of innovative achievements. Many of the completed projects seemed to be successful *despite* the system.

Currently FINCO has an idiosyncratic and inconsistent culture: employees don't have a clear image of the company, its style, or its direction. How managers are treated depends very much on one's boss—one-to-one relationships and private deals carry a great deal of weight. Though the atmosphere of uncertainty creates opportunities for a few, it generally limits risk taking. Moreover, reorganizations, a top-management shake-up, and shuffling of personnel have fostered insecurity and suspicion. It is difficult for managers to get commitment from their subordinates because they question the manager's tenure. Managers spend much time and energy coping with change, reassuring subordinates, and orienting new staff instead of developing future-oriented projects. Still, because the uncertainty creates a vacuum, a few managers in powerful positions (many of whom were brought in to initiate change) do benefit.

Unlike the innovation-producing companies, FINCO features vertical relationships. With little encouragement to collaborate, managers seldom make contact across functions or work in teams. Managers often see formal structures and systems as constraints rather than as supports. Rewards are scarce, and occasionally a manager will break a promise about them. Seeing the company as a follower, not a leader, the managers at FINCO sometimes make unfavorable comparisons between it and other companies in the industry. Furthermore, they resent the fact that FINCO's top management brings in so many executives from outside; they see it as an insult.

UTICO is a very good company in many ways; it is well regarded by its employees and is considered progressive for its industry. However, despite the strong need for UTICO to be more creative and thus more competitive and despite movement toward a matrix structure, UTICO's middle ranks aren't very innovative. UTICO's culture is changing—from being based on security and maintenance to being based on flexibility and competition—and the atmosphere of uncertainty frustrates achievers. Moreover, UTICO remains very centralized. Top management largely directs searches for new systems and methods through formal mechanisms whose ponderousness sometimes discourages innovation. Tight budgetary constraints make it difficult for middle managers to tap funds; carefully measured duties discourage risk takers; and a lockstep chain of command makes it dangerous for managers to by-pass their bosses.

Information flows vertically and sluggishly. Because of limited cooperation among work units, even technical data can be hard to get. Weak-spot management means that problems, not successes, get attention. Jealousy and competition over turf kill praise from peers and sometimes from bosses. Managers' image of the company is mixed: they see it as leading its type of business but behind more modern companies in rate of change.

ORGANIZATIONAL SUPPORTS FOR CREATIVITY

Examination of the differences in organization, culture, and practices in these five companies makes clear the circumstances under which enterprise can flourish. To tackle and solve tricky problems, people need both the opportunities and the incentives to reach beyond their formal jobs and combine organizational resources in new ways.[3] The following create these opportunities:

- Multiple reporting relationships and overlapping territories. These force middle managers to carve out their own ideas about appropriate action and to sell peers in neighboring areas or more than one boss.
- A free and somewhat random flow of information. Data flow of this kind prods executives to find ideas in unexpected places and pushes them to combine fragments of information.
- Many centers of power with some budgetary flexibility. If such centers are easily accessible to middle managers, they will be encouraged to make proposals and acquire resources.
- A high proportion of managers in loosely defined positions or with ambiguous assignments. Those without subordinates or line responsibilities who are told to "solve problems" must argue for a budget or develop their own constituency.
- Frequent and smooth cross-functional contact, a tradition of working in teams and sharing credit widely, and emphasis on lateral rather than vertical relationships as a source of resources, information, and support. These circumstances require managers to get peer support for their projects before top officers approve.
- A reward system that emphasizes investment in people and projects rather than payment for past services. Such a system encourages executives to move into challenging jobs, gives them budgets to tackle projects, and rewards them after their accomplishments with the chance to take on even bigger projects in the future.

Some of these conditions seem to go hand in hand with new companies in not-yet-mature markets. But top decision makers in older, traditional companies can design these conditions into their organizations. They would be wise to do so because, if empowered, innovative middle managers can be one of America's most potent weapons in its battle against foreign competition.

NOTES

1. See my book *Men and Women of the Corporation* (New York: Basic Books, 1977); also see my article, "Power Failure in Management Circuits," *Harvard Business Review,* July–August 1979, p. 65.
2. Tracy Kidder, *The Soul of a New Machine* (Boston: Little, Brown, 1981).
3. My findings about conditions stimulating managerial innovations are generally consistent with those on technical (R&D) innovation. See James Utterback, "Innovation in Industry," *Science,* February 1974, pp. 620–26; John Kimberly, "Managerial Innovation," *Handbook of Organizational Design,* ed. W. H. Starbuck (New York: Oxford, 1981); and Goodmeasure, Inc., "99 Propositions on Innovation from the Research Literature," *Stimulating Innovation in Middle Management* (Cambridge, Mass., 1982).

SECTION III

Managing the Creative Professional

5

THE ROLE OF THE INDIVIDUAL

The Creative Organization

Gary Steiner

DEFINITIONS

First, a few words about what the key terms in this summary mean: "Creativity" has been defined in a number of ways in the psychological literature, in business discussion, in the arts and sciences generally. Within the transcript of this seminar there appear many explicit, and many more implicit, definitions of varying degrees of generality. We make no attempt to frame a master definition at this point. But for purposes of this overview, it is necessary and hopefully sufficient to make this general distinction: *Creativity* has to do with the development, proposal, and implementation of *new* and *better* solutions; *productivity,* with the efficient application of *current* "solutions."

What "better" means, and who is to say, is one of the sticky methodological issues in the field. What it most often means in these pages is better according to professional colleagues or superiors. The meaning of "solution" obviously varies by field; in the following, solutions range from practical answers to specific problems

through new concepts in art, music, or architecture to the most general and abstract conceptualizations that characterize a breakthrough in, say, theoretical physics.

Many of the studies we will cite distinguish "high-creative" from "low-" or "average-creative" groups. It should be clear that "high" and "low" are relative, and not absolute, designations. In most of the samples under investigation, both "high" and "low" groups would qualify as highly creative within the population at large and often even within the profession. It would therefore not have been euphemistic—just too clumsy—to use the designations "more highly" and "less highly" creative. Bear in mind, though, that this is what the shorthand distinction between "high" and "low" means.

I. THE RAW MATERIAL: INDIVIDUAL CREATIVITY

Do individual differences in creativity exist? Does it make sense to speak of more and less creative people in some such way as we speak of more and less intelligent, more or less coordinated, or more or less musical people? Or is

---

personal creativity, like fathering twins, mostly a matter of being in the right place at the right time?

As important as circumstances are in determining who will create what and when, it seems that there are consistent and persistent differences in individual creativity. Holding conditions constant, some people are likely to be more creative than others; and these differences are likely to show up in other situations and at other times. In fact, in most fields, the distribution of creative contributions is something like the distribution of personal income in the United States: a small percentage of people accounts for a large share of the total. (See Guetzkow, p. 35, and Meehl, pp. 28, 127.)

Are these differences in personal creativity specific to particular areas of endeavor, or is there such a thing as general creativity?

That issue involves the distinction between *capacity* and *performance*. Except for a few outstanding historical examples, the most creative people in one field are not likely at the same time to be the most creative in another. But this may be largely a matter of specialization in training and effort. Is an unusually creative architect likely to be highly creative in chemistry also, assuming equal training and opportunity? And are highly creative architects, or chemists, distinguished only by greater creativity in their respective professions, or can they be distinguished from their less creative colleagues in personal capacities and characteristics beyond differential performance on the job?

The results of various testing programs suggest that the qualities and capacities that distinguish more from less creative practitioners of given fields *do* extend beyond the specific area of professional competence. Creative architects, for instance, differ not only in the way they approach architecture but also in the way they approach any number of situations and tasks, some far removed and apparently unrelated to the specific demands of their profession. (See Barron, p. 125.)

What is more, there seem to be at least some differences that hold across diverse fields; for example, some of the same personality characteristics that distinguish between architects of high and average creativity have been observed in studies of creativity not only in industrial research chemists, but even among high school children differing in general creativity.

Granted that people differ in "creativity," are we really talking about anything more than general intelligence?

Yes. General intelligence seems to bear about the same relationship to on-the-job creativity at the professional level as weight does to ability in football. You have to have a lot of it to be in the game at all; but among those on the team—all of whom have a great deal of weight to begin with—differences in performance are only slightly, if at all, related to weight. In short, in the total population, creativity in most fields is associated with high intelligence, probably more so in some (e.g., physics) than in others (art). But within a given group of practitioners, operating at roughly the same professional level, differences in general intelligence provide no significant prediction of differences in creative performance. (See Barron, p. 124; Rokeach, p. 80; and Stein, p. 160.)

What, then, are the characteristics of the creative individual, especially those that might be subject to measurement before the fact so as to make prediction possible?

Although many characteristics of the creative individual, perhaps some of the most important, undoubtedly vary according to the area of creativity, studies of "highs" and "lows" in various fields are beginning to yield some common denominators. The following list concentrates on those differences that are probably more general. In some cases, this assumption of generality stems only from the fact that it seems reasonable on analysis of the characteristics involved vis-à-vis the general demands of the creative process. In others, the generality of the finding is actually supported by research from independent studies in diverse areas.

INTELLECTUAL CHARACTERISTICS

Although measures of general intelligence fail to predict creativity, highs, as a group, typically outscore lows in tests of the following mental abilities:

Conceptual Fluency. The ability to generate a large number of ideas rapidly: List tools beginning with the letter *t;* novel uses for a brick; possible consequences of a situation; categories into which the names of a thousand great men can be sorted—to name just a few of the tasks that have actually been used. (See Barron, pp. 120–21.)

Conceptual Flexibility. The ability to shift gears, to discard one frame of reference for another; the tendency to change approaches spontaneously. (See Rokeach, p. 77, and Ogilvy, p. 206.)

Originality. The ability and/or tendency to give unusual, atypical (therefore more probably new) answers to questions, responses to situations, interpretations of events.

Highs, for instance, are more apt to give rare—as well as more—uses of bricks; they give fewer "popular" interpretations of what an inkblot looks like; in high school, uncommon vs. common career aspirations (e.g., explorer rather than lawyer). (See Barron, p. 121.)

Preference for Complexity. Highs often exhibit a preference for the complex, and to them intriguing, as against the simple and easily understood.

When confronted with complex inkblots, for instance, they tend to seek a more difficult "whole" interpretation that takes the entire blot into account, rather than to identify detailed aspects that clearly resemble certain things. (See Barron, p. 123, and Stein, p. 162.)

The usual interpretation is that highs take complexity as a challenge; that they enjoy the attempt to integrate and resolve it. (See Stein, p. 163.)

PERSONALITY

Several closely related personality characteristics distinguish highs and lows in a number of studies:

Independence of Judgment. Highs are more apt to stick to their guns when they find themselves in disagreement with others.

In a situation where an artificially induced group consensus contradicts the evidence of their own senses, lows more often yield in their expressed judgment. The same is true when the issue at stake is not a factual one but involves voicing an opinion on an aesthetic, social, or political matter. (See Barron, p. 123.)

Deviance. Highs see themselves as more different from their peers and, in fact, they appear to *be* more different in any number of significant as well as trivial characteristics. (See Steiner, p. 257.)

At the extreme, highs sometimes feel lonely and apart, with a sense of mission that isolates them, in their own minds, from average men with average concerns. (See Guetzkow, p. 41, and Rokeach, p. 81.)

Attitudes toward Authority. A related distinction with far-reaching implications for organizations has to do with the way authority is viewed. The difference between highs and lows is a matter of degree, but to make the point we describe the extremes.

Lows are more apt to view authority as final and absolute; to offer unquestioning obedience, allegiance, or belief (as the case may be), with respect approaching deference; to accept present authority as "given" and more or less permanent. Highs are more likely to think of authority as conventional or arbitrary, contingent on continued and demonstrable superiority; to accept dependence on authority as a matter of expedience rather than personal allegiance or moral obligation; to view present authority as temporary. (See Stein, p. 163.)

Attitudes toward subordinates are related in the appropriate direction; those who pay unquestioned allegiance tend to expect it, and vice versa.

Similarly, and in general, highs are more apt to separate source from content in their evaluation of communications; to judge and reach conclusions on the basis of the information itself. Lows are more prone to accept or reject, believe or disbelieve messages on the basis of their attitudes toward the sender. (See Rokeach, p. 71.)

"Impulse Acceptance."   Highs are more willing to entertain and express personal whims and impulses; lows stick closer to "realistic," expected behavior. Highs pay more heed to inner voices, while lows suppress them in favor of external demands. (See Barron, p. 123; Ogilvy, p. 206; and Alexander, p. 237.)

So, for example, highs may introduce humor into situations where it is not called for and bring a better sense of humor to situations where it is. And, in general, highs exhibit a richer and more diverse "fantasy life" on any number of clinical tests. (See Barron, p. 125, and Bruner, p. 210.)

Does the more creative man have more inner impulses or fewer inhibitions, or both, and to what degree? The answer is unknown, but there is at least one intriguing finding that suggests a strange combination of two normally opposing traits:

In the genius and near-genius, a widely used personality test shows "schizoid" tendencies (bi-zarre, unusual, unrealistic thoughts and urges) *coupled* with great "ego strength" (ability to control, channel, and manipulate reality effectively). (See Barron, p. 125, and Alexander, p. 165.) This line of inquiry begins to speak the cliché that the dividing line between madman and genius is a fine one. According to this finding, the line is fine, but firm. (See Alexander, p. 165.)

In sum, highly creative people are more likely than others to view authority as conventional rather than absolute; to make fewer black-and-white distinctions; to have a less dogmatic and more relativistic view of life; to show more independence of judgment and less conventionality and conformity, both intellectual and social; to be more willing to entertain, and sometimes express, their own "irrational" impulses; to place a greater value on humor and in fact to have a better sense of humor; in short to be somewhat freer and less rigidly—but not less effectively—controlled.

APPROACH TO PROBLEMS

The more detailed aspects of the creative process are taken up in the next section, where we see highs at work. We briefly note three distinctions as personal characteristics of creative problem solvers; all are especially significant in the management of creativity and are elaborated upon later.

Motivation.   Highs are more perceptive to, and more motivated by, the interest inherent in the problem and its solution. Accordingly, they get more involved in the task, work harder and longer in the absence of external pressures or incentive, and generally place *relatively* greater value on "job interest" versus such extrinsic rewards as salary or status. (See Barron, p. 126, and Steiner, p. 257.) There is no evidence, however, that the *absolute* importance of external incentives is any less for highs than for lows.

Orientation. Along somewhat the same lines:

Lows are more likely to see their future largely within the boundaries of one organization, to be concerned chiefly with its problems and with their own rise within it, and to develop extensive ties and associations within the community; in short, to be "local" in their loyalties and aspirations. (See Steiner, p. 104, and Merton, p. 101.)

Highs are more apt to think in terms of a larger community, both residential and professional; to view themselves more as members of the profession (whether management, chemistry, or teaching) than as members of Company X; to take their cues from the larger professional community and attempt to rise within it; to be more mobile, hence less "loyal" to any specific organization; in short, to be cosmopolitan in orientation and aspiration. (See Stein, p. 162.)

Hence, the local is more willing to change assignments, even professions (for example, from chemistry or engineering to administration), in the interests of the organization and his own career within it. The cosmopolitan is more likely to change organizations to pursue *his* interests and career within the larger profession. In short, highs change jobs to pursue their interests, not their interests to pursue their jobs. (See Steiner, p. 260.)

Pace. Highs often spend more time in the initial stages of problem formulation, in broad scanning of alternatives. Lows are more apt to "get on with it."

For example, in problems divisible into analytic and synthetic stages, highs spend more time on the former, in absolute as well as relative terms. As a result, they often leave lows behind in the later stages of the solution process, having disposed of more blind alleys and being able to make more comprehensive integrations as a result of more thorough analysis. (See Stein, p. 162.)

One interpretation is that highs have less anxiety to produce, that they are confident enough of their eventual success to be able to step back and take a broad look before making commitments. (See Stein, p. 162, and Steiner, p. 258.)

Can such differences be measured reliably enough to be of use in selection programs?

Many of these qualities can be measured, at least in part, by simple paper-and-pencil tests or other controlled observations. But the instruments are far from perfect and, perhaps more seriously, the correlation between each of these distinguishing characteristics and on-the-job creativity is limited. The characteristics "distinguish" highs from lows only in the sense that highs, on the average, have more of, or more often exhibit, the particular quality. And that is far from saying that all highs have more of each than all lows.[1]

As a result, as with all actuarial predictions of this sort, the procedure becomes more useful as the number of cases to be predicted increases. If many people are to be selected and it is important that some of them will turn out to be highs, a testing program can improve the odds. This would apply, for instance, in the selection of college or graduate students, Air Force Research and Development Officers, or chemists in a major industrial laboratory.

But if few people are being selected and it is important that almost all of them turn out to be highly creative (the chiefs of staff; the top management team; or the scientists to head a project), it is doubtful that, at present, a testing program will improve the odds beyond those of careful personal appraisal and judgment. (See Meehl, p. 25, and Steiner, pp. 129, 256.)

In this connection, there is the interesting suggestion (not documented) that highs may themselves be better judges of creativity in others; that it "takes one to tell one." (See Peterson, p. 93, and Barron, p. 120.)

As the examples suggest, testing to predict

creativity is perhaps least effective where needed most: where the importance of the individual cases is the greatest.

What are the observable characteristics of the creative process; how does it look to an outsider while it is going on?

The appearance of the creative process, especially in its early stages, poses a problem to administrators. Up to a point, it may be hard to distinguish from totally non-productive behavior: undisciplined disorder, aimless rambling, even total inactivity. (See Steiner, p. 258.)

Irregular Progress.   Creativity is rarely a matter of gradual, step-by-step progress; it is more often a pattern of large and largely unpredictable leaps after relatively long periods of no apparent progress. (See Stein, p. 162; Ogilvy, p. 207; and Alexander, p. 238.)

The extreme example is the sudden insight that occurs after a difficult problem is put aside, and at a time of no conscious concern with the matter. Many anecdotes support the film cliché where the great man cries "Eureka!" in the middle of the night or while shaving—or, as in this famous case, while getting on a bus:

> Just at this time I left Caen, where I was then living, to go on a geological excursion under the auspices of the school of mines. The changes of travel made me forget my mathematical work. Having reached Coutances, we entered an omnibus to some place or other. At the moment when I put my foot on the step the idea came to me, without anything in my former thoughts seeming to have paved the way for it, that the transformations I had used to define the Fuchsian functions were identical with those of non-Euclidean geometry. I did not verify the idea; I should not have had time, as, upon taking my seat in the omnibus, I went on with a conversation already commenced, but I felt a perfect certainty. On my return to Caen, for conscience' sake I verified the result at my leisure.—Poincaré

At a level of more immediate concern to most administrators, since few have the problem or the prowess of a Poincaré, the same sort of progress pattern distinguishes creative from merely productive work, and more from less creative activity, in the kind of problem-solving that characterizes the day-to-day activities of the organization. (See Alexander, p. 238, and Steiner, p. 258.)

Suspended Judgment.   The creative process often requires and exhibits suspended judgment. The dangers of early commitment—sometimes to "incorrigible strategies"—are apparent at various levels. In the perceptual laboratory, for example, people who make an early, incorrect interpretation of a picture in an "ambiguitor" (a device that gradually brings a blurred picture into focus), will tend to retain the wrong perception—actually fail to "see"—even when the picture has been fully and clearly exposed. (See Bruner, p. 113.)

Similarly, in the type of small-group problem-solving or decision-making so typical of the modern organization, people will "stick to their guns" to support a position they have taken publicly, beyond its apparent validity and usefulness.

Finally, at the level of the organization itself, financial, technical, or corporate commitments to products, techniques, physical facilities, affiliations, and the like, often stand in the way of change even when it is recognized as necessary and inevitable. (See Peterson, pp. 191, 193; Bruner, p. 196; and Merton, p. 194.)

"Undisciplined" Exploration.   Again, many creators stress the importance of undisciplined thinking, especially in the initial stages, probably because it serves to expand the range of consideration and raw material from which the new solution will emerge.

In this connection, we hear of the use of artificial disorganizers and "boundary expanders," such as alcohol, brain-storming sessions, sometimes even narcotics; and, frequently, the observation that inspiration cannot be willed or worked on, that pressure and preoccupation with the problem are least likely to produce insight—though they may indeed sustain effort in other phases of the process. (See Ogilvy, pp. 203-4, 207, and Barron, p. 166.)

The administrative enigma, then, is to distinguish, before the fact, incubation from laziness; suspended judgment from indecision, "boundary expansion" from simple drinking; undisciplined thinking as a deliberate exploratory step from undisciplined thinking as a permanent characteristic; brain-storming from gibberish by committee. In short, how can one tell the temporarily fallow mind—open and receptive, working subconsciously, and just on the threshold of the brilliant flash—from the permanently idle one? There may, of course, not be an answer. In time, outward predictors and distinguishing characteristics (beyond the individual's past history) may emerge. But for the moment, tolerance for high-risk gambles on creativity is probably one of the prerequisites or costs of playing for the higher stakes creativity provides when it does pay off.

What are the characteristics of the psychological state optimal for creative production?
Motivation. How much should be at stake; how hard should a man be trying, in order to maximize his chances of being creative? There is an apparent paradox:

First, we often hear that the creative process is characterized by a tremendous sense of commitment, a feeling of urgency, even of mission, that results in enormous preoccupation with the problem and perseverance. (See Rokeach, p. 81, and Meehl, p. 27.)

On the other hand, there is evidence that extremely high motivation narrows the focus and produces rigidity, perseveration rather than perseverance, which not only precludes creativity but reduces productivity (freezing up in the clutch). Some go so far as to say that the absence of pressure is a common denominator in situa-

tions conducive to creativity. (See Alexander, p. 238.)

There are two suggested resolutions: One is that the relationship is curvilinear; that creativity first rises, then falls, with motivation—you need enough to maintain effort at high levels but not so much as to produce panic attempts at immediate solution (jumping out of the window instead of looking for the fire escape). And there is, in fact, good evidence of such a relationship in laboratory studies of human and even animal problem-solving.

The other possible resolution involves a distinction in quality of motivation—between "inner" and "outer," "involvement" and "pressure," "drive" and "stress"—related to the earlier observation that highs are more driven by interest and involvement in the task itself than by external incentives. Perhaps external pressure impedes creativity, while inner drive and task-involvement are prerequisites. (See Rokeach, pp. 79, 81.)

In short, it may very well be that "Genius is 90 percent hard work" but that inducing hard work is unlikely to produce genius.

The two resolutions are not mutually exclusive. Motivation of both kinds may have a breaking point, a level where they do more harm than good; although it seems reasonable to suppose that higher levels of "intrinsic" than of "extrinsic" motivation are compatible with creativity.

At any rate, other things being equal, interest in, and commitment to, the problem for its own sake should point to a creative outcome more often than sustained effort purchased by some externally attached reward, simply because the former is more apt to channel energy in the relevant directions.

Open-Mindedness versus Conviction. What intellectual attitude toward one's ideas and suggestions is optimal: how much conviction versus continual reappraisal; self-involvement versus objective detachment? Again, both tendencies appear, and in the extreme.

207

On the one hand, creativity is characterized by a willingness to seek and accept relevant information from any and all sources, to suspend judgment, defer commitment, remain aloof in the face of pressures to take a stand. (See Alexander, p. 239, and Barron, p. 127.) On the other hand, creators in the process of creating are often described as having conviction approaching zeal. (See Shockley, p. 137.)

There may in fact be a sort of simultaneous "antimony" or interaction between "passion and decorum," "commitment and detachment," domination *by* a problem and yet a view of it as objective and external. (See Steiner, p. 257, and Bruner, p. 115.) The process may involve the continual and conflicting presence of both components. (See Peterson, p. 208.) Or it may be a matter of stages. Perhaps the creative process is characterized by open-mindedness in the early, idea-getting phases; then by a bull-headed conviction at the point of dissemination and execution.

There could be at least two reasons. A more open mind, that initially examines more alternatives, is more likely to be convinced of the one it finally selects. An early commitment to a less carefully analyzed approach may be more vulnerable in the face of attack; beliefs developed through more painful and agonizing appraisal are more apt to stand the test of time. (See Bruner, p. 116.)

In addition, creators almost always find themselves on the defensive in the period after the idea has been developed but before it has been "sold." There is an inevitable stepping on toes, effrontery to the status quo and those responsible for it, that usually leads to some rejection of the maverick, especially if the innovation is not immediately, demonstrably superior. And people on the defensive are apt to overstate their case. In short-, open-minded probers may become fervent proselytizers.

As a working summary hypothesis:

In the exploratory, idea-getting stages, there is great interest in the problem; perhaps commit-

ment to its eventual solution but certainly not to any particular approach; an open-minded willingness to pursue leads in any direction; a relaxed and perhaps playful attitude that allows a disorganized, undisciplined approach, to the point of putting the problem aside entirely. But at the point of development and execution, where the selected alternative is pursued, tested, and applied, there is great conviction, dogged perseverance, perhaps strong personal involvement, and dogmatic support of the new way.

II. THE ORGANIZATION ITSELF

What does all this have to do with organization? What are the characteristics of the creative organization; and what are the implications of individual creativity, if any?

There are various ways to approach this question.

One is to reason, deductively, *from* the characteristics of creators and the creative process *to* the kind of environment that ought to be congenial to them and conducive to creative activity. What does the nature of individual creativity imply about the environmental factors that foster or impede it? For the most part, this is the way we proceed in what follows.

Another approach is to treat the organization, as a whole, as the creative unit. Perhaps some of the characteristics that distinguish "high" and "low" individuals also apply to high and low organizations as such.

The characteristics of creative individuals suggest a number of rather direct translations or counterparts at the organizational level; and many of the characteristics independently attributed to creative organizations seem to match items in our description of individual highs.

A brief summary follows. Although this analogizing has serious limitations and may be misleading, the table does serve as an organized index to some of the major characteristics

Gary Steiner

The Creative Individual	The Creative Organization

Conceptual fluency . . . is able to produce a large number of ideas quickly	Has idea men
	Open channels of communication
	Ad hoc devices:
	    Suggestion systems
	    Brain-storming
	    Idea units absolved of other responsibilities
	Encourages contact with outside sources (see

Originality . . . generates unusual ideas	Heterogenous personnel policy Includes marginal, unusual types Assigns non-specialists to problems Allows eccentricity

Separates source from content in evaluating information . . . is motivated by interest in problem . . . follows wherever it leads	Has an objective, fact-founded approach
	Ideas evaluated on their merits, not status of originator
	Ad hoc approaches:
	    Anonymous communications
	    Blind votes
	Selects and promotes on merit only

Suspends judgment . . . avoids early commitment . . . spends more time in analysis, exploration	Lack of financial, material commitment to products, policies Invests in basic research; flexible, long-range planning Experiments with new ideas rather than prejudging on "rational" grounds; everything gets a chance
Less authoritarian . . . has relativistic view of life	More decentralized; diversified Administrative slack; time and resources to absorb errors Risk-taking ethos . . . tolerates and expects taking chances
Accepts own impulses . . . playful, undisciplined exploration	Not run as "tight ship" Employees have fun Allows freedom to choose and pursue problems Freedom to discuss ideas
Independence of judgment, less conformity Deviant, sees self as different	Organizationally autonomous Original and different objectives, not trying to be another "X"

(continued)

209

The Creative Individual

Rich, "bizarre" fantasy life *and* superior reality orientation; controls

The Creative Organization

Security of routine . . . *allows* innovation
"philistines" provide stable, secure environment that allows "creators" to roam
Has separate units or occasions for generating vs. evaluating ideas . . . separates creative from productive functions

attributed to creative organizations; and it is interesting that so many of them sound like the distinguishing characteristics of individual highs.

Finally, there is direct, empirical study of actual creative organizations. This may well turn out to be the most fruitful approach, but it was not the major focus of the seminar. In part, this reflects the state of knowledge; systematic studies of creative organizations, as such, simply do not exist as yet. In part, the composition of the symposium is responsible. A meeting with six psychologists and one psychoanalyst, against three sociologists, inevitably speaks mostly in psychological terms.

At any rate, we make no attempt to represent, let alone do justice to, the sociological investigation and analysis of organizational factors that relate to creativity. In what follows, we reason and abstract mostly from the nature of individual creativity, partly from rather informal observations of actual organizations.

What, specifically, can management do—beyond selecting creative participants—to foster creativity within and on the part of the organization?

Values and Rewards.   What explicit and implicit goals and values characterize the creative organization? What system of rewards and incentives maximizes creativity?

First the creative organization in fact prizes and rewards creativity. A management philosophy that stresses creativity as an organizational goal, that encourages and expects it at all levels, will increase the chances of its occurrence. (See Guetzkow, pp. 43–44.)

But it is one thing to call for creativity, another to mean it, and still another to reward it adequately and consistently when it occurs. More specifically, creativity as a value should find expression in the following:

Compensation.   In most areas of day-to-day functioning, productivity rather than creativity is and should be the principal objective; thus, general reward policies tend to measure and stress regular output. But even where creativity is truly desired and encouraged in good faith, activities that are potentially more creative may be subordinated to those more visibly and closely tied to reward policies. (A familiar academic illustration is the "pressure to publish," which may lead to a plethora of relatively insignificant formula-projects that minimize chances of failure, i.e., nonpublication, but also of creativity.) (See Berelson, p. 103.)

In the business enterprise, a similar grievance centers on discrepancies in reward between the sowing and reaping aspects of the operation; with the greater rewards for work that shows immediate, measurable results (e.g., sales) as against that which may pay off in the longer run (such as basic research).

It may be inevitable that work closer to the balance sheet will be more swiftly and fully compensated than efforts that have tenuous, uncertain, and in any case long-range effects on corporate profits. But creativity and guaranteed, immediate results do not go together; not between, nor within, assignments. If creativity is to be fostered, not impeded, by material incentives, they will have to be applied by a different yardstick. (See Stein, pp. 94–95; Shockley, pp. 96–97; Alexander, pp. 98–99; and Ogilvy, p. 212.)

It is probably this simple: Where creativity and not productivity is in fact the goal, then creativity and not productivity should in fact be measured and rewarded. And if creativity is harder to measure and takes longer periods to assess, then this probably requires some speculative investment on the part of the firm that wants to keep and nurture the few men and the few activities that will eventually be worth it.[2]

Channels for Advancement. Where concern is with creativity in a professional unit or other specialized function operating within the larger organization, there is this related implication: To the extent possible, there should be formal channels for advancement and status within the area of creativity. (See Shockley, p. 97.)

Where it is impossible to promote a creative chemist without taking him out of chemistry, he faces a choice between money and position on the one hand, and chemistry on the other. The company is likely to lose his services as chemist in either case: to administration within its own walls or to another organization where a chemist as such can get ahead. (This is one of the chief organizational advantages and attractions of the major university for the research scientist or scholar: parallel channels for advancement, of at least equal status, exist outside of administration.) (See Alexander, p. 99.)

To some extent this is a matter of size; it is hard to provide for advancement within a department of one or two persons. But size alone is not enough. The nature and number of status levels established, their labels, and especially their actual value within the firm and the larger community, will determine their worth to individuals who hold them. (See Shockley, p. 101.)

"Freedom." Within rather broad limits, creativity is increased by giving creators freedom in choice of problem and method of pursuit. In line with the high's greater interest and involvement in his work, greater freedom is necessary, to maximize those satisfactions that are important to him and that channel his efforts into avenues most likely to prove creative. (See Alexander, p. 239.) Whether and where there is an upper limit is a point of much contention and no evidence. (See Steiner, p. 260.)

But such freedom often puts the appropriate objectives of the organization at odds with the demands of maximum creativity. The symposium itself produced two striking examples.

In one instance, a participant "distracted" himself and the group by working out and presenting an elegant solution to a mathematical problem that had been mentioned only in passing, as a task assigned to subjects in a creativity experiment. From the point of view of the seminar, he was out of bounds. By following his own interests, he was creative. (Would he have arrived at an equally elegant *psychological* insight had he been constrained to the issue as externally defined?) (See Shockley, pp. 88–89, and Steiner, p. 260.)

More dramatically, after the first few hours of the meeting had been spent in rather academic and abstract discussion, one participant reminded us that the purpose of the meeting was to develop useful and understandable guidelines for management and that we had better get on with it. This precipitated a short but heartfelt donnybrook between the advocates of "No nonsense! Keep your eye on the target," and "Take it easy; it's interesting; let's see where it leads"; between "What good is it if you can't tell us what it means for management?" and "Our job is to create, yours to apply."

Both approaches are valid but as means to

different ends. Those responsible for a meeting are rightfully concerned with maximizing its output. By the same token, creative individuals who attend it are not so concerned with the product of the particular conference as with the pursuit of interesting lines of inquiry, whether or not they happen to reach fruition during the session. And curtailing and channeling discussion into areas known to be productive obviously limits the chances of coming up with something outside the range of the ordinary.

This, then, is probably one of the principal costs in the nurture of creativity: Except in the rare and fortunate case where a creative individual's interests exactly match the day-to-day operating objectives of his organization, and continue to do so over time, the organization pays a price, at least in the short run, for giving him his head. What he returns to the organization may or may not compensate it many-fold.

Communication.   Many observations point to the importance of free and open channels of communication, both vertical and horizontal. (See Guetzkow, p. 40, and Bower, pp. 169–70.)

On the one hand, potential creators need and seek relevant information whatever its source, within or without the organization; on the other hand, they are stimulated by diverse and complex input.

Equally important, ideas wither for lack of a grapevine. A possible approach, a feasible but half-baked notion, or even a well worked-out solution must be communicated to those with the power to evaluate, authorize, and implement. (See Guetzkow, p. 40, and Bower, p. 177.)

The presence of formal channels is not enough. People must feel free to use them, and channels must not be clogged by routine paper-flow that ties up time with "programmed trivia," and creates an air of apathy and neglect toward incoming messages because it is so unlikely that they will contain anything of value. (See Guetzkow, p. 41.)

Since highs tend toward cosmopolitan, professional orientation, the organization must at least provide for and perhaps encourage contact and communication with colleagues and associations on the outside. (See Merton, p. 101, and Shockley, pp. 138–39.)

As a special case, there is the matter of scientific and professional publication in the appropriate journals, which is often of great personal importance to creators.

There may be problems of security and the natural jealousy of corporate secrets and employee loyalties. But in many cases, these are unrealistic or exaggerated, given the high rate of horizontal mobility, the discretion of the professional, and the fact that most "secrets" are not. At any rate, there may be no reason to think that the balance of payments will be "out"; there should be at least as much information gained as given away in most external contacts. And in many cases, and within broad limits, the net gain in satisfaction, creativity, and perhaps tenure of highs will probably offset the time and trade secrets lost to the outside.

What, specifically, are the costs of creativity? What must an organization be prepared to give up or tolerate if it wants to increase its creativity?

Answers were scattered throughout the preceding, but it may help to pull them together.

First, creativity, by definition, is a high-risk enterprise, not for society or industry, at large, but for any given unit that attempts it. The greater the departure from present practice, the less likelihood that the innovation will work; the greater the potential payoff, the less the odds of its occurring. Conversely, the larger the number of workers or units independently pursuing any problem, the better the chances that one or more of them will succeed. (See Merton, pp. 59–62.)

In the abstract, then, decisions as to whether and where to attempt creativity, and how much to try for, are much like decisions concerning what to insure, and for how much—although the hopes and fears are reversed. (See Peterson, p. 198.)

Second, within the unit under consideration, fostering creativity assesses costs in assured productivity. To the extent that energy is consumed in investigation and exploration, it does not go into work known to be productive. (See Bensinger, p. 153, and Bower, p. 182.)

Finally, depending on the personal tastes and preferences of management, there may or may not be costs in "security," "comfort," and "congeniality" of the environment: (*a*) Highs are not as deferent, obedient, flattering, easy to control, flexible to *external* demands and changes, conventional, predictable, and so on, through a long list of disiderata in "good" employees. (*b*) In addition, highs are more mobile, less "loyal"—harder to hold by ordinary extrinsic rewards—but easier to acquire by the offer of interesting opportunities. At any rate, they make for a less stable and secure, more challenging but perhaps more disturbing environment. (*c*) A creative organization itself is more committed to change; operates on a faster track; has a less certain or predictable future than the efficient, me-too operation. (See Steiner, p. 259.)

In short, maximizing creativity is not the principal objective of any organization at all times, or even of all organizations at some times. When it is, there are some rough guidelines to how it may be fostered—but not, it is suggested, at no cost.

Consider the organization as a whole, operating within a larger social and economic environment. What type of situation is most likely to produce a creative organization?

The seminar produced little agreement, let alone evidence, on this matter. There was some discussion about the effects of competitive position, size, age, and general success of an organization as they affect its need and chances for creativity. (See Steiner, p. 262.) But nothing approaching a conclusion is visible.

One of the more interesting recurrent debates centered on the relative merits of firmly led, "one-man" organizations versus decentralized corporate entities; on charismatic, inspired leadership by a "great man" versus the greater democracy of the professionally managed organization. (See Hauser, p. 195.) This debate was not resolved, but it does call attention to some distinctions that may be important.

Some Final Distinctions. Last, we take note of some distinctions that may be helpful, suggested simply by the experience of trying to discuss "the creative organization." For instance, the preceding debate may reflect a failure to distinguish between a creative organization and one that produces for a creator.

An organization can be an efficient instrument for the execution of externally created ideas and yet not be in itself creative: for instance, a smooth military unit under a great strategist, a top-notch symphony orchestra, or, in the same terms, a business that hums to the tune of a creative president. These may all implement creativity and yield a product appropriately called creative, but they are not, *ipso facto*, creative organizations. And the characteristics that make for creativity within and on the part of an organization as a whole may in fact be quite different from those that make it the efficient tool of a creative master. (See Alexander, pp. 179, 242.)

Along the same lines, it may be helpful to distinguish between getting people to be more creative and getting creative people to be more productive. The conditions that induce a Frank Lloyd Wright, an Ogilvy, or a Shockley to turn out more of the same—to repeat or elaborate earlier innovations—may be quite different from those that produce the original and subsequent departures.

In short, organizations, like people, may increase their net yield of creative *products* either by the terms that go into their conception or those that enter into their output. And while the net effects may often be the same, the means are probably not.

For the eventual understanding of "the creative organization," it may be important to learn the difference between creating productivity and producing creativity.

NOTES

1. In general, validity coefficients for specific tests at best attain values around .60, which means that they predict about 36 per cent of the variation in observed creativity. (See Barron, p. 125.)
2. High potential pay-off and low risk are, unfortunately, incompatible—just as they are in the stock market and at the gambling tables.

Managing Creative Professionals

Albert Shapero

More than 30 years of research have provided answers to some of the questions technical managers ask about creativity in organizations.

The management of creative workers has become the most critical area faced by management in both the private and public sectors. Without a great deal of fanfare, creative workers, or, more strictly, professionals, have come center stage in the United States and the rest of the developed world. Quantitatively, professionals now surpass all other categories in the U.S. work force. Qualitatively, professionals have a disproportionate effect on all aspects of our society, as the researchers, designers, decision makers and managers who define and direct much of what is done in society. The quality and extent of what is accomplished in the foreseeable future has become a function of the ability of management to harness and channel the efforts of creative workers. The difference in success between one effort and another, one organization and another increasingly depends on whether management understands the differences between the management of professionals and the management relevant to the assembly line.

In trying to evoke and develop creativity in an organization, managers are interested in such questions as: Can creative people be identified for the purpose of hiring? Are there valid and reliable tests that can predict who will be creative? Can creativity be developed or enhanced in employees? Are there creativity techniques that can be taught to employees that will increase creativity within the organization? What kinds of management actions help or retard creativity? What kinds of environments enhance or deter creativity? What differentiates the creative organization from those that aren't creative? Researchers on creativity have generated data that provide some answers to these questions.

From the beginning, much research on creativity has focussed on developing ways of predicting who will demonstrate high creativity in the future. One approach, based on biographical and autobiographical studies of individuals with demonstrated high creativity, attempts to develop predictive profiles. Included among the profile methods is factor analysis. Other attempts have produced psychometric instruments to measure intellectual capabilities considered by the researcher as central to creativity. Most of the latter have measured divergent thinking. Despite several decades of research effort on creativity and highly creative individuals, there is as yet no profile or test that reliably predicts who will be highly creative in the future. Efforts to develop tests to predict later creativity in students have borne little result. Longitudinal studies of the predictive strength of divergent-thinking tests given to students have been disappointing (Howieson, 1981; Kogan, 1974). So far, the only good indication that an individual will be highly creative in the future has been demonstrated high creativity in the past.

THE ENVIRONMENT FOR CREATIVITY

Two aspects of the environment for creativity have been examined by researchers: (1) the kinds of familial and educational environments in childhood that lead to creativity in adulthood, and (2) the kinds of immediate, organizational, and physical environments associated with high creativity. The effect of childhood environments in subsequent creativity is of little utility for managers, although one finding worth noting is that high creatives, unlike those with high IQs, came from families in which parents put little stress on grades (Getzels & Jackson, 1962).

The manager of professionals is concerned with organizational environments associated with high creativity and how they might be generated. Most of the organizational characteristics that appear to enhance creativity relate to the characteristics attributed to highly creative individuals (Steiner, 1965). For example, since nonconformity in both thought and action characterizes high creatives, the organization that is tolerant of a large variety of deviance from the norm is more likely to enhance creativity. It is not surprising to find many "high tech" companies, architectural firms, advertising organizations, and academic faculties are marked by unconventional dress and little rigidity concerning hours of work.

Characteristics of creative organizations (Steiner, 1965) include the following:

- Open channels of communications are maintained.
- Contacts with outside sources are encouraged.
- Nonspecialists are assigned to problems.
- Ideas are evaluated on their merits rather than on the status of their originator.
- Management encourages experiments with new ideas rather than making "rational" prejudgments.
- Decentralization is practiced.
- Much autonomy is allowed professional employees.
- Management is tolerant of risk-taking.
- The organization is not run tightly or rigidly.
- Participative decision making is encouraged.
- Employees have fun.

THE PROCESS OF CREATING

In spite of the apparent uniqueness of the creative process in each individual and the idiosyncratic patterns followed by many creative individuals, studies of the process are in fair agreement that it follows a recognizable overall pattern. The creative process has been variously described, but most descriptions include a series of steps, varying in number, that can be subsumed within the following four steps: (1) preparation, (2) incubation, (3) illumination, and (4) verification.

Preparation. The creative process begins with a problem perceived or experienced. Whenever humans have a problem, and don't know how to solve it by direct action, they resort to thinking, problem-solving, and creativity. The problems that lead to creative responses arise from many sources. They can be thrust upon one or assigned from the outside, be perceived as a threat or opportunity, be encountered, or be sought out because humans are dreaming, restless creatures who enjoy the creative process. Once a problem is perceived, the creative process begins.

Research shows that the conscious "creative" moment comes only after intensive preparation and a period of subconscious incubation. Louis Pasteur put it succinctly: "Chance only favors the prepared mind." Helmholz described his own creative process: "It was always necessary, first of all, that I should have turned my problem over on all sides to such an extent that I had all its angles and complexities "in my head" and could run through them freely without writing" (McKellar, 1957). In a study of highly productive inventors, Rossman (1964) found that they all started the process by "soaking themselves in the problem." Though Rossman reports that some inventors reviewed all previous efforts to solve the problem and others avoided being influenced by previous attempts, all spent time thoroughly exploring the problem to be solved.

The preparation process can include literature searches, talking to many people about aspects of the problem, experimentation, and doodling. Sometimes the preparation process can appear as unplanned, unfocused meandering through a variety of materials. McKellar (1957) considers it as almost a form of "overlearning" to the point where some of the materials become "automatic" in one's consciousness. The gathering of information is a critical part of the process in which the individual examines the materials critically, but not negatively. The creative process requires discriminating criticism that does not reject, but builds upon the materials examined.

Incubation. This is a process that goes on below the level of consciousness. It cannot be commanded. Incubation appears to be a gestation period in which the process goes on subconsciously, and it works best when the individual is inactive with regard to the problem or working on something else. A passage of time, vital to the process, varies with the problem and individual (McKellar, 1957). The philosopher Nietsche spoke of a period of 18 months, and the poetess Amy Lowell spoke of six months. It can be a period of frustration for the individual working against a deadline, for it cannot be pushed or rushed. It is a period when apparently nothing is happening.

One soaks oneself in the problem and then waits. The passage of time is often accomplished by sleep. It is as if sleep provides the time and the opportunity to abandon consciousness of the problem and let the unconscious work. Some great creative discoveries have surfaced in sleep. Kekulé realized his discovery of the benzene ring as the result of a dream of the image of a snake that seized hold of its own tail. Many of Descartes' basic notions of analytical geometry formed in his dreams. Everyone has had the experience of "fighting" a problem to an impasse, and having the solution suddenly crystallize while visiting with friends or discussing other things. The need for a period of incubation may explain why professionals who work on more than one project at a time are more productive than others. Having more than one project permits a person to switch to another project when apparently at an impasse. Switching from one project to another permits the first project to incubate until it is ready, while one is still doing something productive.

The incubation process is recognized but not understood. One plausible explanation is that it is a period in which the mind tests different associations, matches different frames of reference and different conceptual elements to see if they make sense. This explanation fits with the most accepted view of creativity as a process of association.

Probably the most widely held psychological conception is that creativity is the ability to call up and make new and useful combinations out of divergent bits of stored information (Guilford, 1964). The more creative the individual the greater ability to synthesize remote bits of information. The likelihood of a solution being creative is a function of the number and uncommonness of associative elements an individual brings together (Mednick, 1962). The latter notion has been incorporated into a test for creative ability, The Remote Associations test (Mednick & Mednick, 1964). The test taker is asked to "make sense" out of each of 30 sets of three, not obviously related, terms by providing a fourth term related to them (e.g., the fourth term related to "cookies," "sixteen," and "heart" would be "sweet"). Another associationist view is Koestler's "bisociation of Matrices," expressed by the metaphor of creativity as a "dumping together on the floor the contents of different drawers in one's mind" (Koestler, 1964).

Illumination. The Gestalt psychologists refer to illumination as the "aha!" phenomenon. It is that sudden insight, that flash of understanding, in which the solution appears. The mathematician Polya describes it as entering an unfamiliar room in the dark, and stumbling around, falling over pieces of furniture, looking for the light switch. When the switch is found and activated, everything falls into place. All historic examples of the incubation process end with that moment of illumination.

Verification. After the exhilaration of illumination comes the tedious, time-consuming stage of verification. The creative idea must pass the tests of validity, reality, utility, realizability, costs, time, and acceptance in the marketplace.

CREATIVE PROBLEM SOLVING

Rules for creative problem solving can be derived from the data available on the process. They include the following:

1. Soak yourself in the problem. Read, review, examine and analyze any material that you can find on the problem. Talk to people who know about the problem. Look at every side of the problem. Saturate yourself in the subject. Be critical in the positive sense. Don't accept authority. Question the premises. However, insist on finding a way to solve the problem, and do not accept that it cannot be solved.

As a manager, do not easily accept the conclusion that "it can't be done." On hearing all the reasons from his group why something wouldn't work, one successful manager of professionals counters, "I agree it can't be done, but

if we had to do it or be shot what could we do?" It always changes the atmosphere, and turns the group to finding ways to attack the problem rather than judge it. Push the people in your organization to soak themselves in the problem. Provide them with all the information you can. Err on the side of overload. Encourage them to contact a wide variety of sources for information.

2. Play with the problem. Stay loose and flexible in dealing with the problem. Try different assumptions. Leave out one of the conditions that affects the problem, and see what that suggests. Approach the problem from different directions. Turn it over and inside out. Assume different environments. Shift parts of the problem around, physically and spatially. Change the time sequence. Change the order of events. Change the situation.

As a manager, you can help by encouraging your people to explore the problem from every kind of viewpoint. You can do this by discussion, by questioning, by encouraging "wild" approaches in the early stages of a project.

3. Suspend judgment. Fight any tendency to draw early conclusions. You will only lock yourself in, and lose several degrees of freedom. Early fixation on even part of a problem definition keeps you from seeing larger parts of the problem. It foreshortens your perception. Even worse is to get an early fix on part or all of a solution. It cuts you off from a great many possibilities, since you begin to justify your early solution. Suspension of judgment keeps you open to new information, and enables you to see new possibilities as the problem unfolds. If solutions keep suggesting themselves to you, write them down in a notebook, and deliberately put them aside until later in the project. Get them out of your mind.

As a manager, help your people suspend judgment. The manager is probably the biggest obstacle to suspensions of judgment. The manager represents deadlines and budgets, and they must not be forgotten. However, it is important

218

not to push for immediate judgments. Don't pressure your people to come up with solutions in the early stages of a project. Encourage them to note and file any early conclusions as suggested above.

4. Come up with at least two solutions. When you start out with the objective of coming up with two different solutions, it keeps you from fixating on a solution and keeps you thinking about the problem. Studies have shown second solutions tend to be more creative, and trying for two solutions results in more creative solutions. It was found, experimentally, that asking people for two solutions, as compared to one, increased the number of "creative" solutions from 16 percent to 52 percent. When pushed to the limit by being asked for three different solutions, it was found not all responded, but there was an increase by 25 percent in very good, creative solutions (Hyman and Anderson, 1965).

As a manager, insist on two independent solutions to a problem. It is not necessary to work them out in detail, but make sure they are significantly different. The first solution seems to catch all the anxieties and stiffness of an individual, while the second is more free flowing.

5. When stuck. Try more than one way of picturing the problem and solution. Go from a word description to a drawing. Many creative scientists, mathematicians and writers use sketches and diagrams to put the problem into a different perspective. Go from a drawing to abstraction.

Try your problem out on other people. When you discuss your problem with others, you see it differently. You have to make sense out of it.

What the other people say is less important than your own presentation, though unexpected questions can help hook different parts of your brain together.

Give your subconscious a chance to work. Take a break. When you are really up against it, do something else for a while. Remember! It is a ripening process, and you can't force it. Spending round-the-clock sessions will only exhaust you, rather than solve the problem.

As a manager, put yourself in the way of being the person on whom the problem can be tried. Ask your people to "draw you a picture" of the problem to help you understand it. When they get too intense and are not making progress, give them another short assignment to pull them away for awhile, to let their subconscious work.

CREATIVITY FROM THE VIEWPOINT OF THE MANAGER

Can anything systematic be done to increase creativity in individuals and in an organization? Does management really want creativity and the somewhat less controlled conditions necessary to foster it?

To individuals, more creativity carries an implication of special, personally gratifying experiences. To managers, more creativity means new ideas, inventions, and solutions that will do wonderful things for the organization in the marketplace. Few, however, have thought through the consequences of having more creative people and of allowing the conditions that enhance creative behavior in their organizations.

Trying to answer the converse of the question, "Can anything be done to increase creativity?" quickly illustrates how much is generally known about conditions for creativity. Pose the question "Can anything be done to kill creativity in an individual or an organization?" and the mind immediately fills with answers:

- Discourage and penalize risk-taking.
- Discourage and ridicule new ideas.
- Reject and discourage attempts to try unusual methods.
- Make sure all communications follow formal organizational lines and all employees cover themselves.

- Discourage reading and communications with people outside the immediate organization.
- Discourage nonconformity of any kind.
- Discourage joking and humor.
- Provide no recognition.
- Provide no resources.

We easily intuit what it takes to minimize creative behavior, which suggests that it must be possible to improve creativity or, at least, to minimize barriers to creativity. The available information strongly indicates that it is possible to improve one's own creativity and the creativity of employees. It is possible to increase the creative activities and products of an organization. Increasing creativity in an organization is achievable, but it takes a lot more effort than preventing it from occurring. Continuity and stability are important attributes in society, and, of necessity, the dice are loaded against divergence and change.

Highly creative people are attracted by the work, by the problem being worked on, which is good from an organizational viewpoint, but they don't respond in satisfactory ways to the political or organizational constraints that are involved in every problem. Creative people are nonconformists. They are jokers. They have little reverence for authority or procedures. They are short on apparent "loyalty" to the organizations they work for. They don't respond to the kinds of incentives that stir others. They are not moved by status. High creatives don't seem to care about what others think, and they don't easily become part of a general consensus. (Could a preference for consensus management be why the Japanese have recently expressed concern about a lack of creativity in Japan?) In short, creative people can make most managers very uncomfortable. (Teachers and even parents are far more comfortable with students and children with high IQs than with those who are highly creative.)

A case can be always made for creativity, but managers should carefully and honestly think about whether they truly need more creativity and can live with it. If successful at hiring and retaining high creatives, and at generating the conditions needed to keep them creative, management may be creating conditions that make it difficult for its own natural style of doing things. New methods, processes and products can be purchased, copied, and stolen. According to one ironic maxim, it doesn't pay to be first—pioneers get killed. Some years ago, the head of a metal machining company producing thousands of metal fasteners picked through his catalog and fondly indicated product after product that had been invented by other companies. "You know," he said, "we don't know anything about managing creative people, but we're very, very good at designing around other people's designs. What we're really competent at is production and marketing, and we beat the hell out of the creative companies. I can't wait for their next products." Cynical? Perhaps, but it highlights the questions raised here. Many can benefit from the creativity of a few, and there are industries, companies, and fields where creativity is far less needed than in others.

ON THE ROAD TO MORE CREATIVITY

If desired, creativity can be consciously and systematically enhanced in an organization through hiring, motivation, organization, and management actions.

Hiring. The number of highly creative people in an organization can be increased by a hiring policy that deliberately attempts to identify, locate, and hire them. The only valid and reliable way to identify individuals with a high probability of future creative performance is through evidence of past creative performance. The more recent and continuous the past creative performance, the more likely there will be future creative performance.

Where examples of a professional's work are

not as easily demonstrated as in the arts and architecture, the task of determining past creative performance is harder. It is difficult to tease out evidence of the individual creative contributions of an engineer or scientist who has worked on a project that employed scores or hundreds of professionals. One way to tackle the problem is to put the questions directly to the individual: "What are the most creative things you have done on the job in the past three years? What are the most creative things you have ever done?" Similar questions about the individual's work can be asked of others who are familiar with it. In some fields patents, in others publications, may serve the purpose, though they should be examined for their content.

Tests, profiles of traits, and checklists are neither valid nor reliable. No available test can determine who will perform creatively in the future with any reliability. (One may be tempted to follow the example of the author who tried to hire on the basis of the apparent relationship between a good sense of humor and creativity. The rationale was, "If they don't turn out to be creative, at least they'll be a barrel of laughs.")

Motivation. Creative behavior can be maintained and enhanced through incentives that reward creative output and encourage risk-taking, and the use of new methods, processes, and materials. For those who are already highly creative, incentives can maintain and encourage their creative efforts and help retain them in the organization. For other professionals, incentives and positive feedback from management can encourage them to overcome some of the natural blocks to creativity and to take more risks and be more curious. As with any other desired behavior, feedback from management, the performance evaluation system, and the example of management can help stimulate creativity. If a manager smiles on "far out" ideas when they are ventured, lets them be tried (even when he or she is personally sure they won't work), and will even express some extravagant ideas himself, others may feel freer to think and act creatively.

Providing the necessaries. The availability of resources for initial creative efforts is a powerful indicator of management support for creative activities. The resources required to give an idea a preliminary investigation are seldom of any magnitude. Direct provision of resources, or turning a blind and benevolent eye on the inevitable "bootlegging" of an unauthorized project, both serve the purpose of support for creative experimentation. Providing resources for preliminary explorations of ideas without requiring exhaustive justification is a form of intellectual overhead and should be treated as such, formally or informally. (Remember that time is one of the most important resources required for creative activities.)

Some boost to creativity can be obtained through educational programs, though management should be wary of "patented" techniques. All creativity-enhancing techniques have some limited value in terms of stirring up new ideas for a short time. An inherent limitation in almost all of the techniques is that they purport to provide *the* way to the generation of creative ideas or to problem solving. The overall process follows a broad general pattern, but individuals must find their own personal approach.

Managing. Managers should assign tough deadlines but stay out of the operating details of a project. There is no conflict between a deadline and creativity. Creative people resist closure because they see new possibilities as the project unfolds. For all the complaints, deadlines are necessary. Without deadlines few creative projects would ever finish.

Both productivity and creativity can be enhanced by assigning more than one project to a professional. Not all the projects have to be of equal weight, or size, or value. The ability to switch to a second project and let the first project incubate in the subconscious is important to creativity. With only one project and a tough deadline, there is a tendency to try to force the project at times when it can't be forced. Having other projects provides a legitimate (forgivable) and productive way to back off from a stymied project when a pause is needed.

New projects need fresh, unchanneled thinking. Managers might make up project groups to include people of different backgrounds, and refrain from always assigning projects to the individuals who have done that kind of work before and are apparently most suited to it.

Each professional's assignments should provide diversity for that individual. And highly productive groups of five or more years duration should be made more diverse through the addition of new people and by making certain that the individuals in the group get occasional assignments to work with other groups.

Organizations. Organizational mechanisms to assure that new ideas don't get turned down for the wrong reasons (such as middle-management cautiousness) are important. One company set up a new products committee to which any employee, and not just professionals, could submit ideas. The committee, made up of senior scientists, product development people, and a patent lawyer, investigated and discussed each idea and wrote up a decision stating why the idea was accepted, rejected, or recommended for more research. By taking a positive and encouraging stance the company developed a strong flow of ideas from throughout the organization.

There should be a legitimate (nonthreatening) means for taking an idea up the management line if it is rejected by first-line management. The means may be a new product committee, of the type described above, or a procedure for periodic review of ideas people feel strongly about. After many attempts to correlate creativity with personal characteristics, General Electric found that a key variable was the ability not to be dissuaded from their intuitions. The former director of technical systems and materials Jerome Suran believes that high creatives are stubborn types, "because you don't get past the first level of management in a big company unless you feel strongly about your ideas" (Cullem, 1981).

A periodic review of organizational procedures and forms, with a view to identifying and removing those that cannot pass a test of necessity, is often a good idea. Too many required administrative procedures and forms sop up time and energy and impede creative activity. Procedures and forms are pervasive forces for conformity, and the more there are, the less space and time is left for nonconforming, creative thought and effort. Professional organizations should follow the rule that for every procedure or form that is added, at least one should be removed.

REFERENCES

Cullem, T., "Stimulating Creativity," *Electronic Engineering Times,* July 20, 1981.

Getzels, J. W. and P. W. Jackson, *Creativity and Intelligence,* New York, John Wiley and Sons, 1962.

Guilford, J. P., *The Nature of Human Intelligence,* New York, McGraw-Hill, 1964.

Howieson, N., "A Longitudinal Study of Creativity: 1965–1975," *Journal of Creative Behavior,* April–June, 1981.

Hyman, R. and B. Anderson, "Solving Problems," *International Science and Technology,* September 1965.

Koestler, A., *The Act of Creation,* New York, Macmillan, 1964.

Kogan, N. and E. Pankove, "Long Term Predictive Validity of Divergent Thinking Tests. Some negative evidence," *Journal of Educational Psychology,* 66 (6), 1974.

McKellar, P., *Imagination and Thinking,* New York, Basic Books, 1957.

Mednick, S. A., "The Associative Basis of the Creative Process," *Psychology Review,* 69 (3), 1962.

Mednick, S. A. and M. T. Mednick, Remote Associates Test, Boston, Houghton Mifflin, 1964.

Rossman, J., *Industrial Creativity,* New Hyde Park N.Y., University Books, 1964.

Steiner, G. A., *The Creative Organization,* Chicago, University of Chicago Press, 1965.

Autonomy in the Industrial R&D Lab

Lotte Bailyn

Abstract. This article distinguishes between "strategic autonomy" (the freedom to set one's own research agenda) and "operational autonomy" (the freedom, once a problem has been set, to attack it by means determined by oneself, within given resource constraints). The article argues, and presents some preliminary corroborating data, that technical careers in the R&D lab should start lower on strategic than on operational autonomy, that operational autonomy should show initial fairly rapid increase, which should be followed by increases in strategic autonomy, and that thereafter a number of different career paths should be available for technical employees. Most labs, however, seem to espouse a philosophy of strategic autonomy combined with operational controls, which creates dilemmas and contradictions in the technical career, particularly at its start. It is proposed that these two aspects of autonomy can usefully be thought of as a two-dimensional grid. Different positions on this grid seem to fit with different orientations and different tasks, and require different strategies for career management. The article ends with a discussion of these managerial implications.

It has long been assumed that the problem of "professionals" in industrial organizations resides in the conflict between autonomy and organizational goals. It is the thesis of this article, based on intensive studies of employees in a few central R&D labs in the United States and Britain,[1] that this assumption is oversimplified and hides the real issues facing technical employees in industrial R&D. Proper understanding, it is proposed, requires a more differentiated view of the meaning of autonomy, as well as a better ap-

preciation of the orientations of people who populate the professional ranks of the R&D lab.

Symptomatic of the confusion is the issue of nomenclature. What should one call the technical staff employees in such a lab? Some are scientists, others are engineers; some have doctorates, others have various degrees of lesser "professional" standing. The differences between these groups have been well documented (Allen, 1977; Kerr *et al.*, 1977; Bailyn, 1980). The most frequently used term is "professional," but the characterization in some labs of a technical staff, rather than a professional staff, is really more accurate. For these technical employees are not professional in the classic sense: they are not

From *Human Resource Management,* Summer 1985, Vol. 24, No. 2, 129–146, copyright © 1985 John Wiley & Sons, Inc. Reprinted by permission of John Wiley & Sons, Inc.

223

"free"; they have no easily identifiable clients for whom they perform their services; and they are subject to organizational controls of various kinds (Scott, 1965; Child and Fulk, 1982).

One thing these R&D employees do share with the professions is a specialized knowledge base, stemming from their formal technical education. But education alone does not determine people's orientations, and the assumption that these employees both need and desire the autonomy characteristically associated with professional work is not necessarily true. We know, for example, that engineers are unlikely to require or desire professional autonomy. In fact, with the possible exception of those with Ph.D.'s, engineers have been shown to be quite different from scientists in background, interests, values, and orientations (e.g., Ritti, 1971; Allen, 1977; Bailyn, 1980). They neither form a clearly identifiable occupational community (cf. Van Maanen and Barley, 1984), nor do they necessarily fit the assumptions underlying the hierarchical organizational career (Bailyn, 1982). There seems to be no obvious setting in which engineers can readily cash in on their expert knowledge; both organizational and occupational rewards are problematic (cf. Child and Fulk, 1977).

But even among Ph.D. scientists, those who work in industry often do so in part, because of a low priority on professional autonomy. Most do not follow their academic colleagues in espousing the norm of autonomy in the choice of their research agenda. For example, in one R&D lab where I interviewed 16 professionals in depth, only two were oriented to autonomy in this sense; in another lab, where I made 14 such detailed interviews, only three could be classified as desiring such autonomy. Whether through pre-selection or through adaptation to the existing reward structure, or both, it seems that many "professional" employees in the industrial R&D lab do not seek such autonomy. It does not seem to be the case, therefore, that the main issue facing technical specialists in industrial organizations is a conflict between the need for autonomy and bureaucratic control.

I would locate the main issue, rather, in a misunderstanding of the meaning of autonomy in the industrial research career. This misunderstanding stems from the assumption that R&D employees fit the traditional mold of the academic scientist. According to this traditional view, scientific work is guided solely by the curiosity and inclinations of the individual scholar, and is motivated entirely by the activity itself. Science brings its own rewards, it is assumed, and is an activity pursued for its own sake, needing no other recognition. In one lab, for example, during discussion of whether or not to introduce a technical ladder, which would bring the salaries for technical work closer to managerial pay, a manager expressed the fear that "if we do that, no one would want to be a manager." The implication was that the pull of science as an activity is so great that only high salary could induce someone to leave that work and turn to managerial tasks. Further, since the object of science is to add to knowledge and understanding, potential application is not seen to play any role in a scientist's motivation. It is presumed, however, that sooner or later something useful will emerge from experimentally verified scientific theories (Feibleman, 1961). Thus, an atmosphere in which individual creativity has maximum play should maximize the yield, both for knowledge and for application, of scientific research.

Not even academic science is realistically covered by this description (Ziman, 1981). And when applied to industrial R&D, the fit is even less good. Moreover, the assumption that R&D employees fit this mold gives rise to procedures that are clearly counterproductive.

The labs I studied recruit their employees from the top universities, and departments vie with each other for the best people. Thus the recruitment problem gets defined as attracting the best scientists available, against both external and internal competition, which leads recruiters to promise more exploratory work than is usually desired. They thus foster expectations that have a high likelihood of being unfulfilled.

> When I was hired, the department head tried to oversell the job. He did not make it clear that this was a development area, not only research. My first year was very disappointing.

In other words, recruitment procedures that rest on the belief the lab is dealing with the stereotypical scientist whose only interest is the pursuit of inner ideas (Kubie, 1953), may misfire.

The same set of beliefs also guides the initial experiences of these recruits. As stated by managers in a number of different labs:

> We give no orientation. It would be offensive to professionals.

> We don't train professionals. Training is only for mechanics. Ph.D.'s are treated with kid gloves.

And this despite the fact that the work in these labs often depends as much on experience acquired on the job as it does on formal education.

Such behavior, so obviously counterproductive when observed, reflects the deeply held belief that scientists function best when left alone, and the conviction that R&D employees fit this model. That the situation is seen differently by the people affected by these procedures is obvious in the cynical explanation offered by one physicist:

> They seem to think that everybody is so super intelligent that they don't have to tell them anything.

Nor are the practices that emanate from this assumption seen to fit the industrial lab's reward system, which in the end gives high priority to the relevance of technical work for corporate products:

> Management gives you enough rope to hang yourself, for one can do a lot of work without direc-

tion and find out after the fact that that work will not reap rewards.

> They may tell you you are doing well, to carry on, and then in the merit review write that you are not working on a bread and butter project.

> I was never assigned a project and my supervisor failed to communicate to me that there were needs I was failing to meet.

> I found that I could do a perfect job and still be a flop because it was the wrong job to do.

There is irony, therefore, in a situation where management tries to provide an autonomous environment which does not fit the needs of the lab nor of its technical employees. It stems from a misunderstanding of the meaning of autonomy in the industrial R&D lab.

THE MEANING OF AUTONOMY

One of the key norms of academic science is autonomy: the freedom to choose the problems on which to work, to pursue them independently of directives from anywhere except the precepts of a discipline, and to publish freely the results of research. This set of values is inculcated and reinforced by the university, as educator and employer of scientists. Indeed, the central control mechanism of the university—the granting of tenure—evolved in order to protect this freedom from outside pressure.

Such autonomy requires an organizational context geared to its expression, and technical specialists dedicated to the pursuit of science for its own sake. The university provides such a setting and reinforces this orientation in its employees. The industrial research lab, in contrast, is a more "heteronomous" organization (Scott, 1965), subject to controls emanating from the business goals of the parent organization. A different orientation, therefore, tends to be inculcated, which fits the fact, already stated, that most of the lab's employees do not desire such professional autonomy. Indeed, those few who do must confront the costs of the disjunction between orientation and setting. One scientist, for example, who has published papers and has a number of patents to his name, made this point clearly:

> My management respects me and leaves me alone. But this freedom also means that my avenue of movement is closed.

But even here, the effect of the difference in setting was visible. For when this man was finally given a specific assignment by a new supervisor, he found the work very satisfactory:

> Last year I was assigned to the development of a device and it was successful. I enjoyed this. It is a different challenge.

Most R&D employees, in fact, are not concerned with setting their own problems:

> It is not easy to find good problems.

> Supervisors don't tell what to do, but I would prefer to be told. People want to be told; they desire strong management.

And this means being told "what is needed." "We want to have an impact on the corporation."

What they do care about, though, is their lack of "authority," the fact that they have no say over "the light bulbs, the number of people in the projects . . . no say in choosing technicians, or in hiring decisions." What they want, therefore, is to be given some discretion in the process of solving the problems that they are assigned. It is at the level of implementation that they want autonomy, and it is here, often, that controls are imposed through a series of required authorizations and sign-offs. The effect is demoralizing:

> These approval processes destroy initiative. It is the wrong place for controls.

If people get thwarted, if there is over-controlling, one gets the stuffing knocked out.

It is easy to see why such procedures exist. With very few exceptions, industrial R&D labs cannot afford to follow professional norms consistently, and must impose organizational controls at some point (cf. Child and Fulk, 1982). But they do so inappropriately. They emphasize autonomy initially, when intersecting with the university in the search for recruits, which seemingly defines it in accordance with the norms of academic science as the freedom to set one's own problems. But once recruits are established in the lab, controls are imposed in an effort to ensure that the actual work done will contribute to business goals. Managers are responsible for organizationally relevant results. And when, because of the presumed need for an autonomous environment, they do not give clear assignments, then they are inclined to impose controls at the level of implementation. Thus, while seemingly providing *strategic autonomy*—the freedom to set one's own research directions—they withhold *operational autonomy*—the discretion to decide how to pursue this goal.

The psychological distinction between wide basic freedom with constrained options and more directed goals but with many choices on how to reach them, is evident in many spheres of life. Twenty years ago I found a similar situation confronting professional women (Bailyn, 1965). They were given seemingly wide choice on initial decisions: Should they not work? combine work with children? emphasize only career? But if they decided to work, then they were faced with all the constraints that women faced in those days. Men, in contrast, knew they had to find an occupation, but had wide choice in choosing one that suited them. Psychologically, the women's pattern was a more difficult one.

It is important, therefore, to think of autonomy in more differentiated ways than has often been the case. It is the failure to make a distinction between strategic and operational autonomy that creates many of the dilemmas and contradictions confronting the industrial scientist.

RELATION BETWEEN STRATEGIC AND OPERATIONAL AUTONOMY

It is the thesis of this paper that strategic autonomy—the freedom to set one's own research agenda—and operational autonomy—the freedom, once a problem has been set, to attack it by means determined by oneself, within given organizational resource constraints—may be thought of as independent dimensions on a two-dimensional grid on which one can chart the position of R&D tasks and employees (see Figure 1). Further, I would hypothesize that, in general,

the most productive and satisfactory position for the technical staff is to the left of the diagonal, with operational autonomy ≥ strategic autonomy; that the optimum position for the manager of research is to the right of the diagonal, with strategic autonomy > operational autonomy; and that other important roles in the R&D lab (cf. Schriesheim *et al.*, 1977; Roberts and Fusfeld, 1982) can be usefully differentiated according to their position on the grid. Finally, I would suggest that career procedures—particularly systems of evaluation and rewards—should vary according to the position on this grid.

To test some of these ideas, I looked at data from 18 professionals in the central research lab of a large consumer products company. It is a centrally funded lab committed to doing research

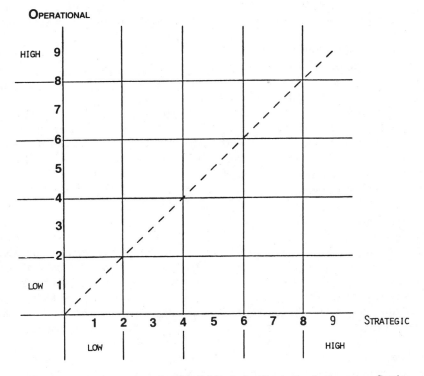

FIGURE 1. *Autonomy in the R&D Lab.* Strategic Autonomy: *Setting Goals; Defining Problems.* Operational Autonomy: *Controlling Means, Modes of Implementation, Solution Procedures*

in a variety of fields, through research that is relevant to its products. These 18 professionals varied in age from 30 to 60, and spanned four technical levels in the lab. The group included two women, and encompassed both science and engineering fields. I asked them all where they would place themselves on the grid, what their position had been when they first entered the lab, and which position they would consider ideal for professionals and for managers in the R&D lab.

These 18 professionals place themselves at many points on this grid: 6 fall on the diagonal line (from low on both to very high on both), 7 to the left (with higher operational than strategic autonomy), and 5 to the right (with higher strategic autonomy). The mean point is close to the middle of the chart (strategic: $\bar{x} = 5.3$ with a standard deviation of 2.4; operational: $\bar{y} = 5.9$ with a standard deviation of 2.6). This group, of course, represents a wide range of experience. Of the four people high on both dimensions, three have been at the lab for more than 15 years, and are at a high technical level—a level to which promotion is a fairly major event. Further, these three are all ranked within the top quarter of their groups in performance. The fourth, who is at a middle level and has been at the lab for five years, describes the current position as 9,8 and reports that "when I first came operational was lower, but strategic would have been the same." And, a further comment is relevant:

> The ideal—and this may be blasphemous—would be to be lower strategic, to have more of an idea of what is relevant, but to be 9 on operational.

In contrast, two of the three people whose strategic autonomy is considerably greater than their operational autonomy are the only newcomers to the lab in the sample. Both have been there less than one year. It would be interesting to know what their view of this position will be after a number of years of work at this lab. The modal characterization of the ideal research manager was found to be one who is pri-

marily strategic (defined as being at least four points higher on strategic autonomy than on operational autonomy, with a mean position of 7.2,1.6), which fits well the hypothesized placement. However, this emphasis on strategic autonomy for the research manager was subscribed to primarily by those technical specialists who themselves were managerially oriented. Those more technically oriented, in contrast, were more likely to believe that the professional should have the greater strategic autonomy.

In general, one finds a complementary relation between the placement of professionals and that of managers. Those who believe that managers in the R&D lab should primarily be strategic give higher operational autonomy to the professional, and those who believe that managers should primarily play an operational role ascribe more strategic autonomy to the professional. This complementarity was stated by a highly rated, technically oriented scientist:

> To start, a professional should be low strategic and low operational. The movement would go up a curve starting with increases in operational, and strategic later. The manager would be the inverse: with respect to a starting recruit the manager would have to be high on both; with an established professional it would depend. The manager is the inverse of the professional. If the professional is high/high, then he would be low on both.

In other words, in the view of these technical professionals, the work of the R&D lab requires both strategic and operational control. It is the distribution of these tasks between the specialists actually performing the technical work and the managers supervising and coordinating it that varies according to experience and orientation.

On ten of these 18 professionals, I had considerably more information, including their performance evaluations. Though I saw no poor performers, five of these ten were rated as top performers, whereas the other five were more av-

Lotte Bailyn

erage. The average length of service of both of these groups is approximately equal (a bit over 13 years), but the top performers are somewhat younger (with mean age of the average performers in the low forties, and in the low thirties for the top performers). Not surprisingly, the top performers placed themselves higher on both strategic and operational autonomy, which is probably an accurate reflection of differences in the actual position of these two groups. What is of greater interest, though, is that the top performers reported that they had started their careers much lower strategically (see Figure 2). In other words, the top performers started closer to the position that has been hypothesized as optimal for technical professionals in an R&D lab. Obviously, one cannot assume causality here.

But it is certainly clear that the top performers have not only moved more than those who are average, but they have moved more in the strategic than in the operational direction. This would seem to be a useful guideline for professional careers: provide increases in strategic autonomy (cf. Dalton *et al.,* 1977). But such movement is only possible if technical recruits start relatively low strategically. One of the implications of this paper is that such a start has many advantages, for the lab and for the technical employee, and is too often not provided in the R&D lab.

On the basis of these considerations, one can hypothesize what the ideal career movement in the R&D lab should be (see Figure 3). At the beginning of a technical career, it is proposed, operational autonomy is more important than stra-

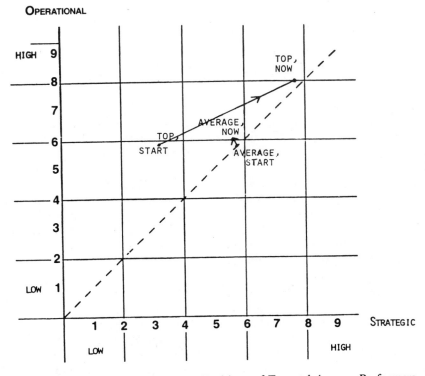

FIGURE 2. *Starting and Present Positions of Top and Average Performers*

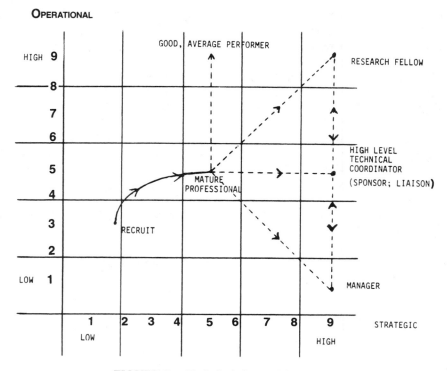

FIGURE 3.   *Technical Career Movement*

tegic autonomy, and increases initially more rapidly. But as the technical employee becomes more experienced, increases in strategic autonomy become critical. The mature professional, therefore, will have considerably more strategic autonomy than the new recruit, and somewhat more operational autonomy. Thereafter, as indicated in Figure 3, technical employees can follow a number of paths. The average technical employee might usefully be embarked on a career consisting of a series of challenging assignments (cf. McKinnon, 1980; Allen, in progress; Epstein, in progress; Bailyn, 1984a). Such a path would consist principally of increases in operational autonomy and would ensure that stagnation based on overspecialization and routinization would not occur. Top performers, in contrast, would continue to be able to achieve increasing strategic autonomy and might go in

one of three directions: to research management (in which case operational control over research decreases); to high level technical coordination (cf. Schriescheim *et al.,* 1977); or to a research fellow position (in which case operational autonomy would also increase). Further, it is proposed that these roles might be thought of as more temporary than permanent, and that high level R&D employees could usefully move among them during their careers.

Autonomy and Setting

The main thrust of the argument so far has been to establish the difference between strategic and operational autonomy, between autonomy and control over ends and over means. But there are other distinctions, already alluded to, that are also important. One of these relates to setting—

the organizational context in which the work takes place.

As has already been indicated, autonomy takes on a different meaning in an "autonomous" professional setting—a setting, like a university, where professionals both set and implement the organizational goals—and a "heteronomous" setting, in which professional work is subordinated to non-professional goals set from within a large administrative framework (Scott, 1965). From the analysis already given, it is clear that most R&D employees do not consider themselves academic scientists. "At the university," claimed a scientist with five years of academic experience, "the most one can do is teach and write, and maybe no one will read it. Here there is the possibility of having an impact." And yet, they also do not feel they should be bound by short-run corporate goals. In one of the labs I studied, the "story" was circulating that "if you can point to a part of a product and say that comes from the research lab, then something is wrong"—that is, you have been overly coopted by business needs.

These comments reflect the dilemma of the central research lab, which is caught between the desire to translate current technical knowledge into profitable product innovations and the need for more basic research in order to produce new ideas with not entirely predictable and certainly more long-range consequences. It is this basic dilemma between long-range research and short-term product improvement that gets translated into the contradictory career procedures already outlined (cf. Bailyn, 1982). A different way of dealing with this dilemma is to build diversity into the R&D lab's procedures. Figure 4 indicates the hypothesized position on the strategic/operational grid of the various technical tasks that comprise research and development, each of which will attract people with different orientations who require different modes of evaluation and rewards. And when one adds to this picture the non-technical requirements of the lab, it is obvious that there is great need for a wide variety

of talent in this setting (cf. Roberts and Fusfeld, 1982).

Unfortunately, however, the career procedures in these labs tend to be narrow and homogenous. They neither respond to the variety of necessary tasks nor to the large differences in career orientations of R&D employees.

Autonomy and Career Orientations

I have already alluded to some of the differences between research employees who are technically oriented and those who are managerially oriented. This distinction—though the most generally acknowledged—does not, however, span the variety of orientations actually present. To get a sense of what these orientations are and how they relate to career procedures, I have taken data from one particular lab in which I had detailed interviews with 16 members of the professional staff. The lab exemplifies the basic R&D dilemma. It prides itself on being a "research site"; had recently hired a number of bright scientists (some attracted from the university); and had just instituted a technical ladder based on well specified criteria of scientific productiveness. At the same time, it was under pressure to show a return on this investment and to justify to the corporation that the work it produced could be translated profitably into improvements in product. The interviews I conducted covered the present work, the career history, and the expectations and hopes for the future of technical employees. Five different orientations emerged from an analysis of these data, each of which was accompanied by different reactions to work experiences and by positive and negative feelings about different aspects of the lab's career procedures. Further, each can be placed at different points on the strategic/operational grid. The lab was obviously in need of the talents of all these orientations. But, at this point in its development,[2] its career procedures seemingly satisfied only a small minority.

This minority consists of the two "academic

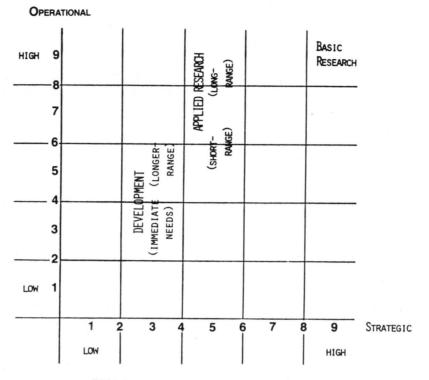

FIGURE 4.   *Position of Various R&D Tasks*

science'' oriented professionals, already referred to, who were oriented to adding to knowledge, giving papers, etc. Their position on the strategic/operational grid would be close to the 9,9 position hypothesized for research fellows. At the time of my interviews, they were the only ones who were fully satisfied with their careers. They were responding, of course, to the recent changes in the lab, but even they had a "wait and see" attitude to the future. They also were fully aware that without others in the lab paying attention to administrative tasks and to the issues involved in making the transfer to production, their bubble might burst. And these others were much less satisfied with their positions.

There were three who were oriented to production—in whose hands, in some sense, the future of the lab could be said to lie. Their position on the strategic/operational grid would seem to be *low* on both dimensions since their output is severely constrained by all kinds of strategic and operational controls. These three were deeply committed to the follow-through on R&D, and worked hard to ensure that the lab's work would get translated into profit for the corporation. They knew they were playing a critical role, and yet they felt unappreciated. Neither the managerial route nor the newly defined technical ladder captured their talents. All three were toying with the idea of trying new fields or new settings at some future time. They would have responded positively, I think, to public recognition of their critical role.

Nor did the lab's career procedures fit the needs of those oriented to administration. There were three in this category, and, according to the discussion above, they would be relatively low on operational autonomy but would need a fair amount of strategic autonomy. These three were less involved with the technical side of their work and more with the lab's administrative tasks: scheduling and budget control of projects; evaluation and development of people. They recognized the importance of these tasks and the inability of many of the more technically oriented to carry them through effectively. But they were concerned about the repetitiveness of these demands; they feared stagnation. They would benefit, I think, from two modifications in career procedures: (1) a more explicit recognition of their interests and concerns with people, by more specific assignments (as mentors to newcomers, for example), or by opportunities to take management oriented courses; and (2) recognition and rewards for group output, not only for individual performance.

Five people were oriented to engineering. They were concerned with technical "craftsmanship," with the development of a product or process that could, in some way, be identified with oneself (cf. Bailyn and Lynch, 1983). Their work depended on a fair amount of operational autonomy but required little strategic autonomy. This orientation is not at all an academic orientation, and hence these people were not eligible for the technical ladder. They were satisfied with their work but felt that, despite a perceived appreciation of what they were doing, the recent emphasis on science had led them to suffer financially. They were more concerned with salary than with status, and would probably respond well to financial recognition.

Finally, there was a group oriented to technical management, who desired a combination of technical/scientific work with real responsibility and authority. What they seemingly needed was high strategic autonomy with a middle range of operational autonomy. All three of these people were among the highly qualified scientists newly recruited by the lab. But, because of other recent hirings, they saw the management road as blocked and felt that the autonomy and recognition of the technical ladder were too circumscribed for them, with too little broad scope. All three anticipated leaving the lab within a few years. And though stock options and other forms of financial recognition might delay this departure, it is unlikely that such rewards could fundamentally alter their reactions.

It is clear, therefore, that each position on the strategic/operational grid needs to be managed differently. And yet all points have their importance for R&D work. In fact, it should be highly advantageous to have this variety in orientations because it would make it possible to easily meet the needs of all the technical and nontechnical tasks of R&D. But the lack of formal recognition of this heterogeneity leads most labs to manage their employees in too homogeneous a way, thus losing the advantage of the very diversity they need.

IMPLICATIONS FOR THE MANAGEMENT OF "PROFESSIONALS"

The most general implication to emerge from this analysis is that the diversity in the R&D lab—in tasks and orientations—requires career procedures based on a variety of criteria of successful performance and encompassing a "cafeteria" of rewards and modes of recognition. This general conclusion has been stated before (e.g., Friedlander, 1971; Bailyn, 1980; Roberts and Fusfeld, 1982; Von Glinow, 1983; Schein, 1986). My purpose in this final section is to suggest, briefly, some ways by which this goal might be reached, and to link these means to the distinction between strategic and operational autonomy.

Elsewhere I have indicated that recognition of such diversity requires a process of negotiation between individual and organization that needs to be renewed periodically (Bailyn, 1984b), and I have talked of the value of temporary and multiple work assignments (Bailyn, 1982, 1984a).

233

These suggestions apply, in my opinion, to all positions on the strategic/operational grid. But the analysis in this paper also points to considerations that vary according to position on the grid. For ease of exposition, I will talk about four general positions: H-H (high on both dimensions); L-L (low on both dimensions); H-L (emphasis on strategic rather than on operational autonomy); and L-H (emphasis on operational autonomy).

The H-H position is likely to be held by only a small number of employees with many years of experience in the lab. It represents the lab's investment in the unforeseeable future, for which a small effort is probably correct. The output of this group would be an addition to knowledge, though with relevance to the needs of the corporation—one might call it *practical knowledge.* Criteria of success would necessarily have to be long-term, and the position represents more a bet on someone's potential than a goal that needs close monitoring. The IBM Fellow is a prototype, and, like that position, a limited term (possibly renewable) would seem to make sense. Such employees probably have ties to a professional community outside the labs, and easy access to professional meetings would seem to be appropriate. Every lab I studied had a few people in this position, and they were generally satisfied and seen to be contributing. A problem arises when the H-H employee requires a position on the managerial hierarchy for the sake of status and compensation. The academically oriented technical ladder, if seen as a viable alternative, could overcome this difficulty. But this would require public recognition of movement up this ladder. In contrast, in one lab I studied, movement up the technical ladder was shrouded in secrecy. The explanation given was that others would be envious and angry. But by trying to deemphasize the disadvantages of envy, one fails to capitalize on the advantages of hope. The psychology here would seem to be more akin to what Hirschman (1973) calls the "tunnel effect," where one gets solace from the fact that one of the lines of traffic approaching the tunnel is moving, even when it is not the one in which one finds oneself.

The L-L position, in contrast, is likely to be held by people at the beginning of their careers. But, as has been indicated, it is also likely to be the appropriate place for production oriented employees, and it is a more problematic position for them than it is for new recruits. These people are more concerned with the transfer of technology into production than with the development of that technology. They would gauge their success by the extent to which the lab's output gets translated into product or process improvements. It is a critical role, dependent on liaison skills for linking the R&D lab to the operating divisions. But, characteristically, it is a role that gets little official recognition from the lab. It makes sense, perhaps, to populate this position by people on a temporary assignment from the production companies, or to see it as a bridging role for R&D employees interested in transferring out of the lab and into an operating division. My sense is that the L-L position would gain in meaning and importance to its mature incumbents if it were part of a career path rooted more in production than in research.

The H-L or strategic position is presumed to be the place for the administration and management of the lab. On the whole, the career procedures of most labs are geared to the selection of people for these roles, and the main rewards and signs of status and recognition are reserved for them. But, as has been indicated, trouble may arise when technical "professionals" are placed in this position. For them, the L-H position, if properly managed, is more appropriate. It is here that most mature professionals would be expected to reside and that the main technical tasks of the lab would get accomplished.

In most labs, however, there is difficulty with the L-H or operational position. In particular, the reward system is problematic. The managerial ladder is clearly not appropriate; nor, in most cases, is the technical ladder since it either does not have commensurate prestige or compensation, or, by emphasizing academic criteria, is applicable primarily to those few employees of the lab who appropriately belong in H-H positions. Continued financial progress is important, naturally, for people in this position, but the main motivation here must come from the work itself. It is for L-H employees that the character of work assignments becomes critical. They must be varying and challenging, and must avoid repetitiveness and overspecialization (cf. Dalton and Thompson, 1971; Zand, 1981; Bailyn, 1984a). One professional, for example, when looking back over his career, commented on the "luck" that forced him to "change fields about every seven years." These "chance events," he felt, made his career considerably more satisfactory than that of most of his peers. It is the *management* of such events, rather than leaving them to chance, that is necessary in order to make the L-H position more generally successful.

These are very general implications. Their successful translation into specific procedures will depend, of course, on the special circumstances in each lab. What is common to all is a clear distinction between strategic and operational autonomy and the realization that tasks require different amounts of each and that different people at different stages of their careers will also span the various positions. Hence the strategic/operational grid may be a useful diagnostic tool for the proper utilization of the talents of R&D employees.

NOTES

1. In order to protect the identity of the companies studied, these labs will not be described in detail. All were parts of central R&D units of large, successful corporations, employing engineers, primarily in electronics, and scientists, primarily in physics. Almost all of the technical professionals in these labs were university graduates, many with Ph.D.'s. The data consist of lengthy individual interviews with people at all levels of the hierarchy and group discussions of preliminary results.

2. Career procedures in the R&D lab fluctuate in response to corporate fluctuations between general support for technical work and the time that it requires, and demands for immediate proof of value by means of profitable products and processes (Kantrow, 1983, p. 72). At the time of my interviews, this lab was coming to the end of a period of strong corporate support for the more scientific aspects of R&D.

REFERENCES

Allen, T. J. *Managing the Flow of Technology: Technology Transfer and the Dissemination of Technological Information within the Research and Development Organization.* Cambridge, MA: MIT Press, 1977.

Allen, T. J. "Career Orientations of R&D Employees." In progress.

Bailyn, L. Notes on the Role of Choice in the Lives of Professional Women. In R. J. Lifton (Ed.), *The Woman in America.* Boston: Houghton-Mifflin, 1965.

Bailyn, L. *Living with Technology: Issues at Mid-Career.* Cambridge, MA: MIT Press, 1980 (in collaboration with E. H. Schein).

Bailyn, L. Resolving Contradictions in Technical Careers. *Technology Review,* October 1982, 40–47.

Bailyn, L. "Careers in High Technology: Notes on Technical Career Progression with Special Reference to Possible Issues for Minorities." Sloan School of Management, 1984a.

Bailyn, L. Work and Family in Organizations: Responding to Social Diversity. In M. B. Arthur, L. Bailyn, D. J. Levinson, and H. A. Shepard (Eds.), *Working with Careers.* Center for Research in Career Development, Graduate School of Business, Columbia University, 1984b.

Bailyn, L., and Lynch, J. T. Engineering as a Life-Long Career: Its Meaning, Its Satisfactions, Its Difficulties. *Journal of Occupational Behavior,* 1983, 4, 263–283.

Child, J., and Fulk, J. Maintenance of Occupational

Control: The Case of Professions. *Work and Occupations,* 1982, 9, 155–192.

Dalton, G. W., and Thompson, P. H. Accelerating Obsolescence of Older Engineers. *Harvard Business Review,* September–October 1971, 57–67.

Dalton, G. W., Thompson, P. H., and Price, R. L. The Four Stages of Professional Careers: A New Look at Performance by Professionals. *Organizational Dynamics,* Summer 1977, 19–42.

Epstein, K. A. Ph.D. dissertation, Sloan School of Management, MIT, in progress.

Feibleman, J. K. Pure Science, Applied Science, Technology, Engineering: An Attempt at Definitions. *Technology and Culture,* 1961, 2, 305–317.

Friedlander, F. Performance and Orientation Structures of Research Scientists. *Organizational Behavior and Human Performance,* 1971, 6, 169–183.

Hirschman, A. The Changing Tolerance for Income Inequality in the Course of Economic Development. *Quarterly Journal of Economics,* 1973, 87, 544–566.

Kantrow, A. M. Management of Technology. *Harvard Business Review,* July–August 1983, 66, 70, 72.

Kerr, S., and Von Glinow, M. A. Issues in the Study of "Professionals" in Organizations: The Case of Scientists and Engineers. *Organizational Behavior and Human Performance,* 1977, 18, 329–345.

Kubie, L. S. Some Unsolved Problems of the Scientific Career. *American Scientist,* 1953, 41, 596–613.

McKinnon, P. "Career Orientations of R&D Engineers in a Large Aerospace Laboratory." Sloan School Working Paper No. 1097–80, MIT, January 1980.

Ritti, R. *The Engineer in the Industrial Corporation.* New York: Columbia University Press, 1971.

Roberts, E. B., and Fusfeld, A. R. Critical Functions: Needed Roles in the Innovation Process. In R. Katz (Ed.), *Career Issues in Human Resource Management,* Prentice-Hall, 1982.

Schein, E. H. Individuals and Careers. In J. Lorsch (Ed.) *Handbook of Organization Behavior,* Englewood Cliffs, NJ: Prentice-Hall, 1986.

Schriesheim, J., Von Glinow, M. A., and Kerr, S. Professionals in Bureaucracy: A Structural Alternative. *TIMS Studies in Management Sciences,* 1977, 5, 55–69.

Scott, W. R. Reactions to Supervision in a Heteronomous Professional Organization. *Administrative Science Quarterly,* 1965, 10, 65–81.

Van Maanen, J., and Barley, S. R. Occupational Communities: Culture and Control in Organizations. In B. Staw and L. Cummings (Eds.), *Research in Organizational Behavior,* Vol. 6, Greenwich, CT: JAI Press, 1984.

Von Glinow, M. A. "Incentives for Controlling the Performance of High Technology and Professional Employees." Technical Report No. G83-3 (34). Graduate School of Business Administration, University of Southern California, Los Angeles, 1983.

Zand, D. E. *Information, Organization, and Power: Effective Management in the Knowledge Society.* New York: McGraw-Hill, 1981.

Ziman, J. What Are the Options? Social Determinants of Personal Research Plans. *Minerva,* 1981, 19, 1–42.

Learning and Problem Solving: R&D Organizations as Learning Systems

Barbara Carlsson

Peter Keane

J. Bruce Martin

In comparison with the relatively systematic, logical, and planned processes of some organizations, R&D processes often appear to be disorderly, and unpredictable—difficult, if not impossible, to manage. However, the hypothesis that the primary output of R&D is *knowledge* (incorporated in formulas and specifications) suggests that its major process is *learning*. We have confirmed that, when R&D activities are viewed as part of a learning process, much of what appears disorderly is seen to have an underlying order. Furthermore, we have determined that this perspective is useful for describing, understanding, and improving the R&D process.

Linear models of technical innovation may be useful in describing key steps in the R&D process and in documenting projects after the fact but are not particularly helpful in understanding the process in real time. Linear models can describe what happened but not *how* it happened, and tend to reinforce the belief in a kind of orderliness which does not exist (see Figure 1).[1]

The model we *have* found to be descriptive

of the way learning occurs in R&D organizations is based on D. A. Kolb's work on individual experiential learning.[2] Kolb postulates a four-step repetitive cycle, which provides the framework for the model shown in Figure 2. This cycle is summarized as follows:

> Immediate concrete experience is the basis for observation and reflection. These observations are assimilated into a "theory" from which new implications for action can be deduced. These implications, or hypotheses, then serve as guides in acting to create new experiences.[3]

We have generalized Kolb's work, which focuses on the individual learning process, to the organizational learning process.

Kolb's learning process requires orientations that are polar opposites: active and reflective; concrete and abstract. The shifting orientation results in four kinds of activity, each of which is required at some stage of the learning process.

1. *Divergence (concrete and reflective).* This kind of activity is required to seek background information and sense opportunities, investigate new patterns, recognize discrepancies and problems, and generate alternatives. Literature browsing and Brainstorming are techniques which may be used to aid this kind of activity.

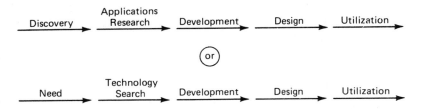

FIGURE 1.   *Linear Models of Technical Innovation*

2. *Assimilation* (*abstract* and *reflective*). This kind of activity is required to develop theory, compare alternatives, establish criteria, formulate plans and hypotheses, and define problems. Grounded Theory techniques are designed to aid this kind of activity.[4]

3. *Convergence* (*abstract* and *active*). This kind of activity is required to select among alternatives, focus efforts, evaluate plans and programs, test hypotheses, and make decisions. Venture Analysis techniques are designed to aid this kind of activity.

4. *Execution*[5] (*concrete* and *active*). This kind of activity is required to advocate positions or ideas, set objectives, commit to schedules, commit resources, and implement decisions. PERT and Critical Path Scheduling are techniques frequently used to aid this kind of activity.

Organizations differ in their capabilities for

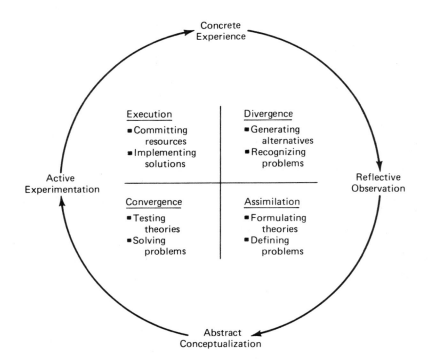

FIGURE 2.   *The Learning Model*

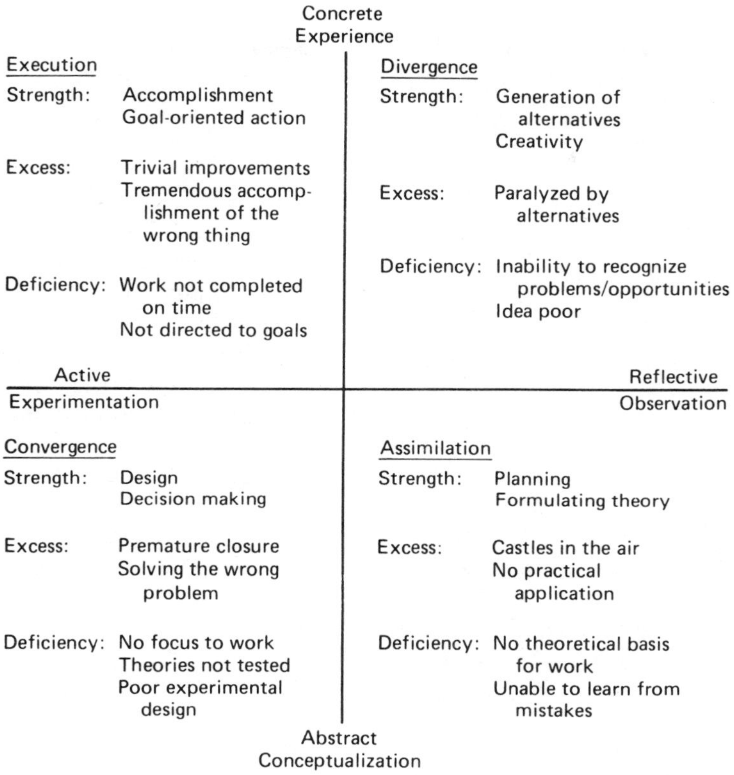

```
                          Concrete
                          Experience
    Execution              |    Divergence
    Strength:  Accomplishment    |  Strength:  Generation of
               Goal-oriented action    |              alternatives
                               |              Creativity
    Excess:    Trivial improvements    |
               Tremendous accomp-    |  Excess:    Paralyzed by
               lishment of the    |              alternatives
               wrong thing    |
                               |  Deficiency: Inability to recognize
    Deficiency: Work not completed   |              problems/opportunities
               on time    |              Idea poor
               Not directed to goals   |
    Active                     |                    Reflective
    Experimentation            |                    Observation
    Convergence                |    Assimilation
    Strength:  Design              |  Strength:  Planning
               Decision making    |              Formulating theory
    Excess:    Premature closure    |  Excess:    Castles in the air
               Solving the wrong    |              No practical
               problem    |              application
    Deficiency: No focus to work    |  Deficiency: No theoretical basis
               Theories not tested    |              for work
               Poor experimental    |              Unable to learn from
               design    |              mistakes
                          Abstract
                          Conceptualization
```

FIGURE 3.   Strengths and Weaknesses

performing the tasks associated with each of the stages. There are predictable strengths associated with an appropriate skill level in each stage and there are predictable weaknesses associated with either an excess or a deficiency in any stage. Figure 3 outlines some of these strengths and weaknesses.

EXPERIMENTAL VALIDATION

In a series of experiments, we have demonstrated that the Learning Method provides a useful description of the R&D process in a way which permits strengths and weaknesses to be assessed, identifies bottlenecks, and provides cues to remedial action. We asked R&D managers what factors inhibited innovation in their individual areas. We found that most of their responses fit into the patterns of strengths or weaknesses predicted in Figure 3. The following are a few examples.

Comment	Corresponding Strength or Weakness
"We're not idea poor, but we do need people to push ideas."	Strength in divergence Lack of execution
"Timetables are sometimes too tight to let people explore."	Excessive execution Too little divergence

239

"We execute well; we need to develop needs." — Sufficient execution. Too little divergence

"We allow ourselves to be diffuse; we need more focus." — Lack of convergence

"We lack conceptualization—fitting all the elements into a full concept." — Lack of assimilation

"We lack good ideas." — Lack of divergence

These data not only suggest that major elements of the R&D process can be expressed in terms of the Learning Model, but also confirm that organizations can develop "flat spots" which may be described in terms of the Learning Model.

In another experiment, we devised a scheme for scoring biweekly progress reports which are written by professional members of our organizations.[6] For each report, this scoring scheme provided a measure of the effort in each stage of the learning process. We applied this scoring scheme to several series of reports written by individual staff members. Our findings, which are summarized below, supported our hypothesis that the Learning Model is descriptive of the dynamics of R&D projects.

1. Most of the subjects appeared to be following a clockwise sequence through the stages of the Learning Model; that is, a report scoring relatively high in Assimilation was likely to be followed by a report relatively high in Convergence, which was likely to be followed by a report high in Execution, etc.

2. A researcher who had no familiarity with the content of the reports or with the authors could from the scores alone predict with accuracy the strengths and weaknesses of the projects. For example, from a series of scores indicating consistently high levels of Assimilation and Execution, and consistently low levels of Divergence and Convergence, one of the researchers correctly predicted that the project would be suffering from a lack of creativity (Divergence) and lack of focusing and testing of hypotheses (Convergence) prior to execution of new activities, and that these deficiencies could result in executions that failed without adding to understanding.

3. The effect of management interventions could be observed in the scores. For example, late in the project cited above there was a sharp but temporary shift into the Convergence stage. Although we observed the shift, we did not know its cause. Subsequent discussions with the manager revealed that the shift was the result of his probing questions about their research design, and confirmed his fear that the effect of his action had been only temporary.

In a third experiment we collected historical data on the progress of a project and extended the data into real time by periodic interviews with members of the project team. We found that key steps in the progress of the project could be interpreted as representing a clockwise sequence through the Learning Model as shown in Figure 4. A list of the activities involved with the project (corresponding to the numbers on the diagram) and a list of the information inputs which occurred during the project (corresponding to the letters on the diagram) follow Figure 4. Critical examination of this analysis by other project managers and their higher-level R&D managers confirmed that the model represented the realities of the project. The higher-level managers were particularly reassured by the sense of order given to a set of events that had not seemed nearly so orderly at the time.

We have subsequently analyzed other projects in the same manner and found less orderly progression around the model. We found instances of stages being skipped, of project teams "stuck" in a stage, and even instances of reverse (i.e., counterclockwise) movement through the stages. The managers involved generally agreed that the pictures were accurate and that the deviations indicated problems deserving of management attention.

USE OF THE MODEL

We can testify to the usefulness of the Learning Model from our own experience. Our individual strengths are in different stages of the model and our efforts to work together often involved more conflict than the task seemed to warrant. As we learned more about the Learned Model, we each developed an appreciation of the contributions of the other members of our group. Our working relationships are greatly improved; now if we find ourselves pulling in different directions, we refer to the Model for resolution.

In the course of our experiments, we have exposed the Learning Model to a large number of R&D managers and project team members, and have received responses suggesting that the Model also has been useful to them. Sharing the Learning Model with others in our organization has been most productive when we have communicated the *concept,* and allowed others to discover applications for themselves. Kolb has developed a Learning Style Inventory which we have found very useful in these discussions.[7] The Learning Style Inventory is a brief pencil-and-paper test which gives the subject an indication of his preference for activity in each of the stages of the Learning Model. Members of work teams who shared their individual results have invariably found important differences among themselves, and usually came quickly to understand how these differences in "Learning Style" have influenced their process of working together. Individuals who prefer Execution are likely to be impatient with Assimilation, and Divergers are likely to find Convergers stodgy and stifling of creativity. An understanding of individual differences has generally led to an interest in understanding the Learning Model, which has in turn led to the kinds of learning and applications reported below.

One project team had been having difficulty in understanding why the character of their interactions with each other shifted sharply from meeting to meeting. In some meetings they found themselves open to new ideas, free to raise questions, and valuing the inputs of other members. In other meetings they found themselves rejecting new ideas, making few significant comments on each other's work, and generally rejecting those ideas which were offered. After being exposed to the Learning Model, they realized that the first condition prevailed when the project was in a Divergence Stage, and the latter occurred when the project required Convergence or Execution.

Discussions with the manager of the same project team provided the basis for a new concept of the role of the project manager. Traditionally the manager's role has been viewed primarily as one of planning, organizing, directing and controlling. When organizations are viewed as learning systems, the manager's role can be viewed as one of providing leadership in the learning process. The following observations developed out of our conversations with the manager of this team.

1. When the development of a product is going smoothly, the manager's role will involve thinking and planning about the next stage, and will be 90° to 135° ahead of that of the team members. For example, if the team is engaged in Execution, the manager will be thinking about the possible alternatives for the project when the results of Execution are known; if the team is engaged in idea generation, the manager's role will involve thinking about the criteria for solution. By concentrating on what is to come, the manager exerts a useful pull on the project.

241

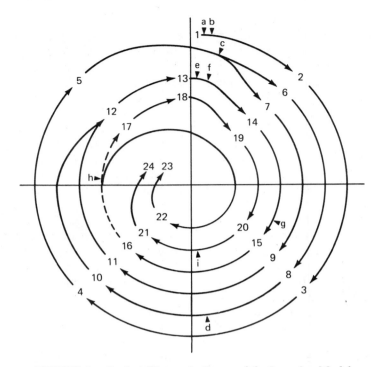

FIGURE 4.   *Project History in Terms of the Learning Model*

2. In time of crisis, when the team is finding it difficult to move through the learning cycle, the role requires the manager to move into the same stage as the project team. For example, the manager may work with the team to develop theories to explain an unexpected result or to help in the pilot plant when there is a critical deadline.

3. The manager must take care that he does not move too far ahead of the project team, thus not only losing sensitivity to their current problems but also confusing them with regard to the path they should take. The manager should avoid pulling the team *across* the Model instead of *around* it.

This same manager used his knowledge of the work team process and his understanding of his role of leadership in the learning process to devise a special plan for supporting the work of one of the team members. The team member had come forward with a proposal to investigate some leads which might result in options which would be alternative or supplemental to those which the team was soon to execute. The manager recognized the merits of the proposal but also recognized that the team member was proposing to involve himself deeply in the Divergence stage of the Model, while the rest of the team was involved in the Convergence and Execution stages. The manager described his strategy to prevent unproductive conflict between the Divergence of the team member and the Convergence of the rest of the team: "I built a fence around the Divergence quadrant and told him to stay in it and the others to stay out." He thus encouraged and supported the team members's independent pursuit of the learning process until

List of the Activities for Figure 4

1. Planning activity initiated by a management question: "What businesses should this division be in?"
2. Generation of nine alternatives.
3. Establishment of criteria for selection made jointly with marketing.
4. Evaluation of the nine alternatives against the criteria resulting in the selection of three projects to pursue.
5. Assignment of staff to activate three projects, one of which is the subject of this study.
6. Identifying the options for positioning the product in the market.
7. Identifying the potential process routes to making the product.
8. Establishing the criteria for deciding the competitive targets.
9. Examining standing criteria in the division for choice of processes, and weighting flexibility higher than normal for this project.
10. Deciding on the specific objective for this product.
11. Choosing the process route to be developed.
12. Making the product and placing a consumer test.
13. Obtaining consumer test results that confirmed that the product targets had been met.
14. Generation of alternatives for obtaining a more favorable economic position in the marketplace.
15. Analyzing the alternatives from the standpoint of the user.
16. Selection of the specific target and the attribute to be optimized.
17. Making the product and placing a consumer test. (The path from 16 to 17 is shown as a broken line because the work was incomplete, i.e., the consumer test was placed without having the optimum product.)
18. Obtaining and analyzing consumer test results which were worse than predicted.
19. Generation of alternatives for the project in view of the outcome of the consumer test.
20. Reexamination of criteria.
21. Optimizing product/process variables.
22. Specifying the process details for the test market production and trimming costs to fit within the appropriation. (The path from "h" to 22 is shown as a solid line, because the intervening steps were obviously taken even though they were not specified as activities, e.g., each item of cost was questioned and trimmed if not justified.)
23. Meeting specific requirements for the test market plant.
24. Making product and placing next consumer test.

List of the Information Inputs for Figure 4

a. Management input—desire to capitalize on a new technology and desire to be of service to society.
b. Consumer input—a generally recognized, unmet consumer need.
c. Technical input—temporary transfer in of a scientist familiar with the new technology.
d. Marketing input—desired product target.
e. Economic input—cost estimate for test market plant much higher than expected.
f. Management input—in view of the projected costs, the business opportunity is seen as unattractive.
g. Marketing input—proposal for new product targets.
h. Management input—appropriation for test market (much lower than original estimate).
i. Management input—top management confirmation of overall market strategy and requirements.

it came into phase with the learning process of the rest of the team.

In still another instance, a group of technical information specialists found the model useful in suggesting ways they could increase their effectiveness in providing technical information to project teams. They realized that the information needs of project teams vary according to the stage of the learning process as shown in the section below.[8]

IMPLICATIONS FOR MANAGEMENT OF R&D

The Learning Model provides a basis for several kinds of action which can be taken by management to improve the R&D process.

Staffing decisions can be made in light of the Learning Model. The assignment of individuals with requisite skills in each of the stages of the learning process should result in improving that process. The balance of skills required is likely to shift over the course of a project. In the earliest cycles through the learning process (e.g., during concept and prototype development), skills in the Divergence and Assimilation stages are likely to be most critical. Later (e.g., when the design is fixed and engineering specifications are being prepared) skills in Convergence and Execution become most critical. Shifts in assignment of individuals during the project life may, in *some* instances, not only improve the progress of the project, but also permit individuals to have assignments which match their preferences and abilities.[9]

Organization policies and reward systems can be used to support an appropriate balance of learning activities. It is our observation (which is supported by research reported by Kolb[10]) that organizations and professional disciplines often develop values which favor activity in one learning stage over the others. When these values are out of balance with the needs of the organization the kinds of problems outlined in Figure 3 can result. Managers can help restore appropriate balance.

Stage	Activity	Information Needs
Divergence	Generation of alternatives Creativity	Specific alternatives Stimulation to the process of generating alternatives (e.g., information about Brain-storming)
	Problem/opportunity sensing	State of the art State of the world
Assimilation	Planning Formulating theory	Policy Planning methodology Strategy models
	Establishing criteria	Evaluation criteria
Convergence	Interpretation of data Narrowing down alternatives	Screening/selection techniques
	Design of experiments Decision making Evaluation of outcome	Experimental design Political science knowledge
Execution	Execution of plan Implementation of decision Goal setting	Feedback on results (Monitoring techniques) Information on need

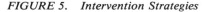

Concrete
Experience

Execution	Divergence
Critical path scheduling	Brainstorming
Goal-setting	Synectics
	Creative problem solving
	Browsing
	Literature
	Visiting
	General consultants

Active Experimentation — Reflective Observation

Convergence	Assimilation
Decision trees	Thinking
Design of experiments	Manipulating data
Calculations	Extracting grounded theory
Methods consultants	Game theory
Experimenting	Management information
	"Expert" consultants

Abstract
Conceptualization

FIGURE 5.   Intervention Strategies

Specific problems can be identified and strategies for remedial action suggested by reference to the Learning Model. The most common specific problems, we expect, will arise when an individual or team is either stuck in or deficient in a learning stage. Some of the techniques which can be used in these situations are shown in Figure 5.

IMPLICATIONS BEYOND R&D ORGANIZATIONS

We believe the experience of the technical information specialists can be generalized to many other support organizations. For example, management science groups are sometimes seen as only helpful in decision making (Convergence), and even then only when risks can be quantified and defined.[11] Another view suggests that management science can provide benefits much more broadly.[12] We believe that the ability of management scientists to provide these benefits is dependent upon their sensitivity to the stage of the learning cycle of the organization (or individual) they are supporting. The table below relates Hammond's categories of benefits to the corresponding stages of the Learning Model.

Potential Benefits of Management Science*	Corresponding Stage of the Learning Model
1. Provides a structure to a situation which is initially relatively unstructured to the manager.	Assimilation
2. Extends the decision maker's information processing ability.	Divergence
3. Facilitates concept formation.	Assimilation
4. Provides cues to the decision maker.	Assimilation/Convergence
5. Stimulates the collection, organization and utilization of data which might not otherwise be collected.	Divergence
6. Frees from mental set.	Divergence/Assimilation

*The list of benefits is taken directly from Hammond (4), pp. 9–11.

While our research and applications have been almost entirely within R&D systems, we believe the Learning Model has parallel applications in other kinds of systems. The importance of the Model to an organization will be proportionate to the importance of production of new knowledge as an organizational goal. To the extent that technical, social and political turbulence is forcing even the most stable organizations and institutions to adopt a learning orientation if they are to survive, we expect the Learning Model to be increasingly useful.[13]

NOTES

1. This paper is no exception. The relatively orderly description of our research bears little resemblance to the actual cycling and recycling, false starts, definition and redefinition of hypotheses and objectives which occurred. However, Harvard Business School Professor Charles J. Christenson has described God as "using an inelegant method to design the world but cleaning up His approach in the published version." At least we are in good company.
2. See Kolb (1973).
3. See Kolb (1973), p. 2.
4. See Glaser and Strauss (1967).
5. We have chosen the term "Execution" rather than "Accommodation," the more precise term used by Kolb, as the label for this stage of the Learning Model. We found that the term "Accommodation" is frequently misunderstood because of its connotations of passivity and compromise.
6. The scoring system was quite complex and specific to the particular reports which were being evaluated. The system consisted essentially of assigning each sentence to a stage of the Learning Model, and totaling the number of sentences in each stage. We are grateful to Sherry Ewald and Paula Miller for their efforts in the sometimes arduous task of scoring the documents.
7. Kolb (1971) describes the development of the Learning Style Inventory, which has been published in Kolb, Rubin, and McIntyre (1974).
8. Thomas J. Allen (private communications) has suggested that the information needs of R&D projects vary with the kind of project (e.g., research, service, engineering) and with the maturity of the project.
9. We caution against the assumption that the learning preferences of individuals are fixed. It has been our observation that for many individuals learning style preference is highly situational.
10. See Kolb (1973).
11. For example, see Arcand (1975).
12. For example, see Hammond (1974).
13. For example, see Bennis and Slater (1968), Schon (1971), and the discussion of the "adaptive-coping cycle" appearing in Schein (1965).

REFERENCES

Arcand, C. G., "Bureaucratic Innovation: The Failure of Rationality." *Chemtech,* 1975, pp. 710–714.

Bennis, W. G., and Slater, P. E. *The Temporary Society,* New York: Harper & Row, 1968.

Glaser, B. G., and Strauss, A. L. *The Discovery of Grounded Theory: Stategies for Qualitative Research.* Chicago: Aldine Publishing Company, 1967.

Hammond, J. S. "The Roles of the Manager and Management Scientist in Successful Implementation." *Sloan Management Review,* Winter 1974, pp. 1–24.

Kolb, D. A. "Individual Learning Styles and the Learning Process." Sloan School Working Paper 535–71. Cambridge, Mass.: Massachusetts Institute of Technology, 1971.

Kolb, D. A. "On Management and the Learning Process." Sloan School Working Paper 652–73. Cambridge, Mass.: Massachusetts Institute of Technology, 1973.

Kolb, D. A.; Rubin, I. M.; and McIntyre, J. M. *Organization Psychology: An Experiential Approach,* 2nd ed. Englewood Cliffs, N.J.: Prentice-Hall, 1974, pp. 23, 25.

Schein, E. H. *Organizational Psychology,* Englewood Cliffs, N.J.: Prentice-Hall, 1965.

Schon, D. A. *Beyond the Stable State,* New York: Random House, 1971.

6

THE ROLE OF THE GROUP AND THE ORGANIZATION

Group Decision Making

Linda Jewell

Joseph Reitz

One of the characteristics of modern organizations of all types is an increasing use of groups for a wide variety of decision-making activities. Planning, forecasting, setting policy, and solving problems are all activities traditionally delegated to individuals in organizations. Now they turn up as the tasks confronting research teams, commissions, task forces, advisory groups, and committees of different structures, sizes, and purposes. Yet it is almost certain that these groups will take longer to deal with these problems than would an individual. And the costs of time guarantee that group decisions will almost certainly cost more than individual decisions. The question may well be asked: Why the increasing trend toward group decision making in organizations? The answer lies in expectations about the quality and acceptance of group decisions.

Reprinted with permission from L. Jewell and J. Reitz, *Group Effectiveness in Organizations,* Scott Foresman, 1981, pp. 80–99.

GROUP VERSUS INDIVIDUAL DECISIONS: QUALITY

We will define a decision-making group as a collection of individuals interacting on a face-to-face basis to solve a problem. Most organizations expect that such groups will make better—more creative, more accurate, or more effective—decisions than individuals. This appears to be common sense. The old saying, "two heads are better than one," states that there should be more information and experience available for a problem when there are more people to work on the problem. Even if one person knows much more about it than anyone else, the limited but unique knowledge of others could serve to fill in some critical gaps. In addition, we have all observed that individuals get into ruts in their thinking. They tend to persist in one approach. By so doing, they fail entirely to see another approach that might solve the problem faster or in a simpler or more efficient manner. While the same tendency holds for individuals in a group, the ruts in which different group members are stuck are likely to be different. Thus a number of approaches to the problem tend to appear relatively quickly.

The greater diversity of information, experience, and approaches to be found in a group seem all the more important as the problems facing organizations become ever more complex. Not only are the organizations themselves becoming larger and more complex, but also issues which could once be ignored must now be factored into the decision-making process. Decision makers must now routinely consider environmental impact, fair employment practices, international implications, and social welfare issues. Clearly, despite the increased costs of so doing, there are some good reasons for organizations to turn problems over to groups. This is particularly true of problems with important consequences.

Group decision making is one aspect of group behavior that has been heavily researched. The first conclusion one can draw from this research is that group decisions are different from the decisions made by the same persons acting as individuals. The "risky-shift" (Stoner, 1961) provides an illustration of the point.

The term *risky-shift* comes from a line of research begun in the early 1960's. Contrary to conventional wisdom, this research found that groups tended to choose riskier solutions than individuals when confronting problems involving uncertainty (Stoner, 1961). The kinds of problems used by Stoner involved questions as to the odds for success a problem solver would require before selecting a high payoff, but uncertain, course of action over a safe, but low payoff, course. Findings showed that when the problem solver was an individual, he or she might require the odds for success to be as high as 50–50. Groups, on the other hand, might select the high payoff alternative when the odds for success were as low as 2 out of 10.

The risky-shift research was exciting because it contradicted the conventional wisdom that groups generally curtail individual tendencies to

take excessive risk. Findings were replicated in a variety of settings and cultures (Cartwright, 1973). The cause of the risky-shift was variously attributed to the leadership in a group, diffusion of responsibility, social comparison, familiarization, extremism, and pluralistic ignorance.[1]

Subsequent risky-shift research incorporated a wider range of problems than those employed by Stoner and results were not so consistent with the idea that groups are always prepared to take more risk than individuals. Problems that gave careful attention to societal values found certain types of decisions upon which groups were consistently less risky than individuals (Stoner, 1968; Marquis & Reitz, 1969). In accordance with these and other findings, the risky-shift became known by the broader label of "group-induced shift" (Pruitt, 1971).

Nature of the Problem

The research which has come to be called the group-induced shift research may be thought of as a special case of the general principle that, following group discussion, individuals tend to make decisions which are different from those they made, or would make, as individuals. Group decisions, as we shall see, may sometimes be better, sometimes be worse, but are almost always different from individual decisions. A primary consideration, as illustrated by the group-induced shift research, is the kind of problem about which a decision must be made. Fifty years of research in problem solving have led to certain well-supported conclusions about the kinds of problems on which groups may be expected to be superior decision makers to individuals and the kind of problems on which they may not.

Multiple-Part Problems. Problems for which groups tend to produce decisions consistently evaluated as better than those of even the best individual in a group have two characteristics: (1) they have multiple parts and (2) these parts are susceptible to division of labor. Selecting a new route for a school bus, for example, may require knowledge about population distribution, traffic flow patterns, safety hazards, street layouts, local politics, state regulations, cost of operation, and a host of other facts that no one individual is likely to possess or have the time to acquire. It is, in fact, not necessary that each individual have all of this information in order to solve the problem. In this situation, a group can generate a satisfactory solution to the problem by putting together or pooling information not commonly held or by combining partial solutions.

Estimation Problems. On certain others kinds of problems, group decisions tend to be above the average performance of individual members[2] but not as good as the decision of the best member of the group. Such problems generally have only a few steps and have judgments or solutions that can be verified in some way by anyone in possession of the original facts of the problem. Estimating the number of persons who would use a branch post office on a particular site, for example, is a type of problem that is not so complex as to call for more information and skills than one person can be expected to possess. Access to information about the population of the area combined with general information as to the percentage of the population in any area that uses a branch office will probably yield a sufficiently accurate estimate. Unless it is impossible, for some reason, to identify an experienced, competent individual to make decisions that fall into this category, it would seem a waste of resources to utilize a decision-making group.

Multiple-Stage Problems. We have stated that groups have been found to produce higher quality solutions than individuals to problems that have multiple parts and allow for division of labor and pooling of the results of this labor. On problems requiring few steps and having verifiable solutions, groups still tend to have the advantage, but only over the average individual problem solver. Problems that violate all of these conditions are problems whose solutions "re-

quire thinking through a series of interrelated steps or stages, analyzing a number of rules at each point, and always keeping in mind conclusions reached at earlier points" (Kelley & Thibaut, 1969, p. 69–70). Such problems might be called multiple-stage problems. They are not amenable to division of labor and the large number of possible lines of reasoning any individual may follow in confronting such a problem makes it difficult to demonstrate the correctness of any given solution. In most organizations long-range planning and major policy decisions fall into this category. On such problems it appears that members of decision-making groups interfere with one another more than they assist one another.

Despite the fact that multiple-stage problems do not lend themselves to effective group decision making, their complexity usually dictates the necessity for inputs from many sources. Not uncommonly these inputs come from a group of specialists and representatives who serve an *advisory function* for the decision maker. The group provides input, alternatives, and suggestions, perhaps even tentative solutions, but a single individual makes the decision.

The advisory group approach to multiple-stage problems described above sounds simpler than it is. A major problem in using such groups effectively is avoiding too much involvement by the leader or ultimate decision maker in early stages of the group interaction, lest that individual completely dominate the group. As Janis (1972) points out, the mere presence of the leader in early stages inclines the group to work toward his or her preferred solution. Janis cites the Bay of Pigs disaster in 1962 as largely resulting from President Kennedy's powerful presence among his advisory group of cabinet officers, C.I.A. officials, and Joint Chiefs of Staff. These advisors sensed that Kennedy's desire to get tough with the Communists meshed with their own invasion plans for Cuba and led them to fail to question their own assumptions. Six major miscalculations resulted in a military and political disaster for the United States. The Bay of Pigs would ap-

249

pear to be a good example of Maier's (1967) contention that a too-strong leader can adversely affect a groups decision processes by using his or her position to promote personal views and to suppress minority or conflicting views.

Do groups produce better solutions to problems than individuals? The answer developed to this point is that they may be expected to do so on certain types of problems. A first consideration, then, for the organization that wishes to make effective use of decision-making groups is to avoid presenting problems to groups that are better solved by individuals. However, even if the cards are stacked in favor of the group by limiting the problems to those on which group performance should be better, additional considerations remain.

Composition of the Group

It should be obvious that the kinds of individuals who make up a decision-making group are an important factor in the effectiveness of that group. A bunch of "goof offs" will probably not produce as good a decision as an individual, no matter what the problem. And groups with very competent, task-oriented members may be expected to produce better decisions than groups without such members. But the characteristics of the particular members of a group do not tell the whole story. Data from a 1960 study by Hoffman and Smith, for example, show that members of a group tend to adopt the decision-making behaviors of the other members. By a continuous mutual adaptation process, a group assumes its own unique problem-solving behaviors and consequently does not respond to problems exactly like any other group. That is, there appear to be individual differences among groups and these differences arise from dynamics within the group as well as from the characteristics of the individual members.

Heterogeneity-Homogeneity. Given the large number of individual characteristics that exist,

there are, of course, an infinite number of different groups that can exist. To examine the specific effects of even a small number of these combinations on the quality of group decisions is both impractical and of questionable value because any one combination may be said to be a unique event. For the organization that uses decision-making groups, however, there is some utility in giving attention to one particular global dimension of group composition—heterogeneity versus homogeneity.

A heterogeneous group is composed of individuals who have different levels or amounts of some trait or characteristic. Homogeneous groups consist of members similar on some trait or characteristic. Obviously, groups will be heterogeneous with respect to some traits and homogeneous with respect to others. A group of female employees chosen at random from the ranks of a large insurance company, for example, will be homogeneous with respect to sex, but heterogeneous with respect to intellectual ability, work experience, and personality characteristics.

The group decision-making literature offers a substantial number of studies that examine the effects of group heterogeneity or homogeneity of some trait on the quality of the solution to a problem developed by a group. Ability, sex, creative potential, general temperament, and a host of specific personality variables have been examined (Sorenson, 1973; Hall, 1975; Laughlin & Bitz, 1975). The implications of these studies are clear. Heterogeneous, or mixed, groups tend to outperform homogeneous groups whatever the trait being studied. In setting up a group to deal with a problem, then, this suggests bringing together competent individuals with a range of experience, backgrounds, perspectives, and temperaments. This suggestion is, of course, entirely consistent with the basic premise that the primary source of the potential advantages of decision-making groups lies in individual differences.

Size. The size of the group can have a number of important implications for decision making.

Clearly, as the size of the group increases, communication becomes more difficult (see, for example, (O'dell, 1968). Opportunities for each member to participate decrease and chances that the discussion will be dominated by a few individuals increase (see Bales & Borgatta, 1955; Hackman & Vidmar, 1970). Chances that cliques or subfactions with different goals will form, especially if there is an even number of group members, also increase as the size of the group increases. As a rule of thumb, it is probably most effective to form decision-making groups of three, five, or seven members depending upon the needs of the situation.

At this point it might be tempting to conclude that if we bring together a small, mixed group of bright individuals and present them with a multiple part problem amenable to division of labor, the decision that the group reaches will certainly be superior to that which any one member might have developed alone. While the group decision certainly might be superior, there are various group processes that can operate to interfere with or block the realization of this potential.

Group Dynamics

As defined earlier a decision-making group is a collection of individuals interacting on a face-to-face basis to solve a problem. The decisions or solutions of these groups of problems are the result of group discussion as to the problem issues, alternatives, and probable outcomes of proposed solutions. Communication processes, therefore, are the means by which a group develops a solution to a problem. If group resources are to be utilized effectively to realize the superior decision-making potential of the group, it is essential that all members having information, perspectives, values, or strategies relevant to the problem have the opportunity to communicate them.

Cooperation. A first condition necessary for varied viewpoints to be heard and considered in the decision-making process is that the group be cooperatively organized. A longtime researcher in group problem solving, Richard Hoffman, makes the basic point that "another contributor to ineffective problem solving is the failure to organize or plan the attack on the problem" (1965, p. 100). In order to "organize or plan an attack," it is necessary that group members be agreed on what is being attacked—that is, that they have a common goal. This cooperative, as opposed to competitive, organization facilitates (but does not guarantee) the communication necessary to the effective use of group resources.

In real life, of course, there are few, if any purely cooperative or competitive situations. In a decision-making group, members have needs and goals relative to their relationships with other group members as well as a stake in the common goal. Unfortunately, the requirements of these two sets of goals may conflict. In this case there exists what Schelling (1960) describes as a *mixed motive situation*. A group member may withhold a valuable insight into a problem, for example, because of a need to appear intelligent and competent in the eyes of the other group members. The risk that the contribution will be laughed at or ignored may be too great.

Status. The nature and strength of the needs which can put individual members of a decision-making group into a mixed motive situation may be expected to vary considerably from one individual and one situation to the next. However, at least one characteristic of many groups—the presence of status differences among the members—has been found to have such consistent effects upon communication patterns that it might be called an almost universal mixed-motive generator.

Status refers to the esteem given individuals position in a social system such as a country, community, organization, or group. High status may be achieved on the basis of individual accomplishment or it may be ascribed simply on the basis of some characteristic possessed by that

251

individual such as age, kinship, or wealth. When an organizational decision-making group is formed, some members may have ascribed status. The nephew of the boss is a familiar example. Other status differences will be based on past achievements such as the attainment of a high position in the company. As group members interact, differential achievement within the group itself may reinforce or weaken initial status differences or create new ones.

The influence of status on communication patterns in a group can be summarized briefly here by noting that the participation and influence of members in groups are directly related to the relative status of the members. People listen more to those with high status and give more credence to what they say. The implications of this line of research for group decision making are considerable. Status differences among members affect the sharing, processing, and evaluation of information. Through its influences on these variables, status differences can considerably affect the quality of the group's decision.

Leadership. Leaders, be they formal (appointed or elected) or informal (emergent) play a particularly critical role in a group. As observed by Maier (1967), a leaders contributions do not receive the same treatment as those of a member of a group. "Whether he likes it or not, his position is different" (p. 247). That is, leadership, by definition, implies status differences.

Because it is influence, the impact of leadership on the quality group decisions is clear. Numerous studies have demonstrated that, unless a group leader takes steps to separate the "discussion leading" function from the functions of contributing and evaluating ideas, the group solution will more likely reflect the preferred solution of the leader than of the group as a whole. The critical steps to be taken include encouraging the free expression of ideas, insisting that minority viewpoints be heard, and discouraging the premature evaluation of ideas (Hoffman, 1965; Janis, 1972; Van de Ven, 1974).

To recapitulate, it has been stated that groups achieve solutions to problems by means of communication. Open communication processes that increase the likelihood that a group will utilize its superior resources are facilitated by cooperative group organization. But even within cooperative groups, distortions in communications are likely to occur as a result of the presence of status differences. The other side of the problem is that, even in group situations where members might feel no status constraints against open communication, the free exchange of ideas, evaluation of suggestions, and consideration of outcomes and alternatives relative to a problem may be considerably hampered by other forces.

Pressures toward Uniformity in Groups.   If we think back on task groups of which we have been members, most of us can recall instances in which the task facing the group was either subtly or explicitly redefined from that of finding the right or best solution to that of simply finding a solution with which everyone would agree. "Bill doesn't like Applicant A, and Fred feels that B doesn't have enough experience, and Susan doesn't think C will fit in. No one seems to have any strong feelings about D one way or the other, so let's offer D the job."

The source of pressure toward uniformity described above may be expected to exert more influence upon the nature of the final solution to a problem than upon the initial communication of ideas about the problem. (Although these will occur automatically as disagreements about some points reduce the time available for raising others). It often becomes a bargaining situation with the final group decision depending upon the balance of power and the relative successes of influence attempts within the group. Clearly there exists here yet another pitfall for effective group decision making. Maier states the problem. "In reaching consensus or agreement, some members of a group must change. If persons with the most (objectively) constructive views are induced to change, the end-product suffers" (1967, p. 243).

Of course, if persons with less constructive views change, the group decision will be improved, or, as noted earlier, the leader may simply carry the day.

The pressures toward uniformity in decision-making groups have particular application to the case of juries. Juries are formal, initially leaderless, closed, noncohesive groups whose only structure is provided by the task: to unanimously agree on the guilt or innocence of the defendant.

Recent research on juries as decision-making groups has produced important findings. Consistent with research on the other decision-making groups, juries make different decisions from those made by individuals, and these decisions are predictably different. The group-induced shift research, for example, indicated that groups make decisions that are more consistent with culturally held values than do individuals (Stoner, 1968). In our society, sociologists tell us, we value individual freedom so much that we prefer to risk freeing a guilty felon than to risk convicting an innocent defendant. Therefore, we would expect juries to be more lenient in criminal cases than individuals.

A research study of 3600 cases by the University of Chicago Law School supported the expectation that juries would be more lenient than individuals. Comparisons in forty-two crime categories of the actual decisions make by juries with the decisions the judge would have rendered found that, in one case out of every five, the jury acquitted a defendant whom the judge would have convicted. In only three percent of the cases did the jury convict a defendant whom the judge would have acquitted. In three out of every four cases, both judge and jury agreed on the verdict (Kalven & Zeisel, 1966).

Defense lawyers make use of the jury research described in two ways. First, they are aware of the kinds of cases in which juries are most likely to be lenient; these include gambling, receiving stolen goods, drunken driving, and indecent exposure. Second, they are aware of certain background and personality characteristics which predict that a juror will likely be biased toward or away from conviction or will be resistant to group pressures. A single holdout against a group's expert power can sometimes reverse the opinion of the group. A single determined juror can sometimes reverse the decision to convict, or at worse, get a hung jury (no verdict).

Juries are pressured to reach unanimity by the definition of their task. But the necessity for reaching an agreed-upon solution is not the only source of pressure that can foster unanimity at the expense of quality.

Group Cohesiveness. Group cohesiveness refers to the extent to which members of a group are attracted to each other and to the group. There are many sources of this attraction, but whatever its source, group cohesiveness is a powerful force for unanimity within groups. Maintenance of the group is simply easier when group members agree. Threats to the group from outside are reduced when the group can present a united front.

The relationship between effective group decision making and pressures for unanimity arising from a desire to keep the group together is complex. Some level of cohesiveness is necessary for a group to tackle a problem at all. If, for example, five individuals from five different departments within an organization are pressed into service as a Founders's Day Committee, the Founder's Day program may never get off the ground. But more cohesiveness is not necessarily better. Just as task groups may redefine (or have it redefined for them) problem solving to be reaching agreement rather than making the best possible decision, so members of highly cohesive groups may redefine it as preserving interpersonal relations and group image. The Bay of Pigs decision described earlier is an example of the negative effects of strong in-group pressures on the quality of a group decision. Janis (1972) coined the term *Groupthink* to describe this phenomenon which is marked by "deterioration of mental efficiency, reality testing, and moral

253

judgement'' (1972, p. 9) in the interests of the group solidarity.

Pressures toward uniformity arising from group cohesiveness need not reach the extremes described by Janis to affect the communication processes by which groups make decisions. Studies have found that there is more communication in groups with higher cohesiveness (Lott & Lott, 1961; Mickelson & Campbell, 1975) and that this communication is more positive than that occurring in less cohesive groups (Back, 1951; Shaw & Shaw, 1962).

It would seem that the increased level of generally positive communication in cohesive groups would facilitate the free expression of ideas necessary to obtaining the facts and evaluating alternatives relative to a problem. To a certain extent this is true. Members or cohesive groups do feel freer to express opinions, especially unpopular opinions, than members of less cohesive groups (Kiesler & Corbin, 1965) but only up to a point. Studies consistently suggest that, once cohesive groups begin to achieve a certain degree of likemindedness, additional information important to the best solution of the problem is likely to be rejected if it is inconsistent with the developing consensus (Hoffman & Maier, 1966). Thus the quality of the end product of group decision-making processes in cohesive groups can vary considerably depending upon the point in time at which group opinion becomes solidified.

GROUP VERSUS INDIVIDUAL DECISIONS: ACCEPTANCE

Many organizational problems require solutions that depend upon the support of others to be effective. The best solution in the world is useless if it is not accepted by those who must implement it. Economists know, for example, that increased saving and reduced spending alleviate inflationary pressures in the long run. The implementa-

tion of this solution, however, depends upon millions of individuals. In the short run, these individuals lose when inflation rates exceed the interest rates on their savings accounts. So they spend rather than save and the ''known solution'' to the problem of inflation is useless.

Recognition of the importance of support for problem solutions provides yet another reason for the increased use of organizational decision-making groups. Insofar as group decision making permits individual participation and influence, it should follow that more individual members are likely to accept decisions when a group develops a solution to a problem than when an individual does so. Even if some or all of those who must implement the solution are not actually part of the group, we would expect increased confidence in the validity of the decision. This confidence comes from the knowledge that it was made by a more than one person and should lead to greater acceptance of the decision.

Attitudes and Behavior

The acceptability argument for using decision-making groups is an argument based upon the concept of attitude. Attitudes are said to have three components—affective (feeling), cognitive (thinking), and behavioral (acting). If a group, rather than an individual, makes a decision, the acceptability argument states that the affective component of individual member's attitudes toward that decision will be positive—feelings of satisfaction with having been part of the process. Likewise, the cognitive component should be favorable—increased confidence and understanding of the decision. Since the three components of an attitude are defined as consistent, the favorable affective and cognitive components of attitudes toward the decision should be followed by behaviors that facilitate implementation of the solution. The argument is less forceful in the case of groups that make decisions for other individuals to implement, but is still based on the general idea that people will be more positive about decisions made by groups than they will be about decisions made by unilateral action.

Satisfaction with Decision. Research generally supports the idea that those who participate in a group decision making are more satisfied with the decision than when a decision is handed down by one individual (Coch & French, 1948; Carey, 1972; White & Ruh, 1973). The extent to which this satisfaction leads to behaviors that are helpful in implementing the solutions is another matter. Reviews of the appropriate literature make it clear that there is no one-to-one correspondence between expressed attitudes and subsequent behavior (Wicker, 1969, 1971; Brigham, 1971). Two studies in which the problem to be solved—absenteeism—was the same are illustrative.

Powell and Schlacter (1971) studied the relationship between degree of participation in decision making about the problem of absenteeism and change in level of absenteeism. They found that employees who participated in groups that developed solutions to the problem expressed greater satisfaction with the solution than did employees who simply received the solution passed down by management. But the subsequent rate of absenteeism for the two groups was the same. On the other hand, Bragg and Andrews (1973) found that participation in decision making was associated with a decrease in absenteeism and an increase in productivity as well as with an increase in reported satisfaction.

Implementation of Decision. Research sometimes supports and sometimes does not support a link between participation in decision making and effective implementation of the decision. This inconsistency probably reflects considerable variation in the kinds of decision-making processes used and in individuals' private opinions as to the quality of the final decision. More basically, it probably also provides evidence for a

fact often overlooked: how he or she feels about the decision making process and the quality of the resultant decision is only one of many factors influencing subsequent behavior of the group member. One individual may believe the problem solution was not very good. Yet this person may be active in implementing the decision because his or her promotion depends upon it. Another person may feel satisfied with the group interaction and confident about the quality of the decision, but fail to do anything about implementation. The problem may simply have low priority.

With respect to the acceptability argument for using groups rather than individuals to make decisions, it must be concluded that individual differences and situational factors make definitive statements about more effective implementation of group-generated decisions impossible. If satisfaction is an issue, however, the argument that group decisions are preferred seems to have some validity.

Responsibility for Decision. Finally, of course, it must be noted that there is another face to acceptability in decision-making groups. This pertains, not to acceptance of the content of the decision, but to acceptance of responsibility for making the decision. Discussion of issues, relevant values, and alternatives can allow each member of a group to feel somewhat less responsible for a decision than if he of she were required to make the decision alone. For certain kinds of decisions, particularly those where a mistake can have serious negative consequences, this *diffusion of responsibility* which is offered by a group may be necessary if the decision is to be made at all. There may be no single individual willing to carry the full weight of responsibility and accountability for his or her judgment. Or it simply may be seen as a more judicious strategy to divide the responsibility for controversial decisions among several individuals, again perhaps because there will be more general confidence in this decision than if it were made by one person.

IMPROVING THE EFFECTIVENESS OF GROUP DECISION MAKING

Groups do have, as we have seen, many potential advantages over individuals as problem solvers or decision makers. Two suggestions for helping to realize this potential have already been made. These suggestion had to do with the selection of members for the group and the choice of the problem presented to the group. There remains, however, the problem of dealing with the various other stumbling blocks to the kinds of communication which will allow the group to effectively utilize these resources.

Interacting Groups

First, a cooperative rather than a competitive group organization is usually more productive in decision-making groups. While it is not always possible to identify them in advance, it may often be possible to avoid combinations of problems and decision-making group memberships that lead to win-lose situations. For example, union-management teams sit down to solve the problem of the next contract. The decision that comes out of this process is unlikely to be the best solution to the particular needs of either group or equally acceptable to both groups. What one side wins, the other loses. Variations in this process occur in many other organizational contexts. Where there is a choice, a situation in which there is a group goal that is larger and more important than individual goals will probably increase the effectiveness of the group. In instances where any decision is very clearly going to be better for some members of the group than for others, it may be better to use the group, or its individual members, as advisors rather than as decision makers.

Second, some degree of group cohesiveness is necessary for effective decision making, but the issue of cohesiveness is tricky when it comes to organizational control. Come decision-making groups are ad hoc; that is they are especially formed to deal with some problem such as the choice of a new plant site. Group cohesiveness takes some time to develop. When an ad hoc group is to be formed, some discretion in selecting members will at least avoid the more obvious barriers to the development of cohesion. It is probably better, for example, not to press individuals into group service against their wills or make persons known to have personality clashes or long-term feuds part of the same group. The opposite side of the coin is to avoid selecting members known to be close friends or individuals who are members of other social or work groups. Clique formation or previously-established camaraderie can also reduce the effectiveness of ad hoc decision-making groups.

The discretion described above may, of course, result in not being able to use certain individuals who would seem to be obvious choices given their knowledge and experience. Further, this strategy requires information that is not always available to those who must set up decision-making groups. Clearly, there are no hard and fast rules here—only guidelines.

Some decision-making groups are long-term or *traditioned,* such as an executive committee, the President's Cabinet (U.S.), or the Joint Chiefs of Staff (U.S.). It is possible, though perhaps unlikely, that cohesiveness has not developed in these groups. If it has not, problems will usually have become obvious and some administrative action such as disbanding the group or changing its membership will already have been taken.

A more likely situation with traditioned groups is that such a group has become too cohesive for purposes of meeting organizational goals. Most long-term decision-making groups have norms, roles, and strategies that are well fixed. Such groups may work along quite effectively. The organization's only real task is to watch for danger signals—clearly superficial treatments of problems; complaints from outsiders about the nature, quality, or feasibility of the decisions; extremely defensive behavior on the part of the group members toward any questions about their activities; or any other signs that the group is more concerned with itself than with its tasks. Should these occur with any regularity, the group has probably outlived its usefulness.

To this point, most of the suggestions for improving the decision making effectiveness of groups are related directly or indirectly to either the task or the composition of the group. There are, however, certain interventions or changes in the decision-making process itself that may prove useful in overcoming certain communication problems.

For the group that redefines its task as simply coming up with some noncontroversial decision, one strategy is to require either interim or final reports in which the reasons for *rejected* alternatives are set forth. In cases where the group has simply gotten a bit careless, such a policy may serve to redirect attention during the decision-making process to the task of reaching a good decision. It also introduces an element of accountability into the process for those groups that may have more deliberately changed the nature of their activities.

The requirement of some form of reporting on group activities is a simple intervention into any decision-making group process. There are really no changes, other than the recording of discussions in some fashion, which the group need make. There are other strategies, however, in which there is intervention directly into the rules of the group discussion.

Alternatives to Interacting Groups

Brainstorming. For the group whose task is to generate imaginative and creative solutions to problems, a Madison Avenue advertising executive developed the process known as brainstorming (Osborn, 1957). The assumption was that group discussion would enhance creative output. A series of rules are the heart of the process, the intent of which is to promote idea generation while avoiding certain of the inhibitory effects of face-to-face groups:

1. Members are encouraged to come up with extreme or outlandish ideas. No idea is too ridiculous.
2. Members are encouraged to use or build upon other's ideas. All ideas generated belong to the group, not to a single individual.
3. Criticism is forbidden. The purpose is to generate ideas, not to evaluate them.

The last rule is particularly important. Stopping to criticize any or all ideas is detrimental to the freewheeling, building creative process that Osborn envisioned.

Despite its popularity and widespread use in advertising and some related fields, two major problems with brainstorming have emerged. First, because there is no evaluation or ranking of ideas, the group lacks a sense of closure on the problem-solving process and members are often dissatisfied. More importantly, research indicates that brainstorming inhibits the creative process, rather than enhancing it (see Bouchard, 1971 for a review of this research). For example, four men working as individuals have consistently produced more unique ideas than four-man brainstorming groups on a variety of problems (Taylor, Berry, & Block, 1958). Apparently the process fails to counteract all the inhibitory characteristics of face-to-face groups discussed earlier.

Delphi Technique. For the group whose task is to confront novel or unusual problems, researchers at the Rand Corporation developed a process aimed at providing members with each others ideas and evaluative feedback while avoiding the inefficiency and inhibitions characteristic of face-to-face groups. In the Delphi method (Dalkey, Rourke, Lewis & Snyder, 1972) it is unnecessary for members ever to meet face-to-face. Instead, the following steps are taken:

1. Each individual member independently and anonymously writes down comments, suggestions, and solutions to the problem confronting the group.
2. All comments are sent to a central location, where they are compiled and reproduced.
3. Each member is sent the written comments of all other members.
4. Each member provides feedback on the others comments, writes down new ideas stimulated by their comments, and forwards these to the central location.
5. Steps 3 and 4 are repeated as often as necessary until consensus is reached (Dalkey & Helmer, 1963).

Obviously the Delphi technique removes the usual group restraints on communication and allows for the full experience, expertise, and critical abilities of the participants to be brought to bear on the problem at hand. It also eliminates the costs of bringing the group together. The technique, however, is time consuming and there is a substantial expenditure of resources involved in carrying out steps 3 and 4 to consensus. Finally, of course, the nature of the process takes it largely out of the control of the organization. Members of the group may procrastinate, get off on tangents that are irrelevant, or come up with a decision that goes outside organizational constraints.

Nominal Group Technique.   Brainstorming and the Delphi technique are modifications of the usual interacting group decision process that have somewhat limited potential. Delbecq, Van de Ven, and Gustafson (1975) describe a technique that would seem to have wider application in that it is basically a control process which can be imposed on any group. In contrast with the typical free-ranging discussion process or with British Parliamentary Procedures, the Nominal Group Technique (NGT) is a structured process specifically designed to balance member participation and to standardize the aggregation of group judgment. The process of decision making in NGT is as follows:

1. The group meets face-to-face, but each member is given the problem in writing and silently and independently writes down ideas on the problem.
2. Each member in turn verbally presents one idea to the group. There is no discussion until all ideas are exhausted.
3. The group discusses ideas, both to clarify and elaborate on them, and to provide evaluation.
4. Each individual independently and anonymously ranks the ideas.
5. The group decision is determined to be the idea with the highest aggregate ranking.

The Nominal technique was designed to incorporate features of both Brainstorming and Delphi. In practice, it has emerged in various forms, and is still being developed and tested. A recent review of the literature (Sullivan, 1978) was optimistic about its promise as a decision-making tool. Of the ten studies reviewed, eight concluded that the Nominal technique was superior to other groups tested in terms of decision accuracy and/or quality.

Leader Training.   Brainstorming, the Delphi method, and the Nominal group technique are three alternatives to the usual approach to group decision making. In some situations, however, the actual structuring of the group process required by these alternatives may be impractical, inadvisable, or inappropriate. An alternative strategy is leader training. In a group, the role of leader, either formal or emergent, is unique. His or her contributions will not be ignored. Maier (1967) has suggested that group advantages will best be utilized when there is a leader who concentrates upon *process* rather than *product*. This suggests that committing some resources to training selected individuals in the skills of listening to understand rather than to evaluate or argue, taking responsibility for accurate communication between members of a group, being sensitive to unexpressed feelings, protecting minority viewpoints, keeping the discussion moving, and summarizing would have a substantial payoff in terms of increasing the effectiveness of decision-making groups. This individual could be the formal or the recognized informal leader of a group. Another possibility is to have one or more such individuals available to all decision-making groups in the special role of communication facilitator. Such facilitators should also be able to help ad hoc decision-making groups through the initial stages of group development and thereby enable these groups to move quickly to the task at hand.

making increases understanding of, satisfaction with, and acceptance of the decision. Understanding, satisfaction, and acceptance in turn are assumed to increase behaviors which will help implement the decision. Research finds that expressed satisfaction with decisions is indeed greater when they are made by groups, but this satisfaction does not necessarily lead to behaviors that facilitate implementation.

Suggestions for improving decision making in the typical interacting group include exercising discretion in group membership, introducing accountability into the process, and leader training. Alternatives to this mode of interaction include Brainstorming, the Delphi technique, and the Nominal group technique.

SUMMARY

Organizations are turning over to groups an increasing number and variety of problems which would formerly have been delegated to individuals. Behind this trend lie two assumptions, the first of which is that the greater resources available to a group will lead to a better decision. The validity of this assumption has been found to depend upon the nature of the task confronting the group, the composition of the group, and the interaction process within the group.

When a group is composed of a mixture of capable individuals confronting a multiple-part problem that lends itself to division of labor and communication within the group allows for utilization of the different opinions, approaches, and pieces of information possessed by the members, groups are likely to produce a better decision than any one member. Whether better or not, however, group decisions are usually different from individual decisions.

Within organizations, as anywhere else, a decision is only as good as its feasibility. The second assumption underlying the use of groups to make decisions is that participation in decision

NOTES

1. See the December, 1971 issue of the *Journal of Personality and Social Psychology* for a review of the literature in this area.
2. For research purposes, *average performance* is a real average—the sum of the individual group member solutions divided by the number of group members. Four individual guesses as to the population of a city, for example, would be added and divided by four to obtain the average group performance. This average is typically less accurate than the best individual guess. For practical purposes, average performance simply refers to the kind of solution most people would be expected to produce in a situation where they have general information and no special expertise.

REFERENCES

Back, K. W. Influence through social communication. *Journal of Abnormal and Social Psychology,* 1951, 46, 9–23.

Bales, R. F., & Borgatta, E. F. Size of group as a factor in the interaction profile. In E. F. Borgatta and R. F. Bales (Eds.), *Small Groups: Studies in*

Social Interaction. New York: Knopf, 1955, 495–512.

Bouchard, T. J. Whatever happened to brainstorming? *Journal of Creative Behavior,* 1971, 5, 182–189.

Bragg, J., & Andrews, I. Participative decision making: An experimental study in a hospital. *Journal of Applied Behavioral Science,* 1973, 9, 727–735.

Brigham, J. C. Ethnic stereotypes. *Psychological Bulletin,* 1971, 76, 15–38.

Carey, R. G. Correlates of satisfaction in the priesthood. *Administrative Science Quarterly,* 1972, 17, 185–195.

Cartwright, D. E. Determinants of scientific progress: The case of research on the risky shift. *American Psychologist,* 1973, 28,223–231.

Coch, L., & French, J. Overcoming resistance to change. *Human Relations,* 1948, 1, 512–532.

Dalkey, N. C., & Helmer, O. An experimental application of the Delphi Method to the use of experts. *Management Science,* 1963, 9, 458–467.

Dalkey, N. C., Rourke, D. L., Lewis, R., & Snyder, D. *Studies in the Quality of Life: Delphi and Decision Making.* Lexington, Ma: Heath, 1972.

Delbecq, A. L., Van de Ven, A. H., & Gustafson, D. H. *Group Techniques for Program Planning: A Guide to Nominal Group and Delphi Processes.* Glenview, Ill.: Scott-Foresman, 1976.

Hackman, J. R., & Vidmar, N. Effects of size and task type on group performance and member reactions. *Sociometry,* 1970, 33, 37–54.

Hall, R. Interpersonal compatibility and work group performance. *Journal of Applied Behavioral Science,* 1975, 11, 210–219.

Hoffman, L. R. Group problem solving. In L. Berkowitz (Ed.), *Advances in Experimental Social Psychology,* Vol. II. New York: Academic Press, 1965, 99–159.

Hoffman, L. R., & Maier, N. R. F. An experimental re-examination of the similarity-attraction hypothesis. *Journal of Personality and Social Psychology,* 1966, 3 (2), 145–152.

Hoffman, L. R. & Smith, C. G. Some factors affecting the behaviors of members of problem solving groups. *Sociometry,* 1960, 23, 273–291.

Janis, I. L. *Victims of Groupthink.* Atlanta: Houghton Miffin, 1972.

Kalven, H., Jr., & Ziesal, H. *The American Jury.* Boston: Little, Brown, 1966.

Kiesler, C. A. & Corbin, L. H. Commitment, attraction, and conformity. *Journal of Personality and Social Psychology,* 1965, 2, 890–895.

Kelley, H. H., & Thibaut, J. W. Group problem solving. In G. Lindzey and E. Aronson (Eds.), *Handbook of Social Psychology,* Vol. IV. Reading, Mass.: Addison-Wesley, 1969, 1–101.

Laughlin, P. R., & Bitz, D. S. Individual vs. dyadic performance on a disjunctive task as a function of initial ability level. *Journal of Personality and Social Psychology,* 1975, 31, 487–496.

Lott, A. J., & Lott, B. E. Group cohesiveness, communication level, and conformity. *Journal of Abnormal and Social Psychology,* 1961, 62, 408–412.

Maier, N. R. F. Assets and liabilities in group problem solving: The need for an integrative function. *Psychological Review,* 1967, 74, 239–249.

Marquis, D. G., & Reitz, H. J. Effects of uncertainty on risk taking in individual and group decisions. *Behavioral Science,* 1969, 4, 181–188.

Mickelson, J. S., & Campbell, J. H. Information behavior: Groups with varying levels of interpersonal acquaintance. *Organizational Behavior and Human Performance,* 1975, 13, 193–205.

O'Dell J. W. Group size and emotional interaction. *Journal of Personality and Social Psychology,* 1968, 8, 75–78.

Osborn, A. F. *Applied Imagination.* New York: Scribner's, 1957.

Powell, R. M., & Schlacter, J. L. Participative management: A panacea? *Academy of Management Journal,* 1971, 14, 165–173,

Pruitt, D. G. Choice shifts in group discussion: An introductory review. *Journal of Personality and Social Psychology,* 1971, 20, 339–360.

Schelling, T. C. *The Strategy of Conflict.* Cambridge, Mass.: Harvard University Press, 1960.

Shaw, M. E., & Shaw, L. M. Some effects of sociometric grouping upon learning in a second grade classroom. *Journal of Social Psychology,* 1962, 57, 453–458.

Sorenson, J. R. Group member traits, group process, and group performance. *Human Relations,* 1973, 26, 639–655.

Stoner, J. A. F. A comparison of individual and group discussions involving risk. Unpublished Master's Thesis. Massachusetts Institute of Technology, School of Industrial Management, 1961.

Stoner, J. A. F. Risky and cautious shifts in group decisions: The influence of widely held values. *Journal of Experimental Social Psychology,* 1968, 4, 442–459.

Sullivan, J. J. An experimental study of a method for improving the effectiveness of the nominal group technique. Unpublished Ph.D. Dissertation, University of Florida, College of Business, 1978.

Taylor, D. W., Berry, P. C., & Block, C. H. Does group participation when using brainstorming facilitate or inhibit creative thinking? *Administrative Science Quarterly,* 1958, 3, 23–47.

Van de Ven, A. H. *Group Decision Making and Effectiveness: An Experimental Study.* Kent, Ohio: Kent State University Press, 1974.

White, J., & Ruh, R. Effects of personal values on the relationship between participation and job attitudes. *Administrative Science Quarterly,* 1973, 18, 506–514.

Wicker, A. W. Attitudes vs. action: the relationship of verbal and overt behavioral responses to attitude objects. *Journal of Social Issues,* 1969, 35,41–78.

Wicker, A. W. Attitude behavior inconsistencies. *Journal of Personality and Social Psychology,* 1971, 19, 18–30.

Teams Which Excel

Patrick J. Sweeney

Douglas M. Allen

One can identify the traits of a research group that functions as a High Performing System. But what causes it to deteriorate?

In 1969, the U.S. Air Force Weapons Laboratory (AFWL) had a critical requirement to solve several major problems in laser technology, which did not appear to have any straightforward, simple solutions. The Air Force Aero Propulsion Laboratory was asked to provide technical assistance in solving these problems and did so by forming a ten-man group to work specifically on the laser problems. In the first year of operation, this group solved more than 12 major problems, won a major technical award, and developed a highly regarded reputation for excellence. This laser group is an example of what Peter Vaill, a behavioral scientist at George Washington University, has described as a "High Performing System" (HPS).

Although an HPS is rare, nearly everyone has been exposed to this type of organization at one time or another. According to Vaill an HPS exists when "a set of men utilizing some collection of technologies is performing, in relation to some predefined goals or standards, in a way which may be described as "excellent" of "outstanding" or "high performing". A method for analyzing the HPS is to observe several such systems and determine the similarity of operations within the systems. Vaill did this by basing his observations on HPSs such as athletic teams, performing arts groups, and the crew of a racing sailboat.[1] He listed 39 such observations which were subsequently summarized into 21 organizational traits in four basic groups by H. Shephard, of Shephard Associates.[2] This list is very important in the understanding of an HPS and is included below with explanations.

HPS ORGANIZATIONAL TRAITS

Behavior

1. *Language.* A private language develops for communication within the system and about its performance and problems. The language is highly functional for communicating system subtleties and complexities and much of it may be nonverbal. Outsiders may experience the language as unintelligible jargon.

2. *Task-Maintenance.* Completing tasks and feeling good are accomplished in unison. The activities involved in doing the work and maintaining team spirit appear to be identical or so intertwined as to be inseparable.

Reprinted with permission from P. Sweeney and D. Allen, "Teams Which Excel," *Research Management,* January-February 1984.

3. *Leadership.* Leaders tend to be viewed by members as experts in the system's basic activity. Generally the leaders are pacesetters and system role models. They tend to work well with others. When a person has been the leader of an HPS for an extended period, he or she becomes a quasi-mythical figure embodying in his person much of the meaning which the system has for its members. Vince Lombardi and Knute Rockne demonstrated this typical leadership characteristic.

4. *Experimentation.* Invariably there exists much tinkering, fiddling, experimenting with different roles, testing, rearranging, and trying new ways of operating the system.

5. *Execution.* Every HPS has its own equivalent of what in sports is termed execution, a set of actions that must be accomplished with great precision in relation to each other action. There must be a cleanness and exactness of performance and an accuracy of timing. Members take great pride in their ability to execute, and failures in execution are dismaying and very upsetting. To observers, members may seem to be taking themselves too seriously.

6. *Process Awareness.* Members of HPSs seem to have a heightened awareness of how things are going. They examine not only what they're doing but how they're doing it. Sometimes there are members in specialized roles who feed back constantly to the members exactly how the process is working.

7. *Fragility.* HPSs are in a way fragile and require some buffering from the external environment. Members also pay a lot of attention to arranging the environment in which they're going to work. Things have to be just right.

System/Environment Relations

8. *System-specific Performance Criteria.* Members often develop a unique set of performance standards for their own system, which may be quite different from the way outsiders evaluate their performance. When the system is not operating well by these special standards, members experience failure and mental anguish.

9. *On/Off.* To observers, HPS systems do not have clear on/off characteristics. The intertwining of task and maintenance (see 2 above) may be a factor of this perception by outsiders.

10. *Communication with Environment.* It is difficult for HPS members to explain to the outside world what they're doing or how they do it. They would rather just say, "Watch me." In fact, members are not highly motivated to tell the outside world, since the meaning of the activity to the member is in the doing, not the explaining.

11. *Environment's Reception of Output.* The HPS's output does not automatically please the environment, for the performance criteria that are important to members tend to be the unique internal criteria mentioned in 8, above.

12. *Boundry Management.* The system needs to be buffered against disturbing interferences. In some fields, agents or managers are employed to negotiate with the outside world.

13. *Interface Management.* When the outputs of several HPSs need to be coordinated, a special system of rules is often developed, which is implemented and policed by individuals or groups that do not have membership in any of the HPSs. In other instances, there is sufficient commitment to superordinate goals to support flexibility and adaptability among HPSs, so that the supersystem becomes an HPS itself.

14. *Rule-Book Modification.* There may be a set of rules or a policy manual, but actual HPS behavior rarely conforms very closely to these because of the tendency to experiment continuously to bring the system closer to some desired state. Performance breakthroughs occur in unplanned ways because members are constantly experimenting and making discoveries about the technology and their personal potentials Thus, with frequent and rapid changes, the rule book is always out of date.

15. *Equipment Modification.* What is true of the set of rules is also true of equipment. Members elaborate and modify it continuously to improve system operation.

16. *Organic Relationship with Equipment.*

263

HPS members experience the system's technology as an extension of themselves.

17. *Biology of Equipment.* Equipment in an HPS develops a perceived psychology and biology. Equipment becomes an animate part of the system and often is given a human or animal name.

Feelings

18. *Intense Commitment.* There is an extremely high level of commitment to the objectives of the activity and to each member's success in the activity. Members don't opt out of an HPS. They freely choose to stay with the people, the activity, and the HPS even when there are supposedly more attractive opportunities elsewhere.

19. *Consciousness of History.* There is a deep consciousness of the lore and history of the activity. New members are recruited with this pride in tradition in mind, looked over very carefully to see if they fit, and indoctrinated in the system's lore.

20. *Varieties of Motivation.* Simplistic theories of motivation just don't account for the behavior of HPS members. Esthetic motivation, the seeking of beauty in the operation of the system, or possibly thrill-seeking, the thrill of victory, may explain the extremely high motivation of HPS members.

21. *Rhythm.* HPSs exhibit a rhythm of operation which members experience and observers can often see. Until the rhythm is achieved members are dissatisfied and continue to strive. After rhythm is achieved an improved performance results with much less apparent effort.

NECESSARY CONDITIONS

With the HPS now defined, the next question is "why?" The theory which is presented here provides a dual answer to the question; that is, there are two conditions which must be present in parallel for an HPS to occur. In general, the first of these deals with the people who make up the organization and the second is concerned with the interfaces between the organization and its environment.

The first condition is composed of two parts—the people in the organization must be both mentally and physically competent to fulfill the basic duties required of them and the people must also be creative. For example, athletes must not only be intelligent enough to thoroughly understand the rules and strategies of the sport, but must also be in peak physical condition to produce an outstanding performance. In a research laboratory, the scientists must understand the basics of the technologies, the state-of-the-art and be able to operate the delicate and precise equipment necessary to perform experiments. These are obvious situations for an HPS. However, in a great majority of cases where these conditions exist, the organization still does not even approach the levels of performance which would qualify it as an HPS.

The second part of this first HPS condition concerns the creativity of the decision makers in the organization. Creativity must exist at the critical level in the organization, where decisions directly affect organization performance. This is at the lowest decision making level. This part of the condition is based upon a comparison of the HPS observations with research upon creative people and the similarities between the two. In fact, the HPS observations mentioned earlier which do not exhibit these similarities (for example, Leadership and Boundary Management) deal with the group only as opposed to the people in the group. The aspect of this theory which deals with creativity benefits as a function of the hierarchy of decision makers in an organization was originally primarily intuitive, but has been substantiated by observation. Returning to the examples of the sports team and the research laboratory, it is evident that creativity has the most benefits at the coaching (or management) level in sports, in which the team strategies are developed, but it has more benefits to the scientists (or "working level") in the research lab. In each case, this is the lowest level of decision making.

Support of this concept was noted in a table developed by John Morse and Jay Lorsch in 1970 which compares the characteristics of a manufacturing and a scientific organization.[3] Both were "high-performing organizations." Their table shows that the freedom to be creative was found only in the management levels in the high performing manufacturing plant, in which those below the management level have little decision making authority. It was noted, however, that the scientific organization appears to allow creativity at all levels.

It is again evident that the above conditions are not complete. There are examples of cases in which these conditions were met and yet an HPS did not occur. Moreover, there are also examples of HPSs which, after a while, ceased to be an HPS although no personnel changes occurred.

The second necessary condition is an environment which *allows* the HPS to happen. The word allow is important because this kind of high performance in an organization cannot be accomplished through any directives, awards, or restrictions; it can only happen if the decision makers are motivated and given the freedom to do what they believe needs to be done.

In order to illustrate this principle of motivation and freedom, let's consider the laser group example which introduced the concept of an HPS at the beginning if this article.[4] The ten people who formed the group were chosen because of their various technical expertise and past R&D performance (or creativity). Most of them had never worked together and they came from several different technical disciplines. In addition to the ten people in the group, the lab designated a manager to function as the link between the group and its environment, and to shelter the group from the external environment. The group agreed to the concept only under the following circumstances, which were granted:

- Time freedom: Flextime (flexible working schedules).
- Travel freedom: Group members would be permitted to travel wherever and whenever they believed it was necessary.
- Top priorities: Supplies and equipment were to be procured as top priority items.
- Administrative activities: Group members were not to have any administrative responsibilities.
- Customer Relations: Group members were permitted to deal directly with the customer, AFWL.

The group office was a single large room which tended to improve interaction. The members of the group usually worked in teams ranging in size from two people to all ten. The group tended not only to work together, but also socialized together during off-duty hours about once a week, usually on Saturdays.

The group constantly exhibited a tremendous amount of creativity and innovation. For example, when it was determined that a laser beam was to be transmitted from a source inside an aircraft to a target outside the aircraft, it was necessary that a hole be created in the aircraft and a turrett be inserted. However, it was not known what effect this would have on the aircraft. There was nothing in the literature but a quick answer was needed. The group drilled a hole in the roof of one member's car and inserted a turrett. They then used a cassette recorder to record the acoustical effects of the hole and turrett as they drove the car on an aircraft runway at 120 MPH. This speed was then translated to a Mach number and results were interpreted to determine the effects.

The group often took other innovative approaches to solving problems. They solved at least 12 of the major problems presented to the group by the AFWL in the first year. They never formalized their results into reports or papers, but instead dealt directly with the Weapons Laboratory, thus "instantly" incorporating their results in the lab's laser systems efforts.

The group quickly gained an outstanding reputation. Internally, the group was characterized as having high group spirit and creativity. Although there were often disagreements, they were always based on technical correctness and not on petty personal differences. The group's manager acted in many ways as the manager of a rock group—he handled all of the group's outside needs while not interfering with its performance.

After its first year the group developed opponents within the Propulsion Lab. These people did not believe the freedom which the group exhibited was proper or fair to the other members of the laboratory.

About this time a newly appointed laboratory commander decided to formalize the group. The group was incorporated into the existing laboratory as one of three branches in one of the laboratory's five divisions. The group then reported to a division director instead of the laboratory director. They were required to document their results, handle administrative duties, and compete for travel and supplies (it should be noted that the group originally operated at a very low cost and its travel was in line with other groups of similar size during the first year).

These changes created large conflicts between the group members and the new structure. During the next three months, the group remained internally compatible, but it was spending time and energy fighting the new environment. The group's productivity dropped substantially. Soon the conflict with the outside world snowballed into the group. Conflict began between group members and also between the group and its customer, AFWL. Eventually, people started leaving the group. When two members had left, the laboratory decided that the group's manager was needed for another position in the lab. His replacement was viewed by the group as an outsider. Eventually, more of the group members moved on. At about two years after the initial formation of the group, it was dissolved due to very low productivity and the conflict which it was causing within the laboratory.

Although impossible to prove that the changes in the environment caused the group to evolve from an HPS to a group with poor productivity, it is possible to hypothesize such a conclusion from the group history. Thus, the freedom which an organization is permitted is an imperative condition for the development and operation of an HPS.

In conclusion, the conditions that must exist for the organization and operation of a high performing system are: 1. Members must be mentally and/or physically competent, 2. Decision makers must be creative, 3. An HPS must be *permitted* (not forced) to happen, 4. Members must be highly motivated and group results must be desired. This theory is not validated outside of what is presented in this article. It is interesting that Vaill made his observations in 1975 and to date, those doing research on this topic can be counted on the fingers of one hand. We would postulate that research and experimentation on HPSs could have a substantial impact on the operations and productivity of many types of organizations.

REFERENCES

1. Notes from P. Vaill, unpublished.
2. Notes from H. Shepard, unpublished.
3. Morse, J. and Lorsch, J., "Beyond Theory Y," *[Harvard Business Review,* May–June 1970: pp. 61–68.
4. Private Conversation with R. Barthelemy, Air Force Wright Aeronautical Laboratories.

A Review of Creativity and Problem Solving Techniques

William E. Souder

Robert W. Ziegler

Here is a catalogue of twenty operational techniques that can serve as a starting point for selecting particular methods for specific needs.

The purpose of this paper is to serve as a quick reference or catalog of operational techniques for stimulating the generation of creative ideas. The reader should note that although the techniques reviewed here can be expected to assist in the generation of embryonic ideas, these techniques must be viewed as only one of several important considerations in the design of a total innovation system. For best results, the techniques need to be combined with organizational methods which provide the necessary care, feeding, and implementation of embryonic ideas.[27, 31]

There are, of course, no formulae for obtaining the right amounts of creativity under various conditions and circumstances. This is due in part to the multitude of factors which can influence the creative process and the dynamic nature of such factors. However, experience[2, 17, 21, 25] suggests that the latent creative potentials of many individuals are often blocked by various perceptual, cultural and emotional factors. There are also many organizational factors that influence creativity. These are described elsewhere, e.g.,

Reprinted with permission from W. Souder and R. Ziegler, ''A Review of Creativity and Problem-Solving Techniques,'' *Research Management*, July 1977.

see 27 and 29. One possible means for unlocking these latent potentials is to utilize some type of ''operational'' creativity technique which aids in circumventing the blockages. Operational techniques are used to mass-produce ideas, as opposed to educational techniques, which are designed to make people more aware of their creative powers. For examples, see.[25] This paper critically reviews a total of twenty operational techniques which the authors feel are among the most effective. Table 4 summarizes the major attributes of the techniques.

BRAINSTORMING

Brainstorming is perhaps the best known operational technique for idea generation.[6, 8, 14] It is an intentionally uninhibited technique that is most frequently used by groups, but has also been successfully employed by individuals. The objective is to generate, in a classroom type setting, the greatest number of alternative ideas from uninhibited responses. Nothing is rejected or criticized. Any attempt to analyze, reject or evaluate ideas is prohibited during the brainstorming process. However, all ideas are written down for subsequent evaluation and development. The brainstorming session is usually carried out under a time constraint, e.g., develop as many ideas as possible in five minutes. In order to have effective brainstorming, Osborn[17] suggests the following "rules" be imposed: judicial judgment (critical evaluation) is ruled out; free-wheeling is welcomed; quantity (not quality) of ideas is the objective; combinations and improvements are sought. Brainstorming thus appears to be most effective when applied to specific rather than general problems. The problem should be limited, simple, open-ended, talkable, and familiar. Also, problems having only one correct solution and/or only a few sensible alternatives do not lend themselves well to brainstorming.

Most authorities feel that group brainstorming is more productive than individual brainstorming.[35, 40] The group brainstorming setting is usually a lively session. Participants eagerly shout out and verbally submit suggestions that are catalyzed and/or build on other ideas that are suggested. Thus, a chain of ideas can often cascade into unique items. Ingenious creations can be brought into existence as the direct result of the mutual support and encouragement of the group. In this regard, Von Fange[40, 41] lists the following reasons why group brainstorming is effective: no one stops to evaluate the ideas that are presented; in the absence of evaluation, no one feels restricted or inhibited; competition evolves from the receptivity of the ideas; praise and encouragement stimulate even greater attainment; idea-finding takes place on what has gone before. However, experience with groups also shows that repression and specious persuasion can lock out some "wallflower" types of personalities, who might otherwise have created contributions to make if they were placed in a more quiet setting. For this reason, cycled individual and group brainstorming sessions have been developed. There is some experience which shows that these cycled settings are superior to either individual or group settings.[29, 30, 32]

REVERSE BRAINSTORMING (TEAR-DOWN, PURGE)

"Reverse" brainstorming (sometimes called the tear-down or purge method) may be useful prior to a brainstorming session, or in conjunction with other methods.[38] It consists of being critical instead of suspending judgment. This initial attack effort is sometimes necessary to pave the way for serious efforts at innovative thinking. Reverse brainstorming prepares one to deliberately go outside the situation to generate so called "idea hooks"—new viewpoints that are often quite remote from the actual situation. A typical approach would be to first list all the things wrong with the operation, process, system, or product. Then, one would systematically take each flaw uncovered and suggest ways of overcoming, improving or correcting it.[4, 6, 8, 25] Care must be exercised to insure that the negative ambience of a tear-down session does not completely overrule a group's optimism.

SYNECTICS

Synectics is a technique that has been developed and modified by Gordon,[11] Prince,[22] and others.[9] It operates like a mental pinball game. Creative solutions to a specific problem are sought through the two-stage process outlined in Figure 1. In the first stage, participants consciously reverse the order of things and "make the strange familiar," through analysis, generalization, and model-seeking. In the second stage, an attempt is made to "make the familiar strange," through personal analogy, direct analogy, symbolic analogy, and fantasy analogy.[21, 31]

A Synectics session is a lively and dynamic maneuver in which rational or obvious solutions are abandoned for what might seem irrelevant or bizarre approaches. Participants act like flints, igniting sparks in other members with their "offbeat" approaches. The intermittent involvement

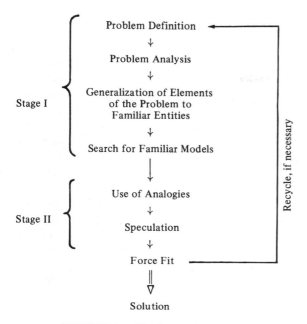

Stage I
- Problem Definition
- ↓
- Problem Analysis
- ↓
- Generalization of Elements of the Problem to Familiar Entities
- ↓
- Search for Familiar Models

Stage II
- Use of Analogies
- ↓
- Speculation
- ↓
- Force Fit

Recycle, if necessary

Solution

FIGURE 1.   The Synectics Process

and detachment brought about by the analogies is subsequently culminated in a "force fit" to the original problem (Figure 1). Through the strain of this new fit, the problem is stretched, pulled and re-focused in order that it may be seen in a new way. A force-fit suggests new contexts and thus provides the raw material for new lines of speculation.[8, 21, 22, 23, 24, 43]

Prince gives an excellent example (see 21, pp. 128–137) of the use of Synectics to develop a bottle closure device. The problem was defined as: "to devise a thermos bottle with an integral closure." The generalization of elements of the problem to familiar entities (stage I, Figure 1) focused the group discussions around the concepts of "tightness" and "effectiveness of closure." The discussions generated several familiar examples of tight, effective closures, such as a clam's shell. The search for familiar models (stage I, Figure 1) swung the discussion to the concept of plastic closure, and the iris of the human eye as an example of a familiar model of an "integral

closure." The group then used elements of personal, symbolic and fantasy analogy (stage II, Figure 1) to speculate on the exact functioning of the iris and to apply this awareness to the thermos bottle problem. A force fit exercise was then undertaken, in which the group was directed to focus on the use of their awareness of the human iris to devise an integral plastic closure. From this exercise, the group suggested a thermos bottle with a rubber sleeve that would close as the top was twisted. One participant developed the key thought: "it's like twisting a long balloon at both ends; if you twist the ends in different directions, you close down the middle" (paraphrased from 21, p. 136).

GORDON METHOD

The Gordon method is a technique for generating new viewpoints (idea hooks). It is used with a small group who is not initially make aware of the exact nature of the actual problem.[12] The intent is to minimize preconceived ideas and habit patterns, so as to avoid a premature solution from being reached before there has been a thorough discussion of the general problem area. The Gordon method forces an unencumbered initial discussion that avoids the danger of a participant becoming so infatuated with his own solution that he ceases to be an effective contributing member. It also avoids inhibitions and/or prejudices that group members may bring to the problem that would adversely affect their performance.[11]

The session leader, who is the only one knowing the actual problem, gets the group to think out loud about a related subject. For example, if the problem were to invent a new toy for a toy manufacturer, the leader might choose the topic play for discussion. He would first focus the discussion on aspects somewhat remote from the actual problem, then on aspects closer to it, and finally on aspects very close to the actual

269

problem. At the end of these discussions, the problem is revealed to the group and then analyze the tape recording of their discussions for possible idea hooks. Each idea hook is then brainstormed (or some other operational creativity method is used) to develop a solution to the actual problem.

Experience suggests[31] that the method works best with a diverse group of persons who are not experts. Moreover, best results seem to be obtained when the group contains some persons whose skills will be required for implementing the solution. One obvious limitation of the Gordon method is that the group leader may be the only participant doing relevant creative thinking. Thus, a great deal depends upon his innate ability to recognize a possibility when it is brought up in a discussion.[14, 25]

CHECKLIST METHOD

In this method, the problem is analyzed against a prepared list of challenges until an idea hook is sparked. Following are a few selected examples of checklists. Osborn: How can we modify, magnify, minify, substitute, rearrange, reverse or combine it.[17] Reise: How can we make it look like something else, animate it, take it literally, make it a parody or imitation.[24] Mortimer: How can we give it convenience of form, time, place, quantity, packaging, readiness, combination, automation, selection.[16] Flesch: What am I trying to accomplish? Have I done this before? How? Could I do it another way? What if I do the opposite? What if I do nothing?[7] Von Fange: What about shape, size? What if reversed, inside out, upside down? What else can it do? What can be left out? What if carried to extremes? Can it be safer? Can it be cheaper?[39] From the nature of these lists, it is apparent that checklists work best when applied to familiar problems or things.

ATTRIBUTE LISTING METHOD

This approach is a variation on the checklist method which is suitable for improving tangible objects. The properties, basic qualities, or attributes of a product are listed. This list is then reviewed, one attribute at a time, with a view toward improving each attribute. For example, consider how the attributes of the common picture frame might be modified by applying this method.[34] Rectangular shape: Could be round, oval, trapezoidal, three-dimensional, continuous. Covered with glass: Why not lucite, plastic film, nothing, a drawn shade? Wooden frame: How about extruded aluminum, plastic, no frame, built-in frame? Opens from back: Why not a slot in top or side, hinge it to open from front, no opening at all, seal completely? Hangs by wire: Could use suction cups, magnetic holder, hooks over a ledge.

The virtue of attribute listing is that it causes an immediate focus on the basic product or problem. It is not based upon historical accumulation of checkpoints, but rather upon an individual analysis of the product or problem in question.[5, 6, 14]

INPUT-OUTPUT TECHNIQUE

The input-output technique is a method for solving dynamic system design problems. General Electric[13] is credited with the development of this scheme, which proceeds by defining the problem in terms of system inputs, outputs and limiting requirements. Then, ways to bridge the gap between inputs and outputs is sought. The object is to produce a number of possible solutions which can then be tested, evaluated, and developed.

As an example, consider the problem of designing a device to automatically shade a room during bright sunlight.[41] The input could be: solar energy (light and heat). The output could be:

making windows alternately opaque and transparent. The specifications could be: must be usable on various sized windows, must admit not more than 20 foot-candles of illumination anywhere in the room, must not cost more than $100 per 40 square foot of window. The input-output procedure would then continue as follows.[13] Step 1: What phenomena respond to the application of heat? Light? Step 2: Can any of these phenomena be used directly to shade the window: Step 3: What phenomena respond to Step 1 outputs? Step 4: Can any of these phenomena be used directly to shade the window? Step 5: What phenomena respond to the Step 3 output? (It must be noted that the most direct path from input to desired output is not always the most economical.) General Electric has found that, given a little practice, this technique is efficient and effective for the solution of the design problems.[13]

Like attribute listing, the input-output technique is based on an analysis of the problem in question. Unlike attribute listing, this technique concentrates on the job to be done. Thus, it seems to be best suited for discovering new or alternative ways to accomplish some desired end.[27, 31]

BUFFALO METHOD

The title of this technique refers to the method developed at the University of Buffalo by S. J. Parnes[18] and others[19] in their creativity training program. In this method, a total approach to problem solving is used. It begins with a difficult and/or complex problem, then proceeds through four major steps: (1) fact-finding; (2) problem-finding; (3) idea-finding; and (4) solution-finding. The procedure also includes steps which are relevant in a social or business setting: acceptance finding, and applying the total process. As in some other methods, the actual route from beginning to end is apt to be disorganized. Feedback, iteration and guidance are essential to success with this approach. The limitation of the approach is its nearly completely dependence upon the quality of leadership and training provided.

FREE ASSOCIATION

Free association is a method of stimulating the imagination to some constructive purpose. The objective of this approach is to produce new combinations, intangible ideas, designs, names, etc. The general approach is to first jot down a symbol—a word, sketch, number, picture—which is related to some important aspect of the problem or subject under consideration. Then, jot down another symbol suggested by the first one. Repeat; ad lib until ideas emerge. This technique can be used effectively by individuals or groups, with ideas "feeding" upon one another, often resulting in imaginative outputs.[6, 25, 34]

FORCED RELATIONSHIP

This is a technique which has essentially the same basic purpose as free association. But it attempts to force associations by the following five-step process.[42] First, isolate the elements and possible forms of the problem at hand. Second, find the relationships between/among these elements and forms (e.g., similarities, differences, analogies, causes and effects). Third, record the relationships in an organized fashion. Fourth, analyze the record of relationships to find ideas or patterns. Finally, develop new ideas from these patterns. As an example, Table 1 illustrates a forced-relationship analysis of the elements "paper" and "soap." The forced relationship technique may be used by itself, or in combination with the Buffalo method and others.[14, 34]

TABLE 1.   Illustration of the Forced Relationships Technique [Adapted from Taylor[34]]

Forms	Relationship/Combination	Idea/Pattern
	Elements: Paper and Soap	
Adjective	Papery soap	Flakes
	Soapy paper	Wash and dry travel aid
Noun	Paper soaps	Tough paper impregnated with soap and usable for washing surfaces.
Verb-correlates	Soaped papers	Booklets of soap leaves
	Soap "wets" paper	In coating and impregnation processes.
	Soap "cleans" paper	Suggests wallpaper cleaner.

COLLECTIVE NOTEBOOK (CNB) METHOD

In the CNB method [14] each participant receives a notebook in which is printed a problem of major scope and a very broad-front presentation of preparative material, including a variety of suggested training aids. Each participant independently records daily in this notebook his thoughts and ideas on the problem for a period of a month. Each then summarizes what he feels are his best ideas on the problem, his suggestions for fruitful directions to explore, and other ideas aside from the main problem. The notebooks are then given to a coordinator (who must be creative-minded and skilled in organizing and summarizing material) who prepares a detailed summary of all the notebooks. These summaries are then discussed by all the parties in a final creative discussion, in which brainstorming, Synectics, etc. techniques may be used. This technique enables a number of individual, independent and open-ended ideas to be developed and documented, which then benefit from a group evaluation. This format—an individual, independent ideational period lasting over a one-month time span, followed by a group evaluation and collective thought exercise—has been found to be superior to other behavioral formats for conducting creativity sessions.[29, 20, 32] However, the obvious dependence on the major role of the coordinator is probably the most significant limitation of the CNB method.

BIONICS

From its very name, Bionics, one realizes that this approach is somehow related to living organisms. In the bionics approach, one asks the question, How is this (the problem, phenomena, etc.) done in nature? Proponents of this technique contend that nature's scheme of things is revealed to those who search. Although often listed as a separate technique, bionics is probably best used at the "Use of Analogies" stage of the Synectics process (Figure 1).[10,38]

MORPHOLOGICAL ANALYSIS

Morphological analysis is a comprehensive way to list and examine all of the possible combinations that might be useful in solving a given problem.[1] These combinations may then be subsequently tested, verified, modified, evaluated and developed.[25, 34] An example is presented in Table 2. The problem was to develop a low cost, fully portable, high validity color TV receiver. The

TABLE 2. *Example of Morphological Analysis*

Function	Tubes	or	IC's	or	LSIC's
			Could be performed using either:		
	Types:		Time frame:		Time frame:
Tuner	Pentodes		2 yrs.		5 yrs.
Picture	Pentodes		Now		5 yrs.
Sound	Pentodes		2 yrs.		Now
Color	Triodes		Now		2 yrs.

Analyses:

Lowest cost	=	Pentode Tuner + IC Picture + Pentode Sound + Triode Color
Lowest weight	=	all LSIC's (5 years away)
Best validity	=	all LSIC's (5 years away)
Compromise	=	Pentode Tuner + IC Picture + LSIC Sound + IC Color

four circuits (tuner, picture, sound and color) could each be achieved in three ways: using all tubes, using all IC's, using all LSIC's. However, at the time this problem arose, it was expected that the IC tuner and sound devices would not be perfected for another two years, and the LSIC tuner, picture and color devices would not be perfected for another five years. As the "analyses" section of Table 2 shows, a compromise product had to be specified until the technology could be developed. The manufacturer entered the market with a less-than-ideal product, to be updated with a new model at a later time. It should be noted that morphological analysis methods have been used to identify emerging technologies and to forecast technical needs, e.g., the analyses in Table 2 point out the need for LSIC's.

INSPIRED (BIG DREAM) APPROACH

This technique is sometimes referred to as a breakthrough approach which can lead to spectacular advancements.[6, 34] It predicates itself on the premise of think-big. The procedure is: think the biggest dream possible. Then, read, study, and think about every subject connected with your big dream. Finally, drop down a dream or so; then engineer your dream into reality.[34] The objective is to make the greatest possible achievement.[6]

SEQUENCE-ATTRIBUTE/MODIFICATIONS MATRIX (SAMM) APPROACH

The SAMM approach[3] is most applicable to sequential situations where step-by-step activities can be listed logically, described briefly and explored for possible creative modifications. An illustration of the SAMM technique is provided in Figure 2, using an actual hot steel slab rolling operation. The operating sequence of activities listed along the left-hand side of the matrix is examined for possible modifications. In the matrix in Figure 2, the analyst has identified (with an "X") several priority areas to look into. For instance, he has noted that the positioning and passing sequences (items 3 and 4) can possibly be combined and rearranged. The SAMM matrix does not describe how this is to be done; it simply identifies the areas. A number of other operational mechanisms, e.g., brainstorming, analogies, etc., can then be employed in the subsequent evaluations. This technique seems to have proven

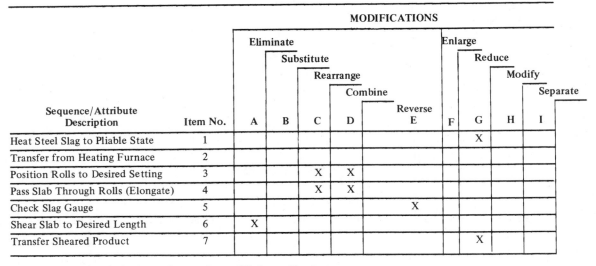

Sequence/Attribute Description	Item No.	MODIFICATIONS								
		Eliminate	Substitute	Rearrange	Combine	Reverse	Enlarge	Reduce	Modify	Separate
		A	B	C	D	E	F	G	H	I
Heat Steel Slag to Pliable State	1							X		
Transfer from Heating Furnace	2									
Position Rolls to Desired Setting	3			X	X					
Pass Slab Through Rolls (Elongate)	4			X	X					
Check Slag Gauge	5					X				
Shear Slab to Desired Length	6	X								
Transfer Sheared Product	7							X		

Key: X = possible priority items that can be modified, combined, etc.

FIGURE 2.   SAMM Illustration

more effective in group settings than in individual settings.[3, 34]

KEPNER-TREGOE METHOD

This method is particularly suited for isolating or finding the problem, and then deciding what to do about it. A systematic outline is made to precisely describe the problem, what lies outside the problem and what is closely related to it. An example is shown in Table 3. This outline then reveals the possible causes of the problem, and facilitates decision-making.[33] Clearly, the technique is geared more to creative problem solving than to far-out ideation.

TABLE 3.   Example of Kepner-Tregoe Method

	Is	Is Not
WHAT		
Deviation:	Carbon Deposit	Blackening
Object:	Filament from Machine A	Other filaments
WHERE		
On object:	On surface	In filament materials
Observed	On Machine A	On other filaments
WHEN		
On object:	After filament is formed	Before filament is formed
Observed:	In trough at 3:50	Before 3:50 P.M.
EXTENT		
How much:	Heavy	Slight
How many:	All Machine A filaments	Machine B filaments

VALUE ANALYSIS

Value analysis is a specialized application of creative problem-solving which may be used to increase the value of a product, process, object, etc. It may be defined as an objective, systematic, and formalized method of performing a job to achieve the necessary functions at minimum cost. To use the value analysis process, one asks the following questions concerning each part:[15] What is it? What must it do? What does it do? What did it cost? What else will do the job? What will that cost? This approach tends to reward the logical thought process. It is very effective in applied areas, e.g., engineering development.[40]

SCIENTIFIC METHOD

Many scientists today do not agree that there is one best scientific method.[10] However, the following general approach is by now regarded as traditional: define the problem; analyze the problem gather data to solve the problem; analyze the data; arrive at potential solutions; test these solutions; select the best one. Clearly, this methodology can serve as a guideline for creative inquiry. The problem analysis and solution testing steps provide opportunities for applying some of the afore-mentioned creativity techniques, e.g., Synectics, etc.

HEURISTICS

Heuristics are methods of demonstration and rules of thumb which tend to lead a person to investigate further. Some operational techniques based upon heuristics are: the techniques of close comparison of neighbors and similar cases the examination of the simplest (naive) case; the examination of special cases; the search for a modified structure to which a rule applies.[14] Heuristics are best suited for the detection of useful preparative material and problem elaboration. Some suggested heuristics are summarized by Polya.[20]

EDISONIAN METHOD

The Edisonian method is an approach consisting principally of performing a virtually endless number of trial-and-error experiments.[34] It is often considered to be a last-ditch approach, resorted to only when more systematic methods have failed to produce the desired results. But it is also useful when one is delving into the unknown,[40, 41] e.g., for exploratory work.

MANAGING A GROUP CREATIVITY SESSION

Successful scientists and engineers are often their own worst enemies in a creativity setting. Their training and prior successes compel them to blot out things that seem silly, or that smack of irrational thinking and fanciful excursions. Yet, these are the very practices that lead one down new alleys and passages that may culminate in creative new solutions. Participants in group ideation sessions are often surprised to listen to their own negativeness in tapes of their sessions. It seems a common trait to pay lip service to openness, and yet to rebuff new ideas. Thus, it is not unusual for participants to feel that group creativity sessions are boring and useless. The group often doesn't come to grips with the real problem, spends most of the time arguing about the problem definition, and generates criticisms of the ideas that do arise. This effectively shuts off further ideation, and only bland ideas emerge. The individuals may go away feeling that they could have done better on their own. Yet, it has become clear that group settings can provide essential stimuli to creativity.[29, 30, 31, 32]

In order to achieve best results, the creativity

275

TABLE 4. Summary of Operational Techniques and Experiences with Them

Problem/Situation Nature	Output or Result Desired	Appropriate Operational Technique	Comments and Experiences
1. Problem is open-ended; Problem is well-defined; Simple solution is sought; Problem is easily understood; Problem has more than one acceptable solution; Participants are able and willing to freewheel and emphasize the positive.	One or more simple, feasible, creative solutions to a well-defined problem that is well understood.	Brainstorming Free Association Heuristics	Methods are often restricted by biases and social inhibitions of one or more participants.
2. Problem is open-ended; Problem is ill-defined; Simple solution is sought; Problem is not well understood; Problem has more than one acceptable solution; Participants are initially unable to freewheel and unable to emphasize the positive.	Analysis of faults, failure modes, things to be corrected in an area that may be incompletely understood.	Reverse Brainstorming Edisonian Method Kepner-Tregoe Method	Methods are often useful starting points for other methods.
3. Problem is open-ended; Problem is fairly well-defined; A complex illogical solution may be sought; Problem is fairly well understood; Problem has one best solution; Participants are able to emphasize the bizarre, analogize and emphasize the positive.	A "far-out" solution, that may be toned down if desired.	Synectics Bionics Inspired (Big Dream) Approach Gordon Method Buffalo Method	These methods require skilled and trained participants for complete success; methods are good for areas where the technology is ill-defined.
4. Problem may not be open-ended; Problem is fairly well-defined; Problem is not well understood; Problem has many acceptable solutions; Participants are able to work in the abstract.	A solution that cannot be visualized, conceptualized or described before the sessions; the elaboration of concepts; dimensions or ideas for further refinement.	Gordon Method Inspired (Big Dream) Approach Synectics	Methods are fully dependent upon the skill of the leader; methods can be good where the technology is ill-defined; methods are good where participants would otherwise rush toward an obvious solution.

#	Conditions	Solution Sought	Methods	Comments
5.	Problem need not be open-ended; Problem is well-defined; Problem is well-understood; Problem has several acceptable solutions, but one best solution; Participants are able to visualize combinations and attributes; Attributes are well-defined; Combinations and variations are meaningful.	New combinations, forms, shapes or means.	Checklists Attribute Listing Morphological Analysis Forced Relationships Input-Output Technique	Methods are limited by ability of participants to visualize combinations, methods work best in well-defined state-of-art technologies.
6.	Problem may be either open or closed-ended; Problem is well-defined; Simple, logical, solution is sought; One best solution is desired; The technology or discipline being studied is well-known; a logical process may be followed to reach a solution; An algorithmic approach may be taken to solution.	A far-out solution is not desired; the bits and pieces of the problem are laying around, waiting to be properly assembled.	Input-Output Technique Buffalo Method CNB (Collective Notebook Method) SAMM (Sequence-Attribute/Modifications Matrix) Value Engineering Scientific Method Heuristics Kepner-Tregoe Method	Methods require that some participants be highly knowledgeable about the technology/discipline under study; group must be heterogeneous (some creative thinkers, some resident experts, some confronters); methods may be good starting points for other methods, e.g., may be followed by synectics, Gordon method or brainstorming.
7.	Problem is closed-ended; Problem is well-defined; A best, logical solution is desired; An engineered solution that can be immediately put into effect is desired; The technology or discipline being studied is highly refined.	Only incremental changes are sought, e.g., a change in form, type or process.	Buffalo Method CNB (Collective Notebook) Method Value Engineering Scientific Method	Methods normally yield success here because the problem is well-defined and there is little uncertainty in recognizing an acceptable solution.

group should be properly constituted, structured, and guided. Experiences[31] indicate that the group should consist of at least one resident expert in the technology being discussed, one persuader, one confronter, one helper, and one dreamer. The resident expert supplies the depth of technological knowledge. The persuader is a friendly personality type who persistently persuades the group to accept ideas and approaches on the basis of their inherent logicalness. The confronter is the bullnosed personality type who won't let anything remain hidden under the rug. The dreamer supplies the far-out fanciful inputs. The helper maintains the group process—by periodically rephrasing and summarizing the work of the group and by smoothing ruffled feelings as needed. The presence of each personality type in the group adds essential ingredients; each offsets and complements the other. Naturally, the selection of these personality types can be an involved trial and error process. However, there are several instruments that can assist in their selection.[30]

In addition to the above members, a process leader and a client should be present. These persons are not grup members; they are outside helpers. The process leader is the expert on dealing with and guiding groups. He formulates the meeting plan and sets the frame-work for the operation of the group process. He gives the group corrective steerage and feedbacks on whether or not they are being too confrontive, too passive, etc. The client is the person who will use the groups' outputs. He supplies factual knowledge to the participants, and provides the criteria for judging the "goodness" of the ideas which the group generates.[30, 31]

REFERENCES

1. Allen. M. S., *Morphological Creativity,* New Jersey: Prentice-Hall, 1962.
2. Arnold, J. E., "Creativity in Engineering," *Society of Automotive Engineers transactions,* Vol. 64, No. 2, 1956, pp. 17–23.
3. Brooks, J. D., *Review of Operational Mechanisms for Innovative Management Course,* Industrial Studies Program, U.S. Steel Corp., Pittsburgh, Pa., (no date), pg. 3.
4. Bujake, Jr., J. E., "Programmed Innovation in New Product Development," *Research Management,* Vol. 12, No. 4, 1969, pp. 279–287.
5. Crawford, R. P., *The Techniques of Creative Thinking,* New York: Hawthorne Books, 1959.
6. Edwards, M. O., "Solving Problems Creatively," *Systems and Procedures Journal,* Jan.–Feb., 1966, pp. 16–24.
7. Flesch, R., *The Art of Clear Thinking,* New York: Harper & Brothers, 1952.
8. Geschka, H.; G. R. Schaude, and H. Schlichsupp, "Modern Techniques for Solving Problems," *Chemical Engineering,* August 6, 1973, pp. 91–97.
9. Gitter, D. L.; W. J. J. Gordon and G. M. Prince, *The Operational Mechanisms of Synectics,* Cambridge, Mass.: Synectics Inc., 1964.
10. Goldner, B. B., *The Strategy of Creative Thinking,* New Jersey: Prentice-Hall, 1962.
11. Gordon, W. J. J., *Synectics,* New York: Harper & Brothers, 1961.
12. Gordon, W. J. J., "Operational Approach to Creativity," *Harvard Business Review,* Vol. 34, 1956, pp. 41–51.
13. Guth, L. W., "Solve Design Problems with a Creative Approach," *General Electric Review,* July, 1953, pp. 5–9.
14. Haefele, J. W., *Creativity and Innovation,* New York: Reinhold Publishing Corp., 1962, pp. 6–7.
15. Miles, L. D. *Techniques of Value Analysis and Engineering,* New York: McGraw-Hill, 1961.
16. Mortimer, C. G., "The Creative Factor in Marketing," *15th Annual Parlin Memorial Lecture,* American Marketing Association, May, 1959.
17. Osborn, A. F., *Applied Imagination,* New York: Charles Scribner's and Sons, 1963, pp. vii–viii (preface).
18. Parnes, S. J., *Description of the University of Buffalo Problem-Solving Course,* Buffalo Creative Education Foundation, 1958.
19. Parnes, S. J., and H. F. Harding (Eds.), *A Source Book for Creative Thinking,* New York: Scribner's & Sons, 1962, pp. 307–324.

20. Polya, G., *How to Solve it,* Princeton University Press, 1945.
21. Prince, G. M., *The Practice of Creativity,* New York: Harper & Row, 1970.
22. Prince, G. M., "The Operational Mechanism of Synectics," *Journal of Creative Behavior,* Vol. 2, No. 1, Winter 1967, pp. 1–5.
23. Raudsipp, E., "Forcing Ideas with SYNECTICS," *Machine Design,* October 16, 1969, pp. 1–6.
24. Reise, O., *How to Develop Profitable Ideas,* New Jersey: Prentice-Hall, 1945.
25. Razik, T. A., *Bibliography of Creativity Studies,* Buffalo, N.Y. S.U.N.Y. University Bookstore, 1965.
26. Souder, W. E. and A. H. Rubenstein, "Some Designs for Policy Experiments and Government Incentives for the R&D Innovation Process," *IEEE Trans. on Eng. Mgt.,* Vol. EM–23, No. 3, August 1976, pp. 129–139.
27. Souder, W. E., "Organizational Methods for Stimulating Innovation," Technology Management Studies Group study paper, University of Pittsburgh, Pittsburgh, PA 15261, February 24, 1976.
28. Souder, W. E., "A Systems Approach to the Integration of R&D Into the Business," Technology Management Studies Group study paper, University of Pittsburgh, Pittsburgh, PA 15261, March 1976.
29. Souder, Wm. E., "Effectiveness of Nominal and Interacting Group Decision Processes for Integrating R&D Marketing," to appear in the February 1977 issue of *Management Science.*
30. Souder, Wm. E., "A Group Process Model for Portfolio Decision Making in Organizational Settings," Technology Management Studies Group study paper, University of Pittsburgh, Pittsburgh, PA 15261, December 10, 1975.
31. Souder, Wm. E., "Some Experiences with Idea Generation and Creativity Groups," Technology Management Studies Group study paper, University of Pittsburgh, Pittsburgh PA 15261, June 15, 1975.
32. Souder, Wm. E., "Achieving Organizational Consensus with Respect to R&D Project Selection Criteria," *Management Science,* Vol. 21, No. 6, February, 1975, pp. 669–681.
33. Stryker, P., "How to Analyze That Problem," *Harvard Business Review,* May–June and July–August, 1965, pp. 61–69.
34. Taylor, J., *"How to Create Ideas,"* New Jersey Prentice-Hall, 1961.
35. Taylor, D. W., P. C. Berry and C. H. Block, "Does Group Participation When Using Brainstorming Facilitate or Inhibit Creative Thinking?," *Tech. Rept. No. 1, Contract Nonr. 609^{20} NR 150–166.* New Haven, Conn., Department of Psychology, Yale University, 1957.
36. "The Silent Crisis in R&D," *Business Week,* March 8, 1976, pp. 90–92.
37. "The Breakdown of U.S. Innovation," *Business Week,* Feb. 16, 1976, pp. 56–68.
38. U.S. Army Management School, *Workbook for Creative Problem-Solving,* Ft. Belvoir, Va., 1964.
39. Von Fange, E. K., "Understanding the Creative Process," *General Electric Review,* July and September, 1955, 9–13.
40. Von Fange, E. K., *The Creative Process in Engineering,* Schenectady, N.Y.: General Electric Corp., 1954, pp. 33–38.
41. Von Fange, E. K., *Professional Creativity,* New Jersey: Prentice Hall, 1959.
42. Whiting, C. S., *Creative Thinking.* New York: Reinhold Publishing Corp., 1958.
43. Xerox Corporation Business Products Group, "It's Spelled SYNECTICS and It Can Mean Success," *The B.P.G. News,* September, 1970, pp. 3–5.

Managers' Misconceptions about Technology

Lowell Steele

Unrealistic assumptions about technology make managing innovation more difficult than it has to be

By any realistic measure, the record of technological innovation by American industry is a magnificent human achievement in the face of immense uncertainty, grinding anxiety, and low odds of success. Nonetheless, unrealistic expectations have kept that technological capability on a roller coaster of corporate funding. For 20 years after World War II, companies and public opinion gave technological innovation virtually universal support. During the next 10 to 12 years, however, it was increasingly seen as a villain that pursued the wrong objectives, was socially unresponsive, and, worst of all, was ineffective.

The scientists and engineers most closely associated with the work of innovation are painfully aware of the consequences of misconceptions about the rate, direction, and character of technological progress. But even they find it difficult to specify what technology can provide, what forces drive and constrain it, and how quickly innovative capacity can respond to those forces. Indeed, to cite but one example, judging correctly when a major technical discontinuity is on the horizon or when extensions of conventional technology will prevail remains a crucial,

difficult decision for business people and scientists alike.

After 29 years of experience in nurturing innovative activity at General Electric, I am still amazed by how fragile and improbable a process innovation really is. More to the point, I am convinced that only if we have a genuinely realistic understanding of the gauntlet an innovation must run in order to succeed will we be more appreciative of the achievement, less vulnerable to disappointment, and better able to manage the process.

Let me, then, identify the most common misconceptions about managing technology and point out their unfortunate consequences.

MISCONCEPTION 1

The criterion for determining the implementation of technology should be "best possible," not "good enough."

"Good enough" may not be elegant, but it accurately reflects the often overlooked fact that social and economic considerations should and do determine the priorities for a technology's application and set the appropriate level of performance. Technology that is not wanted has little market value and so is not worth creating. Similarly, better technical performance than customers desire nearly always incurs a cost penalty. The proper target, therefore, is to create not the best possible technology, but technology that is good enough.

A number of years ago, in an attempt to gain insight into new program opportunities for corporate R&D at GE, I queried engineering managers about their most critical problems. Virtually everyone responded that the principal barriers were not technical—some performance capability they were unable to achieve—but economic.

Familiar definitions of industrial R&D hold that the work inevitable contains risk and uncertainty as to whether the goal can be attained. These definitions rarely make clear, however, that the goal in question includes cost as well as performance targets for the product or process. True, a small fraction of industrial R&D explores technical feasibility with little concern for economic constraints, but all large expenditures must be concerned with both. Especially in a business setting, cost barriers *are* technical barriers.

Every product on the market is the result of a series of compromises among cost, performance, and product life. Obviously, if theses compromises do not reflect the values that customers want, the product does not sell. When, for example, consumers did not care about energy efficiency, materials recycling, or the environment, technologists put their efforts into achieving lower costs in areas that did matter very much to customers. The technology existed at that time to make electrical appliances more energy-efficient, but at a cost that would have priced them out of the market.

Attempts to sell customers on a higher level of performance than they want are also highly problematic. In the late 1940's, GE mounted a campaign to increase public interest in preserving the environment. The response was underwhelming, to say the least. Ford's efforts in the 1950's to push safety-related features met with similar results. In fact, much of what R&D does is develop solutions that are less than technically elegant but that reflect a value for which customers are willing to pay.

When social values change, technology responds, but managers often overestimate the speed of that response and the level of improvement that can be achieved in the short run. Driven by their enthusiasms, technologists themselves may lend credence to these overexpectations. They sometimes forget that trying to make something work correctly *all* the time at a cost-effective price is an excruciatingly detailed task. I well recall the wonderment of one of my associates when charged with putting into operation a new process he had been working on for several years. "Son of a gun," he said, "When my boss tells me to 'make it work,' he means 24 hours a day, 7 days a week, 52 weeks a year!"

Technologists working in the field, however, may underestimate the magnitude of improvement they can achieve over the long term. After all, their reputations are on the line. Given the inherent uncertainty of their work, it is not surprising that they often give conservative estimates of what is possible.

MISCONCEPTION 2

"Good enough" is determined by careful rational choice, *not* by convention—that is, by what consumers have learned to accept or expect.

What R&D produces is rarely as good as what the present level of knowledge about physical laws allows. Instead, it is in Herbert Simon's words what "satisfices"—that is, what meets social expectations.

In health care, for example, where expectations are boundless, science and technology have made nonstop efforts for improvement supported by ample funds from the political system. By contrast, environmental deterioration and energy efficiency were for many years of little concern and so received scant attention from technologists.

Widely shared beliefs, even if mistaken, do much to shape technical effort. At times, what is good enough for the market is actually better than what is physically required to achieve the desired goal. With modern detergents, for instance, cleaning ability is relatively independent of water temperature. Even so, belief in the virtue of hot water in ensuring cleanliness has been slow to change, despite the energy savings that result form using cold water.

Or consider the consequences of the American consumer's view that small household appliance are mainly gifts or impulse purchases. This perception necessarily affects the price, the method of merchandising, and the levels of performance and durability established as design specifications. Technology that is good enough must yield a cost acceptable to a mass market for gift items. In Canada and Europe, however, these appliances are regarded as important additions to household capital, and consumers demand—and are willing to pay for—products that have a longer life and that meet higher performance standards.

Sometimes "good enough" is based on erroneous assumption about costs. Targets for product quality derive from the belief that high volume always incurs a penalty in quality and that, beyond some point, the costs of quality are greater than the savings it generates. The Japanese, by questioning these assumptions, have demonstrated that our beliefs about quality are no more than conventions—and mistaken conventions at that.[1]

MISCONCEPTION 3

Most innovations are successful—and should be.

This distorted perception arises to some extent from the natural tendency of both companies and individual managers to publicize successes while allowing failures to die quietly. In addition, the data needed to analyze a failure—even for an internal study—are usually skimpy and difficult to assemble.

In reality, the failure rate of innovations is high. This fact reflects the intricacy and interdependence of modern advances in technology. To be successful, any attempt to introduce a technical capability must demonstrate that the capability really does offer substantial advantages. Most of the time, however, a new technology either is not enough of an improvement over the old to warrant the effort and the risk it entails, or it has problems and deficiencies that were not apparent initially. As with a jigsaw puzzle, adding a piece to a simple two-dimensional puzzle is not difficult, but fitting a new piece into a complex, three-dimensional puzzle is.

Consider, for example, the interlocking relationships among such products as fabrics, detergents, and washers and dryers, each of which is produced by a different industry. Wash-and-wear fabrics forced the re-design of washers and dryers and the reformulation of detergents. If the advantages of the new fabrics had not been so dramatic, they would not have induced these related changes.

When a single dramatic advance like X-ray tomography or xerography leads to a new level of capability much desired by customers, success is likely to follow. Many technical advances, however, face extended barriers to success.

The need for lower costs in making photovoltaic solar energy available, for instance, is spread uniformly over the entire process—production of high-purity silicon, wafers, and solar cells; assembly into batteries; methods of installation on roofs; and control systems for the resulting electrical output. Hence, no one dramatic improvement can have more than a limited impact on total system costs.

A second reason for the high failure rate of innovations is that the jigsaw puzzle in question changes when threatened with a new piece, thus making a good fit more difficult to achieve. The manufacturers of photoflash bulbs delayed for 20 years the widespread adoption of the electronic flash for amateur use by producing lower cost and more convenient flashbulb systems. The threat to the photoflash business was a powerful stimulus to innovative effort designed to hold off the commercial effects of advances in electronic flashes.

New technology constantly chases the moving target of conventional technology, which is itself goaded to accelerated improvement by the threat. The new technology rarely catches up. In fact, one of the most important economic benefits of innovative activity is the stimulus it gives to conventional technology. For instance, advances in magnetic tape for audio and video recording have prevented the development of thermoplastic recording. Similarly, advances in existing technologies for interrupting high-power circuits have proved an insurmountable barrier to the use of vacuum interrupters, despite their technical elegance and attractive features.

The current competition between video tape and video disk is a good example of one very new technology, video tape, establishing a market position before another. Improvements in the recording length, ease of use, and miniaturization of the tapes have made them a formidable—and moving—obstacle to the success of video disks.

MISCONCEPTION 4

What you do not know about a new technological advance is probably good; Murphy's law rarely applies.

The attractive features of a new discovery must become apparent rapidly, or it will receive no further attention. But as Alec Guinness demonstrated with painful hilarity in the film *The Man in the White Suit,* our ignorance is usually greater than we realize, and even exciting new discoveries can have undesirable attributes.

Sometimes it is possible to discover the fatal birth defect quickly. GE's corporate R&D invented a new fiber that looked and behaved more like wool than any other synthetic material known. Unfortunately, the fiber disintegrated in dry cleaning solvents, and the R&D staff was unable to solve this problem.

Sometimes a limitation elicits, but does not respond to, extended efforts to eradicate it. GE eventually abandoned its program on hydrogen-oxygen fuel cells after years of trying to avoid using platinum as a catalyst. Without platinum, fuel cell life was too short; with platinum, operating costs were uneconomic, and known world supplies of platinum were inadequate to permit its extensive use.

Sometimes, however, a limitation creates immense anxiety but eventually yields to creative effort and luck. It was almost impossible to mold PPO, the key material in Noryl (one of GE's most important engineering plastics), with the technology available at the time. Had GE not discovered PPO's remarkable alloying properties, Noryl would not have survived.

There are also times when a limitation provides applications engineers with an excuse not to use the new invention. Solid-state electronic power devices are vulnerable to voltage surges. Before the development of new circuit techniques and specialized varistors, engineers often cited that vulnerability as a reason not to use such devices.

Achieving consistent, predictable, and cost-effective performance requires a concerted effort to understand how and why an innovation works and to remove or find ways around its undesirable features. All this takes time and costs money. Frequently, the necessary skills are not those of the original inventor, who may be, for instance, an organic chemist with little knowledge of or interest in plastics molding or a solid-state physicist with little knowledge of power circuits and applications.

Understandably, potential users tend to remain skeptics until they have evidence of a technology's successful application to their own needs. Identifying the key leverage point can be critical. For example, the excellent but little-noticed dimensional stability of GE's polycarbonate Lexan proved to be far more attractive to early users, who were beset with plastic warpage and swelling, than did Lexan's dramatic impact resistance. By contrast, the inability to identify and application for the unique information density of thermoplastic recording proved fatal to the technology. The virtues of such pioneering applications cannot, alas, be demonstrated by careful analysis and paper studies. Actual market tests and experimentation are essential.

GE once viewed railroad locomotives as an attractive initial market for heavy-duty gas turbines. The limitations were such that this application still has not proved successful. Not until the turbines were redesigned for lower-cost full-factory—rather than on-site—assembly did they demonstrate their special ability to provide rapid, incremental additions to peaking capacity for electricity generation. It took great skill and ingenuity to shoehorn a package of delicate machinery onto a single railroad car, but there was little doubt that it could be done. Management had to hang tough for many years until it finally became clear what was impeding market acceptance.

As one who has participated in many attempts to match newly discovered technical capability with market pull, I have no patience with those who say, "They should have known better." The market-pull approach, if not used carefully, becomes a meaningless tautology: by definition, innovations that succeed have found market pull. In practice, the pull is usually no more than a barely perceptible tug, which you strain with all your wits to sense and interpret.

MISCONCEPTION 5

In most instances, radically new technology will turn out to be more desirable than advances and extensions of conventional technology.

Despite all the talk of dramatic technological breakthroughs in efforts to attain higher energy efficiency and to reduce environmental damage, most R&D money is going into extensions of conventional technology. Evolutionary advances are less risky, give promise of more timely application, and are, on balance, more cost-effective—that is, they are "good enough."

History may indeed prove me wrong, but I predict that intensification of oil and gas exploration, production in more hostile environments, enhanced recovery methods, cogeneration, combined cycles, and increased attention to efficiency in use will continue to be the most productive responses to our energy problem. Synfuels still wait in the wings, and exotic solar, ocean thermal, and fusion technologies will be many decades in coming along.

We consistently underestimate how much room for improvement is left in a conventional technology. At the same time, we often criticize those who take the opposite course. The people who support evolutionary improvements are not opposed to new technology. Naturally, since they have to bear the odium of being wrong and of seeing an investment prove worthless, they support the development of a technology that promises to be adequate as well as less likely to fail.

After careful study, GE concluded that it knew too little about graphite-reinforced composites, despite their attractive properties, to risk using them in jet engines for wide-bodied aircraft. Consequently, GE decided to use conventional metal alloys. Rolls-Royce went ahead with the graphite fibers, and their limitations eventually forced a costly redesign of the RB211 engine.

As I noted earlier, the demands on today's technology are unforgiving; a close fit is not good enough. Much publicity has surrounded the promise of alternatives to the present automobile engine: the Sterling engine, electric cars, gas turbines, rotary engines, and hybrid electrical/internal combustion engines. Each of these types suffers from inherent limitations in operating performance, life, cost, or maintenance that have not yet yielded to persistent efforts at improvement. In other words, there are sound technical and economic reasons for the adoption—and the long-term survival—of the Otto cycle engine for automobiles.

Enthusiasts predicted for years that AC adjustable drives would replace DC motors, but Exxon's abortive excursion into electrical motors demonstrated once again that such change is difficult. Similarly, enthusiasts have long been predicting that electronic controls would replace electromechanical controls in appliances. The transition has not yet occurred. Pneumatic control devices, highly touted during the 1960's, have found only limited application. Much the same is true of thermoelectric cooling.

Sometimes, of course, a new technology proves irresistible. The Pilkington float process for making plate glass is an example. So, too, is the substitution of radial tires for bias-ply tires. But these are exceptions. In, for example, the emerging competition between electronic photography and silver-halide emulsion-based photography, I predict that silver emulsion will prove hard to dislodge.

MISCONCEPTION 6

The success of a new technology rarely depends on the adequacy of available infrastructure.

Inventing a new substance with dramatic new properties does little good if there are no sources of raw materials, if the means to fabricate it do not exist, or if engineers do not know the design rules for using it.

Here, the history of frozen foods is illuminating. Clarence Birdseye had his flash of insight in 1912, but his development of a satisfactory quick-freezing process was only the first in an excruciatingly drawn-out series of steps. Dietetic information had to be developed on the properties of different frozen foods, and new methods were needed for gathering produce. These changes, in turn, required the location of processing plants closer to sources of supply; new techniques and equipment for transporting, storing, and displaying frozen foods; and willingness on the part of both retailers and homeowners to buy adequate storage systems. Even so, the real catalyzing event was the government's decision after World War II to decontrol the price of frozen foods before that of canned goods. In all, it took some 30 years before all the pieces were in place for a major new technology to flower!

Obviously, not all innovations call for so complex and time-consuming an effort, yet often only large enterprises with their extensive financial reserves and ability to marshal diverse skills can stay the necessary course. Before color television could succeed, to cite a familiar example, more or less simultaneous advances had to happen in studio and broadcast equipment, home TV equipment, and the development of appropriate programs.

Today, those observers who postulate the rapid introduction of solar energy or electric automobiles or paperless offices usually ignore the constraints imposed by infrastructure. A good practice is to assume complete technical success and then ask, "Now what has to happen to get this technology widely adopted?"

Labor practices and application skills can be constraints too. The silicone industry developed a long-lived roofing material that could be applied over old roofs even at very low temperatures. The necessary skills in preparing and applying the material were different from those of customary trade practice, which reflected the hot, dirty, low-skilled work long associated with installing built-up roofing. Territorial boundaries among construction trades precluded the use of painters, whose skills better matched the application requirements. For their part, roofing contractors lacked experience with sophisticated silicone-based materials.

It took additional time and money to train contractors in the application of the new material and to verify that they were indeed following prescribed practice. These considerations held up rapid deployment of the technology, imposed additional costs, and so affected both the size of the potential market and the new product's rate of market penetration.

For a company to make needed investments in infrastructure, not only must it be able to assemble the resources, it must also perceive sufficient opportunity or threat. In the early 1950's, GE scientists invented a polymer with remarkable high temperature properties. Neither the equipment nor the know-how to fabricate the material existed, and GE lacked the capability to develop them. It did not even have effective enough relationships with equipment builders and plastics molders to stimulate action on their part. There was no engineered materials industry at the time, and GE was a novice in plastics.

Because sales were small and the business was peripheral to the company's major growth areas, GE reluctantly abandoned work on the new polymer. DuPont, with its large stake in nylon and long experience in process development and in working with plastic molders, saw the opportunity for a high-performance molded material in a very different light.

A few years later, when Lexan and Noryl came along, GE faced quite a different situation. Both materials presented challenging problems for those seeking to commercialize the technology, but molders were now comfortable with high temperature materials, new equipment had been developed, and the company had ample experience in designing plastic parts for engineering applications. Both Lexan and Noryl became major businesses, thanks in large part to the infrastructure that had meanwhile developed.

MISCONCEPTION 7

Making a technology effective doesn't involve developing routines and standards, achieving greater precision, and working under constraints.

The engineering group in GE's large steam turbine-generator business has a well-deserved reputation for being the best in the world at what it does. The engineers are not easy to work with; they are hard-nosed, doubting, conservative, unforgiving of mistakes, and demanding. To the extent they are resistant to change, scarred as they are from personal encounters with the misconceptions I have been discussing, their resistance helps minimize flawed innovations and costly mistakes. In today's complex technical environment, only the closest attention to detail and the most vigorous insistence on routines and standards make engineering design cost-effective.

In software engineering, for example, programmers have been operating with virtually no constraints on their personal idiosyncrasies or on their preference for "elegant" solutions. The result has been a vast duplication of effort and a proliferation of programs that, save at great expense, only their creators can maintain or modify. This lack of control has led no only to needless cost in writing and debugging software but also to a maddening diversity for the user. Anybody who has struggled with the endless shifts in symbology and keyboard usage that are required by various software packages for personal computers can attest to this Tower of Babel effect.

We must, therefore, learn how to modularize software, to rely on packages already familiar to users, and to impose rules and standards on the free spirits who are writing software. Admittedly, doing so may take some of the fun out of it, but a more systematic and constrained approach will significantly shorten preparation time, reduce errors, simplify future changes, and simplify the user problems.

An inevitable consequence of imposing structure and order on a technology, however, is that the technology itself becomes increasingly resistant to change. It becomes specialized to the task at hand and develops complex interdependencies with other technologies. But it also becomes more precise, efficient, and comprehensive in the solutions it provides.

TAKING STOCK

Where does a sophisticated understanding of these seven misconceptions lead? First of all, it leads to greater conservatism in predicting success for and in deploying new technology. On a probabilistic basis, if you bet "no" most of the time, you will win. Even with the discovery of an important new capability, a whole series of ancillary changes must often occur before market applications can succeed. Do not hesitate to ask, "Even if this new technology is as good as they say, what else has to happen before it can be deployed?" or "How much leverage on the total system does this advance exert?"

From the perspective of the innovator, this understanding focuses attention on the crucial role of a technology's first applications. Because the greatest barriers to innovation are diffusion of effort and uncertainty over performance, there is no substitute for real-life demonstrations in high-leverage applications. Indeed, unless the technology promises a great improvement, it is unlikely even to be tried. Diluting effort by aiming at several potential applications, or seeking refinement of properties without a specific application in mind, is an invitation to failure. To let the learning curve begin to work, you have to get on it.

For those supporting an innovation or debating its potential value, the success of the first application is a crucial bit of information. Once a technological advance has demonstrated its utility and value, the probability that it will "take" soars. In fact, after a technology has begun to demonstrate its value, we have been more prone to underestimate than to overestimate its potential.

Managers must see the process of innovation accurately, not as colored by varied misconceptions. Although the odds are very high that any given innovation attempt will fail, companies must innovate in order to survive. And the benefits of the occasional successes are enormous—not only in direct rewards to the innovator and of gains to society, but also in the ripple effects generated by the process itself. It goads conventional technology into improvement, stimulates adaptability to change, leads a company toward greater self-awareness of its strengths and weaknesses, and responds to one of the most powerful human drives—the urge to try something new.

NOTE

1. See David A. Garvin, "Quality On the Line," *HBR* September–October 1943, p. 64.

Lead User and New Product Development

Eric von Hippel

The organizational field experiment reported in this paper involves predicting the source of innovation, user innovation in this instance, and then outlining a methodology for benefitting from this knowledge. The specific context of the work addresses an important problem facing all innovative organizations, i.e., how can one effectively determine user needs for developing new products (processes and services) in markets that are strongly affected by rapid changes in technology.

The paper begins by exploring in more depth the difficulty faced by traditional methods of market research. It then spells out the lead user methodology I have proposed as a managerial solution for dealing with this problem.[1] A detailed application of this methodology in one industrial setting is subsequently described.

ROOT OF THE PROBLEM: MARKETING RESEARCH CONSTRAINED BY USER EXPERIENCE

One important function of marketing research is to accurately understand user needs for potential new products. Such understanding is clearly an essential input to the success of the new product development process. Nevertheless, users selected to provide input data to consumer and industrial market analysis have an important limitation: their insights into new product (and process and service) needs and potential solutions are constrained by their real-world experiences. Users steeped in the present are, therefore, unlikely to generate novel product concepts that conflict with the familiar.

The notion that familiarity with existing product attributes and uses interferes with an individual's ability to conceive of novel attributes and uses is strongly supported by research into problem solving. Extant studies have shown, for example, that when experimental subjects are familiarized with a complicated problem-solving strategy, they are unlikely to devise a simpler one even when this is appropriate. Moreover, subjects who use an object or see it used in a very normal and familiar way are strongly blocked from using that object in a new or novel manner. In fact, the more recently these objects or problem-solving strategies were used in a familiar way, the more difficult it was for the subject to employ them in a more innovative way.[2] In an R&D setting, Allen and Marquis showed that the success of a research group in solving a new problem was strongly dependent on whether the solutions and experiences it had used in the past fit the demands of the new problem.[3] All of these research studies suggest that typical users of existing products—the type of customer or user-evaluators usually chosen in market research—are poorly situated with regard to the difficult problem-solving tasks associated with assessing unfamiliar product and process needs.

A more extensive discussion of this paper can be found in my recent book entitled *The Sources of Innovation*, Oxford University Press, 1988.

Consider, for example, the difficult problem-solving steps potential users must go through when asked to evaluate their need for a proposed new product. Individually distinct industrial- or consumer-based products are in reality only components in larger usage patterns that involve many such products. Since a change in one component can change perceptions of, and needs for, some or all of the other products in that pattern, users must first identify their existing multiproduct usage patterns in which the new product might play a role and then evaluate the new product's potential contribution within this overall context. (E.g., a change in the operating characteristics of a computer may allow users to solve new problem types if they also make changes in software and perhaps in other, related products and practices.) Users must next invent or select the new (to them) usage patterns that the proposed new product makes possible for the first time and then evaluate the utility of the product in these patterns. And finally, since substitutes exist for many multiproduct usage patterns, the user must estimate how the new possibilities presented by the proposed new product will compete (or fail to compete) with existing options. This problem-solving task is clearly a very difficult one, particularly for typical users of existing products whose familiarity with those products and uses interferes with their ability to conceive of novel products and uses when invited to do so.

The constraint of users to the familiar pertains even in the instance of sophisticated marketing research techniques such as multiattribute mapping of product perceptions and preferences.[4] Multiattribute (multidimensional) marketing research methods, for example, describe users' (buyers') perception of new and existing products in terms of a number of attributes (dimensions). If a complete list of attributes is available for a given product category, the users' perceptions of any particular product in the category can be expressed in terms of the amount of each attribute they perceive it to contain, and the dif-ference between any two products in the category can be expressed as the difference in their attribute profiles. Similarly, users' preferences for existing and proposed products in a category can in principle be built up from their perceptions of the importance and desirability of each of the component product attributes.

Although these methods frame user perceptions and preferences in terms of known attributes, they do not offer a means of going beyond the experience of those interviewed. First, for reasons discussed earlier, users are not well positioned to accurately evaluate novel product attributes or accurately quantify familiar product attributes that lie outside the range of their real-world experience. Second, and more specific to these techniques, there is no mechanism to induce users to identify all product attributes potentially relevant to a product category, especially attributes that are currently not present in any of the given categories.

In similarity-dissimilarity data techniques, for example, users are asked to characterize a product category by comparing products in that category and assessing them in terms of their similarity and dissimilarity. Sometimes the user specifies the ways in which the products are similar or different. In others, the user simply provides similarity and difference rankings or ratings, and the market researcher determines (through his personal knowledge of the product type in question) the important perceptual dimensions that must be motivating the user's data comparisons.

Such similarity-dissimilarity methods clearly depend on the analyst's qualitative ability to interpret the data and correctly identity all the critical dimensions. However, this method can only explore perceptions derived from attributes that exist in, or are associated with, the actual products being compared. Thus, if a group of evaluators is invited to compare a set of cameras and none has a particular feature—say, instant developing—then the possible utility of this feature would not be incorporated in the perceptual dimensions generated. That is, the method would have been blind to the possible value of instant developing prior to Edwin Land's invention of the Polaroid camera.

While other market research techniques, focus group methods for example, need not be limited in principle to identifying only attributes already present in existing products, most of the discussions and associated data are nominally focused on these. Generally speaking, it is very unlikely that these methods can be used to identify attributes not present in the actual set of products being studied, much less a complete list of all relevant attributes. Conventional market research methods simply do not contain an effective mechanism for encouraging these kinds of outcomes, and discussions with practitioners indicate that in present-day practice, identification of any novel attribute is improbable. In sum, then, marketing researchers face serious difficulties when they attempt to determine new product needs that fall outside of the real-world experience of the users they analyze.

LEAD USERS AS A SOLUTION

In many product categories, the constraint of users to the familiar does not lessen the ability of marketing research to evaluate needs for new products by analyzing typical users. In the relatively slow-moving world of steels and autos, for example, new models often do not differ radically from their immediate predecessors. Therefore, even the "new" is reasonably familiar and the typical user can thus play a valuable role in the development of new products.

Contrastingly, in high technology industries, the world moves so rapidly that the related real-world experience of ordinary users is often rendered obsolete by the time a product is developed or during the time of its projected commercial lifetime. For such industries, I propose that lead users, who *do* have real-life experience with

novel product or process needs, are essential to accurate marketing research. Although the insights of lead users are as constrained to the familiar as those of other users, lead users are more familiar with conditions that lie in the future and so, are in a position to provide accurate data on needs related to such prospective conditions.

Lead users of a novel or enhanced product, process, or service are defined as those who display two characteristics with respect to it:

1. Lead users face needs that will be general in a marketplace, but they face them months or years before the bulk of that marketplace encounters them, *and*
2. Lead users are positioned to benefit significantly by obtaining a solution to those needs.

Thus, a manufacturing firm with a current strong need for a process innovation that many other comparable manufacturers will need in two years' time would fit the definition of lead user with respect to that process.

Each of the two lead user characteristics provides an independent contribution to the type of new product need and solution data that such lead users are hypothesized to possess. The first specifies that a lead user will possess the particular real-world experience that the manufacturers must analyze if they are to accurately understand the needs that the bulk of the market will have "tomorrow." Users "at the front of the trend" typically exist simply because important new technologies, products, tastes, and other factors related to new product opportunities typically diffuse through a society over many years rather than impact all members simultaneously.[5]

The second lead user characteristic is a direct application of the hypothesis that the greater the benefit a given user expects to obtain from a needed novel product or process, the greater his investment will be in obtaining a solution. Users who expect high returns from a solution to a need they are experiencing should have been driven by these expectations to attempt to solve their need. This work in turn will have produced insight into the need and perhaps useful solutions that will be of value to inquiring market researchers.

In sum, then, lead users are users whose present strong needs will become general in a marketplace months or years in the future. Since lead users are familiar with conditions that lie in the future for most others, it is hypothesized that they can serve as a need-forecasting laboratory for marketing research. Moreover, since lead users often attempt to fill the need they experience, it is also hypothesized that they can provide valuable new product concept and design data to inquiring manufacturing organizations in addition to need data. As a result, lead users may have a great deal more to contribute than data regarding their unfilled needs; often, they may contribute insights regarding solutions as well. Such "solution" data can range from rich insights to actual working and tested prototypes of the desired novel product, process, or service. Von Hippel has carefully shown, for example, that in some fields users were the actual developers of most of the successful new products eventually commercialized by manufacturers. Users were found to be the actual developers of 82% of all commercialized scientific instruments studied and 63% of all semiconductor and electron subassembly manufacturing equipment innovations studied.[6]

TESTING THE METHOD

To test the usefulness of the lead user concept, a prototype lead user market research study was undertaken in the rapidly changing field of computer-aided-design (CAD) products.[7] (Over 40 firms compete in the $1 billion market for CAD hardware and software. This market grew at over 35% per year over the period 1982 to 1986 and the forecast is for continued growth at this rate for the next several years.) Within the CAD field, we decided to specifically focus on CAD systems used to design the printed circuit (PC) boards used in electronic products, PC–CAD.

Printed circuit boards hold integrated circuit chips and other electronic components and interconnect these into functioning circuits. PC–CAD systems help engineers convert circuit specifications into detailed printed circuit board designs. The design steps that are, or can be, aided by PC–CAD include component placement, signal routing (interconnections), editing and checking, documentation, and interfacing to manufacturing. The software required to perform these tasks is quite complex and includes placement and routing algorithms and sophisticated graphics. Some PC–CAD manufacturers sell only such software, whereas others sell systems that include both specialized computers and software. (Important suppliers of PC–CAD in 1985 included IBM, Computervision, Redac, Calma, Scicards, and Telesis.)

The method used to identify lead users and test the value of the data they possess in the PC–CAD field involved four major steps: (1) identify an important market or technical trend, (2) identify lead users with respect to that trend, (3) analyze lead user data, and (4) test lead user data on ordinary users. I will discuss each in turn.

Identifying an Important Trend

Lead users are defined as being in advance of the market with respect to a given important dimension that is changing over time. Therefore, before one can identify lead users in a given product category of interest, one must specify the underlying trend on which these users have a leading position.

To identify an "important" trend in PC–CAD, we sought out a number of expert users. We identified these by telephoning managers of the PC–CAD groups of a number of firms in the Boston area and asking each: "Whom do you regard as the engineer most expert in PC–CAD in

291

your firm?'' ''Whom in your company do group members turn to when they face difficult PC–CAD problems?''[8] After our discussions with expert users, it was qualitatively clear to us that an increase in the density with which chips and circuits are placed on a board was, and would continue to be, a very important trend in the PC–CAD field. Historical data showed that board density had in fact been steadily increasing over a number of years. And the value of continuing increases in density was clear. An increase in density means that it is possible to mount more electronic components on a given size printed circuit board. This in turn translates directly into an ability to lower costs (less material is used), to decreased product size, and to increased speed of circuit operation (signals between components travel shorter distances when board density is higher).

Very possibly, other equally important trends exist in the field that would reward analysis, but we decided to focus on this single trend in our study.

Identifying Lead Users

To identify lead users of PC–CAD systems capable of designing high-density printed circuit boards, we had to identify that subset of users: (1) who were designing very high-density boards now and (2) who were positioned to gain especially high benefit from increases in board density. We decided to use a formal telephone-screening questionnaire to accomplish this task, and we strove to design one that contained objective indicators of these two hypothesized lead user characteristics.

Printed circuit board density can be increased in a number of ways and each offers an objective means of determining a respondent's position on the trend toward higher density. First, the number of layers of printed wiring in a printed circuit board can be increased. (Early boards contained only 1 or 2 layers but now some manufacturers are designing boards with

20 or more layers.) Second, the size of electronic components can be decreased. (A recent important technique for achieving this is surface-mounted devices that are soldered directly to the surface of a printed circuit board.) Finally, the printed wires, vias, that interconnect the electronic components on a board that can be made narrower and packed more closely. Questions regarding each of these density-related attributes were included in our questionnaire.

Next, we assessed the level of benefit a respondent might expect to gain by improvements in PC–CAD by means of several questions. First, we asked about users' level of satisfaction with existing PC–CAD equipment, assuming that high dissatisfaction would indicate expected high benefit from improvements. Second, we asked whether respondents had developed and built their own PC–CAD systems rather than buy the commercially available systems such as those offered by IBM or Computervision. (We assumed, as we noted previously, that users who make such innovation investments do so because they expect high benefit from resulting PC–CAD system improvements.) Finally, we asked respondents whether they thought their firms were innovators in the field of PC–CAD.

The PC–CAD users interviewed were restricted to U.S. firms and selected from two sources: A list of members of the relevant professional engineering association (IPCA) and a list of current and potential customers provided by a cooperating supplier. Interviewees were selected from both lists at random. We contacted approximately 178 qualified respondents and had them answer the questions on the phone or by mail if they preferred. The cooperation rate was good: 136 screening questionnaires were completed. One third of these were completed by engineers or designers, one third by CAD or printed circuit board managers, 26% by general engineering managers, and 8% by corporate officers.

Simple inspection of the screening questionnaire responses showed that fully 23% of all responding user firms had developed their own in-house PC–CAD hardware and software systems. Also, this high proportion of user-innovators that we found in our sample is probably characteristic of the general population of PC–CAD users. Our sample was well dispersed across the self-stated scale with respect to innovativeness: 24% indicated they were on the leading edge of technology, 38% up-to-date, 25% in the mainstream, and 13% adopting only after the technology is clearly established. This self-perception is supported by objective behavior with respect to the alacrity with which our respondents adopted PC–CAD.

We next conducted a cluster analysis of screening questionnaire data relating to the hypothesized lead user characteristics in an attempt to identify a lead user group. The two cluster solution is shown in Table 1.

Note that this analysis does, indeed, clearly indicate a group of respondents who combine the two hypothesized attributes of lead users and that, effectively, all of the PC–CAD product innovation is reported by the lead user group.

In the two-cluster solution, what we term the lead users cluster is ahead of nonlead users in the trend toward higher density. That is, lead users report more use of surface-mounted components, use of narrower lines, and use of more layers than do members of the nonlead cluster. Second, lead users appear to expect higher benefit from PC–CAD innovations that would allow them even further progress. That is, they report less satisfaction with their existing PC–CAD systems (4.1 vs. 5.3, with higher values indicating satisfaction). Strikingly, 87% of respondents in the lead user group report building their own PC–CAD system (vs. only 1% of nonlead users) in order to obtain improved PC–CAD system performance.[9] Lead users also judged themselves to be more innovative (3.3 vs. 2.4 on the four-statement scale with higher values more innovative), and they were in fact earlier adopters of PC–CAD than were nonlead users. Note that 28% of our respondents are classified in this lead user cluster. The two clusters explained 24% of the variation in the data.

A discriminant analysis indicated that building one's own system was the most important indicator of membership in the lead user cluster. (The discriminant analysis had 95.6% correct

TABLE 1. *Cluster Analyses Revealing Lead and Nonlead User Groups*

	Two-Cluster Solution	
	Lead Users	Nonlead Users
Indicators of user position on PC–CAD density trend		
Use surface mount?	87%	56%
Average line width (mils)	11	15
Average layers (number)	7.1	4.0
Indicators of user-expected benefit from PC–CAD improvement		
Satisfaction[a]	4.1	5.3
Indicators of related user innovation		
Build own PC–CAD?	85%	1%
Innovativeness[b]	3.3	2.4
First use of CAD (year)	1973	1980
Number in cluster	38	98

[a]7-point scale—high value more satisfied.
[b]4-point scale—high value more innovative.

classification of cluster membership. The standardized discriminant function of coefficients were: build own .94, self-stated innovativeness .27, average layers .25, satisfaction −.23, year of adoption −.16, surface mounting .15.)

Analyzing Lead User Insights

The next step in our analysis was to select a small sample of the lead users identified in our cluster analysis to participate in a group discussion to develop one or more concepts for improved PC–CAD systems. Experts from five lead user firms that had facilities located near MIT were recruited for this group. The firms represented were Raytheon, DEC, Bell Laboratories, Honeywell, and Teradyne. Four of these five firms had built their own PC–CAD systems. All were working in high-density (many layers and narrow lines) applications and had adopted the CAD technology early.

The task set for this group was to specify the best PC–CAD system for laying out high-density digital boards that could be built with current technology. (To guard against the inclusion of "dream" features impossible to implement, we conservatively allowed the concept the group developed to include only features that one or more of them had already implemented in their own organizations. No one firm had implemented all aspects of the concept, however.)

The PC–CAD system concept developed by our lead user creative group integrated the output of PC–CAD with numerically controlled printed circuit board manufacturing machines; had easy input interfaces (e.g., block diagrams, interactive graphics, icon menus); and stored data centrally with access by all systems. It also provided full functional and environmental simulation (e.g., electrical, mechanical, and thermal) of the board being designed and could design boards of up to 20 layers, route thin lines, and properly located surface-mounted devices on the board.

Testing Product Concept Perceptions and Preferences

From the point of view of marketing research, new product need data and new product solutions from lead users are only interesting if they are preferred by the general marketplace.

To test this matter, we decided to determine PC–CAD user preferences for four system concepts: the system concept developed by the lead user group, each user's own in-house PC–CAD system, the best commercial PC–CAD system available at the time of the study (as determined by a PC–CAD system manufacturer's competitive analysis), and a system for laying out curved printed circuit boards. (This last was a description of a special-purpose system that one lead user had designed in-house to lay out boards curved into three-dimensional shapes. This is a useful attribute if one is trying to fit boards into the oddly shaped spaces inside some very compact products, but most users would have no practical use for it. In our analysis of preference, we think user response to this concept can serve to flag any respondent tendency to prefer systems based on system exotica rather than practical value in use.)

To obtain user preference data regarding our four PC–CAD system concepts, we designed a new questionnaire that contained measures of both perception and preference. First, respondents were asked to rate their current PC–CAD system on 17 attribute scales. (These were generated by a separate sample of users through triad comparisons of alternate systems, open-ended interviews, and technical analysis.) Each scale was presented to respondents in the form of five-point agree-disagree judgment based on a statement such as "my system is easy to customize."[10] Next, each respondent was invited to read a one-page description of each of the three concepts we had generated (labeled simply, J, K, and L) and rate them on the same scales. All concepts were described as having an identical price of $150,000 for a complete hardware and software workstation system able to support four users. Next, rank-order preference and constant-sum paired comparison judgments were requested for the three concepts and the existing system. Finally, probability-of-purchase measures on an 11-point Juster scale were collected for each concept at the base price of $150,000, with alternate prices of $100,000 and $200,000.

Our second questionnaire was sent to 173 users (the 178 respondents who qualified in the screening survey less the 5 user firms in the creative group). Respondents were called by phone to inform them that a questionnaire had been sent. After telephone follow-up and a second mailing of the questionnaire, 71 complete or near-complete responses were obtained (41%) and the following analyses are based on these.[11]

Lead User Concept Preferred

As can be seen from Table 2, our analysis of the concept questionnaire showed that respondents strongly preferred the lead user group PC–CAD system concept over the three others presented to them: 78.6% of the sample selected the lead user creative group concept as their first choice. The constant sum scaled-preference value was 2.60 for the concept developed by the lead user group. This was 35% greater than users' preference for their own current system and more than twice as great as the preference for the most advanced existing commercially available product offering.

The concept created by the lead user group was also generally preferred by users over their existing systems (significant at the 10% level based on the preference measures: $t = 12$ for proportion first choice and $t = 2.1$ for constant sum). And, the lead user group concept was significantly preferred over the special application user system developed to lay out curved boards. (The lead user concept was significantly better than the user-developed special application system on all measures at the 10% level ($t = 12.3$ for first choice, $t = 7.9$ for preference, and $t = 8.5$ for probability).[12]

Respondents maintained their preferences for the lead user concept even when it was priced higher than competing concepts. The effects of price were investigated through the probability of purchase measures collected at three prices for each concept. For the lead user concept, probability of purchase increases from 52.3% to 63.0% when the price is decreased from $150,000 to $100,000 ($t = 2.3$) and drops to 37.7% when the price is increased to $200,000. Probability of purchase of the lead user concept was significantly higher at all price levels (t greater than 4.4 in all paired comparisons), and it was preferred to the best available concept even when the specified price was twice as high as that of competing

TABLE 2. Test of All Respondents' Preferences Among Four Alternative PC-CAD System Concepts

PC-CAD Concept	% First Choice	Constant Sum[a]	Average Probability of Purchase
Lead user group concept	78.6	2.60	51.7
Respondents current PC–CAD	9.8	1.87	[b]
Best system commercially available	4.9	0.95	20.0
User system for special application	6.5	0.77	26.0

[a]Warren S. Torgerson, *Theory and Methods of Scaling* (New York: Wiley, 1958).
[b]Probability of purchase only collected across concepts.

concepts. All three concepts displayed the same proportionate change in purchase probability as the price was changed from its base level of $150,000. The probability measures indicate substantial price sensitivity and provide a convergent measure on the attractiveness of the concept based on lead user solution content.

Similarity of Lead and Nonlead User Preferences

The needs of today's lead users are typically not precisely the same as the needs of the users who will make up a major share of tomorrow's predicted market. Indeed, the literature on diffusion suggests that in general the early adopters of a novel product or practice differ in significant ways from the bulk of the users who follow them.[13] However, in this instance, as Table 3 shows, the product concept preferences of lead users and nonlead users were very similar.

A comparison of the way in which lead and nonlead users evaluated PC–CAD systems showed that this similarity of preference was deep-seated. An examination of the PC–CAD attribute ratings and factor analyses derived from each group showed five factors that explained the same amount of variation (67.8 for lead users and 67.7 for nonlead users). The factor loadings were also similar for the two groups, and their interpretation suggested the same dimension labels. Also, analyses showed that each group placed a similar degree of importance on each dimension.

DISCUSSION

From the point of view of marketing research, I think that the results of this first test of a lead user method must be seen as encouraging. Lead users with the hypothesized characteristics were clearly identified: a novel product concept was created based on lead user insights and problem-solving activities; and the lead user concept was judged to be superior to currently available alternatives by a separate sample of lead and non lead users. It should be pointed out, however, that the high level of actual product innovation found among lead users of PC–CAD can only be expected in product areas where the returns expected by such users are sufficient to induce user innovation. Where expected user benefit is less, need data available from lead users should still be more accurate and richer in "solution content" than data from nonlead users, but it may not include prototype products such as those we have observed in the study of PC–CAD.

From the point of view of the underlying hypothesis regarding the ability to predict the sources of innovation on the basis of innovators' related expectations of returns and benefits, I think the lead user application has also shown very encouraging results. Users who identified themselves as dissatisfied with existing products were shown more likely to be involved in developing new ones that would be more responsive to their particular needs.

There are, however, certain problematic issues which must be further explored before we

TABLE 3.   Concept Preferences of Lead Versus Nonlead Users

PC–CAD Concept	% First Choice		Constant Sum		Average Probability of Purchase	
	Lead	Nonlead	Lead	Nonlead	Lead	Nonlead
Lead user group concept	92.3%	80.5%	3.20	2.37	53.1	51.2
Respondents' current PC–CAD	7.7	11.1	2.64	1.56	0	0
Best system commercially available	0	2.8	0.67	1.06	10.2	23.9
User system for special application	0	5.6	0.52	0.87	16.3	29.9

have complete confidence in these approaches. One problem in the method is accurate trend identification. Currently we rely on a skillful analyst to select an important trend on the basis of judgement (much as product attributes for use in multi-attribute analysis are selected by market research analysts on the basis of judgement and qualitative data). Clearly, it would be useful to improve this method. Given the present state of the art, one might lessen the chance of error when in doubt by selecting several candidate dimensions and screening lead users on each of them along with the benefit indicators. If the same lead users are identified in each instance, the ideas they generate are likely to span all the candidate dimensions. If they are not, parallel idea generation efforts should be undertaken and the concepts tested with alternative lead user segmentations.

A second problem with the method is that it assumes that the product perceptions and preferences of lead users are or will be similar to non-lead users as a market develops. When this is true, evaluation of the eventual appeal of a lead user product or product concept is straightforward. But what if lead users like the product and non-lead users do not? In this case there are two possibilities: (1) The concept is too novel to be appreciated by non-lead users—but it will later be preferred by them when their needs evolve to resemble those of today's lead users; (2) the concept appeals only to lead users and will never be appreciated by non-lead users even after they "evolve."

In the first case, the high response from lead users and low response from others could be compatible with eventual commercial success for the product; in the latter case it would not be. How can we tell the difference? Analysis can help but we need to develop more reliable indicators that can predict whether lead user perceptions and preferences *do* or *will* foreshadow those of the general user community.

Finally, our study has focused on the identification and study of naturally occurring lead us-

ers. Perhaps lead users can also be created? It is possible for manufacturers to stimulate user innovation by acting to increase user innovation-related benefit. If they can also place users in environments which they judge to foreshadow future general market conditions, they may be able to create lead users. Market research studies which allow users to experience prototypes of proposed new products and then test their reactions are a possible step in this direction.

We have described the implications of lead users for market research in the concept generation and testing phases of new product development. Perhaps they can be useful after product launch as well? Thus, after launch lead users might be employed as opinion leaders; this tactic is now often employed by firms selling medical products and services. Or lead users might be tracked after product launch as a means of identifying important user modifications and improvements to the initial product. Pre-market forecasting of products has received considerable attention in consumer frequently purchased durables markets, but none of these models or methods has integrated the notion of lead users and diffusion of innovation across heterogeneous users.

In sum, it is possible that marketing research methods based on analyses of lead users can offer manufacturers a window on the future customer needs in rapidly-moving fields, and it is our hope that other organizations and researchers will join in further exploring and developing this possibility.

NOTES

1. Eric von Hippel, "Lead Users: A Source of Novel Product Concepts," *Management Science* 32, no. 7 (July 1986): 791–805.
2. R. E. Adamson and D. W. Taylor, "Functional Fixedness as Related to Elapsed Time and to Set," *Journal of Experimental Psychology* 47 (1954): 122–26.

3. T. J. Allen and D. G. Marquis, "Positive and Negative Biasing Sets: The Effects of Prior Experience on Research Performance," *IEEE Transactions on Engineering Management* EM-11, no. 4 (December 1964): 158–614.

4. Alvin J. Silk and Glen L. Urban, "Pre-Test-Market Evaluation of New Packaged Goods: A Model and Measurement Methodology," *Journal of Marketing Research* 15, no. 2 (May 1978): 171–91; Allan D. Shocket and V. Srinivasan, "Multiattribute Approaches for Product Concept Evaluation and Generation: A Critical Review," *Journal of Marketing Research* 16, no. 2 (May 1979): 159–80.

5. For example, when Edwin Mansfield (*The Economics of Technological Change* [New York: Norton, 1968], 134–35) explored the rate of diffusion of 12 very important industrial goods innovations into major firms in the bituminous coal, iron and steel, brewing, and railroad industries, he found that in 75% of the cases it took over 20 years for complete diffusion of these innovations to major firms. Accordingly, some users of these innovations could be found far in advance of the general market.

6. See (1) von Hippel, E. "The Dominant Role of Users in the Scientific Instrument Innovation Process," *Research Policy* 5 (1976): 212–239 and (2) von Hippel, E. "The Dominant Role of the User in Semiconductor and Electronic Subassembly Process Innovation," *IEEE Transactions on Engineering Management* 24 (1977): 60–71.

7. See G. Urban and E. von Hippel, "Lead User Analyses for the Development of New Industrial Products," *Management Science*, 1988.

8. PC–CAD system purchase decisions are made primarily by the final users in the engineering department responsible for CAD design of boards. In this study we interviewed only these dominant influencers to find concepts and test them. If the purchase decision process had been more diffuse, it would have been appropriate to include other important decision participants in our data collection.

9. The innovating users reported that their goal was to achieve better performance than commercially available products could provide in several areas: high routing density, faster turnaround time to meet market demands, better compatibility to manufacturing, interfaces to other graphics and mechanical CAD systems, and improved ease of use for less experienced users.

10. The 17 attributes were: ease of customization, integration with other CAD systems, completeness of features, integration with manufacturing, maintenance, upgrading, learning, ease of use, power, design time, enough layers, high-density boards, manufacturable designs, reliability, placing and routing capabilities, high value, and updating capability.

11. There were 94 individuals (55%) who actually returned the questionnaire, but only 71 returns were judged complete enough to use. This subset consists of 61 respondents who completed all items on both the screening and concept questionnaires, and an additional 10 who completed all items except the constant-sum paired comparison allocations.

12. As part of our analysis we tested for potential nonresponse bias by comparing early and later returns and found none. Returns from the first 41% of respondents showed 77% first choice for the creative group concepts and the last 59% showed 71% first choice. The differences between the early and later returns were not significant at the 10% level ($t = .15$). Thus, there was no evidence of a nonresponse bias. A possible demand-effect bias toward the lead user group concept could have been present, but the low preferences for the best available product and the curved board concepts argues against it. All concepts were presented in a similar format with labels of concept *J, K,* and *L* (the lead user group concept was labeled *K*). We did not expect any differential bias toward concept *K*.

13. Everett M. Rogers with F. Floyd Shoemaker, *Communications of Innovations: A Cross-Cultural Approach* (New York: Free Press, 1971).

SECTION
IV

Issues in Managing Technical Groups and Project Teams

7

ISSUES IN MANAGING TECHNICAL TEAMS AND GROUP PROCESS

Building High Performing Engineering Project Teams

Hans J. Thamhain

David L. Wilemon

Abstract. This article summarizes four years of research into the drivers and barriers of effective teambuilding in engineering work environments. A simple input–output model is presented for organizing and analyzing the various factors which influence team performance. The field survey results supported by correlation analysis indicate that team performance is primarily associated with six driving forces and six barriers which are related to: leadership, job content, personal needs, and general work environment. Specific recommendations are made.

TEAM BUILDING DEFINED

Team building is the process of taking a collection of individuals with different needs, backgrounds, and expertise and transforming them into an integrated, effective work unit. In this transformation process, the goals and energies of individual contributors merge and support the objectives of the team.

The basic concept of team building dates back in history for a long time as summarized in the listing of chronological development shown below. However the onset of modern team building came with the evolution of multidisciplinary management techniques and contemporary organization forms such as the matrix. With these developments, traditional bureaucratic hierarchies declined and horizontally oriented teams and work units became increasingly important.

Today, team building is considered by many management practitioners and researchers to be one of the most critical leadership qualities that determines the performance and success of multidisciplinary efforts. The outcome of these projects ·critically depend on carefully orchestrated group efforts, requiring the coordination and integration of many task specialists in a dynamic work environment with complex organization interfaces. Therefore, it is not surprising to find a strong emphasis on team work and team building practice among today's managers, a trend which, we expect, will continue and most likely intensify for years to come.

Some milestones in the evolution of team building and key contributors to the development of its concepts are shown below:

•4000 BC	Egyptians	Demonstrated ability of formally organizing and controlling work groups.
•1500 AD	Niccolo Macchiavelli	Early explanation of work group structure and functioning. (*The Prince*).
•1930's	Sloan, Mayo, Bernard	Formal organization of work groups in bureaucratic, hierarchical structures. Autocratic behavior.
•1950's	Simon, Lewin, Davis, Drucker	Understanding of group dynamics and behavior in organizations. Translation of established
•1960's	McGregor, Likert, Carzo, Katz, Schein, Lawrence, Lorsch, Jewkes, Blake, Mouton, Fiedler	theories from individuals to work group settings. Increased managerial interest in team building and need for effective team work. Japanese lessons.
•1970's	Benningson, Dyer, Kidder	Specific field studies of technical team work. Attempts to characterize drivers and barriers of high team performance. Theory development.
•1980's	Ouchi, Thamhain, Wilemon.	

ENGINEERING TEAM BUILDING TODAY

Team building is important in any environment which requires the coordination and integration of multidisciplinary activities. It is especially crucial in a technical environment where projects are often highly complex and require the integration of many functional specialties in an often unconventional organizational setting such as the matrix. To manage these multifunctional activities, it is necessary for the managers and their lead engineering personnel to cross organizational lines and deal with resource personnel over whom they have little or no formal authority. Yet another set of challenges is presented by the contemporary nature of the engineering organization with its horizontal and vertical lines of communication and control, its resource sharings among projects and task teams, multiple reporting relationships to several bosses, and dual accountabilities.

Managing technical projects effectively in such dynamic environments requires the understanding of organizational and behavioral variables and their interaction. It is further necessary to foster a climate conducive to multidisciplinary team building. Such a team must have a capacity for innovatively transforming a set of technical objectives and requirements into specific products, system concepts, or services that compete favorably against other available alternatives.

BASIS OF THIS REPORT

The team building concept is not entirely new, as shown in the text insert on evolution, but its application to systematic efforts within a permanent organizational framework—rather than temporary work setting—is relatively recent. Starting with the evolution of formal project organizations in the 1960's, managers in various organizational settings have expressed increasing concern and interest on the concepts and practices of multidisciplinary team building. Responding to this interest, many field studies have been conducted investigating work group dynamics in a general context contributing to the theoretical and practical understanding of team building.[2-4, 6, 13, 14, 18, 20, 38] However, few studies specifically focus on the process and criteria of building effective high-performing engineering teams.[18, 19, 24, 37] Because of this special need and interest the authors have organized and conducted a series of studies over the last four years. These field studies analyzed some 30 companies involving over 500 engineering professionals including 37 managers. All of these companies were U.S. based and were managers as high-technology businesses. The data were gathered primarily by means of interviews augmented by short questionnaires. The results are documented in five research papers listed below:

1. skill requirements for engineering program managers[30],
2. professional needs analysis of engineering personnel versus performance[29],
3. analysis of barriers to teamwork and potential effects on project performance[35],

4. determination of team performance measures and their drivers and barriers, some performance correlates[31],
5. a model for developing high-performing project teams.[37]

This article is an attempt to summarize and integrate the findings from our research and to establish a conceptional framework for effective team building in an engineering/technological work environment.

Originally, a broadly stated proposition was defined to guide our research. It is restated here to focus this paper and to help in guiding the discussion:

P: Engineering team performance is associated with drivers and barriers related predominately to 1) leadership and 2) a professionally stimulating work environment.

MODEL FOR TEAM BUILDING

The characteristics of a project team and its ultimate performance depends on many factors. Using a systems approach, Figure 1 provides a simple model for organizing and analyzing these factors. It defines three sets of variables: 1) *inputs* such as resources and objectives, 2) *outputs* of the workgroups such as the team results or the team characteristics, and 3) *influences* toward effective team work such as leadership, job content, personal goals, and work environment. All of these variables are likely to be interrelated in a complex, intricate form. However, using the systems approach allows researchers and management practitioners to break down the complexity of the team work process which transforms resources into specific results under the influence of managerial, organizational, and other environmental factors. Furthermore, the model can provide a framework for studying

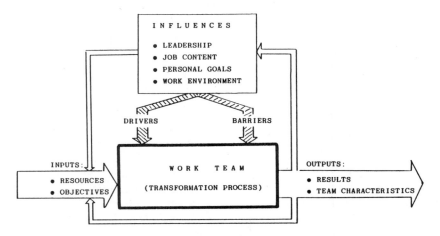

FIGURE 1. *The Transformation of Resources and Objectives into Results Is Affected by a Variety of Drivers and Barriers*

team characteristics and performance at various phases of a project life cycle. Such an investigation has been initiated by the authors. It will include the following project phases: 1) Project Definition and Planning, 2) Project Start-Up, 3) Main Phase, and 4) Project Phase-Out.

FACETS OF TEAM PERFORMANCE

Obviously, each organization has their own way to measure and express performance of a project team. However, in spite of the existing cultural and philosophical differences there seems to be a general agreement among engineering managers on certain factors which are included in the characteristics of a successful technical project team. In fact, over 90 percent of the 500 engineering professionals interviewed over the last four years mentioned three measures as the most important criteria for measuring team performance:

1. technical success,
2. on-time performance,
3. on-budget/within resource performance.

Further, over 60 percent of those who identified these three measures, ranked them in the above order.

When describing the characteristics of an effective, high-performing engineering team, managers point at the factors summarized in Figure 2. These managers stress consistently that a high-performing engineering team not only produces technical results on time and on budget but is also characterized by *specific task-* and *people-related qualities* as shown below.

Task-Related Qualities	People-Related Qualities
• oriented toward technical success;	• high involvement, work interest, and energy;
• committed to the project; result-oriented attitude;	• capacity to solve conflict;
• innovative and creative;	• good communication;
• concern for quality;	• good team spirit;
• willingness to change project plan if necessary;	• mutual trust;
• ability to predict trends;	• self-development of team members;
• on-time performance;	• effective organizational interfacing;
• on-budget performance.	• high need for achievement.

304

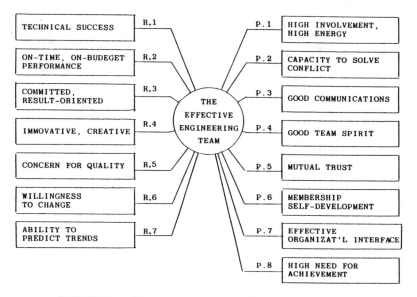

JOB/RESULT-ORIENTED CHARACTERISTICS
(DIRECT MEASURE OF PROJECT PERFORMANCE)

PEOPLE-ORIENTED CHARACTERISTICS
(INDIRECT MEASURE OF PROJECT PERFORMANCE)

FIGURE 2. *Characteristics of an Effective Engineering Team*

In fact, some quantitative analysis, performed during previous studies[31, 32], shows a statistically significant association* between the above team qualities and team performance at a confidence level of $p = 95$ percent or better. Specifically, these measures yielded an average rank-order correlation of $\tau = 0.37$. Moreover, there appears to be a strong agreement between the two professional groups, 1) managers and 2) project team members, on the importance of these characteristics, as measured via a Kruskal-Wallis analysis of variance by ranks at a confidence level of $p = 95$ percent.

The significance of determining team performance characteristics is in two areas. First, it offers some clues as to what an effective team environment looks like. This can stimulate

thoughts of how to foster a work environment responsive to the needs of the people and conducive to team building. Second, the results allow us to define measures and characteristics of an effective team environment for further studies such as the subsequent discussion on drivers and barriers toward team performance.

DRIVERS AND BARRIERS OF HIGH TEAM PERFORMANCE

In 1983 and 84, additional management insight was gained by an investigation of drivers and barriers to high team performance (see 31 and 35). Drivers are factors associated with the project environment that are perceived to be enhancing team effectiveness, while barriers are perceived to be impeding team performance. A listing of the principal drivers and barriers, as

---

*For method and references to statistical modes see Appendix.

perceived by project professionals is shown below:

Drivers, Enhancing Project Performance	Barriers, Impeding Project Performance
• Professionally stimulating and challenging work;	• Different interests and priorities among team members;
• Professional growth potential;	• Unclear project objectives;
• Freedom to choose, decision making;	• Role conflict and power struggle among team members;
• Good overall direction and leadership;	
• Tangible rewards;	• Excessive changes of project scope, spec, schedule and budget;
• Mutual trust, security, and open communications;	
• Proper experience and skills;	• Lack of team definition and structure;
• Sense of accomplishment;	• Wrong capabilities, poor selection of project personnel;
• Good interpersonal relations among team members and with management;	• Lacking commitment from team members or management;
• Proper planning;	
• Sufficient resources;	• Low credibilty of project leader;
• Low interpersonal conflict.	• Poor communications;
	• Poor job security.

Furthermore, studies conducted by Gemmill, Thamhain, and Wilemon between 1974 and 1985[29, 31-33] showed significant correlations and interdependencies among work–environmental factors and team performance. These studies indicate that high team performance involves four primary issues; 1) managerial leadership, 2) job content, 3) personal goals and objectives, and 4) work environment and organizational support.

In addition, a recent follow-up study by Thamhain (in part reported in[33]) used the above typology to collect data and categorize over 60 influence factors which were mentioned by engineering managers as drivers or barriers toward high team performance. The actual correlation of these influence factors to the project team characteristics and performance* provided some interesting insight into the strength and effect of these factors. One of the important findings was that only 12 of the 60 influence factors were found to be statistically significant.** All other factors seem to be much less important to high team performance. Specifically, the findings, summarized in Figure 3, indicate that the *six drivers which have the strongest positive association with project team performance are:*

- Interesting and stimulating work,
- Recognition of accomplishment (of individual or team),
- Experienced engineering management personnel,
- Proper technical direction and leadership,
- Qualified project team personnel, and
- Professional growth potential

while the *strongest barriers to project team performance are:*

- Unclear project objectives and directions,
- Insufficient resources,
- Power struggle and conflict,
- Uninvolved, disinterested senior management,
- Poor job security,
- Shifting goals and priorities.

It is furthermore interesting to note that the six drivers not only correlated favorably to the

---

*Kendall Tan rank-order correlation was used as a measure of association. For method and references to statistical models see Appendix.

**Statistical significance was defined at a confidence level of 95 percent or better.

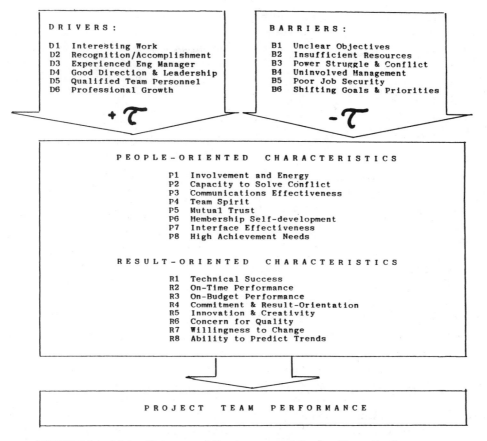

FIGURE 3. *Major Drivers and Barriers toward Project Team Performance*

direct measures of high project team performance, such as technical success and on-time/on-budget performance, but also were positively associated with the 13 indirect measures of team performance shown in Figure 2. The six barriers have exactly the opposite effect. These findings provide some quantitative support to previous exploratory field studies by the authors.[35, 37] What we find consistently is that successful organizations pay attention to the human side. They appear effective in fostering a work environment conducive to innovative work, where people find the assignments challenging, leading to recognition and professional growth. Such a profession-

ally stimulating environment also seems to lower communication barriers and conflict, and enhances the desire of personnel to succeed. This seems to enhance organizational awareness as well as the ability to respond to the often changing project requirements.

In addition, a winning team appears to have good leadership. That is, management understands the factors crucial to success. They are action-oriented, provide the needed resources, properly direct the implementation of the project, plan, and help in the identification and resolution of problems in their early stages.

Taken together, the findings offer support

for the propositions *P* advances earlier and restated here somewhat modified and more specifically in two parts:

P1: The degree of project success seems primarily determined by the strength of six driving forces and six barriers which are related to: 1) leadership, 2) job content, 3) personal needs, and 4) the general work environment.

P2: A professionally stimulating team environment, characterized by 1) interesting challenging work, 2) visibility and recognition for achievements, 3) growth potential, and 4) good project leadership, is strongly correlated with project success. It also leads to low perceived conflict, high commitment, high involved personnel, good communications, change-orientation, innovation and on-time/on-budget performance.

Taken together, the findings show that to be effective in organizing and directing a project team, the leader must not only recognize the potential drivers and barriers but also know when in the life cycle of the project they are most likely to occur. The effective project leader takes preventive actions early in the project lifecycle and fosters a work environment that is conducive to team building as an ongoing process.

The effective team builder is usually a social architect who understands the interaction of organizational and behavioral variables and can foster a climate of active participation and minimal dysfunctional conflict. This requires carefully developed skills in leadership, administration, organization, and technical expertise. It further requires the project leader's ability to involve top management to assure organizational visibility, resource availability, and overall support for the new project throughout its life cycle.

It is this organizational culture which adds yet another challenge to project team building.

The new team members are usually selected from functional resource departments led by strong individuals who often foster internal competition rather than cooperation. In fact, even at the individual contributor level, many of the highly innovative and creative people are high individualistically oriented and often admit their aversion to cooperation. The challenge to the project manager is to integrate these individuals into a team that can produce innovative results in a systematic, coordinated, and integrated *effort* to accomplish the overall project plan. Many of the problems that occur during the formation of the new project team or during its lifecycle are normal and often predictable. However, they present barriers to effective team performance. They must be quickly identified and dealt with. The following section offers specific suggestions.

RECOMMENDATIONS FOR ENGINEERING TEAM MANAGERS

A number of recommendations have been derived from the broader context of this study which can potentially increase the project manager's effectiveness in building high performing teams.

1. Barriers: Project managers must understand the various barriers to team development and build a work environment conducive to the team's motivational needs. Specifically, management should watch out for the following barriers: 1) unclear project objectives, 2) insufficient resources and unclear funding, 3) role conflict and power struggles, 4) uninvolved and unsupportive management, 5) poor job security, 6) shifting goals and priorities.

2. The Project Objectives and their importance to the organization needs to be clear to all personnel who get involved with the project. Senior management can help develop a "priority image" and communicate the basic project parameters and management guidelines.

3. Management Commitment: Project managers must continuously update and involve their managements to refuel their interest and commitment to the new project. Breaking the project into smaller phases and being able to produce short-range results frequently, can be important to this refueling process.

4. Image Building: Building a favorable image for the project, in terms of high priority, interesting work, importance to the organization, high visibility, and potential for professional rewards is crucial in attracting and holding high-quality people. It is also a pervasive process which fosters a climate of active participation at all levels; it helps to unify the new project team and minimizes dysfunctional conflict.

5. Leadership Positions should be carefully defined and staffed at the beginning of a new program. Key project personnel selection is the joint responsibility of the project manager and functional management. The credibility of project leaders among team members, with senior management, and with the program sponsor is crucial to the leader's ability to manage the multi-disciplinary activities effectively across functional lines. One-on-one interviews are recommended for explaining the scope and project requirements, as well as the management philosophy, organizational structure, and rewards.

6. Effective Planning early in the project life cycle will have a favorable impact on the work environment and team effectiveness. Since project managers have to integrate various tasks across many functional lines. Proper planning requires the participation of the entire project team, including support departments, subcontractors, and management. These comprehensive activities, which can be performed in a special project phase such as Requirements Analysis, Product Feasibility Assessment, or Product/Project Definition, usually have a number of team building benefits.

7. Involvement: One of the side benefits of proper project planning is the involvement of personnel at all organizational levels. Project managers should drive such an involvement, at least with their key personnel, especially during the project definition phases. This involvement will lead to a better understanding of the task requirements, stimulate interest, help unify the team, and ultimately lead to commitment to the project plan regarding technical performance, timing, and budgets.

8. Project Staffing: All project assignments should be negotiated individually with each prospective team member. Each task leader should be responsible for staffing his or her own task team. Where dual-reporting relationships are involved, staffing should be conducted jointly by the two managers. The assignment interview should include a clear discussion of the specific task, the outcome, timing, responsibilities, reporting relation, potential rewards, and importance of the project to the company. Task assignments should be made only if the candidate's ability is a reasonable match to the position requirements and the candidate shows a healthy degree of interest in the project.

9. Team Structure: Management needs to define the basic team structure and operating concepts early during the project formation phase. The project plan, task matrix, project charter, and policy are the principal tools. It is the responsibility of the project manager to communicate the organizational design and to assure that all parties understand the overall and interdisciplinary project objectives. Clear and frequent communication with senior management and the new project sponsor becomes critically important. Status review meetings can be used for feedback.

10. Team Building Sessions should be conducted by the project manager throughout the project lifecycle. An especially intense effort might be needed during the team formation stage. The team is being brought together in a relaxed atmosphere to discuss such questions as:

• How are we operating as a team? What is our strength? Where can we improve? What steps are needed to initiate the desired change?

- What problems and issues are we likely to face in the future? Which of these can be avoided by taking appropriate action now? How can we "danger-proof" the team?

11. Team Commitment: Project managers should determine lack of team member commitment early in the life of the project and attempt to change possible negative views toward the project. Since insecurity is often a major reason for lacking commitment, managers should try to determine why insecurity exists, then work on reducing the team members' fears. Conflict with other team members may be another reason for lack of commitment. It is important for the project leader to intervene and mediate the conflict quickly. Finally, if a team member's professional interests may lie elsewhere, the project leader should examine ways to satisfy part of the team member's interests by bringing personal and project goals into perspective.

12. Senior Management Support: It is critically important for senior management to provide the proper environment for the project team to function effectively. Here the project leader needs to tell management at the onset of the program what resources are needed. The project manager's relationship with senior management and ability to develop senior management support is critically affected by his or her credibility, visibility, and priority image of the project.

13. Organization Development Specialists: Project leaders should watch for changes in performance on an ongoing basis. If performance problems are observed, they should be dealt with quickly. If the project manager has access to internal or external organization development specialists, they can help diagnose team problems and assist the team in dealing with the identified problems. These specialists can also bring fresh ideas and perspectives to difficult, and sometimes emotionally complex situations.

14. Problem Avoidance: Project leaders should focus their efforts on problem avoidance. That is, the project leader, through experience, should recognize potential problems and conflicts at their onset and deal with them before they become big and their resolutions consume a large amount of time and effort.

A FINAL NOTE

In summary, effective team building can be a critical determinant of project success. Building the engineering team for a new technical project is one of the prime responsibilities of the program leader. Team building involves a whole spectrum of management skills to identify, commit, and integrate the various personnel from different functional organizations into a single task group. In many project-oriented engineering organizations, team building is a shared responsibility between the functional engineering managers and the project manager, who often reports to a different organization with a different superior.

To be effective, the project manager must provide an atmosphere conducive to teamwork. Four major considerations are involved in the integration of people from many disciplines into an effective team: 1) creating a professionally stimulating work environment, 2) good program leadership, 3) providing qualified personnel, and 4) providing a technically and organizationally stable environment. The project leader must foster an environment where the new product team members are professionally satisfied, involved, and have mutual trust. The more effectively project leaders develop team membership, the higher is the quality of information exchanged, including the candor of sharing ideas and approaches. It is this professionally stimulating involvement that also has a pervasive effect on the team's ability to cope with change and conflict, and leads to innovative performance. By contrast, when a member does not feel part of the team and does not trust others, information will not be shared willingly or openly. One project leader emphasized this point: "There's nothing worse than being on a team when no one trusts anyone else. . . . Such situations lead to gamesmanship and a lot of watching what you say because you don't want your own words to bounce back in your face. . . ."

Furthermore, the greater the team spirit, trust, and quality of information exchange among team members, the more likely the team will be able to develop effective decision-making processes, make individual and group commitment, focus on problem solving, and develop self-forcing self-correcting project controls. These are the characteristics of an effective and productive project team.

Over the next decade we anticipate important developments in team building which will lead to higher performance levels, increased morale, and a pervasive commitment to final results. Areas which should be further investigated include 1) applicability of our findings to engineering teamwork in general, 2) the differences and similarities to nonengineering teams, 3) additional studies into team performance and their correlates, and 4) studies of team performance at various project life cycle stages. These are just a few of the areas that deserve future study, and we hope that this paper will stimulate additional thoughts and research activity.

This paper summarizes several important aspects of team building in an engineering environment. It should help both the professional in the field of engineering management as well as the scholar who studies contemporary organizational concepts to understand the intricate relationships between organizational and behavioral elements. It also provides a conceptional framework for specific research and situational analysis of engineering teambuilding practices.

APPENDIX: STATISTICAL MEASURES AND RANK-ORDER CORRELATION

Association between Team Characteristics and Team Performance

The association was measured by utilizing Kendall's Tau Rank-Order Correlation and Partial Rank-Order Correlation. First, projects were rank-ordered by managers according to their performance. Then the various factors describing the team characteristics were each rank-ordered by both managers and team members according to their strength. Finally, the Tau Coefficients and their significances were calculated for each association. For mathematical procedure see 40.

The Kruskal–Wallis One-Way Analysis of Variance by Ranks

The Kruskal–Wallis analysis is a test for deciding whether K independent samples are from different populations. In our study the test verifies that both managers and other project team members believe in essentially the same qualities that should be present within an effective, high performing project team.

Correlation of Drivers and Barriers to Team Performance

Project team members were asked to rate each of the influence factors, shown as Drivers and Barriers in Figure 3. The rating measured the presence of each of these factors in the team environment, using a five-point scale ranging from "strongly agree" to "strongly disagree." The team rankings based on these scores were then correlated against the team rankings based on performance (P and R scores) as perceived by senior managers (R-scores) and project managers (P-scores). While the correlation factors in Table 1 are based on the perception of managers and team members as indicated respectively, all factors were measured as a perception of both, in

TABLE 1. Drivers and Barriers toward Technical Team Performance

	People-Oriented Characteristics								Result-Oriented Characteristics								Avge
	P1	P2	P3	P4	P5	P6	P7	P8	R1	R2	R3	R4	R5	R6	R7	R8	PR
Drivers (+ τ):																	
D1 Interesting Work	+.45	.55	.35	.40	.30	.10	.20	.55	.30	.30	.20	.50	.25	.25	.25	.10	.32
D2 Recognition/Accomplishment	+.40	.35	.20	.25	.30	.30	.15	.60	.25	.25	.15	.35	.15	.40	.10	.15	.27
D3 Experienced Eng Manager	+.20	.10	.25	.20	.20	.25	.30	.25	.35	.30	.30	.30	.25	.30	.30	.35	.26
D4 Proper Direction & Leadership	+.10	.12	.35	.20	.05	.10	.20	.30	.55	.35	.30	.30	.25	.30	.25	.30	.25
D5 Qualified Team Personnel	+.12	.20	.30	.25	.10	.30	.20	.25	.25	.35	.30	.10	.35	.45	.10	.30	.24
D6 Professional Growth Potential	+.15	.10	.10	.15	.10	.10	.05	.25	.10	.15	.10	.25	.10	.30	.10	.20	.14
BARRIERS (− τ):																	
B1 Unclear Objectives	−.45	.45	.20	.35	.40	.20	.35	.15	−.40	.20	.20	.55	.25	.15	.30	.35	.31
B2 Insufficient Resources	−.30	.35	.05	.35	.25	.05	.10	.20	−.35	.40	.55	.40	.00	.35	.10	.35	.26
B3 Power Struggle & Conflict	−.25	.60	.10	.40	.45	.30	.25	.15	−.20	.15	.20	.35	.20	.30	.20	.10	.26
B4 Uninvolved Management	−.35	.25	.25	.45	.30	.05	.10	.05	−.35	.10	.15	.35	.20	.30	.15	.35	.23
B5 Poor Job Security	−.10	.30	.20	.40	.40	.10	.15	.10	−.30	.20	.15	.35	.15	.35	.20	.30	.23
B6 Shifting Goals & Priorities	−.30	.25	.15	.20	.15	.05	.25	.15	−.20	.35	.35	.15	.15	.40	.25	.10	.22

Significance Levels:
τ≥ .25 . . . p ≤ .05
τ≥ .35 . . . p ≤ .01

P1: Involvement and Energy
P2: Capacity to Solve Conflict
P3: Communications Effectiveness
P4: Team Spirit
P5: Mutual Trust
P6: Membership Self-development
P7: Interface Effectiveness
P8: High Achievement Needs

R1: Technical Success
R2: On-Time Performance
R3: On-Budget Performance
R4: Commitment & Result Orientation
R5: Innovation & Creatively
R6: Concern for Quality
R7: Willingness to Change
R8: Ability to Predict Trends

Kandell Tau Correlation of Team Characteristics and Team Performance fact showing a reasonably high statistical concurrence. Finally, those influences which correlated predominately positive were characterized as drivers, those that correlated predominately negatively were characterized as barriers. The labeling of the variables in Table 1 is according to Figure 3, the statistical significance is indicated as follows: $\tau \geq 0.25$ indicates a 95-percent confidence level ($p \leq 0.05$), and $\tau \geq 0.35$ indicates a 99-percent confidence level ($p \leq 0.01$).

REFERENCES

1. J. R. Adams and N. S. Kirchof, "A training technique for developing project managers," *Project Manag. Quart.,* Mar. 1983.
2. J. J. Aquilino, "Multi-skilled work teams: Productivity benefits," *California Manag. Rev.,* Summer 1977.
3. J. D. Aram and C. P. Morgan, "Role of project team collaboration in R&D performance," *Manag. Sci.,* June 1976.
4. S. Atkins and A. Katcher, "Getting your team in tune," *Nation's Bus.,* Mar. 1975.
5. K. H. Baler, "The hows and whys of teambuilding," *Eng. Manag. Rev.,* Dec. 1985.
6. L. Benningson, "The team approach to project management," *Manag. Rev.,* vol. 61, pp. 48–52, Jan. 1972.
7. R. Carzo, Jr., "Some effects of organization structure on group effectiveness," *Admin. Sci. Quart.,* Mar. 1963.
8. W. J. Conover, *Practical Nonparametric Statistics.* New York: Wiley, 1971.
9. B. A. Diliddo, P. C. James, and H. J. Dietrich, "Managing R&D creatively: B. F. Goodrich's approach," *Manag. Rev.,* July 1981.
10. D. D. Ely, "Team building for creativity," *Personnel J.,* Apr. 1975.
11. R. N. Foster, "A call for vision in managing technology," *McKinsy Quart.,* Summer 1982.
12. P. R. Harris, "Building a high-performance team," *Training Dev. J.,* Apr. 1986.
13. J. L. Hayes, "Teamwork," *Manag. Rev.,* Sept. 1975.
14. D. S. Hopkins, "Roles of project teams and venture groups in new product development," *Res. Manag.,* Jan. 1975.
15. R. J. Howe, "Building teams for increased productivity," *Personnel J.,* Jan. 1977.
16. S. A. Huesing, "Team approach and computer development," *J. Syst. Manag.,* Sept. 1977.
17. J. Jewkes, D. Sawers, and R. Stillerman, *The Sources of Innovation.* New York: Macmillan, 1962.
18. F. E. Katz, "Explaining informal work groups in complex organizations," *Admin. Sci. Quart.,* no. 10, 1965.
19. J. T. Kidder, *The Soul of a New Machine.* New York: Avon, 1982.
20. R. Likert, "Improving cost-performance with cross-functional teams," *Manag. Rev.,* Mar. 1976.
21. D. H. Maister, "The one-firm: What makes it successful," *Sloan Manag. Rev.,* Fall 1985.
22. C. Pincus, "An approach to plan development and team formation," *Project Manag. Quart.,* Dec. 1982.
23. J. B. Quinn, "Technological innovation, entrepreneurship, and strategy," *Sloan Manag. Rev.,* Spring 1979.
24. R. M. Rantfl, "R&D Productivity," Tech. Rep., Hughes Aircraft Co., 1978.
25. E. Raudsepp, "Motivating engineers," *Eng. Manag. Rev.,* Mar. 1986.
26. W. J. Reddin, "Making the team work," *Bus. Manag.* (London), Feb. 1969.
27. L. A. Rogers, "Guidelines for project management teams," *Ind. Eng.,* Dec. 1974.
28. B. A. Salomon, "A plant that proves that team management works," *Personnel,* June 1985.
29. H. J. Thamhain, "Managing engineers effectively," *IEEE Trans. on Eng. Manag.,* Aug. 1983.
30. H. Thamhain and D. Wilemon, "Skill requirements of engineering program manager," in *Proc. 26th Eng. Manag. Conf.,* 1978.
31. H. J. Thamhain and D. L. Wilemon, "Anatomy of a high performing new product team," in *Conv. Rec. 16th Ann. Symp. Project Manag. Inst.*
32. H. J. Thamhain and G. R. Gemmill, "Influence styles of project managers: Some project performance correlates," *Acad. Manag. J.,* June 1974.
33. J. J. Thamhain, "Building a high-performance

technical marketing team," in *Proc. Amer. Marketing Assoc. Conf.,* (Chicago, IL), Aug. 1986.

34. D. J. H. Watson, "Structure of project teams facing differentiated environments: An exploratory study in public accounting firms," *Accounting Rev.,* Apr. 1975.

35. D. L. Wilemon and H. J. Thamhain, "Team building in project management," *Project Manag. Quart.,* July 1983.

36. D. L. Wilemon, *et al.,* "Managing conflict on project teams," *Manag. J.,* 1974.

37. D. L. Wilemon and H. J. Thamhain, "A model for developing high-performance teams," in *Proc. Ann. Symp. Project Management Inst.* (Houston, TX), 1983.

38. J. H. Zenger and D. E. Miller, "Building effective teams," *Personnel,* Mar. 1974.

39. R. C. Ziller, "Newcomer's acceptance in open and closed groups," *Personnel Admin.,* Sept. 1962.

40. S. Seigel, *Nonparametric Statistics.* New York: McGraw-Hill, 1956.

High Performance Research Teams

Ralph Katz

The general neglect of a temporal perspective—the fact that group activities do not take place either at isolated or at random points in time—has been one of the major problems in the study of project groups and teams. Yet until it is addressed, questions about how well a group is doing will receive answers that are, at best, incomplete. As individuals are born, grow up, and grow old—first feeling their way uncertainly, then seeking out new challenges and experiences as they gain confidence, and finally, becoming a bit self-satisfied about their own knowledge and achievements—so the same process seems to occur within groups whose members have worked together for a long time. Research and Development groups seem to have performance curves analogous to the human life cycle—tentative youth, productive energy, and decline with maturity.

The analogy is a convenient one, though subject in both cases to variation: age *need not* mean stagnation in either an individual or a group. Still, a field study of research and development project teams, which I and Professor Tom Allen have been engaged in for some years, does tend to support a general finding of less intense involvement in job demands and challenges with increasing stability in project membership.

It is, of course, natural for both individuals and groups to attempt to structure their work activities to reduce stress and ensure a level of certainty. People like to know, as much as possible, what will happen next. Given this, group members interacting over a long time are likely to develop standard work patterns that are both familiar and comfortable, patterns in which routine and precedent play a relatively large part—perhaps at the expense of unbiased thought and new ideas. On the other hand, an environment devoid of structure and definition, one wholly unfamiliar and enigmatic, is equally undesirable. Without some sort of established pattern or perspective to serve as a basis for action, nothing at all would be accomplished. The task of management, then, is to create and maintain an atmosphere in which employees are both familiar with their job requirements and challenged by them.

THE REQUISITE FAMILIARITY

How long it takes to acquire the requisite familiarity with one's job to function efficiently depends on the length of time it takes an employee to feel accepted and competent in his or her new environment. This feeling is influenced both by the nature of the individual and that of the job. Generally speaking, the time varies according to the level of complexity involved in the job requirements, ranging from as little as a month or two to as much as a year or more on exceptionally skilled jobs as in the engineering and scientific professions.

In engineering, for example, strategies and solutions are usually peculiar to specific settings. Research and development teams in different or-

315

ganizations may face similar problems, yet approach their solutions with widely divergent methods. Thus, even though one may have received an excellent education in, say, mechanical engineering principles, one must still figure out how to be an effective mechanical engineer at Westinghouse, Alcoa, or General Electric.

In the course of long-term job tenure, an individual may be said to pass through three broad stages: *socialization, innovation,* and *stabilization.* A graphic representation of the model is shown in Figure 1.

During the *socialization* period, employees are primarily concerned with understanding and coming to terms with their new and unknown social and task environments. Newcomers must learn the customary norms of behavior within their groups, how reward systems operate, the expectations of supervisors, and a host of other considerations that are necessary for them to function meaningfully. These considerations may vary to a surprisingly large extent even within a single organization. This is important for, while the necessity of such a "breaking-in" period has long been recognized in the case of recently hired members of an organization, it should also be understood that veteran employees assigned to new groups must also "resocialize" themselves since they, too, must now deal with unfamiliar tasks and colleagues. It is in this period that employees learn not only the technical requirements of their new job assignments, but also the behaviors and attitudes that are acceptable and necessary for becoming a true contributing member of the group.

As individuals gain familiarity with their work settings, they are freer to devote their energies and concerns less toward socialization and more toward performance and accomplishment. In the *innovation* stage of a job, employees become capable, to a greater extent, of acting in a responsive and undistracted manner. The movement from socialization to innovation implies that employees no longer require much assistance in deciphering their new job and organizational

surroundings. Instead, they can divert their attention from an initial emphasis on psychological "safety and acceptance" to concerns for achievement and influence. Opportunities to participate and grow within job settings become progressively more pertinent to employees in this stage. As the length of time spent in the same job environment stretches out, however, employees may gradually enter the *stabilization* phase, in which there is a slow shift away from a high level of involvement and receptivity to the challenges in their jobs and toward a greater degree of unresponsiveness to these challenges.

In time, even the most engaging job assignments and responsibilities can appear less exciting, little more than habit, to people who have successfully mastered and become accustomed to their everyday task requirements. It makes sense, then, that with prolonged job stability, employees' perceptions of their conditions at present and possibilities for the future will become increasingly impoverished. If employees cannot maintain, redefine, or expand their jobs for continued change and growth, then their work enthusiasm will deteriorate. If possibilities for development *are* continued, however, then the stabilization period may be held off indefinitely.

The irony of the situation is that employees with the greatest initial responsiveness to job challenges seem to retain that responsiveness for a *shorter* length of time than those expressing less of a need for high job challenge. The greater initial enthusiasm of high-need employees appears to drive them more swiftly through the socialization and innovation period and into stabilization and weariness with routines that are now too familiar to their growth-oriented natures.

Of course, job longevity does not exist in a vacuum. Many other factors may influence the level of job interest. New technological developments, rapid growth and expansion, or strong competitive pressures, or new excited co-workers could all help sustain or even enhance one's involvement in his or her job-related activities. On

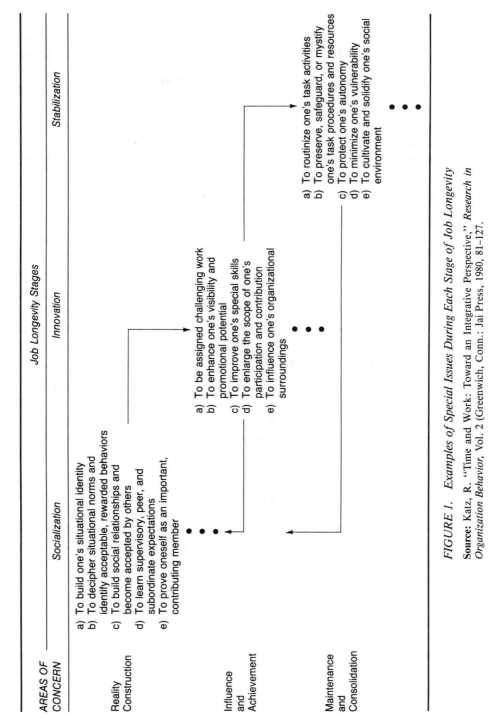

FIGURE 1. *Examples of Special Issues During Each Stage of Job Longevity*

Source: Katz, R. "Time and Work: Toward an Integrative Perspective," *Research in Organization Behavior*, Vol. 2 (Greenwich, Conn.: Jai Press, 1980, 81–127.

the other hand, working closely with a group of unresponsive peers in a relatively unchanging situation might shorten an individual's responsive period on that particular job rather dramatically.

Despite these other influences, though the general trend does hold. In moving from innovation to stabilization, employees who continue to work in the same overall job situation for long periods gradually adapt to such steadfast employment by becoming increasingly indifferent to the challenging aspects of their assignments. And as employees come to care less about the intrinsic nature of the work they do, their absorption in contextual features such as salary, benefits, vacations, friendly co-workers, and compatible superiors tends to increase.

Interestingly, entry into the stabilization period does not necessarily imply a reduced level of job satisfaction. On the contrary, in fact. As employees enter the stabilization stage, they have typically adapted by becoming very satisfied with the comfortableness and predictability of their work environments; for when the chances of future growth and change become limited, existing situations become accepted as the desired. Only when a reasonable gap remains between what individuals desire and what they are presently able to achieve will there be energy for change and accomplishment.

With stability comes a greater loyalty to precedent, to the established patterns of behavior. In adapting to high job longevity, employees become increasingly content with customary ways of doing things, comfortable routines, and familiar sets of task demands that promote a feeling of security and confidence while requiring little exceptional effort or vigilance. The preservation of such patterns is likely to be a prime consideration, with the result that contact with information and ideas that threaten change may be curtailed. Moreover, strong biases may develop in the selection and interpretation of information, in abilities to generate new options and strategies creatively, and in the level of willingness to innovate or implement alternative courses

of action. In a sense, the differences between the innovation and stabilization stages are indicative of the distinctions between creative performance and routine performance; between job excitement and work satisfaction. What is also important to note from the model portrayed in Figure 1 is that individuals can easily cycle between socialization and innovation (with on-going job changes and promotions) or they can slowly proceed from innovation to stabilization over time. Direct movement from stabilization back to innovation, however, is very unlikely without the individual first going through a new socialization (or resocialization) experience in order to unfreeze previously defined and reinforced habits and perspectives. Thus, rotation per se is not the solution to rejuvenation; instead, it is rotation coupled with a new socialization experience that provides the individual with a new opportunity to regain responsiveness to new task challenges and environmental demands. The intensity of the resocialization experience, moreover, must match the strength of the prior stabilization period.

So far, we have described what happens to individual professionals as if they work independently and autonomously. Most of the time, technical professionals function interdependently either as members of specific project teams or specific technology-based groups. It may be more important, therefore, to know not only what happens to an individual over time but also what happens to the performances of teams or groups of individuals who have been working together over time. In any group, there is a changing mix of individuals, some of whom may be in socialization, some in the innovation stage, and still others in stabilization. It is not how this particular mix of individuals act that is important, but how they interact both amongst themselves and outside their group. Towards this end, Professor Tom Allen and I conducted a field study that focused on communication activity as a behavioral index by which to examine the effects of group longevity on project performance,

318

where group longevity measures the average length of time that project members have worked and shared experiences with one another.

Basic data collection for the study took place at the research and development facility of a large American corporation, employing 345 engineering and scientific professionals in 61 distinct project groups or work areas. Each professional belonged to only one project group, and all of the groups remained stable over the course of the data collection period. Project groups were organized around specific, long-term kinds of problem areas such as fiber-forming development and urethane development, and ranged across three broad categories of R&D activity: "Applied Research," "Product & Process Development," and "Technical Service & Support."

The purpose of the study was two-fold. First, to examine the level of communication by project groups at various stages in the group's "life" (that is, its group longevity) and, second, to discover any possible relationship between a lessening of communication and a drop in performance. The focus was on interpersonal communication, which, as many previous studies have demonstrated, is the primary means by which engineering and scientific professionals collect outside information and transfer it into their project groups.

Group longevity, or mean group tenure, was calculated by averaging the individual project tenures of all project members. Therefore, group longevity is *not* the length of time the project has been in existence, nor is it the average time the members have been part of the larger organization. Rather, it represents the length of time group members have been working together in a particular project area.

Participants kept track of all other professionals with whom they had work-related oral communication on a randomly chosen day each week for fifteen weeks. Contacts both inside and outside the research and development facility were measured. Based on this data, three independent measures of project communication were determined by averaging the amount of technical communication per person per project to each of three separate areas of important information:

1. *Intraproject Communication:* The amount of communication reported among all project members.
2. *Organizational Communication:* The level or amount of contact reported by project members with individuals outside the R&D facility but within other corporate divisions, principally marketing and manufacturing.
3. *Professional Communication:* The amount of communication reported by project members with professionals outside the parent organization, including professionals in universities, consulting firms, and professional societies.

For all three areas or sources of information, project groups whose longevity index was five or more years reported much lower levels of actual contact than project groups whose longevity index fell between one and a half and five years. Intraproject, organizational, and outside professional interaction were considerably lower for the longer-tenured groups. Members of these groups, therefore, were significantly more isolated from external sources of new ideas and technological advances and from information within other organizational divisions, especially marketing and manufacturing. Project members were even more isolated from each other in these long-tenured groups.

In addition to these measures of actual communication behavior, a direct measure of the current technical performance of the project groups was developed. All department managers and laboratory directors were separately interviewed and asked to evaluate the overall performance of all projects with which they were technically familiar, based on their knowledge of and experience with the various projects. The managers, in making their evaluations, considered such elements as schedule, budget, and cost performance; innovativeness; adaptability; and the ability to coordinate with other parts of the organization. Each group was independently rated by an average of five higher-level managers; consensus among the ratings was extremely high.

On the average, the association between project performance and group longevity closely paralleled the association of longevity and communication trends. The best performing groups were those with longevities between one and a half and five years. Performance was significantly lower for teams that had been together for less than a year and a half or more than five years. In fact, *none* of the ten project groups in the long-tenured category were among the facility's higher performing project teams, all being rated by the facility's management as either average or below average. It is also interesting to note that none of the managerial evaluators knew which project teams were the long-term ones or whether their organization even had any, since rotations and movements were always ongoing. In reality, over 20 percent of the R&D effort within this organization was being conducted by these ten lower-performing, long-term technical teams.

Almost by definition, projects with higher mean group tenure were staffed by older engineers. This raises the possibility that performance may be lower as a result of the increasing obsolescence of individuals' skills as they aged, rather than because of anything to do with the group's tenure composition. The data, however, do not bear this out. For both the communication and the performance data, it was found that group longevity and not the chronological age of individuals was more likely to have influenced the results.

Another possibility is that long-tenured project teams had simply come to be staffed by less technically competent or perhaps less motivated engineers and scientists. Follow-up visits to this facility, however, show the same proportion of professionals from both the long- and medium-tenured teams being promoted to higher level managerial positions above the project leadership level during the five-year interval since the collection of the original data. Fifteen percent of the engineers who had been working in medium-tenured groups attained managerial positions of either laboratory supervisor or laboratory manager, while the percentage in the longer-tenured groups was 13 percent. In fact, following the introduction of a dual-ladder promotional system designed, according to the company, to reward those whose "technical competency and contributions are well-recognized," the percentage of longer-tenured project members promoted was *greater* than the percentage from medium-tenured groups, 19 percent compared to 12 percent. This seems to indicate a relative parity in the area of competence among the memberships of the respective groups.

Despite the parallel declines in both project communication and performance with increasingly high levels of group longevity, one must be careful not to jump to the conclusion that decays in all areas of communication contributed equally to the lower levels of project performance. Different categories of project tasks require different patterns of communication for more effective performance. Research project groups, for example, have been found to be higher performing when project members maintain high levels of technical communication with outside professionals. Performance in development projects, on the other hand, is related more to contact within the organization, primarily with divisions such as marketing and manufacturing. Finally, for technical-service projects, communication within the team appears most crucial.

Significantly, for each project type, the deterioration in interaction was particularly strong in the area *most* important for high technical performance. This suggests that it is not a reduction in project communication per se that leads to less effective project performance; but rather it is an isolation from sources that can provide the most critical kinds of evaluation, information, and new ideas. Thus, overall effectiveness suffers when research project members fail to pay attention to events and information within the larger technical community outside the organization; or when development project members lose contact with client groups from marketing and manufacturing; or when technical-service project members do not interact among themselves.

Clearly—at least in the case of the groups studied here—there are strong relationships between longevity within a group and decreased levels of communication activity and project performance. In order to develop strategies that circumvent these unfortunate outcomes, the processes through which they occur must be understood in greater detail. What happens in long-term groups that leads to their being relatively cut off from sources of new ideas and information?

Essentially, project newcomers in the midst of socialization are trying to navigate their way through new and unfamiliar territories without the aid of adequate or even accurate perceptual maps. During this initial period, they are relatively more malleable and more susceptible to change, dependent as they are on other project members to help them define and interpret the numerous activities taking place around them. As they become more familiar with their project settings, however, they also become more capable of relying on their own perceptions and knowledge for interpreting events and executing their everyday project requirements. Having established their own social and task supports, their own outlooks and work identities, they become less easily changed and influenced.

If this process is allowed to continue among project members, healthy levels of self-reliance can easily degenerate into problematic levels of closed-mindedness. Rigidity in problem-solving activities—a kind of functional fixedness—may result from this, reducing the group's ability to react flexibly to changing conditions. Novel situations are either ignored or forced into established categories; new or changing circumstances either trigger old responses or none at all.

Furthermore, the longer group members are called upon to follow and justify their problem-solving strategies and decisions, the more ingrained these approaches are likely to become. As as result, alternative ideas that were probably considered and discarded during previous discussions may never be reconsidered even though they may have become more appropriate or feasible. In fact, members may end up devoting much of their efforts to the preservation of their particular approaches against the encroachment of competing methods and negative evaluations. Essentially, they become overly committed to the continuation of their existing ideas and solutions, often without sufficient regard to their "true" applicability.

With this perspective, as one might suspect, the extent to which group members are willing or even feel the need to expose themselves to alternative ideas, solution strategies, or constructive criticism is likely to be diminished. A pattern of *increasing isolation* from external changes and new technological developments, coupled with a growing complacence about work-related challenges may be the result. Project groups with high levels of group longevity, then, appear to behave as if they possess so much expertise in their specialized technical areas that it is unlikely that outsiders might be producing important new ideas or information relevant to the performance of their project tasks. Rather than face the anxiety and discomfort inherent in learning or change, they tacitly assume that their abilities and experienced know-how are far better than those ideas or suggestions coming from outside their group. All of this is part of the well-known "not-invented-here" syndrome in which groups gradually define themselves into a narrow field of specialization and convince themselves that they have a monopoly on knowledge in their area of specialty. Such increased specialization creates an appearance to the outside world of decreased relevance, which leads to a decrease in the team's motivation to communicate with and respond to the outside. It is this isolation and more narrow focus which in turn leads to poorer performance.

Another explanation contributing to the reduced levels of project member interaction is the principle of *selective exposure,* the tendency for group members to communicate only with those whose ideas and outlooks are in accord with their own current interests, needs, and existing attitudes. And group members tend to become more alike over time. Just as it is sometimes said that close friends or husbands and wives seem to grow closer in appearance, so groups may take on a kind of collective viewpoint after interacting for an extended period. As members stabilize their work settings and patterns of communication, a greater degree of similarity is likely to emerge. This, in turn, leads to further stability in communication, and, therefore, even greater isolation from different-thinking others.

There is at least one advantage to this. People who think alike are able to communicate more effectively and economically. This advantage is more than outweighed, however, by the fact that such communication is likely to yield less creative and innovative outcomes than communications containing a variety of differing perspectives.

It should also be recognized that under these kinds of circumstances even the outside information that is processed by long-tenured groups may not be viewed in the most open or unbiased fashion. Many kinds of cognitive defenses and distortions are commonly used by members in *selectively perceiving* outside information in order to support and maintain their decisional policies and strategies. Such defenses can easily be used to argue against any disquieting information and evidence in order to maintain their present courses of action. Such selectivity can also result in a more restricted perspective of one's situation, which can be very detrimental to the group's overall effectiveness, for it often screens out vitally important information cues.

These trends of *increasing isolation, selective exposure,* and *selective perception* can all feed off each other in a kind of vicious circle, leaving group members in a state of greater and greater distance from new advances and ideas, and greater and greater reliance on an increasingly narrow and homogeneous set of alternatives.

MANAGING FOR INNOVATION

Are these processes inevitable? Or can management alter the composition of current R&D groupings in order to minimize the effects of extended group longevity on project performance and still ensure an adequate level of stability for relatively smooth operation? What follows are a few suggestions toward the goal of managing for a continuously high level of innovation.

Employee perspectives and behaviors, and their subsequent effects on performance, can be significantly affected through the systematic and creative use of staffing and career decisions. For example, regular placement of new members into project groups may perform an energizing and destabilizing function—keeping the group longevity index from rising, thereby preventing the group from developing some of the tendencies described here (particularly isolation from critical information areas). New members have the advantage of fresh ideas and approaches, and of a fresh eye for old ones. With their active participation, older members might be kept responsive to the generation of new methods and behaviors as well as the reconsideration of alternatives that might otherwise be ignored. In short, project newcomers create a novelty-enhancing situation, challenging and improving the scope of existing methods and accumulated knowledge.

Clearly, the longevity framework suggests that periodic additions or rotations can help *prevent* the onset of the stabilization processes associated with high longevity. Provided the socialization period is not overly conforming, project groups can simply remain in an innovation cycle. While prevention is clearly easier, it is also suggested that the replacement or reassignment of certain long-tenured professionals to different project groups may be necessary for improving the performance of high longevity teams as well as for keeping such groups stimulated, flexible, and vigilant with respect to their project environments. Continued growth and development comes from adaptations to new challenges, often requiring the abandonment of familiar and stable work patterns in favor of new ones.

Interestingly, managers are usually not aware of the tenure demographics of their project groups. In our studies, managers are usually unable to identify which of their projects have high levels of group longevity. In fact, they are usually surprised that any of their project teams have mean group tenures of five or more years. As part of their project evaluation and human resource planning functions, then, managers might want to generate a more complete picture of their project groups' tenure distributions, from which better staffing and hiring decisions and reassignments of professionals among project activities can be made. While individual age and organizational tenure data are usually available through personnel files, individual project tenure and, more importantly, group longevity data are rarely part of an organization's ongoing information system.

Of course, rotations and promotions are not always possible, especially when there is little organizational growth. As important as job mobility is, it is no doubt equally crucial to determine whether project groups can circumvent the effects of high longevity without new assignments or rejuvenation from new project members. To do this, we must learn considerably more about the effects of increasing job and group longevities. For example, in the study presented here, none of the long-tenured project groups was above average in project performance. Yet different trends might have emerged with different kinds of organizational climates, different personnel and promotional policies, different economic and marketing conditions, or even different types of organizational structures. Can project groups keep *themselves* energized and innovative over long periods, or are certain kinds of structures and managerial practices needed to maintain effectiveness and high performance as a team ages?

In more recent and extensive project data collected from twelve different technology-based organizations involving more than 200 R&D project groups, of which approximately fifty have group longevity scores of more than five years, it turns out that a large number of these long-tenured groups were judged to have a high level of performance. The data are still being processed, but preliminary analyses seem to indicate that the nature of the project's supervision may be the most important factor differentiating the more effective long-tenured teams from those less effective. In particular, engineers belonging to the high-performing, long-tenured groups perceived their project supervisors to be superior in dealing with conflicts between groups and individuals, in obtaining necessary resources for project members, in setting project goals, and in monitoring the activities and progress of project members toward these goals. Furthermore, in performing these supervisory functions, the more effective project managers of long-tenured groups were not very participative in their approaches, instead, they were extremely demanding of their teams, challenging them to perform in new ways and directions. In fact, the most participative managers (as viewed by project members) were significantly less effective in managing teams with high group longevity. Our study also revealed that not all managers may be able to gain the creative performances out of long-term technical groups. Typically, the managers of the higher performing long-term groups had been with their teams less than 3 years and had come to this assignment with a strong history of prior managerial success. It was not their first managerial experience! To the contrary, most were well-respected technical managers who had "made things happen" and who had developed strong power bases and strong levels of senior managerial support within their R&D units or divisions. It was this combination of technical credibility and managerial respect and power that enabled these managers to be effective with their long-term stabilized R&D project teams.

These and other preliminary findings suggest the following strategies for managing professional groups with a longevity index of at least five years:

1. More emphasis should be placed on the particular skills and abilities of the project manager. Members of long-tenured groups are more responsive to the nature of their supervision than to the intrinsic nature of their work content.

2. In terms of managerial style, project managers should place less emphasis on participative management and more emphasis on direction and control. As long as members of long-tenured groups are unresponsive to the challenges in their tasks, participative management will only be related to job satisfaction—not project performance.

3. Project managers, on the other hand, should be very responsive to the challenging nature of their project's work. Consequently, they should be given considerable authority and freedom to execute their project responsibilities, but they, in turn, should be "tight-fisted" with respect to their subordinates.

In a sense, then, traditional managers may be effective for managing high group longevity teams. In a broader context, however, we need to learn how to manage workers, professionals, and project teams as they proceed through different stages of longevity. Clearly; different kinds of managerial styles and practices may be more appropriate at different stages of the process. Delegative or participative management, for example, may be very effective when individuals are highly responsive to their work, but much less successful when employees are not, as in the stabilization phase. As perspectives and responsiveness shift over time, the actions required of managers will vary as well. Managers may be effective to the extent that they can recognize and react to such developments. As in so many areas, it is the ability to manage change that seems most important in providing careers that keep employees responsive and organizations effective.

SUGGESTED READING

Thomas J. Allen, *Managing the Flow of Technology,* MIT Press, 1984. Summarizes more than fifteen years of research conducted by Professor Allen in the areas of technology transfer and technical information flows among professionals.

Ralph Katz, *Career Issues in Human Resource Management,* Prentice-Hall, 1982. Contains ten separate chapters on the management of careers with special emphasis given to the management of professional and technically-based careers.

Intergroup Problems in Organizations

Edgar H. Schein

The first major problem of groups in organizations is how to make them effective in fulfilling both organizational goals and the needs of their members. The second major problem is how to establish conditions *between* groups which will enhance the productivity of each without destroying intergroup relations and coordination. This problem exists because as groups become more committed to their own goals and norms, they are likely to become competitive with one another and seek to undermine their rivals' activities, thereby becoming a liability to the organization as a whole. The overall problem, then, is how to establish collaborative intergroup relations in those situations where task interdependence or the need for unity makes collaboration a necessary prerequisite for organizational effectiveness.

SOME CONSEQUENCES OF INTERGROUP COMPETITION

The consequences of intergroup competition were first studied systematically by Sherif in an ingeniously designed setting (Sherif, Harvey, White, Hood, & Sherif, 1961). He organized a boys' camp in such a way that two groups would form and would gradually become competitive. Sherif then studied the effects of the competition and tried various devices for reestablishing col-

From Edgar H. Schein, *Organizational Psychology,* 3rd edition, copyright © 1980, pp. 172–181. Reprinted by permission of Prentice-Hall, Inc., Englewood Cliffs, NJ.

laborative relationships between the groups. Since his original experiments, there have been many replications with adult groups; the phenomena are so constant that it has been possible to make a demonstration exercise out of the experiment (Blake & Mouton, 1961). The effects can be described in terms of the following categories:

A. What happens within each competing group?

1. Each group becomes more closely knit and elicits greater loyalty from its members; members close ranks and bury some of their internal differences.
2. The group climate changes from informal, casual, playful to work and task oriented; concern for members' psychological needs declines while concern for task accomplishment increases.
3. Leadership patterns tend to change from more democratic toward more autocratic; the group becomes more willing to tolerate autocratic leadership.
4. Each group becomes more highly structured and organized.
5. Each group demands more loyalty and conformity from its members in order to be able to present a "solid front."

B. What happens between competing groups?

1. Each group begins to see the other group as the enemy, rather than merely a neutral object.

2. Each group begins to experience distortions of perception—it tends to perceive only the best parts of itself, denying its weaknesses, and tends to perceive only the worst parts of the other group, denying its strengths; each group is likely to develop a negative stereotype of the other ("they don't play fair like we do").

3. Hostility toward the other group increases while interaction and communication with the other group decreases; thus it becomes easier to maintain the negative stereotype and more difficult to correct perceptual distortions.

4. If the groups are forced into interaction—for example, if they are forced to listen to representatives plead their own and the others' cause in reference to some task—each group is likely to listen more closely to their own representative and not to listen to the representative of the other group, except to find fault with his or her presentation; in other words, group members tend to listen only for that which supports their own position and stereotype.

Thus far, we have listed some consequences of the competition itself, without reference to the consequences if one group actually wins out over the other. Before listing those effects, I would like to draw attention to the generality of the above reactions. Whether one is talking about sports teams, interfraternity competition, labor-management disputes, or interdepartmental competition as between sales and production in an industrial organization—or about international relations and the competition between the Soviet Union and the United States—the same phenomena tend to occur. These responses can be very useful to the group, by making it more highly motivated in task accomplishment, but they also open the door to groupthink. Furthermore, the same factors which improve intragroup effectiveness may have negative consequences for intergroup effectiveness. For example, as we have often seen in labor-management disputes or international conflicts, if the groups perceive themselves as competitors, they find it more difficult to resolve their differences, and eventually both become losers in a long-term strike or even a war.

Let us next look at the consequences of winning and losing, as in a situation where several groups are bidding to have their proposal accepted for a contract or as a solution to some problem. Many intraorganizational situations become win-or-lose affairs, hence it is of particular importance to examine their consequences.

C. What happens to the winner?

1. Winner retains it cohesion and may become even more cohesive.

2. Winner tends to release tension, lose its fighting spirit, become complacent, casual, and playful (the condition of being "fat and happy").

3. Winner tends toward high intragroup cooperation and concern for members' needs, and low concern for work and task accomplishment.

4. Winner tends to be complacent and to feel that the positive outcome has confirmed its favorable stereotype of itself and the negative stereotype of the "enemy" group; there is little motivation for reevaluating perceptions or reexamining group operations in order to learn how to improve them, hence the winner does not learn much about itself.

D. What happens to the loser?

1. If the outcome is not entirely clear-cut and permits a degree of interpretation (say, if judges have rendered it or if the game was close), there is a strong tendency for the loser to *deny or distort the reality of losing;* instead, the loser will find psychological escapes like "the judges were biased," "the judges didn't really understand our solution," "the rules of the game were not clearly explained to us," "if luck had not been against us at the one key point, we

would have won,'' and so on. In effect, the loser's first response is to say "we didn't really lose!"

2. If the loss is psychologically accepted, the losing group tends to seek someone or something to blame; strong forces toward scapegoating are set up; if no outsider can be blamed, the group turns on itself, splinters, surfaces previously unresolved conflicts, fights within itself, all in the effort to find a cause for the loss.

3. Loser is more tense, ready to work harder, and desperate (the condition of being "lean and hungry").

4. Loser tends toward low intragroup cooperation, low concern for members' needs, and high concern for recouping by working harder in order to win the next round of the competition.

5. Loser tends to learn a lot about itself as a group because its positive stereotype of itself and its negative stereotype of the other group are disconfirmed by the loss, forcing a reevaluation of perceptions; as a consequence, the loser is likely to reorganize and become more cohesive and effective once the loss has been accepted realistically.

The net effect of the win-lose situation is often that the losers refuse psychologically to accept their loss, and that intergroup tension is higher than before the competition began.

Intergroup problems of the sort we have just described arise not only out of direct competition between clearly defined groups, but are, to a degree, intrinsic in any complex society because of the many bases on which a society is stratified. Thus, we can have potential intergroup problems between men and women, between older and younger generations, between higher and lower ranking people, between blacks and whites, between people in power and people not in power, and so on (Alderfer, 1977). Any occupational or social group will develop "ingroup" feelings and define itself in terms of members of an "outgroup," toward whom intergroup feelings are

likely to arise. Differences between nationalities of ethnic groups are especially strong, particularly if there has been any conflict between the groups in the past.

For intergroup feelings to arise we need not belong to a psychological group. It is enough to feel oneself a member of what has been called a "reference group," that is, a group with which one identifies and compares oneself or to which one aspires. Thus, aspirants to a higher socioeconomic level take that level as their reference group and attempt to behave according to the values they perceive in that group. Similarly, members of an occupational group upholds the values and standards they perceive that occupation to embody. It is only by positing the existence of reference groups that one can explain how some individuals can continue to behave in a deviant fashion in a group situation. If such individuals strongly identify with a group that has different norms they will behave in a way that attempts to uphold those norms. For example, in Communist prison camps some soldiers from elite military units resisted their captors much longer than draftees who had weak identification with their military units. In order for the Communists to elicit compliant behavior from these strongly identified prisoners, they had to first weaken the attachment to the elite unit—that is, destroy the reference group—by attacking the group's image or convincing the prisoner that it was not a group worth belonging to (Schein, 1961). Intergroup problems arise wherever there are any status differences and are, therefore, intrinsic to all organizations and to society itself.

REDUCING THE NEGATIVE CONSEQUENCES OF INTERGROUP COMPETITION

The gains of intergroup competition may, under some conditions, outweigh the negative consequences. It may be desirable to have work groups pitted against one another or to have departments become cohesive loyal units, even if interdepartmental coordination suffers. Often, however, the negative consequences outweigh the gains, and management seeks ways of reducing intergroup tension. Many of the techniques proposed to accomplish this come from the basic researches of Sherif, Blake, Alderfer, and others; they have been tested and found to be successful. The chief stumbling block remains not so much being unable to think of ways for reducing intergroup conflict as being *unable to implement some of the most effective ways.*

Destructive intergroup competition results basically from a conflict of goals and the breakdown of interaction and communication between the groups. This breakdown in turn permits and stimulates perceptual distortion and mutual negative stereotyping. The basic strategy of reducing conflict, therefore, is to locate goals which the competing groups can agree on and to reestablish valid communication between the groups. Each of the tactical devices that follows can be used singly or in combination.

Locating a Common Enemy

For example, the competing teams in a league can compose an all-star team to play another league, or conflicts between sales and production can be reduced if both can harness their efforts to helping their company successfully compete against another company. The conflict here is merely shifted to a higher level.

Bringing Leaders or Subgroups of the Competing Groups into Interaction

An isolated group representative cannot abandon his or her group position, but a powerful leader or a subgroup that has been delegated power not only can permit itself to be influenced by its counterpart negotiation team, but also will have the strength to influence the remainder of its home group if negotiation produces common

agreements. This is the basis for "summit meetings" in international relations.

Locating a Superordinate Goal

Such a goal can be a brand-new task which requires the cooperative effort of the previously competing groups, or it can be a task like analyzing and reducing the intergroup conflict itself. For example, the previously competing sales and production departments can be given the task of developing a new product line that will be both cheap to produce and in great customer demand; or, with the help of an outside consultant, the competing groups can be invited to examine their own behavior and reevaluate the gains and losses from competition (Walton, 1969).

Experiential Intergroup Training

The procedure of having the conflicting parties examine their own behavior has been tried by a number of psychologists, notably Blake and Mouton (1962), with considerable success. Assuming the organization recognizes that it has a problem, and assuming it is ready to expose this problem to an outside consultant, the experiential workshop approach to reducing conflict might proceed with the following steps:

1. The competing groups are both brought into a training setting and the common goals are stated to be an exploration of mutual perceptions and mutual relations.
2. The two groups are then separated and each group is invited to discuss and make a list of its perceptions of itself and the other group.
3. In the presence of both groups, representatives publicly share the perceptions of self and other which the groups have generated, while the groups are obligated to remain silent (the objective is simply to report to the other group as accurately as possible the images that each group has developed in private).
4. Before any exchange has taken place, the

groups return to private sessions to digest and analyze what they have heard; there is a great likelihood that the representatives' reports have revealed discrepancies to each group between its self-image and the image that the other group holds of it; the private session is partly devoted to an analysis of the reasons for these discrepancies, which forces each group to review its actual behavior toward the other group and the possible consequences of that behavior, regardless of its intentions.

5. In public session, again working through representatives, each group shares with the other what discrepancies it has uncovered and the possible reasons for them, focusing on actual, observable behavior.

6. Following this mutual exposure, a more open exploration is then permitted between the two groups on the *now-shared goal* of identifying further reasons for perceptual distortions.

7. A joint exploration is then conducted of how to manage future relations in such a way as to minimize a recurrence of the conflict.

Interspersed with these steps are short lectures and reading assignments on the psychology of intergroup conflict, the bases for perceptual distortion, psychological defense mechanisms, and so on. The goal is to bring the psychological dynamics of the solution into conscious awareness and to refocus the groups on the common goal of exploring jointly the problem they share. In order to do this, they must have valid data about each other, which is provided through the artifice of the representative reports.

Blake's model deals with the entire group. Various other approaches begin by breaking down group prejudices on an individual basis. For example, groups A and B, each proposing an alternative product (idea), can be divided into pairs composed of an A and a B member. Each pair can be given the assignment of developing a joint product that combines the best ideas from the A product and the B product. Or, in each pair, members may be asked to argue for the product of the opposing group. It has been shown in a number of experiments that one way of changing attitudes is to ask a person to play the role of an advocate of the new attitude to be learned (Janis & King, 1954). The very act of arguing for another product, even if it is purely an exercise, makes the person aware of some of its virtues which he or she can now no longer deny. A practical application of these points might be to have some members of the sales department spend time in the production department and be asked to represent the production point of view to some third party, or to have some production people join sales teams to learn the sales point of view.

Most of the approaches cited depend on a *recognition* of some problem by the organization and a *willingness* on the part of the competing groups to participate in some program to reduce negative consequences. The reality, however, is that most organizations neither recognize the problem nor are willing to invest time and energy in resolving it. Some of the unwillingness also arises from each competing group's recognition that in becoming more cooperative it may lose some of its own identity and integrity as a group. Rather than risk this loss, the group may prefer to continue the competition. This may well be the reason why, in international relations, nations refuse to engage in what may seem like perfectly simple ways of resolving their differences. They resist partly in order to protect their integrity—that is, save face. For all these reasons, the *implementation* of strategies and tactics for reducing the negative consequences of intergroup competition is often a greater problem than the initial development of such strategies and tactics.

PREVENTING INTERGROUP CONFLICT

Because of the great difficulties of reducing intergroup conflict once it has developed, it may be desirable to prevent its occurrence in the first place. How can this be done? Paradoxically, a strategy of prevention challenges the fundamental premise upon which organization through division of labor rests. Once it has been decided by a superordinate authority to divide up functions among different departments or goups, a bias has already been introduced toward intergroup competition; for in doing its own job well, each group must, to some degree, compete for scarce resources and rewards from the superordinate authority. The very concept of division of labor implies a reduction of communication and interaction between groups, thus making it possible for perceptual distortions to occur.

The organization planner who wishes to avoid intergroup competition need not abandon the concept of division of labor, but should follow some of the steps listed below in creating and handling the different functional groups.

1. Relatively greater *emphasis should be given to total organizational effectiveness* and the role of departments in contributing to it; departments should be measured and rewarded on the basis of their contribution to the total effort rather than their individual effectiveness.

2. *High interaction and frequent communication* should be stimulated between groups to work on problems of intergroup coordination and help; organizational rewards should be given partly on the basis of help rendered to other groups.

3. *Frequent rotation of members* among groups or departments should be encouraged to stimulate a high degree of mutual understanding and empathy for one another's problems.

4. *Win-lose situations should be avoided* and groups should never be put into the position of competing for some scarce organizational reward; emphasis should always be placed on pooling resources to maximize organizational effectiveness; rewards should be shared equally with all the groups or departments.

Most managers find the fourth point particularly difficult to accept because of the strong belief that performance can be improved by pitting people or groups against one another in a competitive situation. This may indeed be true in the short run, and may even on occasion work in the long run, but the negative consequences described above are undeniably the product of the win-lose situation. Thus, if managers wish to prevent such consequences, they must face the possibility that they may have to abandon competitive relationships altogether and seek to substitute intergroup collaboration toward organizational goals. The more *interdependent* the various units are, the more important it is to stimulate collaborative problem solving.

Implementing a preventive strategy is often more difficult, partly because most people are inexperienced in stimulating and managing collaborative relationships. Yet observations of organizations using the Scanlon Plan not only reveal that it is possible to establish collaborative relationships, even between labor and management, but also that when this has been done, organizational and group effectiveness have been as high as or higher than under competitive conditions. Training in how to set up collaborative relations may be a prerequisite for any such program to succeed, especially for those managers who have themselves grown up in a highly competitive environment.

THE PROBLEM OF INTEGRATION IN PERSPECTIVE

I have discussed two basic issues in this paper: (1) the development of groups within organizations which can fulfill both the needs of the organization and the psychological needs of its members;

and (2) the problems of intergroup competition and conflict. To achieve maximum integration, the organization should be able to create conditions that will facilitate a balance between organizational goals and member needs and minimize disintegrative competition between the subunits of the total organization.

Groups are highly complex sets of relationships. There are no easy generalizations about the conditions under which they will be effective, but with suitable training, many kinds of groups can function at levels previously unimaginable. Consequently, training in group dynamics by experiential methods may be a more promising approach to effectiveness than attempting a priori to determine the right membership, type of leadership, and organization. Of course, all of the factors must be taken into account, and the training approach, although central, must be carefully chosen to preserve and enhance positive group qualities already present.

The creation of psychologically meaningful and effective groups does not solve all of the organization's problems, however, particularly if such groups compete and conflict with each other. We examined some of the consequences of competition under win-lose conditions and outlined two basic approaches of dealing with this problem: (1) reducing conflict by increasing communication and locating superordinate goals, and (2) preventing conflict by establishing from the outset organizational conditions to stimulate collaboration rather than competition.

The prevention of intergroup conflict is especially crucial if the groups involved are highly interdependent. The greater the interdependence, the greater the potential loss to the total organization of negative stereotyping, withholding of information, efforts to make the other group look bad in the eyes of the superior authority, and so on.

In concluding this section on groups, it should be emphasized that the preventive strategy does not imply absence of disagreement and artificial "sweetness and light" within or between groups. Conflict and disagreement at the level of the group or organizational *task* is not only desirable but essential for the achievement of optimal solutions to organizational problems. By contrast, when the task becomes less important than gaining advantage over the other person or group, interpersonal or intergroup relations suffer the most harmful effects. The negative consequences we described, most notably mutual negative stereotyping, fall into this latter category and undermine rather than aid overall task performance.

Interestingly enough, observations of actual conflictual situations suggest that task-relevant conflict which improves overall effectiveness is greater under collaborative conditions, because groups and members trust each other enough to be frank and open in sharing information and opinions. In the competitive situation, each group is committed to hiding its special resources from the other groups, thus preventing effective integration of all resources in the organization. Potentially constructive task conflict is suppressed under competitive conditions and the danger of groupthink is increased.

Groupthink

Irving L. Janis

"How could we have been so stupid?" President John F. Kennedy asked after he and a close group of advisors had blundered into the Bay of Pigs invasion. For the last two years I have been studying that question, as it applies not only to the Bay of Pigs decision-makers but also to those who led the United States into such other major fiascos as the failure to be prepared for the attack on Pearl Harbor, the Korean War stalemate and the escalation of the Vietnam War.

Stupidity certainly is not the explanation. The men who participated in making the Bay of Pigs decision, for instance, comprised one of the greatest arrays of intellectual talent in the history of American Government—Dean Rusk, Robert McNamara, Douglas Dillon, Robert Kennedy, McGeorge Bundy, Arthur Schlesinger Jr., Allen Dulles and others.

It also seemed to me that explanations were incomplete if they concentrated only on disturbances in the behavior of each individual within a decision-making body: temporary emotional states of elation, fear, or anger that reduce a man's mental efficiency, for example, or chronic blind spots arising from a man's social prejudices or idiosyncratic biases.

I preferred to broaden the picture by looking at the fiascos from the standpoint of group dynamics as it has been explored over the past three decades, first by the great social psychologist

Reprinted with permission from *Psychology Today* magazine, November 1971, copyright © 1971 American Psychological Association.

Kurt Lewin and later in many experimental situations by myself and other behavioral scientists. My conclusion after poring over hundreds of relevant documents—historical reports about formal group meetings and informal conversations among the members—is that the groups that committed the fiascos were victims of what I call "groupthink."

"GROUPY"

In each case study, I was surprised to discover the extent to which each group displayed the typical phenomena of social conformity that are regularly encountered in studies of group dynamics among ordinary citizens. For example, some of the phenomena appear to be completely in line with findings from social-psychological experiments showing that powerful social pressures are brought to bear by the members of a cohesive group whenever a dissident begins to voice his objections to a group consensus. Other phenomena are reminiscent of the shared illusions observed in encounter groups and friendship cliques when the members simultaneously reach a peak of "groupy" feelings.

Above all, there are numerous indications pointing to the development of group norms that bolster morale at the expense of critical thinking. One of the most common norms appears to be that of remaining loyal to the group by sticking with the policies to which the group has already committed itself, even when those policies are obviously working out badly and have unintended consequences that disturb the conscience of each member. This is one of the key characteristics of groupthink.

1984

I use the term groupthink as a quick and easy way to refer to the mode of thinking that persons engage in when *concurrence-seeking* becomes so dominant in a cohesive ingroup that it tends to override realistic appraisal of alternative courses of action. Groupthink is a term of the same order as the words in the newspeak vocabulary George Orwell used in his dismaying world of *1984*. In that context, groupthink takes on an invidious connotation. Exactly such a connotation is intended, since the term refers to a deterioration in mental efficiency, reality testing and moral judgments as a result of group pressures.

The symptoms of groupthink arise when the members of decision-making groups become motivated to avoid being too harsh in their judgments of the leaders' or their colleagues' ideas. They adopt a soft line of criticism, even in their own thinking. At their meetings, all the members are amiable and seek complete concurrence on every important issue, with no bickering or conflict to spoil the cozy, "we-feeling" atmosphere.

KILL

Paradoxically, soft-headed groups are often hard-hearted when it comes to dealing with outgroups or enemies. They find it relatively easy to resort to dehumanizing solutions—they will readily authorize bombing attacks that kill large numbers of civilians in the name of the noble cause of persuading an unfriendly government to negotiate at the peace table. They are unlikely to pursue the more difficult and controversial issues that arise when alternatives to a harsh military solution come up for discussion. Nor are they inclined to raise ethical issues that carry the implication that *this fine group of ours, with its humanitarianism and its high-minded principles, might be capable of adopting a course of action that is inhumane and immoral.*

NORMS

There is evidence from a number of social-psychological studies that as the members of a group feel more accepted by the others, which is a central feature of increased group cohesiveness, they display less overt conformity to group norms. Thus we would expect that the more cohesive a group becomes, the less the members will feel constrained to censor what they say out of fear of being socially punished for antagonizing the leader or any of their fellow members.

In contrast, the groupthink type of conformity tends to increase as group cohesiveness increases. Groupthink involves nondeliberate suppression of critical thoughts as a result of internalization of the group's norms, which is quite different from deliberate suppression on the basis of external threats of social punishment. The more cohesive the group, the greater the inner compulsion on the part of each member to avoid creating disunity, which inclines him to believe in the soundness of whatever proposals are promoted by the leader or by a majority of the group's members.

In a cohesive group, the danger is not so much that each individual will fail to reveal his objections to what the others propose but that he will think the proposal is a good one, without attempting to carry out a careful, critical scrutiny of the pros and cons of the alternatives. When groupthink becomes dominant, there also is considerable suppression of deviant thoughts, but it takes the form of each person's deciding that his misgivings are not relevant and should be set aside, that the benefit of the doubt regarding any lingering uncertainties should be given to the group consensus.

STRESS

I do not mean to imply that all cohesive groups necessarily suffer from groupthink. All ingroups may have a mild tendency toward groupthink, displaying one or another of the symptoms from time to time, but it need not be so dominant as to influence the quality of the group's final decision. Neither do I mean to imply that there is anything necessarily inefficient or harmful about group decisions in general. On the contrary, a group whose members have properly defined roles, with traditions concerning the procedures to follow in pursuing a critical inquiry, probably is capable of making better decisions than any individual group member working alone.

The problem is that the advantages of having decisions made by groups are often lost because of powerful psychological pressures that arise when the members work closely together, share the same set of values and, above all, face a crisis situation that puts everyone under intense stress.

The main principle of groupthink, which I offer in the spirit of Parkinson's Law, is this:

The more amiability and esprit de corps there is among the members of a policy-making ingroup, the greater the danger that independent critical thinking will be replaced by groupthink, which is likely to result in irrational and dehumanizing actions directed against outgroups.

SYMPTOMS

In my studies of high-level governmental decision-makers, both civilian and military, I have found eight main symptoms of groupthink.

1. Invulnerability

Most or all of the members of the ingroup share an *illusion* of invulnerability that provides for them some degree of reassurance about obvious dangers and leads them to become overoptimistic and willing to take extraordinary risks. It also causes them to fail to respond to clear warnings of dangers.

The Kennedy ingroup, which uncritically accepted the Central Intelligence Agency's disastrous Bay of Pigs plan, operated on the false assumption that they could keep secret the fact that the United States was responsible for the invasion of Cuba. Even after news of the plan began to leak out, their belief remained unshaken. They failed even to consider the danger that awaited them: a world-wide revulsion against the U.S.

A similar attitude appeared among the members of President Lyndon B. Johnson's ingroup, the "Tuesday Cabinet," which kept escalating the Vietnam War despite repeated setbacks and failures. "There was a belief," Bill Moyers commented after he resigned, "that if we indicated a willingness to use our power, they [the North Vietnamese] would get the message and back away from an all-out confrontation. . . . There was a confidence—it was never bragged about, it was just there—that when the chips were really down, the other people would fold."

A most poignant example of an illusion of invulnerability involves the ingroup around Admiral H. E. Kimmel, which failed to prepare for the possibility of a Japanese attack on Pearl Harbor despite repeated warnings. Informed by his intelligence chief that radio contact with Japanese aircraft carriers had been lost, Kimmel joked about it: "What, you don't know where the carriers are? Do you mean to say that they could be rounding Diamond Head (at Honolulu) and you wouldn't know it?" The carriers were in fact moving full-steam toward Kimmel's command post at the time. Laughing together about a danger signal, which labels it as a purely laughing matter, is a characteristic manifestation of groupthink.

2. Rationale

As we see, victims of groupthink ignore warnings; they also collectively construct rationalizations in order to discount warnings and other forms of negative feedback that, taken seriously, might lead the group members to reconsider their assumptions each time they recommit themselves to past decisions. Why did the Johnson ingroup avoid reconsidering its escalation policy when time and again the expectations on which they based their decisions turned out to be wrong? James C. Thompson Jr., a Harvard historian who spent five years as an observing participant in both the State Department and the White House, tells us that the policymakers avoided critical discussion of their prior decisions and continually invented new rationalizations so that they could sincerely recommit themselves to defeating the North Vietnamese.

In the fall of 1964, before the bombing of North Vietnam began, some of the policymakers predicted that six weeks of air strikes would induce the North Vietnamese to seek peace talks. When someone asked, "What if they don't?" the answer was that another four weeks certainly would do the trick.

Later, after each setback, the ingroup agreed that by investing just a bit more effort (by stepping up the bomb tonnage a bit, for instance), their course of action would prove to be right. *The Pentagon Papers* bear out these observations.

In *The Limits of Intervention,* Townsend Hoopes, who was acting Secretary of the Air Force under Johnson, says that Walt W. Rostow in particular showed a remarkable capacity for what has been called "instant rationalization." According to Hoopes, Rostow buttressed the group's optimism about being on the road to victory by culling selected scraps of evidence from news reports or, if necessary, by inventing "plausible" forecasts that had no basis in evidence at all.

Admiral Kimmel's group rationalized away their warnings, too. Right up to December 7, 1941, they convinced themselves that the Japanese would never dare attempt a full-scale surprise assault against Hawaii because Japan's leaders would realize that it would precipitate an all-out war which the United States would surely win. They made no attempt to look at the situation through the eyes of the Japanese leaders—another manifestation of groupthink.

3. Morality
Victims of groupthink believe unquestioningly in the inherent morality of their ingroup; this belief inclines the members to ignore the ethical or moral consequences of their decisions.

Evidence that this symptom is at work usually is of a negative kind—the things that are left unsaid in group meetings. At least two influential persons had doubts about the morality of the Bay of Pigs adventure. One of them, Arthur Schlesinger Jr., presented his strong objections in a memorandum to President Kennedy and Secretary of State Rusk but suppressed them when he attended meetings of the Kennedy team. The other, Senator J. William Fulbright, was not a member of the group, but the President invited him to express his misgivings in a speech to the policymakers. However, when Fulbright finished speaking the President moved on to other agenda items without asking for reactions of the group.

David Kraslow and Stuart H. Loory, in *The Secret Search for Peace in Vietnam,* report that during 1966 President Johnson's ingroup was concerned primarily with selecting bomb targets in North Vietnam. They based their selections on four factors—the military advantage, the risk to American aircraft and pilots, the danger of forcing other countries into the fighting, and the danger of heavy civilian casualties. At their regular Tuesday luncheons, they weighed these factors the way school teachers grade examination papers, averaging them out. Though evidence on this point is scant, I suspect that the group's ritualistic adherence to a standardized procedure induced the members to feel morally justified in their destructive way of dealing with the Vietnamese people—after all, the danger of heavy civilian casualties from U.S. air strikes was taken into account on their checklists.

4. Stereotypes

Victims of groupthink hold stereotyped views of the leaders of enemy groups: they are so evil that genuine attempts at negotiating differences with them are unwarranted, or they are too weak or too stupid to deal effectively with whatever attempts the ingroup makes to defeat their purposes, no matter how risky the attempts are.

Kennedy's groupthinkers believed that Premier Fidel Castro's air force was so ineffectual that obsolete B-26s could knock it out completely in a surprise attack before the invasion began. They also believed that Castro's army was so weak that a small Cuban-exile brigade could establish a well-protected beachhead at the Bay of Pigs. In addition, they believed that Castro was not smart enough to put down any possible internal uprisings in support of the exiles. They were wrong on all three assumptions. Though much of the blame was attributable to faulty intelligence, the point is that none of Kennedy's advisers even questioned the CIA planners about these assumptions.

The Johnson advisers' sloganistic thinking about "the Communist apparatus" that was "working all around the world" (as Dean Rusk put it) led them to overlook the powerful nationalistic strivings of the North Vietnamese government and its efforts to ward off Chinese domination. The crudest of all stereotypes used by Johnson's inner circle to justify their policies was the domino theory ("If we don't stop the Reds in South Vietnam, tomorrow they will be in Hawaii and next week they will be in San Francisco," Johnson once said). The group so firmly accepted this stereotype that it became almost impossible for any adviser to introduce a more sophisticated viewpoint.

In the documents on Pearl Harbor, it is clear to see that the Navy commanders stationed in Hawaii had a naive image of Japan as a midget that would not dare to strike a blow against a powerful giant.

5. Pressure

Victims of groupthink apply direct pressure to any individual who momentarily expresses doubts about any of the group's shared illusions or who questions the validity of the arguments supporting a policy alternative favored by the majority. This gambit reinforces the concurrence-seeking norm that loyal members are expected to maintain.

President Kennedy probably was more active than anyone else in raising skeptical questions during the Bay of Pigs meetings, and yet he seems to have encouraged the group's docile, uncritical acceptance of defective arguments in favor of the CIA's plan. At every meeting, he allowed the CIA representatives to dominate the discussion. He permitted them to give their immediate refutations in response to each tentative doubt that one of the others expressed, instead of asking whether anyone shared the doubt or wanted to pursue the implications of the new worrisome issue that had just been raised. And at the most crucial meeting, when he was calling on each member to give his vote for or against the plan he did not call on Arthur Schlesinger, the one man there who was known by the President to have serious misgivings.

Historian Thompson informs us that whenever a member of Johnson's ingroup began to express doubts, the group used subtle social pressures to "domesticate" him. To start with, the dissenter was made to feel at home, provided that he lived up to two restrictions: 1) that he did not voice his doubts to outsiders, which would play into the hands of the opposition: and 2) that he kept his criticisms within the bounds of acceptable deviation, which meant not challenging any of the fundamental assumptions that went into the group's prior commitments. One such "domesticated dissenter" was Bill Moyers. When Moyers arrived at a meeting, Thompson tells us, the President greeted him with, "Well, here comes Mr. Stop-the-Bombing."

6. Self-Censorship

Victims of groupthink avoid deviating from what appears to be group consensus; they keep silent about their misgivings and even minimize to themselves the importance of their doubts.

As we have seen, Schlesinger was not at all hesitant about presenting his strong objections to the Bay of Pigs plan in a memorandum to the President and the Secretary of State. But he became keenly aware of his tendency to suppress objections at the White House meetings. "In the months after the Bay of Pigs I bitterly reproached myself for having kept so silent during those crucial discussions in the cabinet room," Schlesinger writes in *A Thousand Days*. "I can only explain my failure to do more than raise a few timid questions by reporting that one's impulse to blow the whistle on this nonsense was simply undone by the circumstances of the discussion."

7. Unanimity

Victims of groupthink share an *illusion* of unanimity within the group concerning almost all judgments expressed by members who speak in favor of the majority view. This symptom results partly from the preceding one, whose effects are augmented by the false assumption that any individual who remains silent during any part of the discussion is in full accord with what the others are saying.

When a group of persons who respect each other's opinions arrives at a unanimous view, each member is likely to feel that the belief must be true. This reliance on consensual validation within the group tends to replace individual critical thinking and reality testing, unless there are clear-cut disagreements among the members. In contemplating a course of action such as the invasion of Cuba, it is painful for the members to confront disagreements within their group, particularly if it becomes apparent that there are widely divergent views about whether the preferred course of action is too risky to undertake at all. Such disagreements are likely to arouse anxieties about making a serious error. Once the sense of unanimity is shattered, the members no longer can feel complacently confident about the decision they are inclined to make. Each man must then face the annoying realization that there are troublesome uncertainties and he must diligently seek out the best information he can get in order to decide for himself exactly how serious the risks might be. This is one of the unpleasant consequences of being in a group of hardheaded, critical thinkers.

To avoid such an unpleasant state, the members often become inclined, without quite realizing it, to prevent latent disagreements from surfacing when they are about to initiate a risky course of action. The group leader and the members support each other in playing up the areas of convergence in their thinking, at the expense of fully exploring divergencies that might reveal unsettled issues.

"Our meetings took place in a curious atmosphere of assumed consensus," Schlesinger writes. His additional comments clearly show that, curiously, the consensus was an illusion—an illusion that could be maintained only because the major participants did not reveal their own reasoning or discuss their idiosyncratic assumptions and vague reservations. Evidence from several sources makes it clear that even the three principals—President Kennedy, Rusk and McNamara—had widely differing assumptions about the invasion plan.

8. Mindguards

Victims of groupthink sometimes appoint themselves as mindguards to protect the leader and fellow members from adverse information that might break the complacency they shared about the effectiveness and morality of past decisions.

At a large birthday party for his wife, Attorney General Robert F. Kennedy, who had been constantly informed about the Cuban invasion plan, took Schlesinger aside and asked him why he was opposed. Kennedy listened coldly and said, "You may be right or you may be wrong, but the President has made his mind up. Don't push it any further. Now is the time for everyone to help him all they can."

Rusk also functioned as a highly effective mindguard by failing to transmit to the group the strong objections of three "outsiders" who had learned of the invasion plan—Undersecretary of State Chester Bowles, USIA Director Edward R. Murrow, and Rusk's intelligence chief, Roger Hilsman. Had Rusk done so, their warnings might have reinforced Schlesinger's memorandum and jolted some of Kennedy's ingroup, if not the President himself, into reconsidering the decision.

PRODUCTS

When a group of executives frequently displays most or all of these interrelated symptoms, a detailed study of their deliberations is likely to reveal a number of immediate consequences. These consequences are, in effect, products of poor decision-making practices because they lead to inadequate solutions to the problems being dealt with.

First, the group limits its discussions to a few alternative courses of action (often only two) without an initial survey of all the alternatives that might be worthy of consideration.

Second, the group fails to reexamine the course of action initially preferred by the majority after they learn of risks and drawbacks they had not considered originally.

Third, the members spend little or no time discussing whether there are nonobvious gains they may have overlooked or ways of reducing the seemingly prohibitive costs that made rejected alternatives appear undesirable to them.

Fourth, members make little or no attempt to obtain information from experts within their own organizations who might be able to supply more precise estimates of potential losses and gains.

Fifth, members show positive interest in facts and opinions that support their preferred policy; they tend to ignore facts and opinions that do not.

Sixth, members spend little time deliberating about how the chosen policy might be hindered by bureaucratic inertia, sabotaged by political opponents, or temporarily derailed by common accidents. Consequently, they fail to work out contingency plans to cope with foreseeable setbacks that could endanger the overall success of their chosen course.

SUPPORT

The search for an explanation of why groupthink occurs has led me through a quagmire of complicated theoretical issues in the murky area of human motivation. My belief, based on recent social psychological research, is that we can best understand the various symptoms of groupthink as a mutual effort among the group members to maintain self-esteem and emotional equanimity by providing social support to each other, especially at times when they share responsibility for making vital decisions.

Even when no important decision is pending, the typical administrator will begin to doubt the wisdom and morality of his past decisions each time he receives information about setbacks, particularly if the information is accompanied by negative feedback from prominent men who originally had been his supporters. It should not be surprising, therefore, to find that individual members strive to develop unanimity and esprit de corps that will help bolster each other's morale, to create an optimistic outlook about the success of pending decisions, and to reaffirm the positive value of past policies to which all of them are committed.

PRIDE

Shared illusions of invulnerability, for example, can reduce anxiety about taking risks. Rationalizations help members believe that the risks are really not so bad after all. The assumption of inherent morality helps the members to avoid feelings of shame or guilt. Negative stereotypes function as stress-reducing devices to enhance a sense of moral righteousness as well as pride in a lofty mission.

The mutual enhancement of self-esteem and morale may have functional value in enabling the members to maintain their capacity to take action, but it has maladaptive consequences insofar as concurrence-seeking tendencies interfere with critical, rational capacities and lead to serious errors of judgment.

While I have limited my study to decision-making bodies in Government, groupthink symptoms appear in business, industry and any other field where small, cohesive groups make the decisions. It is vital, then, for all sorts of people—and especially group leaders—to know what steps they can take to prevent groupthink.

REMEDIES

To counterpoint my case studies of the major fiascos, I have also investigated two highly successful group enterprises, the formulation of the Marshall Plan in the Truman Administration and the handling of the Cuban missile crisis by President Kennedy and his advisors. I have found it instructive to examine the steps Kennedy took to change his group's decision-making processes. These changes ensured that the mistakes made by his Bay of Pigs ingroup were not repeated by the missile-crisis ingroup, even though the membership of both groups was essentially the same.

The following recommendations for preventing groupthink incorporate many of the good practices I discovered to be characteristic of the Marshall Plan and missile-crisis groups:

1. The leader of a policy-forming group should assign the role of critical evaluator to each member, encouraging the group to give high priority to open airing of objections and doubts. This practice needs to be reinforced by the leader's acceptance of criticism of his own judgments in order to discourage members from soft-pedaling their disagreements and from allowing their striving for concurrence to inhibit criticism.

2. When the key members of a hierarchy assign a policy-planning mission to any group within their organization, they should adopt an impartial stance instead of stating preferences and expectations at the beginning. This will encourage open inquiry and impartial probing of a wide range of policy alternatives.

3. The organization routinely should set up several outside policy-planning and evaluation groups to work on the same policy question, each deliberating under a different leader. This can prevent the insulation of an ingroup.

4. At intervals before the group reaches a final consensus, the leader should require each member to discuss the group's deliberations with associates in his own unit of the organization—assuming that those associates can be trusted to adhere to the same security regulations that govern the policy-makers—and

then to report back their reactions to the group.

5. The group should invite one or more outside experts to each meeting on a staggered basis and encourage the experts to challenge the views of the core members.

6. At every general meeting of the group, whenever the agenda calls for an evaluation of policy alternatives, at least one member should play devil's advocate, functioning as a good lawyer in challenging the testimony of those who advocate the majority position.

7. Whenever the policy issue involves relations with a rival nation or organization, the group should devote a sizable block of time, perhaps an entire session, to a survey of all warning signals from the rivals and should write alternative scenarios on the rivals' intentions.

8. When the group is surveying policy alternatives for feasibility and effectiveness, it should from time to time divide into two or more subgroups to meet separately, under different chairmen, and then come back together to hammer out differences.

9. After reaching a preliminary consensus about what seems to be the best policy, the group should hold a "second-chance" meeting at which every member expresses as vividly as he can all his residual doubts, and rethinks the entire issue before making a definitive choice.

HOW

These recommendations have their disadvantages. To encourage the open airing of objections, for instance, might lead to prolonged and costly debates when a rapidly growing crisis requires immediate solution. It also could cause rejection, depression and anger. A leader's failure to set a norm might create cleavage between leader and members that could develop into a disruptive power struggle if the leader looks on the emerging consensus as anathema. Setting up outside evaluation groups might increase the risk of security leakage. Still, inventive executives who know their way around the organizational maze probably can figure out how to apply one or another of the prescriptions successfully, without harmful side effects.

They also could benefit from the advice of outside experts in the administrative and behavioral sciences. Though these experts have much to offer, they have had few chances to work on policy-making machinery within large organizations. As matters now stand, executives innovate only when they need new procedures to avoid repeating serious errors that have deflated their self-images.

In this era of atomic warheads, urban disorganization and ecocatastrophes, it seems to me that policymakers should collaborate with behavioral scientists and give top priority to preventing groupthink and its attendant fiascos.

Managing Professionals
within Organizational Structures

8

THE ROLE OF CULTURE AND SOCIALIZATION

The Paradox of "Corporate Culture": Reconciling Ourselves to Socialization

Richard Pascale

- An assistant controller at IBM is rehearsed for a stand-up presentation with flip charts—the principal means of formal communication. Each presentation gets "probed"—IBM's secret weapon for training and assessing young professionals. A manager states: "You're so accustomed to being probed you're almost unaware of it. IBM bosses have an uncanny way of pushing, poking, having a follow-up question, always looking for the hidden ball. It's a rigorous kind of self-discipline we impose on ourselves for getting to the heart of problems. It's also management's way of assessing potential and grooming subordinates for the next job. Senior management spends most of its time 'probing.'"[1]
- An MBA joining Bain and Company, the management consulting firm, is surprised by the incredible number of meetings he must attend—company meetings, recruiting meetings, officer meetings, office meetings, case

team meetings, and near-mandatory participation on sports teams and attendance at social events. The objective is to build cohesiveness, participation, and close identification with the firm. There are a set of imperatives for working at Bain: "don't compete directly with peers," "make major conceptual contributions without being a prima donna," "demonstrate an ability to build on others' ideas." In aggregate, these features of Bain's culture are viewed as the underpinnings of success—both internally and with clients.[2]
- An applicant for an entry-level position in brand management at Procter and Gamble experiences an exhaustive application and screening process. His or her interviewer is one of an elite cadre who have been selected and trained extensively via lectures, video tapes, films, practice interviews, and role plays. P&G regards this as a crucial task; it predestines the creative and managerial resources on which the institution's future depends. The applicant is interviewed in depth for such qualities as his or her ability to "turn out high volumes of excellent work,"

"identify and understand problems," and "reach thoroughly substantiated and well reasoned conclusions that lead to action." The applicant receives two interviews and a general knowledge test, before being flown back to Cincinnati for three more one-on-one interviews and a group interview at lunch. Each encounter seeks corroborating evidence of the traits which P&G believes correlate highly with "what counts" for institutional excellence. Notwithstanding the intensity of this screening process, the recruiting team strives diligently to avoid overselling P&G, revealing both its plusses and minuses. P&G actually *facilitates* an applicant's de-selection, believing that no one knows better than the candidate whether the organization meshes with his or her own objectives and values.[3]

• Morgan Guaranty, a bank so profitable and well run that most other bankers use it as a model, competes fiercely for bright and aggressive talent. Once recruited, an extraordinary amount of institutional energy is invested into molding these strong and talented individuals into the Morgan "collegial" style. All employees go through a one year training program that tests their intellect, endurance, and that *requires teamwork* as an essential factor of survival. Constant evaluation assesses interpersonal skills as well as analytical abilities. "The spirit of camaraderie and togetherness" is an explicit objective of entry level indoctrination. Once on the job, frequent rotations provide cross-training and necessitate building an ever-growing network of relationships. Performance evaluations are based not solely upon one's own boss's opinion but upon inputs from every major department with which one interacts. One learns quickly that to succeed one must succeed through the team. Overt political battles are taboo and conflict is resolved directly but never disagreeably. States one officer: "The Morgan traits pro-

vide a basic grammar of understanding that enables divergent elements of our organization to speak a common language."[4]

The common thread of these examples is the systematic means by which firms bring new members into their culture. The technical term is "socialization." It encompasses the process of being made a member of a group, learning the ropes, and being taught how one must communicate and interact to get things done. Mention the term "socialization" and a variety of unsavory images come to mind. Some equate it to the teaching of socialism—an incorrect interpretation—but even when correctly understood as the imposition of social conformity, the concept makes most of us cringe. Americans, dedicated by constitution and conviction to the full expression of individuality, regard "socialization" as alien and vaguely sinister. This taboo causes us to undermanage the forces for cohesion in organizations.

The debate between "individuality" and "socialization," like politics or religion, evokes a strong emotional response. Due perhaps to our hypersensitivity to the topic, most corporations avoid the issue. Most American managers know relatively little about the precise process through which strong culture firms "socialize." There is little written on the subject. Business schools give the subject a passing wink. In fact, business schools find themselves in a particular dilemma since, in extolling management as a profession, they foster the view that a cadre of "professional managers" can move from firm to firm with generic skills that enable them to be effective in each. This runs squarely against the requirements of a strong culture. MIT's Edgar Schein states: "I believe that management education, particularly graduate (business schools), are increasingly attempting to train professionals, and in this process are socializing the students to a set of professional values which are, in fact, in a severe and direct conflict with typical organizational values."[5] It is not surprising that many businesses have become disenchanted with MBAs in line management positions because of their tendency to skip from one firm to the next. It is certainly of interest that most strong culture firms, if they hire MBAs at all, insist on starting them from the ground up and promote exclusively from within. There are no significant MBA programs in Japan—and Japanese students earning MBAs in the U.S. are sent primarily for language skills and the cross-cultural experience.[6]

Consider the fad that currently surrounds the subject of "organizational culture." Many adherents lose enthusiasm when brought face-to-face with the stark reality that "creating a strong culture" is a nice way of saying that an organization's members have to be more comprehensively socialized. Most American firms are culturally permissive. We are guided by a philosophy—initially articulated by Locke, Hobbes, and Adam Smith—which holds that individuals who are free to choose make the most efficient decisions. The independence of the parts makes a greater sum. Stemming from this tradition, American organizations allow members to do their own thing to a remarkable degree. Trendy campaigns "to become a strong culture" encounter resistance when an organization's members are asked to give up their idiosyncrasies and some of their individuality for the common good. The end result is usually the status quo.

Of course, some firms do openly worry about their "culture." Many, however, often err on the side of fostering "pseudo-cultures." (There are numerous examples in Silicon Valley.) Issuing "company creeds" or hosting rituals like "Friday night beer busts" may project the aura of corporate culture; but such elements alone do not facilitate organizational effectiveness. Real changes in style cannot prevail without a carefully thought through and interlocking socialization process.

The crux of the dilemma is this: We are intellectually and culturally opposed to the manipulation of individuals for organizational purposes. At the same time, a certain degree of social uni-

formity enables organizations to work better. The less we rely on informal social controls, the more we must inevitably turn to formal financial controls and bureaucratic procedures. U.S. firms that have perfected and systematized their processes of socialization tend to be a disproportionate majority of the great self-sustaining firms which survive from one generation to the next. Virtually none of these companies discuss "socialization" directly. It occurs as an exercise of the left hand—something that just happens "as the way we do things around here." When we examine any particular aspect (e.g., how the firm recruits, the nature of its entry level training, its reward systems, and so forth), little stands out as unusual. But when the pieces are assembled, what emerges in firms as different as AT&T is from P&G, as Morgan Guaranty is from IBM or Delta Airlines, is an awesome internal consistency which powerfully shapes behavior.

STEPS OF SOCIALIZATION

It is time to take socialization out of the closet. If some degree of socialization is an inescapable necessity for organizational effectiveness, the challenge for managers is to reconcile this with the American insistence upon retaining the latitude for independent action. The solution is neither mind control nor manipulation. It is neither necessary nor desirable to oscillate from extreme individualism to extreme conformity. We can learn from those who have mastered the process. A practical middle road is available. Strong culture firms that have sustained themselves over several generations of management reveal remarkable consistency across seven key steps.

Step One. Careful selection of entry-level candidates. Trained recruiters use standardized procedures and seek specific traits that tie to success in the business. Never oversell a new recruit. Rely heavily on the informed applicant deselecting himself if the organization doesn't fit with his personal style and values.

The earlier Procter and Gamble illustration captures the crucial aspect.[7] Recruitment is the organizational equivalent of "romance." Hiring someone is like marriage—and a broken engagement is preferable to a messy divorce. Recruiters are expected to get deeper than first impressions. Their skill and intuition are developed by intensive training. A great deal of thought is given to articulating precisely and concretely the traits that count. The format for recording these traits is standardized. From the recruit's point of view, the extensive screening sends a signal: "You've got to be special to join." The screening process causes one to reveal oneself and causes most to wonder if they are good enough to get in. This increases receptivity for the second stage.

Step Two.   Humility-inducing experiences in the first months on the job precipitate self-questioning of prior behavior, beliefs, and values. A lowering of individual self-comfort and self-complacency promotes openness toward accepting the organization's norms and values.

Most strong culture companies get the new hire's attention by pouring on more work than can possibly be done. IBM and Morgan Guaranty socialize extensively through training where "you work every night until 2:00 a.m. on your own material and then help others."[8] Procter and Gamble achieves the same result via "upending experiences," sometimes requiring a new recruit to color in a sales territory map—a task for which the novitiate is clearly overqualified.[9] These experiences convey a metamessage: "While you're smart in some ways, you're in kindergarten as far as what you know about this organization." One learns to be humble. Humility tends to flourish under certain conditions: especially long hours of intense work that bring you to your limits. When vulnerability is high, one also becomes close to one's colleagues—and cohesiveness is intensified in pressure-cooker en-

vironments where little opportunity is given to re-establish social distance and regain one's bearings. At the investment banking firm of Morgan Stanley, one is expected to work 12- to 14-hour days and most weekends. Lunches are confined to the firm cafeteria and limited to thirty minutes; trainees are censured for taking lunch outside.[10] Near identical patterns long hours, exhausting travel schedules, and extensive immersion in case work are true at the major consulting firms and law practices. Socialization is a little like exercise—it's easier to reconcile yourself to it when you're young.

Step Three.   In-the-trenches training leads to mastery of one of the core disciplines of the business. Promotion is inescapably tied to a proven track record.

The first phase of socialization aims to attract the right trainees predisposed toward the firm's culture. The second instills enough humility to evoke self-examination; this facilitates "buying in" to the firm's values. Increasingly, the organizational culture becomes the relevant universe of experience. Having thus opened one's mind to the company's way of doing business, the task is now to cement this new orientation. The most effective method for doing so is via extensive and carefully reinforced field experience. While IBM hires some MBAs and a few older professionals with prior work experience, almost all go through the same training and start at the same level. It takes six years to grow an IBM marketing representative, twelve years for a controller. McKinsey consultants and Morgan Stanley analysts must likewise earn their way up from the ranks. The gains from such an approach are cumulative. When all trainees understand there is one step by step career path, it reduces politics. There is no quick way to jump ranks and reach the top. Because the evaluation process has a long time horizon, short term behavior is counterproductive. Cutting corners catches up with you. Relationships, staying power and a consistent proven track record are the inescapable requirements of advancement. Those advancing, having been grown from within, understand the business not as financial abstraction but as a hands on reality. Senior managers can communicate with those at the lowest ranks in the "short hand" of shared experience.

Step Four. Meticulous attention is given to systems measuring operational results and rewarding individual performance. Systems are comprehensive, consistent, and triangulate particularly on those aspects of the business that are tied to competitive success and corporate values.

Procter and Gamble measures three "what counts" factors that have been found to drive brand success. These factors are Building Volume; Building Profit; and Planned Change (defined as changes which simply put, increase effectiveness or otherwise add satisfaction to a job).[11] Operational measures track these factors using Nielsen market share indices as well as traditional financial yardsticks. All performance appraisals are tied to milestones which impact on these factors. Promotions are determined by success against these criteria—plus successful demonstration of management skills.

Another example of comprehensive, consistent, and interlocking systems are those used at IBM to track adherence to its value of "respecting the decency of the individual." This is monitored via climate surveys; "Speak up!" (a confidential suggestion box); open door procedures; skip-level interviews; and numerous informal contacts between senior-level managers and employees.[12] The Personnel Department moves quickly when any downward changes are noted in the above indices. In addition, managers are monitored for percent performance appraisals completed on time and percent of employees missing the required one week a year of training. All first-level managers receive an intensive two-week course in people management and each managerial promotion results in another week-

long refresher. These systems provide a near "fail-safe" network of checks and double checks to ensure adherence to IBM's core value of respecting individual dignity.

Included in IBM's mechanisms for respecting the individual is a device known as the "Penalty Box."[13] Often a person sent to the "penalty box" has committed a crime against the culture—for example, harsh handling of a subordinate, overzealousness against the competition, gaming the reporting system. Most penalty box assignments involve a lateral move to a less desirable location—a branch manager in Chicago might be moved to a nebulous staff position at headquarters. For an outsider, penalty box assignments look like normal assignments, but insiders know they are off the track. Penalty boxes provide a place for people while the mistakes they've made or the hard feelings they've created are gradually forgotten—and while the company looks for a new useful position. The mechanism is one among numerous things IBM does that lend credence to employees' beliefs that the firm won't act capriciously and end a career. In the career of strong, effective managers, there are times when one steps on toes. The penalty box is IBM's "half-way house" enabling miscreants to contemplate their errors and play another day. (Don Estridge, maverick pioneer of IBM's success in personal computers and currently head of that division, came from the penalty box.)

Step Five. Careful adherence to the firm's transcendent values. Identification with common values enables employees to reconcile personal sacrifices necessitated by their membership in the organization.[14]

Of all the steps this is perhaps most essential. It is the foundation of trust between organization and individual. Values also serve as the primary safeguard against our great fear that highly socialized organizations will degenerate into an Orwellian nightmare.[15] Much of our resistance to socialization stems from the suspicion that corporations are fundamentally amoral and their members, once socialized, will pursue inappropriate goals. There are, in fact, significant checks and balances in American society against the extremes of social manipulation. Government, the media, and various other stakeholders such as consumers, environmentalists, and unions become powerfully vocal when corporations cross the line of decorum. And of the great self-sustaining institutions, all over a half century old, little evidence exists of major transgressions despite their strongly socialized cultures. These corporations avoid the undesirable extremes by continually recommitting themselves to shared values that keep them in tune with society.

Placing one's self "at the mercy" of an organization imposes real costs. There are long hours of work, missed weekends, bosses one has to endure, criticism that seems unfair, job assignments and rotations that are inconvenient or undesirable. The countervailing force for commitment under these circumstances is the organization's set of transcendent values which connect *its* purpose with significant higher-order human values—such as serving mankind, providing a first-class product for society, or developing people. Prior to joining Delta Airlines, candidates hear endlessly about "the Delta family feeling." Numerous anecdotes illustrate that Delta's values require sacrifices: management takes pay cuts during lean times; senior flight attendants and pilots voluntarily work fewer hours per week in order to avoid laying off more junior employees.[16] Candidates who accept employment with Delta tend to accept this quid pro quo, believing that the restrictions on individual action comprise a reasonable trade-off. In effect, Delta's family philosophy is seemed worthy enough to make their sacrifices worthwhile. The organization, in turn, needs to honor its values and continually reaffirm their importance. To the outsider, the fuss IBM makes over "respecting the dignity of the individual," the intensity with which Delta Airlines expresses "the Delta

family feeling," may seem like overzealousness. But for those within, these values represent a deeply felt mission. Their credibility and constancy is essential to the socialization transaction.

Step Six.   Reinforcing folklore provides legends and interpretations of watershed events in the organization's history that validate the firm's culture and its aims. Folklore reinforces a code of conduct for "how we do things around here."

All firms have their stories. The difference among firms that socialize well is that the morals of the stories all tend to "point north." Procter and Gamble fires one of their best brand managers for overstating the features of a product. The moral: ethical claims come ahead of making money. Morgan Stanley canonizes partners with legendary skills at "cutting a deal." One of the richest legacies of folklore was found within the former Bell system where numerous stories and anecdotes extolled employees who made sacrifices to keep the phones working.

The Bell folklore was so powerful and widely shared that when natural disaster struck, all elements of a one million member organization were able to pull together, cut corners, violate procedures, make sacrifices against measurement criteria—all in the interest of restoring phone service. This occurred despite extensive bureaucratic obstacles and illustrates how folklore, when well understood, can legitimize special channels for moving an organization in a hurry.[17]

Step Seven.   Consistent role models and consistent traits are associated with those recognized as on the fast track.

Nothing communicates so powerfully to younger professionals within an organization than having peers or superiors who share common qualities and who are formally or informally recognized as winners. Far more can be taught by examples than can ever be conveyed in a classroom. The protégé watches the role model make presentations, handle conflict, write memos—and replicates as closely as possible the traits that seem to work most effectively.

Strong culture firms regard role models as the most powerful ongoing "training program" available. Because other elements of the culture are consistent, those emerging as role models are consistent. Morgan Stanley carefully selects its high-potential cadre for the combination of energy, aggressiveness, and team play that the organization requires.[18] Procter and Gamble exhibits extraordinary consistency among its brand managers across traits such as tough mindedness, motivational skills, enormous energy, and ability to get things done through others.[19]

Unfortunately most firms leave the emergence of role models to chance. Some on the fast track seem to be whizzes at analysis, others are skilled with people, others seem astute at politics: the result for those below is confusion as to what it *really* takes to succeed. The set of companies, formerly parts of the Bell System, have a strong need to become more market oriented and aggressive. Yet the Bell culture continues to discriminate against candidates for the high-potential list who, against the backdrop of the older monopoly culture, are "too aggressive."[20]

The seven dimensions of socialization, while not surprising when examined individually, tend to be overlooked and undermanaged. Many companies can point to isolated aspects of their organizational practices that follow these patterns but rarely is each of the seven factors managed as a concerted and well-coordinated effort. Rarer yet is the firm where all seven hang together. Indeed, it is *consistency* across all seven elements of socialization process that results in a strong cohesive culture that lasts over time.

THE CASE FOR SOCIALIZATION

All organizations require a certain degree of order and consistency. To achieve this, they either utilize *explicit* procedures and formal controls or *implicit* social controls. Great firms tend to do an artful job of blending both. American firms, in aggregate, tend to rely on formal controls. The result is that management often appears to be over-steering, rigid, and bureaucratic. A United Technologies executive states: "I came from the Bell system. Compared to AT&T, this is a weak culture and there is little socialization. But, of course there is still need for controls. So they put handcuffs on you, shackle you to every nickel, track every item of inventory, monitor every movement in production, and head count. They control you by balance sheet."[21]

An inordinate amount of energy in American companies is invested in fighting "the system." (We often find ourselves playing games to work around it.) When an organization instills a strong, consistent set of implicit understandings, it is effectively establishing a common law to supplement its statutory laws. This enables us to interpret formal systems in the context for which they were designed, to use them as tools rather than straitjackets. An IBM manager states: "Socialization acts as a fine-tuning device; it helps us make sense out of the procedures and quantitative measures. Any number of times I've been faced with a situation where the right thing for the measurement system was 'X' and the right thing for IBM was 'Y'. I've always been counselled to tilt toward what was right for IBM in the long term and what was right for our people. They pay us a lot to do that. Formal controls, without coherent values and culture are too crude a compass to steer by."[22]

Organizations that socialize effectively manage a lot of internal ambiguity. This tends to free up time and energy; more goes toward getting the job done and focusing on external things like the competition and the customer. "At IBM you spend 50% of your time managing the internal context," states a former IBMer, now at ITT, "at most companies it's more like 75%."[23] A marketing manager at Atari states: "You can't imagine how much time and energy around here goes into politics. You've got to determine who's on first base this month in order to figure out how to obtain what you need to get the job done. There are no rules. There are no clear values. Bushnell and Kassar stood for diametrically opposite things. Your bosses are constantly changing. I've had 4 in 18 months. We're spread out over 43 buildings over a 20-mile radius and we're constantly reorganizing. All this means that you never have time to develop a routine way for getting things done at the interface between your job and the next guy's. Without rules for working with one another, a lot of people get hurt, get burned out, are never taught the 'Atari way' of doing things because there isn't an 'Atari way.'"[24]

The absence of cultural rules makes organizational life capricious. This is so because success as middle and senior managers not only requires managing the substance of the business, but increasingly involves managing one's role and relationships. When social roles are unclear, no one is speaking the same language; communication and trust break down. Remember, the power to get things done in corporations seldom depends on formal titles and formal authority alone. In great measure, it depends on a person's track record and reputation, knowledge, and a network of relationships. In effect, the power to implement change and execute effectively relies heavily on one's *social* currency, something a person accumulates over time. Strong culture firms *empower* employees helping them build this social currency by providing continuity and clarity. Organizations which do not facilitate this process incur a cost.

Continuity and clarity also yield great dividends in reducing career anxiety. The ebbs and flows of career fortunes attract close scrutiny in organizations. Mixed signals surrounding such things as rewards, promotions, career paths, criteria for being on the "fast track" or a candidate for termination, inevitably generate a lot of gossip, game playing, and counter productive expenditure of energy. Some might feel that these elements can be entirely resolved by the explicit provisions in the policy manual. Fact is, many of

the criteria of success for middle and senior level positions are implicit. It is almost impossible to articulate in writing the nuances and shared understandings that govern the rise or demise of executives. The rules tend to be communicated and enforced via relatively subtle cues. When the socialization process is weak, the cues tend to be poorly or inconsistently communicated.[25]

Look carefully at career patterns in most companies. Ambitious professional strive to learn the ropes but there are as many "ropes" as there are individuals who have, by one means or another, made their way to the top. So one picks an approach and if by coincidence it coincides with how your superiors do things, you're on the fast track. Far more prevalent, however, the approach that works with one superior is offensive to another. "As a younger manager, I was always taught to touch bases and solicit input before moving ahead," a manager of a Santa Clara electronics firm states, "It always worked. But at a higher level with a different boss, my base touching was equated with 'being political.' Unfortunately, the organization doesn't forewarn you when it changes signals. A lot of good people leave owing to misunderstandings over things of this kind. The human cost in weakly socialized organizations tends to go unrecognized."[26]

What about the cost of conformity? A senior vice-president of IBM states: "Conformity among IBM employees has often been described as stultifying in terms of dress, behavior, and lifestyle. There is, in fact, strong pressure to adhere to certain norms of superficial behavior, and much more intensely to the three tenets of the company philosophy—1) respect for the dignity of the individual, 2) providing first-rate customer service, and 3) excellence. These are the bench marks. Between them there is wide latitude for divergence in opinions and behavior." A Procter and Gamble executive adds: "There is a great deal of consistency around here in how certain things are done and these are rather critical to our sustained success. Beyond that, there are very few hard and fast rules. People on the outside might portray our culture as imposing lockstep uniformity. It doesn't feel rigid when you're inside. It feels like it accommodates you. And best of all, you know the game you're in—you know whether you're playing soccer of football; you can find out very clearly what it takes to succeed and you can bank your career on that."[27]

It is useful to distinguish between norms that are central to the core factors that drive business success and social conventions that signal commitment and belonging. The former set is most essential as it ensures consistency around certain crucial activities that link to a firm's strategy. At IBM, people, customers, and excellence have priority. As noted earlier, IBM's format for stand-up presentations and its style of "probing" are seen as vital to keeping the culture on its toes. Bain, Morgan Guaranty, and Procter & Gamble each imposes variations on this theme.

The second set of norms are in effect, organizational equivalents of a handshake. They are social conventions that make it easier for people to be comfortable with one another. One need not observe all of them, but as some conventions count more than others, one strives to reassure the organization that one is on the team. The important aspect of this second set of social values is that, like a handshake, they are usually not experienced as oppressive. Partly, this is because adherence is only skin deep. (Most of us don't feel our individualism is compromised by shaking hands.) In addition, these social conventions are usually self-evident to prospective members and self-selection eliminates many whose integrity would be violated by observing them.

MISCONCEPTIONS

The aim of socialization is to establish a base of attitudes, habits, and values that foster cooperation, integrity, and communication. The most frequently advanced objection is that the companies who do so will lose innovativeness over the long haul. The record does not bear this out.

Many of the companies who socialize most extensively are the ones that have lasted over many generations—at least prima facie evidence of sufficient innovation to cope with the changing environment. Further consider 3M or Bell Labs. Both socialize extensively and both are highly innovative institutions—and they remain so by fostering social rules that *reward* innovation. Another misconception is that socialization necessarily occurs at the expense of maintaining a desirable amount of internal competition. Again, IBM, P&G, major consulting firms, law practices, and outstanding financial institutions like Morgan Stanley are illustrations of strong culture firms where internal competition tends to be healthy but intense. There is, of course, an ever present danger of strong culture firms becoming incestuous and myopic—the "General Motors syndrome." Most opponents of socialization rally around this argument. But what is learned from the firms that have avoided these pitfalls is that they consciously minimize the downside of socialization by cultivating *obsessions*—not just *any* obsession, but ones that serve to continually wrench attention from internal matters to the world outside. The four most common "obsessions" are quality, competition, customer service, and productivity. Each demands an external focus and serves as a built-in way of maintaining vigilance. Positive examples are McDonald's obsessive concern for quality control, Toyota's for productivity, IBM's for customer service, and Morgan Stanley's for competition. These "obsessions" contribute to a lot of fire drills and are regarded as overkill by some. But they also serve as an organizational equivalent of calisthenics. They maintain organizational alertness and muscle tone for the day when real change is required. It should be noted that organizations which tend to be obsessive over internal matters, such as Delta's with "the family feeling," may be riding for a fall.[28]

The underlying dilemma of socialization is so sensitive to core American values that it is seldom debated. When discussed, it tends toward a polarized debate—especially from members of

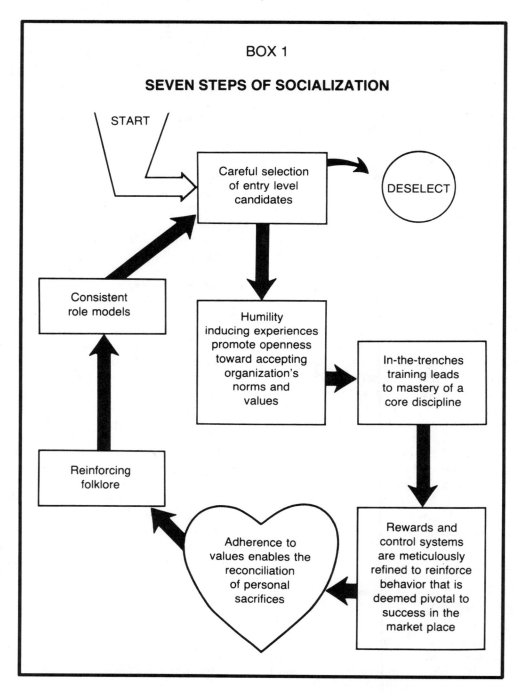

BOX 1

SEVEN STEPS OF SOCIALIZATION

START

Careful selection of entry level candidates

DESELECT

Consistent role models

Humility inducing experiences promote openness toward accepting organization's norms and values

In-the-trenches training leads to mastery of a core discipline

Reinforcing folklore

Adherence to values enables the reconciliation of personal sacrifices

Rewards and control systems are meticulously refined to reinforce behavior that is deemed pivotal to success in the market place

BOX 2. Compute Your "Socialization" Score

Respond to the items below as they apply to the handling of professional employees. Upon completion, compute the total score. For comparison, scores for a number of strong, intermediate, and weak culture firms are to be found below.

	Not true of this company				Very true of this company
1. Recruiters receive at least one week of intensive training.	1	2	3	4	5
2. Recruitment forms identify several key traits deemed crucial to the firm's success, traits are defined in concrete terms and interviewer records specific evidence of each trait.	1	2	3	4	5
3. Recruits are subjected to at least four in-depth interviews.	1	2	3	4	5
4. Company actively facilitates de-selection during the recruiting process by revealing minuses as well as plusses.	1	2	3	4	5
5. New hires work long hours, are exposed to intensive training of considerable difficulty and/or perform relatively menial tasks in the first months.	1	2	3	4	5
6. The intensity of entry level experience builds cohesiveness among peers in each entering class.	1	2	3	4	5
7. All professional employees in a particular discipline begin in entry level positions regardless of prior experience or advanced degrees.	1	2	3	4	5
8. Reward systems and promotion criteria require mastery of a core discipline as a pre-condition of advancement.	1	2	3	4	5
9. The career path for professional employees is relatively consistent over the first six to ten years with the company.	1	2	3	4	5
10. Reward systems, performance incentives, promotion criteria and other primary measures of success reflect high degree of congruence.	1	2	3	4	5
11. Virtually all professional employees can identify and articulate the firm's shared values (i.e., the purpose or mission that ties the firm to society, the customer or its employees).	1	2	3	4	5
12. There are very few instances when actions of management appear to violate the firm's espoused values.	1	2	3	4	5
13. Employees frequently make personal sacrifices for the firm out of commitment to the firm's shared values.	1	2	3	4	5
14. When confronted with trade-offs between systems measuring short-term results and doing what's best for the company in the long term, the firm usually decides in favor of the long-term.	1	2	3	4	5
15. This organization fosters mentor-protége relationships.	1	2	3	4	5
16. There is considerable similarity among the high potential candidates in each particular discipline.	1	2	3	4	5

Compute your score: _____

For comparative purposes:	Scores	
Strongly Socialized Firms................	65–80	...... IBM, P&G, Morgan Guaranty
	55–64	...... ATT, Morgan Stanley, Delta Airlines
	45–54	...... United Airlines, Coca Cola
	35–44	...... General Foods, Pepsi Co.
	25–34	...... United Technologies, ITT
Weakly Socialized Firms................	Below 25	...... Atari

the media and academics who, as a subset of the U.S. population, tend to be among the most pre-occupied with individualism and individual rights. A central premise of this essay is that such polarization generates more heat than light. We will do better if we can advance beyond the extremes of the argument.

Revolutions begin with an assault on awareness. It is time to deal more clear-mindedly with this crucial aspect of organizational effectiveness. Between our *espoused* individualism and the *enacted* reality in most great companies lies a zone where organizational and individual interests overlap. If we can come to grips with our ambivalence about socialization we will undoubtedly make our organizations more effective. Equally important, we can reduce the human costs that arise today as many stumple along ineffectually on careers within companies that lack a sufficient foundation of social rules. This insufficiency is only partly the result of ignorance. In equal measure it derives from our instinctive resistance to social controls—even when some measure of them may be in our own best interest.

REFERENCES

1. Interview with Skip Awalt, Director of Management Development, IBM, Armonk, NY, May 26, 1982.
2. Interviews with Bain Consultants, 1983. Also see: "Those Who Can't Consult," *Harpers* (November 1982), pp. 8–17.
3. N. Kaible, Recruitment and Socialization at Procter and Gamble, Stanford Graduate School of Business, Case II S-BP-236, May 1984.
4. Interviews with professional staff, Morgan Guaranty Trust, New York, 1982.
5. Edgar H. Schein, "Organizational Socialization," in Kolb, Rubin, and McIntire, eds. *Organizational Psychology* (Englewood Cliffs, NJ: Prentice Hall, 1974), pp. 1–15.
6. Richard Pascale and Anthony Athos: *The Art of Japanese Management* (New York, NY: Simon & Schuster, 1981).
7. Kaible, op. cit., pp. 2–6.
8. Interview with recent trainees of IBM's sales development program, Palo Alto, CA, May 1982.
9. Kaible, op. cit., p. 10.
10. Interviews with professional staff, Morgan Stanley, New York, March 1983.
11. Kaible, op. cit., p. 16. *See also* "Readiness Criteria for Promotion to Assistant Brand Manager," unpublished P&G internal document #0689A, pp. 1–2.
12. Interview with Skip Awailt, IBM, op. cit. *See also* T. Rohan, "How IBM Stays Non Union," *Industry Week,* November 26, 1979, pp. 85–96.
13. Interviews with IBM managers, Palo Alto, CA, April 13, 1983. *See also* N. Foy, *The Sun Never Gets on IBM.*
14. See Pascale and Athos, op. cit, Chapter Seven.
15. See for example Zimbardo, "To Control a Mind," *The Stanford Magazine* (Winter 1983), pp. 59–64.
16. J. Guyon, "Family Feeling at Delta Creates Loyal Workers," *Wall Street Journal,* July 17, 1980, p. 13.
17. Interviews with executives of AT&T, Basking Ridge, NJ, February 1982.
18. Interview with professional staff, Morgan Guaranty, Palo Alto, CA, April 1983.
19. Kaible, op. cit, p. 16.
20. Interview with line executives, of Northwestern Bell, Omaha, NE, March 1982.
21. Interview with executives, Pratt & Whitney Division, United Technologies, NY, January 1981.
22. Interview with IBM Marketing and Production managers, Palo Alto, CA, op. cit.
23. Ibid.
24. Interview with product development managers, Atari, Santa Clara, CA, April 1983.
25. Pascale and Athos, op. cit., Chapters 3 & 4.
26. Interview with a production manager of Rolm, Santa Clara, CA, January 1983.
27. Interview with IBM marketing and production managers, Palo Alto, CA, op. cit.
28. M. Loeb, "Staid Delta Air Tries to Stem Losses by Following Other Carriers' Moves," *Wall Street Journal,* July 10, 1983.

Organizational Socialization

Ralph Katz

For many individuals their first year of organizational employment is a very frustrating experience, full of stress, anxiety, and disillusionment. Their struggles to become accepted by others and to function as "true" contributing members within their new work settings are sufficiently dissatisfying that many switch companies within the first couple of years. In fact, Schein (1964) estimated that more than 50 percent of the college graduates entering industrial corporations leave their firms within the first four or five years. Similar high rates of turnover have been found in our own longitudinal studies of young technical professionals. The end result, of course, is a very high rate of organizational turnover among new groups of professional employees—a wasteful outcome, not only economically, but also in terms of lost promise and potential, particularly if the turnover takes place among the most talented individuals.

For other individuals, however, the initial years are a marvelously satisfying experience, full of excitement, achievement, and personal development. Not only are these individuals more likely to remain with their organizations, but it is also likely that they will continue to perform effectively and develop strong commitments to both their job and organizational settings (Steers, 1977).

Given this range of difference in the individual experiences of organizational newcomers, what is it that takes place during one's initial work years that affects the amount of stress one feels and determines one set of outcomes over the other? As discussed by Wanous (1980) and many others, one explanation lies in the perceptual accuracy with which individuals enter their new organizational environments. Generally speaking, the more individuals begin their jobs with unrealistic views and expectations, the more they encounter "reality shock" as they confront the true demands of their everyday task activities. Contrastingly, individuals who assume their new organizational positions with a more realistic understanding and perspective will feel less surprised and disenchanted since they possess, at least initially, more compatible relationships and interactions with both their supervisors and peers.

Based on this argument, if newcomers are given more accurate information about their prospective jobs, they would be able to undertake their new responsibilities with far less discomfort and frustration. They would be, in a sense, better innoculated against the idealistic hopes and expectations that so many young employees form about their upcoming organizational involvements. More "realistic previews" during recruiting, then, can play an important role in preventing disappointments from emerging and disillusioning newcomers as they begin to carry out their daily job assignments.

Although much can be done to educate and prepare new hires for their new world of work, one should also realize that the concerns, reactions, and accomplishments of new employees are eventually shaped by the structure of events and interactions taking place throughout their

355

entire socialization experience within the organization (Katz, 1980; Schein, 1978). A "sink or swim" type of socialization process, for example, evokes conserably more tension and stress than a socialization process that is highly supportive and well structured, even though the actual task demands may be equivalent in both cases. If our ultimate objective is to learn how to provide newcomers with a better "joining-up" process—one that is not only less stressful but also more meaningful and personally developmental—then we need to understand more fully how individual needs and concerns should be met thoughout this important introductory period of organizational careers.

CONTENT OF SOCIALIZATION

During the initial socialization phase, individuals undertaking their first organizational assignments are for the most part very uncertain insofar as organizationally relevant attitudes, behaviors, and procedures are concerned. It is in this early job stage, therefore, that individual newcomers learn not only the specific technical requirements of their jobs but also the socially acceptable attitudes and behaviors necessary for becoming effective organizational members. If new employees hope to direct and orient their own organizational performance in a meaningful and contributive manner, then they must develop a genuine understanding of the events and activities taking place around them. They must build a "situational perspective" within which ideas and assumptions can be tested, interpreted, and interrelated.

As discussed by Louis (1980) and others, creating this perceptual outlook is analogous to building a mental or cognitive map of one's organizational surrounding including its particular cast of characters. To come to know a job situation and act within it implies that the newcomer has developed a sufficiently useful scheme for making sense out of the vast array of experiences associated with his or her participation in the new job setting. The newcomer must come to know what others in the organization are about, how they operate, and how he or she should perform on the job relative to these others. In time, these perceptions provide the new employee with a meaningful way of classifying events and organizing the many interrelationships that exist within the workplace.

In developing this local organizational perspective, every newcomer must accomplish at least three important tasks. They must build their own role identities within their new job contexts; they must discover how to deal with peers and other authority figures, especially their boss; and they must decipher the appropriate reward systems and situational norms of acceptable social and task-related behaviors.

1. *Establishing One's Organizational Role Identity.* As new hires start their organizational careers, they are faced with the problem of developing situational identities that will be viable and suitable both from their own perspectives and from the perspectives of other relevant organizational members. Whether one is aware of it or not, each newcomer must find an answer to the question of "Who and what am I to be in this organization?"

This issue exists simply because all of us have a large repertory of possible roles and behavioral styles that can be enacted in any particular situation. The person who is viewed as influential, aggressive, and helpful in one organizational setting, for example, may be seen by others in a different situation as quiet, reserved, and uninvolved. To some extent, therefore, we can be different people in different situations, depending upon the particular sets of perceptions that come to surround and envelop us.

Newcomers are typically hired into their organizations as the result of some valued educational background or some highly specialized training program. But until they are actually working and participating in their specific job contexts, neither they nor their organizations can really be sure how they will fit into their new work environments. The socialization period, therefore, is a time of mutual discovery between the new employee and the employing organization, each learning more and more about the other. With increasing experience and organizational exposure, the new employee gradually acquires enough self-knowledge to develop a clearer image of his or her own strengths and weaknesses, assessing his or her own preferences, values, talents, and abilities. In a similar fashion, other organizational employees also develop their own perceptual views of the individual newcomer. And as these perceptions and expectations become more firmly established, they function to constrain the role behaviors that the individual is allowed to play within the overall work setting. Thus, it is the intersection among many sets of perceptions that eventually defines the specific role or situational identity of each individual employee. During socialization, then, every newcomer is testing his own self-image against the views and reactions of other organizational employees. The greater the fit between these developing perspectives, the less stress experienced by the new individual since the paths through which he is expected to contribute become increasingly well defined and mutually agreeable.

It is very possible, of course, that not everyone in the work environment will have the same reaction to or will develop the same impression of the new employee. Some may come to value or respect his particular skills and abilities; others may view his areas of expertise as unnecessary and irrelevant. Coworkers or colleagues might also develop a picture of the new employee that is vastly different from the one constructed by his or her supervisor, the one formulated by his or her subordinates, or even the one held by those professionals, customers, or clients outside the organization. All of these types of discrepancies can be operationalized in many different

ways. Nevertheless, in a very general sense, it is extremely difficult for newcombers to break into their new organizations with a well anchored sense of "psychological safety and security" as long as these kinds of differences remain strong or become increasingly diverse and pronounced within the work environment. As many studies have shown (e.g., Katz, 1978a; Hall and Nougaim, 1968), as long as basic personal needs remain conflicted and unfulfilled, new employees will continue to feel very anxious and concerned about their situational roles and organizational identities.

To build this new role identity, socialization must take place along both dimensions of interpersonal and task-related activities. The newcomer has a strong need to obtain answers to a number of important underlying interpersonal questions; while only some of these may be conscious, all need to be answered as quickly as possible. Having entered a strange and unfamiliar social arena, newcomers are strongly concerned with inclusion, that is, becoming a necessary and significant part of the overall organization. According to Schein (1978), Graen (1976), and Katz (1978a), to become accepted and recognized as an important contributing member within one's work setting is one of the major obstacles with which new employees must struggle and which they must eventually overcome. To what extent, then, will they be considered worthwhile? Will they be liked, supported, and appreciated? Will they be kept informed, included, and be given opportunities to make meaningful contributions? These are some of the key interpersonal issues preoccupying employees as their new situational identities become progressively established.

From the technical or task-performance point of view, the newcomer must also figure out whether or not he or she can do the job effectively. As discussed by Schein (1964) and others, to prove or test themselves on the job is another very important concern of new employees. Having spent most of their lives in an educational environment, which has kept them at arm's length from the "real," industrial world, young employees need to discover just what sort of persons they are and of what they are really capable. They need to see how they function on actual work tasks where the outcomes make a significant difference. For this reason the testing of one's skills and abilities is of critical importance. Furthermore, new employees are not only concerned with using their present knowledge, they also want opportunities that enable them to continue to learn and grow—to extend their talents and areas of expertise. One of the inevitable results of prolonged professional education is the expectation that one should continue to self-develop and be given the opportunities and freedom to do so. In short, what is really important to young employees during socialization is the opportunity to clearly demonstrate their work competence and future promise by being meaningfully utilized in some critical aspect of the organization's activities.

2. *Learning to Deal with One's Boss and Other Employees.* A first boss plays a disproportionate role in a young person's career. According to the results of many studies, one of the most critical factors influencing the professional and organizational career success of young employees falls within the mentoring domain of one's immediate supervisor (Kanter, 1977; Graen and Ginsburgh, 1977). Despite the obvious importance of this supervisor-subordinate relationship, very few newcomers are entirely satisfied with their initial boss. One of the major tasks of socialization, then, is to learn how to deal and get along with this individual. He or she may be too Machiavellian, too unstructured, too busy, too fickle, too competent, or even too incompetent. Nevertheless, young employees must learn to adapt to the reality of being dependent upon their particular supervisors.

The newcomer's immediate boss plays a critical role in linking the new employee to the rest of the organization, in making sure his work priorities are consistent with organizational needs, in securing adequate resources, and in providing the additional information and expertise that is necessary to perform well. While some bosses do an excellent job of caring for their new subordinates in these ways, a more reasonable expectation is that only a modest amount of assistance will be forthcoming. In most instances, therefore, newcomers must assume primary responsibility for their own careers and development and must learn to seek the help and information they need to do their work effectively instead of waiting or wishing for their bosses to provide it.

This is not always an easy undertaking. It is often very stressful simply because of the high "psychological costs" that are involved in seeking help from supervisors who are in evaluative and more powerful positions. As summarized by Allen (1977), much research has shown that individuals tend to use information sources that have the least psychological cost instead of using the most effective or most immediate sources of information. However, as in any negotiation or conflict situation, it becomes somewhat easier to approach the "other party" as one generates more meaningful information about those individuals. In a similar fashion it should become easier and less stressful for newcomers to deal with their boss as they acquire a more comprehensive picture of that individual. The more new employees gain insight into the characteristics and perspectives of their supervisor, the easier it will be for them to interact with him or her. Such insight typically requires a very good understanding of his goals, expectations, and work-related values; the personal and task-related pressures that confront him; his areas of managerial strength and weakness; his preferences for different work styles, habits, and so on. In general, then, new employees will become less anxious and will have added control and predictability in dealing with their bosses as they generate increasingly more useful information about them.

In any interpersonal situation, individuals are also more likely to get along and work well together when they are more similar to each other and more compatible in their goals, values, and priority systems. Communication and interaction are always facilitated when individuals have common frames of reference (Rogers and Shoemaker, 1971). Accordingly, one can speculate that organizational socialization will be smoother for those new employees who have the most in common with their immediate supervisors. Lindholm (1983) for example, clearly demonstrated that the single most important determinant of a supervisor-subordinate mentoring relationship resided in the nature of their interpersonal relationship and attraction and not in the nature of their task association or performance.

It is also likely that the very idea of having a boss is inherently uncomfortable to young employees who have recently left the autonomy of university student life. New employees, as a result, are likely to experience considerable conflict as they struggle to balance their desire for professional independence with their more immediate sense of dependence upon their new manager(s) for the definition of their work, their information, their resources, their rewards and promotions, and so forth. This conflict may be even more pronounced for the most creative young professionals who often have low tolerances for formal authority, structure, and procedures. Nonetheless, new hires must first clarify and then learn how to relate to the demands and expectations of their supervisors—how to keep them informed and how to seek their support and approval. At the same time, they must also begin to display an ability to function on their own, to take initiative, to define problems accurately by themselves, and to uncover relevant sources of new and useful information. One of the major accomplishments of socialization, then, in the ability to cope with the creative tension that stems from being dependent, on one hand, yet demonstrating one's independence on the other (Pelz, 1967).

This trade-off between autonomy and con-trol is often one of the major sources of tension between young professionals and their employing work organizations, according to the personal interviews conducted by Bailyn (1982). Quite often, organizations try to create an atmosphere for their young professionals that is very conducive to creative work; one in which professionals are given as much autonomy as possible in choosing problems. This high level of independence, however, is very frustrating to the relatively new professional. In the rapidly changing world of technology, it is not clear to the new employee just what problems or projects are most relevant to the organization's overall goals and objectives. What the young professional really wants is to be placed in a well-defined project that is central to the organization's mission. Having been given this kind of assignment, he or she then expects to be given resources, independence, and discretion to carry out their assignment. Too often, however, the opposite seems to take place. After giving the young professional the autonomous mandate to ''be creative,'' the organization then places a great deal of control on his everyday problem-solving activities. In short, what becomes stressful to young professionals in the early years of work is to be given a very high level of freedom to choose which problems to work on only to be told *how* to work on these problems. In the industrial world of work, young professionals are more likely to welcome the reverse situation; otherwise, they would have remained in university-type settings.

In addition to gaining the acceptance of their boss, newcomers must also learn to deal with other members of the hierarchy and with other peer group members. For those entering with a clear group assignment, the only problem is how to mesh their own needs and abilities with the requirements of the group. For others, however, the problem is to locate the appropriate peer or reference groups with which to align themselves. Much of what goes on in an organization occurs through informal channels and associations that have evolved over time (Allen, 1977; Farris,

1972). Thus, one comes to understand and appreciate the political aspects of different reporting relationships and organizational undertakings primarily through the individual and group contacts of which one has become a part.

The building of relationships within the organization is also important simply because they help us form the coalitions through which we are able to discover new pieces of key information, make important decisions efficiently, and carry out decisions and programs successfully. Very few organizations are completely ruled through omnipotent hierarchies and very few are pure democracies where the majority point of view dominates. Most organizations require the skillful building of interpersonal and political relationships, both formal and informal, in order to function and contribute effectively. All too often, it takes much too long to finally convince newcomers that the organization is composed of many people with whom they must build and cultivate a personal relationship. In a recent study of the socialization process of young technical professionals for example, Lee (1986) discovered that performance was strongly related to the degree to which the newly hired engineer or scientist was communicating and socializing with their more established technical colleagues and not merely interacting only with their peer cohort. Such after work-hour contacts were even more strongly related to performance than grade-point averages per se.

3. *Deciphering Reward Systems and Situational Norms.* As new employees learn to relate to other relevant individuals within the work setting, they must also unravel the customary norms of acceptable social and task related behaviors. If one truly hopes to become a viable, functioning member of the organization and pursue a long-term relationship, then one is required to learn the many attitudes and behaviors that are appropriate and expected within the new job setting. One must discover, for example, when to ask questions, offer new ideas or suggestions,

push for change, take a vacation, or ask for a pay raise or promotion. Newcomers must also align their own assumptions, values, and behavioral modes of conduct against parallel perspectives that are held by their peer and reference groups. Most likely, as employees are able to adopt the collectively held view of things during their socialization, they will be viewed more positively by the organization and will receive more favorable evaluations.

On the other hand, if the new employee finds it difficult to develop a situational perspective that is consistent with those that already exist within the work environment, a high level of stress is likely to result. This dilemma can come about in at least two ways. First, the new employee may strongly disagree with the collectively held view, operating under a very different set of assumptions, values, or priorities. The new assistant professor, for example, may be very excited about teaching and working with graduate students only to discover that his university colleagues value research output almost exclusively. Or there may be strong disagreement concerning the importance of different areas of research, the value of different research methodologies, or the merits of particular application areas. The specific sources of strain will certainly vary with each particular organizational and occupational setting; nevertheless, the more the individual sees oneself as having a "deviant" perspective within the workplace, the more he or she will experience stress in attempting to gain acceptance and prove oneself as a valuable, contributing member.

A second source of discomfort can occur simply when there is no collectively held view of things to guide the new employee. This situation can come about when there is little consensus within the environment, either because the individuals disagree among themselves, or because there has been insufficient time or insufficient stability to develop a collective viewpoint. In either case new employees who find themselves in these situations will experience considerably more stress because of the vast amount of uncertaintly that still exists both within their own roles and within their relevant work environments.

In addition to this general situational perspective, specific beliefs and assumptions about means-end relationships or behavior-outcome contingencies must become clearly defined to help guide and organize the newcomers eventual participation in the workplace (Staw, 1977). From the individual's perspective, he or she must discover what is really expected and what is really rewarded. To what extent can they trust the official formal statements of reward practices and policies? To what extent can they rely on information provided by older, more experienced employees, especially if the situation happens to be changing? New employees must determine for themselves how reward systems actually function so they can comfortably decide where to put their efforts and commitments.

Surprisingly enough, in most organizational settings, the criteria surrounding advancement and other kinds of rewards are very ambiguous especially to young employees in the midst of socialization. Moreover, different employees usually see very different things as being important in getting ahead, covering the full spectrum of possibilities from pure ability and performance to pure luck and politics. Part of the reason for all this ambiguity is that organizational careers are themselves highly variable in that one can succeed in many different ways. Nevertheless, as long as newcomers remain uncertain about the relative importance of alternative outcomes, they will experience considerable tension and stress as they execute their daily activities.

Much of the uncertainty that surrounds reward systems in today's organizations can be traced to the local-cosmopolitan distinctions originally discussed by Gouldner (1957). Having recently been trained in an educational or university-type setting, new professional employees usually enter their organizations with a relatively strong professional orientation. At the same time, however, they must begin to apply this professional knowledge for the good of the organization; that is, they must develop a parallel orientation in which their professional interests and activities are matched against the current and future demands of their functioning organization. This balancing act can lead to a great deal of tension and frustration, particularly if the young employee is forced to allocate his or her time and efforts between two relatively independent sets of interests and rewards. To what extent should they pursue task activities that will be well recognized and rewarded within their profession or within their organization? Can they, in fact, do both relatively easily? All too often, young employees face job situations in which there is too little overlap between the demands, challenges, and rewards of their profession and those of their actual work environments.

By trying to build an accurate picture of the reward system, the young employee is dealing, of course, with only a part of the overall issue. He or she must also begin to question the likelihood of achieving certain results and desired outcomes. An individual's willingness to carry out an action is greatly influenced by whether one feels he or she can perform the action, by one's beliefs concerning the consequences of doing it, and by the attractiveness of the outcomes associated with doing it. To answer these kinds of questions, a reasonable amount of critical performance feedback from supervisors and peers is required. Such feedback provides the newcomer with a clearer sense of how he or she is being viewed and regarded, helping each to find his or her particular "niche" in the overall scheme of things. Unfortunately, in most organizations this kind of useful feedback from supervisors is a rather rare occurrence. In fact, in my own research surveys on engineering professionals, performance feedback was one of the lowest rated behaviors attributed to engineering supervisors in over ten separate RD&E facilities (Katz and Allen, 1978). New employees, therefore, are faced with the problem of obtaining adequate feedback on their own individual performances which can be particularly difficult if one's work is diffused within a larger group or project effort. What becomes most distressing to new employees, then, is that they have entered the organization with an underlying expectation that they would be learning and improving on their first job, yet their supervisors fail to realize that they should act and feel responsible for teaching and helping the employees to accomplish this objective.

Employees need to determine how effectively they are currently performing, how difficult it might be for them to achieve desired outcomes, and how readily they could obtain or develop the various skills and knowledge necessary to meet the demands and expectations of the organization. However, as long as these critical concerns remain unmet and uncertain to new employees, the amount of stress they experience will escalate dramatically. Accordingly, for many employees one of the most important, yet most trying, learning experiences during socialization is how to obtain valid feedback in those particular situations in which it does not automatically or effectively take place. And for many young professionals, the ultimate learning experience is to figure out how to become an excellent judge of one's own individual performance. As a result, socialization is facilitated to the extent that one's supervisor is able to: (1) make an accurate assessment of the new employee's performance and give useful and valid feedback on this performance; (2) transmit the right kinds of values and norms to the new employee in terms of the long-run contributions that are expected of him or her; and (3) design the right mix of meaningful, challenging tasks that permit the new employee to utilize and extend his or her professional skills and build his or her new situational identity.

PROCESS OF SOCIALIZATION

Underlying the tasks represented by the socialization process is the basic idea that individuals are strongly motivated to organize their work lives in a manner that reduces the amount of uncertainty they must face and that is therefore low in stress (Pfeffer, 1981; Katz, 1982). In the words of Weick (1969), employees seek to "enact" their environments by directing their activities toward the establishment of a workable level of certainty and clarity. As they enter their new job positions, they are primarily concerned with reality construction, building more realistic understandings of their unfamiliar social and task environments and their own situational roles within them. They endeavor, essentially, to structure the world of their experience, trying to unravel and define the many formal and informal rules that steer the workplace toward social order rather than toward social chaos.

One of the most obvious, yet most important and often overlooked aspects of new employee socialization is simply that it must take place. By and large, people will not accept uncertainty. They must succeed over time in formulating situational definitions of their workplace with which they can coexist and function comfortably; otherwise, they will feel terribly strained and will seek to leave the given work organization. Until the new employee has created a situational perspective on himself or herself, constructed guidelines regarding what is expected, and built certain situationally-contingent understandings necessary to participate meaningfully within the work setting, the individual cannot act as freely and as fully as he or she would like.

What is very important to recognize here is that stress does not come from the uncertainty itself; it comes from the individual's inability to reduce or lower it. As long as one is making progress in reducing uncertainty, that is, as long as socialization is being facilitated and the individual is making increasing sense out of his or her new work surroundings, stress and anxiety will be lowered and satisfaction will be raised. However, if new employees are somehow prevented from accomplishing any or all of the broad socialization tasks previously discussed, then they are not succeeding in reducing as much of the uncertainty as they need to. This can become highly frustrating and anxiety producing, resulting eventually in higher levels of dissatisfaction and increased levels of organizational turnover. Just as the engineer is highly motivated to reduce technical uncertainty in his or her laboratory activities, the new employee is highly motivated to reduce social and interpersonal uncertainty within his or her new environments. Generally speaking, activity that results in the reduction of uncertainty leads to increasing satisfaction and reduced stress; whereas, activity or change that generates uncertainty creates dissatisfaction and higher stress. Thus, it is not change per se that is resisted, it is the increase in uncertainty that usually accompanies it that is so difficult for individuals to accept.

One must also realize that socialization, unlike an orientation program, does not take place over a day or two. It takes a fair amount of time for employees to feel accepted and competent and to accomplish all of the tasks necessary to develop a situational perspective. How long this socialization period lasts is not only influenced by the abilities, needs, and prior experiences of individual workers, but it also differs significantly across occupations (Feldman, 1977; Katz, 1978b). In general, one might posit that the length of one's initial socialization stage varies positively with the level of complexity of one's job and occupational requirements, ranging perhaps from as little as a month or two on very routine, programmed-type jobs to as much as a year or more on very skilled, unprogrammed-type jobs, as in the engineering and scientific professions. It is generally recognized, for example, that a substantial socialization phase is usually required before an engineer can fully contribute within the organization, making use of his or her knowledge and technical specialty. Even though one might have received an excellent university education in mechanical engineering principles, one must still figure out how to become an effective mechanical engineer at Westinghouse, Dupont or General Electric.

Socialization Is a Social Process

Another very important assumption about socialization is that it must take place through interaction—interaction with other key organizational employees and relevant clientele. By and large, new employees can only reduce uncertainty through interpersonal activities and interpersonal feedback processes.

Newcomers' perceptions and responses are not developed in a social vacuum but evolve through successive encounters with their work environments. Their outlooks become formulated as they interact with and act upon different aspects of their job setting. Their development cannot transpire in isolation, for it is the social context that provides the information and cues with which new employees define and interpret their work experiences (Salancik and Pfeffer, 1977).

One of the more important features of socialization is that the information and knowledge previously gathered by employees from their former colleges or other institutional settings are no longer sufficient nor completely appropriate for interpreting and understanding their new organization domains. As a result, they must depend on individuals within their new situations to help them make sense out of the numerous activities taking place around them. The greater their unfamiliarity, the more they must rely on their new situations to provide the necessary information and interactions by which they can eventually construct their own individual perspectives and situational identities. And it is precisely this situational reliance and social dependence that forces new employees to be more easily influenced during socialization through social interaction (Salancik and Pfeffer, 1978).

Clearly, as employees become increasingly cognizant of their overall job surroundings, they become increasingly capable of relying on their own perceptions for interpreting events and executing their daily task activities. Once they have managed to build a sufficiently robust situational perspective, they are freer to operate more self-sufficiently in that they are now better equipped to determine for themselves the importance and meaning of the various events and information flows surrounding them. On the other hand, as long as new employees have to balance their situational perspectives against the views of significant others within the workplace, frequent interaction with those individuals will be required.

New employees absorb the subtleties of local organizational culture and climate and construct their own definitions of organizational reality—and in particular their own role identities—through interactions with other individuals, including peers, supervisors, subordinates, and customers. Since multiple meanings are likely for any particular event, it is the newcomer's active interpretation of the event, strongly influenced by interacting with one's reference group members, that is so important in constructing his personal view of reality. Furthermore, the more individuals with whom the new employee interacts, the more likely he or she is to put together a view that is both comprehensive and realistic, since different individuals will emphasize different aspects of the work setting and will also differ in the way they interpret events. Recent hires, as a result, formulate their concepts and guide their activities around the anticipated reactions and expectations of the many key employees with whom they are connected.

Of all the concepts that each individual newcomer acquires through the plethora of interpersonal contacts that takes place, perhaps the most important is one's self-concept. It has often been argued that one's fellow workers help to define for each newcomer many of the diverse aspects of the new job setting by the way they act and behave toward these aspects, for example, how they deal with absenteeism, budget overruns, schedule slippages, staff reports, or subordinate suggestions. Similarly, fellow employees help newcomers create perspectives on themselves as particular kinds of individuals by the way the fellow employees act and respond toward these organizational newcomers. As a result, a new em-

ployee's self-image is largely a social product, significantly affected by the behaviors and attitudes of other employees within his or her organizational neighborhood. In essence the newcomer's situational identity is strongly influenced by the self-concept that is gleaned from the eyes of those significant others whom they come to know and with whom they interact.

If newcomers strive to reduce uncertainty by locating and orienting themselves relative to the views and expectations that emerge from those individuals on whom they are most dependent and with whom they are most interactive, then it should not be surprising that some of the most important and most satisfying experiences for new employees are those which attune them to what is expected of them. There is a strong need for newcomers to identify closely with those colleagues and supervisors who can furnish guidance and reassurance concerning such expectations (Graen, 1976). If on the other hand, the individual newcomer is precluded from reducing uncertainty and making increasing sense out of his or her organizational surrounding, then he or she will feel stressed and will be unable to act in a completely responsive and undistracted manner. Many circumstances can arise in any work setting to delay or inhibit a newcomer's socialization, circumstances that invariably prevent the necessary and essential set of interpersonal interactions. Consider, for example, the new employee whose boss is out of town, on vacation, or is simply too busy to help with his or her integration; or the new employee who is assigned to a job location or given an office far away from his or her boss or reference group. Chances are that the reduction of situational uncertainty under these kinds of conditions will be a much prolonged process, perhaps interfering with the newcomer's potential success or even his or her willingness to remain in the organization. Research by Allison (1974) and Lazarsfeld and Theilens (1958) has shown, for example, that when professionals are highly recognized and maintain their strongest links with professionals outside their organization, they are more likely to leave their organizations. In a more recent longitudinal study, Katz and Tushman (1983) found some evidence suggesting that engineers who communicated more often outside than inside their organization were also more likely to leave their organization over the next few years.

Socialization Experiences Are Highly Influential and Long-Lasting

According to the law of primacy expressed by Brown (1963), early socialization experiences are particularly important because they greatly influence how later experiences will be interpreted. The early images and perspectives that are formed in the first year or two of one's organizational career have a strong and lasting influence on one's future task assignments, perceived performances and abilities, and promotional success (Hall, 1976).

More specifically, what has become clear from a large number of studies (e.g., Berlew and Hall, 1966; Bray et al., 1974; Vincino and Bass, 1978) is that the degree to which an employee perceives his or her job as important and challenging by the end of the first year will strongly influence future performance and promotional opportunities. Using overally measures of job challenge, these studies have verified that after one year of employment, young managers who evaluated their jobs more highly or who were viewed more positively by their supervisors were also more likely to have higher performance ratings and higher rates of promotion some five to ten years later. In a similar fashion, Pelz and Andrews (1976) concluded from their cross-sectional study that engineers who were able to utilize more diverse skills and abilities to accomplish an output that became widely known and recognized were more likely to advance within the organization than engineers who were frequently rotated from project to project during their early career years. As a final example, career tracking studies at General Electric have discovered that the best predictor of career success for young professionals at GE was the number of different supervisors who had personal knowledge of the task activities and accomplishments of the young individuals. Given the general consistency in this pattern of findings, it is clear that the newcomer who gets widely known and comes to be seen and sponsored as a valued high performer gains a considerable long-term advantage over the newcomers not so fortunately viewed— the proverbial self-fulfilling prophecy.

In the process of interpreting their early work experiences, young employees begin to observe their colleagues as well as other members who have been labelled as successful or unsuccessful within the organization. They then begin to assess their own careers relative to these individuals. This process of comparison involves many factors, but temporal comparisons represent some of the most critical. By comparing one's progress against these other individuals, the new employee beings to form an implicit "career benchmark" against which both the individual and the organization can start to determine how well he or she is doing. In his large study of British managers, Sofer (1970) shows just how sensitive organizational members can become to their relative career progress. In another example Dalton et al. (1982) strongly argue from their study of R&D professionals that organizations have clearly defined expectations about the behaviors and responsibilities of their more successful engineers at well-defined age-related career stages.

These and many other examples all emphasize that soon after beginning work, employees gradually become concerned about how their progress fits within some framework of career benchmarks. Where are they—are they on schedule, ahead of schedule, behind schedule? The pressure from these kinds of comparisons can become extremely acute especially as the relative judgments become increasingly salient and competitive and their timing increasingly fixed and inflexible. Such events seem to occur in at least

365

two different ways. First, the comparisons can become highly intense as employees enter an organization as part of a well-defined, well-bounded cohort but are then forced to compete amongst themselves for the best individual evaluations, as in the case of many law firms, public accounting firms, consulting companies, universities, and so on. The directness and clarity of these comparisons make the implicit aspects of the career benchmarking process more explicit and, in general, place the young employee under a great deal of stress as he or she competes for the next level of advancement.[1]

For other young employees the occupation or other organization itself can present a fixed timetable for measuring success and career advancement. The tenure process in universities, standardized professional exams (e.g., registered engineer, CPA) or certain apprenticeship periods are all examples of highly structured, well-defined timetables of career progress. These kinds of explicit benchmarks can also place the young employee under severe stress particularly if the employee loses control over the timing of the process or it becomes more like an "up or out" or a "pass/fail" type of system. While the climate that emerges from these more explicit models of career benchmarking may not be very supportive, they may "energize" a great deal of activity and long hours of work on the part of the new employee, at least during his or her early career years.

Because the employee's immediate supervisor influences and controls so many aspects of the communication, task, and career benchmarking factors during socialization, it becomes clear why so many studies have pinpointed the new employee's first boss as being so critical with respect to his or her successful advancements both organizationally and professionally (Kanter, 1977; Schein, 1978; Henning and Jardim, 1977). While supervisors play a critical role in linking their subordinates to other parts of the organization (Likert, 1967), they can also assume a broader role within their work groups, becoming

actively involved in the training, integration, and socialization of their more recently hired members.

By building close working relationships with young subordinates, supervisors might not only improve their group's performance (Katz and Tushman, 1981), but they might also directly affect the personal growth and development of their young professionals. To the extent that supervisors help their new employees participate and contribute more effectively within their work settings, have clearer working relationships with other key organizational individuals, and communicate more easily with outside customers, clients, or professionals, these young professionals will experience less stress and will be less likely to leave the organization. Graen and Ginsburgh (1977) showed, for example, that organizational newcomers who built strong dyadic relationships with their immediate supervisors and who saw a strong relationship between their work and their professional careers were more likely to remain with the organization.

In a much longer longitudinal study, Katz and Tushman (1983) found that young engineers who had high levels of interaction with their first and second level supervisors were significantly less likely to leave the organization over the next 5 years. These supervisors were seen as technically competent and were viewed as valuable sources of new ideas and information. As a result, they became more interactive simply because they were consulted and listened to more frequently on work related matters. At the same time, this high level of interpersonal activity allowed these supervisors to create close working relationships with their younger engineering subordinates, helping them become established and integrated during their early career years. Thus, it may be this high level of interpersonal contact with technically competent supervisors that not only facilitates socialization but also results in more accurate expectations, perceptions, and understandings about one's role in the job and in the larger organization—all of which are important in decreasing turnover and the anxiety levels of new employees.

It has been argued throughout this paper that becoming an integral part of the organization's communication and information processing networks and learning the organization's customs and norms are critically important for reducing stress and fostering more positive attitudes during the early stages of employees' careers. It has also been argued that supervisors play a very direct role in dealing with the initial concerns of young employees, allowing them to reduce uncertainty by helping them understand and interpret the reality of their new settings. In essence, supervisors operate as effective socializing agents and networks builders for their young employees.

In many cases, however, the supervisor is not the only socializing agent of the new employee. The veteran group as a unit can also affect the attachment of new members to the organization. In line with the findings of Katz (1982) and McCain et al. (1981), for example, the larger the proportion of group members with the same group tenure and shared work history, the more distinct that cluster of individuals might become from other organizational members, in general, and from new entering members, in particular. Young employees, for example, might experience a great deal of stress and frustration in trying to integrate themselves into a well-established, older cohort or vice-versa.

Additional conflicts and power issues are also likely to result when there are larger gaps between cohorts within the overall work group. If the group has been staffed on a regular basis, then the new employee's integration is more likely to proceed in a smooth fashion since socialization can be nurtured through the existence of closer, linking cohorts (e.g., Ouchi and Jaeger, 1978). If there are large gaps between cohorts, however, then it is likely that perceptions and beliefs will differ more, resulting in considerable communication difficulty and impedance. The existence of well-differentiated cohorts, according to McCain et al. (1981), increases the possibility of different intragroup norms and expectations which can result in a group atmosphere that is characterized by severe intragroup conflict—a very stressful experience for new employees.

CONCLUSIONS

Perhaps the most important notion in this paper is that individuals undergoing a transition into a new organization are placed in a high anxiety—producing situation. They are motivated, therefore, to reduce this anxiety by learning the functional and social requirements of their new role as quickly as possible. What must be recognized and understood by organizations is that supervisors and group colleagues of new employees have a very special and important role to fulfill in inducting and socializing the new employee. The careful selection of these individuals for young professionals should go a long way toward alleviating many of the problems that usually occur during the ''joining-up'' process. One must recognize that the problems and concerns of young professionals are real and must be dealt with before these young employees can become effective organizational members. Although organizations might want to develop specific training programs to teach managers how to ''break-in'' the young professional more effectively, an alternative strategy would be to make sure that young professionals are integrated and socialized into their job environments only through those particular groups and supervisors who appear especially effective in this function. Rather than allowing all supervisors and groups to recruit and hire new employees as additional staffing needs arise, a more centralized policy of rotating or transferring individuals to some areas in order to hire new employees through other key integrating areas might prove more beneficial to the organization as a whole in the long run. The careful assignment of groups and supervisors to new college recruits, combined with some training for these individuals, should go a long way toward utilizing the great potential in most young professionals, thereby reducing the high levels of frustration, stress, and dissatisfaction that so many of them experience during their initial career years.

NOTE

1. As discussed by McCain et al. (1981), the existence of a well-defined cohort could also lead to a situation in which the cohort develops a strong feeling of group solidarity, competing against the established organization for resources and control. In this instance, however, we are talking about individuals who are more likely to identify with each other than with the joining-up process, perceiving themselves to be distinct from the organization and its members.

REFERENCES

Allen, T. J. *Managing the flow of technology.* Cambridge. MIT Press, 1977

Allison, P. D. Inter-organizational mobility of academic scientists. Paper presented at the meeting of the American Sociology Association. Montreal, 1974

Bailyn, L. Resolving contradictions in technical careers: or, what if I like being an engineer. *Technology Review,* 1982. November–December, 40–47.

Berlew, D. and Hall, T. The socialization of managers: Effects of expectations on performance. *Administrative Science Quarterly,* 1966, 11, 207-223.

Bray, D. W., Campbell, R. J., and Grant, D. L. *Formative years in business: A long-term study of managerial lives.* New York: Wiley, 1974.

Brown, J. A. C. *Techniques of Persuasion.* Baltimore: Penguin Books, 1963.

Dalton, G. W., Thompson, P. H., and Price, R. L. The four stages of professional careers: A new look at performance by professionals. In R. Katz (Ed.), *Career issues in human resource management.* Englewood Cliffs, N.J.: Prentice-Hall, 1982.

Farris, G. The effects of individual roles on performance in innovative groups. *R&D Management,* 1972, 3, 23–28.

Feldman, D. The role of initiation activities in socialization. *Human Relations,* 1977, 30, 977–990.

Gouldner, A. W. "Cosmopolitans and socials: Towards an analysis of latent social roles." *Administrative Science Quarterly,* 1957, 2, 446–467.

Graen, G. Role-making processes within complex organizations. In M. D. Dunnette (Ed.), *Handbook of industrial and organizational Psychology.* Chicago: Rand McNally, 1976.

Graen, G. and Ginsburgh, S. Job resignation as a function of role orientation and leader acceptance. *Organizational Behavior and Human Performance,* 1977, 19, 1–17.

Hall, D. T. *Careers in organizations.* Pacific Palisades, Calif.: Goodyear, 1976.

Hall, D. T., and Nougaim, K. E. An examination of Maslow's need hierarchy in an organizational setting. *Organizational Behavior and Human Performance,* 1968, 3, 12–35.

Henning, M. and Jardim, A. *The managerial woman.* New York: Doubleday, 1977.

Kanter, R. M. *Work and family in the United States.* New York: Russell Sage, 1977.

Katz, R. Job longevity as a situational factor in job satisfaction. *Administrative Science Quarterly.* 1978a, 23, 204–223.

Katz, R. The influence of job longevity on employee reactions to task characteristics. *Human Relations,* 1978b, 31, 703–725.

Katz, R. Time and work: Toward an integrative perspective. *Research in Organizational Behavior,* 1980, 2, JAI Press, 81–127.

Katz, R. The effects of group longevity on project communication and performance. *Administrative Science Quarterly,* 1982, 27, 81–104.

Katz, R. and Allen, T. J. The technical performance of long duration R&D project groups. Technical report to the chief of studies management office, Department of the Army, Grant Number DASG-60-77-C-0134, 1978.

Katz, R. and Tushman, M. An investigation into the managerial roles and careers paths of gatekeeper and project supervisors in a major R&D facility. *R&D Management,* 1981, 11, 103–110.

Katz, R. and Tushman, M. A longitudinal study of the effects of boundary spanning supervision on turnover and promotion in research and development. *Academy of Management Journal,* 1983, 26, 437–456.

Likert, R. *The human organization.* New York: McGraw-Hill, 1967.

Lindholm, J. A study of the mentoring relationship in work organizations. Unpublished MIT Doctoral Dissertation. 1983.

Louis, M. Surprise and sense making: What newcomers experience in entering unfamiliar organizational settings. *Administrative Science Quarterly,* 1980, 25, 226–251.

McCain, B. R., O'Reilly, C. and Pfeffer, J. The effects of departmental demography on turnover. The case of a university. Working Paper, March 1981.

Ouchi, W. G. and Jaeger, A. M. "Type Z organization: Stability in the midst of mobility." *Academy of Management Review,* 1978, 3, 305–314.

Pelz, D. C. Creative tension in the research and development climate. *Science,* 1967, 157, 160–165.

Pelz, D. C. and Andrews, F. M. *Scientists in organizations.* Ann Arbor: University of Michigan, 1976.

Pfeffer, J. Management as symbolic action: The creation and maintenance of organizational paradigms. *Research in Organizational Behavior,* 1981, 3, JAI Press, 1981.

Rogers, E. M., and Shoemaker, F. F. *Communication of innovations: A cross-cultural approach.* New York: The Free Press, 1971.

Salancik, G. R. and Pfeffer, J. An examination of need satisfaction models of job attitudes. *Administrative Science Quarterly,* 1977, 22, 427–456.

Salancik, G. R. and Pfeffer, J. A social information processing approach to job attitudes and task design. *Administrative Science Quarterly,* 1978, 28, 224–253.

Schein, E. H. How to break in the college graduate. *Harvard Business Review,* 1964, 42, 168–76.

Schein, E. H. *Career dynamics.* Reading, Mass.: Addison-Wesley, 1978.

Sofer, C. *Men in mid-career: A study of British managers and technical specialists.* London: Cambridge University Press, 1970.

Staw, B. Motivation in organizations: Toward synthesis and redirection. In B. Staw and G. Salancik (Eds.) *New directions in organizational behavior.* Chicago: St. Clair Press, 1977.

Steers, R. M. Antecedents and outcomes of organizational commitment. *Administrative Science Quarterly,* 1977, 22, 46–56.

Vicino, F. L. and Bass, B. M. Lifespace variables and managerial success. *Journal of Applied Psychology,* 1978, 63, 81–88.

Wanous, J. *Organizational entry,* Reading, Mass.: Addison-Wesley, 1969.

Weick, K. E., *The social psychology of organizing.* Reading, Mass.: Addison-Wesley, 1969.

Does Japanese Management Style Have a Message for American Managers?

Edgar H. Schein

Abstract. Many managers and observers, concerned about U.S. market share and productivity and impressed with Japanese success in these areas, have developed a sudden preoccupation with Japanese management methods. In this article, the author addresses the fundamental issue of what American managers can really learn from the Japanese through an analysis of two current best-sellers on Japanese management. He finds that the books fail to answer the critical question: Can management methods embedded in one culture be effectively transferred to another? As he explains, so little is understood about culture and its relationship to management methods that it is risky to assume that a method that works well in Japan will also work well here.

One of the greatest strengths of U.S. society is our flexibility, our ability to learn. When we see a problem, we tinker with it until we have solved, and we seem to be willing to try anything and everything. One of our greatest weaknesses, on the other hand, is our impatience and short-run orientation. This leads to fads, a preoccupation with instant solutions, a blind faith that if we put in enough effort and money anything is possible, and an inability or unwillingness to see the long-range consequences of some of the quick fixes we try. Complicated solutions that require long-range planning, resolute implementation, and patience in the face of short-run difficulties are harder for us to implement.

The tension between flexibility and fadism can be seen clearly in the current preoccupation with Japanese management. Two recent books, Ouchi's *Theory Z* and Pascale and Athos's *The Art of Japanese Management,* are currently on the *New York Times* best-seller list. Why this sudden interest, and what are the implications of it for management theory? I would like to examine some of the theses of these two books and put these theses into a historical perspective. From this perspective I will draw some tentative conclusions about cultural themes in the U.S. and the implications for U.S. management.

Some Historical Perspective: Indoctrination

In 1961 I published an article called "Management Development as a Process of Influence" attempting to show that many of the socialization methods used by some of our largest corpora-

Reprinted from *Sloan Management Review,* Fall 1981, Vol. 23, No. 1, pp. 55–68 by permission of the publisher. Copyright © 1981 by the Sloan Management Review Association; all rights reserved.

tions (such as IBM and General Electric) were essentially similar to processes of indoctrination that one could observe in many other settings.[1] Such socialization methods were under strong attack by W. H. Whyte (in *The Organization Man*) and others who saw in them a tendency to create "men in grey flannel suits" who would cease to think for themselves and just parrot the corporate line, thus reducing the innovative and creative capacity of the organization and the individuality of the employee.[2] Ironically, the companies that had built such indoctrination centers (such as IBM at Sands Point, N.Y., and General Electric at Crotonville, N.Y.) were very proud of the spirit and common way of thinking that they could induce in their employees and managers. Such spirit was viewed as one of the key sources of strength of these enterprises.

But the pendulum swung hard during the 1960s, and it became the fashion to move away from producing conformity toward stimulating self-actualization. "Indoctrination" either moved underground, was relabeled, or was replaced by "development" programs that emphasized opportunities for the integration of individual goals with organizational goals. Models of development shifted from the engineering model of "molding or shaping people to fit the organization" to more agricultural models of permitting people to flourish according to their innate potential; the obligation of the organization was to provide sunshine, nutrients, water, and other environmental supports. (Little was said in this model about pruning, transplanting, and uprooting, by the way.) The IBM songbook was put away, and managers who used to be proud of their ability to motivate people by inspiring them through common rituals and activities were made to feel ashamed of using "manipulative" tactics.

In the 1970s we discovered the concept of "organizational culture" and have begun to rethink the issue once again. Even if a company does not deliberately and consciously indoctrinate its new employees, its important beliefs, values, and ways of doing things will, in any case, powerfully socialize anyone who remains in the organization and wishes to move upward and inward in it.[3] Such socialization processes and their effects in producing either conformity or innovation have been described and analyzed, and the tactics which stimulate innovation have received special attention.[4]

Now, with the "discovery" that some Japanese companies are effective because of their ability to involve and motivate people, and the assertion that such involvement results from socialization tactics that induce a high degree of loyalty and conformity, we may be headed back toward the ideology of indoctrination so forcefully put aside a mere twenty years ago.

Human Relations and Participation

A similar pendulum swing can be identified with respect to two other human relations values: whether or not one should treat people holistically, and whether or not one should make decisions from the bottom up by participation and consensus mechanisms. Many Americans have grown up with a tradition of bureaucracy, of strong bosses, of hiring people as "hands" to provide certain activities in return for certain pay and benefits. But most students of industrial-relations systems note that there has been a historical trend in such systems from a period of autocracy through a period of paternalism toward the present more consultative and participative models. In the paternalistic phase American companies have treated employees very holistically: building company towns; funding company sports activities; providing country clubs, counseling services, day-care centers, medical facilities, uniforms, and so on. Indeed, one of Ralph Nader's most powerful films deals with the town of Kannapolis, N.C., where the Cannon Mills Co. not only provides lifetime employment but owns all of the housing, uses its own security force as the town police force, and provides all the services needed by the town. What alarmed Nader was the possibility that the citizens of this town were not developing any skills in self-government, which would leave them very vulnerable if the company should move or cease to be so totally paternalistic.

We may also recall that one of the major results of the now historic studies of the Hawthorne plant of the Western Electric Company was the recognition that employees were whole people who brought their personal problems with them to their place of work. In the 1930s the company launched a counseling program that involved company-employed counselors to help employees deal with any personal problems on a totally confidential basis. Though it has been a tradition in our military services that officers not fraternize with the men (presumably because it might be difficult to be objective when individuals must be sent into dangerous situations), there is no such tradition in industry generally. Office parties, company picnics, and other forms of fraternization have been considered legitimate and desirable in many organizations and by many managers, through they are clearly not so institutionalized in the U.S. as they are in Latin America and Japan.

The human relations training programs for foremen that were rampant in the 1940s were clearly aimed at teaching managers to treat their employees as whole people, to consider their needs, to fight for them when necessary, and to build strong loyalty and team spirit. The leadership and sensitivity training which flourished in the 1960s was similarly aimed at truly understanding the needs and talents of subordinates, peers, and bosses, so that appropriate levels of participation could be used in solving increasingly complex problems in organizations. The writings of McGregor on theory Y showed the importance of trust and faith in people; the writings of Argyris showed the necessity of permitting people in organizations to function as adults instead of reducing them to dependent children.[5] Likert argued cogently for System 4, a more participative form of organization in which consen-

sus management plays a big role; and Maslow first introduced the idea of Theory Z, a self-actualizing organization.[6]

Many managers saw the point immediately, and either felt reinforcement for what they were already doing or began to retrain themselves and their organization toward some of the new values and technologies of participative decision making. But as a total ideology this approach clearly has not taken hold. Many organizations discovered:

- That high morale did not necessarily correlate with high productivity.
- That autocratic systems could outproduce democratic systems (at least in the short run).
- That high productivity even when achieved by autocratic methods could build high morale.
- That the costs in terms of time and effort which participation entailed were often not affordable in certain kinds of environments.

Human Relations Japanese Style

Now the pendulum appears to be swinging once again on the issue of paternalism, managing the whole worker, and creating worker involvement through participation. We are told that the Japanese are extremely paternalistic and holistic in their approach to employees, that they tend to employ people for life, and that supervisors take care of the personal as well as the work needs of subordinates (sometimes even helping an employee find a wife). The Japanese use bottom-up consensual decision making and encourage high levels of trust across hierarchical and functional boundaries.

THEORY Z

Ouchi has for some time been arguing that the essential differences between American (Theory

A) and Japanese (Theory J) management systems lie in some key *structural* issues and *cultural* values that make it possible for certain kinds of management styles to flourish. Specifically, he points out that major Japanese companies:

- Employ their key people for "life" (i.e., until forced retirement at the age of fifty-five to sixty).
- Rotate them through various functions.
- Promote them very slow and according to more of a seniority than a merit system.
- Place responsibility on groups rather than on individuals (a value of the Japanese culture).

These determinants make it possible for Japanese companies:

- To treat their employees as total people.
- To build the kind of trust that facilitates bottom-up consensual decision making.
- To control employees in a subtle, indirect manner.

In contrast, Ouchi points out, the bureaucratic model often associated with pure American management methods emphasizes:

- Employment contracts that last only as long as the individual is contributing.
- Specialization of function with rotation reserved only for people on a general managerial track.
- Little concern for the total person.
- Rapid feedback and promotion.
- Explicit formal control systems.
- Individual responsibility (a strong cultural value in the U.S.).
- Individual top-down decision making.

The crucial insight Ouchi provides is to identify another model, which he calls Theory Z, that is found in many American companies, that fits into our culture, and that combines certain features of the A and J models. Such companies have:

- Lifetime employment.
- Slower rates of promotion.
- Somewhat more implicit, less formal control systems.
- More concern for the total person.
- More cross-functional rotation and emphasis on becoming a generalist.
- Some level of participation and consensual decision making.
- A continued emphasis on individual responsibility as a core value.

Though he does not give much evidence in his book, Ouchi has shown in other papers that a U.S. company that approximates the Theory Z criteria generated higher morale, higher loyalty, and generally more healthy, positive feelings at all levels of the hierarchy than did a comparable Theory A company. What is missing, however, is convincing evidence that those companies fitting the Theory Z model are more *effective* than comparable companies operating more on the Theory A bureaucratic model. Furthermore, Ouchi acknowledges that the Theory Z companies he has studied generate less professionalism, have a harder time integrating mavericks into their ranks because they generate strong conformity pressures (leading them to be sexist and racist), and may only be adaptive for certain kinds of technological or economic environments. In fact, the only way a Theory Z company can manage the instabilities inherent in running a successful business in a turbulent environment is to limit lifetime employment to a small cadre of key people and to keep a large percentage of the labor force in a temporary role, policies that resemble more closely the bureaucratic A model. In order to survive, it may be necessary for Theory Z companies to subcontract much of their work or to rely on a set of satellite companies to absorb the instabilities. (The latter is the typical Japanese pattern.)

Implications of Theory Z

After describing how this notion of an industrial "clan" can facilitate certain kinds of long-range involvement on the part of employees, Ouchi argues strongly that U.S. companies should think seriously about becoming more like clans, and lays out a program of how they might do it. Neither the argument that a company should be more like Z, nor the proposed steps for how to get there, are at all convincing, however. The theoretical sophistication displayed in the analysis of types of organizational control is followed by naive and superficial prescriptions about how one might think about a change program designed to help a company to become more like a clan (if, indeed, this is even possible). In effect, the manager is invited to be more open and trusting and to involve his or her people more. Little attention is given to the issue of why a given organization would be less trusting and participative in the first place, or to the problem of transferring managerial values from a culture in which they fit very well to one in which the fit is not at all clear.

But Ouchi makes a strong sales pitch, and it is here that our tendency to embrace the quick fix may get us into trouble. If someone tells us that Theory Z is closer to the Japanese model, and that the Japanese are getting a lot of mileage out of their model, do we all get on the bandwagon and give our employees tenure, push decision making down the hierarchy, and slow down promotions? Do we turn everyone into a generalist, throw out formal control systems, and treat each person as a total human being? If we do, will our productivity shoot right back up, so that we can regain our once dominant economic position? Sounds too simplistic, does it not? Unfortunately, that is just what it is, because it takes into account neither the uniqueness of Japanese culture, the uniqueness of U.S. culture, the technological and environmental conditions that ultimately will dictate wither an A, a Z, or some other form will be the most effective in a given situation. What the Ouchi book leaves out, unfortunately, are criteria to help a manager decide whether or not a Z, and A, or some other form is appropriate.

On the positive side, the analysis focuses on the importance of the human factor, and Ouchi's seven criterion categories are certainly important in assessing the options for managing people. The identification of the clan mechanism as a way of organizing and controlling people brings us back to what many companies know intuitively—"we are one big family in this organization"—and legitimizes the kind of indoctrination that used to be more common. We can see more clearly that between autocracy and democracy there lies a full range of choices, and that a high degree of paternalism is not necessarily incompatible with bottom-up, consensual, participative decision making. The manager can also see that the way people feel about an organization can be explicitly managed even if the relationship to longrange effectiveness is not completely clear. As Etzioni noted long ago, a person can be involved in an organization in a variety of ways, ranging from the "alienated prisoner" or calculative employee to the participating member who is fully and morally involved.[7] Two serious questions to consider are whether U.S. economic organizations can claim moral involvement (as some Japanese firms apparently do) and whether such levels of involvement are even desirable in our culture.

The Ouchi analysis closes with a useful reminder that what ties the Japanese company together is a *company philosophy,* some dominant values that serve as criteria for decisions. What permits bottom-up consensual decision making to occur is the wide sharing of a common philosophy that guarantees a similarity of outlook with respect to the basic goals of the organization. Ouchi provides some case examples and displays a method by which a company can determine its own philosophy.

Edgar H. Schein

INTEGRATING THE SEVEN S's

Pascale and Athos make their argument at a different level of analysis, though they also stress the importance of managing *people* as key resources and the importance of superordinate goals, sense of spirit, or company philosophy. Ouchi is more the social scientist, presenting a theoretically grounded sociological argument for a structural approach to human resource management. Pascale and Athos are less theoretical and more didactic. They are the teachers/ consultants, distilling some of the wisdom from the analysis of the Japanese experience, and they try to transmit that wisdom through a more down-to-earth writing style. The managerial reader will learn more from this book, while the social scientist will learn more from the Ouchi book.

As already indicated, Ouchi has seven basic criteria for distinguishing A from J. Pascale and Athos (with due apologies for the gimmicky quality of the scheme) draw on a formulation developed by the McKinsey Co. that includes the following seven basic variables:

1. Superordinate goals.
2. Strategy.
3. Structure.
4. Systems.
5. Staff (the concern for having the right sort of people to do the work).
6. Skills (training and developing people to do what is needed.
7. Style (the manner in which management handles subordinates, peers, and superiors).

Within this structure, Pascale and Athos identify what they term the "soft S's" and the "hard S's," and explain that the superordinate goals are critical in tying everything together. They argue that Japanese companies are effective because of their attention to such integration and their concern for those variables which have to do with the human factor, the soft S's. These are the factors American managers allegedly pay too little attention to: staff, skills, and, most important, style. The hard S's are strategy, structure, and systems.

Through a detailed comparison of the Matsushita Corp. and ITT under Geneen, the authors bring out the essential contrast between Japanese attention to the soft S's and Geneen's more "American" preoccupation with very tight controls, autocratic decision making, and concern for the bottom line. Yet the Geneen story also illustrates that a system that is as internally consistent as ITT's was and can be very effective. Its weakness lay in its inability to survive without the personal genius of a Geneen to run it.

The Japanese Style

Following this dramatic contrast, Pascale and Athos analyze the Japanese management style and explain how a culture that values "face" and is collective in its orientation can breed managerial behavior that makes the most of ambiguity, indirection, subtle cues, trust, interdependence, uncertainty, implicit messages, and management of process (instead of attempting to develop complete openness, explicitness, and directness in order to minimize ambiguity and uncertainty). "Explicit communication is a cultural assumption; it is not a linguistic imperative," they remind us.[8]

The lesson for American managers is diametrically opposite in the two books. Ouchi's proposal for how to get to Theory Z is to be more open; Pascale and Athos imply (from their positive case examples of U.S. managers who use indirection, implicit messages, and nondecision as strategies) that we might do well to learn more of the arts of how to be less open. Though we in the U.S. often imply that to worry about "face" is a weakness and that it is better to "put all the cards on the table," in fact, there is ample evidence that Americans no less than Japanese respond better to helpful face-saving hints than to sledgehammers. "When feedback is really clear and bad, it's usually too late." "The inherent preferences of organizations are clarity, certainty, and perfection. The inherent nature of human relationships involves ambiguity, uncertainty, and imperfection. How one honors, balances, and integrates the needs of both is the real trick of management."

The analysis of face-to-face communication, drawn from an article by Pascale called "Zen and the Art of Management," is full of valuable insights on the subtleties of how and why indirection, tact, and concern for face are not merely niceties but necessities in human relations. It is crucial to recognize, of course, the distinction between *task* relevant information (about which one should be as open as possible in a problem-solving situation) and *interpersonal* evaluative information (about which it may be impossible to be completely open without running the risk of permanently damaging relationships). Sensitivity training in which people attempted to tell each other what they thought of each other only worked in so-called stranger groups, where people did not know each other before and knew that they would not have to work or live with each other after the program.

Interdependence

Pascale and Athos supplement their analysis of face-to-face relations with an excellent analysis of groups and the dilemmas of interdependence. Noting that the American tradition is one of independence and that the Japanese tradition (based on their limited space and the technology of rice farming) is one of interdependence, they show how groups and meetings can work in this context by members being more restrained, self-effacing, and trusting. As Ouchi points out, getting credit in the long-run, instead of worrying (as Americans often do) about being recognized immediately for any and all accomplishments, is made possible by the knowledge of lifetime employment, i.e., if people have to work with each other for a long time, true contribution will ultimately be recognized. Both books indicate that such group relationships combined with lack of specialization of careers give the Japanese company the ability to integrate better across key functional interfaces, because everyone has more empathy and understanding for other functions.

Superior-Subordinate Relationships

Long-term relationships and a culture in which everyone knows his or her place in the status hierarchy lead to a different concept of superior-subordinate relationships in Japan. The boss is automatically more of a mentor, teaching through subtle cues rather than blunt feedback, exercising great patience while the subordinate learns how to interpret cues and to develop his or her own skills, and reinforcing the basic company philosophy as a conceptual source that helps subordinates to decide what to do in any given situation. This point is critical, because it highlights one of the most important functions of superordinate goals or organizational philosophy. If everyone understands what the organization is trying to do and what its values are for how to do things, then every employee who truly understands the philosophy can figure out what his or her course of action should be in an ambiguous situation. No directives or explicit control systems are needed becuase the controls are internalized.

Individualism and Authority

Pascale and Athos take the issues of power and authority into the cultural realm in a more subtle fashion than does Ouchi, who merely labels J companies as having collective responsibility and A and Z companies as having individual responsibility. But we must ask what individual or collective responsibility means in each culture. Can we assume that the American model of individual rights, independence, equal opportunity under the law, and related values and norms is in any sense the opposite of or even on the same dimension with the Japanese notion of group responsibility? Is the issue simply that the group would be sacrificed for the individual in the U.S., whereas the individual would be sacrificed for the group in Japan?

A more appropriate formulation is to assume that in every culture and in every individual there is a core conflict about how self-seeking or self-effacing to be for the sake of one's group or organization. At the extremes where either nationalism or anarchy is involved, the conflict is easier to reduce, but in a pluralistic society it is a genuine dilemma. (This is exemplified in U.S. sports organizations, which try to create a team while maximizing the individual talents of the players.) In a recent analysis of individualism, Waterman has indicated that in political and social science writings there have always been two versions of individualism: one focuses on selfishness and takes advantage of the group, and one focuses on self-actualization in the interest of maximizing for both the individual and the group the talents latent in the members.[9] Those writers who argue for a humanistic solution to organizational problems are espousing the second definition, which assumes that integration is possible.

In my experience the effective organization is neither individualistic nor collective; rather it attempts to create norms and procedures that extol stardom and teamwork equally. The manager's job (just like the good coach's) is to find a way to weld the two forces together. The Japanese solution to this dilemma appears to be aided immensely by the fact that basic traditions and cultural values strongly favor hierarchy and the subordination of the individual to those above. However, this solution has potentially negative consequences, because it reduces the creative talent available to the organization. One might suspect, however, that the effective organization in Japan finds ways of dealing with this dilemma, and that the highly talented individual is not as pressured to conform as the less talented individual.[10]

The Japanese company in the Ouchi model could be expected to be more innovative on those tasks requiring group solutions, while the American company could be expected to be more innovative on those tasks that require a high level of individual expertise and creativity. Company effectiveness would then depend on the nature of the tasks facing it, its ability to diagnose accurately what those tasks are, and its flexibility in transforming itself—what I have termed an "adaptive coping cycle."[11] Whatever its human virtues and in spite of its ability to integrate better, a Theory Z organization might have more trouble both in seeing changes in its environment and in making the necessary transformations to adapt to those changes. Because of its strong commitment to a given philosophy and the pressure for everyone to conform, it is more likely to produce rigid paradigms for dealing with problems.

Implications for U.S. Management
Both books call for a reexamination of U.S. paradigms of how to organize and how to manage. While one can only applaud this challenge and use the models which the books present to gain perspective for such reexamination, one must be concerned about the glibness of the lessons, recommendations, and advice, given the meager data base on which they are based. Neither book makes much of an effort to decipher what may be happening in our own culture and society that would explain our tendency toward Theory A (if, indeed, it can be shown that such a tendency exists). Why do we have difficulty with some of the solutions the Japanese apparently find natural and easy? And, most important, what are the strengths in the U.S. system that should be preserved and built upon?

For example, Ouchi is quick to point out the negative consequences of the American tendency to try to quantify everything. Most of us would agree that for managing the human system of the organization, quantification may be more of a trap than a help, but one might also argue that our desire to quantify reflects some of the best traditions of Western science and rationalism. The trick is to learn what to quantify and to know why quantification is helpful. In designing quality-control programs or in setting sales targets, it may be crucial to state a goal in quantifiable form in order to measure progress toward the goal. On the other hand, attempting to quantify managerial traits as part of a performance-appraisal system may distort communication and reduce the effectiveness of the whole system, because people would begin to feel like "mere numbers." The effective manager in any cultural system would be the one who knows what to quantify.

Many of the formal control systems that have become associated with the concept of bureaucracy (and that are seen by Ouchi, Pascale, and Athos as dysfunctional relative to the more indirect controls associated with the Japanese style) imply that all organizations face similar control problems. One suspects, however, that controlling the design and building of a large aerospace system might require more formal control mechanisms than the control of an R&D organization in a high-technology industry. Ouchi's comparison of formal bureaucratic with informal clan mechanisms misses the point that Galbraith made so effectively: As any organization evolves, it develops organizational structures that are needed *at that stage* to deal with its information-processing and control problems. A geographically dispersed organization dealing with local variants of a given market has different problems from a high-technology company that has standard products that work more or less in any market. Galbraith's analysis reveals at least six or seven variants of control systems from simple rules to complex matrix structures.[12]

But the most important issue to examine before we race into new organizational paradigms is whether or not we even have the right explanation for Japanese success. Neither Ouchi nor Pascale and Athos presents much evidence to justify the premise that the Japanese organizations cited are successful because of the management system described. In addition, no evidence is shown that such organizations are, indeed, the most successful ones in Japan. For example, it may well be that both Japanese productivity and management style are the reflection of some other common historical, economic, and/or sociocultural factor(s) in Japan. Neither book tells us enough about the following important issues:

- The role of postwar reconstruction.
- The opportunity to modernize the industrial base.
- The close collaboration between industry and government.
- The strong sense of nationalism which produces high levels of motivation in all workers.
- That lifetime employment is possible for roughly one-third of the employees in some Japanese organizations, because of the system of temporary employment for the rest of the employees and the existence of satellite companies that absorb some of the economic fluctuations.
- That all employees retire fairly early by U.S. standards (in their mid-to-late fifties).
- That many of the best companies are family dominated and their strong company philosophies may be a reflection of founder values that might be hard to maintain as these companies age.
- That the cultural traditions of duty, obedience, and discipline strongly favor a paternalistic clan form of organization.

Neither book refers to the growing literature that compares managerial style and beliefs in different countries and that contradicts directly some of the books' assertions about U.S. and Japanese management approaches. For example, although both books extol the virtues of Japanese indirection, subtlety, and ability to live with uncertainty and ambiguity, Hofstede found in a sample of forty countries that U.S. managers reported the highest levels of tolerance of ambiguity, while Japanese managers reported some of the lowest levels. On many dimensions U.S. and Japanese managers are surprisingly similar in their orientation, which suggests that the real answer to organizational effectiveness may be to find those combinations of strategy, structure, and style that are either "culture free" or adaptable within a wide variety of cultures.

KNOWING WHAT IS CULTURAL

If we are to have a theory of organizations or management that is culture free or adaptable within any given culture, we must first know what culture is. This is surprisingly difficult, because we are all embedded in our own culture. What can we learn from Japanese managers if we cannot decipher how their behavior is embedded in their culture? Can we attempt to adapt managerial methods developed in other cultures without understanding how they would fit into our own?

The first and perhaps the most important point is that we probably *cannot really understand another culture* at the level of its basic world view. The only one we can really understand is our own. Even understanding our own culture at this level requires intensive analysis and thought. One cannot suddenly become aware of something and understand it if one has always taken it completely for granted. The true value of looking at other cultures is, therefore, to gain perspective for studying one's own culture. By seeing how others think about and do things, we become more aware of how we think about and do things, and that awareness is the first step in analyzing our own cultural assumptions and values. We can use analyses of Japanese management methods and their underlying cultural presumptions to learn about the hidden premises of U.S. managerial methods and our own cultural presumptions.

If we can grasp and become aware of our own premises and values, we can then examine analytically and empirically what the strengths and weaknesses of our own paradigm may be. This process of self-analysis is subtle and difficult. Not enough research has been done on managerial practices in our own culture; thus, the methods of analysis and tentative conclusions presented below should be treated as a rough first cut at analyzing our own cultural terrain.

Levels of Culture

In thinking about culture, one should distinguish surface manifestations from the essential underlying premises that bind the elements of any given culture. As shown in Figure 1, there are at least three interconnected levels:

1. *Artifacts and creations* are the visible manifestations of a culture (which include its language, art, architecture, technology, and other material outputs) and its visible system of organizing interpersonal relationships, status levels, sex roles, age roles, etc. Though this level is visible, it is often not decipherable in the sense that the newcomer to the culture cannot figure out "what is really going on," what values or assumptions tie together the various visible manifestations.

2. *Values and ideology* are the rules, principles, norms, values, morals, and ethics that guide both the ends of a given society (group) and the means by which to accomplish them. Values and ideological statements usually define what national goals, intergroup relationships, and interpersonal relationships are appropriate to strive for. They are taught to children and reinforced in adults. Generally the level of culture we first encounter is how to achieve the goals (i.e., we encounter the appropriate rules of conduct that govern relationships between nations, groups, and in-

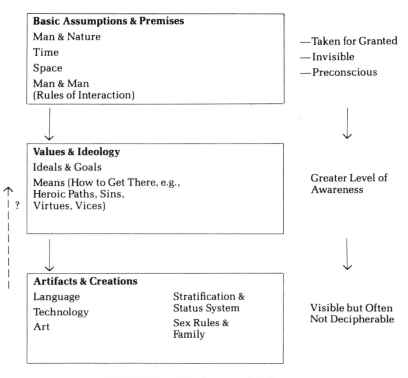

FIGURE 1.   The Levels of Culture

dividuals within the society). This is also where differences are felt most strongly, because of the penalties associated with behaving inappropriately. This level of culture, although partly conscious and partly unconscious, can be revealed if people reflect analytically about their own behavior.

3. *Basic assumptions and premises* are the underlying and typically unconscious assumptions about the nature of truth and reality, the nature of human nature, "man's" relationship to nature, "man's" relationship to "man," the nature of time, and the nature of space. These assumptions create the cultural core or essence, provide the key to deciphering the values and artifacts, and create the patterning that characterizes cultural phenomena. This level is hardest to examine,

because it is taken for granted and, hence, outside of awareness.

If we analyze U.S. culture and managerial assumptions in terms of some of the categories around which basic assumptions are built, what perspective does this provide, and how does this help us to learn from Japanese managerial practices?

SOME KEY ASSUMPTIONS OF U.S. CULTURE

"Man's" Relationship to Nature: Proactive Optimism

It is a premise of most Western societies (particularly of the U.S.) that nature can and should be conquered, that "man" is ultimately perfectible, and that anything is ultimately possible if we put enough effort into it. The philosophy "Where there's a will there's a way," buttressed by "Every day we do difficult things; the impossible just takes a little longer," sets the tone for how we approach tasks. We feel constrained by the environment only if we do not have the knowledge or technology to control or alter it, and then we proactively seek whatever knowledge or technology is necessary to overcome the obstacle.

Such proactive optimism underlies the values surrounding equality of opportunity in that we take it for granted that anyone might be able to accomplish anything, if given the opportunity. In other words, man is ultimately perfectible, as the thousands of self-help books in book stores proclaim. The notion of accepting one's "fate" (limiting one's aspirations according to one's social position or some other nontechnological constraint) is simply not part of the underlying ideology, however much empirical data might argue to the contrary.

Given this core assumption, what kinds of organizational forms are possible in the U.S.? Can an industrial clan (a Theory Z organization) with its intrinsic conservative orientation survive in a cultural environment that emphasizes change, progress, innovation, and novelty? Or would this cultural orientation begin to erode the very core of such an organizational—the stability that produces the comfort?

Similarly, can a culture that encourages people to find better ways to do things independently, to resist arbitrary authority if it interferes with pramatic problem solving, and to value individual accomplishment produce an integrated system like the Pascale/Athos Seven S model? Perhaps the most notable characteristic of U.S. managerial practice is that we are never satisfied and are forever tinkering to find a better way. This will always undermine efforts toward integration. For many U.S. managers, integration equals stagnation. I have observed repeatedly that as soon as a system becomes routine, man-

agers begin to think about "reorganization." Perhaps we deeply mistrust stability and are culturally "pot stirrers."

"Man's" Relationship to "Man": Individualistic Egalitarianism

Every society or group must resolve the issue between individualism and collectivism. The underlying U.S. assumption appears to be that the individual always does and should do what is best for himself or herself, and is constrained only by respect for the law and the rights of others. The rule of law implies that there are no philosophical and moral principles that can ultimately determine when another's rights have been violated, and, therefore, the legislative and judicial process must decide this on a case-by-case basis through a confronting, problem-solving process judged by a jury of peers. Buried in these assumptions is a further assumption that the world can be known only through successive confrontations with natural phenomena and other people; that the nature of truth resides in empirical experience, not in some philosophical, moral, or religious system; and that the ultimate "philosophy," therefore, might as well be one of pragmatism. Ambition, maximizing one's opportunities, and fully utilizing one's capacities become the moral imperatives.

These assumptions, in turn, are related to the Western rational scientific tradition, which emphasizes experimentation; learning from experience; open debate of facts; and a commitment to truth, accuracy, measurement, and other aids to establish what is "real." The openness and pluralism that so many commentators on America emphasize are closely related to the assumption that truth can be discovered only through open confrontation and can come from anyone. The lowliest employee has as good a chance to solve a key problem as the president of the company, and one of the worst sins is *arbitrary* authority ("Do it because I am the boss, even if you think it is wrong'' or ''If I'm the boss, that makes me right'').

Yet teamwork is an important value in U.S. sports and organizational life. It is not clear to me how to reconcile the need for teamwork with the assumptions of individualism, and neither Ouchi nor Pascale and Athos offers much guidance on how consensual methods can be fitted to the notions of individual responsibility that U.S. managers take for granted. One of the greatest fears U.S. managers have of groups is that responsibility and accountability will become diffused. We need to be able to identify who is accountable for what, even when the realities of the task make shared responsibility more appropriate. According to Ouchi and Pascale and Athos, the Japanese deliberately blur individual responsibility and adapt their decision making to such blurring. If that is so, their version of the consensus method may have little to teach us.

Participatory methods can work in the U.S., but they must be based on a different premise: the premise that teamwork and participation are better ways to solve problems, because knowledge, information, and skills are distributed among a number of people. We must, therefore, involve those people who have relevant information and skills. But the goal in terms of U.S. assumptions is better problem solving and more efficient performance, not teamwork, consensus, or involvement per se. Unless Japanese consensus methods are built on the same premise of effective problem solving, they are in many senses culturally irrelevant.

Similarly, the Japanese concern for the whole person may be based on premises and assumptions that simply do not fit our core assumptions of individualism and self-help. U.S. managers are scared of paternalism and excessive involvement with subordinates, because they see them as ''invasions of privacy.'' If an individual is taken care of by an organization, he or she may lose the ability to fight for himself or herself. Our whole system is based on the assumptions that one must ''be one's own best friend''

and that the law is there to protect each and every one of us. Dependency, security orientation, and allowing others to solve our problems are viewed as signs of failure and lack of ambition and are considered to be undeserving of sympathy. On the other hand, if it is necessary to take care of the whole family in an overseas transfer in order to enable to primary employee to function effectively, then we do it. Pragmatism, necessity, and efficiency override issues of what would be more humane, because of the underlying belief that we cannot philosophically agree on basic standards of what is ''best'' for everyone. What is best for people must be decided on the basis of negotiation and experience (ultimately expressed in laws, safety codes, and quality of work-life standards).

A culture based on such premises sounds harsh and cold, and the things we are told we should do to ''humanize'' organizations sound friendly and warm. But cultures are neither cold nor warm, because within any given culture both warmth and coldness have their own meaning. We may not like certain facets of our culture once we discover their underlying premises, and we may even set out to change our culture. However, we cannot produce such change simply by pointing to another culture and saying that some of the things they do *there* would be neat *here*. We have not yet begun to understand our own culture and the managerial paradigms it has created. This article is a beginning attempt to stimulate such self-understanding, which is a prerequisite for any ''remedial'' action.

REFERENCES

1. See: E. H. Schein, ''Management Development as a Process of Influence.'' *Industrial Management Review* (now *Sloan Management Review),* May 1961, pp. 59–77. E. H. Schein, *Coercive Persuasion* (New York: Norton & Co., 1961).

2. See W. H. Whyte, Jr., *The Organization Man* (New York: Simon & Schuster, 1956).

3. See: E. H. Schein, "The Individual the Organization, and the Career: A Conceptual Scheme," *Journal of Applied Behavioral Science* (1971): 401–426; E. H. Schein, Career Dynamics: Matching Individual and Organizational Needs (Reading, MA: Addison-Wesley, 1978).

4. See: J. Van Maanen and E. H. Schein, "Toward a Theory of Organizational Socialization" in *Research in Organizational Behavior* (Vol. 1) B. Staw, ed. (Greenwich, CT: JAI Press, 1979).

5. See: C. Argyris, *Integrating the Individual and the Organization* (New York: John Wiley & Sons, 1964): A. H. Maslow, *Motivation and personality* (New York: Harper & Row, 1954): D. M. McGregor, *The Human Side of Enterprise* (New York: McGraw-Hill, 1960).

6. See: R. Likert, *The Human Organization* (New York: McGraw-Hill, 1967): A. H. Maslow, *The Farthest Reaches of Human Nature* (New York: The Viking Press, 1971).

7. See: A. Etzioni, *Complex Organizations* (New York: Holt, Rinehart, and Winston, 1961).

8. See: R. T. Pascale and A. G. Athos, *The Art of Japanese Management: Applications for American Executives* (New York: Simon & Schuster, 1981), p. 102.

9. See: A. S. Waterman, "Individualism and Interdependence." *American Psychologist* (1981): 762–773.

10. See J. McLendon, *Rethinking Japanese Groupism: Individual Strategies in a Corporate Context* (unpublished paper, Harvard University, 1980).

11. See E. H. Schein, *Organizational Psychology,* 3rd. ed. (Englewood Cliffs, NJ: Prentice-Hall, 1980).

12. See J. Galbraith, *Designing Complex Organizations* (Reading, MA: Addison-Wesley, 1973).

That's Easy for You to Say

Lucien Rhodes

An obsession with "corporate culture" can be worse than no culture at all. Just ask the man who wrote the book on the subject.

It all began on Labor Day weekend in 1982. Allan A. Kennedy was sitting in a low beach chair on the shore in front of his cottage on Cape Cod. Next to him was his friend and fellow consultant Tony Merilo. As they relaxed there, watching the sailboats drift across Cape Cod Bay, drinking beer, and listening to a Red Sox game on the radio, Kennedy turned to Merilo and, with the majestic eloquence suited to great undertakings, said: "Gee, Tony, you know, we ought to start some kind of business together."

This identical thought has, of course, passed between countless friends ever since the discovery of profit margins. Coming from most people, it would have fallen into the general category of loose talk. But Kennedy was not most people. For one thing, he was a 13-year veteran of McKinsey & Co., the management consulting firm, and partner in charge of its Boston office. More to the point, he was the coauthor of a recently published book that offered a startling new perspective on corporate life—one that challenged the whole way people thought about business.

The book was entitled *Corporate Cultures,* a term that was itself new to the language, and it

dealt with an aspect of business that, up to then, had been largely ignored. Broadly speaking, that aspect involved the role played by a company's values, symbols, rites, and rituals in determining its overall performance. Citing examples from some of the country's most dynamic companies, Kennedy and co-author Terrence E. Deal showed that these "cultural" factors had a major effect on the attitudes and behavior of a company's employees, and were thus of critical importance to its long-term success.

By any measure, the book was a groundbreaking work, challenging, as it did, the rational, quantitative models of corporate success that were so popular in the 1960s and '70s. But its impact had as much to do with its timing as its content. Published in June 1982, during a period of economic stagnation—with unemployment at 9.5%, the prime over 16%, and trade deficits soaring to record levels—*Corporate Cultures* offered a welcome antidote to the doom and gloom that was abroad in the land. Like *In Search of Excellence,* which appeared a few months later, it suggested that Japan was not the only nation capable of producing strong, highly motivated companies that could compete effectively in the international arena. America could produce—in fact, was already producing—its own.

What the book did not detail, however, was how corporate cultures were actually constructed. The authors could describe a particular culture and demonstrate its effects, but they offered few clues as to how a company might develop a culture in the first place. So the news that Allan Kennedy was going into business was greeted with more than passing interest among the followers of corporate culture. Here was an opportunity to find out how a living, breathing culture could be created, and the creator would be none other than the man who wrote the book.

After an extensive survey of business opportunities, Kennedy and Merilo decided to develop microcomputer software for sales and marketing management. They felt this was their most promising option, given the anticipated growth of the microcomputer market and their own experience as consultants. Acting on that assessment, they resigned from McKinsey and, in February 1983, formally launched Selkirk Associates Inc. with four of their friends.

Kennedy had lofty ambitions for Selkirk. More than a business, he saw it as a kind of laboratory for his theories. He wanted it to function as a society of professional colleagues committed to building a culture and a company that would stress collaboration, openness, decentralization, democratic decisions, respect, and trust. In this society, each individual would be encouraged to devise his or her own entrepreneurial response to the challenges of the business.

For Kennedy, this was not a long-term goal, something that would evolve naturally in the fullness of time. On the contrary, it was a pressing, immediate concern. Accordingly, he focused all his attention on creating such a culture from the start. "I spent lots of time," he says, "trying to think about what kind of values the company ought to stand for and therefore what kind of behavior I expected from people." These thoughts eventually went into a detailed statement of "core beliefs," which he reviewed and amplified with each new employee. In the same vein, Kennedy and his colleagues chose a "guiding principle," namely, a commitment to "making people more productive." They would pursue this ambition, everyone agreed, "through the products and services we offer" and "in the way we conduct our own affairs."

And, in the beginning at least, Selkirk seemed to be everything Kennedy had hoped for. The company set up shop in Boston, in an office that consisted of a large, rectangular room, with three smaller attachments. Each morning, staff members would pile into the main room and sort themselves out by function—programmers and systems engineers by the windows; administrators in the middle, sales and marketing folk at the other end. In keeping with Kennedy's cultural precepts, there were no private offices or, indeed, any physical demarcations between functions.

It was a familial enterprise, informed with the very qualities Kennedy had laid out in his statement of core beliefs. The work was absorbing, the comradeship inspiring. Most mornings, the staff feasted on doughnuts, which they took to calling "corporate carbos," as a wordplay on "corporate cultures." They began a scrapbook as an impromptu cultural archive. Included among the memorabilia was "The Ravin," an Edgar Allan Poe takeoff that commemorated Selkirk's first stirrings in earlier temporary headquarters:

Once upon an April morning,
  disregarding every warning,
In a Back Bay storefront,
  Selkirk software was begun:
True, it was without a toilet,
  but that didn't seem to spoil it.

To strengthen their bonds even further, the staff began to experiment with so-called rites, rituals, and ceremonies—all important elements of a corporate culture, according to Kennedy's book. Selkirk's office manager, Linda Sharkey, recalls a day, for example, when the whole company went out to Kennedy's place on Cape Cod to celebrate their common purpose with barbecues on the beach. "The sun was shining, and we were all there together," she says. "It was a beautiful day. That's the way it was. We didn't use the terms among ourselves that Allan uses in the book. With us, corporate culture was more by seeing and doing." Sharkey remembers, too, Friday afternoon luncheons of pizza or Chinese food, at which everyone in the company had a chance to talk about his or her accomplishments or problems, or simply hang out.

Kennedy was pleased with all this, as well he might be. "We were," he says, "beginning to develop a real culture."

Then the walls went up.

The problem stemmed from the situation in the big room, where the technical people were laboring feverishly to develop Selkirk's first product, while the salespeople were busy preselling it. The former desperately needed peace and quiet to concentrate on their work; the latter were a boisterous lot, fond of crowing whenever a prospect looked encouraging. In fact, the salespeople crowed so often and so loudly that the technicians complained that they were being driven to distraction. Finally, they confronted Kennedy with the problem. Their solution, which Kennedy agreed to, was to erect five-foot-high movable partitions, separating each functional grouping from the others.

In the memory of Selkirk veterans, "the day the walls went up" lives on as a day of infamy. "It was terrible," say Sharkey. "I was embarrassed."

"It was clearly a symbol of divisiveness," says Kennedy.

"I don't know what would have been the right solution," says Reilly Hayes, Selkirk's 23-year-old technical wizard, "but the wall certainly wasn't. It blocked out the windows for the other end of the room. Someone [in marketing] drew a picture of a window and taped it to the wall. The whole thing created a lot of dissension."

Indeed, the erection of the walls touched off a feud between engineering and marketing that eventually grew into "open organizational warfare," according to Kennedy. "I let the wall

stand, and a competitive attitude developed where engineering started sniping at marketing. We had two armed camps that didn't trust each other."

As if that weren't bad enough, other problems were beginning to surface. For one thing, the company was obviously overstaffed, having grown from 12 people in June 1983 to 25 in January 1984, without any product—or sales—to show for it. "That was a big mistake," says Kennedy. "We clearly ramped up the organization too fast, particularly given the fact that we were financing ourselves. I mean, for a while, we had a burn rate of around $100,000 per month."

Even more serious, however, was the problem that emerged following the release of the company's initial product, Correspondent, in February 1984. Not that there was anything wrong with the product. It was, in fact, a fine piece of software, and it premiered to glowing reviews. Designed as a selling tool, it combined database management, calendar management, word processing, and mail merge—functions that could help customers organize their accounts, track and schedule sales calls and follow-ups, and generate correspondence. And it did all that splendidly.

The problem had to do with the price tag, a whopping $12,000 per unit. The Selkirk team members had come up with this rarefied figure, not out of greed, but out of a commitment to customer service—a goal to which they had pledged themselves as part of their cultural mission. In order to provide such service, they figured, a Selkirk representative might have to spend two or three weeks with each customer, helping to install and customize the product. Trouble was, customers weren't willing to *pay* for that service, not at $12,000 per unit anyway. After a brief flurry of interest, sales dropped off.

"We just blew it," says Kennedy. "We were arrogant about the market. We were trying to tell the market something it wasn't interested in hearing. We took an arbitrary cultural goal and tried to make it into a strategy, rather than saying we're a market-driven company and we've got to find out what the market wants and supply it." Unfortunately, six months went by before Kennedy and his colleagues figured all this out and began to reduce Correspondent's price accordingly.

By then, however, Selkirk's entire sales effort was in shambles, a victim of its commitment to employee autonomy. Sales targets were seldom realized. Indeed, they were scarcely even set. At weekly meetings, salespeople would do little more than review account activity. "If a salesman said each week for three weeks in a row that he expected to close a certain account, and it never happened," say Merlo, "well, we didn't do anything about it. In any other company, he would probably have been put on probation." As it was, each of the participants entered the results of the meeting in a red-and-black ledger book and struck out once again to wander haphazardly through uncharted territory. "The mistake we made," reflects Merlo, "was using real money in a real company to test hypotheses about what sales goals should be."

Finally, in June 1984, Kennedy took action, laying off 6 people. In July, Correspondent's price was dropped to $4,000 per unit, but sales remained sluggish. In September, Kennedy laid of 5 more people, bringing the size of the staff back to 12.

One of those laid off was the chief engineer, a close friend of Kennedy's, but a man whose departure brought an immediate ceasefire between the warring factions. That night, the remaining staff members took down the walls and stacked them neatly in the kitchenette, where they repose to this day. "We felt," says Sharkey, "like we had our little family back together again."

With morale finally rebounding, Selkirk again cut Correspondent's price in the early fall, to $1,500. This time, sales responded, and, in November, the company enjoyed its first month in the black.

But Selkirk was not yet out of the woods.

What remained was for Kennedy to figure out the significance of what had happened, and to draw the appropriate conclusions. Clearly, his experiment had not turned out as he had planned. His insistence on a company without walls had led to organizational warfare. His goal of providing extraordinary service had led to a crucial pricing error. His ideal of employee autonomy had led to confusion in the sales force. In the end, he was forced to fire more than half of his staff, slash prices by 87%, and start over again. What did it all mean?

Merlo had one answer. "We're talking about an experiment in corporate culture failing because the business environment did not support it," he says. "The notion of corporate culture got in the way of tough-minded business decisions." He also faults the emphasis on autonomy. "I don't think we had the right to be organized the way we were. I think we should have had more discipline."

Kennedy himself soon came around to a similar view. "Look in [the statement of core beliefs] and tell me what you find about the importance of performance, about measuring performance or about the idea that people must be held accountable for their performance," he says. "That stuff should have been there. I'm not discounting the importance of corporate culture, but you have to worry about the business at the same time, or you simply won't have one. Then you obviously won't *need* a culture. Where the two come together, I think, is in the cultural norms for performance, what kind of performance is expected of people. And that's a linkage that wasn't explicit in my mind three years ago. But it is now." He adds that, if the manuscript of *Corporate Cultures* were before him today, he would include a section on performance standards, measurement systems, and accountability sanctions.

On that point, he might get an argument from his co-author, Terrence Deal, a professor at Vanderbilt University and a member of Selkirk's board of directors since its inception. Deal does not disagree about the importance of discipline and performance standards, but he questions the wisdom of trying to impose them from above. The most effective performance standards, he notes, are the ones that employees recognize and accept as the product of their own commitment, and these can emerge only from the employees' experience. "One of the things that we know pretty handsomely," says Deal, "is that it's the informal performance standards that really drive a company."

In fact, Kennedy may have gotten into trouble not by doing too little, but by doing too much. Rather than letting Selkirk's culture evolve organically, he tried to impose a set of predetermined cultural values on the company, thereby retarding the growth of its own informal value system. He pursued culture as an end in itself, ignoring his own caveat, set down in his book, that "the business environment is the single greatest influence in shaping a corporate culture." Instead, he tried to shape the culture in a vacuum, without synchronizing it with the company's business goals.

In so doing, Kennedy reduced corporate culture to a formula, a collection of generic "principles." It was a cardinal error, if not an uncommon one. "There are a lot of people," says Deal, "who take our book literally and try to design a culture much as if they're trying to design an organization chart. My experience across the board has been that, as soon as people make it into a formula, they start making mistakes." By following the "formula," Kennedy wound up imposing his own set of rules on Selkirk—although not enough of them, and not the right kind, he now says. The irony is that a real corporate culture allows a company to manage itself *without* formal rules, and to manage itself better than a company that has them.

Deal makes another point. Kennedy, he observes, might be less concerned with performance today if he had not hired so many friends at the beginning. Friends are nice to have around, but it's often hard to discipline them, or subject them to a company's normal sanctions. Over the long run, Deal says, their presence at Selkirk probably undermined the development of informal performance standards.

Kennedy himself may have played a role in that, too. He estimates that, over the past year, he has spent only one day a week at Selkirk. The rest of the time he has been on the road as a consultant, using his fees to help finance the company. In all, he has sunk some $1 million of his own money into Selkirk, without which the company might not have survived. But it has come at a price. "Nobody had to pay attention to things like expenses, because there was a perception of an infinite sink of money," Kennedy says.

The danger of that perception finally came home to him last summer, when three of Selkirk's four salespeople elected to take vacations during the same month. The result was that sales for the month all but vanished. Kennedy had had enough. "I told the people here that either you sustain the company as a self-financing entity, or I will let it go under. I'm unwilling to put more money on the table."

And yet, in the end, it was hard to avoid the conclusion that a large part of Selkirk's continuing problem was Allan Kennedy himself—a thought that did not escape him. "I've got a lot to learn about running a business successfully," he says, "about doing it myself, I mean. I think I know everything about management except how to manage. I can give world-class advice on managing, but—when it comes right down to it—I take too long and fall into all the traps that I see with the managers I advise."

Whatever his shortcomings as a manager, there is one thing Kennedy can't be faulted for, and that is lack of courage. Having drawn the inevitable conclusion, he went out looking for someone who could help him do a better job of managing the company. For several months, he negotiated with the former president of a Boston-based high-tech firm, but the two of them were unable to come to terms. Instead, Kennedy has made changes at Selkirk, that he hopes will achieve the same effect. In the new structure, Merlo is taking charge of the microcomputer end of the business, while Betsy Meade—a former West Coast sales representative—has responsibility for a new minicomputer version of Correspondent, to be marketed in conjunction with Prime Computer Corp. As for Kennedy, he will concern himself with external company relations, product-development strategies, and, of course, corporate culture.

Kennedy is full of optimism these days. He points out that, despite its checkered history, Selkirk has emerged with a durable product and an installed base of about 1,000 units. In addition, the company will soon be bolstered with the proceeds from a $250,000 private placement. Meanwhile, he says, some of the company's previous problems have been dealt with, thanks to the introduction of a reliable order-fulfillment process, the decision to put sales reps on a straight commission payment schedule, and the establishment of specific sales targets for at least the next two quarters. "I think we have much more focused responsibility," he says, "and much more tangible measures of success for people in their jobs."

Overall, Kennedy looks on the past three years as a learning experience. "There are times when I think I should charge up most of the zigs and the zags to sheer rank incompetence," he admits. "But then there are other times when I look back and say, 'Nobody's that smart, and you can't do everything right.' In life, you have to be willing to try things. And if something doesn't work, you have to be willing to say, 'Well, that was a dumb idea,' and then try something else." Now, he believes, he has a chance to do just that.

In the meantime, he is in the process of writing another book. He already has a proposal circulating among publishers. In his idle moments, he occasionally amuses himself by inventing titles. One of those titles speaks volumes about where he has been: *Kicking Ass and Taking Names.*

9

COMMUNICATIONS, TECHNOLOGY TRANSFER, AND THE ROLE OF TECHNICAL GATEKEEPER

Communication Networks in R&D Laboratories

Thomas J. Allen

Abstract. Communication networks in R&D laboratories are shown to have structural characteristics, which when properly understood can be employed to more effectively keep the laboratories' personnel abreast of technological developments. Informal relations and physical location are shown to be important determinants of this structure. Informal relations can be developed through formation of project teams and intergroup transfers and loans. The effect of physical location on communications is especially strong and should be given serious consideration when designing research facilities.

INTRODUCTION

To date, attempts to automate the transmission of scientific and technological information have been most notable for their failure. The reason for this does not lie in any lack of attention or inadequate effort allocated to the problem, since very large sums of money have been expended on storage and retrieval systems for scientific and technological information. Rather, it is due to the nature and complexity of the information itself, and to the uncertainty and very personal nature of each user's needs.

For this reason, the human being is still the most effective source of information, communication with a technically competent colleague being conducted on a two-way basis, with the output of the source tracking and responding to the expressed needs of the user. In this manner, the ability of the source to adapt flexibly and re-

Reprinted with permission from T. J. Allen, "Communication Networks in R&D Labs," *R&D Management,* 1971, Vol. 1, 14–21.

spond rapidly to communicated needs enables it to cope effectively with the uncertain nature of those needs.

A large number of recent studies show that increased use of organizational colleagues for information is strongly related to scientific and technological performance. The relation to performance is, perhaps, demonstrated most clearly in a recent study by a group at M.I.T. Some of the results of this study are presented in this paper as a basis for a discussion on strategies for properly structuring the flow of technical information in research and development organizations.

THE INTERNAL CONSULTING STUDY

Eight pairs of individuals in different organizations, but working on identical problems, were compared on the extent to which each of them consulted with organizational colleagues. Since there were always two individuals attempting to solve the same problem, their solutions could be compared for relative quality and the sample split between 'high' performers and 'low' performers. Performance evaluations were made by competent technical evaluators in the government laboratories that had sponsored the projects. Dividing the sample into high and low performers allowed a further comparison to be made, now on an aggregate basis, of behaviour leading to high or low performance.

When such a comparison was made with respect to the number of times organizational colleagues were consulted during the project, it showed that high performers made far greater use of this source of technical information (Figure 1). As a matter of fact, high performers not only reported a significantly greater frequency of consultation with organizational colleagues, they also spent significantly more time in their discussions with colleagues.

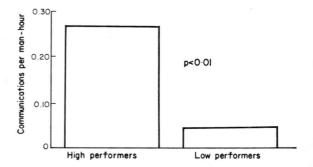

FIGURE 1. *Extent of Communication between R&D Project Members and Organizational Colleagues Not Assigned to the Project*

Furthermore, they relied on more people both within their own technical specialty and on other specialties (Figures 2a and 2b). The high performer was in closer touch than the low performer with developments in his own field. Through his wide range of contact within his specialty he is less likely to miss an important development which might have some impact on the problem to which he is assigned. He also had wider contact with people in specialties other than his own. In fact, it was only the high per-

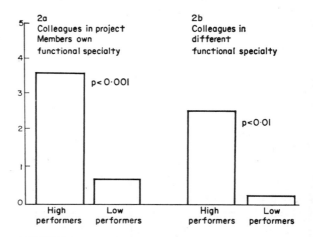

FIGURE 2. *Number and Location of Organizational Colleagues with Whom Project Members Communicate*

formers who showed any real contact outside of their specialty (Figure 2b). The low performers seldom ventured outside of their field. These findings agree with those of Pelz & Andrews (1966) who noted that colleague contacts both within the immediate work group and with other groups in the organization were positively related to a man's performance and that the variety of contacts and their frequency each contributed independently to performance.

One cannot of course determine very easily whether communication causes high performance or whether high performers merely communicate more. Pelz & Andrews (1966), in their study, obtained data on which of the two parties initiated the contact. They then assumed that a man's high performance would be more likely to attract contact from others than to induce him to initiate contacts himself. They then looked only at contacts initiated by the information user and found that the relation with performance remained strong. They concluded:

> large amounts of colleague contact tended to go with high performance even when one looked only at scientists who themselves were the primary initiators of the contacts. Under these conditions it was difficult to believe that the contacts were primarily the *result* of previous high performance. Thus the hypothesis that contacts with colleagues stimulated performance seemed to be supported (p. 47).

SUPPORT FROM OUTSIDE THE PROJECT: A PARADOX

Given the benefits to be derived from internal consultation, one would expect project members to rely heavily upon their technical staff for information. In fact, this is not the case. During the nineteen projects studied by Allen (1966), project members actually obtained more of their ideas from outside of their firms than from their own technical staff—although in general a poor performance was shown by sources outside of the firm. In fact, when individuals inside and outside of the firm were compared as sources of ideas, there was an inverse relation between frequency of outside use and performance.

Those information sources that reward the user by contributing more to his performance are used less than those that do not. Such a situation would seem to conflict with the principles of psychological learning theory. One might expect a person to return more frequently to those channels that reward him most consistently. The data show just the opposite to be true. The paradox can, however, be resolved with the introduction of an additional parameter. It can be safely predicted that an individual will repeat a behaviour that is rewarded more frequently than one that is unrewarded, only if the cost to him of the rewarded behaviour is less than or equal to the cost of the unrewarded behaviour. In other words, both cost and benefit may be taken into consideration when deciding upon a source of information.

Gerstberger and Allen (1968) actually studied this decision process in some detail. They found no relation at all between the engineers' perception of the benefits to be gained from an informal information channel and the extent to which the channel was used. However, a very strong relation existed between extent of use and the engineers' perception of the amount of effort that it took to use the channel. Cost in that case was the overriding determinant of the decision. Working back from this finding, one might speculate that the failure to consult with organizational colleagues is attributable to a high cost associated with such consultation. In fact, there is evidence to indicate that the organizational colleague is a high cost source of information for research and development project teams (Allen *et al.*, 1968). It can, for example, be very costly for a project member to admit to a colleague that he needs his help.

TECHNOLOGICAL 'GATEKEEPERS'

A number of recent studies have indicated that technologists do not read very much, and one might conclude that literature is not a very effective vehicle for bringing new information into the organization; and while it is found that outside personal contact is used very heavily by organizational technologists, further analysis suggests that this means of transfer is not much more instrumental than literature. The reason for this is that the average technologist cannot communicate effectively with outsiders. This is reflected in the results of several research studies which are consistent in their discovery of an inverse relation between outside personal contact and technical performance (Allen, 1964; Shilling & Bernard, 1964).

How then does information enter the organization? First of all, it is clear that entry does occur, because without it no R&D organization could long survive. No R&D organization, no matter how large, can be fully self-sustaining. In order for the organization to survive its members must maintain themselves abreast of current developments in those technologies which are central to the organization's mission. It must, in other words, constantly import technical information. Not only were the organizations under study surviving; they were, to all appearances, thriving. They were extremely successful, and highly regarded technically. They must, therefore have been successful, somehow, in acquiring information from outside, and disseminating it within their borders. The question remains, how?

The first important clue lies in the observation that, of all possible information sources, only one appears to satisfactorily meet the needs of R&D project members. That one source is the organizational colleague. This has been shown in the case of R&D proposal competitions (Allen, 1964) for preliminary design studies (Allen, 1966; Allen *et al.,* 1968); for 'idea generating groups' (Baker, *et al.,* 1967); for engineers and scientists

in a wide variety of industrial, governmental and university settings (Pelz & Andrews, 1966); and for the members of 64 laboratories in the biological sciences (Allen, 1964).

Following this clue, Allen & Cohen (1969) discovered that the process by which organizations most effectively import information is an indirect one (Figure 3). There existed, in the organizations that they studied, a small number of key people upon whom others relied very heavily for information. These key people, or 'technological gatekeepers', differ from their colleagues in their orientation toward outside information sources. They read far more, particularly the 'harder' literature. Their readership of professional engineering and scientific journals is significantly greater than that of the average technologist (Figure 4). They also maintain broader-ranging and longer-term relationships with technologists outside of their organizations (Figure 5). The technological gatekeeper mediates between his organizational colleagues and

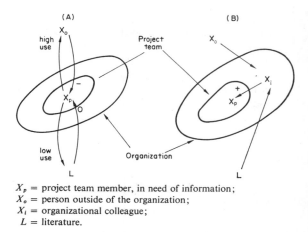

X_p = project team member, in need of information;
X_o = person outside of the organization;
X_i = organizational colleague;
L = literature.

FIGURE 3. *The Dilemma of Importing Information into the Organization (Direct paths do not work (A), because literature is little used by the average technologist and because the direct contact with outside persons is ineffective. An indirect route, through the technological gatekeeper (B) has been shown to be more effective. Symbols next to incoming arrows indicate the polarity of the correlation with performance)*

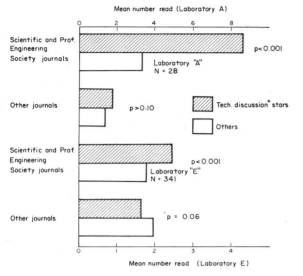

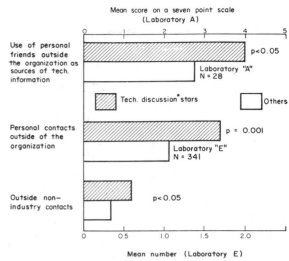

*Persons receiving one standard deviation or more above the mean number of technical discussion choices per person in their laboratory (Laboratory 'A') or in their department (Laboratory 'E').

FIGURE 4. *Journal Readership by Technical Discussion Stars (Laboratory 'A' is the original laboratory reported in Allen & Cohen (1969). Laboratory 'E' is the advanced technology component of a large aerospace firm)*

*Persons receiving one standard deviation or more above the mean number of technical discussion choices per person in their laboratory (Laboratory 'A') or in their department (Laboratory 'E').

FIGURE 5. *Personal Contact Outside of the Organization by Technical Discussion Stars (Laboratory 'A' is the original laboratory reported in Allen & Cohen (1969). Laboratory 'E' is the advanced technology component of a large aerospace firm)*

the world outside, and he effectively couples the organization to scientific and technological activity in the world at large.

NETWORKS OF GATEKEEPERS

Using the techniques of the earlier study (Allen & Cohen, 1969), the structure of the communication network in the research and advanced technology division of a large aerospace firm was measured. The laboratory under study was organized on a functional basis around five engineering specialties and three scientific disciplines.

The gatekeepers in each specialist department were identified, as well as the structure of the communication network in that department.

Because of the complexity of the networks in such a large organization (Figure 6), an attempt was made to simplify them through graph-theoretic reduction.

A communication network (or portions thereof) can be characterized according to the degree of interconnectedness that exists among its nodes. There are several degrees of interconnectedness or 'connectivity' that can exist in a network (Flament, 1963). In the present analysis, only that degree of connectivity which Flament has called 'strong' will be considered. A strongly connected component, or strong component in a network, is one in which all nodes are mutually reachable. In a communication network, a potential exists for the transmission of information between any two members of a strong component (Flament, 1963; Harary *et al.,* 1965). For

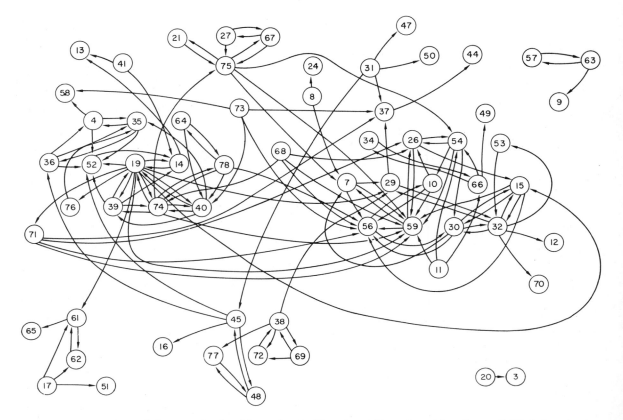

FIGURE 6.   Typical Communication Network of a Functional Department in a Large R&D Laboratory

this reason, the laboratory's communication network was reduced into its strong components and their membership was examined.

When the departmental networks of the organization are reduced in this manner, two things become apparent. First of all, the formation of strong components is not aligned with formal organizational groups, and second, while there were in each functional department anywhere from one to six non-trivial strong components, nearly all of the gatekeepers can be found together as members of the same strong component (see, for an example, Figure 7). On the average, 64% of all gatekeepers can be found in eight strong components, one for each of the five technological and three scientific specialties. In each

technical specialty, there is one strongly connected network in which most of the gatekeepers are members. The gatekeepers, therefore, maintain close communication among themselves, thus increasing substantially their effectiveness in coupling the organization to the outside world.

In fact, if one were to sit down and attempt to design an optimal system for bringing in new technical information and disseminating it within the organization, it would be difficult to produce a better one than that which exists.

New information is brought into the organization through the gatekeeper. It can then be communicated quite readily to other gatekeepers through the gatekeeper network and disseminated outward from one or more points to other

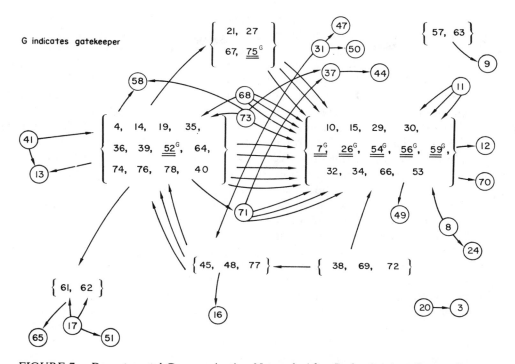

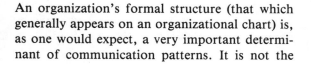

FIGURE 7. *Departmental Communication Network After Reduction into Strong Components (Strong components are shown in brackets, and gatekeepers are shown by underlining with 'G' superscript)*

members of the organization (Figure 8). Perhaps the most interesting aspect of this functioning of the organizational communication network is that it has developed spontaneously, with no managerial intervention. In fact, there was scarcely a suspicion on the part of management that the network operated in this way.

THE INFLUENCE OF NON-ORGANIZATIONAL FACTORS ON THE STRUCTURE OF COMMUNICATION NETWORKS

An organization's formal structure (that which generally appears on an organizational chart) is, as one would expect, a very important determinant of communication patterns. It is not the

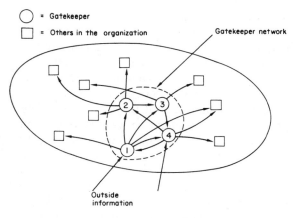

FIGURE 8. *The Functioning of the Gatekeeper Network (New information is brought into the organization by 1. It can be transmitted to 2, 3, and 4 via the gatekeeper network. It reaches its eventual users [squares] through their contacts with gatekeepers)*

397

sole determinant, however. In addition to formal organizational structure, there are available to management at least two other factors that can be used to promote (or discourage) communication. The first of these operates through the extension of informal friendship-type relations within the organization. Allen & Cohen (1969) have shown how informal relations influence the structure of communication networks, and Allen *et al.* (1968) explore in detail how this influence comes about. Simply stated, people are more willing to ask questions of others whom they know, than of strangers. The key lies in the expected damage sustained by the ego if one's question is met with a critical response. To be told that you have asked a dumb or foolish question is the ultimate in rebuffs. Few people are willing to entertain such a risk. Now, out of all the people in the world, there are hopefully only a small percentage who would meet even a truly stupid question with such a retort. Even given that this percentage is very small, however, many people will follow the strategy of minimum regret and assume that everyone belongs to this set unless proven otherwise. This results in a situation in which, of all people who are known, only a small percentage are unapproachable, but all unknowns are unapproachable. To increase the proportion of people in the organization, who can be approached for information, management would be well advised to increase the number of acquaintanceships among its technical personnel. This it can do very easily. People will not become acquainted until they first meet. There are, however, a number of ways through which technical people can come to meet one another. Interdepartmental projects are one such device. People who come to know one another through service on projects or other inter-functional teams retain their effectiveness as channels between departments for some time even after the project or team had been disbanded. Interdepartmental teams can, and do, provide an indirect benefit, through the persistence of the relations that they establish, over and above their direct contributions to coordination. The same thing can be said for transfers within the organization. For a period of time following a transfer, the transferred individual will provide a communication path back to his old organization. His influence extends far beyond this direct link, though. Probably the most important contribution of the transferred person lies in his ability to make referrals. The number of communication paths that potentially become available when a man is transferred is the product of the number of acquaintanceships which he developed in the two parts of the organization. For some people this can be a very large number. So with only a very few transfers, a large number of communication paths can be created and coordination thereby improved.

Of course, the effect diminishes with time, since both people and activities will change in the old group, and the transferred person will gradually lose touch. Kanno (1968) has shown that following a transfer between divisions of a large chemical firm, the transferred persons provided an effective communication link back to their old divisions for $1\frac{1}{2}$ years. The duration over which communications remain effective following a transfer is determined by many factors; principal among these are the rate of change of activities and turnover of personnel in the old organization. If projects are of short duration, with many new ones constantly being initiated and the turnover of personnel is high, one would expect that the effect of a transfer in promoting communication would be short-lived. Where the activity is more stable and turnover low, the transfer can be effective over a longer period of time. With estimates of these parameters and of the number of people (and their work) with whom the average transfer is acquainted, a systematic program of intra-organizational transfer can be developed. Such a program would contribute directly to communication, coordination and empathy among the sub-elements of the organization.

THE EFFECTS OF GEOGRAPHICAL LOCATION

In addition to formal organizational and information relations there is a third very important factor that can be used to influence the structure of organizational communication networks, i.e. the physical configuration of the facilities in which that organization is placed.

The data on the effect of spatial separation to be presented now were obtained in three very different organizations. The first organization is a 48-man department in a medium-sized aerospace firm. The 48 people were all engineers and scientists, primarily in electrical and mechanical engineering and applied physics. The second organization that was studied is a 52-man section of a medical school laboratory. The third organization comprised 57 social psychologists, economists and applied mathematicians in a management school.

To determine the influence of physical separation on the probability of two people communicating, the distance between every possible pair of people was measured. Moving outward in 5-yard intervals from each person, a measurement was made of the proportion of people within each interval with whom the focal person communicated. The measurement of distance was the actual distance that the focal person would have to walk in order to reach another person's desk. All measurements were taken on a single floor.

The proportion of people with whom an individual communicates, or the 'probability of communication' as it is labelled in the figure, decays with the square of distance outward from the focal person (Figure 9). The fact that the probability of communication decays with the distance separating people is not too surprising. Nor is the fact that it follows an inverse square law. What is surprising is the extreme sensitivity of probability to distance. The function, naturally, must become asymptotic beyond the minimum point of the parabola. The striking thing is

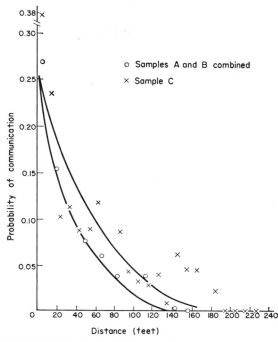

FIGURE 9. *Probability of Communication as a Function of the Distance Separating Pairs of People*

that it reaches this asymptote within 25 yards. This was true in all three organizations. In fact, for the first two organizations, the curves fall so close together that the data are combined in Figure 9. The result, therefore, appears to be general and independent of the nature of the technical work being performed.

As though, by itself, physical separation were not serious enough, there appear to be circumstances which can exacerbate its effect. The amount of difficulty, by way of corners to be turned, indirect paths to be followed, etc., encountered in traversing a path intensifies the effect of separation on communication probability. One index of this difficulty, something which might be called a 'nuisance factor' is the difference between the straight line and actual travel distances (Figure 10) separating two people.

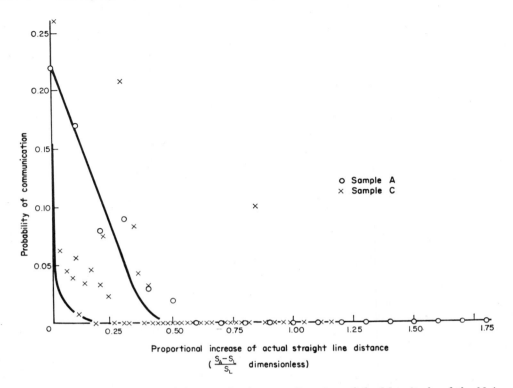

FIGURE 10.   *Probability of Communication as a Function of the Magnitude of the Nuisance Factor (O = Sample A; X = Sample C)*

When communication probability is plotted as a function of the magnitude of the 'nuisance factor' (Figure 10) the effect is quite startling. This effect holds true whether the nuisance factor is computed on an absolute basis or as a proportion of straight line separation distance.

ORGANIZATIONAL STRUCTURE

To encourage communication between project teams and the supporting technical staff, separation distances must be kept to a minimum. To locate a project in a separate facility is essentially to cut it off from support by the rest of the laboratory staff. There is a trade-off that must be

made in locating project members. Effective coordination of all elements of project activity may require that all or most of the team members be located together in a specially assigned place. On the other hand, to maintain the specialists assigned to the project abreast of developments in their technical fields demands that they be kept in contact with the specialist colleagues. This, in turn, favours locating them with their specialist groups. Marquis (1969) has argued for the latter alternative on very large projects. All of the projects in Marquis's sample were of fairly long duration; several years. This may well hold the key to the trade-off. For long-term projects, technical personnel should remain in the same location with their specialist colleagues. Assignment to a project of long duration can force a man to lose touch with his field unless steps are taken to enable his free interaction with colleagues in the field. The result is technical obsolescence and difficulty for both the man and the organization in dealing with future assignments. In the case of a brief project, the length of separation will be too short to have these results, and the balance swings in favour of locating all project members together.

Long projects demand functional organization, while short-duration projects may be organized on a project basis with all team members located together.

Functional organization has the undesirable consequence of making intra-project coordination difficult. A possible solution to this problem lies in overlaying a coordinating team across the functional departments in what has come to be known as a matrix organization. This is not always as easy to accomplish as it first sounds, but when it functions properly it can achieve the desired goals of the functional organization without the loss in project coordination.

Project and matrix organization have the undesirable consequence of making communication between functional departments difficult. Transfers, where possible, and short-duration interdepartmental projects, assist in countering this problem. In addition, the overall configuration of the laboratory should be structured in such a way that inter-functional communication is eased. Where it is desirable to have communication between groups, they should be located near each other. Where this is impossible they can be made to share certain facilities that will force interaction. The nature of the facility is secondary. It may be as humble as a coffee pot or men's room or as grandiose as a computer or an expensive instrument. What matters is that it brings people into contact who would otherwise not meet. It is quite easy, in any organization, to think of a large number of such facilities for promoting interaction. Where possible they should be located where they will promote the desired patterns of group interaction. In those cases in which it is not feasible to manipulate the position of the interaction facility, then desired patterns of interaction should be given serious consideration in allocating the use of the facility among groups and in positioning groups around it. In the latter situation it must be borne in mind that the extent to which a facility will be used is also an inverse function of distance. Frohman (1968), for example, found the principal determinant of use of a technical library in an industrial firm to be the distance separating users from it. Interaction facilities must be positioned in such a way that they promote interaction among groups that would not otherwise interact, while at the same time they are not so far removed from any of the groups that they lose their effectiveness.

SUMMARY AND CONCLUSIONS

The importance to research and development projects of technical staff support cannot be overstressed. Seldom, if ever, is management able satisfactorily to predict and obtain all of the talents that will be needed in a project and incorporate them in the project team. The project must, therefore, obtain much of its required information from sources beyond its own membership.

Research shows very clearly that the best source for this support lies in the technical staff of the laboratory itself. Attempts to bring information to the project directly from outside of the organization usually have been ineffective. The process by which an organization imports and disseminates outside information is more complex than people normally assume. The best way to maintain the project team abreast of outside developments lies in understanding and making proper use of existing information systems. This includes the use of technological gatekeepers for project support. Outside information can then be delivered to the project quite effectively, albeit by an indirect route. Research evidence indicates quite strongly that the indirect approach is far more effective than any direct approach to coupling project members to outside sources, whether personal or written.

There are available a wide variety of techniques for improving communication and coordination between projects and their supporting staff. A number of formal organizational mechanisms have been described in detail. In addition to these, use may also be made of the informal relationships that will develop when people come into contact with one another. A very effective means for increasing the level of acquaintanceships in an organization is the inter-group transfer. Physical location is also a very strong determinant of interaction patterns. People are more likely to communicate with those who are located nearest to them. Individuals and groups can therefore be positioned in ways that will either promote or inhibit communication. Architectural design thus becomes an important determinant of the structure that an organization's communication network will assume. Shared facilities or equipment can also be used to promote interaction between groups.

All of these factors must be taken into account and properly arranged in order to effectively couple the research and development project to its supporting information system.

REFERENCES

Allen, T. J. (1964) 'The Use of Information Channels in R&D Proposal Preparation', Cambridge, Mass.: M.I.T. Sloan School of Management, Working Paper No. 97-64.

Allen, T. J. (1966) 'Managing the Flow of Scientific and Technological Information, Ph.D. Dissertation, Cambridge, Mass.: M.I.T. Sloan School of Management.

Allen, T. J., Gerstenfeld, A. & Gerstberger, P. G. (1968) 'The Problem of Internal Consulting in the R&D Laboratory', Cambridge, Mass.: M.I.T. Sloan School of Management, Working Paper No. 319-68.

Allen, T. J. & Cohen, S. I. (1969) 'Information flow in two R&D laboratories', Administrative Science Quarterly, Vol. 14.

Baker, N. R., Siegmann, J. & Rubenstein, A. H. (1967) 'The effects of perceived needs and means on the generation of ideas for industrial research and development project', I.E.E.E. Transactions on Engineering Management, Vol. 14.

Flament, C. (1963) 'Applications of Graph Theory to Group Structure', New York: Prentice Hall.

Frohman, A. (1968) 'Communication problems in an industrial laboratory', Unpublished term paper, Cambridge, Mass.: M.I.T. Sloan School of Management.

Gerstberger, P. G. & Allen, T. J. (1968) 'Criteria used in the selection of information channels by R&D engineers', Journal of Applied Psychology, Vol. 52.

Harary, F., Norman, R. S. & Cartwright, D. (1965) 'Structural Models', New York: Wiley.

Kanno, M. (1968) 'Effect on Communication Between Labs and Plants of the Transfer of R&D Personnel', S.M. Thesis, Cambridge, Mass.: M.I.T. Sloan School of Management.

Marquis, D. G. (1969) 'Organizational factors in project performance', Program Management (ed. J. Galbraith), Cambridge, Mass.: M.I.T. Press.

Pelz, D. C. & Andrews, F. M. (1966) 'Scientists in Organizations', New York: Wiley.

Shilling, C. W. & Bernard, C. W. (1964) 'Informal Communication Among Bio-Scientists', George Washington University Biological Sciences Communication Project, Report 16A-64.

An Investigation into the Managerial Roles and Career Paths of Gatekeepers and Project Supervisors in a Major R&D Facility

Ralph Katz

Michael L. Tushman

Abstract. This study investigates the role of gatekeepers in the transfer of information within a single R&D location by comparing directly the performance of project groups with and without gatekeepers. The results show that gatekeepers performed a linking role only for projects performing tasks that were 'locally-oriented' while 'universally-oriented' tasks were most effectively linked to external areas by direct project member communication. Gatekeepers also appear to facilitate external communication by their locally-oriented project colleagues. A follow-up study five years later showed that almost all gatekeeping project leaders had been promoted up the managerial ladder; in contrast, one half of the non-gatekeeping project leaders had ascended the technical ladder. This implies that higher managerial levels demand strong interpersonal as well as technical skills.

R&D project teams must process information from outside sources in order to keep informed about relevant external developments and new technological innovations (Myers & Marquis, 1969). Furthermore, empirical studies over the past 15 years have demonstrated that oral communications, rather than written technical reports or publications, are the primary means by which engineering professionals collect and disseminate important new ideas and information

Reprinted with permission from R. Katz and M. Tushman, "An Investigation into the Managerial Roles and Career Paths of Gatekeepers and Project Supervisors in a Major R&D Facility," *R&D Management,* 1981, Vol. 11, 103–110.

into their project groups (Allen, 1977). While such personal contacts may be essential, there are alternative communication structures by which R&D groups can effectively draw upon information outside their organizations (Katz & Tushman, 1979). In particular, the research reported here focuses explicitly on the role played by gatekeepers in the effective transfer and utilization of external technology and information. (Gatekeepers are defined as those key individual technologists who are strongly connected to both internal colleagues and external sources of information (Allen & Cohen, 1969).) Since most gatekeepers are also project supervisors, this study also contrasts the managerial roles and subsequent career paths of gatekeeping supervisors against project supervisors not functioning as gatekeepers.

COMMUNICATION AND PERFORMANCE

Generally speaking, previous research has shown that project performance is strongly associated with high levels of technical communication by all project members to information sources within the organization (i.e., high levels of internal communication). The positive findings of Allen (1977), Pelz & Andrews (1966), and Farris (1972) strongly argue that direct contacts between project members and other internal colleagues can enhance project effectiveness.

While direct communication by all project members may be effective for internal communications, the particular method for effectively keeping up-to-date with technical advances outside the organization are probably very different. Numerous studies, for example, have shown that project performance is not positively associated with direct project member communication to external information areas. In fact, most studies have found them to be inversely related (e.g., Allen, 1977; Katz & Tushman, 1979; Baker, Siegmann & Rubenstein, 1967). It seems that most engineers are simply unable to communicate effectively with extraorganizational information sources.

One explanation for these significant differences stems from the idea that technological activities are strongly local in nature in that their problems, strategies, and solutions are defined and operationalized in terms of particular strengths and interests of the organizational subculture in which they are being addressed (Katz & Kahn, 1978; Allen, 1977). Such localized definitions and shared language schemes gradually unfold from the constant interactions among organizational members, the tasks' overall objectives and requirements, and the common social

and task related experiences of organizational members. These idiosyncratic developments are a basic determinant of attitudes and behaviours in that they strongly influence the ways in which project members think about and define their various problems and solution strategies.

Such localized perspectives eventually become a double-edged sword. As long as individuals share the same common language and awareness, communication is rather easy and efficient. Conversely, when individuals do not share a common coding scheme and technical language, their work-related communications are less efficient, often resulting in severe misperceptions and misinterpretations (Dearborn & Simon, 1958). Thus, the evolution of more localized languages and technological approaches enables project members to deal effectively with their more local information processing activities within the organization; yet at the same time, it hinders the acquisition and interpretation of information from areas outside the organization. This lack of commonality across organizational boundaries serves as a strong communication impedance causing considerable difficulty in the communications of most engineers with external consultants and professionals (Allen, 1977; Price, 1965).

Given this burden in communicating across differentiated organizational boundaries, how can project groups be effectively linked to external information areas? One way is through the role of project gatekeeper; that is, certain project members who are strongly connected to outside information domains but who are also capable of translating technical developments and ideas across contrasting coding schemes (Allen & Cohen, 1969). Through these key members, external information can be channelled into project groups by means of a two-step communication process (Coleman, Katz & Menzel, 1966). First, gatekeepers gather and understand outside information, and subsequently they translate it into terms that are more meaningful to their locally constrained colleagues. Gatekeepers, as a result, perform an extremely valuable function, for they may be the principal means by which external ideas and information can be effectively transferred into R&D project groups.

While substantial literature applauds this gatekeeper concept, there is virtually no direct evidence that gatekeepers enhance project performance. Support has to be inferred indirectly either from the empirical findings of Katz & Tushman (1979) and Allen, Tushman & Lee (1979) or from the case studies in project SAPPHO (Achilladeles, Jervis & Robertson, 1971). Our initial research question, then, concerns the association between project gatekeepers and technical performance. Is this relationship positive across all forms of R&D activity or are some project areas more effectively linked to external technology through direct contact by all project members rather than through a gatekeeper? Moreover, if gatekeepers are necessary for effective technology transfer, must they then be the primary source for collecting outside information, or can they also serve to facilitate the external communication of their more locally constrained colleagues?

GATEKEEPERS, PERFORMANCE, AND THE NATURE OF THE TASK

The need for a two-step process of information flow depends on a strong communication impedance between the project group and its external information areas. To the extent that different technical languages and coding schemes exist between project members and their external technical environments, communication across organizational boundaries will be difficult and inefficient. In particular, most technological activities (unlike the sciences) are strongly local in nature. The coupling of bureaucratic interests and demands with localized technical tasks and coding schemes produces a communication boundary that differentiates these project groups

from their outside areas. Product development groups in different organizations, for example, may face similar problems yet may define their solution approaches and parameters very differently (Katz & Tushman, 1979; Allen, 1977). As a result, it becomes increasingly difficult for most technologists to integrate external ideas, suggestions and solutions with internal technology that has become locally defined and constrained. It is hypothesized, therefore, that locally oriented projects (i.e., development and technical service projects) will require gatekeepers to provide the necessary linkages to external information areas—without gatekeepers, direct external contacts by members of local projects will be ineffective.

In contrast, if external information sources do not have different language and coding schemes from members of the project group, then a significant communication impedance will not exist. Work that is more universally defined (scientific or research work, for example) is probably less influenced and constrained by local organizational factors, resulting in less difficulty *vis-à-vis* external communications. Under these conditions, project members are more likely to share similar norms, values, and language schemes with outside professional colleagues, thereby, permitting effective communication across organizational and even national boundaries. They are simply more capable of understanding the nature of the problems and corresponding solution approaches employed by their relevant external colleagues. Hagstrom (1965), for instance, found a strong positive correlation between the productivity of scientists and their levels of contact with colleagues from other universities. For universally defined tasks, therefore, it is hypothesized that gatekeepers are not required to link projects with their relevant external information areas; instead, direct outside interaction by all project members is more advantageous. The nature of a project's work, therefore, should be a critical factor affecting the development of localized languages and orientations and consequently will moderate significantly the relationship between project performance and the usefulness of gatekeepers.

ROLE OF GATEKEEPERS

If gatekeepers enhance the performance of project groups working on locally defined tasks, then what specific information processing activities of gatekeepers contribute to higher project performance? There are at least two alternatives. The more traditional explanation is that gatekeepers function as the primary link to external sources of information and technology—information flows through these key individuals to the more local members of the project team (Allen & Cohen, 1969). Relevant external information is transferred effectively into a project group because of the capable boundary spanning activities of the project's gatekeeper.

Another possibility is that gatekeepers also assume an active training, development, and socialization role within their work groups. From this perspective, gatekeepers not only gather, translate, and encode external information, but they also facilitate the external contacts of their project colleagues. By helping to direct, coach, and interpret the external communications of their fellow project members, gatekeepers act to reduce the communication boundary separating their projects from outside information areas.

If gatekeeping permits other project members to communicate effectively with external areas, then for localized projects with gatekeepers, there should be a positive association between a project's external communication and its performance. On the other hand, if gatekeepers do not play this more active role, then an inverse relation is more likely to exist between the external communications of locally oriented group members and project performance. Because gatekeepers work and interact so closely with other project members about technically related problems, it is hypothesized that gatekeepers fulfill this large role of both gathering outside information and facilitating the external communications of their project colleagues.

GATEKEEPERS AND PROJECT SUPERVISORS

If most gatekeepers are also first-level project supervisors (Allen, 1977), then to what extent can any project supervisor substitute as a gatekeeper and play this linking role to external areas? Supervisors of locally oriented projects who are not gatekeepers face the same communication impedance as their project subordinates when communicating externally. As a result, without the benefit of a gatekeeper, the communications of non-gatekeeping supervisors outside the organization will be inversely related to project performance. In contrast, supervisory gatekeepers are capable of communicating effectively across organizational boundaries and consequently will show a positive association between external communication and project performance.

Finally, if there is a significant distinction between the information processing activities and capabilities of project supervisors who are gatekeepers and those who are not, then to what extent will they also have different career paths within the technical organization? Are gatekeeping supervisors, for example, more likely to be promoted to particular laboratory positions than non-gatekeeping supervisors? From an exploratory point of view, this research describes the career paths of these different kinds of project supervisors over a 5-year period. The key issues are whether gatekeeping and non-gatekeeping supervisors were promoted and utilized differently within the organization over this time period, and whether they are currently effective in their respective career positions.

METHODOLOGY

This study was conducted at the R&D facility of a large American corporation. Employing a total of 345 professionals, the laboratory was organized into 7 departments, each containing its own set of projects. At the time of our study, 61 separate project groups existed across the 7 departments. These groups remained stable over the data collection period, and each professional was a member of only one project group.

Communication

To measure actual communications, each professional kept track of all other professionals with whom he or she had work-related oral communication on a randomly chosen day each week for 15 weeks. The sampling of days was arranged to allow for equal numbers of weekdays. Respondents reported all contacts both within and outside the laboratory's facility, including to whom they talked and how many times they talked with that person. Social and written communications were not reported. An overall response rate of 93% was achieved over the 15 weeks. In addition, 68% of all communication episodes reported within the laboratory were reciprocally mentioned by both parties. Given these high rates of response and mutual agreement, these sociometric methods provide a rather accurate picture of the verbal interactions for all laboratory professionals.

For each project member, internal communications was measured by summing the number of work-related contacts reported over the 15 weeks between that member and all other professionals within the organization. External or outside communication was measured by summing the member's reported communications to other professional individuals outside the organization, including R&D consultants, professors, vendors, customers, and the like. As discussed by Katz & Tushman (1979), these individual scores were also aggregated to obtain project measures of internal and external communication.

Conceptually, project gatekeepers are defined as those members who are high internal communicators and who also maintain a high degree of outside communication. In line with previous studies (see Allen, 1977), this study operationalized gatekeepers as those project members who were in the top fifth of both the internal and external communication distributions. Gatekeepers were identified in 20 project groups while 40 projects had no gatekeepers within their memberships.

Project Type

R&D tasks differ along several dimensions, including time span of feedback, specific vs. general problem-solving orientation, and the generation of new knowledge vs. utilization of existing knowledge and experience (Rosenbloom & Wolek, 1970). Based on these dimensions, distinct project categories were defined ranging from research to development to technical service. Such a categorization also forms a universal (research) to local (technical service) project continuum. As discussed by Katz & Tushman (1979), respondents were asked to use these specific project definitions and indicate how well each category represented the objectives of their task activities. A second question asked respondents to indicate what percentage of their project work fell into each of the project categories. A weighted average of these two answers was calculated for each respondent (Spearman-Brown reliability = 0.91).

To categorize projects, however, the homogeneity of members' perceptions of their task characteristics had to be examined to check for the appropriateness of pooling across individual project members (see Tushman, 1977 for details). As pooling was appropriate, individual responses were averaged to get final project scores, yielding 14 Research, 23 Development, and 23 Technical

Service projects. Research projects carried out more universally oriented scientific work (discovering new knowledge in glass physics, for instance) while development and technical service projects were more locally oriented in that they worked on organizationally defined problems and products.

Project Performance

Since comparable measures of project performance have yet to be developed across different technologies, a subjective measure was employed. Each department and laboratory manager ($N = 9$) was separately interviewed and asked to evaluate the overall technical performance of all projects with which he was technically familiar. Whenever an informed judgment could not be made, they were asked not to rate the project. From these interviews, each project was independently rated by an average of about 5 managers using a seven-point scale ranging from very low to very high. These individual ratings were averaged to yield overall project performance scores (Spearman-Brown reliability = 0.81).

Follow-up Study

Approximately 5 years after these previously described data were collected, we returned to this R&D facility to locate the current laboratory positions of the original set of project supervisors. During this time interval, a dual ladder promotional system had been installed. According to the company, the technical ladder was introduced to reward individual professionals whose 'technical competency and contributions are well-recognized'. All technical ladder positions were above the original project supervisory level. As a result, we were able to determine from our follow-up analysis whether a project supervisor had either (1) been promoted up the managerial ladder, (2) been promoted up the technical ladder, (3) had not been promoted above the project level, or (4) had left the R&D facility.

Finally, a very high-level manager currently investigating problems associated with the dual ladder system was asked to evaluate the particular project supervisors who had been promoted up the technical ladder ($N = 12$). Based on his knowledge of the *current* technical contributions of these individuals, each was rated on a 4-point scale ranging from low to high. Unfortunately, similar performance ratings for project supervisors promoted up the managerial ladder could not be obtained.

RESULTS

Gatekeeper Presence and Project Performance

The performance means reported in the first row of Table 1 clearly indicate that, in general, the performances of projects with gatekeepers were not significantly different from the performances of projects without gatekeepers. As previously discussed, however, locally oriented projects (i.e., development and technical service) should display a positive association between gatekeeper presence and project performance. Universal-type or research projects, on the other hand, should show an inverse relation between gatekeeper presence and project performance.

The breakdown of performance means by project type strongly supports these differences in the appropriateness of the gatekeeping function. As shown by Table 1, research projects *without* gatekeepers were significantly higher performing than research projects *with* gatekeepers. It may be that research projects are more effectively linked to external information areas through direct member contacts.

In sharp contrast, development projects *with* gatekeepers were significantly more effective than development projects *without* gatekeepers. Unlike research groups, then, development proj-

TABLE 1. *Project Performance as a Function of Gatekeeper Presence and Project Type*

Project Type	Mean Performance for Projects:		
	With Gatekeepers	Without Gatekeepers	Mean Difference in Performance
All projects	4.70	4.53	0.17
	(N=20)	(N=40)	
Project type			
Research	4.22	4.92	−0.70**
	(N=5)	(N=9)	
Development	4.91	4.15	0.76***
	(N=8)	(N=15)	
Technical service	4.80	4.67	0.13
	(N=7	(N=16)	

**$p < 0.05$ and ***$p < 0.01$ indicate significant mean differences in project performance.

ects are linked to outside information areas more effectively through the use of gatekeepers. No significant differences in project performance, however, were discovered between technical service groups with and without gatekeepers. As a result, the mechanisms used by technical service projects to import external information effectively remain unclear.

Role of Gatekeepers

It was suggested that on locally oriented tasks, gatekeepers may do much more than simply channel outside information into their project groups. They may also act to reduce communication impedance, facilitating the external communications of their fellow project colleagues. In contrast, locally oriented projects without gatekeepers will have no clearly effective link to external areas.

Results reported in Table 2 support these ideas. For local projects without gatekeepers, there was a consistent inverse association between members' external communication and project performance. For projects with gatekeep-

ers, however, a significantly different pattern emerged—external communication was positively associated with project performance. Furthermore, these correlational differences were strong even after the direct communication effects of gatekeepers were removed. For both development and technical service groups, gatekeepers and their project colleagues were able to communicate effectively with outside professionals.

The significant correlational differences between projects with and without gatekeepers strongly support the argument that gatekeepers influence the ability of local project members to communicate effectively with external sources of technical information. Members of research projects, on the other hand, do not seem to face a communication impedance when communicating externally, for Table 2 shows that the level of outside interaction by all research project members was positively associated with performance independent of a gatekeeper's presence within the group. Gatekeepers as a result, may not play an important information processing role in the more universally oriented research projects, but they appear to play a vital role in the more lo-

TABLE 2.   *Correlations between Project Performance and External Communication by Project Type and Gatekeeper Presence*

Measures of External Communication for:	Correlation with Performance for Projects:	
	With Gatekeeping Leaders	Without Gatekeeping Leaders
Research projects:		
(a) All project members	0.53	0.46*
(b) All members excluding project leaders[†]	0.37	0.70**
(c) Project leaders	0.55	0.29
	(N=5)	(N=9)
Development projects:		
(a) All project members	0.31	−0.45**
(b) All members excluding project leaders	0.55*	−0.21
(c) Project leaders	0.37	−0.51**
	(N=8)	(N=15)
Technical service projects:		
(a) All project members	0.31	−0.19
(b) All members excluding project leaders	0.64*	−0.03
(c) Project leaders	0.77*	−0.34*
	(N=7)	(N=16)

[†]In the first column of correlations, project leader refers to the project's gatekeeper, 75% of whom were also project supervisors. In the second column, project leader simply refers to the project's supervisor.

*$p < 0.10$; **$p < 0.05$; pairwise correlations that are significantly different at the $p < 0.10$ level or less have been underlined.

cally defined development and technical service projects.

Gatekeepers and Project Supervisors

Can project supervisors substitute for gatekeepers in linking their projects to external information areas? The correlations reported in Table 2 do not support this position. For development and technical service projects, the greater the external communication of project supervisors who were not gatekeepers, the lower their project's performance. Generally speaking, therefore, supervisors are not necessarily an effective link to external domains. In contrast, the association between outside contact and project performance was very positive for supervisors who were also gatekeepers. Such significant correlational differences strongly imply that supervisory status alone cannot effectively deal with the demands for keeping in touch with outside information sources.

In light of these significant role differences, were gatekeeping and non-gatekeeping supervisors likely to receive the same kinds of promotions? The results of Table 3 suggest they did not. The follow-up study of the facility some 5 years later reveals that almost all of the gatekeeping supervisors had been promoted up the managerial ladder. Of the 12 gatekeeping supervisors remaining with the company, 11 are in higher-level managerial positions. Although non-gatekeeping

TABLE 3.   Comparison of Promotions of Gatekeeping and Non-gatekeeping Project Supervisors along the Dual Ladder over a 5-year Period

	Supervisory Role	
Laboratory Position of Project Supervisors after 5 Years	Project Supervisors Who Were Also Gatekeepers	Project Supervisors Who Were Not Gatekeepers
(a) Percent promoted to *managerial* positions above the project level	73.4	37.3
(b) Percent promoted to *technical* positions above the project level	6.6	27.9
(c) Percent not promoted to positions above the project level	0.0	16.2
(d) Percent no longer employed	20.0	18.6
Totals	100.0% ($N=15$)	100.0% ($N=43$)

supervisors were almost as likely to be promoted, they were not as likely to receive managerial promotions. Almost as many non-gatekeeping supervisors were promoted up the technical ladder as were promoted up the managerial ladder. In fact, of the 13 project supervisors who had made it up the technical ladder, only one had been a technical gatekeeper. (This particular gatekeeper was initially promoted up the managerial ladder but was switched to a technical ladder position when it became clear that he was not functioning effectively as a laboratory manager.)

While gatekeeping supervisors were essentially promoted up the managerial ladder, could one have differentiated between non-gatekeeping supervisors promoted managerially and those promoted technically? The means reported in Table 4 indicate that there were significant communication differences between these two promotional categories. Project supervisors promoted up the technical ladder had only half as many internal interactions as project supervisors selected for managerial positions. Interestingly enough, there were almost identical levels of in-

TABLE 4.   Comparisons of Mean Internal and External Communications of Project Supervisors Promoted over the Next 5 Years

Promotional Positions above the Project Level	Mean Internal Communication (per Person per Week)	Mean External Communication (per Person per Week)
(a) Gatekeeping supervisors promoted to managerial positions ($N=11$)	74.3[a]	4.8[a]
(b) Non-gatekeeping supervisors promoted to managerial positions ($N=16$)	70.6[a]	1.5[b]
(c) Supervisors promoted to technical positions[†] ($N=12$)	39.7[b]	1.4[b]

[†]Of these 12 project supervisors, only one had functioned as a project gatekeeper.
Note: In each column, means with superscript 'a' are significantly greater than means with superscript 'b' at the $p < 0.01$ level.

ternal communications for gatekeeping and non-gatekeeping supervisors promoted to managerial positions. External communications did not differentiate between the promotional ladders of non-gatekeeping supervisors. Thus, the level of interpersonal activity and skills that one has demonstrated within the organization may have been a strong factor in shaping one's promotional ladder within this dual ladder system.

Finally, it is important to mention that neither of our original measures of internal or external communication could significantly predict the current contributions of project supervisors now positioned on the technical ladder. Instead, as shown by Table 5, the current performances of professionals on the technical ladder are significantly lower for project supervisors who had headed technical service activities than for project supervisors who had been in charge of either development or research project work. Given their relatively low level of outside contact in the first place (at least when compared with their gatekeeping counterparts), these findings suggest that the technical ladder (at least as presently operationalized in this and in similar facilities) may be less appropriate for R&D professionals whose work experiences, activities, and orientations have been on the 'local' side of the technological continuum. In light of the small number of cases in Table 5, however, considerably more research is needed to corroborate these results.

DISCUSSION

In engineering and scientific environments, there are at least two distinct methods by which R&D project groups can keep abreast of technical ideas and developments outside their organizations: (1) by direct contact by all project members and (2) by contact mediated by project gatekeepers. Our findings suggest that the effectiveness of these two alternatives is strongly affected by the communication impedance separating project groups from their external

information areas. Universally-oriented research projects, for example, face little communication impedance when processing outside ideas and information since their work is less constrained by local organizational factors. Therefore, instead of relying on gatekeepers to keep informed about outside developments and advances, members of higher performing research groups were able to rely on their own external contacts. In fact, a significant inverse relationship between project performance and gatekeeper presence was uncovered among the facility's 14 research groups.

As project activities become more specialized and locally defined, however, language and cognitive differences between project members and external professionals increase, creating substantial communication impedance and more tendentious information flows. As a result, individual interaction across organizational boundaries becomes more difficult and ineffective. To wit, higher performing development and technical service groups had significantly less outside contact by all project members. Nevertheless, important technical information must be acquired from relevant outside sources. Gatekeeping, as a result, can be a necessary and effective process for transferring external technology into localized project groups. In particular, within our sample of development projects, those with gatekeepers were considerably more effective than those without gatekeepers. Thus, what are needed to introduce outside information effectively into development projects are specialized project individuals who keep current technically, are readily conversant across different technologies, and who are contributing to their project's work in direct and meaningful ways, i.e., technical gatekeepers (Allen, 1977).

Unlike development projects, the performances of technical service projects were not positively related to the presence of gatekeepers even though their project members could not communicate effectively with outside information areas (see Table 2). One possible explanation for these differences stems from differences in the nature

TABLE 5. *Performance Ratings of Project Supervisors Promoted up the Technical Ladder by Project Type*

	Prior Type of Project Supervision		
	Research (N=4)	Development (N=5)	Technical Service (N=3)
Mean performance ratings**	3.75	3.40	1.67

**These mean performance ratings are significantly different at the $p < 0.05$ level.

of their work. In contrast to development projects which typically involve dynamic technologies, new knowledge, and/or new products, technical service work tends to deal with more mature technologies, existing knowledge, and/or existing products. Because these technologies are more stable and can be understood more easily by the organization's management (Frost & Whitley, 1971), the specialized gatekeeper role may not be necessary. Instead, the managerial hierarchy may be able to keep members sufficiently informed about external events and information through formal operating channels (Walsh & Baker, 1972; Allen, Tushman & Lee, 1979).

Generally speaking, the particular method by which R&D projects can effectively connect with external technical information appears to differ significantly across the research, development, and technical service spectrum of R&D activities. The particular method is strongly contingent on both the nature of the project's work and the stability of the involved technologies. Thus, it seems that the combination of localized yet dynamic technologies necessitates the active presence and participation of gatekeepers within engineering project groups.

The Gatekeeping Role and Project Supervision

In linking local project groups to extra-organizational areas, our results indicate that gatekeepers not only bring in outside information, but just as important, they facilitate the external communication of their more locally oriented colleagues. As a result, localized engineering projects with gatekeepers are in a better position to take advantage of external technology since other members are now capable of communicating effectively across organizational boundaries. This additional capacity lessens the project's complete dependence on gatekeepers for gathering and disseminating all important outside information.

In research-type tasks, on the other hand, gatekeepers are not an effective method for obtaining external information; nor does it appear that they serve in any communication facilitating capacity. In higher performing research projects, members did not rely on gatekeepers for their external information; in a sense, they functioned as their own technical gatekeepers.

One should also note that many supervisors of locally-oriented projects could not adequately perform a gatekeeping role in linking their projects to outside technology. In contrast to gatekeeping supervisors, the external interactions of supervisors who were not gatekeepers were negatively associated with project performance. While these non-gatekeeping supervisors may have developed important internal linkages, they are unable to fulfill the same external function as their gatekeeping peers. Such findings suggest distinguishing between two types of project leaders: (1) locally oriented supervisors who may be appropriate for more administrative and technical support activities and (2) gatekeeping supervisors who may be more contributive on product and process development activities.

These different capabilities also seem to have led to different kinds of career paths. All project gatekeepers remaining in the organization over a

5-year period were promoted along the managerial ladder. Almost all non-gatekeeping supervisors were also promoted during this interval. However, only about half were positioned on the managerial ladder—the other half being promoted along the technical ladder. While there were no strong differences between the technical performances of project groups which had supervisors promoted managerially versus those which had supervisors promoted technically, there had been very strong differences between their communication activities. Those selected for managerial positions had been high internal communicators; in fact, they were as high as project gatekeepers. In sharp contrast, supervisors promoted along the technical ladder had been extremely low internal communicators. Thus, what differentiated between these two alternative career paths for non-gatekeeping supervisors was not technical competence but interpersonal competence. (This is particularly important since most companies with technical ladders 'claim' to reward individuals for outstanding technical contributions. Gatekeepers as individuals, moreover, typically represent the most technically competent first-level supervisors within laboratories (see Allen, 1977), and they were promoted managerially. Thus, supervisors promoted along the technical ladder were probably not the most technically competent individuals, nor were they keeping in touch with external technology to the same extent as gatekeepers. Perhaps it is these deficiencies that cause many companies to have substantial difficulty with their dual ladder systems.) Supervisors who had behaviourally demonstrated their ability to interact effectively with other professionals within the organization were given higher level managerial responsibilities and positions. Such findings strongly argue that technical skills were not sufficient for attaining high level managerial positions; rather technical and interpersonal skills had to be combined. As emphasized by Mintzberg (1973) and Schein (1978), high level R&D managers should not only be technically competent, but they should also be able to communicate and interact effectively with other individuals, especially since many of their work responsibilities are either carried out or interfaced with these people.

Finally, of the technically promoted project supervisors who are now poor contributors, proportionately more have come from supervising technical service work. One explanation is that in most organizations, individuals promoted up the technical ladder are given considerably more freedom to define where and how they will make their technical contributions. As a result, it becomes very difficult to manage and integrate them with other project colleagues and activities. Over time, therefore, their work becomes increasingly independent and self-contained. In some sense, they are asked to function like a creative research scientist but in a local technological work environment. This new role may be particularly troublesome for professionals who had become accustomed to technical support work in which the technologies were often well understood and more stable and in which the tasks were often more structured (Allen, Tushman & Lee, 1979).

CONCLUSIONS

In conclusion, gatekeepers perform a critical role within R&D settings that often goes unrecognized. By realizing the importance of the gatekeeping role within development tasks, R&D managers can link their product or process efforts to sources of external technology more effectively. A manager could examine, for example, the extent to which important technologies utilized within various development projects are actually 'covered' by a gatekeeping type person. However, the degree to which these communication activities can be managed may be limited. Gatekeeping is an informal role in that other project engineers must feel sufficiently secure and comfortable psychologically to approach gatekeepers with their technical problems, mistakes, and questions without fear of personal evaluation or other adverse considerations (Allen, 1977). Therefore, to the extent that the organization tries to formalize such a gatekeeping function, it runs the risk of inhibiting the very kinds of interaction it wishes to promote.

This is not meant to imply that gatekeeping cannot be managed or helped; on the contrary, it can. In fact, a number of R&D facilities have instituted formal gatekeeper programmes. What is important to recognize is that the interest and ability of individuals to link with external technology cannot be suddenly 'decreed' by management. Typically, such outside professional interests are a 'given' and are not easily influenced by the organization, although they can be made easier to pursue. What can be more easily influenced is the degree to which gatekeepers are actually present and participating in project tasks as well as their accessibility to other project members. Their work positions, for example, could be located close to other project engineers to foster easier and more frequent communication. However, the development of sufficient internal contacts and communications to be an effective gatekeeper takes time. In the present sample, for example, all of the gatekeepers had been working in their present project groups for a period of at least two years. In short, the external side of the gatekeeping role is usually being performed by the gatekeeper anyway. It is the internal side that can be facilitated and made more effective.

REFERENCES

Achilladeles, A., Jervis, P. & Robertson, A. (1971) *Success and Failure in Innovation.* Project Sappho, Sussex: University of Sussex Press.

Allen, T. J. (1977) *Managing the Flow of Technology.* Cambridge, MA: M.I.T. Press.

Allen, T. J. & Cohen, S. (1969) 'Information flow in R&D laboratories', *Administrative Science Quarterly,* Vol. 14, 12–19.

Allen, T. J., Tushman, M. & Lee, D. (1979) 'Technology transfer as a function of position on research, development, and technical service continuum', *Academy of Management Journal,* Vol. 22, 694–708.

Baker, N., Siegmann, J. & Rubenstein, A. (1967) 'Effects of perceived needs on the generation of ideas in R&D projects', *IEEE Transactions on Engineering Management,* Vol. 14, 156–163.

Coleman, J., Katz, D. & Menzel, I. (1966) *Diffusion of Innovation.* New York: Free Press.

Dearborn, R. & Simon, H. (1958) 'Selective perceptions in executives', *Sociometry,* Vol. 21, 140–144.

Farris, G. (1972) 'The effects of individual roles on performance in innovative groups', *R&D Management,* Vol. 3, 23–28.

Frost, P. A. & Whitley, R. D. (1971) 'Communication patterns in a research laboratory', *R&D Management,* Vol. 1, 71–79.

Hagstrom, W. (1965) *The Scientific Community,* New York: Basic Books.

Katz, D. & Kahn, R. (1966) *The Social Psychology of Organizations,* New York: Wiley Co.

Katz, R. & Tushman, M. (1979) 'Communication patterns, project performance, and task characteristics', *Organizational Behavior and Human Performance,* Vol. 23, 139–162.

Mintzberg, H. (1973) *The Nature of Managerial Work.* New York: Harper & Row.

Myers, S. & Marquis, D. (1969) 'Successful industrial innovation', Washington, D.C.: *National Science Foundation.*

Pelz, D. & Andrews, F. M. (1966) *Scientists in Organizations,* New York: Wiley Co.

Price, D. (1965) 'Is technology historically independent of science?', *Technology and Culuture,* Vol. 6, 553–568.

Rosenbloom, R. & Wolek, F. (1970) *Technology and Information Transfer.* Boston, MA: Harvard Business School.

Shilling, C. & Bernard, J. (1964) 'Informal communication among bioscientists', Report 16A, George Washington University, Washington, D.C.

Schein, E. H. (1978) *Career Dynamics.* Reading, MA: Addison-Wesley.

Tushman, M. (1977) 'Technical communication in R&D laboratories: the impact of project work characteristics', *Academy of Management Journal,* Vol. 20, 624–645.

Walsh, V. M. & Baker, A. G. (1972) 'Project management and communication patterns in industrial research', *R&D Management,* Vol. 2, 103–109.

A Longitudinal Study of the Effects of Boundary Spanning Supervision on Turnover and Promotion in Research and Development

Ralph Katz

Michael L. Tushman

Abstract. An investigation of the influence of boundary spanning project supervisors on the turnover and promotion of engineering professionals found that, in general, boundary spanning supervisors had little direct effect on the careers of all project subordinates. However, project supervisors who also were technical gatekeepers significantly affected the organizational careers of young engineers.

What factors influence turnover and promotion in research, development, and engineering (RD&E) settings? One research stream has looked at the effects of job experiences and formal supervision on turnover, performance, and promotion (Andrews & Farris, 1967; Berlew & Hall, 1966); others have looked at the norms and climate created in the laboratory (Barth & Vertinsky, 1975; Pelz & Andrews, 1966); and still others have looked at the effects of informal communication networks and boundary spanning roles (Allen, 1977; Katz & Tushman, 1981). In RD&E settings, boundary spanning individuals are key actors in the laboratory's communication and information processing activities (Tushman

& Nadler, 1980). The present study focuses on formal and informal aspects of leadership by investigating (over a 5-year period) the influence of boundary spanning supervisors on the turnover and promotions of their project subordinates. Underlying the study is the basic idea that career decisions are strongly affected by how well individuals are linked into their organization's formal and informal networks (Graen & Ginsburgh, 1977; Organ & Greene, 1972).

LITERATURE REVIEW AND HYPOTHESES

To keep informed about relevant external developments as well as new work requirements, project teams must gather information from a variety

From the *Academy of Management Journal*, 1983, Vol. 26, No. 3, 437–456. Reprinted by permission.

of outside sources. Such contact is especially critical for RD&E project teams, given their dependence on new technological advances within the larger professional community as well as their need to coordinate with other organizational areas (Roberts & Fusfeld, 1982; Utterback, 1974).

Although RD&E groups must acquire outside information, considerable research has shown that widespread direct contact by all engineering project members is *not* an effective method for communicating outside the project group. Instead, boundary spanning project members are needed to link project teams effectively to outside sources of relevant information. As discussed by Allen (1977) and Katz and Tushman (1979), special project members, labelled gatekeepers, are needed to link project colleagues to key sources of information both inside and outside the organization. Other project members, labelled internal liaisons, link project colleagues only to sources of information within the organization. These kinds of outside information are transmitted effectively into project groups through both types of boundary spanning individuals (Tushman, 1977). First, gatekeepers and internal liaisons gather and understand relevant outside information; subsequently they channel it in more meaningful terms to their project colleagues. Boundary spanning individuals, then, perform an extremely valuable function, for they are the principal means by which outside ideas and information are transferred effectively into RD&E project groups (Allen & Cohen, 1969; Katz & Tushman, 1981). Although both gatekeepers and internal liaisons connect project colleagues to important outside information sources within the organization, *only* gatekeepers provide an effective interface with technical knowledge and advancements *outside* the organization (Tushman & Scanlan, 1981).

Most boundary spanning individuals in RD&E are also project supervisors, although supervisory status per se does not automatically result in high communication activity either within or across organizational boundaries. Rather, project supervisors who are seen as technically competent, who keep up-to-date, and who are seen as valuable sources of ideas and information are likely to become boundary spanning individuals simply because they will be consulted and listened to more frequently on work-related matters (Rosen, Billings, & Turney, 1976). Previous research, in fact, has shown that between 70 and 80 percent of the boundary spanning individuals are also first level project supervisors. In contrast, only about half of the project supervisors perform a boundary spanning function (Allen, 1977; Schwartz & Jacobson, 1977; Tushman & Scanlan, 1981).

Even though boundary spanning has been recognized as one of the more important elements of effective leadership and managerial behavior (Graen & Ginsburgh, 1977; Likert, 1967; Mintzberg, 1973), very little is known about how boundary spanning activity relates to other important managerial functions. In addition to enhancing project effectiveness, would boundary spanning project supervisors also be more likely to affect the work activities and careers of those project members reporting to them?

Research over the past 15 years has demonstrated that interpersonal communications are the primary means by which engineering professionals acquire and disseminate important ideas and information (Allen, 1977; Katz, 1982a; Menzel, 1966). Moreover, it is through such social processes that most professionals come to learn the norms, values, and operating rules of their organization (Katz, 1980; Kerr, 1977). Rather than relying on written technical reports, publications, or other formal structures, professionals in RD&E keep abreast of new technical developments and organizational demand through informal contact and personal associations with other RD&E professionals (Allen, 1977; Farris, 1972).

If interpersonal contact and interaction are key determinants of integration and socialization in RD&E and if boundary spanning supervisors are critical players in the laboratory's communication and information processing network, then these supervisors are doing much more than simply channeling outside information into their projects' groups. Most likely, they are assuming a broader role within their work groups, becoming actively involved in the training, integration, and socialization of their subordinates. Katz and Tushman (1981) found, for example, that gate-keeping supervisors not only gathered and disseminated external information, but they also improved the external interface of their engineering subordinates by helping to direct, coach, and interpret their external communications.

As a result of their elaborate outside contact and close working relationships with project subordinates, boundary spanning supervisors not only improve their group's technical performance (Tushman & Katz, 1980), but they also may directly affect the personal growth and development of project members. To the extent that boundary spanning supervisors help project members participate and contribute more effectively within their work settings, have clearer working relationships with other corporate areas, and communicate more easily with outside professionals, project members are less likely to leave the organization (Farris, 1971; Graen & Ginsburgh, 1977; Pelz & Andrews, 1966).

Boundary spanning supervisors also are highly influential in technical, administrative, and personnel decision making (Tushman & Romanelli, 1983). Consequently, engineers assigned to work with these supervisors have better chances at gaining increased exposure and more extensive work opportunities. If boundary spanning supervisors are influential and provide their subordinates with better opportunities, then engineers working for these particular supervisors should have a greater rate of promotion. Based on these arguments, the following are hypothesized:

1. Project members working for boundary spanning supervisors are more likely to remain with the organization than are project members working for supervisors who are not boundary spanners.

2. Project members working for boundary spanning supervisors are more likely to receive promotions to management than are project members working for supervisors who are not boundary spanners.

These turnover and promotion effects are proposed for project members in general. Young employees, however, are more likely to benefit from the socialization and developmental role played by boundary spanning supervisors (Berlew & Hall, 1966). Most turnover occurs within the first few years of organizational employment (Schein, 1978). In addition, engineers usually expect promotions to managerial rank sometime between the ages of 30 and 40 (Dalton, Thompson, & Price, 1982; Ritti, 1971). It therefore is expected that the proposed relationships will be particularly strong for younger project members. Accordingly, the hypotheses will be tested for the full sample of professionals and for project members of different age groups.

Project Task Characteristics

Although the importance of boundary spanning has been well demonstrated, recent research indicates that not all RD&E projects are alike in the way they function or in the way they should be managed (Allen, Tushman, & Lee, 1979). Because of differences in work requirements, there are substantial information processing differences among groups engaged in research, development, and technical service kinds of activities.

In research activity, project members are less constrained by local organizational circumstances because the nature of their work is more universally defined. As a result, research project members can communicate effectively with professional colleagues outside the organization without the help of gatekeepers. In fact, Tushman & Katz (1980) found that research teams relying on boundary spanning gatekeepers were significantly less effective than research teams in which members kept themselves up-to-date and maintained their own external contacts. Nevertheless, research teams must be linked to other organizational areas; and evidence suggests that given the researcher's more cosmopolitan perspective, boundary spanning supervisors are an effective way to ensure their organizational coordination (Allen et al., 1979).

Development projects, on the other hand, involve less universally defined tasks in that their problems and solution strategies are defined and operationalized in terms of the organization's particular strengths, interests, language schemes, and cultural norms. Because of this local orientation, communication across organizational boundaries becomes extremely difficult and ineffective for most development project members (Allen, 1977; Baker, Siegmann, & Rubenstein, 1967). Despite this difficulty, development groups must stay well informed about technical developments outside their organization and must maintain close ties with other organizational areas, marketing and operations in particular. Boundary spanning project members are needed for effective linkage of development groups with these critical information areas (Katz & Tushman, 1981).

Although technical service projects are more local in nature, their work deals with more mature technologies and existing knowledge and products (Rosenbloom & Wolek, 1970). As a result, members of technical service projects can rely more easily on established practices and procedures. In technical service work, therefore, boundary spanning individuals are not necessary because project members can be kept sufficiently informed about external events and information through formal hierarchies and operating procedures (Tushman & Katz, 1980; Walsh & Baker, 1972).

If boundary spanning supervisors are more critical and influential in development work than in either research or technical service, then their influence on the career outcomes of engineering subordinates also should be particularly important in development projects. As a result, the following hypothesis is suggested:

3. Project work characteristics will moderate the effects that boundary spanning supervisors have on the turnover and promotion of engineering subordinates. The influence of such supervisors will be stronger in development projects than in either research or technical service.

Alternative Comparisons

To what extent are promotions simply a function of working for supervisors who are themselves promoted to higher managerial positions? Webber (1976) suggested that working for highly promotable supervisors enhances one's own chances of promotion. Boundary spanning supervisors usually are promoted (Allen, 1977; Katz & Tushman, 1981), but they comprise only a subset of supervisors who receive promotions over a given time frame. The present study investigates whether there is a particular benefit in working for boundary spanning supervisors rather than for any project supervisor who gets promoted. Furthermore, it is possible that being assigned to a high performing project group affects the turnover and promotion opportunities of young project members more than do the technical and interpersonal skills of their boundary spanning supervisors. The hypothesized relationships, therefore, also are tested and compared against the effects of working in high performing project teams.

METHOD

Setting

This study was conducted among all project members working in a large corporate RD&E facility. At the start of the study, the facility's professionals ($N = 345$) were divided into seven separate functional departments, which in turn were subdivided into 61 projects organized around specific, long term types of discipline and product focused problems. Each professional was a member of only one project group.

Five years after the initial data collection period, the titles and positions of those professionals still employed by the organization were obtained. Although the RD&E facility nearly doubled in size during this interval, longitudinal examinations reported here focus on the career histories of only those professionals employed at the start of the study. In addition, 8 percent of the project members retired during the 5-year period and consequently were excluded from all analytical investigations.

Communications, Gatekeepers, and Internal Liaisons

To measure communication activity, project members reported (on specially provided lists) those individuals with whom they had work-related oral communication on a randomly chosen day each week for 15 weeks, including whom they talked to and how many times they talked to that person during the day. Social and written communications were not reported. During the 15 weeks, the overall response rate was 93 percent. Moreover, 68 percent of all communications within the RD&E facility were reciprocally reported by both parties. As discussed by Katz and Tushman (1979), all communication data were used as reported. Given systematic bias in self-report data (e.g., supervisors overreport communication from subordinates), a 68 percent reciprocity rate over many thousands of communications represents a high level of internal reliability and provides a clear, accurate picture of each project member's communication patterns.

For each project member, six mutually exclusive communication measures were operationalized as follows:

1. *Departmental communication:* The amount of communication with other nonsupervi-

sory engineering colleagues within his or her functional department including project colleagues.

2. *Laboratory communication:* The amount of communication with other engineering colleagues within the remaining six functional departments.

3. *Immediate supervisory communication:* The amount of communication with his or her immediate project supervisor.

4. *Departmental supervisory communication:* The amount of communication with his or her departmental supervisor.

5. *Corporate communication:* The amount of communication with other individuals outside the RD&E facility but within other corporate divisions, primarily marketing and manufacturing.

6. *External professional communication:* The amount of communication with other RD&E professionals outside the parent organization, including professionals within universities, consulting firms, and various professional societies.

For each project engineer, the amount of communication to these two horizontal, two vertical, and two outside sources of information was calculated by summing the number of interactions reported during the 15 weeks (see Katz and Tushman, 1979, for details). Except for the high positive correlation between departmental and immediate supervisory communication ($r = .34$), the six measures were not significantly associated with one another.

Conceptually, gatekeepers are defined as those project members who are very high internal communicators and who also maintain very high external contacts with outside professionals. This study operationalized gatekeepers as those project members whose departmental and external professional communications were both in the top fifth of their respective distributions (Katz & Tushman, 1981; Whitley & Frost, 1973). Internal liaisons, on the other hand, were defined as those project members who were in the top fifth of both their departmental communication distribution and their communications to other functional departments and organizational divisions (Allen & Cohen, 1969; Tushman & Scanlan, 1981). Based on these definitions, 18 percent ($n = 11$) of the project supervisors functioned only as internal liaisons, 13 percent ($n = 8$) functioned only as gatekeeping supervisors, and 11.6 percent ($n = 7$) fulfilled both the gatekeeping and internal liaison roles. The remaining project supervisors ($n = 35$) were not performing a boundary spanning function either as a gatekeeper or as an internal liaison. Finally, in one of these 35 cases, the position of project manager was held temporarily by the departmental supervisor. Engineers from this group, as a result, were not included in any statistical comparisons involving prior reporting relationships.

Project Characteristics

As previously discussed, RD&E projects differ widely with respect to the generation of knowledge versus the utilization of existing knowledge and experience. Based on this dimension, project categories were organized around research, development, and technical service kinds of project activities. Using definitions described in Katz and Tushman (1979), project members indicated how well each category represented the objectives of their project work. As in Pelz and Andrews (1966), project members also indicated the percentage of their project activities that fell into each of the possible project categories. A weighted average of the answers to these two questions was calculated for each project member (Spearman-Brown reliability = .91).

To categorize projects empirically, project member responses were averaged to yield 14 research, 24 development, and 23 technical service project groupings. As discussed by Tushman (1977), the homogeneity of members' perceptions of their project characteristics also was checked to ensure the appropriateness of aggregating across individual scores.

Project Performance

To get comparable measures of project performance across significantly different technologies, all departmental and laboratory managers ($N = 9$) were interviewed individually and asked to evaluate the overall technical performance of all projects with which they were sufficiently familiar. When they could not make an informed judgment, they did not rate that project. Each project was independently evaluated by an average of five managers using a 7-point Likert type scale ranging from (1) very low to (7) very high. Individual ratings were averaged to yield overall project performance scores (Spearman-Brown reliability = .81). To classify project members according to whether they were working in a high or low performing project team, project groups were split at the sample mean of 4.59.

Promotion and Turnover

Almost five years after the collection of the preceding data, data on managerial promotions and turnover were gathered. Despite the facility's strong growth, 31 percent of the project members and 19 percent of the project supervisors had left the company during this time interval. Furthermore, among the 15 gatekeepers and 18 internal liaison supervisors, the turnover rates were 20 and 17 percent, respectively.

In this organization, managerial positions and titles start within the department above the project supervisory level. During the 5-year interim period, 11 percent of the project members and 46.5 percent of the project supervisors had been promoted to management positions. Although less than half of the project supervisors had received management positions, 73.3 percent of the gatekeeping subset and 67 percent of the internal liaison subset had been promoted to management levels.

RESULTS

Turnover

The first hypothesis was concerned with the influence of boundary spanning supervisors on the turnover rates of project engineers. Table 1 reports the percentages of project members who remained with the organization over the 5-year period as a function of their prior type of supervision. For the sample as a whole, project members who reported to gatekeeping supervisors had a significantly lower rate of organizational turnover than did engineers assigned to supervisors who were either nonboundary spanners or only internal liaisons. Engineers who reported to internal liaisons had the lowest retention rate

over the 5-year period (only 62 percent); those who reported to gatekeeping supervisors or supervisors who were *both* gatekeepers and internal liaisons had the highest retention rates (82 and 85 percent, respectively). Clearly, gatekeepers had a more positive effect on retention rates than did internal liaisons. Furthermore, project members assigned to those supervisors who received promotions did not stay with the organization any longer than did members who worked for unpromoted supervisors (Table 1B). Similarly, engineers who worked in high performing projects did not remain with the organization any longer than did those who worked in low performing projects.

Because 70 percent of the turnover occurred for project members less than 36 years of age, additional comparisons were carried out for separate age groupings. Except for gatekeeping supervisors, these additional comparisons failed to uncover any significant turnover differences

TABLE 1. *Supervisory Influence on the Proportion of Engineers Remaining in the Organization over a 5-year Period*

	A. Prior Type of Reporting Relationship: Engineer Worked for a Supervisor Who Was:			
	Internal Liaison	Gatekeeper	Gatekeeper and Internal Liaison	Neither a Liaison nor a Gatekeeper
% Remaining in organization after 5 years (N)	62%[b] (45)	82%[a] (28)	85%[a] (20)	70%[b] (115)

	B. Did Engineer Work for a Supervisor Who Was Subsequently Promoted to a Managerial Position?		C. Did Engineer Work in a Project That Was:	
	Yes	No	High Performing	Low Performing
% Remaining in organization after 5 years (N)	67.6% (102)	71.7% (106)	73.7% (114)	63.5% (104)
	Not significantly different		Not significantly different	

[a,b]Based on *T*-tests, percentages superscripted "a" are significantly greater than those superscripted "b" ($p < .10$).

N: The *N*'s in sections A and B are based on engineers from only 60 projects. In section *C, N* is based on engineers from all 61 projects.

among prior types of reporting relationships of high and low project performance. To pinpoint the influence of gatekeepers on subordinate turnover, Figure 1 plots as a function of age the cumulative retention rates of project members reporting to gatekeeping supervisors (Group A) and those members not reporting to gatekeeping supervisors (Group B). In Figure 1, as well as in the rest of this paper, the term gatekeeping supervisors refers to supervisors who were either functioning only as gatekeepers or functioning simultaneously as gatekeepers and internal liaisons. Nongatekeeping supervisors refers to the rest of the supervisory population.

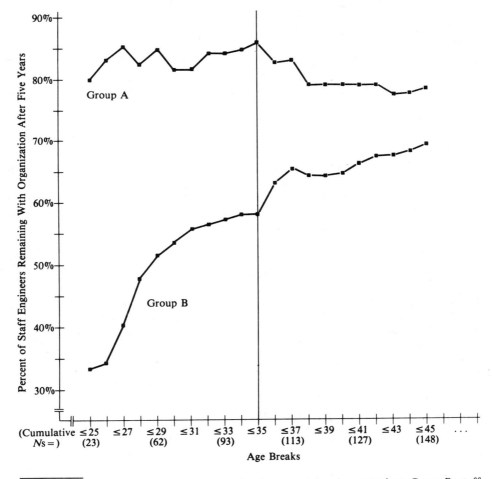

^aGroup A: staff engineers who reported directly to a gatekeeping supervisor; Group B: staff engineers who reported directly to a nongatekeeping supervisor. The vertical line indicates that pairwise percentages between Groups A and B remained significantly different (p < .05) through an age break of 35 years. Ns represent the total number of engineers within both groups at six representative age breaks.

FIGURE 1.   *Retention of Engineers after Five Years by Prior Type of Reporting Relationships at Successive Age Breaks*^a

Of those project subordinates who were age 25 or less, only 33 percent remained in the organization if they had *not* reported to a gatekeeping supervisor. The comparable percentage for project members assigned to a gatekeeping supervisor was almost 80 percent. Similarly, of those project subordinates who were 35 years old or less, only 57 percent remained with the organization if they had *not* been working with a gatekeeping supervisor. The comparable percentage in Group A was 84 percent. Although this difference is statistically significant, the figure clearly shows that most of the difference in retention rates between Groups A and B occurs among members between the ages of 25 and 29. Retention rates between the two groups converge rather quickly after age 35.

Based on the curves in Figure 1, there appear to be at least three distinct age breaks: (1) less than 30; (2) 30–35; and (3) 36 or more. Using these age breaks, Table 2 shows that project subordinates less than 30 years of age were significantly more likely to remain in the organization if they had been working with a gatekeeping supervisor. Over 84 percent of these engineers were still with the organization after five years versus only 51 percent for the parallel group of young engineers not reporting to gatekeeping supervisors. Similar significant differences in turnover, however, did not emerge between project members for each of the two remaining age categories.

In project groups, individuals functioning as gatekeepers are not always the project's supervisor. In the sample, there were five projects in which one of the members, and not the project supervisor, was functioning as a gatekeeper. Although this number of cases is rather small, the turnover pattern of engineers from these five groups was nearly the same as the turnover pattern from projects without any gatekeeper. For members less than 35 years of age, for example, the 5-year retention rate from projects without gatekeepers was 56 percent; the comparable retention rate from the five projects that had only a nonsupervisory gatekeeper was also low, only 58 percent. The retention rate with a gatekeeping supervisor was significantly higher at 84 percent. Although collegial gatekeepers are important in obtaining needed technical information, apparently only a gatekeeping supervisor has strong positive effects on early socialization and developmental processes.

Although gatekeeping supervisors may have led to reduced turnover levels among young project subordinates, Hypothesis 3 suggests that these effects might be stronger for members of development project groups. This possibility was reported in Table 3, which compares the turnover rates of project engineers less than 30 years of

TABLE 2.   *Proportion of Engineers Remaining in the Organization after Five Years by Prior Age and Reporting Relationship*

Prior Age of Engineers	Prior Reporting Relationship Percent		Proportional Differences
	Assigned to a Gatekeeping Supervisor	Not Assigned to a Gatekeeping Supervisor	
Less than 30	84.6 ($n=13$)	51.0 ($n=49$)	33.6*
Between 30 and 35	83.3 ($n=12$)	66.7 ($n=27$)	16.6
Greater than 35	78.3 ($n=23$)	78.6 ($n=84$)	.3

*$p < .05$

TABLE 3. *Proportion of Young Engineers (<30) Remaining in the Organization After Five Years by Prior Reporting Relationship and Project Task Areas[a]*

	Prior Reporting Relationship Percent		
Prior Project Areas	Assigned to a Gatekeeping Supervisor	Not Assigned to a Gatekeeping Supervisor	Proportional Differences
Applied research	83.3	44.4	38.9
	($n = 6$)	($n = 9$)	
Product/process development	75.0	53.8	21.2
	($n = 4$)	($n = 26$)	
Technical service	100.0	50.0	50.0
	($n = 3$)	($n = 14$)	

[a]Because of small sample sizes, statistical tests are not used; instead, the focus is on the overall consistent pattern of positive proportional differences.

age for each project category. The turnover differences between project subordinates with and without gatekeeping supervisors was consistently positive for each project area, although the small number of cases precludes statistical testing. For each project area, approximately half of the young project members not reporting to a gatekeeping supervisor had left the company within five years despite substantial growth within the RD&E facility. In sharp contrast, none of the corresponding turnover rates for project members reporting to a gatekeeping supervisor exceeded 25 percent.

Clearly gatekeeping supervisors had considerable influence over the turnover rates of young professionals within this facility. What is it about gatekeeping supervisors that brings about these lower levels of turnover? As previously discussed, turnover may be a function of how well young professionals get integrated into their organization's formal and informal networks. Because gatekeepers are key individuals in these networks, reporting to a gatekeeping supervisor may well facilitate the young professional's linkages to important information sources both within and outside the organization. An investigation was made as to whether young project members reporting to gatekeeping supervisors had different interaction patterns than did project members reporting to nongatekeeping supervisors. Table 4 reports mean communication scores broken down by supervisory relationships and turnover. Separate comparisons are reported for communication to each of the six information sources used in the study.

As shown in Table 4, there were no significant differences between the communication patterns of young engineers who worked for gatekeeping supervisors and those who worked for nongatekeeping supervisors. Their levels of interaction were very similar in each communication area. Furthermore, regardless of their supervisory reporting relationship, project members who either stayed or left did not differ in the intensity of their prior horizontal collegial interactions or in their contacts with individuals and professionals outside the RD&E facility. What differentiated young stayers from leavers was their level of contact with their project and departmental supervisors; that is, their degree of vertical communication and integration. For both gatekeeping and nongatekeeping relationships, project subordinates who remained over the five years had significantly more communication with their departmental supervisor than did project members who left. Stayers also had more interaction with their project supervisors, although the difference was not quite significant

TABLE 4.   *Mean Communications of Young Engineers (<30 years) Broken Down by Prior Reporting Relationship and Subsequent Turnover*

Prior Measures of Communication (per Month)	Prior Reporting Relationship	
	Assigned to a Gatekeeping Supervisor	Not Assigned to a Gatekeeping Supervisor
Horizontal communications with:		
1. Departmental colleagues		
a. Engineers who remained	117.8	104.8
b. Engineers who left	110.2	113.4
2. Laboratory colleagues		
a. Engineers who remained	28.2	26.3
b. Engineers who left	27.1	24.8
Vertical communications with:		
3. Immediate supervisor		
a. Engineers who remained	30.1[a]	27.6
b. Engineers who left	8.8[b]	19.0
4. Department supervisor		
a. Engineers who remained	4.9[a]	3.6[a]
b. Engineers who left	0.0[b]	1.2[b]
Outside communications with:		
5. Other corporate areas		
a. Engineers who remained	17.9	20.8
b. Engineers who left	25.8	17.4
6. External professionals		
a. Engineers who remained	1.1	2.1
b. Engineers who left	5.8	2.0

[a,b]For each pair, communication means superscripted "a" are significantly greater than those superscripted "b" ($p < .05$). *N*s can be found in Table 2.

for members who reported to nongatekeeping supervisors.

What are the relative effects of prior communication and reporting relationships on subsequent turnover? A hierarchical discriminant analysis was run on the turnover outcomes of the 62 project members less than 30 years of age using the six communication measures and the prior reporting relationship (coded "1" and "0" for working with and without a gatekeeping supervisor) as possible differentiating variables. After both measures of vertical communication entered the discriminant analysis significantly, none of the remaining independent variables, in-cluding reporting to a gatekeeping supervisor, accounted for any significant amount of additional discrimination between stayers and leavers. Using the Wilks Lambda criterion, the discriminant function containing both vertical communication variables was significant at the $p < .05$ level ($x^2 = 6.13; DF = 2$) and correctly classified 74 percent of the project subordinates. Thus, it is not the assignment of young project members to a gatekeeping supervisor per se that enhances long term retention. What really makes the difference is the high level of vertical interaction that takes place between gatekeeping supervisors and their young engineering subordinates.

In testing the hypotheses, it is important to mention that age really serves as a surrogate means for examining employees at similar career stages. Strictly speaking, several cohorts of employees at different career stages would be the most advantageous method for testing the influence of gatekeeping on project subordinates. In a field study of the sort, however, such cohorts are unavailable. Furthermore, there simply were not enough turnover cases, especially with gatekeeping supervisors, even to begin to determine whether age, tenure, or some other career variable is most appropriate. In any event, age and tenure are so highly congruent for very young employees that any distinction would be primarily conceptual rather than yielding any clear empirical differences.

Managerial Promotions

During the five years, 23 of the project members were promoted to managerial positions. Table 5

reports promotion percentages for different types of prior reporting relationships. As with turnover, project members who reported to gatekeeping supervisors had a significantly higher rate of promotion than did project members who reported to other kinds of supervisors, including internal liaisons. Furthermore, individuals assigned to supervisors who were subsequently promoted were no more likely to get promoted than were individuals who worked for unpromoted supervisors. Similarly, individuals from high performing projects did not receive proportionately more promotions than did individuals from low performing projects.

Because almost 70 percent of the project members promoted to managerial positions were between the ages of 27 and 32 at the start of our study, the data within this more limited age range were reanalyzed. As before, the various types of reporting relationships revealed no important effects on promotion rates within this restricted subsample, except for the comparison of gate-

TABLE 5. *Supervisory Influence on the Proportion of Engineers Promoted to Managerial Level Positions over a 5-year Period*

	A. Prior Type of Reporting Relationship: Engineer Worked for a Supervisor Who Was:			
	Internal Liaison	Gatekeeper	Gatekeeper and Internal Liaison	Neither a Liaison nor a Gatekeeper
% Promoted to managerial positions after 5 years	11.1%[b]	14.3%[a]	15.0%[a]	11.3%[b]

	B. Did Engineer Work for a Supervisor Who Was Subsequently Promoted to a Managerial Position?		C. Did Engineer Work in a Project That Was:	
	Yes	No	High Performing	Low Performing
% Promoted to managerial positions after 5 years	11.8%	10.4%	9.6%	12.5%
	Not significantly different		Not significantly different	

[a,b]Based on *T*-tests, percentages superscripted "a" are significantly greater than those superscripted "b" ($p < .10$).

N: The *N*s in sections A and B are based on engineers from only 60 projects. In section C, *N* is based on engineers from all 61 projects.

keeping versus nongatekeeping supervisors (Table 6). For this comparison, the difference was significant; for project members who reported to a gatekeeping supervisor, the promotion rate was 41.2 percent, whereas only 17.4 percent of the engineers reported to a nongatekeeping supervisor were similarly promoted.

Although proportionately more engineers who had reported to gatekeepers were promoted to management within this general subsample, Table 6 shows that most of this difference can be found in the area of product and process development. No significant advantage was found in the promotion rates of project engineers reporting to gatekeepers in either research or technical service areas. On the other hand, two-thirds of the engineers reporting to gatekeepers in development projects received management promotions, in contrast to only 18.5 percent of the engineers reporting to nongatekeepers, although once again the number of cases is rather small. Nonetheless, development work is precisely the project area in which gatekeepers presumably are most necessary and influential and in which they were hypothesized to have the strongest influence over managerial promotions.

As in the turnover analyses, the communication patterns of project members within the 27–32 year old age range were examined to see if those promoted also had differential patterns of contacts and interactions within their work settings. None of the communication measures, however, was significantly related to managerial promotions for these individuals.

Discussion

The research findings presented here support the idea that supervisory behavior is an important factor in the making of one's organizational and professional career. Not all supervisors in the study, however, had comparable relationships with the career outcomes of their engineering subordinates. Only boundary spanning gatekeeping supervisors were significantly associated with reduced turnover rates and higher rates of subordinate promotion to management. These associations, moreover, were particularly strong for

TABLE 6.   *Proportion of Engineers Promoted to High Level Managerial Positions over the Next Five Years by Prior Reporting Relationship and Project Task Areas*[a]

| | Prior Reporting Relationship Percent | | |
Prior Project Areas	Assigned to a Gatekeeping Supervisor	Not Assigned to a Gatekeeping Supervisor	Proportional Differences
Across all areas	41.2 ($n=17$)	17.4 ($n=46$)	23.8*
By project area			
Applied research	33.3 ($n=6$)	20.0 ($n=10$)	13.3
Product/process development	66.7 ($n=6$)	18.5 ($n=27$)	48.2**
Technical service	20.0 ($n=5$)	11.1 ($n=9$)	8.9

[a]Table includes only those engineers in the age range (27 through 32) in which almost 70 percent of the promotions took place.
*$p<.10$
**$p<.05$

young professionals. They disappeared for older, more experienced engineers.

On a percentage basis, more young engineers who had gatekeeping supervisors remained with the firm than did those whose supervisors were not gatekeepers. Why were these gatekeepers so strongly related to lower levels of turnover? Was it the result of their supervisory status, their technical ability, or their outside professional contacts? These characteristics certainly are important, but the results on communication suggest that gatekeepers were related to the low turnover among their young project subordinates because of the high levels of hierarchical interaction and activity that took place between them. Because gatekeeping supervisors are technically competent, interpersonally active, and they readily identify with the professional orientations of young engineers, they establish close working relationships with most of their project subordinates, almost 85 percent in the study. It was this high level of hierarchical activity and concern that discriminated between young engineers who stayed and those who left. In the relatively few cases in which gatekeeping supervisors either failed to communicate or denied access to their young subordinates, these individuals probably became disenchanted, gave up, and left. Thus, it may not be the gatekeeping role or supervisory status per se that is related to turnover. In line with the findings of Graen and Ginsburgh (1977), what seems most beneficial are high levels of work-related contact and involvement with relevant competent supervisors—interactions that occur most frequently with gatekeeping supervisors.

In addition to these turnover relationships, gatekeeping supervisors were linked to the managerial promotions of project subordinates who were between the ages of 27 and 32 at the start of the study. Within this age range, project members working for gatekeeping supervisors attained a significantly higher rate of promotion to management than did project members working for nongatekeeping supervisors. Furthermore,

the promotion rate for young project members reporting to gatekeepers in development areas was more than three times the promotion rate of development project members assigned to non-gatekeeping supervisors. In development work, gatekeepers are highly influential individuals who strongly enhance project performance by connecting engineers to more useful ideas and information outside the project. Having better access to critical information, along with working for influential supervisors, may be associated with greater work opportunities and organizational visibility which, in turn, lead to higher rates of management promotion.

IMPLICATIONS AND CONCLUSIONS

From a broader perspective, the relationship between lower turnover and high interpersonal involvement with gatekeeping supervisors affirms the important role that project supervisors can and should play during the early socialization years of young professionals. As discussed by Schein (1978) and Katz (1980), young employees build perceptions of their work environment and establish their new organization identities through the plethora of interactions and interpersonal activities that take place during the early years of their laboratory integration. Young engineers, therefore, not only need to interact with their colleagues and peers, but they also require considerable interaction with and feedback from relevant supervisors to learn what is expected of them and to decipher how to be a high performing contributor.

Because they are well-connected professionally and organizationally, gatekeepers are particularly qualified to meet the breaking-in concerns of young professionals, directing and coupling the professional orientations of young engineers with a more appropriate organizational focus. Most likely, the high level of interpersonal contact between gatekeeping supervisors and young project engineers not only facilitates socialization but also results in more accurate expectations, perceptions, and understanding about one's role in the project and in the larger organization—all of which are important in decreasing the turnover of newcomers (Katz, 1980; Pondy, 1978; Wanous, 1980).

These results, then, combined with other research evidence—for example, Dalton et al. (1982), Graen and Ginsburgh (1977), and Vicino and Bass (1978)—indicate that becoming an integral part of an organization's communication and information processing networks and learning the organization's customs and norms are critically important during the early stages of employees' careers. Although socialization can take place in many different ways, gatekeeping supervisors appear particularly important in the organizational integration of young engineering subordinates, helping them understand and interpret the reality of their new settings in order to function more fully and meaningfully within the organization. Gatekeeping supervisors, then, fulfill an important leadership and training function for young engineers, operating effectively as important socializing agents and network builders for these young employees.

Organizations have to recognize that the problems and concerns of young engineers are real and must be dealt with before they become effective organizational members. Although specific training programs could be developed to teach project managers how to "break-in" the young engineer more effectively, the careful selection of supervisors for young professionals also would go a long way toward alleviating many of the problems that usually occur during this joining-up process.

It is also important to note that gatekeeping supervisors were not related to the career outcomes of their older employees. Individuals in the innovation or stabilization phases of their careers have a more clearly developed sense of personal identity and organizational reality—their reputations and areas of contribution being more

firmly defined (Katz, 1982b). As a result, the turnover and promotion rates of these more established veterans may be influenced more by individual differences and by task and organizational factors than by the characteristics of their immediate supervisors.

Finally, one should realize that in a longitudinal field study of this sort, the random assignment of project members to gatekeeping and nongatekeeping supervisors was not possible. Although the thinking here emphasizes the direct role that gatekeepers might play in influencing project members' careers, it also is possible that gatekeepers either attracted or were assigned members who were more likely to stay or were of higher promotion potential. Furthermore, other uncontrolled organizational factors could have influenced the results. For example, data were not collected on how long project members worked for their respective supervisors. What is known is that project members who reported to gatekeeping supervisors early in their careers had more successful organizational outcomes. It remains for future research to look even more closely at these types of relationships. Even with these traditional caveats, substantial research and practice strongly indicate that gatekeepers are extremely important in RD&E settings, not only for the effective transfer and processing of outside technical information, but also in the socialization and development of young engineers.

REFERENCES

Allen, T. J. *Managing the flow of technology.* Cambridge: MIT Press, 1977.

Allen, T. J., & Cohen, S. Information flow in R&D labs. *Administrative Science Quarterly,* 1969, 14, 12–19.

Allen, T. J., Tushman, M., & Lee, D. Technology transfer as a function of position on research, development, and technical service continuum. *Academy of Management Journal,* 1979, 22, 694–708.

Andrews, F., & Farris, G. Supervisory practices and innovation in scientific teams. *Personnel Psychology,* 1967, 20, 497–515.

Baker, N., Siegmann, J., & Rubenstein, A. Effects of perceived needs on the generation of ideas in R&D projects. *IEEE Transactions on Engineering Management,* 1967, 14, 156–163.

Barth, R., & Vertinsky, I. The effect of goal orientation and information environment in research performances. *Organizational Behavior and Human Performance,* 1975, 13, 110–132.

Berlew, D., & Hall, T. The socialization of managers: Effects of expectations on performance. *Administrative Science Quarterly,* 1966, 11, 207–223.

Dalton, G., Thompson, P., & Price, R. The four stages of professional careers: A new look at performance by professionals. In R. Katz (Ed.), *Career issues in human resource management.* Englewood Cliffs, N. J.: Prentice-Hall, 1982, 129–153.

Farris, G. A predictive study of turnover. *Personnel Psychology,* 1971, 24, 311–328.

Farris, G. The effect of individual roles on performance in innovative groups. *R&D Management,* 1972, 3, 23–28.

Graen, G., & Ginsburgh, S. Job resignation as a function of role orientation and leader acceptance. *Organizational Behavior and Human Performance,* 1977, 19, 1–17.

Katz, R. Time and work: Toward an integrative perspective. In B. Staw & L. L. Cummings (Eds.), *Research in organizational behavior* (Vol. 2). Greenwich, Conn.: JAI Press, 1980, 81–127.

Katz, R. The effects of group longevity on project communication and performance. *Administrative Science Quarterly,* 1982a, 27, 81–104.

Katz, R. Managing careers: The influence of job and group longevities. In R. Katz (Ed.), *Career issues in human resource management.* Englewood Cliffs, N. J.: Prentice-Hall, 1982b, 154–181.

Katz, R., & Tushman, M. Communication patterns, project performance and task characteristics: An empirical evaluation and integration in an R&D setting. *Organizational Behavior and Human Performance,* 1979, 23, 139–162.

Katz, R., & Tushman, M. An investigation into the managerial roles and career paths of gatekeepers and project supervisors in a major R&D facility. *R&D Management,* 1981, 11, 103–110.

Kerr, S. Substitutes for leadership: Some implications for organizational design. *Organization and Administrative Sciences,* 1977, 2, 135–146.

Likert, R. *The human organization.* New York: McGraw-Hill, 1967.

Menzel, H. Information needs and uses in science and technology. In C. Cuadra (Ed.), *Annual review of information science and technology.* New York: Wiley, 1966, 41–69.

Mintzberg, H. *The nature of managerial work.* New York: Harper and Row, 1973.

Organ, D., & Greene, C. The boundary relevance of the project manager's job. *R&D Management,* 1972, 3, 7–11.

Pelz, A., & Andrews, F. M. *Scientists in organizations.* New York: Wiley, 1966.

Pondy, L. Leadership is a language game. In M. McCall & M. Lombardo (Eds.), *Leadership: Where else can we go?* Durham, N.C.: Duke University Press, 1978, 87–99.

Ritti, R. *The engineer in the industrial corporation.* New York: Columbia University Press, 1971.

Roberts, E. B., & Fusfeld, A. R. Critical functions: Needed roles in the innovation process. In R. Katz (Ed.), *Career issues in human resource management.* Englewood Cliffs, N.J.: Prentice-Hall, 1982, 182–207.

Rosen, N., Billings, R., Turney, J. The emergence and allocation of leadership resources over time in a technical organization. *Academy of Management Journal,* 1976, 19, 165–183.

Rosenbloom, R., & Wolek, F. *Technology and information transfer.* Boston: Harvard Business School, 1970.

Schein, E. *Career dynamics: Matching individual and organizational needs.* Reading, Mass.: Addison-Wesley, 1978.

Schwartz, D., & Jacobson, E. Organizational communication network analysis: The liaison role. *Organizational Behavior and Human Performance,* 1977, 18, 158–174.

Tushman, M. Communication across organizational boundaries: Special boundary roles in the innovation process. *Administrative Science Quarterly,* 1977, 22, 587–605.

Tushman, M., & Katz, R. External communication and project performance: An investigation into the role of gatekeepers. *Management Science,* 1980, 26, 1071–1085.

431

Tushman, M., & Nadler, D. Communication and technical roles in R&D laboratories. In B. Dean & J. Goldhar (Eds.), *Management of research and innovation.* New York: TIMS, North Holland Publishing Co., 1980, 91–112.

Tushman, M., & Romanelli, E. Uncertainty, social location, and influence in decision making: A sociometric analysis. *Management Science,* 28, 1983.

Tushman, M., & Scanlan, T. Boundary spanning individuals: Their role in information transfer and their antecedents. *Academy of Management Journal,* 1981, 24, 289–305.

Utterback, J. Innovation in industry and the diffusion of technology. *Science,* 1974, 183, 620–626.

Vicino, F. L., & Bass, B. M. Lifespace variables and managerial success. *Journal of Applied Psychology,* 1978, 63, 81–88.

Walsh, V., & Baker, A. Project management and communication patterns in industrial research. *R&D Management,* 1972, 2, 103–109.

Wanous, J. *Organizational entry.* Reading, Mass.: Addison-Wesley, 1980.

Webber, R. Career problems of young managers. *California Management Review,* 1976, 18, 19–33.

Whitley, R., & Frost, P. Task type and information transfer in a government research lab. *Human Relations,* 1973, 25, 537–550.

10

THE ROLE OF STRUCTURE AND CLIMATE

A Skunkworks Tale

Thomas J. Peters

Innovation is unpredictable. It thrives in the chaos of "skunkworks," where product champions go scrounging for success.

Yellow Post-it Note Pads have quickly become as commonplace in the American office as paper clips. The product is a $100 million winner for 3M. The idea behind it came from a 3M employee who sang in a choir. The slips of paper he used to mark the hymnals kept falling out, and it dawned on him that adhesive-backed pieces of paper might solve his problem.

The requisite technology existed, and a prototype was soon available. "Great story," you say—but wait, this tale's not quite over yet. Major office-supply distributors thought the idea was silly. Market surveys were negative. But 3M secretaries got hooked on the product once they actually used it. Post-it's breakthrough finally came when 3M mailed samples to the personal secretaries of Fortune 500 CEOs, using the letterhead of the 3M chairman's secretary.

The Post-it story would amount to nothing more than a charming tale were this development process not repeatedly played out at companies across the U.S. The course of innovation (idea generation, prototype development, contact with an initial user, and breakthrough to the final market) is highly uncertain. Moreover, it will always be sloppy, disorganized, and unpredictable, and that is the important point. It's important because we must learn to design organizations that explicitly take into account the unavoidable sloppiness of the process and use it to their advantage rather than fight it.

From America's best-run companies come tales of incredible perseverance, countless experiments, perverse and unusual product-users, five-person "skunkworks" sequestered in dingy warehouses for 60 days, plans gone awry, inventions made in the wrong industry at the wrong time for the wrong reason, and specifications for complex systems scrawled across the backs of en-

From *The Stanford Magazine,* 1983. Reprinted by permission.

velopes. Innovation just doesn't happen the way it's supposed to.

THE 10 MYTHS OF INNOVATION

The hyperorganized approach leads companies to fall prey to the 10 myths of innovation management, which have already hampered many a firm. These false beliefs must be put to rest, and the sloppy side of innovation must be exploited. The 10 myths are as follows:

1. Specs and a market plan are the first steps to success.
2. Detailed strategic and technological plans greatly increase the odds of a no-surprises outcome.
3. Only a big team can blitz a project, especially if it is a complex one.
4. Contemplation stimulates creativity.
5. Big projects are inherently different from small projects and must be managed differently.
6. An organization must have a rigid hierarchy if would-be innovators are to get a fair hearing.
7. Product compatibility is the key to economic success.
8. Customers will tell you only about yesterday's needs.
9. Technology push is the cornerstone of success.
10. Perfectionism pays off.

Some companies love to make plans more than they love to make profitable new products. In these bureaucratic behemoths, someone's bright idea is turned into a six-month, $2 million study—a paper study. A paper evaluation of the study by various interested parties takes another three months. Some sort of design go-ahead is given, and writing the technical specs, at a cost of $3 million, takes six more months. The specs are evaluated in the four months after that.

During this last stage, a prototype is finally built. It costs $5 million to $10 million and takes four to six months to complete. And guess what? It doesn't work. Throughout the history of successful corporate innovation—from the development of French-fries seasoning at McDonald's to faded jeans at Levi Strauss & Company to the System 360 computer at IBM—neither the first nor the second prototype has *ever* worked. The successful innovators just go back to the drawing board.

But now the people in charge of the project really begin to sweat. By this time, careers are on the line and a lot of time, money, and pride has been invested in the design. So now they enter the ''ignore the misfit data and make the damn thing work'' stage. Meanwhile, the competitors have introduced three or four new products, each with several new features. As time goes by, the plodding planners fall further behind. So they recomplicate the product. ''We're going to get it exactly right,'' they boast. But when they finally get it to the marketplace, it's adorned with so many bells and whistles that it doesn't work well.

This mentality is the antithesis of the Wee Willie Keeler approach. Wee Willie Keeler was a consummate opportunist who played baseball from 1892 to 1910. He once said, ''Hit 'em where they ain't,'' and he proved that strategy's worth by making it into the Baseball Hall of Fame even though he stroked only 34 home runs in 19 seasons. His approach is imitated to a T by firms like Hewlett-Packard, 3M, McDonald's, Wang Laboratories, PepsiCo, Citicorp, Johnson & Johnson, Digital Equipment, and others like them. This philosophy says, in effect: *Start out by spending $25,000, or even as much as a quarter of a million dollars. Build a prototype, or a big hunk of one, in the first 60 to 90 days. And then poke it to see if it moves.*

Whether projects like these involve aircraft, missiles, or French fries, the results achieved by scores of companies suggest that something can always be built in this length of time. The evaluation of the prototype should take another 60 days. (Even at such an early stage, firms following this approach may decide—explicitly or not—to start up a second team doing roughly the same work as the first, just to get a different look.)

"We're already playing with something tangible," say project leaders at these companies. "Now we take the next little step. We build another new version in 90 days. It's a more developed prototype that will cost a little more, around $100,000 to $200,000. After it's built, we can probably get it, or part of it, into a user's hands—not an average user (that's still years away), but a lead user who's willing to experiment with us. Even an in-house lead user might do the trick." And on goes the process, always involving investments that increase little by little and time-frames that do the same.

At each step the innovators learn a little more, because they set up harsh reality tests with hard products and real users. If something doesn't work, they weed it out quickly before career lock-in and irreversible psychological addiction to hitting home runs take place.

In the aircraft manufacturing industry, one such harsh confrontation with reality is known as the chicken test. Aircraft engines have to be built to withstand possible ingestion of flocks of birds. To determine what would happen in that unlikely event, engineers buy 15 or 20 gross of chickens, stuff some into a cannon with a barrel four feet in diameter, and fire them at engines running full throttle. It's the ultimate pragmatic test. Rolls-Royce spent several years and several hundred million dollars on a new graphite-material engine. After all that, it failed the chicken test.

What the Wee Willie Keeler, or experimental, approach boils down to is getting your inevitable chicken test out of the way early. Every new product fails a chicken test or two at some point. The burning issue is, when does it fail? At the end of four years, by which time the competitors have a new array of products on the market? Or at the end of 90 days?

BUREAUCRACY UNDER ATTACK

Strategic planning is being attacked on all fronts. Many claim that it is too rigid. Others say it's too bureaucratic. Some believe that corporations should at least decentralize such planning (General Electric and Westinghouse, who were early pioneers in strategic planning, are doing just that). A few even suggest that we get rid of it altogether.

But do we really want to do that? The new "in" terms are *technology* and *production*. "Technology planning" and "manufacturing planning" are the preferred substitutes for strategic planning. Before heading off down a new trail, though, let's look at the record of technology planning. It's hardly spotless.

Think of recent inventions that we're all familiar with. "We do not consider that the aeroplane will be of any use for war purposes," declared the British minister of war in 1910. In the late 1940s, market research predicted that the total sales of mainframe computers would be about a dozen. Even though the robotics industry is crowded with such competitors as United Technologies Corporation, General Electric, Westinghouse Electric, and IBM, the first "intelligent mobile robot" will come from a less-than-household name—Denning Systems Inc. of Washington, D.C., a classic three-inventors-in-a-garage operation.

A highly systematic analysis of this phenomenon may be found in the book *The Sources of Invention* by John Jewkes, a professor of economic organization at Oxford University. After studying the development of 58 of this century's major inventions, Jewkes concluded that at least 46 of them occurred in "the wrong place." Note the unusual origins of the following inventions:

- Kodachrome film was invented by a couple of musicians.
- A watchmaker fooling around with brass castings came up with the process involved in the continuous casting of steel.
- The developers of the jet engine were told by reciprocating-aircraft-engine people that it was useless. (They finally peddled their invention not to engine-makers but to air-frame-makers.)

According to Jewkes, there is no industry group in which much innovation has taken place as or when it was supposed to. On top of this, "the initial use and vision for a new product is virtually never the one that is ultimately of the greatest importance commercially," reports Jim Utterback, an MIT associate professor of engineering who for more than a decade has studied the development of inventions. He has concluded that users play a special role in this process. To support his point, he recounts the path to success of invention after invention.

His analysis of incandescent lighting is typical. Its first use was on ships, which in retrospect seems natural enough: it's dangerous to keep gas lamps on a seafaring vessel, whose rolling motion can upset them. Thus the incandescent light found its first home in a highly specialized market niche. Then, in a move that *every* market-research department could easily have predicted, incandescent lighting spread to—baseball parks! Night games have been with us ever since. From there the invention moved to neighborhoods, where it replaced gas streetlamps, and only 15 years later did incandescent lights begin to make it into homes. As a more recent example of this pattern, transistors were first used for missile guidance systems; their use by home consumers lagged 20 years behind.

The role of corporations in all this is truly frightening. Organizations have an apparently inherent tendency to make exactly the wrong moves in trying to stimulate innovation, accord-ing to Utterback, who states, "In 32 of 34 companies, the current product leaders reduced investment in the new technology in order to pour more money into the old."

Not only, then, does the leader *not* embrace the new, he actually reduces his investment in the new to hold on to the old. The problems involved in switching to a new technology are manifold. First, there's scientific hubris (the engineer knows best, he can predict the use of the product most accurately); then comes marketing hubris (how could all those tons of data on the Edsel be wrong?). Jewkes offers three rules of thumb regarding technological planning, all of which are well worth heeding:

- Peering into the future is a popular and agreeable pastime that, if not taken seriously, is also comparatively innocuous.
- There is a great virtue in picking and choosing from a variety of available options.
- The industrial laboratory does not appear to be a particularly favorable environment for the inducement of innovation.

Does this mean that corporations should do away with central planning? Should centralized R&D activity be abolished? The answer is no. First, one does need to make general bets on technological directions: it's important to know the difference between, say, north and northwest. That's fine. What isn't sensible is trying to prespecify the difference between a course of 43 degrees and a course of 46 degrees. As a former managing director at the consulting firm McKinsey & Company liked to argue, "About the best you can hope for is to get the herd heading roughly west." And this is a task that centralized research can do.

"As a regimen or discipline for a group of people, planning is very valuable," notes Fletcher Bryom, the iconoclastic former chairman of Koppers Company. "My position is, go ahead and plan, but once you've done your planning, put it on the shelf. Don't be bound by it. Don't use it as a major influence on the decision-making process. Use it mainly to recognize change as it takes place.''

QUICK-AND-DIRTY SOLUTIONS

When the U-2 spy plane emerged as the country's most sophisticated airborne surveillance system 30 years ago, many experts said that it would never fly. It's still doing yeoman service. The developers were a retired aeronautical engineer named Kelly Johnson and a small band of Lockheed Corporation mavericks. They called their off-line group "the Skunk Work"—the original business use of an apt term that (as far as I can determine) may have been coined by Al Capp, who drew the comic strip *Li'l Abner.*

Lockheed is not unique. At GE the same activity is called "bootlegging"; at 3M they label it "scrounging." It would not be difficult to argue that 3M, Hewlett-Packard, Digital Equipment, and Johnson & Johnson are today nothing more than collections of skunkworks.

The finding stands out more and more clearly as the evidence rolls in: whenever a practical innovation has occurred, a skunkwork, usually with a nucleus of six to 25 people, has been at the heart of it. Most skunkworks seem to do things in an incredibly short period of time. While visiting a Westinghouse lab, General Curtis LeMay, then Chief of Staff of the Air Force, found a pencil sketch of what was at the time a beyond-the-state-of-the-art product: a side-mounted radar. He asked if he might have one within 90 days. The next day he sent Westinghouse an airplane to hang it on. He got his device less than 90 days later. In the recent book *The Soul of a New Machine* by Tracy Kidder, Data General's computer-project leader, Tom West, speculates that the company's crucial breakthrough in microcoding may have taken place in less than a week. [*Editor's note:* Microcoding builds into a computer the instructions that make it operate.]

But what happens with a quick-and-dirty skunkwork product? Is the quality as high? Does it ever fit into the rest of the product line? The record shows, delightfully, that the stuff that comes from skunkworks is often of high quality, even though it was invented in a fraction of the so-called normal time.

The creative impetus behind skunkworks boils down to ownership and commitment. In *The Soul of a New Machine,* West describes the phenomenon: "There are 30 guys out there who think they've invented it; I don't want that tampered with." Firms like 3M, Johnson & Johnson, and Hewlett-Packard all agree that in creating the sense of ownership, intense commitment, and unbounded energy that comes from turned-on teams, a surprisingly small group is optimal.

A struggle against others is also important. It, too, engenders feelings of ownership and commitment. Interestingly, its most important form is rivalry with others *inside* the company, not with an outside competitor. Few companies are really familiar with their competitors, but their divisions sure know one another. Constructive internal competition is difficult to manage. There are a great number of subtleties and traps. The net result, however, is almost always positive.

The skunkwork cannot do all things. On the other hand, the empirical indications seem to say, loud and clear, "Ignore this form of organization for innovation at your own peril." The alternative is *de novo* design of the tiniest parts, excessively long product-development cycles, large teams in which ownership and commitment are missing, do-everything-inside attitudes, over-complexity, and situations in which competing central staffs make the decisions on technical issues or delay them endlessly on the basis of the most tenuous market or financial projections. The show just doesn't get on the road.

HELL-BENT ON SUCCESS

If big, well-orchestrated teams were at the heart of successful innovation, we would expect to find them populated with powerful thinkers who regularly ascended to their mountaintop retreats to look out over the pines. As a result of such reflection, they would accomplish the necessary breakthroughs, presumably on schedule. If, on the other hand, rough-and-tumble skunkworks, hell-bent on outproducing some formal group, were the norm, we would expect to find bleary-eyed folks staring at computer screens or test tubes in dirty, forgotten basement corners.

It does turn out that bleary eyes play quite a large role in innovation. When a year's worth of work is routinely accomplished in five weeks, someone called a "champion" will be found at the heart of the operation. Formal IBM in-house studies of research projects always unearth a champion. National Science Foundation studies suggest that the champion's role in pushing an idea to fruition is crucial. When the brand manager of a consumer-goods company, even in a highly structured system, becomes a determined champion, the odds of success go up tenfold. Looking back over his career in *Adventures of a Bystander,* Peter Drucker, the noted business expert, remarks, "Whenever *anything* is accomplished, it is being done, I have learned, by a monomaniac with a mission."

A crucial corollary is that the corporation that would nourish inventors must also tolerate, even praise, failure. Going through 3M's roster of senior officers with one of the company's executives a couple of years ago, I discovered that virtually every 3M officer had reached the top because he himself had introduced several important new products. Moreover, each story, as it was recounted in conventional form, focused on the rough places in the road: the 10 years of ups and downs when the product was too advanced for the marketplace, when it had to be reformulated, when the manufacturing scale-up didn't work. Setbacks are considered standard operating procedure. Above all else, the winners are those who persist.

SMALL WITHIN BIG

Massive projects like the manned space program or the development of the transistor at AT&T Bell Labs aren't that different from less complex undertakings; they're just bigger. They too can be treated, to a substantial degree, as collections of skunkworks. In an important sense, the principle "small within big" turns out to be essential to the success of big projects. Most of the breakthroughs in these cases are the results of champions' operating off-line. Charles Brown, chairman of AT&T, said recently, "Today the long-distance network looks like one big, perfectly conceived solution. The reality that we often forget when we think about innovation planning is that the network is a collection of thousands of small breakthroughs that occurred here and there, and certainly not according to schedule or by courtesy of a flawless master plan."

The story of Boeing's recent development of the air-launched cruise missile is even more pertinent. The system is complex. Undoubtedly it should have been developed all at once, with the aid of a 100,000-bubble PERT chart (a "program evaluation and review technique" diagram that indicates the relationships among the phases of a project). The missile-development program was in fact broken down into seven major pieces. Modest-size teams were assembled to deal with the seven projects. Each task was then accomplished in a remarkably short period of time relative to the norm. Each had a champion. Each was in competition with all the others on several vital fronts.

Then what happened? You guessed it. Put the seven pieces together and they don't fit exactly right. So you have to spend some time, as much as a few months, getting the interfaces just right, despite the prior effort that went into interface specifications. (Twice-a-week meetings of a "tie-breaker" group sorted out many of the issues in question.) The final design isn't as technically beautiful as ideals of theoretical perfection suggest is possible. But multiple passes usually take less time and result in the development of simpler, more practical systems than a single everything-at-once pass. (Boeing's cruise missile was delivered more than a year ahead of schedule and well under budget.)

But back to the question of whether big differs from small. There is no question that it does. The Boeing 767 and the French-fries seasoning change at McDonald's are not the same. On the other hand, commitment, championing, small within big, piece-versus-piece competition, the overtight deadline, and the turned-on modest-size group are the keys to breaking down a big, forbidding task into smaller, more manageable ones.

CHARGED-UP TEAMS

The conventional wisdom holds that only a strong functional monolith will keep the engineers' (and innovators') viewpoint to the fore. It's a nice argument on paper, but it doesn't hold much water in practice. What actually happens is that engineers lose out to marketing and finance people in divisional organizations. The divisions are interested only in short-term profit.

By definition, the functional monolith is almost always bureaucratic; it's not oriented to commitment and small-team action. Too many firms force creative people to work on five or six projects that span three or four divisions. But my experience on this one is crystal-clear. No one with one-seventh of the responsibility for anything ever felt committed to it. Peter Drucker's "monomaniacs with missions" were not monomaniacs with *seven different* missions.

Under some forms of management, divisional organizations that grow too big become hopelessly bureaucratic. On the other hand, "the division is the solution" (and the strategy) for Hewlett-Packard, 3M, Johnson & Johnson, Emerson Electric, and the like. Johnson & Johnson constantly creates new divisions. Its corporate watchword is simple: "Growing big by staying small."

These companies carefully monitor the size of their divisions. At HP, divisions are kept to less than a thousand people so that, in president and CEO John Young's words, "the general manager will know all his people by their first names." Bill Gore, chairman of W.L. Gore & Associates, comments, "As the number of people in an organization approaches 200, the group somehow becomes a crowd in which individuals grow increasingly anonymous and significantly less cooperative." The low numbers, whether 200 or 1,000, are all aimed at enhancing ownership and commitment.

Another vital part of the small-team, small-division mentality is the ability to manage, with relatively little muss and fuss, the bureaucratic conflicts that fatally delay much development. As an old hand at skunkworking once said, "Let's be clear about the magnitude of the effects that small teams have. The charged-up team that contains 10 to 50 people isn't in the '10 percent productivity improvement' game. Its results are often 300, 400, even 700 percent beyond those achieved by larger groups."

GET IT OUT THE DOOR

Some firms don't believe in meeting product-release dates. First the date is pushed back three months; then it gets shoved back another 45 days. All the while the bosses are thinking, "We've got to make sure that the software is totally compatible with all the rest of the product family." So the logic goes.

Compatibility is important, particularly in the case of systems-related high-technology products. But sometimes the last 2 percent that's needed for 100 percent compatibility takes 12 months to achieve. Meanwhile, 10 competitors have found a solution to the problem and gotten their products to the marketplace. In such extremely fast-paced markets as data handling, computers, and telecommunications, though, there are literally thousands of entrepreneurs who will fill in the spaces and do the last 2 percent of the work for you.

Digital Equipment's products overlap; users occasionally find that some of its products are incompatible with products that they're supposed to be compatible with. HP's engineers, marketers, and salesmen also lament the incompatibility of some of their products. But companies that wait, trying to achieve the last percentage point of compatibility, may well go belly-up.

The same principle holds true in many other markets, although they show a little less intensity. That's the reason Proctor & Gamble, 3M, Mars, and Johnson & Johnson are so insistent about spurring competition among their own divisions and brand managers. Bloomingdale's does the same thing with buying and floor-space assignments in its stores, and Macy's has done extremely well emulating Bloomingdale's. In most markets, new things are happening all the time. The lion's share is often virtually invisible—that is, you frequently don't see it until it's too late. To keep up with the competition, you have to keep getting new items into the market.

Errors of premature release can be (and frequently are) disastrous. Often a product hits the marketplace before the bugs have been worked out. Its technical superiority is blunted by poor reliability or insufficient support. This type of nightmare must be avoided at all costs. But getting that last possible feature, that last degree of complexity (read "overcomplexity"), that last percentage of compatibility, may cost you more of the market than you would have gained by making a perfect product. Unfortunately, the perfectionists tend to get their way because they always use the argument "It'll only take us

another 30 days." But we all know that those 30-day projects always seem to take 120 days—if you're lucky.

CUSTOMERS GENERATE IDEAS

The evidence is overwhelming: the great majority of ideas for new products come from the users. Eric von Hippel, a professor at MIT's Sloan School of Management, has studied scientific-instrument equipment manufacturers, and his results are revealing. He reviewed 160 inventions and found that more than 70 percent of the product ideas originated with users. And these weren't just bells-and-whistles ideas, either. Sixty percent of the minor modifications came from users, as did 75 percent of the major modifications. But astonishingly, *100 percent* of the so-called "first of type" ideas for sophisticated devices like the transmission electron microscope were user-generated. According to von Hippel's studies, users that got their ideas across to the producers did a lot more than whisper into their ears. The users came up with the ideas, they prototyped them, they debugged them, and they had them working. Only then did they tap the producers for their experience in reliable production of multiple copies.

Lead users don't have to be Ph.D.'s or work in germ-free labs. One classic lead user was a housewife whose husband worked at the Corning Glass labs. One day he took home a new glass container that he was going to store acid in. She accidentally used it to heat some food in the oven, and it didn't break. Such is the origin of Pyrex cookware!

Stay in touch with users. It's important in every industry from fast food to computers. Hewlett-Packard has coined the term MBWA—"Management by Wandering Around." Wandering around should mean listening to the user in a direct, not an abstract or shorthand, way. A general manager who designed a major new computer describes a neat trick he pulled off: "I bought my uncle a computer store. I spent nights and weekends working there. My objective was to stay close to the ultimate user, to observe his frustrations and needs firsthand and incognito." What he learned was reflected in the eventual computer design in a thousand little ways and several big ones.

SERVICE AND QUALITY COUNT

"More scientists in bigger labs" seems to be the conventional watchword, along with "Better planning, better tools." The heck with skunkworks. But it's more than skunkworks. It's more than listening to users, too. Service and quality hold as much value as gee-whiz technology—or more.

Recently I talked with the president of a technology company about commodities. He was disturbed by some people's unfortunate tendency to call high-technology products (chips, instruments, personal computers) "commodities." The problem with this is that if you label a specific product a commodity, you'll start to behave as if it is one, neglecting service and quality. For instance, let's take a mundane product: toilet paper. If you go to your local grocery store and purchase a four-roll, 220-square-foot package of one-ply generic-brand toilet paper, the price will be around 79 cents. But if you go to a Seven-Eleven-type grocery, a package of Procter & Gamble's Charmin will cost you $1.99. The difference in distribution channels (Seven-Eleven) and the quality difference (P&G) is obviously enough to add $1.20 to a 79-cent product—or, more accurately, to add $1.20 to a product that cost about a quarter to produce.

Technology push is crucial, but it is not the principal reason that America is undergoing so many industry setbacks. User-unfriendliness, the inability to realize that the customer perceives a product in his own terms, is at least as big a weakness. If you don't believe me, ask 'em in Detroit.

PERFECTIONISTS FINISH LAST

If it weren't for people, 10,000-person research groups would be the most efficient. If it weren't for people, execution via 100,000-bubble PERT charts would be the most efficient. If it weren't for people, huge amounts of money invested in technical forecasting would allow companies to anticipate competition, customer-related problems, and technological surprises. If it weren't for users, in-house development of every part that went into every invention would be the best way to assure quality.

Optimization. What's optimal? It's hard to believe, but the "suboptimal" system is often the most truly optimal. Go back to the big-versus-small debate. As a way to do the job, skunkworking is faster, cheaper, and higher-quality than the optimization route. Getting 90 percent compatibility and letting the marketplace do the rest turns out to be optimal, not suboptimal. Getting the last 10 percent may cost you 60 percent of the market.

Tom West of Data General didn't care a whit about building a machine that the "technology bigots" would like. He was interested in people who "wanted to get a machine out the door with their name on it." The stories about the U-2, the missile-development program broken down into seven parts, and the Post-it pads seem to be the same. Committed people, people competing against the market and other corporations and other divisions, those are the people who get the job done. Hail to the skunkworks!

Organizational Issues in the Introduction of New Technologies

Ralph Katz

Thomas J. Allen

1. INTRODUCTION

More than ever before, organizations competing in today's world of high technology are faced with the challenges of "dualism," that is, functioning efficiently today while planning and innovating effectively for tomorrow. Not only must these organizations be concerned with the success and market penetration of their current product mix, but they must also be concerned with their long-run capability to develop and incorporate in a timely manner the most appropriate technical advancements into future product offerings. Research and development-based corporations, no matter how they are organized, must find ways to internalize both sets of concerns.

Now it would be nice if everyone in an organization agreed on how to carry out this dualism or even agreed on its relative merits. This is rarely the case, however, even though such decisions are critically important to a firm competing in markets strongly affected by changing technology (Allen, 1977; Roberts, 1974). Amidst the pressures of everyday requirements, decision makers representing different parts of the organization usually disagree on the relative wisdom of allocating resources or particular RD&E talents among the span of technical activities that might be of benefit to today's versus tomorrow's organization. Moreover, there are essentially no well-defined principles within management theory on how to structure organizations to accommodate these two sets of conflicting challenges. Classical management theory with its focus on scientific principles deals only with the efficient production and utilization of today's goods and services. The principles of high task specialization, unity of command and direction, high division of labor, and the equality of authority and responsibility all deal with the problems of structuring work and information flows in routine, predictable ways to facilitate production and control through formal lines of authority and job standardization. What is missing is some comparable theory that would also explain how to organize innovative activities within this operating environment such that creative, developmental efforts will not only take place but will also become more accepted and unbiasedly reviewed, especially as these new and different ideas begin to "disrupt" the smooth functioning organization. More specifically, how can one structure an organization to promote the introduction of new technologies and, in general, enhance its longer-term innovation process, yet at

Reprinted with permission from P. R. Kleindorfer (ed.), *The Management of Productivity and Technology in Manufacturing*. Plenum Press, 1985, pp. 275–300.

the same time, satisfy the plethora of technical demands and accomplishments needed to support and improve the efficiency and competitiveness of today's producing organization?

Implicit in this discussion, then, is the need for managers to learn how to build parallel structures and activities that would not only permit these two opposing forces to coexist but would also balance them in some integrative, meaningful way. Within the RD&E environment, the operating organization can best be described as an "output-oriented" or "downstream" set of forces directed towards the technical support of the organization's current products and towards getting new products out of development and into manufacturing or into the marketplace. Typically, such pressures are controlled through formal structures and through formal job assignments to project managers who are then held accountable for the successful completion of product outputs within established schedules and budget constraints.

At the same time, there must be an "upstream" set of forces that are less concerned with the specific architectures and functionalities of today's products but are more concerned with the various core technologies that might underlie the industry or business environment not only today but also tomorrow. They are, essentially, responsible for the technical health and excellence of the corporation, keeping the company up-to-date and technically competitive in their future business areas.

In every technology-based organization, as discussed by Katz and Allen (1985), the forces that represent this dualism compete with one another for recognition and resources. The conflicts produced by this competition are not necessarily harmful; in fact, they can be very beneficial to the organization in sorting out project priorities and the particular technologies that need to be monitored and pursued, provided there are mechanisms in place to both support and balance these two forces.

If the product-output or downstream set of forces becomes dominant, then there is the likelihood that sacrifices in using the latest technical advancements may be made in order to meet budget, schedule, and immediate market demands. Given these pressures, there are strong tendencies to strip the organization of its research activities and to deemphasize longer-term, forward-looking technological efforts and investigations in order to meet current short-term goals which could, thereby, mortgage future technical capabilities. Under these conditions, requirements for the next generation of new product developments begin to exceed the organization's in-house expertise, and product potentials are then oversold beyond the organization's technical capability.

At the other extreme, if the research or upstream technology component of the organization is allowed to dominate development work within R&D, then the danger is that products may include not only more sophisticated but also perhaps less proven, more risky, or even less marketable technologies. This desire to be technologically aggressive—to develop and use the most attractive, most advanced technology—must be countered by forces that are more sensitive to the operational environments and more concerned with moving research efforts into some final physical reality. Technology is not an autonomous system that determines its own priorities and sets its own standards of performance. To the contrary, market, social, and economic considerations eventually determine priorities as well as the dimensions and levels of performance necessary for successful commercial application (Utterback, 1974).

To balance this dualism—to be able to introduce the new technologies needed for tomorrow's products while functioning efficiently under today's current technological base, is a very difficult task. Generally speaking, the more the organization tries to operate only through formal mechanisms of organizational procedures, structures, and controls, the more the organization will move towards a functioning organization

443

that drives out its ability to experiment and work with new technological concepts and ideas. More informal organizational designs and processes are therefore needed to influence and support true innovative activity, countering the organization's natural movement towards more efficient production and bureaucratic control. These informal mechanisms are also needed to compensate for the many limitations inherent within formal organizational structures and formal task definitions. In the rest of this paper, we will describe three general areas of informal activity that need to take place within an RD&E environment (in parallel with the formal, functioning organization) in order to enhance the innovation process for the more timely introduction of new technologies into the corporation's product portfolio. The general proposition is that these areas of informal activity need to be managed within the RD&E setting, strengthening and protecting them from the pressures of the "productive" organization in order to increase the organization's willingness and ability to deal with the many advancements that come along, especially with respect to new areas of technology.

2. PROBLEM SOLVING, COMMUNICATIONS, AND THE MOBILITY OF PEOPLE

To keep informed about relevant developments outside the organization as well as new requirements within the organization, R&D professionals must collect and process information from a large variety of outside sources. Project members rarely have all the requisite knowledge and expertise to complete successfully all of the tasks involved in new technical innovations; information and assistance must be drawn from many sources beyond the project both within and outside the organization. Furthermore, if one assumes that the world of technology outside the organization is larger than the world of technology inside the

organization, then one should also expect a great deal of emphasis within R&D on keeping in touch with the many advancements in this larger external world. Allen's (1977) 20 years of research work on technical communications and information flows clearly demonstrates just how important this outside contact can be in generating many of the critical ideas and inputs for more successful research and development activity.

At the same time, the research findings of many studies, including Katz and Tushman (1981), Allen (1977), and Pelz and Andrews (1966), have consistently shown that the bulk of these critical outside contacts comes from face-to-face interactions among individuals. Interpersonal communications rather than the formal technical reports, publications, or other written documentation are the primary means by which engineering professionals collect and transfer important new ideas and information into their organizations and project groups, In his study of engineering project teams, for example, Allen (1977) carefully demonstrated that only 11% of the sources of new ideas and information could be attributed to written media; the rest occurred through interpersonal communications. Many of these "creative" exchanges, moreover, were of a more spontaneous nature in that they arose not so much out of formal project requirements and interdependencies but out of factors relating to past project experiences and working relationships, the geographical layouts of office locations and laboratory facilities, attendances at special organizational events and social functions, chance conversations with external professionals and vendors at conferences and trade shows, and so on. Anything that can be done to stimulate informal contacts among the many parts of the organization and between the organization's R&D professionals and their outside technology and customer environments is likely to be helpful in terms of both technology development and technology transfer.

Since communication processes play such an important role in fostering the creative work activities of R&D members, it would be nice if each individual or project team were naturally willing or always motivated to expose themselves to fresh ideas and new points of view. Unfortunately, this is usually not the case as engineering individuals continue to work in a particular project area or in a given area of technology. In fact, one of the more important assumptions underlying human behavior within organizations is that people are strongly motivated to reduce uncertainty (Katz, 1982). As part of this process, individuals, groups, and even organizations strive to structure their work environments to reduce the amount of stress they must face by directing their activities and interactions toward a more predictable level of certainty and clarity. Over time, then, engineers and scientists are not only functioning to reduce technical uncertainty, they are also functioning to reduce their "personal and situational" uncertainty within the organization (Katz, 1980). In the process of gaining increasing control over their task activities and work demands, three broad areas of biases and behavioral responses begin to emerge. And the more these trends are allowed to take place and become reinforced, the more difficult it will be for the organization to consider seriously the potential, long-term advantages of the many new and different technologies that are slowly being developed and worked on by the larger outside R&D community.

2.1 Problem-Solving Processes

As R&D professionals work together in a given area for a long period of time and become increasingly familiar with their work surroundings, they become less receptive toward any change or innovation that threatens to disrupt significantly their comfortable and predictable work patterns of behavior. In the process of reducing more and more uncertainty, these individuals are likely to develop routine responses for dealing with their frequently encountered tasks in order to ensure predictability, coordination, and economical in-

formation processing. As a result, there develops over time increasing rigidity in their problem-solving activities—a kind of functional stability that reduces their capacity for flexibility and openness to change. Behavioral responses and technical decisions are made in fixed, normal patterns; and consequently, new or changing situations that may require technical strategies that do not fit prior problem-solving modes are either ignored or forced into these established molds. R&D professionals interacting over a long period, therefore, develop work patterns that are secure and comfortable, patterns in which routine and precedent play a relatively large part. They come, essentially, to rely more and more on their customary ways of doing things to complete project requirements. In their studies of problem-solving strategies, for example, Allen and Marquis (1963) show that within R&D there can be a very strong bias for choosing those technical strategies and approaches that have worked in the past and with which people have gained common experience, familiarity, and confidence; all of which inhibit the entry of competing tactics involving new technologies, new ideas, or new competencies.

What also seems to be true is that as engineers continue to work in their well-established areas of technology and develop particular problem-solving procedures, they become increasingly committed to these existing methods. Commitment is a function of time, and the longer individuals are asked to work on and extend the capabilities of certain technical approaches, the greater their commitment becomes toward these approaches. Furthermore, in accumulating experience and knowledge in these technical area, R&D has often had to make clear presentations, showing progress and justifying the allocation of important organizational resources. As part of these review processes, alternative or competing ideas and approaches were probably considered and discarded, and with such public refutation, commitments to the selected courses of action become even stronger. Individuals become known for working and building capability in certain technical areas, both their personal and organizational identities become deeply ensconced in these efforts, and as a result, they may become overly preoccupied with the survival of their particular technical approaches, protecting them against new technical alternatives or negative evaluations. All of the studies that have retrospectively examined the impact of major new technologies on existing organizational decisions and commitments arrive at the same general conclusion: those working on and committed to the old, invaded technology fail to support the radical new technology; instead, they fight back vigorously to defend and improve the old technology (e.g., Cooper and Schendel, 1976; Schon, 1963). And yet, it is often these same experienced technologists who are primarily asked to evaluate the potential effects of these emerging new technologies on the future of the organization's businesses. It is no wonder, therefore, that in the majority of cases studied, the first commercial introduction of a radical new technology has come from outside the industry's traditional competitors.

2.2 Communication and Information Processing

One of the consequences of increased behavioral and technical stability is that R&D groups also become increasingly isolated from outside sources of relevant information and important new ideas. As engineers become more attached to their current work habits and areas of technical expertise, the extent to which they are willing or even feel they need to expose themselves to new ideas, approaches, or technologies becomes progressively less and less. Instead of being vigilant in seeking information from the outside world of technology or from the market place, they become increasingly complacent about external events and new technological developments. After studying the actual communication behaviors of some 350 engineering professionals in a

major R&D facility, Katz and Allen (1982) found that as members of project teams worked together, gained experience with one another, and developed more stable role assignments and areas of individual contribution, the groups also communicated less frequently with key sources of outside information. Research groups, for example, failed to pay sufficient attention to events and information in their external R&D community while product development and technical support groups had reduced levels of communication with their internal engineering colleagues and with their downstream client groups from marketing and manufacturing. Such low levels of outside interaction also result in stronger group boundaries, creating tougher barriers to effective communication and more difficult information flows not only among R&D groups but also to other organizational divisions and to other areas outside the organization.

Another set of forces that affects the amount and variety of outside contact that R&D employees may have is the tendency for individuals to want to communicate only with those who are most like themselves, who are most likely to agree with them, or whose ideas and viewpoints are most likely to be in accord with their own interests and established perspectives. Over time, R&D project members learn to interact selectively to avoid messages and information that might be in conflict with their current dispositions toward particular technologies or technical approaches, thereby restricting their overall exposure to outside views and allowing themselves to bias the interpretation of their limited outside data to terms more favorable to their existing attitudes and beliefs. Thus, the organization ends up getting its critical and evaluative information and feedback not from those most likely to challenge or stretch their thinking but from those with whom they have developed comfortable and secure relationships, i.e., friends, peers, long-term suppliers and customers, etc. And it is precisely these latter kinds of relationships that are least likely to provide the inputs and thinking necessary to stimulate the organization's movement into new technical areas.

2.3 Cognitive Processes

One of the dilemmas of building in-house capability in particular areas of technology is that engineers responsible for the success of these technical areas become less willing to accept or seek the advice and ideas of other outside experts. Over time, these engineers may even begin to believe that they possess a monopoly on knowledge in their specialized areas of technology, seriously discounting the possibility that outsiders might be producing important new ideas or advances that might be of use to them. And if this kind of outlook becomes mutually reinforced within a given R&D area or project group, then these individuals often end up relying primarily on their own technical experiences and know-how, and consequently, are more apt to dismiss the critical importance of outside contacts and pay less attention to the many technical advances and achievements in the larger external world. It is precisely this attitude, coupled with the communication and problem-solving trends previously described, that helps explain why most of the successful firms in a very new area of technology had never participated in the old or substituted area of technology.

This rather myopic outlook within R&D is also encouraged as technologists become increasingly specialized, that is, moving from broadly defined capabilities and solution approaches to more narrowly defined interests and specialties. Pelz and Andrews (1966) argue from their study of scientists and engineers that with increasing group stability, project member preferences for probing deeper and deeper into a particular technological area becomes greater and greater while their preferences for maintaining technical breadth and flexibility gradually decrease. Without new challenges and opportunities, the diversity of skills and of ideas generated are likely to become progressively more narrow. They are, essentially, learning more and more about less and less. And as engineers welcome information from fewer sources and are exposed to fewer alternative points of view, the more constricted their cognitive abilities become, resulting in a more restricted perspective of their situation and a more limited set of technological responses from which to cope. One of the many signs of obsolescence occurs when engineers retreat to their areas of specialization as they feel insecure addressing technologies and problems outside their direct fields of expertise and experience. They simply feel more comfortable and creative when they can see their organizational contributions in terms of their past performance standards rather than on the basis of future needs and requirements.

Finally, there is not only a strong tendency for technologists to communicate with those who are most like themselves, but it is just as likely that continued interaction among members of an R&D project team will lead to greater homogeneity in knowledge and problem-solving behaviors and perceptions. The well-known proverb "birds of a feather flock together" makes a great deal of sense, but it is just as accurate to say that "the longer birds flock together, the more of a feather they become." One can argue, therefore, that as R&D project members work together over a long period, they will reinforce their common views and commitments to their current technologies and problem-solving approaches. The group not only tries to hire or recruit new members like themselves, thereby exacerbating the trend towards greater homogeneity and consensus and less diversity. Such shared values and perceptions, created through group interactions, act as powerful constraints on individual attitudes and behaviors and provide group members with a strong sense of identity and a great deal of assurance and confidence in their traditional activities. At the same time, however, these shared systems of meaning and beliefs restrict individual creativity into new areas and isolate the group even further from important outside contacts and technical developments, thereby causing the old technologies to become even more deeply entrenched.

2.4 Mobility of People and the "Not Invented Here" Syndrome

What is implied by all of this discussion is that R&D managers need to learn to observe the strong biases that can naturally develop in the way engineers select and interpret information, in their willingness to innovate or implement radically new technological approaches, or in their cognitive abilities to generate or work with new technical options so that appropriate actions can be undertaken to encourage R&D to become more receptive and responsive to new ideas and emerging technological opportunities. The trends described here are observable; one can determine the extent to which project groups are communicating and interacting effectively with outside information sources, whether project groups are exposing themselves to new ideas and more critical kinds of reviews, or whether a project group is becoming too narrow and homogeneous through its hiring practices.

In the best-selling book, *In Search of Excellence,* organizations are encouraged by Peters and Waterman to practice the Hewlett Packard philosophy of MBWA (Management by Wandering Around). But managers have to know what to look for as they wander around. In particular, technical managers can try to detect the degree to which these different trends are materializing, for the way engineering groups come to view their work environments will be very critical to the organization's ability to introduce and work with new technologies. The more the perceptual outlook of an R&D area can be characterized by the problem-solving, informational, and cognitive trends previously described, the more likely it has internalized what has become known in the R&D community as the "Not Invented Here" (NIH) or the "Nothing New Here" (NNH) syndrome. According to this syndrome, project members are more likely to see only the virtue and superiority of their own ideas and technical activities while dismissing the potential contributions and benefits of new technologies and competitive ideas and accomplishments as inferior and weak.

It is also argued here that the most effective way to prevent R&D groups from developing behaviors and attitudes that coincide with this NIH syndrome is through the judicious movement of engineering personnel among project groups and organizational areas, keeping teams energized and destabilized. Based on the findings of Katz and Allen (1982), Smith (1970), and several other studies, new group members not only have a relative advantage in generating fresh ideas and approaches, but through their active participation, project veterans might consider more carefully ideas and technological alternatives they might otherwise have ignored. In short, project newcomers represent a novelty-enhancing condition, challenging and improving the scope of existing methods and accumulated knowledge.

The mobility of people within the organization is a most fruitful approach for keeping ideas fresh, building insights, and maintaining innovative flexibility. Japanese organizations, for example, assume that the best course of development for capable individuals is lateral rotation across major functional areas of the firm before upward advancement takes place. In a Japanese company, an engineer progressing well may move from R&D into marketing, then into manufacturing, and perhaps back into R&D at a higher level. This is seldom the kind of career track that American firms find appropriate; yet, we all know for sure the kinds of problems one is avoiding as well as the benefits that would accrue over the long run through the greater use of rotation programs even if rotation were limited to between research and development and engineering groups.

In an additional attempt to foster new thinking and to build stronger intraorganizational bridges and communication networks, some companies hold special meetings in which organizational areas report on what they have been doing and on the kind of capability they have. The 3M Corporation, for example, holds a proprietary company fair at which there are presentations of technical papers, exhibits, and demonstrations of projects and prototypes. The fair enables the rest of the people in the company to begin to learn about what is taking place in other divisions for laboratories. The Monsanto Company uses what it calls the Monsanto technical community to bring together technical people, trained in similar disciplines but employed in different divisions of the firm, and it convenes these people in different workshops and groups, encouraging them to exchange ideas and information. These kinds of programs can be very helpful in fostering communication and in stimulating the identification of new technical capabilities as well as the identification of new market and technical needs throughout the firm.

3. ORGANIZATIONAL STRUCTURES

Unlike productivity, which is the efficient application of current solutions, innovation usually connotes the first utilization of a new or improved product, process, or practice. Innovation, as a result, requires both the generation or recognition of a new idea followed by the implementation or exploitation of that idea into a new or better solution. So far, we have discussed organizational processes to the extent that they primarily affect the idea-generation phase of the innovation process. It is just as important, of course, for an organization to plan for the idea-exploitation phase, where exploitation includes the appraisal, focusing, and transferring of research ideas and results for their eventual utilization and application. To say that one is managing or organizing for the introduction of new technologies within the innovation process implies that one is "pushing" the development and

movement of new technical ideas and capabilities downstream through the organization from research to development to engineering and even into manufacturing and perhaps some phase of customer distribution.

Innovation, then, is a dynamic process involving the movement and transfer of technologies across internal organizational boundaries. Formal organizational design, on the other hand, is a static concept, describing how to organize collections of activities within well-defined units and reporting relationships, e.g., research, advanced development, product development, engineering, quality assurance, etc. Formal organizational structures tell us what to manage and with whom to interact within certain areas of interdependent activity; they tell us little about how to move information, ideas, and in particular technologies across different organizational areas, divisions, or formal lines of authority. In fact, formal structures tend to separate and differentiate the various organizational groupings, making the movement of ideas and technologies particularly difficult across these groupings, especially if there are no compensating integrating mechanisms in place. And it is in the movement of new technological concepts from research to advanced development to successful product development that we are particularly interested.

The effective organization, therefore, needs to cause the results of R&D to be appropriately transferred. Technically successful R&D, especially if it embraces new radical technologies, is very likely to pose major problems of linkages with the rest of the firm, particularly product development, engineering, manufacturing, marketing, sales, field service, and so on. A company can do a terrific job of R&D and a terrible job of managing the innovating process overall simply because the results of R&D have never been fully exploited and successfully moved downstream. Witness, for example, the problems of Xerox, where the R&D labs have generated and surfaced many major new advances and approaches only to discover that the company has failed to fully exploit and capture benefit from many of them. Other corporations, on the other hand, have benefited extremely well from Xerox's research activities—so many in fact that some have quipped that Xerox's research facilities should be declared a national resource instead of a resource for Xerox (see *Fortune* magazine, September, 1983).

Over the past decade or so, Roberts (1979) has been studying the problems of moving R&D results through the organization. From carrying out these studies, he has found that most large organizations have been dissatisfied with the degree of transfer of their own R&D results and feel very uncomfortable about how little of their good technical outcomes ever reach the marketplace and generate profitable pay-back for the firm. The R&D labs he studied seemed to have broad enough charters to do almost anything they chose, but ended up being quite narrow as to what they in fact implemented within their own organizations. To enhance the transfer of R&D results across the barriers of organizational structures, Roberts (1979) advocates the building of bridges; and in particular, he recommends three different groups of bridges: procedural, human, and organizational.

The procedural approaches, according to Roberts, try to tie together both the R&D unit and the appropriate receiving units by joint efforts. In the case of new technological concepts, the most immediate receiving unit is typically some advanced development group or some divisional product development organization that receives the output from a centralized research and development lab. The kinds of procedural bridges that have been suggested include joint planning of R&D programs and joint staffing of projects, especially immediately before and after transfer, for those are the most critical phases of the process in which key know-how and information can easily slip through the cracks.

Joint appraisal of results by research, development, and any other appropriate downstream unit or customer is also employed in some labs.

From the viewpoint of generating useful information, the best time to carry out joint appraisal of results is when failure has occurred, for there is usually something objective to look at from which one might be able to learn and improve. At the same time, however, this exercise must be done carefully and sensitively to prevent this opportunity from becoming a situation of mutual fingerpointing, showing why the other group is really at fault and how those people caused the failure. In these joint appraisals, the attributions of failure should be centered around substantive issues that can be dealt with behaviorally, structurally, or procedurally; otherwise, intergroup conflicts and differences will be strengthened, which is likely to cause even greater difficulty in future technological handoffs. Joint appraisal of successes should also not be overlooked, for they can be very helpful in generating the goodwill and trust necessary to strengthen organizational linkages, especially after a history of prior difficulty or failure.

The establishment of human bridges also helps to cope with transfer issues. Interpersonal alliances and informal contacts inevitably turn out to be the basis of integration and intraorganizational cooperation that really matter. The human approaches focus on the relationships that convey information between people, that convey the shift of responsibility from one person to another, and that convey enthusiasm for the project. Roberts argues strongly, in fact, that the building of human bridges is by far the best way to transfer this vital enthusiasm and commitment.

Technology moves through people, and the most effective of these human bridges is the actual movement of people in two directions. Upstream movement of development engineers to join the R&D effort well in advance of the intended transfer is a very important step. This transfers information from the product development areas into the research process, creates an advocate to bring the research results downstream, and builds interpersonal ties for the later assistance that will inevitably be needed as the technology encounters problems. Downstream movement of research individuals will also be helpful in providing the technical expertise necessary for development to build up its own understanding and capability.

In addition to the specific movement of people, human bridges are also built through the interpersonal communication systems that have developed over time through the history of working relationships, rotation programs, task force participation, and other organizational events and activities. Another important device to be considered is the joint problem-solving meeting in which development individuals are asked to sit down with research colleagues to let them explain their difficulties and initial problem-solving thinking. Such meetings are not only helpful in dealing with specific project problems, but will also be useful in building stronger human bridges between the related R&D areas and may even be helpful in solving additional related problems that were not initially put forth.

The final area for considering the movement of R&D results towards development and eventual commercialization consists of organizational changes and organizational bridges. According to Roberts, these are the toughest kinds to create and implement effectively in an organization. It is far easier to alter procedures or to try to build human bridges across groups than it is to change organizational arrangements and relationships. Nevertheless, several different structural approaches can be effective under different organizational conditions. Some organizations have developed specialized transfer groups, created solely for the purpose of transferring important technical advances or important new processes. Under this approach, the transfer group is like the licensor of a technology who is not just sending equipment and documentation but who is also responsible for training others to work with the technology, for installing the equipment, etc. If used, the specialized transfer group should consist of at least a few of the key technical players. Senior management should not be allowed to argue that they cannot spare the superstars of the research organization to support development or manufacturing engineering.

Another organizational approach is to employ integrators or integrating groups that are given responsibility for straddling the various parts of the RD&E organization. This is a very uncomfortable and a very difficult job to assume because it is extremely difficult to ask someone to take care of an integrating function across two separate suborganizations when he or she does not have responsibility for either the sending or the receiving organization. To perform this function successfully requires someone who can cope with the political sensitivities of multiple groups and who has built substantial informal influence and credibility within the organization.

Finally, a variety of corporate venture strategies can be considered by companies that are concerned with developing new technical approaches, new product lines, or want a stronger emphasis on technical entrepreneurship. Roberts (1980) suggests a large variety of possible venture strategies, ranging from the high corporate involvement of internal venturing to low corporate involvement through venture capital investments in outside firms for the purpose of gaining windows on technology and new market opportunities. Additional venture strategies are also described by Roberts, including the coupling of R&D efforts from both the large corporation and the small independent firm. In general, there is no single best way to organize for the effective introduction of new technologies; but the more informal mechanisms one puts in place to foster both the idea generation and the idea exploitation phases, the more one is likely to be successful at managing the innovation process.

4. ORGANIZATIONAL CONTROLS

All of these organizational attempts at stimulating new technological innovation will fall flat, of course, if organizational controls are not consistent with the innovation process. In looking at many case histories of successful versus unsuccessful innovations based on radical new technologies, Cohen *et al.* (1979) and several other studies have identified a number of factors as being critically important for trying to influence the generation and successful movement of new technologies through the organization.

4.1 Technical Understanding

One of the most important issues in working with new technologies is that the research function must fully understand the main technical issues of the technology before passing it on. Although this point seems obvious, it is often overlooked. The research function must focus not only on the benefit of the new technology in and of itself; it must also deal with the technology's limitations relative to conventional technologies and to other new technological approaches. In the early days of transistors, for example, one large electronics company spent a great deal of money and many years of research effort on understanding the materials and processing problems of germanium for point contacts and junction transistors. Unfortunately, the research organization failed to compare the use of germanium to silicon, whose own development was continuing to make a great deal of progress. Only after many years did the organization finally realize the limitations in the advantages of germanium over silicon and these limitations had less to do with the devices themselves and more to do with device implementation in packaging and circuitry.

It is also important, therefore, to make sure that research understands where the new technology might fit in with respect to the product line or at least what requirements must be met to reach this fit. Research should not waste its time solving problems that do not exist or producing technologies that cannot be sold. Whirlpool, for example, invested substantial research resources

in making appliance motors more energy efficient long before the oil crisis, but of course, the marketplace was not yet interested in these kinds of advances. Similarly, GE conducted a great deal of research in environmental concerns in the 1940s but at that time there was very little interest in improving the ecology of our environment. As a last example, DuPont developed Corfam as a synthetic substitute for leather, but unfortunately for DuPont, the public was perfectly satisfied with leather and saw no need for the manmade substitute.

Full understanding also means that research must begin to examine the means of manufacturing, the availability of key materials and technical talents, the ease of use, and so on. Air Products and Chemicals, for example, spent millions of dollars to develop a fluorination process so that textile manufacturers could make fabrics, especially polyesters, more resistant to oil and grease. Unfortunately, textile manufacturers did not want fluorine—a poisonous and corrosive gas—anywhere near their plants and refused to buy the system. Research should also be able to make, at the very least, preliminary cost estimates. One of the most basic elements of a technology is its cost. In fact, a study of technology programs at GE concluded that most of the barriers to the introduction of new technologies (even hardware and software) were cost constraints and not technical feasibility; it was getting the technology to perform capably at a marketable cost.

To help ensure these kinds of requirements, some labs have begun to hire full-time marketing representatives and cost estimators as a regular part of the R&D organization. Previously, corporate R&D organizations were completely dependent on product line divisions for both marketing and sales effort and for business and economic analysis as well. These dependencies, especially the latter, were harmful in getting research projects justified, supported, and accepted by the divisions who were supposed to be the eventual customer of the research results.

4.2 Technical Feasibility

All too often, a technology is transferred before there has been sufficient time within research to demonstrate true feasibility. Such pressures can come from the downstream organization or they can arise from the "unbridled enthusiasm" of the researchers themselves. In either case, it would be more beneficial to discuss what constitutes feasibility and for research to strive to achieve it.

Most new technical concepts do not succeed simply because they must run a gauntlet of barriers as they enter the main part of the functioning organization. In many cases, the new technology is embedded within a system of established technologies. The question then is whether the new technology will offer a sufficient competitive advantage to warrant its incorporation into this interdependent system, perhaps changing drastically the tooling and the overall manufacturing process. Experienced technologists will typically warn you that what you do not yet know about the workings of a new technical advance will probably come back to haunt you. What often appears to be a simple technical issue turns out to be more complicated than we realize. GE discovered a fiber, for example, that looked and behaved more like wool than any synthetic yet known. Unfortunately, the fiber disintegrates in today's cleaning solvents, and the problem has yet to be solved.

4.3 Research and Development Overlap

As previously discussed, it is very helpful to the movement of a new technology if development, or some other appropriate receiving organization, also has a group of technical people who have been getting up to speed on the technology before the actual transfer, e.g., the presence of "ad tech" groups. Such advanced technical activities within development can greatly aid the movement of technology and the smoothing of conflicts.

In a similar fashion, it is also important for research to maintain some activity to support and defend the new technology or to find new ways to extend the technology. Research must not be allowed to feel that it is "finished" at the time of transfer, for if this feeling is present, their willingness and enthusiasm to support the technology will be minimal. Most new technologies are relatively crude at first. Ball-point pens, for example, blotted, skipped, stopped writing all together, and even leaked in consumers' pockets when they first appeared on the market. The first transistors were expensive and had sharply limited frequencies, power capabilities, and temperature tolerances. Such experiences are very typical of new technologies, especially radical new technologies. And the more prepared research is to help "push" the technology, the less likely it will be for the new technology to be dismissed prematurely as a "fad" or as a technology with very limited application.

4.4 Growth Potential

As a related point, all too often a research program sells itself short by being too narrow and not showing a clear path towards technical growth and growth in product applicability. In almost every instance, when the new technology appears on the scene, the old technology is forced to "stretch" itself, often with major advances being achieved in the threatened technology. Under these circumstances, the new technology is in the position of trying to chase or catch a "changing target." Moreover, this new potential in the old technology often holds back the entry of the new technology. Advances in flashbulbs, for example, held off the widespread use of electronic flash for quite some time, while advances in magnetic tape audio and video recording have prevented the emergence of thermoplastic recording. In their well-known study of strategic responses to technological threats, Cooper and Schendel (1976) indicate that in the majority of cases, sales of the old technology did not decline after the introduction of a new technology. To the contrary, sales of the old technology expanded even further. It is for these reasons that the diffusion and substitution of a radical new technology must be viewed as a long-term process and research and development must carefully prepare to argue and demonstrate why the pressured organization should be patient during this time period.

4.5 Organizational Slack and Sponsorship

When an organization pushes too hard for productivity within the RD&E environment, trying to measure and control all aspects of the innovation process, there is little room or slack for experimenting or pursuing novel ideas and concepts. The environment is simply too tightly run and the climate becomes unfavorable for very new or long-term innovation. Engineers and scientists become anxious, restrict the depth of exploration along new paths, and center their attention upon issues closely related to the company's immediate output. Creative innovation, on the other hand, is harder to measure and takes a longer period to assess. It requires speculative investments on the part of the firm that wants to nurture the ideas and the experimenting activities that will eventually be worth it.

Given all of the resistance and testing that a new technological idea will eventually encounter from the functioning organization and from operational review committees, strong corporate sponsorship is needed to protect new technological innovations. And the more radical the new technology, the stronger the corporate sponsorship has to be. One of the observations we have made from working and consulting with many technology companies is that most (and in some high technology companies, all) radical new technologies have had to have well-identified sponsorship at the corporate level in order to succeed.

Another important finding from retrospective studies of radical innovation is that new technologies are not really new! By this, we mean that technological change is a relatively continuous and incremental process which casts shadows far ahead. According to Utterback and Brown (1972), the information incorporated in successful new innovations has been around for roughly 5–30 years prior to its use. They further argue that there are many multiple signals within the external environment that can be used to predict the direction and impact of future technological changes and development. Von Hippel (1983), for example, argues that one can often anticipate future innovations by identifying what he calls "lead users," that is, users whose needs today foreshadow the needs of the general marketplace tomorrow. Nevertheless, even if particular areas of new technology were identified as extremely important, without strong sponsorship it is unlikely that sufficient resources would be diverted to it, that engineers would be isolated from other pressures or tasks to work on it, or that they would be given sufficient uninterrupted time to complete it. One of the reasons why so many new technologies are introduced through the emergence or spin-offs of new firms is that in these situations, the new technology does not encounter resistance from or have to fight against already existing businesses and entrenched technical approaches.

Another benefit of strong sponsorship is that it helps protect the individual risk taker who is willing to take on the entrepreneurial burden of moving the new technology through the organization. No matter how beneficial the new technology appears to be, someone must be willing to sell the effort and make it happen. Schon's (1963) analysis of successful radical innovation is quite clear. At the outset, the new technological concept encounters sharp resistance, which is usually overcome through vigorous promotions by one emerging champion. What is important to recognize here is that these champions are typically self-selected; it is extremely difficult to appoint someone to withstand all of the pressures,

454

hassles, and risks associated with being an idea champion and then to expect him or her to do it excitedly for a long period.

Finally, we also know from research studies that the ultimate use of a new technology is often not known or may change dramatically as the technology becomes further developed. The new technology, moreover, often invades traditional industry by capturing a series of submarkets, many of which are insulated from competition for some extended period. The earliest application of the transistor, for example, was in hearing aids, but its use was not immediately transferred to the organization's defense divisions. Because of these more limited niche markets (and consequently, relatively low sales volume), R&D often concludes that it does not have to work closely with marketing; nor does it want to subject its technological concept to the typical market screens of revenue and volume. Such a conclusion, however, does not help to build the strong harmonious relationship between marketing and R&D that has been shown to be so important for successful commercialization of new innovations (e.g., Souder, 1978). The key to success in these kinds of situations may be to find a pioneering application where the advantages of the new capability are so high that it is worth the risks. This would require the coupling of technical perspective with creative marketing development to identify such pioneering applications. On this basis, early involvement of marketing could be very helpful in providing inputs and market perspective (but not market screens) to the new technological effort.

4.6 Organizational Rewards

Ultimately, we all know that those activities which are measured or get rewarded are those which get done. If the managerial and organizational recommendations and suggestions discussed in this chapter are to be effectively implemented, then the reward systems must be consistent and commensurate with the hoped-for behaviors. One of the most important of these is that research engineers and scientists must come to see that part of their reward system is not just the generation of publication of new technological concepts and advances, but that part of their responsibilities is also the successful transfer of their work. A few high-technology companies we know have been making such reward systems explicit within their corporate labs, and although it has taken some time to take hold, it has been quite effective in moving technology through the development cycle. It has also resulted in research seeking more joint sponsorship of its activities, especially with the development divisions—all of which has helped to strengthen the communications and bridging mechanisms within the corporation.

Finally, in most areas of day-to-day functioning, productivity rather than creativity is and should be the principal objective. Even where innovation and creativity are truly desired and encouraged, activities that are potentially more creative may be subordinated to those activities of higher organizational priority or more closely tied to identified organizational needs. Nevertheless, organizations exhibit simultaneous demands for routinization and for innovation. And it is in the balance of these countervailing pressures that one determines the organization's true climate for managing and encouraging the introduction of new technological opportunities.

REFERENCES

Allen, T. J., and Marquis, D. G. (1983). Positive and negative biasing sets. The effect of prior experience on research performance, *IEEE Trans. Eng. Manag.* 11, 158–162.

Allen, T. J. (1977). *Managing the Flow of Technology,* MIT Press, Cambridge, Massachusetts.

Cooper, A. C., and Schendel, D. (1976). Strategic responses to technological threats, *Bus. Hor.* February, 61–69.

Cohen, H., Keller, S., and Streeter, D. (1979). The transfer of technology from research to development, *Res. Manag.* May, 11–17.

Katz, R. (1980). Time and work: Toward an integrative perspective, *Res. in Organ. Behav.* 2, 81–127.

Katz, R. (1982). The effects of group longevity on project communication and performance, *Admin. Sci. Q.* 27, 81–104.

Katz, R., and Allen, T. J. (1982). Investigating the not invented here (NIH) syndrome, *Res. Dev. Manag.* 12, 7–19.

Katz, R., and Allen, T. J. (1985). Project performance and the locus of influence in the R&D matrix, *Acad. Manag. J.* 26, 67–87.

Katz, R., and Tushman, M. (1981). An investigation into the managerial role and career paths of gatekeepers and project supervisors in a major R&D facility, *Res. Dev. Manage.* 11, 103–110.

Pelz, D. C. and Andrews, F. M. (1966). *Scientists in Organizations,* Wiley, New York.

Roberts, E. B. (1974). A simple model of R&D project dynamics, *Res. Dev. Manage.* 5, 1–15.

Roberts, E. B. (1979). Stimulating technological innovations: Organizational approaches, *Res. Manage.* 22, 26–30.

Roberts, E. B. (1980). New ventures for corporate growth, *Harv. Bus. Rev.* July—August, 58, 134–142.

Schon, D. D. (1963). Champions for radical new inventions, *Harv. Bus. Rev.* 41, 76–84.

Souder, W. E. (1976). Effectiveness of product development methods, *Ind. Market. Manage.* 7, 299–307.

Utterback, J. M. (1974). Innovation in industry and the diffusion of technology, *Science* 183, 620–626.

Utterback, J. M., and Brown, J. W. (1972). Monitoring for technological opportunities, *Bus. Hor.* 15, 5–15.

von Hippel, E. (1983). *Novel Product Concept from Lead Users: Segmenting users by Experience,* Massachusetts Institute of Technology Working Paper No. 1476–83.

The One-Firm Firm:
What Makes It Successful

David H. Maister

What do investment bankers Goldman Sachs, management consultants McKinsey, accountants Arthur Andersen, compensation and benefits consultants Hewitt Associates, and lawyers Latham & Watkins have in common? Besides being among the most profitable firms (if not *the* most profitable) in their respective professions? Besides being considered by their peers among the best *managed* firms in their respective professions? The answer? They all share, to a greater or lesser extent, a common approach to management that I term the "one-firm firm" system.

In contrast to many of their competitors, one-firm firms have a remarkable degree of institutional loyalty and group effort that is clearly a critical ingredient in their success. The commonality of this organizational orientation and management approach among each of these firms suggests that there is indeed a "model" whose basic elements are transferable to other professions. The purpose of this article is to identify the elements of this model of professional firm success, and to explore how these elements interact to form a successful management system.

METHODOLOGY

The information on specific firms contained in this article has been gleaned from a variety of "public domain" sources, as well as selected interviews (on and off the record) at a number of professional service firms, including but not restricted to those named herein. However, none of the information presented here represents "official" statements by the firms involved. As with most professional service organizations, the firms discussed here are private partnerships with no requirement, and with little incentive, to expose their inner workings. Consequently, public information on the management practices (and economic results) of such firms is difficult to obtain.

This situation is regrettable because the professional service firm represents the confluence of two major trends in the U.S. (and worldwide) economy: the growing importance of the service sector, and the increasing numbers of "knowledge workers." As a result, any lessons that can be learned about successful management of such enterprises could potentially be of importance not only to the professions but also to other service entities and organizations grappling with the problems of managing large numbers of highly educated employees.

In an attempt to discover the principles of

"good management" of professional service firms, I have worked very closely with a broad array of service firms in a variety of capacities. My research has been driven by two propositions: first, that professional service firms are sufficiently different from industrial corporations to warrant special study; and second, that the management issues faced by professional service firms are remarkably similar, regardless of the specific profession under consideration. I have chosen in this article to concentrate on the second proposition.

WHAT IS MEANT BY "WELL MANAGED"?

The firms chosen for discussion were identified in the following way. In the course of my research and consulting work, I have made it my practice to ask repeatedly the question, "Which do you consider the best managed firm in your profession?" The question is, of course, ambiguous. In any business context, "well managed" can be taken to refer, alternatively, to profitability, member satisfaction, size, growth, innovativeness, quality of products or services, or any of a number of other criteria. The difficulty in identifying "successful" firms is particularly acute in the professions because many of the conventional indicators of business success do not necessarily apply. For example, since there are few economies of scale in the professions,[1] neither size nor rate of growth can be taken as unequivocal measures of success: many firms have chosen to limit both. Even if "per-partner" profit figures were available (which they are not), they would also be unreliable measures, since many professional firms are prepared to sacrifice a degree of profit maximization in the name of other goals such as professional satisfaction and/or quality of worklife. Finally, since "quality" of either service or work product is notoriously

difficult to assess in professional work,[2] few reliable indicators of this aspect of success are obtainable.

In spite of these difficulties, it has been remarkable how frequently the same names appear on the list of "well-managed" firms in the professions, as judged by their peers and competitors. The firms discussed here were on virtually everyone's list of admired firms, often together with the comment, "I wish we could do what they do." It should be noted that other firms, not discussed here, were also mentioned frequently. However, as expressed earlier, what makes Arthur Andersen, Goldman Sachs, Hewitt Associates, and Latham & Watkins worthy of some special attention is not only that they are successful and well respected, but that, in spite of being in different professions, they appear to share a common approach to management (the one-firm firm system) that is readily distinguishable from many of their competitors. This approach is clearly not the only way to run a professional service firm, but it is certainly *a* way that is worthy of special study.

THE "ONE-FIRM FIRM" SYSTEM

Loyalty
The characteristics of the one-firm firm system are institutional loyalty and group effort. In contrast to many of their (often successful) competitors who emphasize individual entrepreneurialism, autonomous profit centers, internal competition and/or highly decentralized, independent activities, one-firm firms place great emphasis on firmwide coordination of decision making, group identity, cooperative teamwork, and institutional commitment.

Hewitt Associates (described along with Goldman Sachs in a recent popular book as one of "The 100 Best Companies in America to Work For")[3] says that, in its recruiting, it looks for "SWANs": people who are *S*mart, *W*ork hard, are *A*mbitious, and *N*ice. While emphasis on the first three attributes is common in all professional service firms, it is the emphasis on the last one that differentiates the one-firm firm from all the others. "If an individual has ego needs that are too high," notes Peter Friedes, Hewitt's managing partner, "they can be a very disruptive influence. Our work depends on internal cooperation and teamwork."

The same theme is sounded by Geoffrey Boisi, the partner in charge of mergers and acquisitions at Goldman Sachs: "You learn from day one around here that we gang-tackle problems. If your ego won't permit that, you won't be effective here."[4] By general repute, Goldman has achieved its eminence with a minimum of the infighting that afflicts most Wall Street firms. In contrast to many (if not most) of its competitors on the street, Goldman frowns upon anything resembling a star system.

Downplaying Stardom
The same studied avoidance of the star mentality is evidenced at Latham & Watkins. As Clinton Stevenson, the firm's managing partner, points out: "We want to encourage clients to retain the firm of Latham and Watkins, not Clint Stevenson."[5] Partner Jack Walker reinforces this point: "I don't mean to sound sentimental, but there's a bonding here. People care about the work of the firm."[6] The team philosophy at McKinsey, one senior partner explained to me, is illustrated by its approach to project work: "As a young individual consultant, you learn that your job is to hold your own: you can rest assured that the team will win. All you've got to do is do your part."

Above all else, the leaders and, more important, all the other members of these firms view themselves as belonging to an *institution* that has an identity and existence of its own, above and beyond the individuals who happen currently to belong to it. The one-firm firm, relative to its competitors, places great emphasis on its institutional history, broadly held values, and a reputation that all actively work to preserve. Loyalty to, and pride in, the firm and its accomplishments approaches religious fervor at such firms.

Teamwork and Conformity
The emphasis on teamwork and "fitting in" creates an identity not only for the firm but also for the individual members of the firm. This identity, for better or worse, is readily identifiable to the outside world. References by others in the profession to members of one-firm firms are not always flattering. Members of other Big-8 firms, particularly those where individualism and individual contributions are highly valued, often make reference to "Arthur Androids." The term "A McKinsey-type" has substantive meaning in the consulting profession—sometimes even down to the style of dress. In the 1950s, I am told by a McKinsey-ite, a set of hats in the closet of a corporation's reception room was an unmistakable sign that the McKinsey consultants were in. The hats have disappeared, but the mentality has not. Goldman Sachs professionals are referred to by other investment bankers as the "IBM clones of Wall Street."

Long Hours and Hard Work
For all the emphasis on teamwork and interpersonal skills, one-firm firm members are no slouches. All of the firms discussed here have reputations for long hours and hard work, even above the norms for the all-absorbing professions in which they compete. Indeed, the way an individual illustrates his or her high involvement and commitment to the firm is through hard work and long hours. Latham & Watkins lawyers are reputed to bill an *average* of 2,200 hours apiece, with some heroic performers reaching the heights of 2,700 hours in some years: this con-

trasts with a professionwide average of approximately 1,750. At Goldman Sachs, sixteen-hour days are common. It has been said: "If you like the money game, here's [Goldman's] a good team to play on. If you like other games, you may not have time for them."[7] James Scott, a Columbia Business School professor, has commented: "At Goldman, the spirit is pervasive. They all work hard, have the same willingness to work all night to get the job done well, and yet remain in pretty good humor about it."[8] Similarly, McKinsey, Hewitt, and Arthur Andersen are all hard-working environments, above the norms for their respective professions.

Sense of Mission

In large part, the institutional commitment at one-firm firms is generated not only through a loyalty to the firm but also by the development of a sense of "mission," which is most frequently seen as client service. *All* professional service firms list in their mission statement what I call the "3 S's": the goals of (client) Service, (financial) Success, and (professional) Satisfaction. What is recognizable about one-firm firms is that, in their internal communications, there is a clear priority among these.

Within McKinsey, a new consultant learns within a very short period of time that the firm believes that the *client comes first,* the firm second, and the individual last. Goldman Sachs has a reputation for being "ready to sacrifice anything—including its relations with other Wall Street firms—to further the client's interests."[9] At Hewitt Associates, firm ideology is that the 3 S's must be carefully kept in balance at all times; however, client service is clearly number one. None of this is meant to suggest that one-firm firms necessarily render superior service to their clients compared with their competitors; nor that they always resolve inevitable day-to-day conflicts among the 3 S's in the same way. The point is that there *is* a firm ideology which everyone understands and which no one is allowed to take lightly.

Client Service

The emphasis at one-firm firms is clearly one of significant attention to managing client relations. In these firms, client service is defined more broadly than technical excellence: it is taken to mean a more far-ranging attentiveness to client needs and the quality of interaction between the firm and its clients. Goldman Sachs pioneered the concept on Wall Street of forming a marketing and new business development group whose primary responsibility is to manage the interface between the client and the various other parts of the firm that provide the technical and professional services. In most other Wall Street firms, client relations are the responsibility of the individual professionals who do the work, resulting in numerous (and potentially conflicting) contacts between a single client and the various other parts of the firm. Hewitt Associates, alone in its profession, has also pioneered such an "account management" group.[10] At McKinsey, in the words of one partner, "Here everyone realizes that the (client) *relationship* is paramount, not the specific project we happen to be working on at the moment."

The high-commitment, hard-working, mission-oriented, team-intensive characteristics of one-firm firms are reminiscent of another type of organization: the Marine Corps. Indeed, one-firm firms have an elite, Marine Corps attitude about themselves. An atmosphere of a special, private club prevails, where members feel that "we do things differently around here, and most of us couldn't consider working anywhere else." While all professional firms will assert that they have the best *professionals* in town, one-firm firms claim they have the best *firm* in town, a subtle but important difference.[11]

SUSTAINING THE ONE-FIRM FIRM CULTURE

Up to this point, we discussed a type of firm culture, a topic much discussed in recent management literature.[12] Our task now is to try and identify the management practices that have created and sustained this culture. Not surprisingly, since human assets constitute the vast majority of the productive resources of the professional service firm, most of these management practices involve human resource management.

A good overview of the mechanisms by which an "elite group" culture, with emphasis on the *group,* can be created is provided by Dr. Chip Bell,[13] a training consultant, who suggests that the elements of any high performance unit include the folowing:

- Entrance requirements into the group are extremely difficult.
- Acceptance into the group is followed by *intensive* job-related training, followed by team training.
- Challenging and high-risk team assignments are given early in the individual's career.
- Individuals are constantly tested to ensure that they measure up to the elite standards of the unit.
- Individuals and groups are given the autonomy to take risks normally not permissible at other firms.
- Training is viewed as continuous and related to assignments.
- Individual rewards are tied directly to collective results.
- Managers are seen as experts, pacesetters, and mentors (rather than as administrators).

As we shall see, all of these practices can be seen at work in the one-firm firms.

Recruiting

In contrast to many competing firms, one-firm firms invest a significant amount of *senior* professional time in their recruitment process, and they tend to be much more selective than their competition. At one-firm firms, recruiting is either heavily centralized or well coordinated centrally. At Hewitt Associates, over 1,000 students at sixty-five schools were interviewed in 1980. Of the seventy-two offers that were made, fifty accepted. Each of the 198 invited to the firm's offices spent a half-day with a psychologist (at a cost to the firm of $600 per person) for career counseling to find out if the person was suited for Hewitt's work and would fit within the firm's culture. At Goldman Sachs, 1,000 MBAs are interviewed each year; approximately thirty are chosen. Interviewing likely candidates is a major responsibility of the firm's seventy-three partners (the firm has over 1,600 professionals). Goldman partner James Gorter notes, "Recruiting responsibilities almost come before your business responsibilities."[14] At Latham & Watkins, all candidates get twenty-five to thirty interviews, compared to a norm in the legal profession of approximately five to ten interviews. As a McKinsey partner noted:

> In our business, the game is won or lost at the recruiting stage: we take it very seriously. And it's not a quantity game, it's a quality game. You've got to find the best people you can, and the trick is to understand what *best* means. It's not just brains, not just presentability: you have to try and detect the potentially fully developed professional in the person, and not just look at what they are *now*. Some firms hire in a superficial way, relying on the up-or-out system to screen out the losers. We do have an up-or-out system, but we don't use it as a substitute for good recruiting practices. To us, the costs of recruiting-mistake turnover are too high, in dollars, in morale, and in client service, to ignore.

Training

One-firm firms are notable for their investment in firmwide training, which serves both as a way to add to the substantive skills of juniors and as an important group socialization function.[15] The best examples of this practice are Arthur Andersen and McKinsey. The former is renowned among accounting students for its training center in St. Charles, Illinois (a fully equipped college campus that the firm acquired and converted to its own uses), to which young professionals are sent from around the world. In the words of one Andersen partner: "To this day, I have useful friendships, forged at St. Charles, with people across the firm in different offices and disciplines. If I need to get something done outside my own expertise, I have people I can call on who will do me a favor, even if it comes out of their own hide. They know I'll return it."

Similarly, McKinsey's two-week training program for new professionals is renowned among business school students. The program is run by one or more of the firm's senior professionals, who spend a significant amount of time inculcating the firm's values by telling Marvin Bower stories—Bower, who ran the firm for many years, is largely credited with making McKinsey what it is today. The training program is not always held in the U.S. but rotates between the countries where McKinsey has offices. This not only reinforces the one-firm image (as opposed to a headquarters with branch offices) but also has a dramatic effect on the young professionals' view of the firm. As one of my ex-students told me: "Being sent to Europe for a two-week training program during your first few months with the firm impresses the hell out of you. It makes you think: 'This is a class outfit.' It also both frightens you and gives you confidence. You say, 'Boy, they must think I'm good if they're prepared to spend all this money on me.' But then you worry about whether you can live up to it: it's very motivating." All young professionals are given a copy of Marvin Bower's history of the firm, *Perspectives on McKinsey,* which, unlike many professional firm histories, is as full of philosophy and advice as it is dry on historical facts.

"Growing Their Own" Professionals

Unlike many of their competitors, all of the one-firm firms tend to "grow their own" professionals, rather than to make significant use of lateral hiring of senior professionals. In other words, in the acquisition of human capital, they tend to "make" rather than "buy." This is not to say that no lateral hires are made—just that they are done infrequently, and with extreme caution. "I had to meet with the associates (i.e., not only the partners) before the firm [Latham & Watkins] took me on," Carla Hills [former Secretary of Housing and Urban Development] recalls. "Lateral entry is a big trauma for this place. But that's how it should be."[16]

Avoiding Mergers

A related practice of one-firm firms is the deliberate avoidance of growth by merger. Arthur Andersen, unlike most of the Big-8 firms, did not join in the merger and acquisition boom of the 1950s and early 1960s, in an attempt to become part of a nationwide accounting profession network. Instead, it grew its own regional (and international) offices. Similarly, the decade-long merger mania in investment banking has left Goldman Sachs, which opted out of this trend, as one of the few independent partnerships on the street. In contrast to many other consulting firms, McKinsey's overseas offices were all launched on a grow-your-own basis, initially staffed with U.S. personnel, rather than on an acquisition basis. With one recent exception, all of Latham & Watkins's branch offices were all grown internally.

It is clear that this avoidance of growth through laterals or mergers plays a critical role in both creating and preserving the sense of institutional identity, which is the cornerstone of the one-firm system.

Controlled Growth

As a high proportion of the professional staff shares an extensive, common work history with the one-firm firm, group loyalty is easier to foster. Of course, this staffing strategy has implications for the *rate* of growth pursued by the one-firm firm. At such firms (in contrast to many competitors), high growth is not a declared goal. Rather, such firms aim for *controlled* growth. The approach is one of, "We'll grow as fast as we can train our people." As Ron Daniel of McKinsey phrases it: "We neither shun growth nor idolize it. We view it as a by-product of achieving our other goals." All of the one-firm firms assert that the major constraint on their growth is not client demand, but the supply of qualified people they can find and train to their way of practicing.

Selective Business Pursuits

Related to this issue is the fact that one-firm firms tend to be more selective than their competitors in the type of business they pursue. It has been reported that an essential element of the Goldman culture is its calculated choosiness about the clients it takes on. The firm has let it be known, both internally and externally, that it "adheres to certain standards—and that it won't compromise them for the sake of a quick buck."[17] At McKinsey, the firm's long-standing strategy is that it will only work for "the top guy" (i.e., the chief executive officer) and, as illustrated internally with countless Marvin Bower stories, will only do those projects where the potential value delivered is demonstrably far in excess of the firm's charges. Junior staff at McKinsey quickly hears stories of projects the firm has turned down because the partner did not believe the firm could add sufficient value to cover its fees. Similarly, while Andersen has been an aggressive marketer (a property common to all the one-firm firms), Andersen appears to have taken a more studied, less "opportunistic" approach to business development than have their competitors.

Consequently, one-firm firms tend to have a less varied practice-mix and a more homogeneous client base than do their more explicitly individualistic competitors. Unlike, say, Booz, Allen, McKinsey's practice is relatively focused on

three main areas: organization work, strategy consulting, and operations studies. In the late 1970s, the heyday of "strategy boutiques," many outsiders commented on the firm's reluctance to chase after fast-growing new specialties.[18] But McKinsey, like all of the other one-firm firms, enters new areas "big, or not at all." Andersen's strategy in its consulting work (the fastest growing area for all of the Big-8) has been more clearly focused on computer-based systems design and installation than has the variegated practices of most of its competitors. Goldman has been notably selective in which segments of the investment market it has entered, and has become a dominant player in virtually every sector it has entered.

Outplacement

One of the fortunate consequences of the controlled growth strategy at one-firm firms and the avoidance of laterals and mergers is that these firms, in contrast to many competitors, rarely lose valued people to competitors. At each of the firms named above, I have heard the claim that, "Many of our people have been approached by competitors offering more money to help them launch or bolster a part of the practice. But our people prefer to stay." On Wall Street, raiding of competing firms' top professionals has reached epidemic proportions; yet, this does not include Goldman Sachs. It is said that one of the rarest beasts on Wall Street is an *ex*-Goldman professional: very few leave the firm.

Turnover at one-firm firms is clearly more carefully managed than it is among competitors. Those one-firm firms that do enforce an up-or-out system (McKinsey and Andersen) work actively to place their alumni/ae in good positions preferably with favored clients. McKinsey's regular alumni/ae reunions, a vivid demonstration of its success in breeding loyalty to the firm, are held two or three times a year. In part, due to the "caring" approach taken to junior staff, one-firm firms are able to achieve a very profitable high-leverage strategy (i.e., high ratio of junior to senior staff) without *excessive* pressures for growth to provide promotion opportunities.[19]

Compensation

Internal management procedures at one-firm firms constantly reinforce the team concept. Most important, compensation systems (particularly for partners) are designed to encourage intra-firm cooperation. Whereas many other firms make heavy use of departmental or local-office profitability in setting compensation (i.e., take a *measurement*-oriented, profit-center approach), one-firm firms tend to set compensation (both for partners *and* juniors) through a *judgmental* process, assessing total contribution to the firm. Unique among the Big-8, Andersen has a single worldwide partnership cost-sharing pool (as opposed to separate country profit centers): individual partners share in the joint economics of the whole firm, not just their country (or local office). "The virtue of the 'one-pool' system, as opposed to heavy profit-centering, is that a superior individual in an otherwise poor-profit office can be rewarded appropriately," one Andersen partner pointed out. "Similarly, a weaker individual in a successful office does not get a windfall gain. Further, if you tie individual partner compensation too tightly to departmental or office profitability, it's hard to take into account the particular circumstances of that office. A guy that shows medium profitability in a tough market probably deserves more than one with higher profitability in an easy market where we already have a high market share."

Hewitt Associates sets its partner compensation levels only after all partners have been invited to comment on the contributions (qualitative *and* quantitative) made by other partners on "their" projects and other firmwide affairs. Vigorous efforts are made to assess contributions to the firm that do not show up in the measurable factors. Peter Friedes notes:

We think that having no profit centers is a great advantage to us. Other organizations don't realize how much time they waste fighting over allocations of overhead, transfer charges, and other mechanisms caused by a profit-center mentality. Whenever there are profit centers, cooperation between groups suffers badly. Of course, we pay a price for not having them: specific accountability is hard to pin down. We often don't know precisely whose time we are writing off, or who precisely brought in that new account. But at least we don't fight over it: we get on with our work. Our people know that, over time, good performance will be recognized and rewarded.

Goldman Sachs also runs a judgment-based (rather than measurement-based) compensation system, including "a month-long evaluation process in which performance is reviewed not only by a person's superiors but by other partners as well, and finally by the management committee. During that review, 'how well you do when other parts of the firm ask for your help on some project' plays a big part."[20] At Latham & Watkins, "15 percent of the firm's income is set aside as a separate fund from which the executive committee, at its sole discretion, awards partners additional compensation based on their general contribution to the firm in terms of such factors as client relations, hours billed, and even the business office's 'scoring' of how promptly the partner has logged his or her own time, sent out and collected bills, and otherwise helped the place run well."[21]

Investments in Research and Development

In most professional service firms, particularly in those with a heavy emphasis on short-term results or year-by-year performance evaluations, any activity that takes an individual away from direct revenue-producing work is considered a detour off the professional success track within the firm and is therefore avoided. This is not the case with one-firm firms.

As the one-firm culture is based on a "team-player'' judgment-system approach to evaluations and compensation (at both the partner and junior level), it is *relatively* easier (although it is never easy) for one-firm firms to get their best professionals to engage in nonbillable, stafflike activities such as research and development (R&D), market research, and other investments in the firm's future. For example, McKinsey is noted in the consulting profession for its internally funded R&D projects, of which the most famous example is the work that resulted in the best seller, *In Search of Excellence*. This book, however, was only one of a large number of staff projects continually under way in the firm. An ex-student of mine noted that ''at McKinsey, to be selected to do something for the firm is an honor: it's a quick way to get famous in the firm if you succeed. And, of course, you're expected to succeed. Firm projects are treated as seriously as client work, and your performance is closely examined. However, my friends at other firms tell me that firm projects are a high-risk thing to do: they worry about whether their low chargeable hours will be held against them later on.''

Andersen likewise invests heavily in firmwide activities. For instance, it conducts extensive cross-office and cross-functional industry programs, which attempt to coordinate all of the firm's activities with respect to specific industries. In fact, it is rumored, although no one has the statistics, that Andersen invests a higher proportion of its gross revenues in firmwide investment activities than does any other firm.

Goldman's commitment to investing in its own future is illustrated by the firm's policy of forcing partners to keep their capital in the firm rather than to take extraordinarily high incomes. Hewitt's commitment to R&D is built into its organizational structure. Rather than scatter its professional experts throughout its multiple office system (staffed predominantly with account managers), it chose to concentrate its professional groups in three locations in order to promote the rapid cross-fertilization of professional ideas. Significant investments of professional time are made in nonbillable research work under the guidance of professional group managers who establish budgets for such work in negotiation with the managing partner.

Communication

Communication at a one-firm firm is remarkably open and is clearly used as a bonding technique to hold the firm together. All the firms described above make *heavy* use of memorandums to keep everyone informed of what is happening in other parts of the firm, above and beyond the token efforts frequently made at other firms. Frequent firmwide meetings are held, with an emphasis on cross-boundary (i.e., interoffice and interdepartmental) gatherings. Such meetings are valued (and clearly designed) as much as for the social interaction as for whatever the agenda happens to be: people *go* to the meetings. (At numerous other firms I have observed, meetings are seen as distractions from the firm's, or the individual's, business, and people bow out whenever they can.)

At most one-firm firms, open communication extends to financial matters as well. At Hewitt, they believe that ''anyone has a right to know anything about the firm except the personal affairs of another individual.'' At an annual meeting with all junior personnel (including secretaries and other support staff), the managing partner discloses the firm's economic results and answers any and all questions from the audience. At Latham & Watkins, junior associates are significantly involved in all major firm committees, including recruiting, choosing new partners, awarding associate bonuses, and so on. All significant matters about the firm are well known to the associates.

Absence of Status Symbols

Working hard to involve nonpartners in firm affairs and winning their commitment to the firm's success is a hallmark of the one-firm firm and is reinforced by a widely common practice of sharing firm profits more deeply within the organization than is common at other firms. (The ratio between the highest paid and lowest paid partner tends to be markedly less at one-firm firms than it is among their competitors.) There is also a suppression of status differentials between senior and junior members of the firm: an important activity if the firm is attempting to make everyone, junior and senior alike, feel a part of the team. At Hewitt Associates, deemphasizing status extends to the physical surroundings: everyone, from the newest hire to the oldest partner, has the same size office.

The absence of status conflicts in one-firm firms is also noticeable across departments. In today's world of professional megafirms composed of departments specializing in vastly different areas, one of the most significant dangers is that professionals in one area may come to view *their* area as somehow more elite, more exciting, more profitable, or more important to the firm than another area. Their loyalty is to their department, or their local office, and not to the firm. Yet the success of the firm clearly depends upon doing well in all areas. On Wall Street, different psychological profiles of, and an antipathy between, say, traders and investment bankers is notorious: many attribute the recent turmoil at Lehman Brothers (now Shearson Lehman) to this syndrome. In some law firms, corporate lawyers and litigators are often considered distinct breeds of people who view the world in different ways. In some accounting firms, mutual suspicion among audit, tax, and consulting partners is rampant. In consulting firms, frequently there are status conflicts between the "front-room" client handlers and the "back-room" technical experts.

What strikes any visitor to a one-firm firm is the deeply held mutual respect across departmental, geographic, and functional boundaries. Members of one-firm firms clearly *like* (and respect) their counterparts in other areas, which makes for the successful cross-boundary coordination that is increasingly essential in today's marketplace. Jonathan Cohen of Goldman Sachs notes that out-of-office socialization among Goldman professionals appears to take place more frequently than it does at other Wall Street firms. Retired Marvin Bower of McKinsey asserts that one of the elements in creating the one-firm culture is mutual trust, both horizontally and vertically. This atmosphere is created primarily by the behavior of the firm's leadership, who must set the style for the firm. Unlike many other firms, leaders of one-firm firms work hard not to be identified with or labeled as being closer to one group than another. Cross-boundary respect is also achieved at most one-firm firms by the common practice of rotating senior professionals among the various offices and departments of the firm.

Governance: Consensus-building Style

How are one-firm firms governed? Are they democracies or autocracies? Without exception, one-firm firms are led (*not* managed) in a consensus-building style.[22] All have (or have had) strong leaders who engage in extensive consultation before major decisions are taken. It is important to note that all of these firms do indeed have leaders: they are not anarchic democracies, nor are they dictatorships. Whether one is reading about Goldman's two Johns (Weinberg and Whitehead), McKinsey's (retired) Marvin Bower and Ron Daniels, Latham & Watkins's Clinton Stevenson, or Hewitt's Peter Friedes, it is clear that one is learning about expert communicators who see their role as preserver of the "true religion." Above all else, they are cheerleaders who suppress their own egos in the name of the institution they head. Such firms also have continuity in leadership: while many of them have electoral systems of governance, leaders tend to stay in place for long periods of time. What is more, the firm's culture outlasts the tenure of any given individual.

Of course, the success of the consensus-building approach to firm governance and the continuity of leadership at one-firm firms is not fortuitous. Since their whole philosophy (and, as I have tried to show, their substantive managerial practices) is built upon cooperative teamwork, consensus is more readily achieved here than it is at other firms. The willingness to allow leaders the freedom to make decisions on behalf of the firm (the absence of which has stymied many other "democratic" firms) was "prewired" into the system long ago, since everyone shares the same values. The one-firm system *is* a system.

CONCLUSION: POTENTIAL WEAKNESSES

Clearly, the one-firm firm system is powerful. What are its weaknesses? The dangers of this approach are reasonably obvious. Above all else, there is the danger of self-congratulatory complacency: a firm that has an integrated system that *works* may, if it is not careful, become insensitive to shifts in its environment that demand changes in the system. The very commitment to "our firm's way of doing things," which is the one-firm firm's strengths, can also be its greatest weakness. This is particularly true because of the chance of "inbreeding" that comes from "growing-your-own" professionals. To deal with this, there is a final ingredient required in the formula: self-criticism. At McKinsey, Andersen, Goldman, and Hewitt, partners have asserted to me that "we have no harsher critics than ourselves: we're constantly looking for ways to improve what we do." However, it must be acknowledged that, without the diversity common at other professional service firms, one-firm firms with strong cultures run the danger of making even self-criticism a proforma exercise.

Another potential weakness of the one-firm firm culture is that it runs the danger of being insufficiently entrepreneurial, at least in the short run. Other more individualistic firms, which promote and reward opportunistic behav-

ior by individuals and separate profit centers, may be better at reorganizing and capitalizing on emerging trends early in their development. Although contrary examples can be cited, one-firm firms are rarely "pioneers": they try to be (and usually are) good at entering emerging markets as a late second or third. And because of the firm-wide concentrated attack they are able to effect, they are frequently successful at this. (The similarity to IBM in this regard, as is much of what has been discussed above, is readily noticeable.)

The one-firm approach is *not* the only way to run a professional service firm. However, it clearly is a very successful way to run a firm. The "team spirit" of the firms described here is broadly admired by their competitors and is not easily copied. As I have attempted to show, the one-firm firm system is *interally* consistent: all of its practices, from recruiting through compensation, performance appraisal, approaches to market, governance, control systems, and above all, culture and human resource strategy, make for a consistent whole.

REFERENCES

1. D. H. Maister, "Profitability: Beating the Downward Trend," *Journal of Management Consulting,* Fall 1984, pp. 39–44.
2. D. H. Maister, "Quality Work Doesn't Mean Quality Service," *American Lawyer,* April 1984.
3. R. Levering, M. Moskowitz, and M. Katz, *The 100 Best Companies to Work for in America* (Reading, MA: Addison-Wesley, 1984).
4. B. McGoldrick, "Inside the Goldman Sachs Culture," *Institutional Investor,* January 1984.
5. S. Brill, "Is Latham & Watkins America's Best Run Firm?" *American Lawyer,* August 1981, pp. 12–14.
6. Ibid.
7. Levering et al. (1984).
8. McGoldrick (January 1984).
9. Ibid.
10. D. H. Maister, *Hewitt Associates* (Boston, MA:

Harvard University, Graduate School of Business, HBS Case Services).

11. D. H. Maister, "What Kind of Excellence?" *American Lawyer,* January–February 1985, pp. 4–6.

12. See, for example, V. J. Sathe, *Culture and Related Corporate Realities* (Homewood, IL: Richard D. Irwin, Inc., 1985).

13. C. Bell, "How to Create a High Performance Training Unit," *Training,* October 1980, pp. 49–52.

14. McGoldrick (January 1984).

15. D. H. Maister, "How to Build Human Capital," *American Lawyer,* June 1984.

16. Brill (August 1981).

17. McGoldrick (January 1984).

18. See, for example, "The New Shape of Management Consulting," *Business Week,* 21 May 1979.

19. For a discussion of the role of turnover on professional service firm success, see D. H. Maister, "Balancing the Professional Service Firm," *Sloan Management Review,* Fall 1982, pp. 15–29.

20. McGoldrick (January 1984).

21. Brill (August 1981).

22. For a discussion of governance in professional firms, see D. H. Maister, "Partnership Politics," *American Lawyer,* October 1984.

Project Performance and the Locus of Influence in the R&D Matrix

Ralph Katz

Thomas J. Allen

Abstract. This study examines the relationship between project performance and the relative influence of project and functional managers in 86 R&D teams in nine technology-based organizations. Performance relationships are investigated for three areas of influence within the project team and for influence in the overall organizations. Analyses show higher project performance when influence over salaries and promotions is perceived as balanced between project and functional managers. Performance reaches its highest level, however, when organizational influence is centered in the project manager and influence over technical details of the work is centered in the functional manager.

The matrix structure was first developed in research and development organizations in an attempt to capture the benefits and minimize the liabilities of two earlier forms of organization, the functional structure and the project form of organization (Allen, 1977; Kingdon, 1973; Marquis, 1969).

The functional alternative, in which departments are organized around disciplines or technologies, enables engineers to stay in touch more easily with new developments in those disciplines or technologies than does the project form. It has, however, the disadvantage of creating separations between technologies, which makes interdisciplinary projects more difficult to coordinate.

The project form of organization overcomes the coordination problem by grouping engineers together on the basis of the problem or project on which they are working, regardless of their disciplines. Although it eases the integration of mutildisciplinary efforts, the project structure removes individuals from their disciplinary departments. The detachment involved makes it more difficult for professionals to keep pace with the most recent developments in their underlying disciplines and results in poorer performance on longer-term technical efforts than occurs in functionally grouped organizations. (Marquis & Straight, 1965).

FORCES INHERENT IN THE MATRIX

The matrix, by creating an integrating force in a program or project office, attempts to overcome

From the *Academy of Management Journal,* 1985, Vol. 28, No. 1, 67–87. Reprinted by permission.

the divisions that are inherent in the basic functional structure. In the matrix, project or program managers and their staffs are charged with the responsibility of integrating the efforts of engineers who draw upon a variety of different disciplines and technical specialties in the development of new products or processes (Galbraith, 1973). The managers of functional departments, on the other hand, are responsible for making sure that the organization is aware of the most recent developments in its relevant technologies, thereby insuring the technical integrity of products and processes that the program or project office is attempting to develop.

These disparate responsibilities often lead to conflict between the two arms of the matrix. Project managers are often forced by market needs to assume a shorter range view of the marketing function than functional managers need to have (Lawrence & Lorsch, 1967). Since they are responsible for developing a product that can be successfully produced and marketed, project managers take on a perspective that is sometimes more closely aligned to that of persons in marketing or manufacturing than to the perspective held in the research and development organization. Functional department heads, with their closer attachment to underlying technologies, are inclined to take a longer term view and consequently may be more concerned with the organization's capability to use the most up-to-date technologies than with meeting immediate customer needs.

Both of these perspectives are necessary to the survival of the organization. Someone has to be concerned with getting new products out into the market, and someone has to be concerned with maintaining the organization's long-term capability to develop and incorporate technical advancements into future products. Research and development organizations, no matter how they are organized, always have both of these concerns. The matrix structure merely makes them explicit by vesting the two sets of concerns in separate managers.

In formalizing these two distinct lines of managerial influence, the R&D organization is generating "deliberate conflict" between two essential managerial perspectives as a means of balancing these two organizational needs (Cleland, 1968). Project managers whose prime directive is to get the product "out the door" are matched against functional managers who tend to hold back because they can always make the product "a little better," given more time and effort (Allen, 1977; Marquis, 1969). When these two opposing forces are properly balanced, the organization should achieve a more nearly optimum balance, both in terms of product completion and technical excellence. Unfortunately, a balanced situation is not easy to achieve. Often one or the other arm of the matrix will dominate, and then, what appears to be a matrix on paper becomes either a project or a functional organization in operation.

These two conflicting forces of a matrix affect R&D project performance principally through their respective influences on the behaviors and attitudes of individual engineers. It is the engineers who perform the actual problem-solving activities that result in new products or processes. How they view the relative power of project and functional managers over their work lives will strongly influence how they respond to the different sets of pressures and priorities confronting them in the performance of their everyday tasks.

In any matrix organization, there are at least three broad areas of decision making in which both project and functional managers are supposed to be involved: (1) technical decisions regarding project work activities and solution strategies; (2) determination of salaries and promotional opportunities; and (3) staffing and organizational assignments of engineers to particular project activities. These are critical areas in which project and functional managers contend for influence, for it is through these supervisory activities that each side of the matrix attempts to motivate and direct each engineer's efforts and

470

performance (Kingdon, 1973). The degree to which each side of the matrix is successful in building its power and influence within the R&D organization will have a strong bearing on the outcomes that emerge from the many interdependent engineering activities (Wilemon & Gemmill, 1971).

Although a great deal has recently been written about matrix organizations (e.g., Hill & White, 1979; Souder, 1979), very little is actually known about the effectiveness of these structures (Knight, 1976). In particular, there has been no research investigating the relationships between project performance and the distribution of power and influence within the organization. Will a balance in power between project and functionally oriented forces result in higher project performance? In an attempt to answer this question, the present study examines the relationships between project performance and the relative dominance of project and functional managers for 86 matrix project teams from nine technology-based organizations.

HYPOTHESES

Details of Project Work

This is the arena in which project and functional interests are most likely to come into direct conflict. The project manager has ultimate responsibility for bringing the new product into being and is, therefore, intimately concerned with the technical approaches used in accomplishing that outcome. However, if the project side of the matrix is allowed to dominate development work, two quite different problems can develop. At one extreme, there is the possibility that sacrifices in technical quality and long-term reliability will be made in order to meet budget, schedule, and immediate market demands (Knight, 1977). At the other extreme, the potential of products is often oversold by making claims that are beyond the organization's current technological capability to deliver.

To guard against these shortcomings, functional managers can be held accountable for the overall integrity of the product's technical content. If the functional side of the matrix becomes overly dominant, however, the danger is that the product will include not only more sophisticated, but also perhaps less proven and riskier technology. The functional manager's desire to be technologically aggressive—to develop and use the most attractive, most advance technology—must be countered by forces that are more sensitive to the operational environment and more concerned with moving developmental efforts into final physical reality (Mansfield & Wagner, 1975; Utterback, 1974).

To balance the influence of both project and functional managers over technical details is often a difficult task. While an engineer may report to both managers in a formal sense, the degree to which these managers both actively influence the direction or clarification of technical details and solution strategies will vary considerably from project to project, depending on the ability and willingness of the two managers to understand and become involved in the relevant technology and its applications. Nonetheless, project performance should be higher when team members can take both perspectives into account. Accordingly, the following is proposed:

Hypothesis 1. Project performance will be higher in a matrix structure when both project and functional managers are seen to exert equal influence over the detailed technical work of engineers.

Salaries and Promotions

Advocates of matrix organizations (e.g., Davis & Lawrence, 1977; Kingdon, 1973; Sayles, 1976) have long agreed on the importance of achieving balanced influence over salary and promotion decisions. Both Knight (1976) and Goggin (1974) explicitly emphasize that matrix organizations require matching control systems to support their multidimensional structures; otherwise, they would be undermined by reward systems that are based on assumptions of unitary authority. The underlying argument is that when engineers view either their project or their functional managers as having more control over chances for salary increases and promotions, the engineers' behaviors and priorities are more likely to be influenced and directed solely by the side with that control.

This is one of the key issues in what are often described as "paper matrix" situations: management assumes that by drawing overlapping structures and by prescribing areas of mutual responsibility, balance will be achieved among appropriate supporting management systems. In practice, however, one of the two components of the matrix comes to dominate or appears to dominate in key areas such as determination of salaries or of promotions. It is important to stress here that it is the engineer's perception that counts. Unless engineers see both managers as controlling their progress in terms of income and status, there will be a natural tendency for them, particularly in conflict situations, to heed the desires of one manager to the neglect of the other. The matrix then ceases to function, resulting in a structure that is more likely to resemble either the pure project or the pure functional form of organization despite any "paper" claims to the contrary. We therefore expect that:

> *Hypothesis 2. Project performance will be higher in a matrix structure when both project and functional managers are seen to exert equal influence over the promotions and rewards of engineers than it will be when one or the other manager is seen as dominating.*

Personnel Assignments

Personnel assignments often provide the focus for the priority battles that frequently afflict matrix organizations. With the pressure on them from both management and customers to produce, project managers often find themselves in tight competition for the resources necessary to provide results (Knight, 1977; Steiner & Ryan, 1968). One of the most critical of these resources is technical talent. Each functional department employs engineers of varying technical backgrounds, experiences, and capabilities. (Allen & Cohen, 1969). Every project manager learns quickly which engineers are the top performers and naturally wants them assigned to his project. As a result, an intense rivalry develops among project managers, with each attempting to secure the most appropriate and most talented engineers for his project (Cleland & King, 1968). Functional managers, on the other hand, have a different motivation. They have no difficulty finding resources to support their top performers, but they also have to keep the rest of their engineering staff employed. They must therefore allocate or market the services of their less talented engineers to all project groupings.

At this point we must make a distinction between performance at the project level and performance at the level of the entire R&D organization. Organizational performance might be higher when project and functional managers have equal influence over personnel assignments. The performance of a single project, however, will probably be higher when that project's manager has greater influence over personnel assignments, since presumably that project will then obtain the best talent. Since our study is at the project level, and although we realize that high individual project performance may be suboptimal for the entire R&D organization, we expect that:

> *Hypothesis 3. Project performance will, on the average, be higher when project managers are seen to exert greater influence over personnel assignments to their projects than functional managers.*

Organizational Influence

We must consider more than the bases of supervisory influence that exist within a project group. Considerable research has shown that managers of high performing projects are also influential outside their project teams (e.g., Katz & Allen, 1982; Likert, 1967; Pelz, 1952; Steiner & Ryan, 1968). According to these studies, managers affect the behaviors and motivations of subordinates not only through leadership directed *within* the project group but also through their organizational influence *outside* the project (Katz & Tushman, 1981; Pfeffer & Salancik, 1978). The critical importance of organizational influence on project outcomes has also been confirmed by many studies of technological innovation (e.g., Achilladelis, Jervis, & Robertson, 1971; Myers & Marquis, 1969). In almost every instance, successful innovation required the strong support of organizationally powerful managers who could provide essential resources, mediate intergroup conflicts, and were positioned to protect the developmental effort from outside sources of interference.

Based on these findings, if engineers see either arm of the matrix as having greater power in the organization at large, their behavior should be affected, particularly in situations of conflict. Engineers want to be on the "winning team" (Kidder, 1981). Perceptions of organizational influence, therefore, will be an important determinant of what actually occurs in a project, for an imbalance would probably result in engineers' paying greater attention and attributing greater importance to the more powerful side of the matrix.

This does not mean that the locus of organizational influence necessarily determines the loci of influence over work, rewards, and assignments. There may be, for example, many instances in which the less organizationally powerful manager exerts greater influence over one of the other dimensions. Such incongruences place engineers in uncomfortable positions, particularly if there is strong disagreement between their two managers. As discussed by Allen (1966), discomfort over technical direction often leads to postponement of critical technical decisions and failure to narrow the scope of technical alternatives, resulting in lower project performance. From an exploratory standpoint, our research examines two important questions involving organizational and project influence. First, is there a strong association between perceived organizational influence and the relative dominance of project and functional managers over the rewards, personnel assignments, and technical work of project engineers? And second, to what extent do these dimensions of organizational and internal dominance interact to affect project performance? Do they independently relate to project performance or do they interact in determining performance?

The basic model (Figure 1) underlying our

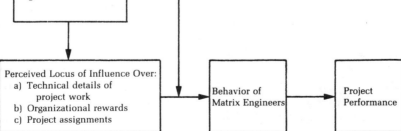

FIGURE 1. *A Model of the Relationships between Project Performance and Loci of Influence*

473

study, then, is that the loci of power between project and functional managers relate to project performance through their respective effects on the behaviors and efforts of engineers in matrix situations. More specifically, how professionals perceive the distribution of influence between their functional and project managers over the technical details of their project work, over their chances for organizational rewards, and over their assignments to particular project activities will significantly affect their performances on their project teams, as hypothesized. These perceived loci of influence, moreover, may be strongly related to how engineers in a matrix organization see the relative power of the two managers within the larger organization.

On the other hand, the locus of organizational influence may not be associated with any of these three measures of internal influence; instead, it may be an additional factor that interacts with these measures to affect project performance. Most likely, the locus of organizational influence will interact with a particular measure of internal project influence only when the two influence measures are not strongly interconnected; otherwise, it is more likely that they will covary with project performance.

RESEARCH METHODS

Setting

The data presented in this paper derive from a study of R&D project teams in nine major U.S. organizations. Although the selection of participating organizations could not be made random, they were chosen to represent several distinct work sectors and markets. Two of the sites are government laboratories; three are not-for-profit firms receiving most of their funding from government agencies. The four remaining companies are in private industry, two in aerospace, one in electronics, and one in food processing.

In each organization, we first met with higher level managers in order to gain an understanding of how the R&D organization was structured, identify the project assignments of all R&D professionals, and learn the multiple reporting relationships of all project members. Short meetings were then scheduled with the R&D professionals to explain the broad purposes of our study, to solicit their voluntary cooperation, and to distribute individual questionnaires to all professionals. To insure the accuracy of data on project assignments, we told respondents to answer all questions in terms of the project assignment identified on the questionnaire's front page. If this was incorrect or out of date, the respondent was told to replace it with the correct project assignment. We also tailored questionnaires to the particular reporting structure by using language appropriate to each project group. Project managers, appropriate functional managers, and staff engineers and scientists received slightly different questionnaires; the managers were not asked questions about their own influence or about the influence of their managerial counterparts.

We asked individuals to complete their questionnaires as soon as possible, and gave them stamped, return envelopes so that they could mail completed forms directly to us. (These procedures not only insured voluntary participation, but also enhanced data quality since respondents had to commit their own time and effort.) Response rates across organizations were extremely high, ranging from a low of 82 percent to a high of 96 percent. Data from the nine organizations were collected over a period of 21 months during the 1979 and 1980 calendar years.

Although these procedures yielded over 2000 respondents from 201 project teams, only 86 projects involved engineers and scientists in matrix dual-reporting relationships. A total of 486 engineers worked in matrix relationships in the 86 projects, an average of almost 6 engineers per project. Responses of these engineers, averaged to provide project measures, are the basic data analyzed. The proportion of the project team working in dual-reporting relationships varied from 20 percent (1 project) to 100 percent (18 projects); 19 projects had 70–99 percent, 21 projects had 60–69 percent, 20 projects had 50–59 percent, and 7 projects had 21–49 percent in matrix dual-reporting relationships. Results reported here are based only upon responses of engineers in matrix dual-reporting structures. Since the percentage of matrix engineers within projects varies considerably across the sample, significant findings will be reexamined as a function of these variations.

Matrix Relationships

We asked respondents in matrix structures to indicate on 7-point Likert-type scales the degree to which their project and functional managers influenced: (1) the technical details of their project work; (2) their salary increases and promotions; (3) their having been selected to work on the project; and (4) the overall conduct of the organization. For each of these dimensions of influence, scale responses ranged from 1 for "my project manager dominates" to 7 for "my functional manager dominates"; the middle point, 4, indicated that influence was balanced between the two. For each question, we averaged individual member responses to calculate overall project scores for the four influence areas.

For each measure of influence, we employed a one-way ANOVA to compare within-project variance to between-project variance (cf. Katz & Tushman, 1979) and used Bartlett's M-test to examine the homogeneity of intraproject variance. Following these two broad tests, separate F-tests insured that the variance of each measure within each project was not significantly greater than the pooled variance. Except for a few isolated instances, the four influence measures for these projects passed all three tests, thereby strongly supporting the procedure of combining individual perceptions to derive aggregated project scores. Results from such statistical methods—as discussed by Oldham (1976), Sheridan and Vredenburgh (1978), and others—suggest a very high level of consensus or reliability by project for each of our influence measures, although the reliability of individual responses is certainly limited by the 1-item scales. All of our analyses, however, were conducted at the project level; responses of individual engineers were averaged to provide project measures. Also, project measures reflected only the responses of project engineers in matrix reporting relationships. For each dimension of influence, lower scores were taken to indicate project manager dominance and higher scores to indicate functional manager dominance. Because some questions were not included in early versions of the questionnaire, the number of project teams from which complete data were obtained ranged from 63 to 86.

Project Performance

Since measures of objective performance that are comparable across different technologies have yet to be developed, we used a subjective measure similar to that of many studies, including Lawrence and Lorsch (1967) and Katz and Tushman (1981). In each organization, we measured project performance by interviewing managers who were at least one hierarchical level above the project and functional managers, asking them to indicate on a 5-point Likert-type scale whether a project team was performing above, below, or at the level expected of them, given the particular technical activities on which they were working. Managers evaluated only those projects that they were personally familiar with and knowledgeable about. Evaluations were made independently and submitted confidentially to the investigators. As in the previously mentioned studies, the managers considered—but were not limited to—criteria that included schedule, budget, and cost performance; innovativeness; adaptability; and the ability to cooperate with other areas of the organization. On the average, between four and five managers evaluated each project. The evaluations showed very strong internal consensus within each organization (Spearman-Brown reliabilities range from a low of .74 to a high of .93). It was therefore safe to average the ratings of individual managers to yield reliable project performance scores. However, performance data were missing from two projects. Right after we collected our data, an expert panel of independent, outside R&D professionals exhaustively evaluated a small subset of our project base ($N=$ 8). The ordering of their project performance evaluations agreed perfectly with the ordering of our own aggregated measures of performance. Such agreement between two separate sources provides considerable support for the validity of our project performance measures. Finally, our measures of relative project performance were not confounded with size of project groups; they were not significantly related to the overall number of project members, to the number of matrix project members, or to the proportion of project members in matrix reporting relationships. To clarify the distinction between high and low project performance, performance measures were converted to normalized scores, with a mean of 0 (the original sample mean was 3.32).

RESULTS

As previously explained, we averaged responses to classify projects according to the degree to which project of functional managers exerted influence over each of four activity areas. Project scores of 1 through 3 were coded as signifying dominant influence by the project manager, while scores of 5 through 7 were taken to indicate functional manager dominance. Intermediate values, greater than 3 and less than 5, were considered as signifying balanced influence.

The locus of influence, as shown in Table 1, varies considerably both among projects and across dimensions of influence. Influence over technical details of work and over personnel assignments is balanced in the majority of cases. On the other hand, over half of the functional managers are seen as having greater influence over salaries and promotions: functional managers are viewed as controlling these rewards in almost 60 percent of the projects, project managers in only 7 percent. It is important to remember that it is the perceptions of engineers in matrix-reporting relationships that was measured, for it is perceived reality—not the reality itself—that influences engineers' behavior. Project managers may in fact have equal influence over salaries and promotions, but unless this equality is clearly apparent to engineers, it cannot affect their behavior.

Organizational influence, in contrast, is almost equally distributed across the three influence categories, with 30 percent of the projects having a more dominant functional side, 31 percent a more dominant project side, and 38 percent a reasonably balanced situation.

TABLE 1. *Distribution of Managerial Influence by Area as Perceived by Project Members*

| | Locus of Influence | | | |
Area of Influence	Functional Manager	Balanced	Project Manager	N[a]
Influence within the project				
Technical content of project work	14.0%	50.0%	36.1%	86
Salaries and promotions	58.1	34.9	7.0	86
Personnel assignments	28.6	54.0	17.5	63
Influence within the organization	30.2	38.3	31.4	86

[a]As previously explained, *N* varies by area of influence.

Because the projects under investigation come from government, not-for-profit, and industrial organizations, it is also important to see if there are major differences among these sectors. Generally speaking, there are no significant differences in the distributions of managerial influence for the dimensions of technical content and personnel assignments. In each sector, the distributions are consistent with the percentages reported in Table 1. For the other two loci of influence, however, there are significant variations from the distributions of Table 1 by the type of organization. In the not-for-profit sector, functional managers are seen as having considerably more influence within their organizations than their project management counterparts and are perceived as dominating rewards in over 80 percent of the projects. In sharp contrast, project managers are viewed as having stronger organizational influence than functional managers in over half of the projects in the industrial and government sectors. These differences are not surprising, since not-for-profit organizations are somewhat more oriented to academic research and probably place greater emphasis on the disciplines than either industry or government organizations; industry and government organizations, in turn, probably put more emphasis on project management and the clear-cut product or system that must be brought into being. We present these descriptive distributions not to test any specific hypothesis, but simply to give the reader a better view of our data base, especially since we could not undertake randomized sampling of organizations. Given these variations, we will investigate the robustness of any significant findings from the whole sample across these different work sectors.

Project Performance

As the above distributions show, it is very clear that the degree to which project or functional managers exert influence over dual reporting engineers differs considerably among projects. The locus of influence also differs for each dimension of influence. The next step, therefore, was to test our hypotheses by seeing how project performance varied with these loci of influence. To examine the proposed relationships, we performed an analysis of covariance on each dimension of internal project influence. In each analysis, project performance was the dependent variable, and the categories of managerial dominance and balance (i.e., the locus of influence) were the independent variables. Since the number of engineers in dual reporting relationships differed substantially among the projects, the number of such engineers within each project was used as a covariate.

Technical Details of Project Work. Table 2 presents results on the relationship between project performance and the locus of influence over the technical details of project work. Performance does not vary significantly with the locus of influence over technical content. Although there is a slight tendency toward higher performance when the project manager is perceived to have moderately high influence or the functional manager to have strong influence, neither of these tendencies is significant. Also, the latter result stems from only 11 development projects. In any event, balanced involvement in technical matters of both sides of the matrix is not related to higher project performance; the data do not support hypothesis 1.

TABLE 2. *Project Performance as a Function of the Locus of Influence over Technical Content of Project Work*

Locus of Influence	Number of Projects	Project Performance[a]
Project manager	31	0.07
Balanced	42	−0.08
Functional manager	11	0.10

[a]Normalized means; a one-way analysis of covariance indicated that mean performance did not differ significantly ($F = 1.43$)

Salaries and Promotions.   In the area of salaries and promotions, the ANCOVA results of Table 3 show that project performance varies significantly across the loci of managerial influence. The mean performance levels in Table 3 indicate that project performance is highest when influence is either balanced or when project managers are viewed as controlling organizational rewards, although there are only six project cases in this latter category. Nevertheless, mean performance is significantly lower when functional managers are seen by project members as having more influence over their salaries and promotion opportunities.

Because the distribution of projects along the influence continuum is so extremely skewed towards functional control, we used Tukey's (1977) smoothing procedures as most appropriate for obtaining a more complete descriptive picture of the association between project performance and the locus of managerial influence over salaries and promotions. An examination of the resulting plot of smoothed performances (Figure 2) reveals a fairly regular pattern of decreasing performance with increasing functional control over monetary and career rewards. Although Tukey's smoothing procedures do not yield specific statistical tests, the pattern that emerges from Figure 2, together with the results from Table 3, support the hypothesis that project performance is directly associated with the degree to which project managers are seen as influ-

ential over the salaries and promotions of their subordinates.

Personnel Assignments.   Project performance does not vary significantly with the locus of influence over personnel assignments (Table 4). Although we hypothesized that project performance would be higher when the project manager was seen to have greater influence than the functional manager over the staffing of project work, this does not turn out to be the case—at least not to the extent that its effects are evident in the different project groupings. It is interesting to note, however, that the lowest-performing set of projects are those in which the functional managers are seen as controlling the allocation of project personnel.

Organizational Influence.   To what extent is organizational influence associated with the three measures of internal influence within the project? The correlations in Table 5 show that the locus of organizational influence is closely related to the locus of influence over salaries and promotions and to the locus of influence over personnel assignments. The way in which engineers in a matrix structure view the relative power of project and functional managers within the organization is not independent of how they view their managers' relative power over organizational rewards and staffing decisions. The locus of organizational influence is, however, inde-

TABLE 3.   *Project Performance as a Function of the Locus of Influence over Salaries and Promotions*

Locus of Influence	Number of Projects	Project Performance[a]
Project manager	6	0.40
Balanced	29	0.37
Functional manager	49	−0.27

[a]Normalized means; one-way analysis of covariance indicated that mean performance differed significantly at the .02 level ($F = 4.69$).

TABLE 4.   *Project Performance as a Function of the Locus of Influence over Personnel Assignments*

Locus of Influence	Number of Projects	Project Performance[a]
Project manager	10	0.04
Balanced	33	0.08
Functional manager	18	−0.41

[a]Normalized means; one-way analysis of covariance indicated that mean performance did not differ significantly ($F = 1.07$).

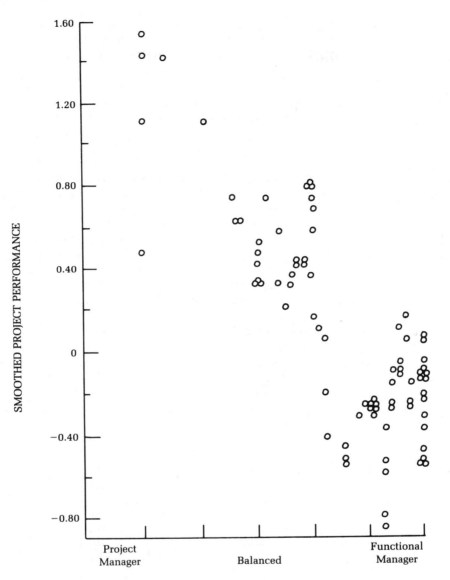

aSmoothed by 3 RSSH method used twice (Tukey, 1977)

FIGURE 2.   Smoothed Project Performance[a] as a Function of Locus of Influence over Salaries and Promotions

TABLE 5.   Correlation of Locus of Organizational Influence and Loci of Internal Influence

Internal Influence Over:	r
Technical content of work	−.02
Salaries and promotions	.65*
Personnel assignments	.49*

*$p < 0.001$

pendent of how they see their project and functional managers' influencing the detailed technical content of their work. The correlation between these two areas of influence is close to zero.

Since there is not a strong connection between organizational influence and influence over technical content of the work, the final question is whether the loci of influence in these two areas operate separately on performance or whether they interact to affect project performance. A two-way analysis of variance (Table 6) reveals once again that influence over the technical details of project work is not related, at least as a main effect, to project performance. The locus of organizational influence, on the other hand, is significantly associated with project performance in that projects with relatively more powerful project managers are somewhat higher performing than are other projects.

More important, however, the ANOVA results also reveal an interaction effect on project performance between these two modes of influence. As shown by the performance means at the top of Table 6, project performance is higher when project managers are seen as having relatively more influence within the organization and functional managers are seen as having relatively more influence over the technical content of what goes into the project. Performance is lowest when functional managers are seen as dominant in both of these areas. Additional analyses did not uncover any interference with these findings by project size or organization sector; nor did they uncover any other significant interaction effects on project performance among the other influence combinations.

As previously discussed, it is important to investigate the robustness of the results from Table 6 since projects varied widely in their percentages of matrix engineers. It is possible, for example, that the relationships between project perform-

TABLE 6.   Project Performance^a as a Function of the Loci of Influence over Technical Content of Project Work and Influence in the Organization

	Locus of Influence over Technical Content	
Locus of Influence within the Organization	Project Manager	Functional Manager
Project Manager	0.10	0.80
	(N=30)	(N=12)
Functional manager	−0.05	−0.59
	(N=30)	(N=12)
Sources of Variation for Two-Way ANOVA:	df	F	p
Influence over technical content	1	0.36	N.S.^{b}
Influence in organization	1	4.88	.03
Interaction	1	6.45	.01

^{a}Normalized means
^{b}N.S. = not significant

ance and the distributions of power will be significantly different for projects with high proportions of matrix engineers than for projects in which the proportion of matrix engineers is relatively low. To test this possibility, the sample was divided based on the distribution described in the first part of the methods section. Projects in which at least 70 percent of the engineers were in dual-reporting relationships constituted the high subsample ($n = 37$) while projects with less than 60 percent of engineers in dual-reporting relationships constituted the low subsample ($n = 26$). The 21 intermediate projects were not assigned to either of the subsamples in order to keep a reasonable separation between the categories.

The 2 sets of ANOVA results presented in Table 7 parallel the pattern of means in Table 6. For both the high and low project categories, there is a similar interaction effect on project performance between the two loci of influence. In both subsamples, project performance is highest when project managers are seen as having relatively more influence within the organization and functional managers are seen as having relatively more influence over the technical details of project work; in both instances, project perform-

ance is lowest when functional managers are seen as dominant along both of these influence dimensions. These patterns of performance means among the cells are comparable to those in Table 6, suggesting a rather consistent set of results within the overall data base.

DISCUSSION

Our findings suggest an appropriate separation of roles between the managers of R&D professionals in matrix structures. The project manager should be concerned with external relations and activities. He should have sufficient power within the organization to gain the backing and continued support of higher management, to obtain critical resources, and to coordinate and couple project efforts with marketing and manufacturing (cf. Achilladelis et al., 1971). The concern of functional managers, on the other hand, should be more inward-directed, focusing chiefly on the technology that goes into the project. They are usually more closely associated with the necessary technologies, and consequently, should be better able than project managers to make informed decisions concerning technical content.

TABLE 7. *Project Performance[a] as a Function of Locus of Influence by Proportion of Matrix Engineers*

Proportion of Engineers in Matrix Relationships	Locus of Influence within Organization	Locus of Influence over Technical Content	
		Project Manager	Functional Manager
High ($\geq 70\%$)[b]	Project Manager	0.22 ($N=17$)	0.89 ($N=6$)
	Functional Manager	0.07 ($N=11$)	−0.60 ($N=3$)
Low ($<59\%$)[c]	Project Manager	−0.38 ($N=7$)	0.80 ($N=4$)
	Functional Manager	−0.31 ($N=10$)	−0.73 ($N=5$)

[a]Normalized means

[b]Based on a 2-way ANOVA, the main effect for organizational influence and the interaction effect between the two loci of influence for this subsample are significant at the .09 and .06 levels, respectively.

[c]For this subsample, neither of the main effects is significant at the .10 level or less while the interaction effect between them is significant at the .08 level.

But these roles can never be completely separate since, for example, relations with marketing and manufacturing have critical implications for technical content, and vice-versa. A strong working relationship must therefore exist between project and functional managers. However, the results of this study suggest that clearer distinction of managerial roles leads to more effective project performance than does managers' sharing responsibilities and involvement. Performance appears to be highest when project managers focus principally on external relations and the output side of the project work, leaving the technological input side to be managed primarily by the functional side of the matrix.

Despite this finding, most of the projects in our sample do not have this role separation pattern, at least as judged by the project members themselves. In more than half of our project groups, for example, members report their project managers have substantially more influence over the technical content of project work than their functional counterparts. Perhaps this is not too surprising since it is the project manager who manages the output and who is ultimately responsible for the project's success. It is, moreover, the project manager's reputation and career that are most intimately tied to project outcomes. Nevertheless, according to our study, overall performance might be improved if functional managers, who know more than project managers about the technologies involved, had greater influence over the technical activities of personnel assigned to project managers.

An enhanced role for the functional manager might also provide some additional benefit in mitigating one of the problems characteristic of matrix organizations. Functional managers have often felt threatened by the introduction of the matrix. Where they formerly had power and visibility in their functional structures, they see, under the matrix, a drift of all of this "glamour" to the project side of the organization. As a result, the matrix has often been undermined by recalcitrant or rebellious department heads, who saw the technical content of their responsibilities diminishing, and their careers sinking into an abyss of personnel decisions and human relations concerns. A clearer delineation of technical responsibilities and an explicitly defined contributive role for functional managers in the technical content of project work may well alleviate this problem.

Over the years, there has been considerable discussion concerning the need to maintain a balance of power in matrix organizations. Very little has been done, however, to investigate the elements or components of power and influence that should be balanced. Using project performance as our criterion, the present study's results provide very little support for the theories of balanced responsibility. Except for joint influence over the areas of salary and promotion, higher project performance is not associated with a balanced state of influence within any of the other three areas of supervisory activity.

Where does this leave all of the theories and propositions regarding matrix balance? The final set of results in Tables 6 and 7 suggests a better understanding of how balance of power might be achieved to make the matrix more effective. The findings imply that it is *not* through mutual balance or joint responsibilities along single dimensions of influence that the matrix should be made to work, but rather that the matrix should be designed and organized around more explicit role differentiation among dimensions of influence. The project manager's role is distinctly different from that of a functional manager. The two have very different concerns and should relate to both project team members and the larger organization in distinctly different ways. It therefore makes sense that the influence which each should exert over the behaviors of matrix project members to bring about effective project performance will be along different dimensions.

Project performance appears to be higher when project managers are seen as having greater organizational influence. Theirs is an outward orientation. As a result, they should be concerned with gaining resources and recognition for the project and with linking it to other parts of the business to insure that the project's direction fits the overall business plan of the organization. Functional managers, on the other hand, should be concerned with technical excellence and integrity, seeing that the project's inputs include state-of-the-art technology. Their orientation is inward, focusing on the technical content of the project. Detailed technical decisions should be made by those who are closest to the technology. The localization of technical decision-making in functional departments, however, implies an important integrating role for project managers, who are responsible for making sure that the technical decisions overseen by several different functional managers all fit together to yield the best possible end result. Clearly, the greater project managers' organizational influence, the easier it will be for them to integrate and negotiate with functional managers whose technical goals are often in conflict.

CONCLUSIONS

This paper has discussed a few of the factors that might be important in developing a better perspective about matrix structures and relationships. Our findings imply that balanced authority need not exist along each dimension of managerial influence. Instead, the distribution of influence seems better accomplished through differentiation of input- and output-oriented roles to functional and project managers, respectively—although the joint involvement of both managers in the area of organizational reward was significantly related to higher project performance.

Since the data reported in this study are cross-sectional, we cannot really be sure of what happens to a project team as its member continue to interact throughout the different innovative phases of a project (Roberts & Fusfeld, 1982).

For example, the locus of influence that is most effective in the "upstream" or early phases of an innovation process may be very different from what is required as R&D efforts move further "downstream" into the engineering and manufacturing stages. Furthermore, while our discussion has emphasized the direct role that project and functional managers can play in influencing the overall performance of matrix project groups, the reverse situation is just as possible. With higher project performance, for example, project managers may come to be seen as more powerful and influential within an organization. Clearly, it remains for future research to look even more closely at these kinds of relationships.

Even with these caveats, the findings presented here indicate that the distribution of power both within and outside the project group is important in matrix settings. Perhaps it has been the lack of a clear understanding of how to differentiate and integrate the different areas of internal and external influences that has led to so much role conflict, stress, and frustration in the implementation and on-going management of matrix-type designs (e.g., Hill & White, 1979). Although it is relatively easy to create formal matrix structures by establishing two separate lines of reporting relationships, a great deal more research is needed to understand the different staffing requirements and the specific kinds of leadership and management systems necessary to influence and effectively support matrix relationships in R&D organizations. We hope the findings presented here will encourage additional research in these directions.

REFERENCES

Achilladelis, A., Jervis, P., & Robertson, A. 1971 *Success and failure in innovation: Project Sappho.* Sussex, England: University of Sussex Press.

Allen, T. J. 1966. Performance of information channels in the transfer of technology. *Industrial Management Review,* 8 (1): 87–98.

Allen, T. J. 1977. *Managing the flow of technology,* Cambridge, Mass.: MIT Press.

Allen, T. J., & Cohen, S. 1969. Information flow in R&D labs. *Administrative Science Quarterly,* 14: 12–19.

Cleland, D. I. 1968. The deliberate conflict. *Business Horizons,* 11 (1): 78–80.

Cleland, D. I., & King, W. R. 1968. *Systems analysis and project management.* New York: McGraw-Hill.

Davis, S., & Lawrence, P. 1977. *Matrix,* Reading, Mass.: Addison-Wesley.

Galbraith, J. 1973. *Designing complex organizations.* New York: Addison Wesley.

Goggin, W. C. 1974. How the multidimensional structure works at Dow Corning. *Harvard Business Review,* 52 (1): 54–65.

Hill, R. E., & White, R. J. (Eds.) 1979. *Matrix organization and project management.* Ann Arbor, Mich.: University of Michigan Press.

Katz, R., & Allen, T. J. 1980. *The technical performance of long duration R&D project groups.* Technical report to the Chief of Studies Management Office, Department of the Army.

Katz, R., & Allen, T. J. 1982. Investigating the "not invented here" syndrome. *R&D Management,* 12 (1): 7–19.

Katz, R., & Tushman, M. 1979. Communication patterns, project performance, and task characteristics: An empirical evaluation and integration in an R&D setting. *Organizational Behavior and Human Performance,* 23: 139–162.

Katz, R., & Tushman, M. 1981. An investigation into the managerial roles and career paths of gatekeepers and project supervisors in a major R&D facility. *R&D Management,* 11 (3): 103–110.

Kidder, T. 1981. *The soul of a new machine.* New York: Little Brown.

Kingdon, O. R. 1973. *Matrix organization: Managing information technologies.* London: Tavistock.

Knight, K. 1976. Matrix organization: A review. *Journal of Management Studies,* 13 (2): 111–130.

Knight, K. 1977. *Matrix management.* London: Gower.

Lawrence, P. R., & Lorsch, J. W. 1967. *Organization and environment.* Boston: Harvard Business School.

Likert, R. 1967. *The human organization.* New York: McGraw-Hill.

Mansfield, E., & Wagner, S. 1975. Organizational and strategic factors associated with probability of success in industrial research. *Journal of Business,* 48: 179–198.

Marquis, D. G. 1969. Ways of organizing projects. *Innovation,* 5 (7): 26–33.

Marquis, D. G., & Straight, D. L. 1965. *Organizational factors in project performance.* M.I.T. Sloan School of Management Working Paper No. 1331, Cambridge, Mass.

Myers, S., & Marquis, D. G. 1969. *Successful industrial innovations.* Technical report No. 69–17, National Science Foundation, Washington, D.C.

Oldham, D. R. 1976. The motivational strategies used by supervisors: Relationships to effectiveness indicators. *Organizational Behavior and Human Performance,* 15: 66–86.

Pelz, D. 1952. Influence: A key to effective leadership in the first-line supervisor. *Personnel,* 29: 209–226.

Pelz, D., & Andrews, F. M. 1976. *Scientists in organizations.* Ann Arbor, Mich.: University of Michigan Press.

Pfeffer, J., & Salancik, G. R. 1978. *The external control of organizations: A resource dependence perspective.* New York: Harper and Row.

Roberts, E. B., & Fusfeld, A. R. 1982. Critical functions: Needed roles in the innovation process. In R. Katz (Ed.) *Career issues in human resource management:* 182–207. Englewood Cliffs, N.J.: Prentice-Hall.

Sayles, L. R. 1976. Matrix management: The structure with a future. *Organizational Dynamics,* 5 (2): 2–17.

Sheridan, J. E., & Vredenburgh, D. J. 1978. Predicting leadership behavior in a hospital organization. *Academy of Management Journal,* 21: 679–689.

Souder, W. E. 1979. Special issues on project management. *IEEE Transactions on Engineering Management.* 26 (3): 49–87.

Steiner, G., & Ryan, W. 1968. *Industrial project management.* New York: Macmillan.

Tukey, J. 1977. *Exploratory data analysis.* Reading, Mass.: Addison-Wesley.

Utterback, J. M. 1974. Innovation in industry and the diffusion of technology. *Science,* 183: 620–626.

Wilemon, D. L., & Gemmill, G. R. 1971. Interpersonal power in temporary management systems. *Journal of Management Studies,* 8: 315–328.

SECTION
VI

Managing Human Resources

11

ORGANIZATIONAL AND PROFESSIONAL CAREERS

How "Career Anchors" Hold Executives to Their Career Paths

Edgar H. Schein

Some executives hunger for managerial promotion. Others, equally talented, reject managerial power for functional autonomy. A Sloan School of Management study suggests that companies need to know more about key executives' motivational drives and needs.

Certain motivational/attitudinal/value syndromes formed early in the lives of individuals apparently function to guide and constrain their entire careers. These basic combinations of needs and drives act, in effect, as "career anchors" that not only influence career choices, but also affect decisions to move from one company to another, shape what the individuals are looking for in life, and color their views of the future and their general assessments of related goals and objectives.

This concept of career anchors emerges directly from a lengthy—and continuing—study of

a representative group of Alfred P. Sloan School of Management alumni who completed their graduate work in the early 1960s and are now more than a decade into their life careers. Periodic contact with these young men and analysis of their postgraduate activities has provided extensive insights and intimate details of both their professional and personal lives. The evidence at hand strongly suggests that, in addition to exerting strong influences on the career paths and career satisfactions of the individuals themselves, career anchors—as a concept—also carry important implications for business, industrial, and other employing organizations. For example:

- If career anchors do indeed function as stable syndromes in the personality, it becomes important for employing organizations to identify these syndromes early. It does little good, for example, to offer promotion into management to someone who basically does not want to be a manager but whose basic goal is attainment of technical/functional competence or who is anchored instead to entrepreneurial, creative, or primarily autonomous activities. The organization stands to gain by creating career opportunities that are congruent with the basic anchor needs of its human talent.

· Within the context of the career anchor concept, organizations thus will have to learn to think more broadly about the different kinds of contributions people can make. This means development of multiple reward systems as well as multiple career paths that will permit full development of diverse kinds of individuals.

ORIGINS AND SCOPE OF THE SLOAN MANAGEMENT PANEL STUDY

Launched in 1961, a panel study covering the careers of 44 Sloan School graduates was initiated to assess the interaction of personal values and career events in the lives of managers in organizations. The project had the original goal of determining the mechanisms and effects of organizational socialization. Some of the key questions it was designed to answer included:

In what manner and through what means would the values of Sloan students be influenced by their organizational experiences? Would certain sets of individuals with certain sets of values be more or less socialized? Could one determine what kinds of value syndromes would lead to careers in which the individual would innovate, that is, change organizations rather than be changed by them?

Participants in the study were selected on the basis of random sampling techniques and were invited to participate in order to eliminate the bias of volunteering. The panel of 44 men who agreed to cooperate is believed to be reasonably representative of the graduating classes from which its members were drawn. (The panel originally consisted of 15 men each from the Sloan classes of 1961, 1962, and 1963, but was reduced to 44 by the withdrawal of one member after a point where it was too late to replace him.)

Beginning with interviews and various attitude and value surveys administered prior to graduation, contact has been maintained with each of the 44 panelists at various points during their subsequent careers. A major review and resurvey of the panel was completed in 1973–1974, and various aspects of that effort will be spelled out in later reports. On the basis of the initial analysis, however, it was determined that the career histories of the panelists could be understood best in terms of the concept of "career anchors."

THE ANCHOR CONCEPT: SPOTLIGHTING COMMON THEMES AND NEEDS

A career can be thought of as a set of stages or a path through time that reflects:

1. An individual's needs, motives, and aspirations in relation to work.
2. Society's expectations of what kinds of activities will result in monetary and status rewards for the career occupant.

Work careers thus reflect both individual and societal (or organizational) definitions of what is a worthwhile set of activities to pursue throughout a lifetime. In a sense, then, one can speak of two sets of "anchors" for a career.

- On one hand, a career is anchored in a set of job descriptions and organizational norms about the rights and duties of a given title in an organization. The "head of production," for example, is expected to perform certain duties; he carries certain sets of responsibilities and is held accountable for certain areas of organizational performance.
- On the other hand, the career is anchored in a set of needs and motives which the individual is attempting to fulfill through the work he does and the rewards he obtains for that work—money, prestige, organizational membership, challenging work, freedom, and other satisfactions. The rewards he seeks thus can be thought of as his job values— what he is looking for in a job. These values, in turn, also reflect an underlying pattern of needs that the individual is trying to fulfill.

Thus, as head of production, he may seek to exercise his basic need for influencing and controlling numbers of people and resources. Or he may be trying to meet the challenge of successfully building something or getting something accomplished that is proof of his competence.

For others, the underlying need serving as a career anchor is the exercise of a certain talent such as quantitative analysis; for still others it is a need to find security—to link oneself with a stable and predictable future via an occupation or an organization. The drive for money, as many previous analyses have shown, is perhaps more difficult to unravel because it often masks other underlying needs. The career anchor categories as defined here must take these needs into account.

The 44 interviews revealed a number of common themes in what people are fundamentally looking for in their careers. And these common themes can be defined as the underlying individual career anchors that function to pull a person back if he strays too far from what he *really* wants.

ANCHOR 1. MANAGERIAL COMPETENCE

The panelists who were classified in this category made it clear that their fundamental motivation is to be competent in the complex set of activities that comprise the idea of "management." The most important components of this concept are:

1. *Interpersonal competence*—the ability to influence, supervise, lead, manipulate, and control people toward the more effective achievement of organizational goals.
2. *Analytical competence*—the identification and solving of conceptual problems under conditions of uncertainty and incomplete information.
3. *Emotional stability*—the capacity to be stimulated by emotional and interpersonal crises rather than exhausted or debilitated by them, the capacity to bear high levels of responsibility, and the capacity to exercise authority without fear or guilt.

In other words, the person who wants to rise in the organization, who is seeking higher and higher levels of responsibility, must be good in handling people, an excellent analyst, and emotionally able to withstand the pressures and tensions of the executive suite. In terms of organizational categories, he is usually thought of as a line or general manager, depending on his rank. Occasionally a senior functional manager fits this concept if he gets his prime satisfaction from managerial and related human relations responsibilities rather than from the technical part of his job.

ANCHOR 2. TECHNICAL-FUNCTIONAL COMPETENCE

A number of respondents left no doubt that their careers are motivated by the challenge of the actual work they do—financial analysis, marketing, systems analysis, corporate planning, or some other area related to business or management. Their anchor is the technical field or functional area, not the managerial process itself. If a member of this group holds supervisory responsibility, he is usually supervising others in the same technical area, and he makes it clear that it is the area, not the supervising, that turns him on. This kind of person is not interested in being promoted out of his technical area; his roots are in the actual analytical work he is doing. In terms of organizational titles, such people are spread over a wide range of functional managers, technical managers, senior staff, junior staff, and some external consultants and related activities. People with this set of needs will leave a company rather than be promoted out of their technical/functional area.

ANCHOR 3. SECURITY

Other respondents have tied their careers to particular organizations. Although one must infer the assumption, it is reasonable to postulate that their underlying need is for security, and that they seek to stabilize their careers by linking them to given organizations. The implications are that an individual in this grouping will accept, to a greater degree than the other types, an *organizational* definition of his career. Whatever his private aspirations or competence areas, this individual must rely increasingly upon the organization to recognize these needs and competencies and do the best possible by him. But he loses some degree of freedom because of his unwillingness to leave a given organization if his needs or talents go unrecognized. Instead, he must rationalize that the organization's definition of his career is the only valid definition.

If such an individual has technical/functional talent, he may rise to a senior functional manager level; but if his psychological makeup includes a degree of insecurity, that very insecu-

rity could make him "incompetent" with respect to higher levels of management where emotional security and stability become prime requisites for effective performance.

Length of time with a given organization is not a sufficient criterion for defining this career anchor. One must know something of the reasons why an individual has remained with a given organization before one can judge whether the holding force is insecurity or a pattern of constant success.

By the same logic, we find some individuals who are security-oriented yet who move from one company to another. In these cases strong similarities mark the types of companies and the career slots that the individual exchanges. To cite an example, one panelist's pattern of seeking security and stability expressed itself partly in seeking to remain in a given community where his family was very happy. Over a period of years he switched companies three times, but in each case he picked a similar company and started in that company at an equal or lower level in terms of rank. He is quite willing to sacrifice some autonomy in his career to stabilize his total life situation.

ANCHOR 4. CREATIVITY

Some respondents expressed a strong need to create something on their own. This is the fundamental need operating in an entrepreneur, and it expresses itself in the desire to invent a new business vehicle, find a new product, develop a new service, or in some way create something that can be clearly identified with the individual.

On the Sloan graduate panel, for example, one participant has become a successful purchaser, restorer, and renter of town houses in a large city. Another, who developed a string of financial service organizations that use computers in a new and more effective way in a region where such services were not available, also is purchasing and developing large tracts of land and is co-owner of a large cattle ranch.

One gets the impression that the creativity/entrepreneurial pattern is also closely related to the need for autonomy and independence. All of the entrepreneurs strongly expressed the desire to be on their own, free of organizational restraints, but the decisive factor is that they did not leave the world of business to achieve their autonomy. Instead they chose to try to express their business and managerial skills by building their own enterprises.

This commitment to business also shows up in this group's ambition to acquire a great deal of money. But money is not sought for its own sake or for what it will buy. Instead, one gets the distinct impression that total financial assets are only a measure used to define one's degree of success as an entrepreneur.

ANCHOR 5. AUTONOMY AND INDEPENDENCE

The respondents who were primarily concerned about their own sense of freedom and autonomy had found organizational life to be restrictive, irrational, and/or intrusive into their private lives. Some left the world of business altogether, seeking careers that provided more autonomy; others became consultants operating on their own.

One became a university professor in areas related to business. Another has become a free-lance writer who not only has rejected business as an arena but also has rejected the success ethic he associates with it. For him it has become more important to develop himself—he lives frugally, working as a ghost writer when he needs the money; he travels; and he works on his creative writing when the mood strikes him.

The consultants in the sample include several who are plainly in that line of endeavor because they seek autonomy although, as noted previously, not all consultants have that need. Some consultants are motivationally entrepreneurs; some are technical/functional specialists; and some are in transition toward a managerial role.

RELATIONSHIP OF CAREER ANCHORS TO OCCUPATIONAL/ ORGANIZATIONAL TITLES

Career anchors are *personal* motivational/attitudinal/value syndromes. For that reason, the areas in which a person wants to become competent or sets the goals of his career will not necessarily be reflected in his occupational or organizational titles as shown in the boxed summary.

Of the eight panelists anchored in managerial competence, not all have made it to higher levels of management. But their interviews clearly indicated that they seek higher levels and that they get their primary satisfactions out of managerial activities per se. Within that group are two career patterns—working one's way up within large organizations, and seeking larger jobs within smaller organizations.

Both pattern groups include individuals who have moved from one company to another and who sometimes have interrupted the pattern with stints in management consulting. But in the first group the individual always ended up in another large organization; in the second group there was a clear decision to move toward smaller organizations.

Almost half of the panelists (19) were classified as anchored in technical/functional competence, reflecting their major concern that they be able to continue the kind of work they enjoy and are apparently good at. We should not assume, however, that members of the other groups are less concerned about developing their expertise or that they care less about the kind of work they do. We can say that in each person one can find a predominant concern that will function as an anchor in the sense of pulling him back if he strays too far from fulfilling that concern.

JOB TITLES AND ORGANIZATIONS OF PANELISTS IN CAREER ANCHOR GROUPS

Anchor 1—Managerial Competence

Manager of factoring systems: corporate headquarters, large financial corporation
Sales manager and part owner: family furniture business
Sales manager: industrial foods division, large conglomerate
Director of corporate plan administration: large airline
President and part owner: small manufacturing firm
Manager of marketing and assistant to general manager: large division of large corporation
Director of administration: insurance services division of large financial corporation
Vice-president for finance and administration: medium size service organization

Anchor 2—Technical/Functional Competence

Manager of data processing and part-founder: large consulting R&D firm
Research associate to vice-president for academic affairs: medium size university
Director of required earnings studies: large national utility
Manager of engineering: large product line of medium size manufacturing company
Member of technical staff: R&D division of large national utility
Principal programmer: technical unit of large systems design and manufacturing company
Market development engineer: new venture group, chemical corporation
Project manager: aero-space division of large electronics corporation
Treasurer: small growth company
Commerce officer: large government department, Canadian government
Assistant professor of operations research: management department, U.S. Naval Academy
Senior consultant: small management consulting firm
Assistant director: White House Office of Telecommunications
Plant manufacturing engineer: large consumer products division of large corporation

Manager, market support systems, Europe: information services division of large corporation
Teacher and department head: regional rural Canadian high school
Project supervisor: technical division of large chemical company
Director, cost analysis group: large technical systems consulting firm
Principal in large management consulting firm

Anchor 3—Organizational Security

Manager, forward product planning research: large auto company
Marketing sales representative: large data services company
Advisory marketing representative: large computer manufacturer
Chief engineer: small family steel fabricating company

Anchor 4—Creativity

Founder of several financial, service, and real estate businesses
Founder of one firm and developer of second firm in chemical industry
Marketing development staff: overseas development of new ventures for industrial protein products of large consumer company
Marketing consultant: self-employed, searching for new enterprises to buy or develop (one previous unsuccessful venture)
Senior vice-president: media services, large advertising firm; real estate owner and developer
President and co-founder: planning and consulting firm

Anchor 5—Autonomy and Independence

Senior consultant: small management consulting firm
Communication consultant: self-employed, looking for entrepreneurial opportunity in communications field
Proprietor and owner: retail hardware and wholesale pumping equipment business
Assistant professor of business and economics: regional campus of a large state university system
Self-employed consultant: operations research field emphasizing applications to health care
Senior consultant: specialist in taxation work, large accounting firm
Self-employed free lance writer

In the autonomy group, for example, the professor is certainly concerned about his area of specialization. But if given a chance to pursue that line of work in a large organization at a much higher salary and with much better equipment or resources, he probably would not take it if he viewed that organizational setting as one in which he would have to sacrifice his autonomy.

In the technical/functional competence group, we find several middle level functional or technical managers; several people in senior or middle staff roles; some in straight consulting; and two in teaching (one at a university, the second at high school level).

It must be remembered that if the concept of career anchors is valid, the 19 men in this group are *not* in transition toward managerial roles per se. They may climb within functional/technical management, but the theoretical assumption is that they would refuse to be promoted into a role that would entail giving up the kind of work they are doing.

Many of the panelists in this group sense that they are violating the "success ethic" of the business world and feel somewhat guilty and in conflict about their lack of success and ambition. And while they talk of their work and family as being important to them and claim that they enjoy their life as it is, they wonder, nonetheless, whether they are missing something and whether they are doing as well as their peers. But our prediction is that none of these men will move out of their present orientations and will find ways to deal with their conflicts.

Of the four men who can be classified as security oriented, three have spent most of their careers within a single organization. One has moved frequently, but he always remained within the same geographical area and always took similar types of jobs (with one exception—an abortive venture into trying to start a company with a group of associates). These men talk of their work, their families, their overall satisfaction with the geographical area where they have settled, and their sense of having achieved enough to satisfy themselves.

The group concerned with creativity has proved to be the most interesting because it includes the entrepreneurs. Four have launched successful enterprises which have brought them fame or fortune, or both. Their activities vary greatly, but each activity is a clear extension of the person behind it.

The autonomy group—four consultants, one owner/proprietor of a small business, one professor, and one freelance writer—resembles the technical/functional competence group in many respects—except that no functional managers or staff roles are represented in it. This group is distinguished by the fact that its members display little conflict about missed opportunities or failure to aspire higher. All are happy in their work and enjoy their freedom. All have a sense of their own professionalism and can link the results of their work to their own efforts, a feeling they share with the creativity group.

On the surface it is not easy to differentiate the autonomy and creativity group members because the entrepreneurs also enjoy autonomy and freedom. But when one listens to the entrepreneurs, it becomes obvious that they are preoccupied with building something, whereas the primary need of the autonomy oriented panelists is to be on their own, with no concerns about making money or building empires.

BACKGROUND CHARACTERISTICS OF THE ANCHOR GROUPS

If career anchors are formed fairly early in life, even though they may not be recognized by the person, will one find symptomatic relationships between panelists' background characteristics and the anchor groups they ended up in? Several key background characteristics were considered—intellectual aptitude and performance, and parental education and occupation. Because of the small number of men involved in the study sample, it is difficult to do more than draw attention to a few trends.

The data shown do not yet permit spelling out the nature of the mechanisms in operation, though a more detailed analysis of the original interviews with the panelists should illuminate these findings. However, there appear to be consistent patterns of intellectual performance, particularly in the autonomy and creativity groups, and all groups show some biases in terms of the educational and occupational status of mothers and fathers. To summarize:

Grade point averages and business aptitude test scores (See Table 1): In terms of undergraduate grade point averages (GPA), the managerial and technical/functional groups scored highest, while the creativity group had the lowest grades. Similarly, in terms of aptitude as measured by the Admissions Test for Graduate Study in Business (ATGSB), the autonomy group scored highest and the creativity group again had the lowest scores. In terms of grade point averages at Massachusetts Institute of Technology, the groups resemble each other closely—except for the lower average of the creativity group.

This difference could reflect real intellectual aptitude differences, but it is more likely a reflection of early biases in the entrepreneurial group toward breadth of interest and creative activities.

Perhaps this group put more energy into developing skills of leadership and creation of opportunities than into narrow academic pursuits.

Parental education and occupations: Motivational syndromes should be related to parental values and aspirations, and from the objective data available, several interesting patterns emerge.

The managerial competence group is average in fathers' education, low in mothers' education, high in business and managerial fathers, and high in percentage of housewife mothers. In contrast, the technical/functional competence group is high in parental education but is more diversified in parental occupations. The security group is low in fathers' education and high in mothers' education, high in percentage of business and managerial fathers, and average in number of housewife mothers. One can conjecture that the security orientation reflects a feeling on the part of the alumnus that once he has completed graduate school and made it into some level of management, he already has achieved success by climbing higher on the socioeconomic ladder than his father.

The creativity group shows high levels of education for both fathers and mothers and a high percentage of business/managerial fathers. Perhaps the broad interests of this group derive from the breadth that is associated with the higher level of education of *both* parents.

TABLE 1.   *Undergraduate Grade Point Averages, Business, Aptitude Test Scores, and Graduate Grade Point Averages of Anchor Groups*

Career Anchor	Undergraduate G.P.A.	ATGSB Total	Verbal	Quantitative	Graduate G.P.A.
Managerial Comp. (N = 8)	4.0	574	29	39	4.4
Tech./Funct. Comp. (N = 19)	3.9	590	34	38	4.2
Security (N = 4)	3.7	573	31	38	4.2
Creativity (N = 6)	3.2	555	31	36	4.0
Autonomy (N = 7)	3.5	628	37	41	4.2
Total	3.9	587	33	38	4.2

The autonomy group, average for parental education and level of mothers' occupation, stands out in having the lowest percentage of business/managerial fathers and the highest percentage of professional fathers. The autonomy pattern may already have been set in these families in that among the fathers' occupations were farmer, associate professor, chief engineer of a company, electrical contractor, insurance agency owner, and executive vice president of a family business. Only the latter two jobs are business and managerial, and they both involve ownership: none of the fathers was a manager in the traditional sense.

MEASURING CAREER SUCCESS OF ANCHOR GROUPS

Success is a complex and difficult variable to define and measure. It can be defined objectively by societal standards or subjectively by personal standards and goals. The data reported here focus on one indicator of *objective* success—the income of panelists. Table 2, which is based on incomes reported in the 1973–1974 interviews, in many cases shows only baseline numbers that exclude annual bonuses, value of stock options, and other perquisites. Annual incomes of the entrepreneurs would have to be supplemented with figures on the total value of assets that they said they have accumulated.

As might be expected, the most successful in pure income terms is the managerial competence group; climbing of the managerial ladder is congruent with society's definition of success. The successful entrepreneurs are similarly high if one includes their assets, but even the most successful of them reports an annual *income* of only $40,000. For this group it perhaps is more important to build total assets than to consume what they have amassed. At the low end of one income scale we have the autonomy-oriented group who have left large organizations.

ASSESSING THE ANCHOR CONCEPT

In introducing and elaborating on the concept of career anchors, we have viewed them as syndromes that, while formed fairly early in life, effectively influence one's entire career. In classifying the panelists into career anchor groups, the groupings were made on the basis of reasons they gave for career choices, why they shifted from company to company and job to job, and how they assess their future work careers. Data from the earlier (precareer) interviews were not used in order to minimize bias. The relationships reported between career anchors, intellectual aptitude, school performance, parental background, current jobs, and current income are therefore real relationships because the classification into career anchor groups was made before any of the correlative data were examined.

TABLE 2.   *Income of Career Anchor Groups*

Career Anchor	Mean	Median	Range
Managerial Competence* (N=6)	$35,500	$31,000	$27,000–$50,000
Tech./Funct. Competence (N=19)	25,800	26,000	16,000– 42,000
Security (N=4)	23,000	24,500	18,000– 25,000
Creativity** (N=6)	29,000	26,000	17,000– 40,000
Autonomy (N=7)	19,000	17,000	10,000– 25,000
Total	26,600	25,000	

* One person has over $50,000 per year in supplemental income from real estate ventures.
**The two successful entrepreneurs report assets in excess of a half million dollars.

Accepting this overall correlation as an indication of the stability of career anchors as influential syndromes in the personality underscores a need for organizations, on the one hand, to help employees recognize their anchors and, on the other hand, to create multiple paths and reward systems to permit effective utilization of managerial, technical, and other professional talents. Organizational efforts to identify underlying career anchor orientations and to channel them toward fulfillment of individual's indicated needs and goals should generate greatly improved rewards and benefits for both the organization and its managers.

Improving Professional Development by Applying The Four-Stage Career Model

Paul H. Thompson

Robin Zenger Baker

Norman Smallwood

The four stage career model is an essential element in the career development of employees at all levels.

Following the recession, the management of the Chemco Company felt strongly that operations could be streamlined and human resources used more effectively. Marcus Nordlin, vice-president of administration, had the task of interviewing managers and senior professionals to determine what could be done to get the company back up to speed. After about 40 interviews, Nordlin had received many useful suggestions for streamlining operations. But he noticed, too, that one complaint, in particular, kept cropping up among his professional staff:

> I feel stifled in my current position.

> If I want to get ahead, I'll have to leave.

> My management responsibilities don't leave me any time for technical work I really enjoy.

Nordlin believed that these employees had a point: The company needed to focus more on professional development to make full use of its technical workforce. For additional input, Nordlin pulled together a committee to address the issue.

The professional development task force tackled the problem enthusiastically. They read articles on careers, contacted other companies to find out what they were doing, and interviewed over 100 professionals in groups of 12 to 15. They discovered that their employees were intensely interested in career development—and that they wanted answers. The most frequently asked questions were:

- What is my job? (Why do priorities change so often?)
- How am I doing? (I get too little feedback.)
- What are the career paths in the division?
- How do I get ahead?

In response to the intensity of feeling turned up by their study, the task force recommended an ambitious program of professional development. Nordlin was impressed by the quality of data and recommendations in their report, but didn't know quite how to proceed. Other executives felt it was risky to start a professional development program. They were afraid of raising unrealistic expectations, losing valuable people to transfers, and disrupting the organization. Nordlin and his management team struggled with the problem for 18 months before approving a small pilot program.

In our experience, the preceding example is not an isolated case. Despite a recognized need and interest in career development programs, efforts to implement them have a hard time getting past the planning stages. Our research has led us to the following conclusions:

1. Employees are very interested in knowing more about factors affecting their performance and their careers.
2. Managers are reluctant to discuss these issues.
3. Most managers and human resource professionals haven't found a direct approach to professional development issues.

If all three of these conclusions are correct—and there is considerable evidence to suggest they are—then a great deal of frustration surrounding career development is inevitable. We have found, however, that if the third issue is resolved (providing managers with a framework to approach career growth) then the other two problems can be greatly alleviated.

A 1977 article in *Organizational Dynamics,* "The Four Stages of Professional Careers—A New Look at Performance by Professionals" (by P. H. Thompson, G. W. Dalton, and R. L. Price) introduced a model of professional career development. This model has been applied in various organizations and has proved a useful way to set up effective career development programs.

HOW THE FOUR-STAGE MODEL WORKS

In the article, Thompson, Dalton, and Price suggest that there are four stages in the career of a professional employee. Each stage differs from the others in the *tasks* that individuals perform, the types of *relationships* that they form, and the *psychological adjustments* that they need.

Performance requirements vary from stage to stage. For example, new employees generally spend a period of time in an apprentice role taking care of detail work. As employees progress through their careers, they usually take on more responsibility for projects and leadership tasks. Exhibit 1 outlines some of the central features of each stage.

As professionals get older, they tend to maintain higher performance ratings if they can move at least to Stage III. This notion that performance is linked to progress through career stages is crucial to a discussion of how organizations can help employees with their professional development. Time and again organizations focus their career development efforts on Stage II employees while paying less attention to appropriate rewards, training, and job assignments for those in other stages.

APPLYING THE FOUR-STAGE MODEL

The four-stage career model can be a useful tool in providing an accurate and insightful profile of the workforce because it looks at more than just formal titles and pay scales. The model can shed light on other helpful information such as who's contributing, who's blocked, and what's causing a lack of progress.

Some executives may feel that such detailed diagnosis is unnecessary because it merely generates information already widely known in the organization. Managers often respond to such proposals with comments like: "I know the workforce; I've been with the company for 25 years." However, situations can change so gradually that even long-time managers may not be aware of developing problems.

Marcus Nordlin heard about the four-stage

model after the task force had worked together for more than three years. By using the career-stage concepts, Nordlin and the task force were able to pursue a logical, focused program of career development. The four-stage model served as a framework for applying the more conventional methods of career development: organizational diagnosis, job assignments, training, compensation, and career discussions. Following is a description of these methods and how they can be used in conjunction with the four-stage model.

Organizational Diagnosis

Diagnosing an organization involves several steps outlined below.

Business diagnosis.   Begin with a clear understanding of the strategy or business plan of the organization. Focus on such questions as: What human resources are needed to implement this strategy or business plan? What performance issues are critical to assure that the organization will have the committed efforts of individuals with the training and experience needed to implement the organization's strategy? What would be the impact of having Stage III and IV people who really knew how to use the system to make things happen?

Another way to explore the organization's needs is to compare the organization with its closest competitors. Look for any competitive advantages that these organizations enjoy because of more loyal or dedicated employees. Many recent books on culture and excellence point out a common factor in companies like IBM, Procter and Gamble, and Hewlett Packard: They have committed, long-service employees and generally promote from within. These companies have developed employee loyalty into a strategic business advantage.

Workforce Diagnosis.   First on the list of this phase of the organizational diagnosis is to obtain demographic data about the employee pool: age, seniority, length of job assignment, education level, and field of degree. It may also be beneficial to examine recent employee educational activity such as evening classes and company courses. Performance data and salary information are also relevant.

We recommend examining the current career stages of the organization's professionals. Such examination typically yields a different picture of the workforce than the demographics provide. Dividing up employees according to their career stage is relatively easy. Our method has been to put the name of each employee in a department (50 to 70 professionals) on a small index card, and then arrange a meeting with the manager. Describe the four-stage model to the manager (see Exhibit 1) and then ask him or her to place each staff member's card in the stage that most nearly fits that employee's contribution. Most managers can complete an exercise like this for about 50 employees in 30 minutes.

It is also helpful to ask employees about their career concerns through interviews or questionnaires. An effective way to obtain employee input is to conduct group interviews. One way to come up with groups of manageable size is to divide the workforce according to tenure (less than five years, five to fifteen years, over fifteen years). These three groups can be broken down further until a number suitable for interviewing is reached.

The interview format need not be complex. Below are some questions to help generate discussion.

1. What does this organization do to promote career growth?
2. What does the organization do that hinders career development?
3. What does it mean to be a high performer in this job?
4. Who has been most helpful to you in your career?

EXHIBIT 1. *Characteristics of Career Stages*

Stage I	Stage II
Works under the supervision and direction of a more senior professional in the field.	Goes into depth in one problem or technical area.
Work is never entirely his or her own, but assignments are given that are a portion of a larger project or activity being overseen by a senior professional.	Assumes responsibility for a definable portion of the project, process, or clients.
	Works independently and produces significant results.
Lacks experience and status in organization.	Develops credibility and a reputation.
Is expected to willingly accept supervision and direction.	Relies less on supervisor or mentor for answers, develops more of his or her own resources to solve problems.
Is expected to do most of the detailed and routine work on a project.	Increases in confidence and ability.
Is expected to exercise "directed" creativity and initiative.	
Learns to perform well under pressure and accomplish a task within the time budgeted.	

Stage III	Stage IV
Is involved enough in his or her own work to make significant technical contributions but begins working in more than one area.	Provides direction for the organization by:
	"Mapping" the organization's environment to highlight opportunities and dangers.
Greater breadth of technical skills and application of those skills.	Focusing activities in areas of "distinctive competence."
Stimulates others through ideas and information.	Managing the process by which decisions are made.
Involved in developing people in one or more of the following ways:	Exercises formal and informal power to:
Acts as an idea leader for a small group.	Initiate action and influence decisions.
Serves as a mentor to younger professionals.	Obtain resources and approvals.
Assumes a formal supervisory position.	Represents the organization:
Deals with the outside to benefit others in organizations—i.e., works out relationships with client organizations, develops new business, etc.	To individuals and groups at different levels inside the organization.
	To individuals and institutions outside the organization.
	Sponsors promising individuals to test and prepare them for key roles in the organization.

5. What could the organization do to improve career development?

Managers can also be interviewed to see how they feel about employee's careers. Are people being transferred too often or not often enough? Do employees have adequate training to do their jobs? If managers report being too busy to be concerned about helping their staff, that information is also useful.

The final step involves analyzing the acquired data. Conclusions can be drawn, for example, simply by analyzing the links between the following sets of statistics: age and performance

501

rankings; age and salary levels; age, performance, and career stage; education level and performance; age and length of job assignments; and stage and length of job assignments.

While looking at the data, be aware of signals that may indicate problem areas. You may find a large proportion of employees in one age or tenure group, for example. One company had 40 percent of its managers in the 55-to 65-year-old group. In another company 35 percent of the employees had worked with the company for three years or less.

Another signal to look out for is an over-abundance of employees in one stage. In an organization with a young staff, too many employees may be corralled into Stage II while very few have been moved to Stage III or IV. A low correlation between stage and salary is also a reliable clue that career development is not progressing as it should.

Job Assignments

The four-stage model is also useful in determining which job assignments are best for developing an employee's career at various points in his or her professional development. Employees in different stages may need different kinds of assignments. In Stage I, for example, challenging assignments are critical to the development of the employee. In Stage II, variety of job experiences is more important. As employees move into Stages III and IV, assigning jobs becomes more complex. Employees who are clear about the way careers develop may well choose an assignment that provides them with new options instead of electing to be promoted to a narrower field. Some may even want to repeat a phase to gain skills or pursue interests. Let us examine some of the job assignment issues that typically arise in each stage.

Stage I.   Professionals in Stage I are generally concerned about their initial job assignments. They want assignments that will allow them to test themselves, make a meaningful contribution, and learn new skills. The amount of challenge in first assignments can have a significant impact on the employee's entire career. In a study of AT&T employees, David Berlew and Douglas T. Hall found that those who had been given more challenging assignments in their first year were more likely to be evaluated as effective employees for as long as seven years thereafter.

But despite its powerful effect in individual careers, a high level of challenge is usually not built into initial job assignments. In another study of 22 research and development organizations, Hall and Edward E. Lawler III found only two organizations in which employees felt they had been given moderately or highly challenging first-job assignments. This common practice of cautiously starting new recruits on simple projects can be frustrating to graduates and wasteful for the company. Organizations may err in providing too little challenge for competent new employees.

Stage II.   When professionals begin to seek independence, take responsibility for projects, and broaden their experience, it is usually time to make a variety of job assignments available. The amount of time employees spend in one assignment can make a big difference in their effectiveness and satisfaction. Many employees indicate that after three to five years on the same assignment, little new learning or challenge takes place. If professionals are not learning, growing, and gaining greater competence on their job, they can become bored, frustrated, and eventually less effective. Many professionals note this phenomenon in their own careers:

> In the first year I am just getting used to the job. I work hard, but I am not at the peak of performance. In the second year I know what I am doing, and I am still interested, so I'm pretty productive. By the third year I begin to lose a sense of challenge, and I am not as productive.

Research supports the notion that the length of time in a position can influence employee effectiveness. Ralph Katz suggests that there are three periods in any assignment: socialization, innovation, and stabilization. During the socialization period, employees become familiar with their environment in preparation for the highly involved innovation stage when they are most effective. As the individual becomes accustomed to the demands of the position, he or she may enter a less productive stabilization stage. Katz recommends moving employees periodically into new groups or positions to maintain an optimal level of productivity.

Companies that ignore their employees' need for a breadth of job assignments risk losing those employees. In the computer department of one company, for example, programmers were hired to work on three distinct types of projects. Although each project required specialized training, many of the skills were transferable across projects. Several employees at various times expressed an interest in transferring to one of the other projects to broaden their experience. But the supervisors refused to let their valuable people go. One reason was that there was no departmental program or model that clearly articulated the value of developing employees. Although management talked about the advantages of developing employees, supervisors were not sure how to go about it. They did not share information about openings with people inside the department. Instead, they hired from the outside to fill openings. Turnover skyrocketed among programmers who felt they had to go elsewhere to broaden their career experience.

Contrast this example with the sales manager in a Fortune 500 organization who kept a chart for the career development of each staff member. She had developed a system of listing each person's name along with their assignments under her jurisdiction. By tracking who held each assignment and for how long, she could easily see which employees needed new assignments to round out their experience. She actively developed her employees by literally trading them in and out of jobs and transferring them to other areas to broaden their backgrounds.

One dilemma organizations face is not having enough developmental positions to go around. Even though top employees may need to broaden their experience, sometimes there are no positions in the part of the organization that will give them the development they need. This problem can be solved in part by arranging interdepartmental transfers or job rotation.

It is important to recognize that the final responsibility for determining new assignments for professionals should not be left to the immediate supervisor. Often the supervisor has little knowledge of other available positions within the organization. Also, supervisors have a vested interest in keeping good performers in their own departments. Losing competent people, no matter how beneficial to the individual or the organization as a whole, is seldom easy for the immediate supervisor.

One way of facilitating interdepartmental transfers is to set up a board of managers, two or three levels removed from the employees who would benefit from transfers, to review potential candidates for positions that open up. One organization holds a semiannual personnel review attended by second- and third-level managers. At that meeting, the managers review the career progress of each professional in the division. If it is decided that an employee needs a transfer to develop new skills, the personnel manager is directed to work out the arrangements for such a move. Because all the managers are involved in the meeting, they have information about the developmental needs of individuals and the available opportunities in the organization. Also, since these managers are not working directly with the employees eligible for transfer, they wouldn't be inclined to keep a talented employee on a particular assignment if doing so would be detrimental to that person's career development.

Stages III and IV. While most agree that good job assignments are important to employees early in their careers, they don't always recognize the importance of job assignments for those in Stages III and IV. But they, too, often need the benefit of a new job assignment. Over-forty employees are also susceptible to boredom, the itch to start over in another career, or the idea of leaving the frustrations of the organization to start their own companies. These "happy dropouts," as a recent article in *Forbes* magazine describes them, still have the "guts, imagination, and ability" to throw themselves wholeheartedly into new and sometimes vastly different positions. Unfortunately, these top performers are often limited by "up-or-out" attitudes. Unless managers broaden their thinking about the feasibility and acceptability of lateral moves or even "demotions" to facilitate the career development of senior employees, they will lose one of their most valuable resources.

Beverly Kaye, author of *Up Is Not the Only Way,* suggests that alternatives to "moving up," such as "moving across," "moving down," or "staying put," can be attractive both to the organization and to the employee. Moving across, for example, has the advantage of providing a "way of demonstrating adaptive abilities and broadening skills, learning about other areas of the organization, and developing new talents." One computer company encourages lateral moves by requiring each professional employee to spend two weeks of every year working in another division. This requirement exposes employees to other areas of the company where they are better able to explore their interests; it also opens doors to possible transfers.

Moving down can also provide an opportunity for those who seek fulfillment in work outside the office or who wish to try a new focus. One 50-year-old manager who had successfully supervised 300 employees for eight years felt he had reached a dead end in his career until he was given an opportunity to make a unique career shift.

> I was asked to do a major study for the president that would require my full time and effort. I was reluctant to accept the assignment if it meant giving up my position as department manager, be-

cause I didn't know where it would lead. In order to do the study, I had to go back and learn a lot about surveys, interviews, analyzing questionnaire data, and so on.

> After I finished the study, the president asked if I would take a position in which some of the things proposed in the report would be implemented. He invited me to become his assistant and work out of the office of the president. I decided to take the new position, and it has been a very good experience. It has enabled me to have an impact on the whole organization and to work with issues and people I've genuinely enjoyed.

Although moving from a highly visible position to a nonsupervisory spot can carry the stigma of failure with it, the benefits for both the individual and the organization can be so great that fear of the stigma should not paralyze efforts to make such changes. By entering into honest dialogue, by using imagination, and by creating new roles that may not currently exist in the organization, moves can be made which use everyone's talents more fully.

Another option for employees in Stages III and IV is to explore new dimensions of their current-jobs. By dealing directly with customers, supervising increasing numbers of employees, or taking on new areas of responsibility, their experience can be broadened. Organizations that ignore the developmental needs of their professionals risk losing their competitive edge. Unless management keeps a watchful eye over job assignments given their professionals, productivity and innovation may suffer.

Training

An additional career development avenue that can benefit from an awareness of the four-stage framework is training. In some organizations, training constitutes the entire career development program. But despite the millions of dollars American organizations spend each year on training, the results are often disappointing. Characteristics of training programs that contribute to this problem include the following:

1. Providing the same training for everyone. Many organizations decide what skills should be taught during the year and then run everyone through the same programs.
2. Repetition of subject matter. In many corporate training programs we've heard people complain, "This is the fourth time in the last five years that I've been told about McGregor's Theory X and Theory Y. Why don't they do a better job of coordinating what's covered in these training programs?"
3. Last minute quota-filling. Many organizations specify the amount of training employees should receive (five days each year, for example). Unless managers are careful, these policies can lead to poor planning. As the year draws to a close, managers may begin to send their employees to whatever courses happen to be offered at that time. Little consideration is given to what would be most useful to the employee.

To avoid these problems, developers of training programs need to consider what type of training can most benefit individuals at various points in their careers. Some organizations have successfully used the concept of the four-stage career model to design courses geared to employees who face critical transitions in their careers. For example, one organization designed a training session for Stage II managers about to take on some of the mentoring responsibilities critical to Stage III.

The career-stage model has also been useful in identifying gaps in the overall training program. After applying the model one organization found that it had programs for new hires, new supervisors, and those about to retire, but lacked training for anyone in between.

Compensation

Compensation is another area in which looking at the stages of career progress can help create a system that fosters professional performance and development. Ironically, our research showed that many organizations have compensation systems that fail to reward the most productive employees. Many pay systems base rewards on the number of employees supervised, instead of the value of a staff member's contribution to the firm. Such systems discriminate against the highly productive nonsupervisory employees who contribute as much to organizational performance as do managers.

One company has taken steps toward solving this problem by acknowledging the contributions of their technical staff in later career stages.

> At Analog Devices, a computer components company in Norwood, Massachusetts, managers are not the only ones who receive top perks, salaries, stock options, and autonomy. Purely technical engineers called corporate fellows, division fellows, and senior staff engineers are compensated very much the way management is compensated. Division fellows can have the same perks and salary enjoyed by a division or general manager.
>
> Senior staff engineers at Analog are given flexibility in their working hours, the option of working at home or the office, and the same salary as senior managers. Senior engineers are given a great deal of leeway on the types of design projects they tackle, and are encouraged to suggest improvements on current products.

Most compensation systems could be improved greatly by a conscientious attempt to reward those in later stages who may not have a formal supervisory position but whose technical contribution is nevertheless equally valuable to the organization. Such modifications have the potential to help organizations attract and retain top-quality professionals.

Career Discussions

For several reasons career discussions between employees and supervisors are one of the most critical elements of an effective performance-improvement process. First, it is the employee's responsibility, not the organization's, to develop his or her career. Managers are interested in their unit's performance level and, as they are often rewarded for a short-term focus, they do not always consider what would be best for each individual. Even if they had the time and the inclination, managers are not omniscient and do not know what each individuals' career goals are. Employees must take responsibility for deciding what they would like to do and ensuring that they are not stuck in jobs below their capacity, Career discussions allow employees to talk about their aspirations and ideas for becoming more valuable to the organization. They also give managers the opportunity to tell employees how they are perceived.

Second, careers are no linear or static, nor are organizations clear-cut hierarchies. Employees move in and out of jobs constantly, and continually have opportunities to take on new tasks. Career discussions can help keep employees abreast of emerging opportunities and managers aware of their employees' emerging interests.

Third, individuals who understand the organization can contribute more effectively to it. Managers can help their employees a great deal by being frank about "how things work around here."

Finally, even though immediate supervisors usually do not make ultimate decisions on assignment changes, it is through the supervisor that an employee's interests and capabilities are usually transmitted to those who do decide on new assignments. Therefore, one of the most useful things a company can do to help employees manage their careers is to train both managers and professionals in the art of holding fruitful career discussions. A few lessons can help remove three of the most common blocks to open discussions about careers:

1. Lack of an adequate language or vocabulary to discuss careers.
2. Failure to distinguish the responsibilities of the manager and the professional in career discussions.

3. Inadequate preparation by the professional for a discussion of his or her career.

Let us note briefly how training has helped overcome each of these blocks. Where both managers and professionals have been introduced to a career model and have been given an opportunity to discuss it, the vocabulary problem has been resolved. Both are then able to approach their discussion from common ground. The failure to distinguish the responsibilities of each party in a career discussion can best be understood by examining Exhibit 2.

A CASE IN POINT

For a clearer picture of how the four-stage model works, the following example outlines the changes that take place in an organization using the career-stages framework. Managers in the exploration division of a large multinational oil company decided that they needed to address some critical performance issues in their organization. One of the managers involved created a task force on the subject and used the idea of four stages. The activities the task force envisioned and began to promote were quite ambitious and could be classified in three distinct phases.

Phase A: Initiation

A business and workforce diagnosis showed that the turnover of geologists and geophysicists had reached alarming levels (18 percent among professionals with five to ten years of experience). Many older professionals and managers pointed out that the exploration division had become a training ground for the small oil companies in the region. By the time employees had gained five to seven years of experience they were lured away by small companies that were offering lucrative financial packages.

EXHIBIT 2. *A Realistic Division of Responsibilities in Career Discussions*

Dimension	Professional Employee	Manager
Responsibility	Assumes responsibility for individual career development.	Assumes responsibility for employee development.
Information	Obtains career information through self evaluation and data collection. What do I enjoy doing? Where do I want to go?	Provides information by holding up a mirror of reality: How manager views the employee. How others view the employee. How "things work around here."
Planning	Develops an individual plan to reach objectives.	Helps employee assess plan.
Follow-through	Invites management support through high performance on the current job, by understanding the scope of the job and taking appropriate initiative.	Provides coaching and relevant information on opportunities.

To further define the problem, the task force charted the career progression of employees using the stages concept and language. Then a one-day workshop for a group of 20 managers of geologists and geophysicists was held introducing the four-stage model and how it could be applied to career discussions. The workshop was followed by a half-day seminar attended by all professionals. Here, senior managers expressed commitment to, and support for, a career management effort. The concept of career stages was also introduced and its implications discussed. Over the next six months, managers and professionals tried to use the model in discussions about performance, compensation, and career development. They found it provided the necessary language for addressing touchy issues like promotions and salary raises.

The effectiveness of this initial phase became apparent as geologists and geophysicists were finally able to describe some of their aspirations and frustrations. With their superior they explored possibilities for achieving their aspirations within the framework of their own company. Managers came to understand the professionals' frustrations and took steps to eliminate some of the sources. These measures brought a decline in turnover, and the objectives of the original program began to be met.

Phase B: Innovation

The most significant effect of this initial effort was the creation of a context for managers and employees in the division to make major changes in the organization, moving from human resource concerns to a focus on business productivity.

The exploration division might not have moved beyond their initial program if the economic situation in the oil industry had remained stable. However, in 1981, profits declined rapidly, and a decision was made to reduce the exploration division staff by 20 percent. Rumors circulated that management commitment to the career program was over. The initial business need for the career program had been to reduce turnover; there was now a need to reduce the number of employees.

At this critical point, a senior manager took an interest in the program and pointed out a new business need. He had been involved in a research project analyzing successful oil companies. The data indicated that successful oil finds often resulted when professionals spent several years in the same geographical area—a length of stay that enabled them to better understand the business and technical challenges there. (By contrast, the exploration division typically moved professionals between geographical areas on a regular basis.) When this finding was linked to the career management effort, a new business need was identified.

Instead of laying off employees, the department instituted an early retirement program that was so attractive that almost all who were eligible took advantage of it. But the large number of early retirees, along with the recent high turnover of experienced staff, left an inexperienced workforce; 70 percent of the remaining professionals had less than five years' service. When this information was presented to the vice-president, he authorized funds to continue the career development program. A key objective was to retain the remaining Stage III professionals and to cultivate high-potential Stage II employees for promotion to Stage III as soon as possible.

With an increased emphasis on taking individual responsibility for their own careers, some of the nonmanagers in Stage III started taking more initiative and began using their contacts in other departments to do more cooperative projects. During this period, a few of the nonmanagers in Stage IV recognized the link between career stages and the literature on innovation. They read about product champions with executive sponsorship.

A series of workshops were conducted to discuss product champions and encourage more risk taking. Many of the Stage III professionals responded enthusiastically, and the number of new ideas and projects increased substantially. Unfortunately, this increased conflict between Stage III nonmanagers and a number of the supervisors in the department. One area of tension revolved around resources. A professional would request resources for a project and the supervisor

would turn it down. In the past this would effectively have killed the project. Under the new circumstances, however, the professional would take the idea on to other Stage III and Stage IV professionals in the hope of rallying support so the project could be continued. The supervisors called this process "end running"—and they didn't like it. Others considered this kind of initiative a sign of success.

Phase C: Institutionalization

The lack of agreement between the various levels of the organization provided the impetus to move into Phase C. Many managers were quite traditional and felt comfortable only when decisions were made in the formal hierarchy. Those pushing the new ideas about career stages and innovation wanted to place more emphasis on informal methods of doing business. They wanted to encourage mentor relationships and develop ways to bypass bureaucracy.

The general manager, who supported the new direction, initiated a meeting of several key people. At the meeting, they first tried to envision what was critical for the future success of the division. They asked questions concerning the ideal future: "What would be the role of professionals and managers? How would jobs and work be different?" Their discussion led them to restructure the division along the lines of a professional team concept. It was agreed that a change of structure would signal to everyone that senior management wanted to move in new directions. Teams were organized around geographical business areas. Each team was assigned professionals from Stages I, II, and III. Support people such as business analysts and computer specialists were assigned to teams on a full-time basis. The teams were given a budget with full responsibility to manage it. If they were "successful," they could get additional resources from the divisionwide "slush fund." Perhaps the most controversial issue concerned supervision. Some district managers elected to set up project teams to which no formal leader was assigned. Where this occurred, either the team shared the administrative load or someone emerged to provide leadership. In either case, the teams usually felt that the process was effective and preferred it to having an assigned project leader.

All of these organizational innovations were triggered by allowing career-stage concepts to take root. Upper management and professionals alike were pleased with the results. Productivity increased and employees were strongly in favor of the new entrepreneurial climate. The chief geologist said: "This is what I've been trying to convince management to do all along. These ideas have minimized bureaucracy, and they keep managers off the backs of professionals. It avoids the problem of managers making technical decisions they don't really understand anymore."

By describing the experience of this organization in detail, we do not suggest that all organizations introducing the career-stage model will end up completely restructured. We present this example because it shows how the different elements of the four-stage model are applied and what the implications are for the rest of the organization.

THE CHALLENGE

There is a great opportunity for managers to increase the productivity and performance levels of professionals. For managers, the four-stage model provides a common language in which to discuss performance and career issues with employees. Managers can help professionals identify and overcome blocks to their progress and develop strategies for improvement. The model can help both professionals and managers understand what they must do to become and remain high performers in their current assignments. For organizations, the model provides a basis for the planning and development of professional resources, a way to more fully utilize existing capabilities, and a framework for reassessing policies and practices that impact professional performance.

The Dual Hierarchy in Research

Herbert A. Shepard

In recent years, industry has become increasingly dependent on technological innovation as an instrument of competition. Within the individual firm, power tends to shift to those who possess the skills most needed for survival and growth. Over the past half-century, this distinction has passed from manufacturing to sales and thence to research and development. Staff-line organization idealogy, which developed as a tribute to the preeminence of manufacturing, has slowed and obscured shifts of power, has been modified to become a theory of organization applicable to the structure of subunits of the firm, and has tended to give way to functional ideology which allows power to flow more freely in response to changing environmental demands.

The shift of power to research and development has been hampered by staff-line theory which defined it as an advisory service rather than an innovative force or a higher center of intelligence. A more ancient ideology which developed as a tribute to the rise of the bourgeoisie, based on the classical economic theory, also hampered the shift of power by defining monopoly as evil and a short time perspective as good. The innovative process is a delayed response system: research requires that the firm have a cushion of monopoly to support it and survive the period until another cushion can be provided by innovation; thus, the firm must have a long time perspective. The shift of power has been further

hampered by the ideology of science which denies the relevance of power to scientific work and by the social norms of physical science which exclude and deny the validity of certain types of knowledge and skill required for innovation—political, economic, organizational, social, psychological, cultural, etc.

The relatively weak position of the research and development laboratories of many firms is reflected in their acceptance of the organizational traditions of the rest of the firm, even though these traditions are adapted to the requirements of production rather than research. Until recently, few industrial laboratories have abandoned the organizational model suited for efficient repetition of operations and sought a model more in keeping with the requirements of innovation or the mobilization of intelligence.

It is by no means certain that solutions to problems of coordination, control, evaluation, program formulation, personnel maintenance, decision-making, and the provision of administrative services can be found which do not, of themselves, interfere with the mobilization of intelligence. However, the process which produces these problems also produces a managerial class which is concerned with them and with the mobilization of intelligence. Research managements are experimenting with new organizational arrangements intended to resolve the dilemmas of laboratory organization which confront them.

The problems of research and development organization which confront research managements are not necessarily defined by them in the terms used in this paper. Problem definition is

Reprinted with permission from H. Shepard, "The Dual Hierarchy in Research," *Research Management,* August 1958, 177–187.

influenced by the situation of the definer. The experience of a research manager is more likely to be organized as follows. As a technical organization grows in size, problems of coordination, control, evaluation, program formulation, personnel maintenance, decision-making, and the provision of administrative services become more complex and burdensome. A managerial class develops which is concerned primarily with these matters. The class is hierarchically differentiated as is the custom in most large-scale organizations. Since its responsibility entails control over the activities of scientists and engineers, it is logical that technical competence be one criterion for entry into the class. However, entering the managerial class removes the technical man from direct participation in technical work, and he comes to devote himself to many matters not recognized as technical. When a good scientist is made a manager a good scientist is lost. Yet, promotion to management is the reward for competence in scientific work. Hence, the laboratory becomes a school for making nonscientists of its scientists.

This anomaly having been recognized, the intelligent managerial action is to seek a corrective device, a means of preventing the undesirable outcome. Getting rid of an undesired consequence without, at the same time, destroying the institution that produces it or producing other, equally undesirable consequences in its place, is, however, rarely an easy undertaking. Research managements have experimented with a number of methods and approaches. Two of these will be described and discussed in the following pages.

THE CONCEPT OF TECHNICAL DIRECTION

In simplest terms, the problem appears to be to find a way of rewarding scientists for good scientific performance without removing them from scientific work. One approach to this problem emphasizes the concept of technical direction.

For example, administrative assistants, whose duties are to perform nontechnical functions for research supervisors and managers, may be provided to enable the latter to spend their time directing technical activities and thus to continue to make a scientific contribution. At the same time, it is felt that, by having a high degree of technical competence represented in the laboratory management, better results will be assured.

Emphasis on the concept of technical direction produces new problems. Commonly experienced difficulties include the following.

(1) The search for inspirational leaders. The skills involved in technical leadership are not well understood, nor do they appear to be readily transferable. Some scientists are gifted in this respect, but the demand appears to exceed the supply.

(2) The productive scientist who is not acceptable to others. When there is evidence that a scientist lacks the aptitude for technical direction, there is no alternative way to reward him for excellent scientific performance.

(3) The morale of administrative assistants. If the administrative assistant is a scientist by training, he is likely to regard his administrative post as evidence of failure as a scientist. If he were a successful scientist, he would be a technical director, or at least a practicing research worker. If he is a nonscientist, he is likely to sense disparagement of his skills on the part of the scientific staff. In either case, a satisfying career is difficult to work out.

(4) The effect of a hierarchy of technical directors. Emphasis on the concept of technical direction implies that technical directors have a responsibility for technical decisions. Inspirational technical leadership is one side of the coin; control is the other. The inspirational leader need not be a controlling figure, but it is difficult to avoid producing a system of authoritarian control where there is a hierarchy of technical directors.

The most serious criticism of emphasis on the concept of technical direction is that it is wasteful of the laboratory's scientific resources. The exercise of technical judgment by a technical director may be regarded as top company management's way of decreasing the likelihood of erroneous technical decisions, since top management must usually accept the technical aspects of laboratory reports on faith. But the technical director's knowledge is inevitably inferior to the combined resources of his scientific staff. Hence, his contribution is likely to be redundant, at best, or negative. The greater his knowledge, the more likely is this danger to be overlooked, and the more likely is his staff to be dependent on his scientific resources rather than on their own. The danger that poor decisions may be made does not derive from the danger that the director may be technically incompetent, but from the danger that he may not know how to ensure that the scientific intelligence of his staff is brought to bear on problems.

THE DUAL HIERARCHY
OR TECHNICAL LADDER

Some of the difficulties associated with emphasis on the concept of technical direction have led research managements to experiment with another approach to the problem of mobilizing scientific intelligence. This approach is called the "dual hierarchy" or "technical ladder" method. It springs partly from the same problem definition as do the experiments which emphasize the concept of technical direction: namely, that the best scientists are lost when they are rewarded by being made managers. A companion problem, namely, that some able scientists are, in their own opinion or in the opinion of their associates or of management, singularly unfitted for carrying managerial responsibilities, also motivates the dual ladder approach. It is intended to make the practice of research as rewarding or attractive as the practice of management.

The dual ladder approach is roughly as follows: The laboratory, let us assume, is divided into departments, each with a department head. Each department is divided into sections under section heads, and each section is further subdivided into work groups of scientists and engineers, under group heads. This constitutes the managerial ladder. Now, another set of positions is established, roughly paralleling the department head, section head, and group head positions in terms of salary, job luxuries, and freedom of decision on work matters. Terms are invented to label these positions, for example, Scientific Advisor, Senior Research Associate, and Research Associate, in descending order. This constitutes the technical ladder. Research Associates report to Section Heads, Senior Research Associates to Department Heads, and Scientific Advisors to the chief executive of the laboratory. No managerial responsibilities encumber the freedom of persons occupying these positions. This makes it possible to give recognition and reward to scientists who do outstanding work by promoting them in the technical ladder, at the same time providing them with opportunity to continue in scientific work. The scientist has two ways to advance in the organization.

There are several variations of the above approach, but they share in common the idea of acquiring and maintaining productive scientists in scientific work by rewarding them with prestige, freedom, and job luxuries (special parking spaces, comfortable offices, secretaries, private laboratories, etc.) As with the approach previously discussed, certain difficulties are associated with the dual ladder method. Some common ones include the following.

(*1*) *Role definition for the technical ladder position.* Usually, the keynote of upward movement in the technical ladder is meant to be freedom in research. According to scientific mythology, such freedom is highly valued. In the context of the industrial laboratory, however, it may not be desired by the scientist, for any of several reasons. For some, such freedom is loneliness, rejection, the feeling of not belonging. It is valued highly only by relatively autonomous people. Frequently, the technical ladder position seems appropriate for those members of the staff who are regarded as "prima donnas," that is, for people who are already experiencing rejection by their associates. The reward of a technical ladder position confirms their worst suspicions. A decrease in productivity is sometimes noted after the appointment of a scientist to a technical ladder position; while this may be attributed to his resting on his laurels or to inadequate supervision, it may also be his reaction to discovering that the means he has been using to impress others and gain recognition and acceptance have failed, and that he has been formally isolated from the rest of the staff. In some dual ladder systems, the incumbent is expected to serve as a consultant to others in matters affecting his specialty. The provision of consultant aid requires a high degree of skill, sensitivity to the feelings and needs of others, and ability to help without damaging the other's self-esteem. An appointment to a technical ladder position is, however, rarely accompanied by training in consulting methods; moreover, there is a tendency to appoint scientists who show skill in human relations to positions in the managerial ladder. Once again, the technical ladder incumbent is likely to experience rejection and to react in ways which are not serviceable to himself or the organization.

(2) *The technical ladder position as reward rather than opportunity.* When the emphasis in promoting a scientist to a technical ladder position is reward for past service, certain difficulties may be encountered. Scientific mythology tells us that the scientist is motivated by curiosity. The picture is usually presented of the scientist as one possessed by a burning desire to undertake some favorite projects, from which undertaking he has been prevented by the requirements of his present job. Appointment to a technical ladder position may succeed primarily in revealing the scientist to himself and his associates to be lacking in the independence and commitment which he was formerly free to pretend.

(3) *The technical ladder position as a shelf.*

The reward aspect of appointment to a technical ladder position, together with its capacity for isolating the individual from the rest of the organization, makes it a convenient shelf for senior staff members whose managerial or technical skills are outmoded or wanting, but who occupy influential positions. To the scientific staff, such appointments are an admission by management that promotion to a technical ladder position is a punishment rather than a reward.

(4) *The technical ladder position as an ambiguous status symbol.* Within his profession, there is no universality of title meaning for the industrial scientist as there is for the academic scientist. While ambiguity may occasionally serve purposes of face-saving or making an impression, it is a source of stress when the scientist is trying to identify himself relative to other members of his profession. The problem of identification may be more stressful in the nonscientific community of neighbors and family, where status and worth are identified by widely recognized labels and by such criteria as the size of organization the individual commands.

(5) *The technical ladder position as proof of inadequacy.* The scientist who is gifted in his ability to inspire and lead others as well as in his science belongs logically in the managerial ladder. The technical ladder is usually reserved for competent and brilliant scientists who are regarded as lacking in managerial potential. In our society, leadership skills and leadership positions are highly valued. The technical ladder incumbent is only half a man. Under these circumstances, promotion to a technical ladder position is a dubious honor: it is as much stigma as reward.

(6) *Promotion in the technical ladder as mobility up and out.* The characteristics that make the technical ladder a convenient shelf make it unattractive to many scientists. It is peripheral rather than central. It removes the scientist from the main stream of organization. It gives freedom in place of power, but power is needed to remain free. Moreover, as noted above, appoint-

513

ment to a technical ladder position is, in many laboratories, a judgment that the incumbent is unfit to exercise power. This permanent exclusion from the main stream of organization means that the technical ceiling, in terms of income and prestige, is low in comparison with the managerial ceiling. A combination of managerial and technological skill is highly valued in modern corporations. The research scientist or engineer may well aspire to a position in top management if he begins to move up the managerial ladder; but a step up the technical ladder is towards a point of no future and no return.

(7) *A shortage of rungs in the technical ladder.* In some laboratories, the growth of a technical ladder has been topsy-like. In these cases, it often happens that there are only one or two prestige and income categories, with the result that a scientific career is out of the reach of scientists who are only competent but not brilliant or, alternatively, that the ceiling for advancement in the technical ladder is so low as to be unattractive to ambitious scientists.

(8) *Technical ladder positions are less secure.* The productivity of the scientist in a technical ladder position is more easily assessed, or at least more open for inspection, than the productivity of a manager. Especially if he is doing independent work, where he is relatively isolated from the rest of the staff, there is no difficulty in fixing the responsibility on him if his results do not come up to the expectations of management. In evaluating a supervisor or manager, there are many considerations and many areas of irreducible uncertainty. Unless the scientist in the technical ladder has been able to take a valued consultant role, however, his situation is uncomfortably simple. Moreover, much more is expected of the scientist in a technical ladder position than performance of the routine tasks that comprise the bulk of scientific work: he is expected to be creative. Persons in the managerial ladder, however, may be highly regarded for providing leadership to groups performing work that is largely routine.

That the dual ladder is a sensitive system, not subject to breakdown from many causes, down not demonstrate that it is unworkable, but rather that, to thrive, it requires conditions which are hard to establish and maintain. Some prescriptions and proscriptions can be inferred from the foregoing list of pitfalls.

First, the opportunity rather than the reward aspect of the technical ladder position should be stressed. It should be determined whether the candidate does have a burning desire to do some independent work. This consideration suggests that the technical ladder position should be a temporary, rather than a permanent commitment.

Second, it suggests that research workers who are primarily oriented to success in their profession rather than in the company are the most appropriate candidates for technical ladder positions. If the scientist regards the laboratory simply as a convenient place to do his work, he is more likely to feel liberated than isolated in the technical ladder.

Third, it suggests that training in consulting skills and the provision of consulting opportunities are important integrating elements. The scientist in the technical ladder can still be an influential member of the organization.

Fourth, it suggests that great care should be taken in the selection of candidates for technical ladder positions, since the prestige of the technical ladder rests only on the willingness of good scientists to accept positions in it. Relegation of deadwood to the technical ladder destroys its potential value.

THE PROBLEM OF ORGANIZATIONAL INFLUENCE

The most important issue is the problem of organizational influence or power. It is interesting to note that, in the British Scientific Civil Service, the assumption appears to be made that anyone can manage, but that it requires rare talent to do research. There, the equivalent of our technical ladder positions are highly prized, and high scientific rank achieved largely through managerial advances is regarded as less valid than high rank achieved by climbing the technical ladder. In the United States, however, it is doubtful that we can ever support, with enough evidence for it to become reality for scientists, the myth that science is a more important or more valid activity than management. Some laboratories have been successful in removing the stigmata from the technical ladder positions by transferring scientists from one ladder to the other in accord with research requirements, research workers' inclinations, and career consideration.

More fundamentally, however, it may be desirable to reevaluate the functions of members of the managerial hierarchy. Emphasis on control and direction of a professional group seems almost a contradiction in terms. In the professional mythology, a research manager can scarcely accept responsibility for the work of his staff; that responsibility is their own. Professional mythology is, however, no match for the realities of American life. For many young scientists and engineers, the practice of their professions is primarily a means of getting a management position.

The denial of desire for power in the official version of the scientific career is a source of confusion for the scientist, rather than a valid basis for a calling. The young scientist has not acquired the self-image or the skills required for sharing responsibility. Dependency pays off in the laboratory; it makes a cooperative subordinate, suitable for promotion to a position of responsibility. Thus, authority and dependency are the bases of laboratory organization, and a technical ladder must be added to free some scientists for creative work. There is needed a new concept of research management, which helps nominally professional workers to acquire the self-image and skills required before they can accept professional responsibility. Unless scientists are able to participate responsibly in decision-making, to use each other's resources, to engage in mutual evaluation, and to work autonomously, a controlling, centralized management is necessary.

The Dual Ladder:
Motivational Solution or Managerial Delusion?

Thomas J. Allen

Ralph Katz

Abstract. The 'Dual Ladder' reward system has been used for years by industry as an incentive system to motivate technical performance. Its effectiveness has been called into question on many occasions. This paper will report the results of a survey of nearly 1,500 engineers and scientists in nine U.S. organizations. In this survey, engineers were asked to indicate their career preferences in terms of increasing managerial responsibility, technical ladder advancement or more interesting technical work. Responses indicate marked age-dependent differences in response, particularly a strong increase in the proportion preferring more interesting project work over either form of advancement.

INTRODUCTION

The effectiveness of so-called 'dual ladder' career systems has long been debated in both industrial and academic circles (Moore and Davies, 1977; Smith and Szabo, 1977; Sacco and Knopka, 1983). The idea was conceived somewhere in the dim past by a research manager or personnel administrator, who hoped to increase the number of career opportunities available to high performing technical professionals and thereby to sustain their motivation.

The original idea held to the implicit assumption that productive engineers and scientists were being 'forced' into administrative roles in order to attain higher salary levels and organizational prestige. Their technical talents were thereby lost to their organizations. The assumption that productive scientists and engineers had to be 'forced' into management was shown to be invalid. Many studies (Ritti, 1971; Krulee and Nadler, 1960; Bailyn, 1980) have shown that a very high proportion of scientists and engineers in industry see their career goals in terms of eventual progress in management. In fact, a recent survey of MIT freshmen shows fully 20 percent of those choosing engineering majors citing management as their ultimate career goal.

Nevertheless, there remains some proportion of the technical staff of most organizations who prefer to remain in full contact with technical problem solving, for whom management has no

Reprinted with permission from T. J. Allen and R. Katz, "The Dual Ladder: Motivational Solution or Managerial Delusion?," *R&D Management*, 1986, Vol. 16, 185–197.

attraction, and who could potentially find a technical ladder career rewarding. The basic question is just how large this proportion is.

Companies vary widely in their estimates. Some restrict technical ladder entry severely, while others promote a relatively high proportion of their staff into technical ladder positions. Companies also vary widely in their enthusiasm over the concept. A representative of one company, who requested anonymity, reported to the authors that when his company was recently considering the possibility of such a system, he informally polled the management of 13 other companies that already had such a system. Most reported varying degrees of satisfaction, but when asked if, given the chance, they would do it over again, 12 of the 13 replied definitely not.[1]

The problems underlying the dual ladder concept are several. First there is a general cultural value which attaches high prestige to managerial advancement. Managers are seen as important in our society in general. Vice presidents are accorded high prestige. Someone working for an industrial organization with the title of Senior Research Fellow is not accorded the same degree of prestige by society at large. As a result, technical staff begin very early to think about eventually attaining a management position. Consequently when told that they have been selected for promotion to a technical ladder position, such a person hears a very different message. He hears that the organization does not think that he will make a good manager. The technical ladder promotion then becomes a consolation prize, and very often de-motivates an otherwise productive member of the staff.

Second, despite many organizations' attempts to equate pay and perquisites for the two ladders, there is one key ingredient of the managerial ladder which is missing from the technical ladder, viz., power. As an individual progresses on the managerial ladder, the number of employees reporting to that individual generally increases. When that manager requests action, those subordinates generally mobilize to accom-

plish the action. This is a strong external indicator of power, hence also prestige. As an individual progresses on the technical ladder, neither the number of subordinates nor visible power increase. Hence a technical ladder position is viewed inside the organization as less important than its supposedly equivalent management counterpart.

Finally, organizations tend, over time, to diverge from the initial design and intent of the system. For the first few years, the criteria for promotion to the technical ladder may well be followed rigorously, but they gradually become corrupted. The technical ladder often becomes a reward for organizational loyalty rather than technical contribution. Equally damaging is the even more prevalent tendency to use the technical ladder as a repository for failing managers (Smith and Szabo, 1977). Either of these practices will destroy whatever reward value there may be in the dual ladder system.

Given all of this, two key questions develop. First of all, what proportion if any of a laboratory's technical staff will find the technical ladder career an attractive one? Second, for those others who will never be promoted to the limited number of managerial positions, and who are not necessarily inclined toward the technical ladder, what can be done to reward and continue to motivate them?

To address these questions, technical staff from nine organizations were asked, along with a number of questions, to indicate their career preferences, whether toward management, technical ladder, or whether they might simply be interested in project assignments of challenging and exciting nature irrespective of promotion (Table 1).

RESEARCH METHODS

The data presented in this paper were collected in a study of engineers and scientists in nine major U.S. organizations. The selection of partici-

TABLE 1.   Format of the Question

To what extent would you like your career to be:	
a) a progression up the technical professional ladder to a higher-level position?	1 2 3 4 5 6 7
b) a progression up the managerial ladder to a higher-level position?	1 2 3 4 5 6 7
c) the opportunity to engage in those challenging and exciting research activities and projects with which you are most interested, irrespective of promotion	1 2 3 4 5 6 7

pating organizations could not be made random, but they were chosen to represent several distinct sectors and industries. Two of the organizations are government laboratories, one in the U.S. Department of Defense, the other in the National Aeronautics and Space Administration; three are not-for-profit firms doing most of their business with government agencies. The four remaining organizations are in private industry: two in aerospace, one in the electronics industry and one in the "packaged-goods" industry.

In each organization short meetings were scheduled with the members of the technical staff to explain the general purposes of the study, to solicit their voluntary cooperation and to distribute questionnaires to each engineer individually. In addition to the usual demographic questions, the questionnaire included a number of questions about the ways in which each individual viewed his future career and the ways in which the organization structured its reward system around career factors. There are also a number of questions addressing the way in which engineers view their jobs and the importance that they attach to various features in their jobs. The central questions around which the present paper is developed are those shown in Table 1. These questions ask engineers their preference in terms of progression on either the managerial or technical ladders or in lieu of these, the opportunity to engage in challenging and exciting projects irrespective of promotion. The third question was included just for what was expected to be those few engineers who might not be interested in the traditional paths of organizational progress.

Individuals were asked to complete their questionnaires as soon as possible. Stamped, return envelopes were provided so that completed forms could be mailed to the investigators directly. These procedures not only ensure voluntary participation, but they also enhance data quality since respondents must commit their own time and effort. The response rate across organizations was extremely high ranging from 82% to a high of 96%. A total of 2,157 usable questionnaires were returned.

RESULTS

Respondents varied in age from 21 to 65 with a mean of 43 and standard deviation of 9.6 years. Managers and those holding technical ladder positions are included. There are 374 managers and 351 engineers in technical ladder positions among the 2,157 who completed the survey.

Respondents were initially classified as being oriented toward a technical, managerial, or project-centered career if their response on one of the three scales exceeded the response on the other two by at least one scale point. Those who reported equally favouring any two of the three options were left out of the analysis. A total of 1,495 respondents indicated a preference for one of the three options. Of these, 488 (32.6%) preferred the managerial ladder over the two alternative career paths, 323 (21.6%) preferred the technical ladder and a surprising 684 (45.8%) reported a preference for having the, 'opportunity to engage in those challenging and exciting research activities and projects with which (they) are most interested, irrespective of promotion.'

Such a large proportion of respondents preferring a somewhat non-traditional form of reward arouses suspicions that the wording in the question may have made the alternative more attractive than was intended. It would seem reasonable that, were this the case, the induced preference would not be as strongly felt as preferences based on the more substantial conviction. Increasing the margin of preference required in defining orientation does not, however, decrease the proportion of those preferring interesting projects (Table 2).

In fact, the number of engineers reporting the project preference is not as sensitive to the increased margin of specification as are the numbers preferring managerial or technical ladders. It would certainly appear from this that the project preference is relatively strongly held and is unlikely to have resulted to any significant degree from the wording of the question.

In addition, a more recent study (Epstein, in preparation), using a less strongly worded third alternative, has produced nearly identical results.

Orientation as a Function of Age
Career preferences, as one might expect, are significantly related to age (F = 18.25; df = 2, 1399; p < 0.001). The proportion of engineers citing a preference for interesting projects increases almost monotonically with age (Figure 1). This may be due, partially, to a realization that advancement opportunities along the two traditional ladders are diminishing with age. This can be only partially true, since such a high proportion of those in their twenties indicate this preference. In fact, it is the most preferred alternative for all engineers, save those from 25 to 30.

The technical ladder career attracts the smallest proportion of engineers in all ages. The proportion indicating this preference hovers around 20 percent showing only a mild peak among those in their thirties. The proportion preferring a managerial career peaks in the late twenties and declines steadily thereafter.

Career Preference as a Function of Position
As one might expect, managers report a marked preference for a managerial career. There is some diminution with age (Figure 2) with a concomitant increase in preference for interesting projects. Only for a brief period in their late thirties do managers show any interest in the technical ladder.

Most of the engineers, who are on the technical ladder, prefer one of the other two alternatives. The younger ones tend to prefer management over the technical ladder. Older technical ladder engineers indicate a preference for interesting projects.

TABLE 2. *Sensitivity Analysis of the Scale Margin Used in Defining Career Orientation*

Margin of Preference (Scale Point)	Number of Respondents Preferring:		
	Managerial Ladder	Technical Ladder	Interesting Projects
1	458 (32.7%)	302 (21.5%)	642 (45.8%)
2	290 (35.8%)	128 (15.8%)	393 (48.4%)
3	151 (36.5%)	50 (12.1%)	213 (51.4%)

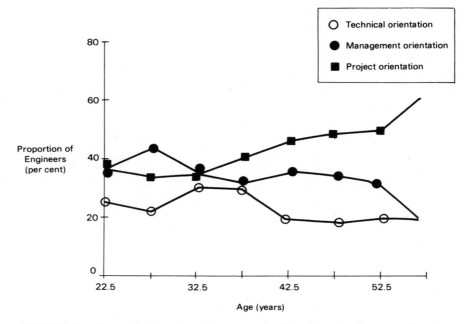

FIGURE 1.   *Career Preferences of Engineers in Nine Organizations as a Function of Age (N = 1402)*

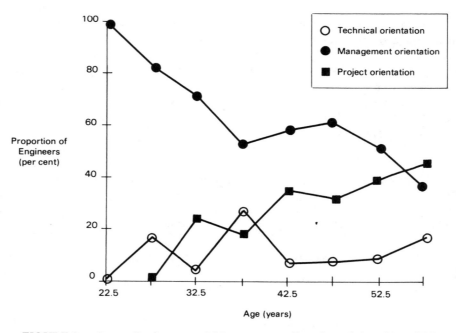

FIGURE 2.   *Career Preferences of Managers as a Function of Age (N = 374)*

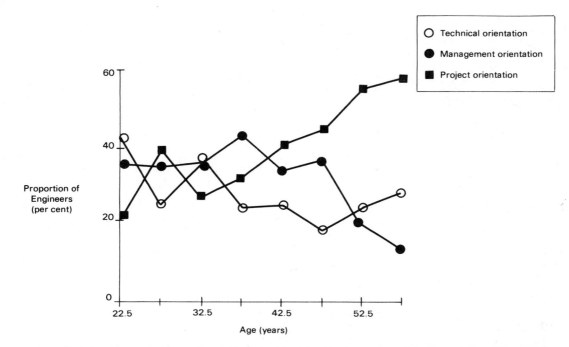

FIGURE 3.   *Career Preferences of Technical Ladder Engineers as a Function of Age (N = 351)*

Characteristics of Engineers as a Function of Orientation

Those engineers, citing different career preferences, differ in a number of other interesting ways as well (Table 3). As expected, those preferring the technical ladder are more concerned with their professional reputation, while those preferring management are more concerned with organizational matters. They prefer more to work on projects of importance to the organization and on those they see as having a potential for advancement.

The project oriented engineers are apparently not so concerned with the externalities. They seem much more influenced by the intrinsic nature of the task. They prefer technically challenging projects, having the freedom to be creative and original and working with competent colleagues.

The three orientations seem to appeal to very different kinds of people. Of course if individuals shift their orientation over time, as the data of Figure 1 suggest, then it is certainly possible that all of these other preferences change as well in order to preserve a logical system. The present data, being cross-sectional, cannot determine whether actual changes in individual orientation of engineers preferring management have increased in recent years with a concomitant decrease in those who are interested more in engineering work. If there is a change over time, it would seem to be a major reorientation of the individual's motivational base. It is important to note the positioning of the questions in the questionnaire. Those dealing with motivational issues were intentionally placed several pages ahead of the career orientation questions. So the responses to those questions were not prompted by any thought on the part of the engineer as to career preferences.

TABLE 3.   *Importance of Job Characteristics as a Function of Career Orientation*

Perceived Importance of:	Managerial	Technical Ladder	Project	p
being able to pursue own ideas	5.72	5.70	5.82	NS
building a professional reputation	5.74	5.82	5.26	0.001
working with competent colleagues	5.77	5.83	5.94	0.05
working on technically challenging tasks	6.04	6.29	6.32	0.001
working on organizationally important projects	5.36	4.74	4.70	0.001
working on projects leading to advancement	5.94	5.06	4.09	0.001
working on professionally important projects	4.92	5.11	4.81	0.01
having freedom to be creative and original	5.78	5.99	6.07	0.001

Choosing two of the motivational variables, which show a significant difference across orientations, we see a fairly stable preference by orientation across different ages (Figures 4 and 5). Young engineers with a project orientation value the freedom to be creative and original at least as much as their older colleagues. Similarly, those with a management orientation prefer to work on organizationally important projects without regard to age.

Perception of the Reward System

Following the question about career orientation respondents were asked to indicate the most likely form of reward for high performance in their job. They were given the same three alternatives, management promotion, technical ladder advancement or interesting project assignments.

A relatively high proportion of the younger engineers see the technical ladder as the most likely reward. For those over 30, this diminishes considerably and interesting project assignments are seen to be the most likely form of reward (Figure 6). Only about 20 to 25 percent of respondents see a management promotion as the

most likely reward. This is less sensitive to age than either of the other two alternatives and doesn't decrease much in likelihood with age, at least before the age of 50.

Examining the reward value of each form of promotion separately produces some very interesting results. The technical ladder promotion is seen by young people of all three orientations to be a reward for high performance. Naturally it is those with a technical ladder orientation who themselves feel more strongly about this (Figure 7). After the age of 40 however, there is, on the average, general disagreement with the proposition that high performance will lead to a technical ladder promotion. This is true to some degree even for those oriented toward the technical ladder career.

As for a management promotion coming as a reward for performance only the managers really believe this to be true (Figure 8), and even their belief diminishes with time. At no point, however, do they disagree with the proposition. Everyone else, particularly those engineers with a project orientation, disagrees that a management promotion would result from high job performance.

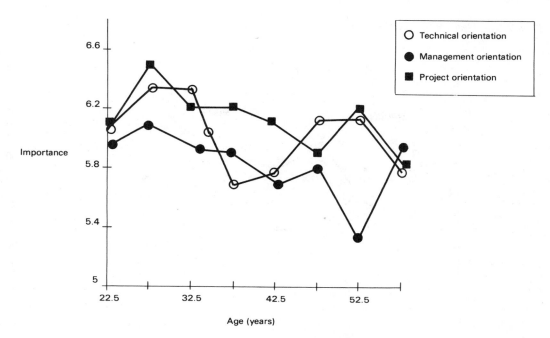

FIGURE 4.   *Importance of Having Freedom to Be Creative and Original*

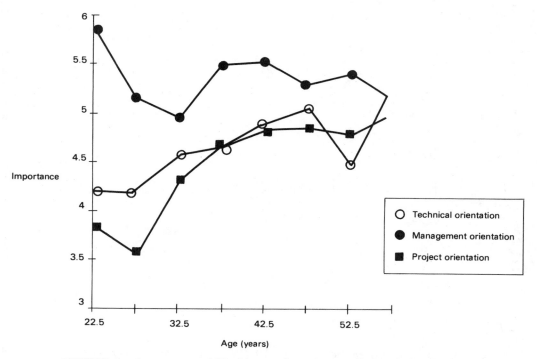

FIGURE 5.   *Importance of Working on Organizationally Important Projects*

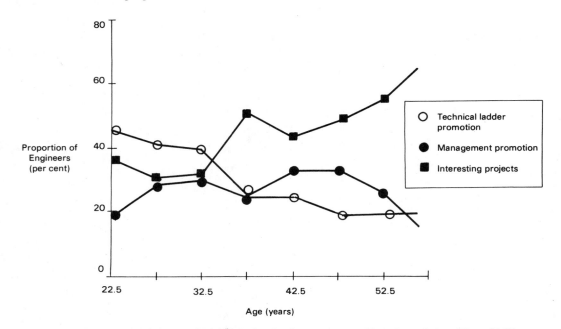

FIGURE 6.   Perception of Rewards for Performance as a Function of Age (N = 1061)

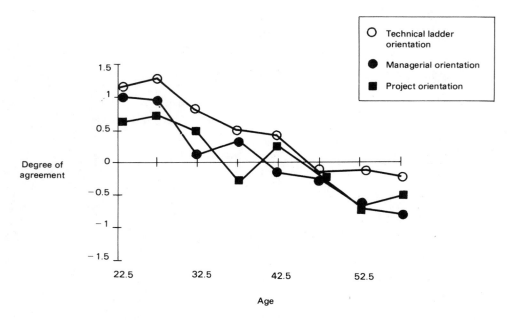

FIGURE 7.   Agreement with the Statement That High Performance Leads to Technical Ladder Promotion as a Function of Career Orientation

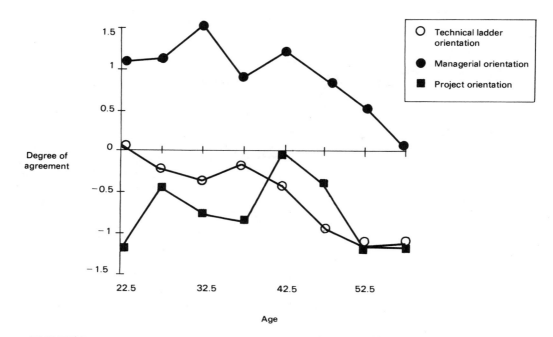

FIGURE 8. *Agreement with the Statement That High Performance Leads to Managerial Promotion as a Function of Career Orientation*

Interesting projects are seen as a reward for performance by those with the project orientation and by young engineers with a technical ladder orientation (Figure 9). At no point do those with a managerial orientation agree with this possibility.

In general, with the possible exception of the technical ladder oriented engineers, those with different orientations tend to see performance rewarded in the direction favoured by their orientation. In the case of those inclined toward the technical ladder this is true while they are young but diminishes considerably with time. Of course there is no way of filtering cause from effect in these observations. It may be that the perceived reward system is the basis for the orientation. On the other hand it may very well be that the orientation is acquired for other reasons and through a rationalization process the engineer comes to believe that high performance will advance him in the desired direction.

Perceptions as a Function of Position

Finally, grouping individuals as a function of their actual position rather than orientation produces some interesting results. Roughly 30 percent of the engineers already on the technical ladder indicate a preference for that type of career trajectory. On a seven-point scale, their degree of preference averages between 5.0 and 5.5 (Figure 10). Only about 10 percent of managers would prefer a technical ladder career. Only for a brief period in their late thirties do managers seem attracted by the relative freedom of the technical ladder, but they recover from that fairly quickly.

When it comes to preference for a managerial career, managers are unequivocal (Figure 11). They rate it higher than anyone. Interestingly, the technical ladder staff rate the managerial career higher than the category of other engineers, particularly as they become older.

Interesting project assignments increase in desirability for all engineers, managers included,

525

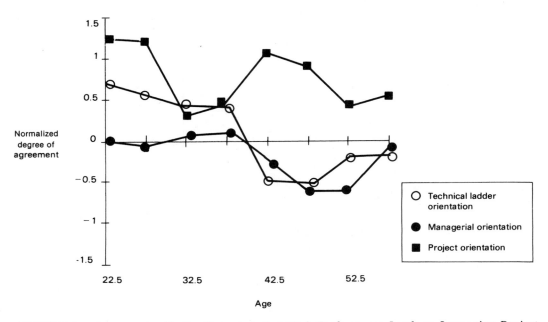

FIGURE 9. *Agreement with the Statement that High Performance Leads to Interesting Project Assignments as a Function of Career Orientation*

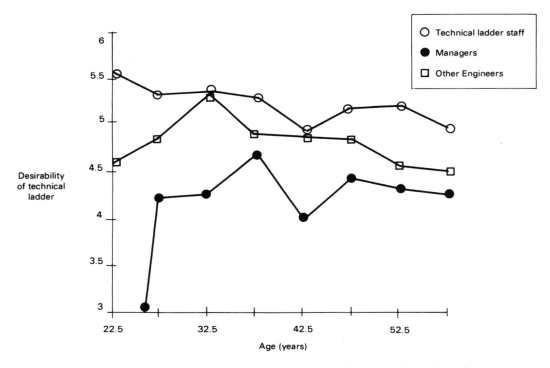

FIGURE 10. *Preference for Technical Ladder as a Function of Job Classification*

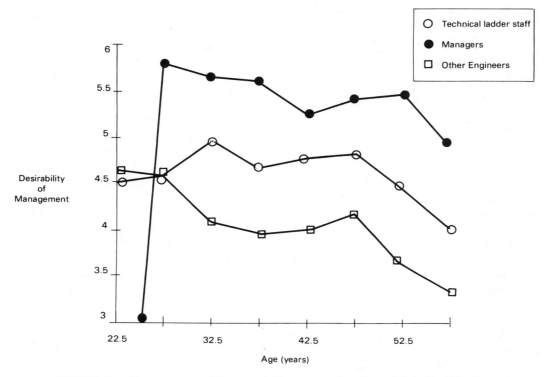

FIGURE 11. *Preference for Managerial Career as a Function of Job Classification*

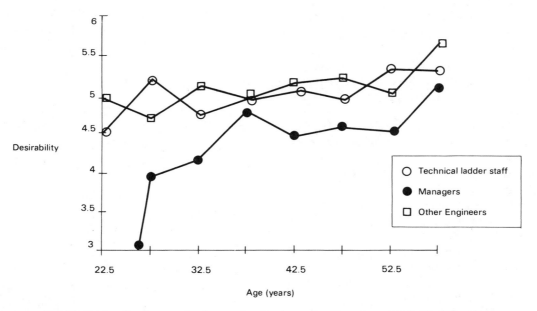

FIGURE 12. *Preference for Interesting Projects as a Function of Job Classification*

as they age (Figure 12). Although younger managers do not seem to place a very high value on the nature of the work that they are asked to do, they eventually come to feel almost as strongly about this as do their subordinates.

CONCLUSIONS

It is very clear from the data that, while young engineers generally seek managerial advancement, a substantial proportion report a preference for what has come to be known as 'technical ladder' advancement in the organization. Both of these more career-oriented motivations decline with age and are replaced with a desire for more interesting work content, without regard to organizational standing.

An open question remains over the degree to which this result from rationalizations by those who have given up on the possibility of promotion or whether it is a real change of attitude with age. The latter could be the result of an increased awareness of the costs (increased travel, longer hours, administrative burden, etc.) that are often associated with organizational advancement.

The existence of a substantial proportion of young engineers who indicate the 'interesting project' preference and the fact that engineers with this orientation differ significantly on several other parameters, indicates that there is some underlying substance distinguishing this group. Managerially-oriented engineers differ from those with a technical orientation, and project-oriented engineers differ significantly from both of them.

The increasing concern for work is very important and largely neglected in the case of older engineers. Work assignments for older engineers are often made with the implicit assumption of the inevitability of technical obsolescence. That inevitability has been seriously challenged in recent years (Cf. Cole, 1979; Kaufman, 1975). Furthermore such an assumption leads to work as-

signments that are inherently less challenging and thereby creates a self-fulfilling prophecy, guaranteeing obsolescence. Recent research (Felsher, et. al., 1985) shows that instead of age being the cause of obsolescence, the failure of management to provide challenging work and to emphasize the need for technical currency is the more liely cuse. If older engineers seek more challenging work and seldom find it, can there be any wonder that they often allow themselves to sink into obsolescence?

The present research results reinforce the formula for career growth proposed by Katz (1982). Older engineers can be challenged by modifying job assignments and thereby forcing the acquisition of new knowledge. That they seek this type of challenge is quite evident in the data.

ACKNOWLEDGMENTS

The authors wish to acknowledge the assistance of the U.S. Army Office of Research, which supported the research on which this analysis is based, and the management and personnel of the nine firms that collaborated in the research.

NOTES

1. Conversations which one of the authors has had recently with managers of the thirteenth company question its status as an exception.

REFERENCES

Bailyn, L. (1980) *Living with Technology: Issues at Mid-Career.* Cambridge, MA: MIT Press.

Cole, S. (1979) Age and scientific performance. *American Journal of Sociology. 84,* 958–977.

Epstein, K. A. (In preparation) *Performance of the Dual Ladder in Industry.* Doctoral Dissertation, MIT Sloan School of Management.

Felsher, S. M., Allen T. J. and Katz R. (1985) *Technical Obsolescence: Inevitability or Management Direction?*. M.I.T. Sloan School of Management Working Paper, No. 1640–85.

Katz, R. (1982) Managing careers: The Influence of job and group longevities, in Katz *Career Issues in Human Resource Management*. Englewood Cliffs, N.J.: Prentice-Hall.

Kaufman, H. (1975) *Career Management: A Guide to Combatting Obsolescence*. New York: IEEE Press.

Krulee, G. K. and Nadler, E. B. (1980) Studies of education for science and engineering: Student values and curriculum choice. *IEEE Transactions on Engineering Management. 7*, 146–518.

McKinnon, P. (1980) *Career Orientations of R&D Engineers in a Large Aerospace Laboratory*. M.I.T. Sloan School of Management Working Paper 1097–80.

Moore, D. C. and Davies, D. S. (1977) The dual ladder—establishing and operating it. *Research Management. 20,* 14–19.

Ritti, R. R. (1971) *The Engineer in the Industrial Corporation*. New York: Columbia University Press.

Sacco, G. J. and W. N. Knopka (1983) Restructuring the dual ladder at Goodyear, *Research Management. 26*, 36–41.

Smith, J. J. and Szabo, T. T. (1977) The dual ladder—Importance of flexibility, job content and individual temperament, *Research Management, 20*, 20–23.

12

PERSONNEL PRACTICES AND POLICIES

Stimulating and Managing Ideas

William E. Souder

Effective organizational climate, careful adherence to five guiding principles, and an efficient idea flow system are necessary for the successful birth and growth of ideas.

Ideas are the life-blood of any organization. Yet maintaining the constant flow of this life-blood is an enormous challenge for most R&D departments.

How do successful firms keep high-quality ideas flowing? To answer this question, 50 *Fortune* 250 firms were surveyed as portions of larger studies of new product development.[1,2] When integrated with practices described in the literature, the following picture emerged: successful idea flow requires that management develop a finely-tuned system like Figure 1. This paper discusses the components and principles of that system.

The generation of useful ideas depends largely on individual abilities. However, research managers can stimulate theses abilities through the following policies:

- Sabbaticals
- Release time
- Providing guidance and guidelines
- Award programs
- Idea campaigns and contests
- Job rotation, involvement and exposure

1. *Sabbaticals, release-time and guidelines.* Sabbaticals and release-time arrangements can be effective mechanisms for stimulating scientists to develop their embryonic ideas.[3] But great care is required in the implementation of these policies. Participants take the risk that their pet idea will turn out to be a failure in management's eyes, while the assigned work they left behind is pushed to accolades of success.[3,4] Moreover, management may not feel they can afford the luxury of releasing anyone from the crush of current assignments to work on pet ideas. Under these circumstances, a release-time program can become a frustratingly elusive gem for the scientist.[4] On the whole, however, such policies con-

Reprinted with permission from W. Souder, "Stimulating and Managing Ideas," *Research Management*, May–June 1987, 13–17.

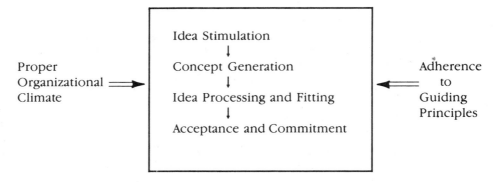

FIGURE 1.   *Idea Flow System*

vey a message that management is interested in fresh new ideas, even if no one avails themselves of the privilege. The mere presence of the policy telegraphs a message that management supports ideation.

Many organizations pay lip service to idea generation, but then fail to effectively communicate specific guidelines on the *types* of ideas wanted. Nothing is more disappointing and morale-sapping, to both the managers and the scientists, than to have a large number of irrelevant ideas being generated. Ideas that are generated in isolation from top management involvement or without a plan for their utilization are likely to lead to disappointment for all parties.

2. *Awards, campaigns and contests.* Numerous kinds of tangible and intangible awards have been used. Awards for patentable ideas, for significant technical ideas, for cost-saving ideas and for product improvement ideas are common.[5, 6, 7] The nature of these awards ranges from salary adjustments to certificates of appreciation, as illustrated in Table 1. The merit of such programs is open to conjecture. Properly administered award programs enhance the production of useful ideas.[5] However, whether the award should be money or some intangible, the size or value of the award, who should confer the award, whether or not peers should vote on the candidates, how to decide when an idea merits an award and who shall get the award, what

to do about co-inventors and other contributors, and how to distinguish major ideas from ideas of lesser potential—these are some of the difficulties in formulating and administering an idea awards program.[5]

Some companies have found that the above issues are best decided by the engineers and scientists themselves, through rotating membership, "awards committees." This approach has a dual advantage. Through service on the committee, the professionals acquire an awareness of management's problems and perspectives in evaluat-

TABLE 1.   *Examples of Idea Awards*

- Outstanding Innovation Award—up to $50,000 bonus awarded annually for ideas that significantly impact the company

- Best Annual Patent Award—$500 plus certificate and/or plaque for significant patents

- Most Creative Idea Award—up to $15,000 bonus and/or plaque awarded annually for creative ideas

- Team Achievement Award—certificate and/or plaque or bonuses for most outstanding team efforts

- Hall of Fame Room Award—recipients' pictures and list of achievements placed in a Hall of Fame room or corridor

ing ideas. And, as committee members, they necessarily interact with other idea submitters and management. They thereby serve as two-way communicators and translators of needs, guidelines, objectives, and goals.

Periodic contests or campaigns for new ideas may be staged. These can be directed at a particular need or a particular type of idea. An intangible or tangible reward may be offered as an incentive. If they are well-focused and well-planned, such campaigns can be highly successful. For example, a well-known consumer goods producer engaged in a campaign aimed at soliciting a name for a new household cleanser. Employees were given samples of the prototype product, told to try it out and asked to submit their ideas. A panel of managers and employees was assembled to select the best ones. The winners were given their choice of a year's supply of one of the company's products. Nearly all the employees submitted suggestions for names, along with suggested new uses for the product. Numerous technical and non-technical ideas were received for ways to improve the product, and many new technical ideas were received for related new products.

3. *Job Rotation, involvement and exposure.* The most productive idea generators are often people who have experienced a diversity of work assignments and environments. Moving personnel around the organization to develop their experience base and their total understanding of the company are important ingredients. Involvement in all phases of the work—the planning, the execution, the finalizing, and the transfer of the results to the user—also appear to be key ingredients. When the individuals are exposed to all the aspects of the work, they are much more able to see the interconnections and interrelationships, and to find significant gaps and needs.

This type of total involvement is highly motivating. Most scientists and engineers want to generate useful ideas that will have a significant impact on the company. Involvement in all phases affords them the best opportunity for

this.[1,2,3] Thus, the most effective idea policy may be just the opposite of release time: mainstream involvement. The work itself can be more motivating than any extrinsic award or reward program.

CONCEPT GENERATING TEAMS

The use of brainstorming, Synectics or think-tank teams has now become commonplace. Much has been written about the techniques for carrying out such activities.[8] Still, they often fail. Why? Because these teams are not properly managed.

Successful scientists and engineers are often their own worst enemies in an idea-generating session. Their training and prior successes may compel them to blot out things that seem silly, or that smack of irrational thinking and fanciful excursions. Yet these are the very practices that lead one down new passages that may culminate in creative new ideas. Participants in group ideation sessions are often surprised to listen to their own negativeness in tapes of their sessions. It seems common to pay lip service to openness while rebuffing new ideas

Thus, it is not unusual for participants to feel that group ideation sessions are boring and useless. The group often doesn't come to grips with the real problem, spends most of the time arguing about the problem definition, and generates premature criticisms of the ideas that arise. This effectively shuts off further ideation and only bland ideas emerge. The individuals may go away feeling that they could have done better on their own. Yet, it has become clear that group settings can provide essential stimuli to creativity.

In order to achieve the best results, idea generating groups should be properly constituted, structured and guided. Experiences indicate that the group should consist of at least one resident expert on the technology being discussed, one

533

persuader, one confronter, one helper and one dreamer. The resident expert supplies the depth of technological knowledge. The persuader has a friendly personality. He persistently persuades the group to accept ideas and approaches on the basis of their inherent logic. The confronter has a bull-nosed personality that won't let anything remain hidden under the rug. The dreamer supplies the far-out, fanciful inputs. The helper maintains the group process, by periodically rephrasing and summarizing the work of the group and by occasionally smoothing ruffled feelings.

The presence of each personality type in the group adds essential ingredients; each offsets and complements the other. Selection of these personality types can be an involved trial and error process. However, several instruments can help.[9, 10]

In addition to the above members, there should be a process leader and a client. They are *not* group members but, rather, outside helpers. The process leader is the expert on dealing with and guiding groups. He formulates the meeting plan and sets the framework for operation of the group process. He gives the group corrective steering and feedback on whether or not they are being too confrontive, too passive, etc. The client is the person who will use the group's outputs. He supplies factual knowledge to the participants, and provides feedback and encouragement.[9, 10]

IDEA PROCESSING AND FITTING

Idea submitters often feel that their ideas are fragile extensions of themselves, to be properly protected until they can make their own way in a hostile world. Like a mother bear and her cub, idea submitters can react with great emotion if they perceive that their ideas are being mishandled.

The "care and feeding of ideas" is a delicate and sensitive matter. What happens to an idea after it is submitted will have a significant impact on the rate of generation of other new ideas. Here are six approaches that have often been used to handle ideas:

- Idea inventories
- Idea clearing houses
- Idea brokers
- Fitting teams
- Screening teams
- Review teams

1. *Idea inventories.* Many organizations maintain a running inventory of ideas. Such an inventory can serve as a central file, to be retrieved and searched in response to specific idea needs. It can also insure that all ideas are properly recorded and documented, so that they are less likely to become lost. And it can provide the data base for monitoring the organization's idea generating productivity.

An idea inventory may make an important contribution to the development and embodiment of embryonic or unclear ideas. To enter an idea into most inventories, its nature must be fully spelled out and a short abstract written. This facilitates the retrieval and future use of the idea. The documentation process generally results in the idea being categorized by its salient attributes and characterized in a variety of ways. Thus, putting ideas into the inventory forces participants to comprehend the ideas well enough to restate them for the data base, and to maintain more complete information systems.

2. *Idea clearing houses and brokers.* Many organizations have developed procedures for directing ideas to potential users and clients. These procedures need not be elaborate. A comprehensive "want" list of the types of ideas and technologies of interest to each department may be kept. With this list, a central clearing-house staff can shuttle incoming ideas to potentially interested departments.

Clearing houses depend greatly on the abilities of the clearing house staff. The staff must interact frequently with potential clients and stay up to date on their needs and wants. In effect, the clearing house staff serves as idea brokers. They attempt to match existing ideas with existing wants, and to encourage the generation of new solutions to emerging problems. Clearing houses and brokerage functions are most effective when used in conjunction with idea inventories and/or idea fitting and screening teams.

3. *Idea fitting teams.* Many firms often find themselves with ideas that are not relevant to the nature of their business, or that simply do not fit the company personality. One potential solution to such misfit problems is to set up in-house idea fitting teams.

A fitting team operates somewhat like an idea or concept generation team, and it must be managed similarly. However, this is where the similarity ends. A fitting team's charter is to massage, bend, twist and fit previously generated ideas to the company. The fitting team's role is to convert high-quality irrelevant ideas into high-quality relevant ideas. Note that there is an idea generating aspect to this task. But the emphasis in operation is quite different from the brainstorming, free association or similar approaches used to mass-generate new ideas. Rather, reverse brainstorming, means-ends and attribute modification techniques are commonly used by fitting teams.[9] In fitting, the emphasis is on disassembling the idea into its components, then stretching or recombining these components into more relevant ideas.

Idea fitting is a complex psychological and group behavioral process that is not fully understood.[8, 9] Fitting does not seem to be as natural a process as idea generation. Effective idea generators do not seem to be effective idea fitters, and vice versa. Fitting teams often oscillate between periods of high output and enthusiasm, and periods of protracted wandering and dejected introspection. Thus, fitting teams usually require constant positive reinforcement and encouragement. The group dynamics of a fitting team are often very subtle, and it is wise to have a group behavior expert present to help guide the team efforts.

Experience has shown that it is essential for the idea inventor to be present when his idea is being fitted. Most new ideas are embryonic in nature and often incompletely documented. They are likely to be incompletely revealed, and quite possibly misrepresented or misunderstood by the fitting team. The idea inventor must be present to elaborate, explain, embellish, and convey the full flavor of his idea to the fitting team. Moreover, the experience of interacting and dialoguing with the team is usually an enlightening and educational process for all parties. Insights into group dynamics, idea selling and evaluation processes, and project selection criteria are often gleaned by the participants. Futhermore, the idea handling principles (see below) of fairness, credit, confidence and shelter require that the idea inventor be present at the idea fitting session.

4. *Idea screening and review teams.* New ideas should be screened for relevance early in their life cycles. This provides the idea submitter with definitive feedback in whether or not the organization is interested, thus giving him a basis for deciding whether or not to proceed. This is a vastly superior alternative to permitting the idea submitter to invest further time in an idea that is likely to be rejected.

There are two keys to effective review teams: criteria and membership. The consensus list of criteria used to assess and screen the ideas should be simple but relevant, and the system for rating the projects should be equally uncomplicated. Team members who evaluate and assess the ideas should include representatives from the management, production, scientific, engineering and marketing staffs of the company.

It is important that the idea submitter be present at the screening session where his idea is assessed. As in the case of fitting teams, the idea submitter must be present to interact with the group and convey the essence of his idea. Although many different models and procedures may be used to screen ideas, experience shows that Q-sorting and nominal-interacting processes are especially effective.[9]

ACCEPTANCE AND COMMITMENT

Most good ideas take several years to mature into commercially successful products. Some managers find the temptation to shelve or even terminate immature ideas during business cycle downturns irresistible. But recessionary R&D budget cuts always have a high cost in terms of the loss of scientific morale and creative enthusiasm. Shelving or terminating good ideas for temporary economic reasons can irreparably damage or even shut off the flow of all future good ideas.

In general, the continual flow of high-quality ideas is fostered by top management commitment to R&D over the long term. Putting R&D on a five-year budget cycle (as opposed to an annual budget period), committing funds to projects for a specified planning horizon (as opposed to an annual renewal basis) and providing discretionary funding so that work on important ideas can continue during troubled business times— these are all prerequisites for an effective idea flow system.

GUIDING PRINCIPLES

The five principles listed in Table 2 should be carefully adhered to in designing any idea handling system. Confidence is very important. If the idea submitters are not confident that their ideas will be treated properly, then they are unlikely to submit them. If the supervisor maintains a positive, receptive posture toward new ideas and makes a sincere effort to assist the submitter, this will significantly contribute to a sense of confidence in the entire system.

TABLE 2.   *Five Principles of Idea Handling*

Confidence of the idea submitter in the system

Credit for the idea to the idea originator

Shelter the idea from its natural enemies

Responsiveness of the system to the idea submitter

Fairness in judging the idea

Every idea submitter needs assurance that he will be credited with the idea. There is an ever-present danger that the inventor's name will become disassociated from the idea once it is communicated to others. In most cases the only credit the inventor requires is that others know the idea was his. Peer recognition as a productive contributor is a key reward.

All young ideas must be carefully sheltered from several natural enemies, including the human proclivity to reject the fanciful and irrational and to engage in premature evaluations. An effective idea handling system makes provision for sheltering an idea. Sheltering can take many forms. For example, the idea handling system may have a pool of discretionary funds or seed money that the idea inventor can use to support the further development, elaboration, and testing of his idea. Sheltering may take the form of coaching and counseling the idea inventor on how to best get his idea accepted. Or sheltering may take the form of a team of enthusiastic personnel, on whom the idea inventor can safely try out his ideas without the risk of prejudgment.

Responsiveness is an essential quality of any idea handling system. Nothing can be more discouraging to an idea submitter than to have no follow-up action taken on his idea. Every idea submitter deserves an acknowledgment that his idea has been received, and periodic reports on its status. Nothing shuts off the flow of ideas faster than to have an idea simply vanish or become "lost in the system."

Fairness is vital. Every idea submitter must believe that his idea will receive a fair trial. What constitutes fairness may, of course, vary from one organization to another and from one person to another. Generally, a fair trail will not pit an idea against an unequal opponent, e.g., judge an embryonic idea for a radical new technology against an idea for improving the cost of an old product. A fair trial implies a complete, detailed evaluation of the idea, using criteria that are relevant for the idea.[9]

ORGANIZATIONAL CLIMATE

The techniques and approaches discussed above can enhance the idea outputs of any organization. However, they cannot compensate for ineffective organizational talents, communication patterns and objectives.

Having the proper mix of human talents and role-persons is vital for idea generation. If the organization does not have enough creative scientists and idea generators, then there simply will not be enough ideas coming forth. If there are many new ideas being generated but these ideas do not fit the organization, then there are not enough idea fitters or idea translators. If the organization has pools of unexplored ideas, then there are not enough coaches, mentors or "grand old men" in the organization. Thus, a mix of human talents and role-players is needed to carry out the idea flow process. Personnel can be selected and trained to play these roles as part of their regular functions.[9, 11]

Since most projects will be interdisciplinary in nature, they will cut across many parts of the organization. The willingness of interdepartmental personnel to work together as a team, and to formulate projects based on embryonic ideas, is very important. Without this willingness, it is unlikely that the organization will be highly successful in idea generation and selection.

It is essential that the organization have a set of consensus criteria for distinguishing good from bad candidate ideas. It is equally important that the criteria be closely related to company goals. Otherwise, personnel are likely to develop ideas that do not fit the organization. A consensus exercise—in which various persons throughout the organization are invited to participate in the listing, ranking, and rating of criteria—can be used to establish a consensus set of criteria.

Another effective approach is to involve personnel at the scientific level in a variety of standing task forces and committees for long range planning. The advantage of this approach is that the participants carry away a feeling that they have participated in the goal setting process for the whole organization.[9]

REFERENCES

1. Souder, Wm. E., *et al,* "An Exploratory Study of the Coordination Mechanisms Between R&D and Marketing as an Influence on the Innovation Process," final report, NSF Grant 75-17195, August 26, 1977.
2. Souder, Wm. E., *et al,* "A Comparative Analysis of Phase-Transfer Methods for Managing New Product Developments," final report, NSF Grant 79-12927, August 15, 1983.
3. Pelz, D C. and F. M. Andrews. *Scientists in Organizations.* Institute for Social Research: University of Michigan, 1976.
4. Souder, Wm. E. "Effects of Release-Time on R&D Outputs and Scientist Gratification," *IEEE Trans. on Engineering Management,* Vol. EM-28, No. 1, February 1981, pp. 8–12.
5. Souder, Wm. E. "Award Programs for R&D Personnel," *Research Management,* Vol. 28, No. 6, 1985, pp. 13–18.
6. Turner, W. J. "How the IBM Awards Program Works," *Research Management,* Vol. 12, No. 4, July 1979, pp. 2–27.
7. "Alcoa's Awards Program," *Wall Street Journal,* April 5, 1984, p. 12.

8. Van Gundy, Arthur. *Techniques of Structured Problem Solving.* Van Nostrand Reinhold. New York, 1981.

9. Souder, Wm. E. "*Project Selection and Economic Appraisal.* Van Nostrand Reinhold, New York, 1984.

10. Souder, Wm. E. "A Group Process Model for Portfolio Decision Making in Organizations," *Proceedings of the Western AIDS Meeting,* March 17–18, 1977, pp. 56–58.

11. Frohman, A. L., "Critical Mid-Management Functions for Innovative R&D." *Research Management,* Vol. 19, No. 4, July 1976, pp. 7–13.

Performance Appraisal: Dilemmas and Possibilities

Michael Beer

It completely refused to run (a) when the waves were high, (b) when the wind blew, (c) at night, early in the morning, and evening, (d) in rain, dew, or fog, (c) when the distance to be covered was more than 200 yards. But on warm, sunny days when the weather was calm and the white beach close by—in a word, on days when it would have been a pleasure to row, it [the outboard motor] started at a touch and would not stop.

—John Steinbeck

Steinbeck's description of an outboard motor is a very apt introduction to an article on performance appraisal. When performance and potential are good, when superior and subordinates have an open relationship, when promotions or salary increases are abundant, when there is plenty of time for preparation and discussion—in short, whenever it's a pleasure—performance appraisal is easy to do. Most of the time, however, and particularly at the times when it is most needed and most difficult to do, performance appraisal refuses to run properly.

The difficulties managers and subordinates experience in the appraisal interview may be traced to the quality of their relationship, to the manner and skill with which the interview is conducted, and to the appraisal system itself—that is, the objectives the organization has for it, the administrative system in which it is embedded, and the forms and procedures that make up the

system. This article will explore the difficulties, the many causes of these difficulties, and what might be done about them.

GOALS OF PERFORMANCE APPRAISAL

Both the organization and the individual employee want the performance appraisal to meet particular objectives. In some cases these objectives or goals are compatible, but in many cases they are not. The potential for conflict between the employee's goals and the organization's objectives for performance appraisal has been discussed by Lyman W. Porter, Edward E. Lawler III, and Richard J. Hackman and the subject will be reviewed and expanded in this article.

The Organization's Goals
Performance evaluation is an important element in the information and control system of most complex organizations. It can be used to obtain

539

information about the performance of employees—so that decisions about placement, promotions, terminations, and pay can be made.

Performance appraisal systems and, more important, discussions between supervisor and subordinate about performance, can also influence the employee's behavior and performance. This is true of management by objectives (MBO) systems, as well as various performance rating systems. The process of influencing behavior is an important part of the organization's efforts to develop future human resources, and it is of utmost importance to managers in their attempts to obtain the results for which they are accountable. From the manager's and the organization's points of view, the performance appraisal process is a major tool for changing individual behavior.

The following lists summarize the organization's objectives for performance appraisal. First, the *evaluation goals:*

1. To provide feedback for subordinates so that they will know where they stand.
2. To develop valid data for pay (salary and bo-

nus) and promotion decisions and to provide a means for communicating these decisions.
3. To help the manager in making discharge and retention decisions and to provide a means for warning subordinates about unsatisfactory performance.

Next, the *coaching and development goals:*

1. To counsel and coach subordinates so they will improve their performance and develop future potential.
2. To develop commitment to the larger organization through discussion with subordinates of career opportunities and career planning.
3. To motivate subordinates through recognition and support.
4. To strengthen supervisor-subordinate relations.
5. To diagnose individual and organizational problems.

Note that this list includes many goals and, as the vertical arrow on the left of Figure 1 shows, they are in conflict. When the perform-

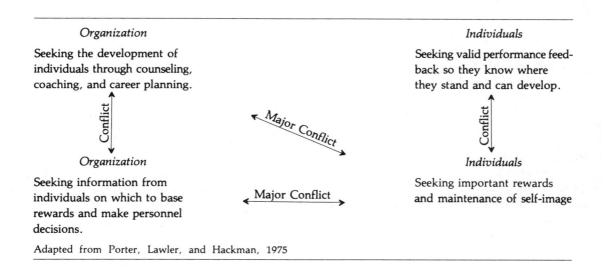

Organization

Seeking the development of individuals through counseling, coaching, and career planning.

Conflict

Organization

Seeking information from individuals on which to base rewards and make personnel decisions.

Major Conflict

Major Conflict

Individuals

Seeking valid performance feedback so they know where they stand and can develop.

Conflict

Individuals

Seeking important rewards and maintenance of self-image

Adapted from Porter, Lawler, and Hackman, 1975

FIGURE 1.   *Conflicts in Performance Appraisal*

ance appraisal is being conducted to meet evaluation goals, the system is a tool by which managers make difficult judgments that affect their subordinates' futures. When they communicate these judgments, they may well have to justify their appraisal in response to, or in anticipation of, subordinates' disagreement. The result can be an adversary relationship, faulty listening, and low trust. None of these are conducive to the coaching and development objectives of performance appraisal. When coaching and development are the goals, managers must play the role of helper. If they are to help, they must draw out subordinates, listen to their problems, and get them to understand their own weaknesses. The different communication processes required to achieve the conflicting goals of performance appraisal create difficult problems for the manager involved.

The Individual's Goals

As the vertical arrow on the right of Figure 1 shows, the employee also has conflicting goals for the performance appraisal. Employees want and desire feedback about their performance because it helps them learn about themselves, how they are doing, and what management values. If this information is favorable, it helps satisfy their psychological needs for competence and success; if it is not, they tend to experience failure, and the feedback may be difficult to accept. Thus, even when people in organizations ask for or demand feedback, they are really looking for favorable feedback that will affirm their concept of themselves. When rewards, such as pay and promotion, are tied to the evaluation, employees have even more reason for wanting to avoid unfavorable evaluations.

An employee's self-development goals require him or her to be willing to accept feedback and ideas for alternative approaches to the job. Subordinates must be willing to drop their defenses and consider accepting the manager's view of their performance. They need an inquisitive attitude about their performance and what might be done to improve it. However, to protect their self-image or to obtain valued rewards, subordinates may gloss over, if not deny, problems. Often without realizing it, individuals may present themselves in a more favorable light than warranted by the facts. The simultaneous needs to be open and to be protective create difficult problems for the individual.

Conflicting Individual and Organizational Goals

The biggest conflict however, is between individual and organizational goals or objectives. The individual desires to confirm a positive self-image and to obtain organizational rewards, such as promotion or pay. The organization wants individuals to be receptive to negative information about themselves in order to improve their performance and promotability. It also wants individuals to be helpful in supplying necessary information. The conflict is over the exchange of valid information. As long as individual employees see the appraisal process as having an important influence in their reward (pay, recognition), on their career (promotions and reputation), and on their self-image, there will be a reluctance to engage in the kind open dialogue required for valid evaluation and personal development. The poorer the employee's performance, the worse the potential conflict, and the less likely that there'll be an exchange of valid information. Major conflicts between the individual and the organization are shown by the diagonal and horizontal arrows in Figure 1 and are the reasons why performance appraisals run like Steinbeck's outboard motor.

PROBLEMS WITH PERFORMANCE APPRAISAL

Several identifiable problems develop around the performance appraisal process. Some of the most troublesome follow.

Ambivalence and Avoidance

Given the conflicts that are present in the performance appraisal process, it is not surprising that supervisors and subordinates are often ambivalent about participating in it.

Supervisors are uncomfortable because their organizational role places them in the position of being both judge and jury. They must make decisions that affect people's careers and lives in significant ways. Futhermore, most managers are not trained to handle the difficult interpersonal situations that are likely to arise when feedback is negative. This is a problem particularly because managers must maintain good relations with their subordinates to preform their own jobs effectively. All this leads to uncertainty about their subjective judgments and anxiety about meeting with subordinates to discuss performance. Yet supervisors also know they must have performance discussions because the organization expects it and subordinates want it. Finally, supervisors often feel personally and legally bound to let people know where they stand. If they are not open with their subordinates, mutual trust suffers because subordinates usually sense when supervisors have been less than truthful. Then, too, there's the growing threat that supervisors' actions can lead to legal action against the organization if an individual feels he or she has been treated unfairly. Furthermore, as I have already pointed out, subordinates usually want constructive feedback, but they're very ambivalent about receiving negative feedback.

The ambivalence of both superiors and subordinates has led to what some behavioral scientists have called the "vanishing performance appraisal." In many organizations, supervisors report that they hold periodic appraisal interviews and give honest feedback, while their subordinates report they have not had a performance appraisal for many years or that they heard nothing negative. The appraisals conducted by the supervisors seem to "vanish." What probably happens is that supervisors, fearful of the appraisal process, have talked in very general terms to the subordinates, alluding only vaguely to problems. There are many ways this can occur. One of the most common is the "sandwich approach"—that is, the supervisor provides negative feedback between heavy doses of positive feedback. He or she may choose to conduct an appraisal on an airplane or during a car ride where the setting blurs its serious purpose. There are other ways, too, to obscure the process—for example, the supervisor makes very general statements and doesn't refer to specific problems. Or when the supervisor's own anxiety or the subordinate's defensiveness signals potential problems, the supervisor does provide negative feedback, but immediately counterbalances it with positive statements.

The subordinate's fear of learning things that will diminish his or her self-image often leads to the lack of initiative in seeking negative feedback and an unconscious collusion with the supervisor that results in avoidance. Thus the supervisor and subordinate engage in long conversations that are only marginally related to the purpose of the appraisal interview. Or they may engage in small talk or humor that conveys an oblique message, or they may develop a pattern of communication in which phrases do not convey a clear meaning to either of them. Thus there is no in-depth exploration of negative feedback, and it is not fully understood and internalized by the subordinate.

Defensiveness and Resistance

The conflict between the organization's evaluation objectives and its coaching and development objectives tends to place the manager in the incompatible roles of judge and helper during the appraisal interview. Some managers feel obligated to fulfill their organizational role as judge by explaining to the employee all facets of his or her evaluation. They want to be sure they fulfill their obligation to let the subordinate know where he or she stands by going down a rating form or discussing all "short falls" in performance. This tactic can naturally elicit appraisee's resistance as they defend against threats to their self-esteem.

Defensiveness may come in a variety of forms. Subordinates may try to explain away their "short falls" by blaming others or uncontrollable events; they may question the appraisal system itself; they may minimize the importance of the appraisal process; they may demean the source of the data; they may insincerely apologize and say they will not do it again just to cut short their exposure to negative feedback; or they may seem to agree readily to the information while inwardly denying its validity or accuracy.

The core of the problem is that the supervisor's organizational role as judge can lead them into communicating and defending their evaluation to subordinates at the very time they are trying to develop an open two-way dialogue for a valid information exchange and development. The defensiveness that results may take the form of open hostility and denials, but it may also take the form of passivity and "surface" compliance. In either case, the subordinate doesn't really accept or understand the feedback. Thus, those subordinates who may need development the most may learn the least.

The Worst of All Interviews:
Avoidance and Defensiveness Combined
The problems created by ambivalence and avoidance can combine with the problems of defensiveness and resistance in the same appraisal interview. For example, when managers go through a perfunctory performance appraisal to fulfill their supervisory duty, ambivalence leads them to avoid direct and meaningful talk about performance, while the need to fulfill the judge's role leads them to a complete but mechanical review of the evaluation form. Thus even though they avoid delving into subordinates' performance problems, they elicit defensive behavior from subordinates by going through the evaluation form in detail. Thus neither the benefits of avoidance (that is, maintenance of good relations

and personal comfort) nor the benefits of accurate feedback (that is, clear understanding and development) are reaped, and none of the problems of avoidance are resolved.

Nonevaluative Evaluation
The basic dilemma of the appraisal process is how to have an open discussion of performance that meets the employee's need for feedback and the organization's need to develop employees, yet prevents damage to the employee's self-esteem and to his or her security about organizational rewards. This is, of course, a paradox, and thus both goals are not fully achievable. In the rest of this article, I will offer some ideas and suggestions on dealing with this paradox.

POTENTIAL SOLUTIONS
TO APPRAISAL PROBLEMS

There are three major ways in which the problems I have outlined can be dealt with. First, the appraisal system can be designed to minimize the negative dynamics outlined above. (The manager often has only marginal control over these matters.) Second, more attention can be paid to the ongoing relationship between supervisors and subordinates. Third, the interview process itself—that is, the quality of communication between supervisor and subordinate—can be improved. Let's look at how these approaches can be directed toward solving appraisal problems.

Designing the Appraisal System
The following corrective steps can improve performance appraisal systems.

Uncoupling Evaluation and Development. Herbert Meyer and his associates have suggested that less defensiveness and an open dialogue result when the manager splits her or his role as helper from that as judge. This can be done by

543

having two separate performance appraisal interviews: one that focuses on evaluation and the other that focuses on coaching and development. The open problem-solving dialogue required for building a relationship and developing subordinates should be scheduled at a different time of the year than the meeting in which the supervisor informs the subordinate about her or his overall evaluation and its implications for retention, pay, and promotion. Such a split recognizes that managers cannot help and judge at the same time without the behavior required by one role interfering with the behavior required by the other.

Many performance appraisal systems inadvertently encourage managers to mix the role of judge and helper by providing only one evaluation form that ends up in the subordinate's personnel record. What is needed are two distinct forms and procedures. The evaluation form becomes part of the personnel record while the form that guides the development discussion does not.

Choosing Appropriate Performance Data. A manager can minimize defensiveness and avoidance by narrowly focusing feedback in specific behaviors or specific performance goals. For example, rating a person as unsatisfactory on a characteristic as broad as motivation is likely to be perceived as a broadside attack and as a threat to self-esteem. Feedback about specific incidents or aspects of "how" a person is performing the job is more likely to be heard than broad generalizations, and it will be more helpful to the individual who wants to improve performance. Thus an appraisal discussion that relies on a report-card rating of traits or performance is doomed to failure because it leads the supervisor into general evaluative statements that threaten the subordinate.

Fortunately, some appraisal techniques are available to guide the supervisor toward more specific behavioral observations. One example is the behavioral rating scale that asks supervisors to indicate the degree to which subordinates fulfill certain behavioral requirements of their job (for example, participating actively in meetings or communicating sufficiently with other departments). Another technique is the critical incident method in which the supervisor records important examples of effective or ineffective performance.

Similarly, there are various management-by-objectives (MBO) techniques that can be used to guide the appraisal discussion toward reviewing specific accomplishments.

Robert Ruh and I have suggested elsewhere that a comprehensive performance management system include both MBO and behavioral ratings. MBO is a means of managing *what* the individual should do, while behavioral ratings are a means for helping employees examine *how* they should do it. They are different but complementary tools in managing and appraising performance. A behavioral rating form might very well be the tool an organization can provide to managers as a guide for the developmental interview.

Separating Evaluations of Performance and Potential. Current performance, as measured by the attainment of results, is not necessarily correlated with potential for promotion. Yet many appraisal systems do not adequately provide for separate evaluations of these dimensions. In the case of a subordinate who rates high in current performance and low in potential for advancement (or vice versa), a manager is placed in the situation of averaging his or her unconscious assessment of these qualities and then defending an evaluation that may be inconsistent with his or her perception and the subordinate's self-perception of either performance or potential alone. Even if separate evaluations of these dimensions do not reduce subordinate defensiveness, they can reduce the manager's need to defend a composite rating that he or she cannot justify. Systems that separate assessments of performance and potential increase the likelihood of a constructive dialogue and therefore reduce the likelihood of avoidance.

Recognizing Individual Differences in System Design. Individuals differ in their needs for performance evaluation and development. Upwardly mobile employees may desire and need more feedback about performance and promotability than less upwardly mobile employees. They will also need longer and more frequent developmental discussions. Similarly, more confident and open employees will be able to handle these discussions better than will employees who lack self-esteem and are defensive. Performance appraisal policies should permit managers to use different methods depending on the particular employee being appraised. An appraisal every two or three years may be enough for an employee who has reached the peak of his or her capabilities. Such an appraisal could be limited to a rating and discussion of current performance, but omit any discussion of promotion potential. Uniform systems and procedures stand in the way of such differential treatment.

Upward Appraisal. The appraisal dynamic that contributes most to defensiveness and/or avoidance is the authoritarian character of the supervisor-subordinate relationship. The simple fact that one person is the boss and responsible for evaluation places him or her in a dominant role and induces submissive behavior on the part of the subordinate. Futhermore, the boss holds and controls rewards. In order to develop the open, two-way dialogue required in the coaching and developmental interview, power must be equalized or at least brought into better balance during the interview. One way to achieve this is to ask subordinates to appraise their supervisor.

An upward appraisal can help a supervisor create the conditions needed for an effective performance appraisal interview for several reasons. It gives subordinates a real stake in the appraisal interview and an opportunity to influence a part of their environment that ultimately influences their performance. Thus it makes them more equal and less dependent, increasing their motivation to enter the appraisal process with an open frame of mind. It also offers the supervisor an opportunity to demonstrate nondefensive behavior and a willingness to engage in a real two-way dialogue (assuming the supervisor is capable of behaving nondefensively).

Organizations can encourage the use of upward appraisals by providing forms and developing policies that support this approach. If the organization doesn't do so, the supervisor can develop his or her own form or seek informal feedback sometime during the appraisal interviews.

Self-appraisal. Experience with self-appraisal suggests that it often results in lower ratings than the supervisor would have given. Subordinates appraising themselves before an interview do so with the knowledge that an unrealistic or obviously self-serving rating will affect their manager's perception of them. Thus performance appraisal systems that include self-appraisal before either the coaching or evaluation interview are likely to result in a more realistic rating and a greater acceptance of the final rating by subordinates and supervisors.

Some or all of the system design elements described in this section can be used to minimize manager avoidance and subordinate resistance. But by themselves they are not sufficient. Good relationships and interpersonal competence are also required.

Improving Supervisor-Subordinate Relationship

Not surprisingly, the quality of the appraisal process depends on the nature of the day-to-day supervisor-subordinate relationship. First, an effective relationship means that the supervisor is providing feedback and coaching on an ongoing basis. Thus the appraisal interview is merely a review of issues that have already been discussed. Second, the appraisal interview is only a small segment of the broader supervisor-subordinate relationship, and expectations for it are likely to be shaped by the broader relationship. If a relationship of mutual trust and supportiveness exists, subordinates are more apt to be open in discussing performance problems and less defensive in response to negative feedback.

There is no substitute for a good supervisor-subordinate relationship. Without such a relationship, no performance appraisal system can be effective. Although the development of such a relationship is not the subject of this article, it is important to understand that the appraisal interview itself can be used to build a relationship of mutual trust, provided the interview is modeled after some of the ideas discussed in the next section.

Improving the Appraisal Interview

The appraisal interview has multiple objectives. Therefore, it isn't surprising that different objectives are best met by somewhat different interview methods.

Directive Interviews.   If the interview's objective is to communicate a performance evaluation or pay decision that has already been made, the interview should take a more directive form. The manager tells the subordinate what the evaluation is and, to assure the subordinate about its fairness, the process by which it was determined. The manager then listens actively, accepting and trying to understand the employee's reactions and feelings without signaling that the performance evaluation is open to change.

If the manager has already evaluated the subordinate, any attempt to conduct an open and participative dialogue to motivate the subordinate will fail. Such an approach encourages the subordinate to try to influence the manager's rating—a move that puts the manager in the position of defending a final decision. In this situation, the subordinate not only has to accept an evaluation that may be inconsistent with his or her self-perception, but may also have to leave the interview frustrated by unsuccessful attempts to influence the manager.

As stated earlier, managers may be drawn into this situation by systems that provide only one form for evaluation. An open dialogue cannot occur because the manager follows the form mechanically in an effort to communicate accurately judgments that he or she has already committed to paper. Corporate procedures that require the manager's boss to review the evaluation before the appraisal interview only increase the manager's need to defend the rating and reduce even further the likelihood of an open dialogue.

Participative Problem-solving Interview.   If the interview's objective is to motivate subordinates to change their behavior or improve their performance, an open process that includes mutual participation is required. This approach takes the manager out of the role of judge and puts him or her into the role of helper. The objective is to help subordinates discover their own performance deficiencies and help them take the initiative to develop a joint plan for improvement. The problem-solving interview makes no provision for communicating the supervisor's unilateral evaluation. The assumption underlying this type of interview is that self-understanding by subordinates and motivation to improve performance cannot occur in a setting where the manager has already made judgments and psychologically separates her- or himself from the subordinate to avoid being swayed. The problem-solving interview is therefore less structured, relies on the subordinate to lead the discussion into problem areas, and relies on the manager to listen, reflect, care, guide, and coach.

Individual Differences and the Interview.   The subordinate's characteristics should also determine the interview method. Subordinates differ in their age, experience, sensitivity about negative feedback, attitude toward the supervisor, and desire for influence and control over their destiny. For example, if the subordinate is young, inexperienced, and dependent and looks up to the supervisor, a more directive interview in which the supervisor does most of the talking may be appropriate—unless, of course, it is the supervisor's objective to help the subordinate become more independent. On the other hand, if the subordinate is older, more experienced, and sensitive about negative feedback, and has a high need for controlling his or her destiny, the same objective is best met by a less directive approach.

Mixed-model Interviews. When situational factors such as corporate policies, practices and forms, available time, and subordinate expectations prevent separate evaluation and developmental interviews, it is possible to design one interview to achieve both purposes. The most effective way of implementing a mixed-model appraisal interview is to start the appraisal process with the open-ended problem-solving approach and end with the more directive approach. If the supervisor starts off with one-way communication, real two-way communication and in-depth exploration of personal and job performance issues is unlikely to occur. Thus, as Table 1 shows, the interview should start with an open-ended exploration of perceptions and concerns with the subordinate taking the lead, and it should finish with a more closed-ended agree-

TABLE 1.   *Mixed-Model Interview*

Interview Begins

1. Open-ended discussion and exploration of problems, in which the subordinate leads and the supervisor listens.

2. Problem-solving discussion, in which the subordinate leads, but supervisor takes somewhat stronger role.

3. Agreement between supervisor and subordinate on performance problems and a plan for improvements.

4. Closing evaluation, in which the supervisor gives his or her views and final evaluation if the subordinate has not dealt with important issues.

Interview Ends

ment on what performance improvements are expected. Performance problems and improvements are agreed to jointly, but if such agreement is not possible, ultimate responsibility rests with the supervisor. The supervisor may choose to tell the subordinate what is expected if crucial problems have not been discussed or solutions agreed on.

There are many ways in which a mixed-model interview can be implemented. I have outlined one possible pattern for an effective appraisal interview with multiple purposes below. The following assumptions underlie the recommended interview process:

1. It is possible to defuse the potential negative effects of corporate systems and traditional expectations through joint supervisor-subordinate agreement on interview content and process before the interview.

2. Joint planning of the interview enhances the probability that the interview goals and process will be compatible.

3. Joint supervisor-subordinate agreement on ground rules for effective communication before the interview increases control over the process.

4. It is necessary to equalize the power of the appraiser and appraisee to achieve developmental objectives and maintain good relations. However, this should not prevent the supervisor from taking a more directive role later in the interview if it is necessary.

5. A good appraisal interview can occur only in a context of good supervisor-subordinate relations or when both parties are motivated to use the interview as a means of improving relations.

6. Managers can mix the inherently incompatible judging and helping roles only if the latter is the primary role and goal.

7. A mixed interview requires the manager to assume a substantial range of styles and to have the ability to shift between them quickly and appropriately.

The following proposed interview sequence is only illustrative:

1. *Scheduling.* Notify the subordinate well in advance when the appraisal discussion is scheduled. The interview should be set at a time when both parties are alert and undisturbed by external organizational or personal matters. The discussion should be scheduled as long after the salary review as possible.

2. *Agreeing on content.* Before the interview, discuss the nature of the interview with the subordinate and work toward agreement on the goals of the interview and what will be discussed (for example, rating forms to be used or performance issues to be discussed). This gives the subordinate a chance to prepare for the interview (including self-rating or rating the supervisor if this is to be part of the session), and to come to the interview on a more equal footing with the supervisor. If necessary, it also permits supervisor and subordinate to devise a form and procedure compatible with their goals for the interview.

3. *Agreeing on process.* Agree on the process for the appraisal discussion with the subordinate before the interview. For example, agreement should be reached on the sequencing of interview phases. If an open exploratory discussion is to come first, followed by problem solving, action planning, and upward appraisal, this is the time to tell the subordinate about these phases. Similarly, ground rules for communications can be established that will ensure constructive feedback and good listing. (See step 7.)

4. *Setting location and space.* If possible, meet on neutral territory or in the subordinate's office. In this way, a relationship of more equal power that's so crucial to open communication can be established.

5. *Opening the interview.* Review the objectives of the appraisal interview that were previously agreed to. This review sets the stage and allows supervisor and subordinate to prepare themselves psychologically.

6. *Starting the discussion.* Give the initiative to the subordinate in the discussion that follows the opening statement. Specifically start the discussion by asking, "How do you feel things are going on the job? What's going well and what problems are you experiencing? How do you see your performance?" Such general questions will stimulate the subordinate to take the initiative in the problem identification and solving discussion. To facilitate this, a subordinate may be asked to appraise his or her own performance. If the manager starts by expressing views about the employee's performance, the interview inevitably becomes directive.

7. *Exchanging feedback.* Follow well-accepted ground rules for giving and receiving feedback. A supervisor who sets up these methods for effective communication encourages the exchange of valid information.

In giving feedback, a supervisor can reduce employee's defensiveness by being specific about the performance and behavior-causing problems (that is, what was said and done?). Citing specific examples of observed behavior and describing the consequences of that behavior in terms of effects on others, on the supervisor's feelings, and on the department's performance can help an employee identify what needs to be changed. To prevent defensive reactions, the supervisor should avoid making general statements, imputing motives to behavior (that is, you are lazy or you aren't committed), blaming, or accusing.

The supervisor should set up ground rules for receiving feedback and encourage the subordinate to follow them. Defensiveness should be avoided at all costs; negative feedback is usually cut off by the giver when signs of defensiveness appear in the receiver and this reduces the amount of information transmitted. Active listening can encourage receptiveness to and understanding of negative feedback. The receiver should paraphrase what is being said, request clarification, and summarize the discussion periodically. The receiver can maintain openness and keep information coming by exploring the negative feedback and showing a willingness to examine him- or herself critically. On the other hand, feedback is usually cut off and understanding reduced by justifying actions, apologizing, blaming others, explaining, and "building a case."

The ground rules for receiving feedback are not meant to imply that supervisors and subordinates should not help each other understand why they are doing what they are doing. However, the timing of explanations is critical in stimulating openness instead of defensiveness. Active listening first, followed by explanations later, is a better sequence than the reverse.

8. *Presenting the supervisor's views.* The supervisor should provide a summary of the subordinate's major improvement needs based on the previous discussion. This summary sets the agenda for the next phase of the discussion in which plans for improvement are developed jointly. However, the summary should also include the subordinate's strengths—those things that should be continued.

9. *Developing a plan for improvement.* Let subordinates lead with what they think is an adequate plan for improvement on the basis of the previous discussion and summary. It is much easier to prevent defensiveness if the supervisor reacts to and perhaps expands on the subordinate's plans for changing instead of making such suggestions directly. A problem-solving rather than blame-placing approach should be maintained. However, if subordinates cannot formulate good action plans, or seem to be unmotivated to do so, the supervisor can take a more directive approach at this point. It is critical that the interview end in a concrete plan for performance improvement or else no change is likely to occur.

10. *Closing the discussion.* Close the discussion with a view of the individual's future. However, this is relevant only in organizations where opportunities for promotion exist and for individuals who clearly have potential—unless, of course, the individual brings it up and wants to know. If the individual needs to be told what his or her evaluation is, this should be done at the very end of the interview if it cannot take place in a separate interview.

SUMMARY

This article attempts to summarize what is known about the underlying causes of problems experienced with performance appraisal and to suggest some means for overcoming these. The central thrust has been to find means for dealing with the main barrier to effective appraisals—that is, avoidance by the supervisor and defensiveness from the subordinate. We have suggested a number of ways in which supervisors and subordinates might negotiate the difficult dilemma of discussing an evaluation of performance in a nonevaluative manner.

SELECTED BIBLIOGRAPHY

A discussion of the many organizational and contextual factors affecting performance appraisal can be found in Morgan W. McCall and David L. DeVries's "Appraisal in Context: Clashing with Organizational Realities," presented in symposium "Performance Appraisal and Feedback: Fleas in the Ointment," David DeVries, Chair, *84th Annual Convention of the American Psychological Association,* Washington, D.C., September 5, 1976.

The section on performance appraisal goals draws extensively on discussions of this subject in Lyman W. Porter, Edward E. Lawler III, and Richard J. Hackman's *Behavior in Organizations* (McGraw-Hill, 1975).

An example of a performance appraisal system designed to deal with some of the dilemmas discussed in this article can be found in Michael Beer and Robert A. Ruh's "Employee Growth Through Performance Management," *Harvard Business Review,* July–August 1976.

The phenomenon of the "vanishing performance appraisal" was first discussed by Douglas T. Hall and Edward E. Lawler III in "Job Characteristics and Pressures and Organizational Integration of Professionals," *Administrative Science Quarterly,* Third Quarter 1970.

The effects of performance feedback on a person's self-esteem were discussed by Alvin Zander in "Research on Self-Esteem, Feedback and Threats to Self-Esteem," in A. Zander (Ed.), *Performance Appraisals: Effects on Employees and Their Performance,* (The Foundation for Research in Human Behavior, 1963).

The classic study of performance appraisal that first posited the importance of splitting evaluation from developmental interviews is Herbert H. Meyer, Emanuel Kay, and John R. P. French, Jr.'s "Split Roles in Performance Appraisal," *Harvard Business Review,* January–February 1965.

The critical incident technique in which managers record incidents of effective or ineffective performance by subordinates as data for appraisals was first discussed by John C. Flanagan and Robert K. Burns in "The Employee Performance Record," *Harvard Business Review,* September–October 1955.

The idea that different types of individuals have different performance appraisal purposes was articulated by Norman R. F. Maier in "Three Types of Appraisal Interviews," *Personnel,* March–April 1958.

Problem-solving performance appraisal interviews that rely heavily on nondirective counseling were first discussed by Carl R. Rogers in "Releasing Expression," *Counseling and Psychotherapy* (Houghton Mifflin Company, 1942).

A number of ideas in this article about methods for improving the performance appraisal interviews were discussed by Herbert H. Meyer in "The Annual Performance Review Discussion—Making it Constructive" (University of South Florida, unpublished and undated paper).

Guidelines for giving and receiving feedback are cited in this article as important in guiding a constructive dialogue between boss and subordinate. This was discussed in more detail in John Anderson's "Giving and Receiving Feedback" in G. W. Dalton, P. R. Lawrence, and L. E. Greiner's (eds.) *Organizational Change and Development* (Richard D. Irwin and Dorsey Press, 1970).

Determinants of R&D Compensation Strategies in the High Tech Industry

David B. Balkin

Luis R. Gomez-Mejia

Abstract. This study indicates that sales volume, stage in the product life cycle, profitability and turnover are all important predictors of the method and magnitude of financial rewards provided by high tech firms to R&D employees. The most favorable situational factors for R&D incentive compensation are a low sales volume high tech company, operating in the growth stage of the product life cycle, with high turnover rates, and capable of linking profitability to incentive rewards such as bonuses.

The so called "high tech revolution" has recently been the focus of much attention in the U.S. as the number of new high tech firms and products entering the market grows exponentially each year (Thorne, 1982). This explosive growth is viewed by many as important to the welfare of most Americans in terms of generating jobs, creating a plethora of new consumer goods, increasing labor's productivity, and strengthening U.S. competitive edge in world markets (Smilor, 1982).

High tech firms share certain unique attributes that distinguish them from other companies (Balachandra, 1982). These features include the following: (1) a product at the cutting edge of technology; (2) a high priority placed in research and development; (3) numerous innovations being introduced at frequent intervals; (4) a high rate of turnover for R&D personnel; (5) geographic concentration as these firms are usually located in "technology centers" such as Silicon Valley or Route 128 in Boston; and (6) high mortality rates as a result of strong competitive pressures. These characteristics in turn pose numerous challenges to the human resource function such as attracting and retaining R&D talent in the midst of severe industry wide turnover rates; keeping up with rapidly expanding market rates for scientists and engineers; and rewarding the performance of essential R&D employees who function in high pressure jobs that demand long hours, commitment, teamwork, and creativity to meet company objectives.

Suprisingly, little attention has been devoted in the academic management literature to many of these issues. This lack may be the result of the recency of the "high tech revolution" and the

Reprinted with permission from D. B. Balkin and L. R. Gomez-Mejia, "Determinants of R&D Compensation Strategies in the High Tech Industry," *Personnel Psychology,* 1984, Vol. 37, 635–650.

551

difficulties faced in data gathering since secrecy is highly valued by these firms (Balkin, 1983).

The objective of this paper is to shed light on some of these issues by analyzing the determinants of R&D compensation policies and practices in the high tech industry. A number of hypotheses are posited and empirically tested on data collected from 33 high tech firms and 72 non-high tech companies with research and development units in the Boston area.

HYPOTHESES AND RATIONALE

The theoretical framework described below argues that high tech firms will design compensation strategies to effectively cope with unique environmental and organizational forces impacting the attraction, retention, and motivation of R&D personnel. The independent variables in the model include sales volume, stage in the product life cycle, profitability, and the attrition rate. The dependent variables include base compensation (salaries and fringe benefits) and incentive-based reward systems for R&D employees.

Sales Volume
A large number of studies over the last 60 years have generally shown that, within a given industry, sales volume has a positive effect on the compensation level of managerial and professional personnel (e.g., Agarwal, 1981; Lewellen and Huntsman, 1970; McGuire, Chiu, and Elbing, 1962). Factors used to explain this relationship include differences in marginal productivity (Roberts, 1959); separation of control from ownership (Baumol, 1959); variations in organizational structures (Simon, 1957); degree of job complexity (Agarwal, 1981); the existence of multiple "wage contours" (Dunlop, 1957); and the greater availability of slack resources in larger organizations (Gomez-Mejia, Tosi and Hinkin, 1983).

It should not come as a surprise in the present study to find a positive relationship between sales volume and the base compensation of R&D personnel in high tech firms. On the other hand, this correlation by itself is likely to be misleading since a major portion of high tech pay may be in the form of incentive rewards not being included in the base compensation measure. One would expect smaller high tech firms, dependent on new innovations, to rely on the incentive component of their R&D compensation mix. Such a practice may allow them to be competitive in the labor market against larger firms in the industry. Most of the smaller high tech firms are led by entrepreneurs who are risking their capital on a new product (Graves, 1982). These small firms cannot afford to pay competitive salaries and benefits relative to larger firms (such as IBM), yet they need to attract and retain top scientific and engineering talent to work in their R&D labs. Small high tech firms can offer an R&D compensation mix more heavily weighted towards incentive pay and thereby share part of the risks of success with their employees. By providing a lower base compensation (which would act as a fixed cost in the short run) in exchange for a wide array of incentive pay programs, smaller high tech companies can buffer themselves against short term financial pressures. Given the fact that in smaller high tech firms the proportion of labor costs to total costs is greater (Balkin, 1983), such a compensation strategy will allow the firm to survive while attracting and retaining essential R&D personnel.

Hypothesis 1. While sales volume in the high tech industry will have a positive effect on base pay and fringe benefits for R&D personnel, sales level will be inversely related to the use of incentive based compensation strategies for R&D employees.

Stage in the Product Life Cycle
A number of studies have found that the stage in the product life cycle for a firm is highly related

to the emphasis it places on innovation. This is particularly true for high tech firms (Balachandra, 1982). Firms at the growing stage suffer from high mortality rates and view product innovation as the best way to get established in a particular industry (Bell, 1982). These firms actively search for new products involving significant deviations from existing technology, in order to penetrate those areas in which more mature firms control markets (Goodman and Abernathy, 1978; Rothwell, 1978; Utterback and Abernathy, 1975) and in which established companies have large investments in existing routine technologies (Morison, 1966).

Growth firms are thought to be more responsive to market trends and shifts since fixed overhead costs involving standardized technology are relatively minor as compared to more mature firms (Morison, 1966). In other words, mature organizations tend to be more conservative because the risk of changing well established technologies is greater than at the growth stage of the product life cycle. Finally, in their sociotechnical system, firms at the growth stage would tend to attract younger, more risk-taking managerial and technical personnel; which probably also stimulates innovation (Ettlie, 1983).

A high tech firm's stage in the product life cycle is expected to influence the extent to which it relies on incentive-based compensation for scientists and engineers. Firms at the growth stage are heavily involved in R&D as they are busy trying to launch new products into the market. For example, data presented by Hambrick (1983) indicates that in a random sample of 318 firms at the growth stage, 221 (72%) could be categorized as "innovative" (i.e., when more than five percent of the revenues are derived from products introduced in the last three years). The offering of incentive pay may be a useful strategy to attract and retain talented scientists and engineers at this stage of the product life cycle. These R&D employees may be willing to accept the immediate risks inherent in working for a struggling firm, in exchange for anticipated long term rewards. On the opposite end, firms at the mature stage are less likely to use an incentive pay strategy as part of their compensation policies. For these companies, growth is less rapid, routing manufacturing technology becomes predominant, and the search for product innovations does not play such a major role (Mueller, Culbertson, and Peckham, 1979).

Hypothesis 2. High tech firms at the growth stage of the product life cycle are more likely to follow and R&D incentive based reward strategy than companies at the mature stage.

Profitability

A substantial body of research has shown that a firm's profitability, in addition to sales volume, tends to be related to the compensation level of its employees (e.g., Agarwal, 1981; Lewellen and Huntsman, 1970; Reynolds, 1982). This should by true as well for high tech and traditional firms employing scientists and engineers. However, one would expect to find a major distinction between high tech and traditional firms on the extent to which profitability relates to the use of R&D incentive compensation. Since technological breakthroughs and innovations play a larger role in the profitability of high tech firms, and incentive pay should be based on the rate of innovations and the firm's performance, one would expect to find a positive relationship between the use of incentive programs and profitability in the high tech industry.

Hypothesis 3. In the high tech industry, profitability will be positively related to both base compensation and the use of incentive pay programs for R&D personnel.

Attrition Rates

Studies investigating relationship between employees' performance and turnover suggest that the strength and direction of the correlation between those two variables depends on how easy performance can be observed and measured. When performance is visible to others inside and outside the firm, leavers are predominantly better performers (Dreher, 1982; Martin, Price and Mueller, 1981). The model of voluntary turnover provided by March and Simon (1958) suggests that employees with the best work records are most likely to find alternative employment opportunities. Their perceived and actual ease of mobility from the organization should be enhanced, resulting in high turnover rates among the best performers. A positive relationship between performance and turnover has been repeatedly shown for scientists, engineers, and academic personnel since professional contributions can be more easily measured in these occupations. For example, Allison's data in the mobility patterns of 2,248 scientists in university departments supported this conclusion. He found that the ''higher one's productivity, the more likely one is to leave his job'' (1974, p. 14). Martin et. al. (1981) and Price (1977) provide an extensive review of this literature.

In addition to performance, another factor affecting the turnover rates of scientists and engineers is the labor market demand-supply interaction. To the extent that demand exceeds supply for these groups, the more likely turnover is to occur (Mobley, 1980).

For high tech firms, one of the major challenges, if not the most critical one, is how to attract and retain key technical talent. This industry is plagued by vicious ''pirating'' of scientists and engineers from one firm to another, leading to notoriously high turnover rates (Reynolds, 1982). The fact that these firms tend to be concentrated in a few ''technology centers'' adds to the turnover problem because the moving costs incurred when changing jobs are minimized.

Since retaining high performers for R&D labs is critical to the firm's survival, and the replacement of these people (most of whom are performing tasks requiring extended project spe-

cific training) is both expensive and difficult, one would expect high tech companies to offer a wide array of incentive based reward programs. Likewise, one would expect to find a positive relation between turnover and incentive pay. Interviews with high tech compensation managers curing the course of this study indicated that long term incentives such as profit sharing, and stock purchase schemes are designed partially to enable a high tech firm to retain key technical people. In other words, high attrition rates induce management to establish a reward package that helps to ''lock in'' people to the organization. In addition, by clearly tying accomplishments to short term incentives (such as bonuses), high performing scientists and engineers are also less likely to look for a job elsewhere.

Although the use of incentive programs should be positively related to turnover, R&D attrition rates should in turn be negatively related to salary level and benefits. Employees who feel that their compensation is not comparable to what they could receive elsewhere are more likely to leave the company (Lawler, 1971). In a very tight market, such as that of scientists and engineers in high tech, the likelihood of an inverse relation between base compensation and turnover is even greater.

Hyphothesis 4. While the attrition rate in high tech firms will be negatively related to base compensation, it will be positively correlated with the use of incentive based reward strategies for R&D personnel.

In summary, the model presented here argues that high tech R&D compensation strategies are contingent on organizational, environmental, and technological factors. The hypothesized effects of sales, profitability, and turnover on base compensation are an extension of earlier research in other industries. The theoretical linkages between sales, stage in product life cycle, profitability, and turnover with R&D incentive based regard systems, and the influence of the product life cycle on R&D base compensation, have never been explored before.

METHOD

Sample

The firms in the study were selected in two stages. First, over 150 in-person and by-phone interviews were held with compensation managers in Route 128 "technology center," Boston, Massachusetts. These interviews were used to identify a large sample of firms that employ significant numbers of scientists and engineers in the area. A total sample of 223 firms was identified in this manner. The criteria for sample selection included: (a) at least three percent of all employees must be scientists and engineers; (b) all firms must have at least one R&D unit; (c) all firms must be within a 70 mile radius to ensure that they are all exposed to a similar environment, e.g., cost of living, unemployment rate, ease of mobility; (d) the sample must include a representative mix of "growing" and "mature" firms; (e) the sample must include a large number of both "high tech" and "traditional" firms to be used for comparison; (f) there should be a good distribution of companies in terms of dollar sales for both high tech and traditional samples; and (g) the sample should have a representative mix of firms in terms of main product lives such as computers, telecommunications, and semiconductors.

Of the original 223 firms, 105 (47%) agreed to collaborate in the project after being assured that company private data would be kept strictly confidential by the authors and that a free copy of the tech report would be made available to participants. As can be seen in Table 1, the resulting sample distribution consists of 33 "high tech" firms and 72 "traditional" firms. The sample of traditional firms was used as a control group to determine whether or not the findings in the high tech group are company or industry specific.

Operational Measures

The data collection tool used in the study was developed based on interviews with over 100 compensation managers in these companies. The survey was pre-tested with a sample of these managers to ensure that it was easy to understand, and that the items were not ambiguous. The survey, conducted through the mail in August, 1983, included questions pertaining to organizational characteristics (see Table 1) and compensation policies/practices (see Table 2) in these firms. The operational measures for the independent and dependent variables are described in more detail below.

High Tech vs. Traditional Firms. The high tech sample was identified as companies who reported that their research and development budgets consisted of five percent or more of their 1982 sales revenues. This is the Massachusetts High Technology Council definition of a high tech firm.

Sales Volume. This variable was operationalized as annual sales revenues during 1982.

Stage in Product Life Cycle. This variable was defined in a manner similar to that of Hambrick (1981; 1983) and Hofer, (1975). A company's stage was coded into a dummy variable according to one of the following categories (as indicated by respondents):

Mature Stage: Products or services familiar to vast majority of prospective users. Technology and competitive structure are reasonably stable.

Growth Stage: Sales growing at 10% or more annually in real terms. Technology and competitive structure are still changing.

In the present sample, stage in the product life cycle and sales volume correlated at .21, indi-

TABLE 1.   *Summary of Company Characteristics for High Technology and Traditional Samples (N = 105)*

Company Characteristics	Sample Distribution		
	Hi Tech (N = 33) %	Traditional (N = 72) %	Total (N = 105) %
1. Number of Employees:			
0–499	63.6	50.0	54.4
500–599	0	16.7	11.4
1000–5000	36.4	20.8	25.7
more than 5000	0	12.5	8.6
2. Scientists and Engineers as			
a Percentage of all Employees:	20.5	14.5	16.4
3. Yearly R&D Turnover (%):	15.1	7.0	10.0
4. Sales Revenues for 1982:			
Up to $10 M	54.5	30.0	38.1
$10–99.9 M	9.1	39.0	29.6
$100–999.9 M	36.4	17.0	23.8
$1 B or more	0	13.0	8.6
5. Average Growth Rate in Sales for 1977–82 (Mean):	31.6	27.0	28.3
6. Stage in Business Life Cycle			
Growth	54.5	54.2	54.3
Mature	45.5	45.9	45.8
7. R&D Expenditure as a Percentage of Sales, 1982:			
less than 1%	0	9.0	6.0
1–2.9%	0	55.0	36.0
3–4.9%	0	36.0	24.0
5–6.9%	36.4	0	12.0
7% or more	63.6	0	21.0
8. Profit Rate During 1982 (Mean):	7.6	8.2	8.0
9. Company Product Line:			
Computers	9.1	4.2	5.7
Semiconductors	0	4.2	2.9
Electronics	36.4	25.0	28.6
Communications	9.1	4.2	5.7
Chemicals	18.2	4.2	8.6
Drugs	0	4.2	2.9
Instruments	9.1	0	2.9
Other	18.2	54.2	42.9

cating that these two measures are fairly independent.

Profitability.   Profitability in this study was defined as the ratio of net income for 1982 compared to annual sales revenues for 1982. While total profits is generally a function of sales volume, the profit rate (profitability) need not be so (Eatwell, 1971; Marris, 1971). This was corroborated in the present sample since sales volume

TABLE 2. *Summary of R&D Compensation Practices in High Technology and Traditional Samples* (N = 105)

Compensation Items	Hi Tech (N = 33) %	Traditional (N = 72) %	Total (N = 105) %
1. Midpoints of Salary Grades:			
25th percentile	0	5.0	3.0
50th percentile	63.6	71.0	69.0
75th percentile	27.3	14.0	19.0
over 75th percentile	9.1	9.0	9.0
2. Benefits as % of Payroll:	35.2	34.8	35.0
3. Equity Pay Adjustments:	72.7	54.2	60.0
4. Average Percent Merit Raise:	8.0	8.3	8.2
5. Bonus Compensation to R&D Employees:	81.8	33.3	48.6
6. Profit Sharing for R&D Employees:	54.5	33.3	40.0
7. Stock Options for R&D Employees:	72.7	25.0	40.0
8. Profit Sharing for Key R&D Employees:	63.6	33.3	42.9
9. Stock Bonus for Key R&D People:	27.3	4.2	11.4
10. Long Term Stock Options for Key R&D People:	54.5	33.3	40.0
11. Stock Purchase Plan for Key R&D People:	36.4	20.8	25.7

and profitability showed a very modest correlation of .27.

Attrition. The turnover rate was measured as the percent of R&D personnel that left the company during 1982.

Compensation. This variable has three components: salary, fringe benefits, and incentive pay. Base salary is measured by a four-point interval scale that represents the quartile position in the labor market for scientists and engineers used by the firm to position its R&D salary grades. This scale (see Table 2) captures differences in compensation policies between those firms that pay above the going rate (at the 75th percentile or higher), at the going rate (50th percentile), or below the going rate (25th percentile or lower) for scientists and engineers in the labor market. Individual employee salary levels are highly related to a company's compensation policy for base salaries (Henderson, 1982). Fringe benefits are mea-

sured as a percentage of total payroll costs for R&D units. The higher the percentage, the greater the scope of benefits offered to the employee. The measure of incentive based rewards is the number of such programs available to scientists and engineers in the business. These may range from zero to seven for a given firm (see Table 2). Interviews with compensation managers during this study revealed that as the number of incentive pay programs increases, the importance of incentive pay with respect to the total compensation package also increases.

Analysis

A multiple regression model was utilized to test for the significance of sales volume, stage in the product life cycle, profitability and turnover on salaries, fringe benefits, and incentive pay. Separate regressions were calculated for the high tech sample, the traditional sample, and the total sample. In the total sample regression, the high tech measure is a dummy variable coded one for high tech and zero for other firms.

RESULTS

Table 3 summarizes the regression results for the high tech, traditional, and total samples. For the high tech firms, the regression model explains 69 percent of the variance in base salary, 24 percent of the variance for benefits, and 47 percent of the variance for incentive pay. As hypothesized, sales volume and profitability showed a significant positive effect on salary, while attrition rate showed a significant negative coefficient. For fringe benefits, only sales volume was a significant predictor. Incentive pay, as hypothesized, was negatively related to company size, and positively related to stage in product life cycle and profitability. Stage in product life cycle had a positive effect on base compensation ($p \leq .01$). This suggests that mature high tech firms may not be willing to offer generous salaries and benefits to attract top technical talent since R&D is not as crucial to them.

Among the traditional firms, the explained variance in all three regression equations was much lower than in the high tech sample. In this group, the R^2 for salary, benefits, and incentive pay were .13, .18, and .14 respectively. Unlike the high tech sample, stage in product life cycle was not statistically significant, and the effect of sales volume only reached significance for benefits but not for salary and incentive pay.

When the regression equation is calculated in the total sample, the high tech variable is significant and positive for base salary and incentive pay. These findings indicate that high tech firms are associated with higher base salaries and a greater emphasis on incentive pay programs when compared to other companies that employ scientists and engineers, even after controlling for sales, stage, profitability, and attrition rate. The high tech coefficient for benefits was not sta-

tistically significant. However it should be noted that benefits are measured as a percent of base salary; therefore, even when this index is similar between the two samples, in absolute dollars the outlay in fringe benefits would be greater for the high tech group.

The turnover variable is significant and positive for incentive pay in the traditional and total sample regressions, but not for the high tech group. This indicates that across different firms the turnover rate, as predicted, is positively associated with incentive pay programs. The nonsignificant results in the high tech sample for turnover may be due to the restriction of range for that variable among these firms. The standard deviation for turnover is much lower in the high tech sample (3.88) than in other firms (9.24).

Table 2 provides summary data about R&D compensation policies and practices in high tech and traditional firms. The practice of giving "equity pay adjustments," which is a euphemism for periodic across the board raises, is used most often by high tech firms (i.e., 73 percent versus 57 percent in the traditional sample). The magnitude of the equity pay adjustment for R&D units is also greater in the high tech group (i.e., 12 versus 8 percent for traditional firms). Interviews with several compensation managers indicated that the greater turnover rate for R&D personnel in high tech firms (i.e., 15 percent versus 7 percent for the traditional sample) creates a constant need to bring more people in from the outside at rapidly expanding market rates. This situation results in severe salary compression for R&D personnel, providing the impetus for frequent "equity pay adjustments."

The percent of salary increases based on "merit" is virtually identical for both high tech and traditional firms. However, dramatic differences between the two samples can be seen for short term and long term incentives offered to R&D employees. Reliance on these incentive programs, as hypothesized earlier, is much greater for high tech firms. These rewards are provided

TABLE 3. Regression Analysis of the Determinants of R&D Compensation for High Tech, Traditional, and Total Samples (N = 105)

Independent Variables	High Tech Firms (N = 33)			Traditional Firms (N = 72)			Total Sample (N = 105)		
	Base Compensation		Incentive Rewards	Base Compensation		Incentive Rewards	Base Compensation		Incentive Rewards
	Salary	Benefits		Salary	Benefits		Salary	Benefits	
Sales Volume	.125* (.064)	.462** (.176)	-.475** (.132)	.014 (.016)	.286* (.137)	-.070 (.093)	.024 (.087)	.344** (.109)	-.240* (.120)
Stage in Product Life Cycle	.893** (.141)	.189 (.334)	2.038** (.504)	.219 (.244)	.016 (.290)	.061 (.198)	.450** (.178)	.004 (.220)	.575** (.239)
Profitability	.057** (.014)	-.039 (.034)	.113* (.051)	.046** (.019)	.047* (.023)	.025 (.016)	.022* (.012)	.039* (.019)	.008 (.020)
Attrition Rate	-.014** (.005)	.016 (.014)	-.013 (.021)	-.014 (.016)	-.030 (.019)	.034** (.013)	-.019** (.009)	-.004 (.012)	.023 (.011)
High Tech Firm (Total Sample Only)	N.A.	N.A.	N.A.	N.A.	N.A.	N.A.	.618** (.193)	.147 (.242)	.867** (.261)
R^2	.69	.24	.47	.13	.18	.14	.18	.17	.18
Constant	2.60	3.13	1.60	2.60	3.09	1.98	1.63	3.06	1.72

Standard Errors in Parentheses
*$p \leq .05$
**$p \leq .01$

on top of "equity adjustments" and "merit" pay increases.

DISCUSSION AND CONCLUSIONS

The purpose of this paper has been to explore the determinants of compensation policies and practices for R&D personnel working in high tech firms. The results reported here indicate that sales volume, stage in the product life cycle, profitability, and turnover are all important predictors of the method and magnitude of financial rewards provided by these firms to R&D employees. Over half of the variance in R&D salary, benefits, and incentive pay in high tech firms can be accounted for by these factors.

The compensations items with the most interesting implications for this study are those pertaining to incentive based reward systems, which clearly differentiate between high tech and traditional firms. The most favorable situational factors for R&D incentive compensation are a low sales volume high tech company, operating in the growth stage of the product life cycle, with high turnover rates, and capable of linking profitability to incentive rewards such as bonuses. This study also suggests that there is a different tradeoff in the mix of the R&D compensation package by sales volume. A large volume high tech firm will offer higher salaries to R&D personnel but less incentive pay such as profit sharing, stock options, or bonuses. The small volume high tech firm will offer lower salaries, but a wider array of incentive based rewards. These policies enable the small and growing high tech firm to attract and retain scarce technical talent while buffering itself from short term financial pressures. These companies are usually new ventures that offer key scientists and engineers a share of the company in the form of stock ownership. If the company succeeds, these employees may derive a sizeable amount of capital from the sale of their stocks. In addition to stock options, profit sharing and bonuses are available based upon the reaching of company objectives.

This study only represents a first step in understanding some of the unique challenges and responses of high tech firms in coping with their R&D human resource problems. Many questions will remain unanswered that should be dealt with in the future. For example: To what extent are incentive based systems successful in attracting and retaining key technical talent? Do incentive based rewards for scientists and engineers in high tech actually increase the rate of innovation and profitability of the firm? Are there any differences in the background, personal characteristics, and quality of R&D personnel attracted to the growing, small high tech firms versus other companies? Are there any differences in the compensations systems of those high tech firms that failed versus those that survived the competition? Over 80 percent of the high tech compensation managers participating in the survey reported that they "strongly agree" that incentive-based rewards increase the number and quality of R&D hires, improve the retention of key R&D talent, and enhance the productivity of scientist and engineers. Perhaps existing compensation practices as summarized in Table 2 may be partly the result of these ingrained beliefs. However, only through a carefully designed study can we come up with a more solid answer as to the ultimate effectiveness of these practices.

With some notable exceptions, the compensation literature tends to emphasize applied techniques for job evaluation, methods for establishing external equity, and the development of procedures to administer pay systems. While techniques are important, there is the danger of overlooking the broader organizational context when designing compensation systems. As argued by Milkovich and Newman (1984) examining and dissecting techniques is so seductive that it often becomes the only interest of compensation specialists: "The mechanisms become the focus, ends in themselves. The purposes of the pay system are often forgotten. Such questions as 'So what does this technique do for (to) us?', 'How does this help achieve pay objectives'?, 'Why bother?' are not asked.'' (Milkovich and Newman, 1984, p. 11). This study takes a broader or more macro view of compensation design issues than is commonly the case. There are at least three implications for compensation specialists emanating from the general framework and findings presented here.

First, the compensation system should be designed to reinforce the overall strategy of the organization. Therefore, the system should be guided by the strategic stage of the firm. While only two stages of the product life cycle are represented in this study (growth and stability), the results shown here indicate that there are significant differences in the form of compensation package between these stages. These differences would be even more pronounced at the extreme stages of the product life cycle. At the start up stage, the employee would be expected to receive a pay mix with relatively low base pay (to conserve cash), strong emphasis on incentive pay (to emphasize unit and individual performance and to share the results of growth), and low benefits (to control costs). An organization in a declining stage of the product life cycle is likely to have high fixed costs, including base salary and benefits, and lose the flexibility to offer pay incentives (Milkovich and Newman, 1984).

Second, the compensation system should be tailored to the type of organization. The pay system is likely to be ineffective unless it is congruent with the needs of the firm. For instance, high tech firms place a greater emphasis on incentive pay programs, even after controlling for sales volume, product life cycle, profitability, and attrition rates. This emphasis on high tech is the result of a research and development orientation where innovation is pivotal, and where the contributions of scientists and engineers can be more easily discerned. In this type of environment, tra-

ditional job evaluation schemes (e.g., point, factor comparison) are less appropriate because their unit analysis is jobs rather than individuals.

Third, the pay system should be designed for target employee groups that would best respond to a particular compensation package. The type of employee attracted to a pay system that relies heavily on incentives is likely to be young, risk taker, achievement oriented, and willing to trade off long term gratification for short term sacrifices. A firm that does not take this into account is likely to suffer from high turnover rates. As indicated earlier, in the case of high tech firms the risk of turnover of best performers is higher since individual contributions are more easily recognized.

There are several limitations to this study that should be recognized. First, the composition of the sample of high tech firms is heavily weighted with electronics companies. Other high tech product lines such as genetic engineering or drugs were not represented in the sample. Since compensation patterns may reflect practices within the industry product groups, it may be risky to generalize the findings of this study beyond the computer and electronics industries which form a subset of high tech.

One other limitation of the study is that not all the factors that affect compensation were posited in the model. Some interesting variables to look at in the future would be age of industry, company, and workforce (high tech tends to be young); skill levels required of the workforce; and product life cycles in years (high tech products have short life cycles). Since older workers tend to have different compensation needs (i.e., they prefer more security) than younger workers (who tend to be greater risk takers), age may affect the form of the compensation package. For example, older workers may prefer a pension plan while younger workers may prefer to put those dollars into more stock options or profit sharing with a lump sum annual payout.

REFERENCES

Agarwal, N. (1981). Determinants of executive compensation. *Industrial Relations, 20,* pp. 36–46.

Allison, P. D. Inter-organizational mobility of academic scientists. Paper presented at the meeting of the American Sociological Association, Montreal, 1974.

Baumol, W. J. (1959). *Business behavior, value, and growth.* New York: Macmillan.

Balachandra, R. (1982, November). *Characteristics of high tech firms.* Unpublished paper presented at New England Business and Economic Association, Springfield, Massachusetts.

Balkin, D. (1983, September). *Compensation practices in the high tech industry.* Unpublished Technical Report, Northeastern University.

Bell, M. J. (1982). The entrepreneur, the market, and venture capital. In R.W. Similor (Ed.), *Small business and the entrepreneurial spirit.* Institute for Constructive Capitalism, University of Texas at Austin.

Dreher, G. F. (1982). The role of performance in the turnover process. *Academy of Management Journal, 25,* 137–147.

Dunlop, J. (1957). The task of contemporary wage theory. In G. Taylor and C. Pierson (Eds.), *New concepts in wage determination.* New York: McGraw-Hill.

Eatwell, J. L. (1971). Growth, profitability and size: The empirical evidence. In Robin Marris and Adrian Atwood (Eds.), *The corporate economy: Growth, competition, and innovative potential* (pp. 389–421). Cambridge, Mass.: Harvard University Press.

Ettlie, J. E. (1983). Organizational policy and innovation among suppliers to the food processing sector. *Academy of Management Journal, 26,* 27–44.

Goodman, R. A., and Abernathy, W. J. (1978). The contribution of new boy phenomena to increasing innovation and improvement in new technology. *R and D Management, 9,* 33–44.

Gomez-Mejia, L. R., Tosi, H., and Hinkin, T. (1983). *Determinants of executive compensation.* Unpublished Technical Report, University of Florida, Gainesville, Florida.

Graves, G. T. (1982). The technology based small business. In R. W. Smilor (Ed.), *Small business and the entrepreneurial spirit.* Institute for Constructive Capitalism, University of Texas at Austin.

Hambrick, D. C. (1981). Environment, strategy, and power within top management teams. *Administrative Science Quarterly, 26,* 253–275.

Hambrick, D. C. (1983). Some tests of the effectiveness and functional attributes of Miles and Snow's strategic types. *Academy of Management Journal, 26,* 5–26.

Henderson, R. I. (1982). *Compensation management.* Reston, Virginia: Reston Publishing Company.

Hofer, C. W. (1975). Toward a contingency theory of business strategy. *Academy of Management Journal, 18,* 784–810.

Lawler, E. E. (1971). *Pay and organizational effectiveness.* New York: McGraw-Hill.

Lewellen, W. G., and Huntsman, B. (1970). Managerial pay and corporate performance. *American Economic Review, 60,* 710–720.

March, J. C., and Simon, H. (1958). *Organizations.* New York: Wiley.

Marris, R. (1971). Some new results on growth and profitability. In Robin Marris and Adrian Atwood (Eds.), *The corporate economy: Growth, competition, and innovative potential* (pp. 421–427). Cambridge Mass.: Harvard University Press.

Martin, T. N., Price, J. L., and Mueller, C. W. (1981). Research note on job performance and turnover. *Journal of Applied Psychology, 66,* 116–119.

McGuire, J. W., Chiu, J. S., and Elbing, A. O. (1962). Executive incomes, sales, and profits. *American Economic Review, 60,* 753–761.

Mobley, W. H. (1980). *Some unanswered questions in turnover and withdrawal research.* Paper presented at the meeting of the Academy of Management, Detroit.

Morison, E. E. (1966). *New machines and modern times.* Cambridge Mass.: MIT Press.

Mueller, W. F., Culbertson, J., and Peckham, B. (1979). *Market structure and technological performance in the food manufacturing industry.* Washington, D.C.: National Science Foundation.

Milkovich, G. T., and Newman, J. M. (1984). *Compensation.* Business Publications, Inc.

Price, J. L. (1977). *The study of turnover.* Ames Iowa: The Iowa State University Press.

Roberts, D. R. (1959). A general theory of executive compensation based on statistically tested propositions. *Quarterly Journal of Economics, 70*, 270–294.

Reynolds, L. G. (1982). *Labor economics and labor relations.* Englewood Cliffs, N. J.: Prentice-Hall, Inc.

Rothwell, R. (1978). The characteristics of successful innovators and technically progressive firms. *R and D Management, 7,* 415–424.

Simon, H. A. (1957). Compensation of executives. *Sociometry, 20,* 32–35.

Smilor, R. W. (1982). *Small business and the entrepre-neurial spirit.* Institute for Constructive Capitalism, University of Texas at Austin.

Thorne, J. R. (1982). Entrepreneurs, technology, and the nurturing environment. In R. W. Smilor (Ed.), *Small business and the entrepreneurial spirit.* Institute for Constructive Capitalism, University of Texas at Austin.

Utterback, J. M., and Abernathy, W. J. (1975). A dynamic model of process and product innovation. *Omega, 3,* 639–656.

Managing a Diverse Work Force: Women in Engineering

Kate Kirkham

Paul Thompson

In competing for quality engineers, it will pay to have your people develop the awareness and skills necessary to manage a diverse work force.

Prior to 1975, very few women obtained degrees in engineering in the United States. However, that situation began to change, and by 1980 over 10 percent of all bachelor degrees in engineering were awarded to women (a total of 5,948).[1] Women now make up 4.3 percent of total engineers with percentages as high as 11.3 percent in some fields.[2]

The major influx of women into engineering in an encouraging development when many people are forecasting a shortage of engineers in the United States in the next decade.[3] As more women seek employment in engineering organizations, managers face a greater challenge to effectively manage an integrated work force which reflects a wider range of work styles and diversity of individuals not now found in many engineering organizations. Although qualifications of women are similar, often their values, experiences and professional expectations are different.

In an effort to find out how organizations were responding to the increasing number of

women entering engineering, we interviewed men and women in eight engineering organizations. Our interest was in understanding the total impact of the increasing diversity in engineering, rather than in evaluating compliance with basic requirements of equal employment opportunity laws. We wanted to identify what helps or hinders working relationships, as well as expand our ways of thinking about this issue. The organizations sampled included companies in a variety of industries, including basic metals, defense, electronics, and energy.

The interviews included individual contributors and managers, as well as staff people in personnel or employee relations. The small sample of responses included in the box (next page) illustrates the wide range of options on how well women were being accepted. Most of the men we interviewed said there was no problem with women being accepted in their organizations. However, almost all of the women and a few of the men had quite a different view. They see a number of situations that make acceptance of women as peers and professionals quite difficult.

In one organization we saw a dramatic example of those different views. In that company

From *Research Management,* March–April 1984, 9–16. Reprinted by permission.

we held individual interviews and group discussions with 44 engineers and managers, exploring several topics including the acceptance of women engineers. Thirty-nine of those interviewed said there was no problem—women were completely accepted and were treated just the same as men. Only five people said that women were not being treated equally. It was interesting that all three of the women in the sample indicated that women were not being treated equally. After gathering additional information about practices in the company, it became clear that there were significant problems in the lack of opportunities for women engineers in terms of job assignments, travel, and promotions. The surprising finding was that only 2 out of 41 men were able to see (or perhaps were willing to admit) these problems.

As we analyzed all of the interviews, we realized that the words "acceptance" and "equal treatment" were being used quite differently by the respondents. Some people were thinking about men and women receiving equal pay and being called engineers; others were looking at job assignments and opportunities to travel to field sites or professional conferences; still others were concerned about informal relationships, including going to lunch together or being accepted as one of the "boys." A number of organizations did not grant us permission to interview because the topic itself was viewed as "too sensitive," either by the employee or the employer. In other cases, we were discouraged by personnel staff from talking about differences because of the legal implications. Apparently, some people were thinking about the issues of diversity only in terms of violations of EEO laws.

We concluded that there are significant challenges facing managers who want to be effective in managing women and men in engineering, and that there isn't just "one problem" that can be located at one level of the organization or can be attributed only to women or only to men. The important issue is understanding the total dynamics of the demographic changes in the engineering profession—what helps or hinders working relationships and how to think about these issues in order to better manage a diverse work force.

A FRAMEWORK FOR UNDERSTANDING

In our interviews we heard many managers express an interest in improving their effectiveness in managing a diverse work team of men and women. Unfortunately, many of them did not have useful ways to think about the issue. Some of the men were only dealing with very elementary questions related to their interactions with women, such as, "Should I open the door for them or not?"

We want to expand the thinking on these issues by considering three different perspectives: interpersonal, group and organizational. Each level of this framework has a primary expression of differences that can negatively affect the management of diversity:

1. *Interpersonal dynamics involve interactions between individuals who are different.* At the individual level, it is prejudice—the voiced attitudes or non-verbal behaviors that indicate personal bias.
2. *Group dynamics involve a group identity.* They may involve an individual interacting with a different group of others or an individual's stereotypes about a group of others. At the intergroup level, the collective appearance of prejudice is expressed as stereotyping or discrimination. Even individuals who should consider themselves non-prejudical can unintentionally contribute to discrimination initiated by a larger group.
3. *Organizational dynamics involve the impact of a company's policies and practices—intended or not—on individuals who are different.* When we combine individual prejudicial attitudes with discriminatory acts, they can produce policies and practices at the or-

ganizational level that can alter the climate and "terms and conditions" of employment. This produces what is referred to as institutional patterns of sexism.

Learning to think critically about the dynamics at each level can aid a manager in *selecting* appropriate responses. Invariably, there are more alternatives than "is this legal to do or not to do?" For example, friction may be occurring between men and women on the same work team. Examination from the perspective of the three levels reveals that the problem is not originating from a biased supervisor, but from the supervisor's role implementing a long-standing company practice about travel.

The framework not only introduces a broader perspective for thinking about and understanding the complexities of a diverse work force, but it also suggests the need for different management strategies on each level.

DYNAMICS BETWEEN INDIVIDUALS

This level of analysis focuses on the relationship between individual male and female employees, where personal prejudice is the main problem in managing diversity. Most men have not worked with women professionals before and, as a result, they are not sure how to relate to women engineers. Prejudice can be a product of just such a lack of experiences and hence unintentional, or it may be an expression of intended attitudes about another because of his/her gender. Let's examine some examples from our interviews

The women that we interviewed said that many of their male colleagues had adjusted quite well to working with women, but that others were having problems. Unfortunately, a few men who have difficulty treating women as professionals can create significant problems for women entering engineering. The most obvious

examples of inappropriate behavior toward a professional woman include:

- Calling female engineers "girls."
- Making frequent jokes about women not being as smart as men or that "they should be home having babies."
- Seeing a woman engineer primarily as someone to flirt with or tease.

We were surprised at the number of men who continue to refer to females with college degrees as "girls." Many of these "girls" are 30 or 40 years old. But for most women engineers, this is a minor issue compared to other things. One woman said, "I don't care what they call me as long as they give me a good job assignment." This view was somewhat typical of the response on that issue, but other women indicated that they are getting tired of not being treated as professionals. In some cases, the joking was seen as more serious. One woman said:

> My boss is very sexist. He makes a lot of jokes about women drivers, women staying at home, etc. When a mistake is made, he'll say, "Some dumb broad probably did it." I try to get him to stop by joking back, but he doesn't stop. His boss is aware of the problem, but he doesn't do anything about it.

It's obvious that this woman sees her boss's behavior as more than a minor irritation. She was quite unhappy about the treatment she was receiving and felt that it interfered with her work. Women are particularly concerned about these "minor" problems when they represent an attitude that women are not full-fledged professionals. Less obvious examples of prejudice occur as a form of "helping" or protecting. One woman described her concern about her boss's overconsideration of her dual role as engineer and wife:

> My manager tells me that I should go home every day before six o'clock so I can fix dinner for my

---

**A WIDE RANGE OF OPINIONS ON HOW WELL WOMEN
ARE ACCEPTED**

- We're quite successful in our efforts to recruit women and they are working out very well. Most of the women are assigned to work with young supervisors because they are more likely to accept women engineers. (Male engineering manager)

- We've worked very hard to help women gain acceptance and to make sure they're given challening work assignments, but we've got a long way to go in this company. Some men try to avoid women professionals. Managers often give women work that isn't challenging. A woman has to prove herself much more than a man does. Only after she's proven herself can she expect to get meaningful work. (Female employee relations manager)

- I make it a point to not treat women engineers differently. They are given the same assignments and the same treatment as men. If a woman is given special treatment, the men complain. We hired a woman chemical engineer. She's a great little girl and has worked out very well. (Male engineer manager)

- Sexism is rampant in my department. The men play racquetball together. I play racquetball, but I'm never invited to play with them. The boss and the men go to lunch together; I'm never invited. The boss has had all of the men in the department over to his house, but I've never been invited to his house. They seem to be trying to isolate the women engineers. (Female engineer)

---

husband. I know he means well, but it still upsets me because I don't want to get the reputation that I can't be relied on to stay and complete a project when we have a tight deadline.

Another example came from a helpful executive who hired a management consultant to conduct a team-building seminar with the people who reported directly to him. Of his 14 immediate subordinates, the one woman was not invited to attend the session. When the consultant discovered the situation and asked why she had not been invited, the executive replied, "I thought Ann would feel uncomfortable being the only woman in the session." The consultant replied, "How do you think she will feel when she finds out she was the only one of your subordinates who was not invited to the session?" She was included in the next session. The executive was "protecting" the woman from what he saw as an awkward situation for her based on his values of how men and women interact, without realizing that the work situation required a different attitude on his part.

Problems that arise in interpersonal relations are often difficult to handle because when women bring up the issue, they are often accused of being too sensitive. One woman commented:

> It bothers me when someone makes a negative comment about women. But I've been told that I'm too sensitive. I don't know if I'm too sensitive. There is quite a bit of stereotyping here. At school there was a more liberal atmosphere. But coming to work here was like stepping back ten years. Here men compare you with their wives, not to other engineers. It's a subtle influence, but it's there.

DYNAMICS INVOLVING GROUP IDENTITY

This level of analysis enables us to look at employee interactions that are a product of group dynamics. A great deal of the activity in organizations takes place in groups including both work groups and social groups. While some of the women we interviewed were quickly integrated into the on-going groups in their organizations, many women, unfortunately, did not find such a supportive environment. The quote in the box about "Sexism is rampant in my department . . ." illustrates this problem of a woman who feels excluded.

When we consider group behavior, several facets of male/female interactions are sharpened:

- Sometimes men are not able to clearly see the individual characteristics of a specific woman because they hold stereotypic views of women in general which block their perception.
- Women may experience a collective impact from the behavior of a group of men that individual men in that group are not aware of.
- A non-prejudiced man in a group of men may not be aware that he is part of the collective impact which restricts a woman's performance.

For example, in one organization a group of male professionals played basketball together during the lunch hour several days a week. In those sessions, a lot of information was shared about joint projects, developments in the group, etc. When two women were hired into the group, they were not involved in the basketball games and hence did not have access to the information exchanged in those informal sessions. Individually, the men expressed no intent to discriminate against the women, but their collective behavior had a negative impact on the women's ability to perform. Unfortunately, the manager didn't handle the situation very well. In trying to give the women access to the information, he caused the men to feel that they were being asked to give up their noon-time recreation to accommodate the women, or else invite them into the locker room. Few women are asking for that type of a response. However, whey would like access to information that's important to their work.

Some people have not been too sympathetic when we've described this problem, because it doesn't seem to relate to work. They argue that the organization can't be responsible for regulating the social activity of it employees. But, as is evident, these group activities are not just social get-togethers. Many times important work takes place in social settings.

Another aspect of this problem concerns womens' participation in informal discussions in their own departments. One woman engineer reported that when she entered a room and a group of men were talking, the conversation often changed abruptly. Where the conversation had been focused on important business or technical problems they would switch to lighter subjects which they assumed would be of interest to her.

These stereotyped assumptions about women which the men were imposing on her prevented her from having access to important information which affected her job. She added:

> When I first came to work here, I noticed that conversations with me were different than with

the young men—not as open about how the organization works and how you get ahead. With men, they discuss the secrets of how the system works, but with women that was taboo. I felt that they didn't even take me seriously. They may not have meant to exclude me, but they didn't tell me how to publish or where to publish. I had to do it on my own. Once I had some articles published, then they began to respect me. Now I'm doing joint research and publishing with men, but they wouldn't work with me until I had developed a reputation outside the lab.

It's not clear why some men will not take women engineers seriously, but that behavior puts the women at a disadvantage. And it often takes exceptional effort and ability to overcome that disadvantage, as these women discovered.

Another example of the tendency for men to rely on stereotypes about women as a group, rather than to look at *individual* qualifications, is in their assumptions about relationships among women in an organization. Many women are assigned ''women's work'' simply because superiors assume that all women have certain women's skills. One woman computer scientist was assigned by her boss to handle all communications with the women in the typing pool. The department was having some problems in its relationship with the typing pool and the boss assumed that a woman would be more effective in communicating with other women. The computer scientist resented this because it gave her less time in the area where she was trained.

But even for women who have succeeded in gaining acceptance from the men in their group as a professional engineering woman, there are still dilemmas which they must contend with on the job in order to *maintain* their group's acceptance. Many women are afraid to confront problems because they don't want to be seen as troublemakers or ''women's libbers.'' One woman described her dilemma on this issue as follows:

I work with a group of male engineers. One of them is quite obnoxious in the way he talks about

women. I sit at the desk next to his and sometimes when a secretary walks by, he describes in great detail what he'd like to do sexually with her. I have to decide whether to speak up and lose my effectiveness with the group, or remain silent. I have to neuter myself to get along with the men in engineering.

This woman has decided that confronting male engineers about their language is too costly to her effectiveness in the group, so she says nothing. Eventually, she may decide that silence is too high a cost to pay and she may leave the organization. Managers need to become aware of the impact of such situations. Male engineers need to be cognizant of how their behavior and attitude is affecting the lone woman in the group. Women in groups of men benefit from male ''allies'' who, by voicing their similar opinions, help change the tendency to stereotype.

Unfortunately, two traps operate at the group level to immobilize many men who could be effective in confronting stereotypes. First of all, many men rely on their personal experience as the only criteria for checking on the legitimacy of an issue. In effect, they are saying, ''If I haven't observed that, it probably didn't happen.'' Secondly, they use the entire group as a reference to support their rationalizations. ''Well, not everyone here, Jane, is like that.''

While both of these statements contain some truth, they do not contribute to gaining insight into the experience of someone else, nor to effectively solving problems in organizations.

IMPACT OF ORGANIZATIONAL POLICIES AND PRACTICES

This level of analysis focuses on policies and practices that may impact men and women differently. Since women are newcomers to professional jobs in most organizations, managers may not have taken a careful look at policies which may have a negative impact on women. For example, a chief engineer in a large company in the defense industry reported that he was unsuccessful in getting his company to adapt its policies to accommodate women. He said they had hired "a very competent woman engineer" who after two years decided to have a baby and wanted to take a one-year maternity leave. "Our company policy wouldn't permit that, so I tried to get them to change it. The company had nothing to lose by approving a one-year leave. We wanted her back and we're having trouble finding engineers these days. It was a leave without pay, but they still wouldn't approve it. No wonder we have difficulty attracting women to our organization."

At a time when engineers are in short supply, it seems logical that engineering firms could only help themselves by adapting their policies and practices to accommodate women.

A common attitude toward organizational level problems is, "We have an EEO office and they'll handle this issue." Unfortunately, the EEO office can't handle all of these problems alone. We are not opposed to an organization having a separate EEO office which can provide technical resources, but the existence of such an office should not be used as an excuse for managers and individual contributors to ignore their on-going responsibility for skill development in this important area, or delay action until the issues require attention by the EEO office. Too often, managers use organizational policy as an excuse not to take action.

When there is no specific organizational policy to direct managers as they make decisions about women, they tend to rely on assumptions. One supervisor decided that all the engineers on his project needed to travel to the plant to get a better understanding of production problems. His boss approved the trip, but said none of the women should go. The supervisor was very upset because the women had important assignments on the project.

Managers should take responsibility for their role in reviewing the impact of internal policies, or lack of policy, especially those which concern traveling and working in the field. Managers may be uneasy about women traveling alone (or traveling with a man, for that matter). One manager said:

> We have a dilemma about assigning women to some jobs—for example, jobs that require a lot of traveling alone. Some of the projects are in areas where it's not very safe. Should we send women to work in areas where they might get raped?

This last problem is a real dilemma and not all women want to travel alone or travel into unsafe areas. However, almost all women would like to be involved in the decision. They would like an opportunity to consider the assignment and decide for themselves whether they would like to accept it.

Official policies regarding work and travel are not the only problems women face; the organizational climate can often hinder women's informal support. Since there are few women in the top management of companies, most senior executives are not aware of the issues on other levels of the organization and do not have an effective way of understanding the situations which women encounter. One woman who tried to organize a women's support group within her company encountered unwarranted negative reactions from top management.

> A few weeks ago, three of us (all women) got together to discuss the problems women face here due to lack of awareness and support. Later, we met with the V.P. of Industrial Relations to talk about creating a women's support group. He went straight to the president. The president was very concerned and told the V.P. to stop it before it got started. He said if we get a women's support group, before very long we'll have a Ku Klux Klan group, etc. It got blown all out of proportion. We just wanted a chance to discuss some issues. We weren't planning to picket the plant.

Attitudes of people in influential positions can have a major impact on the management of diversity in organizations. The organization can be blocked on these issues when those in key positions assume that no problem exists until it is objectively proven to them, or when they believe that the outcome of a policy will be experienced by everyone the way it was intended.

THE INTERLOCKING LEVELS

Our examples have been an effort to illustrate the three different levels of diversity and the traps that can block effective behaviors. It is important before we begin examining the implications for change to look at two issues that consistently surfaced during our study. These issues emphasize the importance of diagnosis, because they appear across all three levels. They are job assignment and availability of feedback.

Job assignment can be simultaneously influenced by personal bias, by stereotypic assumptions about women in general, and by organizational practices. Consider these examples:

- A woman chemical engineer was assigned to a supervisor who did not want a woman working for him. He assigned her to paint the floor in the department. The woman got very upset and told her supervisor's boss. A review was conducted and the supervisor was fired.
- A manager of employee relations said some managers are reluctant to give a woman work that is challenging. They are afraid the woman will get pregnant or leave when her husband gets transferred. As a result, they give women routine jobs where they can be easily replaced, independent of their personal situation.
- Some organizations have unwritten policies that women will not be assigned to jobs that involve traveling to the field. As a result, they do not get field experience, which af-

fects the kind of job assignments they get later in their careers.

Almost all of the women that we interviewed indicated that job assignment was very important to them. They were very concerned that organizations take whatever action was necessary to see that they were given equal access to challenging jobs. They did not want a biased manager, group dynamics, or organizational policies to stand in the way of their receiving meaningful work.

The second issue that surfaced across all levels was the availability of feedback. Many of the women we interviewed indicated that it was hard for them to get concrete feedback about their performance. They would like specific information about job expectations, an evaluation of their work on a specific project, etc. A variety of explanations were given for the apparent reluctance of males managers to give female engineers critical feedback. One woman suggested that men don't believe that women are generally willing to change in order to get ahead in the organization. She said:

> Recently I was talking with a department manager about the development plans for one of his female subordinates. He reported that she is bright and articulate, but she would not become a supervisor because she isn't aggressive enough. I asked, "Have you told her that?" He said he hadn't, because he didn't think she wanted to change. Later, the department manager described a male subordinate in very similar terms and said that he was working with the man to help him become a supervisor.

The woman reporting this incident could not understand why the department manager would insure that the man was getting feedback on his shortcomings and allow his own unchecked assumptions to prevent the woman from getting the same constructive feedback.

Another explanation was presented by Kanter in her book, *Men and Women in the Corporation:*

There were instances in which women trainees did not get direct criticism in time to improve their performance and did not know they were the subjects of criticism in the company until told to find jobs in other divisions. They were not part of the buddy network that uncovered such information quickly, and their managers were reluctant to criticize a woman out of uncertainty about how she would receive the information. (One man put quite simply how he felt about giving negative feedback to a woman: "I'm chicken.") Here, feelings that it is impossible to level with a different kind of person stood in the way.[4]

One of the men in our study had a different perspective on this issue. He said the male managers that he worked with complained that women always wanted more feedback than the men in the department. His view is that men and women both get the same amount of formal feedback, but the women are dissatisfied because they feel a need for more than they are receiving.

It is clear from the multiple explanations about why women aren't getting the kind of feedback they want, that the issue has many causes and influencing factors from all three levels. Those managers who want to effectively handle diversity will explore the issue of feedback beyond their own personal behavior to understand how stereotypes or policy interfere with this process.

IMPLICATIONS FOR ACTION

In our interviews, we often encountered attitudes which make it difficult to solve problems that stand in the way of women becoming productive engineers. One supervisor, for example, told us he didn't see what he could do about it. "I'm just a supervisor. I can't control what my subordinates say or change the policies of the company. The women will just have to prove themselves and then they'll be accepted."

We disagree with that view. In many of the examples described in this article, the first-line supervisor had adequate power and influence to improve the situation if he or she had only used that influence. Supervisors can do a great deal to create a climate where both men and women are given challenging job assignments, critical feedback, access to important job information, etc. They can also be allies for women in awkward situations or involve them in informal activities.

Another attitude that blocks progress in this area is the idea that we should let the men and women who are on the same work team deal with these problems. This implies that issues would only be addressed at the group level. Unfortunately, many men have not had experience in working with women as peers, and lack the skills to deal with problems that arise in this area. A group or interpersonal level problem often needs to be resolved with support from the large organization. In our research, we found several organizations that were not passive on this issue, but had taken the initiative to deal with many of the problems that we identified. Some concrete examples may illustrate what organizations can do.

A large research organization, which was praised by one woman employee for having a progressive outlook toward placing women in non-traditional jobs, has had a Women's Association for more than ten years. This association functions as an educational, discussion and action group that is primarily concerned with the problems women face in employment. The association sponsors monthly noontime programs for all women as well as a committee on science and engineering, which aids the company's scientists and engineers in forming a network.

Most companies are just starting to take an interest in networks and seminars for women. For example, one of the electronics firms in our study was interested in assisting men and women to understand and manage greater diversity. Therefore, they developed two seminars to address these issues. The first seminar was offered for professional women and was two days in length. It focused on the unique challenges fac-

WOMEN IN R&D MANAGEMENT

In October 1982, IRI ran an experimental Management Study Group entitled "Management Study Group—For Women Only." Management Study Groups are one of the IRI Management Development Programs, and are intended for first-line managers; i.e., scientists and engineers who are in their first position as supervisor or manager. These groups discuss many of the problems that first-line managers encounter, under the general headings of Projects, Motivation, and Communications. This experimental group, for women only, discussed these general topics, and also some of the problems unique to women managers in industrial research. Discussion leader was Mary L. Good, vice president and director of research, U O P Inc., and designated as "1982 IR&D Scientist of the Year" by *Industrial Research & Development Magazine.* This first group was monitored by Arline Lewis, IRI's coordinator of education services, and the following are some of her observations.

- In the past few years, there has been an increase in the number of women moving from the bench into R&D management.

- Women research managers face the same problems as their male counterparts. However, in moving into a field still dominated by males, additional problems exist peculiar to women.

- A woman who wishes to advance her career in research management has to make some basic decisions. Is she willing to make the same sacrifices that men traditionally have made to gain advancement? The primary sacrifice appears to be time, is she willing to contribute those extra hours so necessary in the research establishment? She shouldn't expect any privileges except those extended to her male counterparts.

- Many of the women in this group had single-parent responsibilities in addition to their job responsibilities. In order to meet both sets of responsibilities, and not sacrifice either, many have resorted to the concept that "money buys time" which means that they use a portion of their increased income as a manager to pay for household assistance.

- Since she is functioning in a predominantly male world, there is no doubt that she will be surrounded by male subordinates. It was the hope of the group that women managers would handle resentments by all subordinates in the same manner as their male counterparts, by establishing a management style that permits their labs to function smoothly and efficiently.

- What about relationships with other females? There is a tendency for some women to become overly critical of their female co-workers, both supervisors and subordinates. The consensus was that it is necessary to judge other women on ability alone, judgment should not become clouded by emotional issues.

- The group expressed concern about the difficulty in attending management training programs under company sponsorship. This difficulty occurs because of the very small number of women managers in any R&D department, so that when people are selected to attend seminars, meetings, and the like, the choice usually goes to the majority population. In this special IRI group, which only women could attend, the participants felt that by being segregated in this way, they were working against some of the ideas previously expressed. However, their attendance could prove advantageous by giving them management training, an opportunity to meet peers from other companies and industries, and at the same time bring them to their managers' attention.

- Only a relatively small portion of time was spent on those problems unique to women managers. This reflected the attitude of the group that they would like to be treated in the same fashion as their peers— The Editor of *Research Management*.

ing women in the work place and discussed such issues as advancement, communication with men, etc. The most important aspect was the opportunity for women to meet and discuss common experiences. The second seminar focused on men and women working together. Ten men and ten women were assigned to each discussion group during the one-day seminar. The central issue was why women do not advance as fast as men in the organization when all other variables are equal. Male managers of the female engineers participated in the seminar. The major outgrowth of these seminars was increased awareness by both men and women of the organizational issues facing women.

For example, after one engineering manager participated in the seminar, he initiated a discussion with the women in his department to see if they were experiencing any of the problems he had heard about. His interest and openness encouraged them to speak candidly about things that were bothering them. Several of them admitted that they felt handicapped because of their lack of experience with some of the tools they were expected to know how to use. As a result of this discussion, the engineering department is planning to assess new engineers' skills with tools and offer a short training program for both men and women in the use of tools and equipment. This manager's willingness to listen and the company's willingness to change assumptions about engineers will benefit both men and women.

In the first example, we described a formal program of seminars that was quite visible in the organization. But low-key activities that lack visibility can also be effective. One company with a small engineering department was seen as very supportive. We interviewed two women in the department who were hired a year apart. The first woman hired reported being more frustrated by teasing than her co-worker, who was hired a year later. She said:

> When the men used to joke about women not being as smart as men, I felt they were making fun of me personally. Now that there are two of us, I feel more comfortable about joking back. The two women in our department are both on the same work team (4 people), so we have an equal vote in all of our work. It's a lot easier now that there are two of us.

Research indicates that a lone woman in a professional organization often gets isolated. This company was sensitive to this issue and solved the problem by putting the two women in the department on the same work team.

This company was also willing to modify formal policies to meet special circumstances created by the presence of women in the organization. The company had a policy against family members working in the same department. When one of the women engineers married a man in the same department, that presented a problem. Rather than insisting that one of them leave the company or move to a non-engineering department, their supervisors counseled them about potential problems and then arranged for them to continue working for the same department, but on different projects and under different supervisors. These activities lacked the visibility of major programs or seminars, but they produced significant results. The women we interviewed in that organization were quite positive about the organization and its responsiveness to their needs.

In summary, those managers who learn to think critically about the dynamics which are occurring on each of the three levels of the organization will be far more effective in sorting out strategies that will contribute to employee effectiveness. By examining individual relationships between men and women, a manager can identify disruptive, prejudicial behaviors on the individual level and provide assistance to improve understanding and communication between employees. On a group level, a manager can become sensitive to the impact which stereotypical attitudes have on employee effectiveness. Finally, by examining organizational policies, the manager can sort out those practices which discriminate and be a catalyst in initiating the necessary changes.

In the next decade, engineering organizations will be hiring many more white women and women of color. Those organizations which encourage their employees and managers to develop the awareness and skills to manage a diverse work force will have the advantage in the competition for quality engineers.

REFERENCES

1. *Manpower Comments,* Scientific Manpower Commission, Vol. 18, No. 8, October 1981, p. 20.
2. *Employment and Earnings,* U.S. Department of Labor, Bureau of Labor Statistics, Vol. 29, No. 1, January 1982, p. 165.
3. For example, Kahne, Stephen, "A Crisis in Electrical Engineering Manpower." *IEEE Spectrum,* June 1981, pp. 50–52.
4. Kanter, Rosabeth Moss. *Men and Women of the Corporation,* New York: Basic Books, Inc., Publishers, 1977, p. 227.
5. Rose, Clare, Sally Ann Menninger, and Glenn F. Nyre. "The Study of Women in Science and Engineering." Summary Report, Los Angeles: Evaluation and Training Institute, 1978, p. 21.

Human Resource Policies for the Innovating Organization

Jay R. Galbraith

Innovation is currently sought by most organizations. Somewhere in their strategic plans they all discuss the importance of searching for new businesses, fostering new products, or new processes. But despite the fact that innovation is so revered, it remains very difficult to achieve. Why is something so desirable so elusive?

There are several reasons. First, innovation is *destructive*. It destroys investments in capital, careers, and installed basis of power. It is always interesting to see the "about face" of someone who urges innovation but finds one which renders a personal specialty obsolete. These cheerleaders quickly become Luddites.[1] Second, innovation is a *political process*. It is political in part because of its potential destructiveness, but also because new ideas raise issues of charters, territories, missions, and future direction. With the advent of microcomputers and user-friendly languages many innovations are discovered by users in manufacturing, engineering, or marketing. The innovation, if discovered, immediately raises territorial issues with the data-processing department. Therefore, almost every new idea runs counter to the established ways of doing business. The new and unproven ideas get killed very often by the Luddites and the politicians. The third reason that innovation is so difficult is that it requires an innovative organization specifically designed to produce commercially successful ideas. Most of our organizations are operating organizations. They are designed to do something well for the millionth time. Organizations that efficiently produce the millionth product are not very good at doing something for the first time. That is the task of the innovating organization. Thus to be innovative a firm needs two organizations—one to operate the current business and one to innovate into new businesses. This chapter describes the structure of the innovative organization and the human resource policies and systems needed to support it. Again, most human resource policies are designed for the operating organization. Because the task of innovating is inherently different than operating, an innovating organization needs human resource policies that support innovation.

The innovating organization need not be an expensive, duplicate structure. For some organizations it may simply be an occasional effort wherein a half-dozen people are set up in a trailer in the parking lot. The point is that even in these temporary ventures there is structure, some key processes, special rewards, and a type of person that must be blended into an innovating organization. The next sections describe this structure and the key processes consistent with it. Then the human resource policies to fit this structure and process are discussed in greater detail. Before describing the innovating organization, a case example of an innovation is presented from which a number of lessons can be drawn.

Jay R. Galbraith

THE INNOVATING PROCESS

This section presents a typical process by which innovations occur in organizations. The organization is a new venture that was started in the early 1970s. A group of engineers developed a new electronics product while working for a well-known innovative electronics firm. Because they were in a division that did not have the charter for this product, however, a political battle ensued and, as is frequently the case, the engineers left to form their own company. They successfully found venture capital and introduced their new product. Initial acceptance was good, and within several years they were growing rapidly and had become an industry leader.

However in the early 1970s, Intel invented the microprocessor. By the mid to late 1970s the Intel innovation began to spread through the electronics industries. Manufacturers of previously "dumb" products now had the capability to infuse "intelligence" into their product lines. A competitor who understood computers and software introduced just such a product into the new venture firm's market. It met with initial high acceptance. The president of the firm in point responded by hiring someone who knew something about microcomputers, some software people, and instructed the engineering department to respond.

The president spent most of his time raising capital to finance the venture's growth. Realizing one day that the engineers had not made much progress, he instructed them to get a product out. They did, but it was a half-hearted effort. The new product had a microprocessor in it but was less than the second generation product that was needed.

The president then pursued international opportunities. He started up in Europe and Singapore, but there again he noticed that his main competitor was growing faster than his company was and had begun to steal market share. The competitor quickly became the industry leader.

The president decided that he had better take charge of the product development effort.

Upon his return he found that the hardware and software groups were locked in a political battle in engineering. Each felt its "magic" was the more powerful. Since the lead engineer and cofounder had a hardware background, the hardware establishment prevailed. But they then clashed head-on with the marketing department who agreed with the software group. The result was a set of studies and presentations but no new product. The situation as it presents itself is that of a young, relatively small (1200 people) entrepreneurial firm that cannot innovate. The president wanted innovation and provided resources to produce it. That was not enough. Much more was needed.

The president became more involved. One day he received a call from his sales manager in the New England territory. The sales manager said, "I think you should come up here. A field service engineer has made some modifications to our product and programmed it in a way that my customers are asking us to do. We may have something here."

The president was impressed with what he saw. The engineer wanted to use the company's product to track his own inventory. He wrote to the company headquarters for programming instructions. The response from headquarters was that it was against company policy to send instructional materials to field engineers. Undaunted, the engineer bought a home computer and taught himself to program. He then modified the product in the field and programmed it to solve his problem. When the sales manager happened to see what was done, he recognized its significance and immediately called the president.

The field engineer accompanied the president back to headquarters. He presented his work to the engineers who had been working on the second generation product for so long. Their response was that the application was nice but

577

idiosyncratic. They said that their planned product would be superior. Again, the hardware group prevailed. The field engineer was thanked and returned to his position.

Weeks later, the same sales manager called the president again. He said that the company would lose this talented guy if something wasn't done. Besides, he thought that the field engineer was right and not the engineering group. The president recalled that he had been impressed and that the field engineer had produced something more valuable than his entire engineering department had. He brought him back to headquarters and tried to find something for the field engineer to do while he decided what should be done. Within a few days, the president received a request from the European sales manager to assign the engineer to him.

The European sales manager was visiting headquarters for a period of training. During that time he heard of the field engineer, sought him out, and listened to his story. It turned out that the sales manager had a French bank that wanted the kind of application that the field engineer had created for himself. A successful application would be worth an order for several hundred machines. The president gave the go-ahead and sent the field engineer to work in Europe. The engineering department said it wouldn't work. Three months later, the field engineer successfully developed the application and the bank signed an order for several hundred machines.

When the field engineer returned, the president assigned him to a trusted marketing manager who was told to protect him and get a product out. The engineers were told to support the manager and reluctantly did so. They created some applications software and a printed circuit board which could easily be installed in all existing machines in the field. The addition of this board and the software temporarily saved the company and made its current product slightly superior to that of the competitor.

The president was elated. He congratulated the young field engineer and gave him a good position on the staff working in special assignments to develop software. Then he began encountering problems. The president tried to get personnel to give the engineer a special cash award. Personnel was reluctant. "After all," they said, "other people worked on the effort, too. It will set a precedent."

Then the finance department wanted to withhold $500 from the engineer's pay. He had received an advance of $1000 for his European trip but only turned in vouchers for $500 upon return.

The young engineer didn't help himself very much either. He was hard to get along with and refused to accept supervision from anyone except the European sales manager. The president, therefore, arranged to have him permanently transferred to Europe. The personnel department had prepared the necessary paperwork three times and three times the engineer had changed his mind about going at the last minute. Today the president is still wondering what to do with him.

In this not uncommon story we have a number of lessons we can use to construct the characteristics of an innovating organization. The next section takes these lessons and elaborates upon them in order to develop the structure and processes that constitute the innovating organization. The reward systems and people practices that make up the human resource policies of the innovating organization are then described.

THE INNOVATING ORGANIZATION

The innovating organization is no different from an operating organization in the make-up of its component parts. It consists of a task, structure, processes, reward systems, and people as shown in Figure 1.[2] Each component must fit with each other component and with the task. A basic premise of this chapter is that the task of the in-

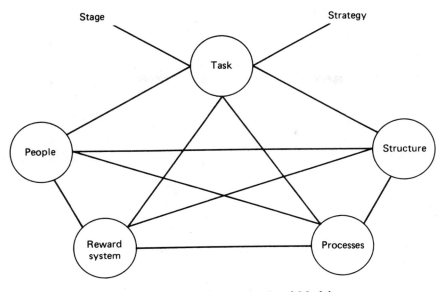

FIGURE 1. *An Organizational Model*

novating organization is fundamentally different from that of the operating organization. The innovating task is more uncertain and risky, takes place over longer time horizons, assumes failure is good in the early stages, and so on. Therefore, the organization that performs that task should be different as well. A firm wishing to innovate needs both an operating organization and an innovating organization. But what is the innovating organization? The next sections describe the structure, processes, rewards, and staffing practices of the innovating organization.

The Structure of the Innovating Organization
The innovating organization has a structure of its own, and can be described in terms of several roles. These roles define one of the three structural dimensions of the innovating organization. Each dimension incorporates a lesson from the example presented in this section.

Roles. Like the result of all organized phenomena, innovation occurs from a combination of roles, whether the innovation occurs inside or outside a formal organization. Innovation is rarely an individual phenomenon.[3] There are three main roles in the commercialization of any new idea. The three roles are well illustrated in the case example.

Every innovation starts with an *idea generator* or idea champion. In the preceeding example the field engineer was the person who generated the new idea. This is the inventor, the entrepreneur, or risk taker on whom much of our research attention has been focused. The main conclusion of this research is that an idea champion is needed at each stage of an idea's development into an innovation. That is, at each stage, a dedicated, full-time individual whose success or failure depends on developing the idea is necessary for innovation. Very little more need be added here. It is the other roles—traditionally ignored—that will receive most of our attention.

The need for other roles begins because the idea generator is usually a low-level person who experiences a problem and develops a new response to it. The lesson here is that many ideas originate down where "the rubber meets the road." The lost status and authority level of the idea generator creates a need for the next role.

Every idea needs at least one *sponsor* to promote it. In order to carry an idea into implementation, someone has to discover it and fund the increasingly disruptive and expensive development and testing efforts that shape it. Thus idea generators need to find sponsors for their ideas in order to perfect them. In our example, the New England sales manager, the European sales manager, and finally, the marketing manager sponsored the idea of the field engineer. Thus one of the functions of the sponsor is to lend his or her authority and resources to an idea to carry it down the road toward commercialization.

The other function of the sponsor is to recognize the business significance of an idea. In any organization there are hundreds of ideas being promoted at any one time. The sponsor must select among these ideas those that might become new business ideas. Thus it is best that sponsors be generalists. That is not always the case, as the case example illustrates.

Sponsors are usually middle managers who are distributed throughout the organization. They frequently work for both the operating and innovating organization. Some of the sponsors run divisions or departments and it is their task to balance the operating and innovating needs of their business or function. Other sponsors work full-time for the innovating organization when the firm can afford the creation of venture groups, new product development departments, and the like. In the example, the sales managers spontaneously played the sponsor role. The third sponsor, the marketing manager, was formally designated. The point here is that by formally designating the role or recognizing it, funding it with money earmarked for innovation, creating innovating incentives, and developing and selecting sponsorship skills, the organization can improve its chances of successfully innovating. Little attention has been given to sponsors. They are fundamental for innovation to take place.

The third role illustrated in the case example is that of the *orchestrator*. The president played this role. An orchestrator is needed because new ideas are never neutral. In fact, truly innovative ideas are destructive. Innovation destroys investments in capital equipment and affects people's careers. The management of ideas is a political process.[4] The problem is that the political struggle is biased toward the establishment who have significant authority and control of resources. The orchestrator must be a power balancer if the new idea is to have a chance to get tested. The orchestrator's role involves protecting idea people, promoting the opportunity to try out new ideas, and backing them when proven effective. This person has to legitimize the whole process. The president did exactly that with the field engineer. Before he became involved, the hardware establishment prevailed.

Orchestrators play their role by using the processes and rewards described in the following sections. That is, one orchestrates by funding innovating activities and creating incentives for middle managers to sponsor innovating ideas. Orchestrators are the top managers of the organization. It is their task to design the innovating organization.

The typical operating role structure of a divisionalized firm is shown in Figure 2. The hierarchy consists of operating functions reporting to division general managers who, in turn, report to group executives. The group executives report to the chief executive (CEO). Some of these people play roles in both the operating and the innovating organization.

The role structure of the innovating organization is shown in Figure 3. The chief executive and a group executive function as orchestrators. Division managers are the sponsors who work in both the operating and the innovating organization. In addition several "reservations" are created in which managers of R&D, corporate development, product development, market development, and new process technology function as full-time sponsors. These reservations

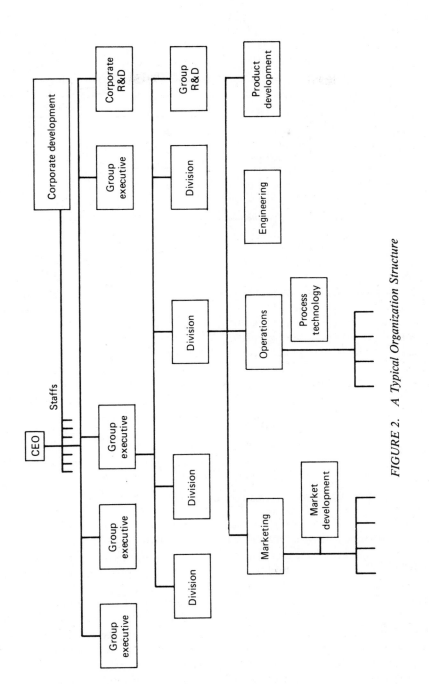

FIGURE 2. A Typical Organization Structure

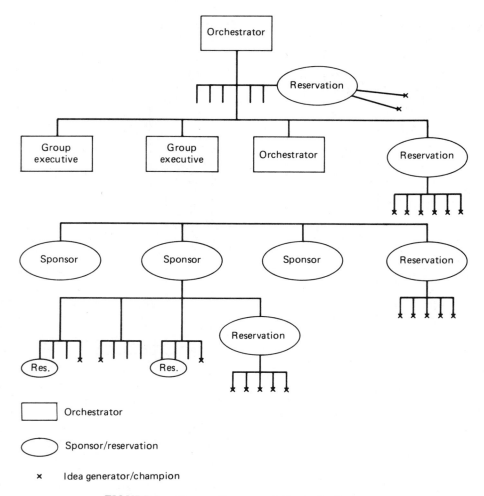

FIGURE 3.   Human Resource Roles in the Structure

allow the separation of innovating activity from the operating core. This separation is an organizing choice we label *differentiation,* and is described in the next section.

Differentiation.   In the case example, the innovation was perfected at a remote site and was relatively advanced before it was ever discovered by management. It suggests that if one wants to stimulate new ideas, the odds are better if the

early effort is differentiated from the operating organization in order to perfect and test "crazy" ideas. An effort is differentiated when it is separated physically, financially, and/or organizationally from the day-to-day activities likely to disrupt it. Had the field engineer worker worked within the engineering department or at company headquarters, his idea probably would have been snuffed out prematurely.

Another kind of differentiation is to free initial idea tests from staff controls designed for the operating organization. At one company, they used to make decisions on whether to buy a new oscilloscope in about 15 or 30 minutes with a shout across the room. After being acquired, that same decision would take 12–18 months because the purchase required a capital appropriation request. Controls based on operating logic and current business logic reduce the ability of the innovating organization to rapidly, cheaply, and frequently test and modify new ideas. Thus the more differentiated an initial effort is, the greater the likelihood of innovation.

The problem with differentiation, however, is that it decreases the likelihood of transferring a new proven idea back into the operating organization. Herein lies the differentiation/transfer dilemma. *The more differentiated an effort, the greater the likelihood of having to manage the transfer of the new idea into the operating organization for implementation.* The dilemma occurs only when the organization needs both invention and diffusion for innovation. That is, some organizations may not need transfer to an operating organization. When Exxon started up its information systems business, there was no intention to have the products implemented by the petroleum company. They had to grow their own operating organizations. Therefore, they maximized differentiation in the early phases. However, when Intel started on the 64K RAM, the effort was consistent with their current business, and transfer into fabrication and sales was critical. Therefore, the effort was only minimally separated from the implementing division producing the 16K RAM. The difficulty arises when a new product or process is different from the current ones, but must be implemented through the existing manufacturing and sales organizations. These organizations need both invention and diffusion. The greater the need for invention and the greater the difference between the new idea and the existing concept of the business, the greater the degree of differentiation that is

needed to perfect the idea. The only way to accomplish both is to proceed stagewise. That is, differentiate in the early phases and then start the transition so that little differentiation exists at implementation. The transition process is described in the section on key processes.

In summary, invention occurs best when initial efforts are separated from the operating organization and its controls. Separation is needed because innovating and operating are fundamentally different and opposing logics. Separation allows both to be preformed simultaneously. Separation also prevents the establishment from prematurely snuffing out a new idea. The less the dominant culture of the organization supports innovation, the greater is the need for separation.[5] Often this separation occurs naturally as in the example, or clandestinely, such as in "bootlegging." If a firm wants to foster innovation, then it can create reservations where innovating activity can occur as a matter of course. Let us now turn to the third and last structural dimension of the innovating organization.

Reservations. Reservations are organizational units (such as R&D) that are totally devoted to creating new ideas for future business. Their purpose is to reproduce the garagelike atmosphere of inventors where people can rapidly and frequently test their ideas. Reservations are meant to be havens for "safe learning." When innovating, one wants to maximize early failure to promote learning. On reservations, separate from operations, this cheap, rapid screening can take place.

Reservations consist of people who work solely for the innovating organization. The reservation manager works full-time as a sponsor. Reservations permit differentiation to occur. They are also located both in the divisions and at corporate headquarters to permit various degrees of differentiation.

Reservations can be internal or external. Internal reservations are like research groups, product and process development labs, market development, new ventures, corporate development and some staff groups. They are organizational homes where idea generators can contribute without becoming managers. This was one of the intentions of staff groups. However, staffs often assume control responsibilities or are narrow specialists who contribute to the current business idea. Because these groups can be expensive, outside reservations such as universities, consulting firms, and advertising agencies are often used to tap nonmanagerial idea generators.

Reservations can also be permanent or temporary. The reservations described such as R&D units are reasonably permanent entities. Others can be temporary. Members of the operating organization can be relieved of operating duties to develop a new program, a new process, or a new product. When developed they take the idea into operating organization and resume their operating responsibilities. But for a period of time they are differentiated from operations in varying degrees in order to innovate, fail, learn, and ultimately perfect a new idea.

Collectively, the roles of orchestrators, sponsors, and idea generators working with and on reservations constitute the structure of the innovating organization. Some of the people such as sponsors and orchestrators play roles in both organizations, whereas reservation managers and idea generators work only for the innovating organization. Virtually everyone in the organization can be an idea generator and all middle managers are potential sponsors. However, not all choose to play these roles. People vary considerably in their innovating skills. By recognizing these roles, developing people for them, giving them opportunity to use their skills through key processes, and rewarding innovating accomplishments, the organization can do considerably better than just allowing the spontaneous process to work as described in the example. Across this structure of the innovating organization are several key processes. These are described in the next section.

Key Processes in the Innovating Organization

In our case example, the idea generator and the first two sponsors found each other through happenstance. The odds of such match-ups can be significantly improved through the explicit design of processes to help sponsors and idea generators find each other. Processes of funding, idea getting, and idea blending are key ones for improving match-ups. In addition, transitions and program management are processes for taking ideas from reservations into operations. Each of these processes is described in the following.

Funding.   One of the key processes to increase an organization's ability to innovate is an explicit funding process for the innovating organization. A leader in this field is Texas Instruments. TI budgets and allocates funds for operating and separate funds for innovating. In essence the orchestrators make the short run-long run tradeoff at this point. They then orchestrate by choosing where to allocate the innovation funds: to division sponsors or corporate reservations. The funding process is a key tool for orchestration.

A lesson from the case example was that it often takes multiple sponsors to launch a new idea. The field engineer's idea would never have been brought to management's attention without the New England sales manager. It would never have been tested in the market without the European sales manager. Multiple sponsors keep fragile ideas alive. If engineering had been the only sponsor for technical ideas, there would have been no innovation.

Some organizations purposely create a multiple sponsoring system and make it legitimate for an idea generator to go to any sponsor that has funding for new ideas. Multiple sponsors duplicate the market system of multiple bankers for entrepreneurs. At 3M, an idea generator can go to his or her division sponsor for funding. If refused, the idea generator can go to any other division sponsor or even to Corporate R&D. If the idea is outside the current businesses, the idea generator can go to the New Ventures group for support. By this point if the idea is rejected by all sponsors, it must not be a very good idea. However, the idea is kept alive and given several opportunities to be tested. The presence of multiple sponsors keep fragile, young ideas alive.

Idea Getting. The idea-getting process occurs in all organizations, as it did in the example. The premise of this section is that the odds of matchups can be improved by organization design. First, the natural process can be improved by network building actions such as multidivision or multireservation careers, companywide seminars, and conferences. All these practices plus a common physical location facilitate matching at 3M.

The process is formalized at TI through an elaborate planning process called the OST System (Objectives, Strategies, and Tactics) which is an annual harvest of new ideas. Innovating funds are distributed to managers of Objectives (sponsors) who fund projects from idea generators which become tactical action programs. Ideas not funded go into a creative backlog to be tapped throughout the year. Whether formally, as at TI, or informally, as at 3M, there is a known system for matching ideas with sponsors.

Ideas are also obtained by aggressive sponsors. Sponsors sit at the crossroads of many ideas and often arrive at a better idea as a result. They then pursue an idea generator to champion it. Good sponsors know where the proven idea people are located and attract them to come and perfect an idea on their reservation. Sponsors will go inside or outside to pursue these idea people.

Finally, formal events can be scheduled for matching purposes. At 3M there is the annual fair at which idea generators can set up booths to be viewed by shopping sponsors. Exxon Enterprises held a "shake the tree event" at which idea people could throw out ideas to be pursued by attending sponsors. Any number of such events can be created. The point is that by devoting time to ideas and making innovation legiti-

mate, the odds of having sponsors find new ideas are increased.

Idea Blending. An important lesson to be derived from our scenario is that it is no accident that a field engineer produced the new product idea. Why? Because the field engineer spends all day working on customer problems and also has knowledge of the technology. Within the mind of a single person, there is a blending of two vital elements of innovation: knowledge of a need and a means for satisfying that need. In addition, our field engineer had a personal need for which the technology could be designed. The premise being espoused here is that innovation is more likely to occur when knowledge of technologies and user requirements are combined in the minds of as few people as possible, with one person the optimal.

On other occasions it is often debated whether innovations are need-stimulated or means-stimulated. Do you start with the disease and look for a cure or start with a cure and find a disease for it? Research shows that two-thirds of the innovations are need-stimulated (Tushman and Moore, 1981). But this argument misses the point. As shown in Figure 4(*a*), the debate is over whether use or means drives the downstream efforts. This kind of thinking is linear and sequential. Instead, the model suggested here is shown in Figure 4(*b*). That is, for innovation to occur, the knowledge of all key components must be simultaneously coupled, and the best way to maximize communication among the components is to have the communication occur intrapersonally. If not intrapersonally, then as few people as possible will effectively communicate interpersonally. The point is that initial innovative ideas occur when knowledge of the essential specialities is coupled in as few heads as possible. This coupling can occur intrapersonally by growing or selecting people. These practices are discussed in the people section.

There is a variety of processes that are employed to match knowledge of need and knowl-

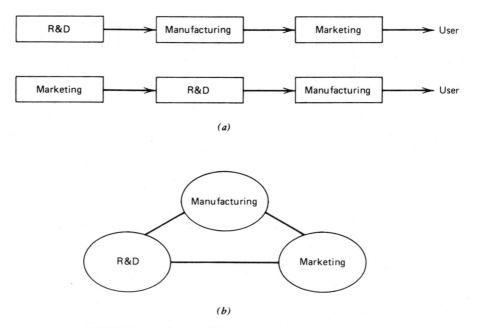

FIGURE 4.   *Nature of Functional Interdependence*

edge of means. AT IBM, marketing staff are placed directly in the R&D labs where they interpret the market requirements documents. People are rotated through this unit and a network is created. Wang holds an annual users' conference at which customers and product designers interact over the use of Wang products. Lanier insists that all top managers, including R&D management, spend one day per month selling in the field. It is said that British scientists made remarkable progress on developing radar after actually flying missions with the RAF. In all these cases there is an explicit matching of the use and the user with knowledge of a technology to meet the use. Again, these processes are explicitly designed to get a user orientation among the idea generators and sponsors. They increase the likelihood that inventions will be innovations. The more complete a new idea or invention is at its inception, the better the likelihood of transfer into the operating organization and the communication of the innovation.

Transmitting.   The most crucial process is the transition of an idea from a corporate reservation to an operating organization for implementation. This process occurs stagewise as in the case example. First, the idea was formulated in the field before management ever knew about it. Then it was tested with a customer, the French bank. And, finally, development and full-scale implementation was the third stage. In other cases several stages of testing and scale-up may occur. Transitions should be planned stagewise. At each stage the orchestrator has several choices that balance the need for further invention with the need for diffusion. The choices and stages of idea development are shown in Figure 5.

The choices facing the orchestrator at each stage are: Who will be the sponsor? Who will be the champion? What is the source of the staff for the effort? At what physical location will work be performed? Who will fund the effort? How much autonomy or how differentiated should the effort be? An idea must go through a transition

Choice/Stage	I	II	. . . .Nth	Implementation
Sponsor	Corporate	Corporate		Division
Champion	Corporate	Corporate		Division
Staffing	Corporate	Corp.-Div.		Division
Location	Corporate	Corporate		Division
Funding	Corporate	Corporate		Division
Autonomy	Corporate	Complete		Minimal

FIGURE 5.   Choices and Stages of Idea Development

from a reservation into an operating division in this stagewise manner. For example, at the initial stage of new idea formulation the sponsor could be the corporate ventures group with the champion working on the corporate reservation. The effort would be staffed with other corporate reservation types and funded by corporate. The activity would be fully separate and autonomous. If the results were positive, the next stage would be entered, but if the idea needed further development, some division people would be brought in to round out the needed specialties. If the data were still positive after the second stage, then the effort could be transferred physically to the division but the champion, sponsor, and funding would still be corporate. In this manner, by orchestrating through choice of sponsor, champion, staff, location, funding, and autonomy, the orchestrator balances the need for innovation and protection with the need for testing against reality and diffusion.

This is an all too brief outline of the transition process. Entire books have been written on the subject of technology transfer (Rogers and Rogers, 1976). The goal here is to highlight the stagewise nature of the process and the decisions to be made by the orchestrator at each stage. The process is crucial because it is the link between the two organizations. That is, in order to consistently innovate, the firm needs an operating organization, an innovating organization, and a process for the transition of ideas from one to the other.

Program Management Process.   Finally, equally critical to the innovating organization is the program management process of implementing new products and processes within a division. That is, the idea generator usually hands the innovation over to a product/design/program manager at the time of implementation, who follows it across the functional organization within the division. Although the systems and organizational processes for project management have been discussed elsewhere (Galbraith, 1977), the point is that a program management process is vital.

In summary, across the innovating structure run several key processes. These are the funding, idea getting, idea blending, transition, and program management processes. Many of these occur naturally in all organizations. The implicit hypothesis of this section is that the odds for successful innovation can be increased by the explicit design of these processes and the devotion of corporate resources to them.

HUMAN RESOURCE POLICIES

To complete the design of the innovating organization, the human resource policy areas of rewards, selection, and people development need to be addressed. In this section human resource policies for idea generators and sponsors are specifically addressed. In many cases these policies are different from the systems needed in the operating organization.

Reward System

The innovating organization, like the operating organization, needs an incentive system of its own to motivate innovating behavior. Since the task of innovating is different from the task of operating, the innovating organization needs a different reward system. The innovating task is riskier, more difficult, and takes place over longer time horizons. These factors usually require some adjustment to the reward system of the operating organization. The amount of adjustment depends on how innovative the operating organization is, and on the attractiveness of outside alternatives.

The functions of the reward system are threefold. First, the rewards are to attract and hold idea people in the company and in the reservations. As firms have different attraction and retention problems, they will vary in the reward systems they use. Second, the rewards should motivate the extra effort needed to innovate. After failing 19 times, something has to motivate the idea generator to make the twentieth attempt. And, finally, rewards should be given for successful performance. These rewards should accrue to idea generators primarily. However, the reward measurement system for the sponsors is equally important, and each is discussed in the next section.

Rewards for Idea Generators.
The choice of reward system consists of encouraging internal motivation by providing opportunity to pursue one's ideas, promotion, recognition, and special compensation. People can be attracted and motivated intrinsically by simply giving them the opportunity and the autonomy to pursue their own

ideas. Autonomy is provided by placing them in a reservation. Many idea people are internally driven as was the field engineer in the case example. As such, the provision of opportunity to an idea generator to come to a reservation, pursue his or her own ideas, and be guided and evaluated by reservation manager constitutes a minimal level or reward. If the minimal level attracts and motivates idea people, the innovating organization should go no further in creating a separate reward system.

Additional motivational leverage can be obtained if needed through promotion and recognition for innovating performance. The dual ladder is the best example where an individual contributor can be promoted and given increased salary without becoming a manager. At 3M a contributor can rise in the organization to an equivalent level of a group executive and not be a manager. The dual ladder has always existed in R&D but is now being extended to other functions as well. Other firms use special recognition for career performance. AT IBM there is the IBM Fellows program in which a Fellow is selected and can then work on projects of his or her own choosing for the next five years. At 3M there is the Carlton Award which is described as an internal Nobel Prize. The promotion and recognition systems reward innovation and aid in building an innovating culture.

When greater motivation is needed and/or the organization wants to signal the importance of innovation, special compensation is used in addition to providing opportunity and recognition. Different systems have been used. They are discussed in order of increasing motivational impact and of increasing dysfunctional ripple effects.

Some companies reward successful idea generators with one-time case awards. For example, International Harvester's share of the combine market jumped from 12% to 17% due to the introduction of the axial flow combine. The scientist whose six patents contributed to the product development was given $10,000. If the product continues to succeed, he may be given another award. IBM uses the "Chairman's Outstanding Contribution Award." The current program manager on the 4300 series was given a $5000 award for her breakthrough in coding on her last assignment. These awards are post hoc and serve to reward rather than to attract and motivate.

Stronger motivation is achieved through programs that offer a "percentage of the take" to the idea generator and early team members. Toy and game companies give a royalty to inventors, internal and external, of toys and games that are introduced. Apple Computers claims to give employees a royalty for software programs they write and which will run on Apple equipment. A chemical company started a pool which was created by putting 4% of the first five years of earnings aside from a new business venture. The pool was to be distributed to the initial venture team. Other companies create pools from percentages (2–20%) of cost savings created by process innovations. In any case, a predetermined contract is created to motivate the idea generator and early joiners of the risky effort.

The most controversial effort to date are those attempts to duplicate free market rewards inside the firm. A few years ago, ITT bought a small company named Qume which made high-speed printers. The founder became a millionaire. He had to quit his initial organization to found the venture capital effort. If ITT can make an outsider a millionaire, why not give the same chance to entrepreneurial insiders? Many people agree with that premise but have not found the formula to implement the idea. One firm created some five-year milestones for a venture, the accomplishment of which would result in a cash reward of six million dollars to the idea generator. However, the business climate changed after two years and the idea generator, not surprisingly, tried to make the plan rather than adapt to the new, unforeseen reality. Another scheme is to give the idea generator and the initial team some phantom stock. That stock gets evaluated at sale time the same way any acquisition would be eval-

uated. This process duplicates the free market process and gives internal people the same venture capital opportunities and risks as they have on the outside.

Although the special compensation programs produce motivation, they also have dysfunctional consequences. Other people often contribute at later stages and feel like second-class citizens. Also, any program that discriminates among people produces perceptions of inequity and possible fall-out in the operating organization.[6] Care should be taken to manage the fall-out if the benefits are judged to outweigh the costs.

Rewards for Sponsors. Sponsors also need incentives. In the case example the sales people had an incentive to adopt a new product because they were being beaten in the market. Sponsors will not sponsor innovating ideas unless the sponsor has innovating incentives. The task of the orchestrator is to create and communicate those incentives.

Sponsor incentives take many forms At 3M, division managers have a bonus goal that 25% of their revenue should come from products introduced in the last five years. When the percentage falls and the bonus is threatened, these sponsors become amazingly receptive to new product ideas. The transfer process becomes much easier as a result. Sales growth, percent revenue increase, number of new products, and so on are all bases for creating incentives for sponsors to adopt innovating ideas.

Another controversy occurs when the idea generators get phantom stock. Should the sponsors who supervise these idea people get some phantom stock, too? Some banks have created separate subsidiaries so that sponsors can get stock in the new venture. To the degree that sponsors contribute to idea development, they will need to be given the stock options as well.

Thus the innovating organization needs its own reward system for idea generators and sponsors. The firm should start with as simple a reward system as possible and move to more motivating, more complex, and possibly more upsetting rewards as attraction and motivation problems require.

Staffing the Innovating Organization
The last policy area of the innovating organization is that of staffing practices. The assumption is that some people are better at innovating than others and these other people are necessarily those who are good at operating. Therefore, the ability of the innovating organization to generate new business ideas can be increased by systematically developing and selecting those people who are better at innovating than others. But first the attributes must be identified. They are discussed in the following for the idea generators and the sponsors.

Attributes of Idea Generators. The field engineer in the case example is the quintessential inventor. He is not mainstream. He is hard to get along with and breaks company policy in order to perfect an idea. These people have strong egos which allow them to persist in swimming upstream. They generally are not the kind of people who get along well in an organization. However, if there are reservations, innovating funds, and dual ladders, these people can be attracted and retained.

The psychological attributes of successful entrepreneurs are those of *high need for achievement and risk taking*. But several other attributes are needed to translate that need onto innovation. First, there is usually an irreverence towards the status quo. These people often come from outcast groups such as immigrants. They are less satisfied with the way things are and have less to lose with a change in the current business idea.

Another attribute is that of *previous programming in the industry*. Successful innovation requires indepth knowledge in the industry gained either through experience or formal education. Hence the innovator needs to obtain the knowledge of the industry, though not the "religion." Previous start-up experience is also associated with successful business ventures. Attracting people from incubator firms (high technology) and areas (Boston, Silicon Valley) can increase the odds of finding innovators.

The amount of organizational effort required to select these people varies with the ability to attract them to the organization in the first place. If idea people are attracted through reputation, then by funding reservations and employing idea-getting processes, idea people will select themselves and over time earn a reputation for idea generation. If the firm has no reputation for innovation, then idea people must be sought out or external reservations used for initial idea generation. One firm made extensive use of outside recruiting. A sponsor would develop an idea and then attend annual conferences of key specialties to determine who was best in the area, interview them, and then offer the ones with entrepreneurial interests the opportunity to develop the venture.

Another key attribute of successful business innovators is *varied experience*. This variety creates the coupling of knowledge of means and use in the mind of a single individual. It is the generalist not the specialist who creates an idea outside the current business idea. Specialists are inventors; generalists are innovators. These people can be selected or developed. One firm selects the best and the brightest from the ceramics engineering schools and places them in central engineering in order to learn the system. Then they are assigned to field engineering where they spend three to five years with clients and client problems. Then they return to central engineering product design. Only then do they get to design products for those same customers. The internal coupling can be created by role rotation. Some aerospace firms rotate engineers through manufacturing liaison roles.

Thus there are some known characteristics of idea generators. These people can be attracted or selected. By role rotation a varied experiential

Jay R. Galbraith

background can also be created. These people will be retained, however, only if there are reservations for them and sponsors to champion them.

Attributes of Sponsors and Reservation Managers. The people who manage the idea development process must also be attracted, developed, retrained, and trained, as well as those who generate and test ideas. Again, some attributes and skills are better for managing ideas than other, and the innovating organization needs those who have learned the idea management skills. The attributes to be selected and developed are a management style for idea people, early experience in innovating, idea-generating capabilities, skills at putting together deals, and generalist business skills. A description of these attributes follows.

One of the key skills of the innovating organization is to manage and supervise the kind of person who is likely to be an idea generator and champion. In the last section these idea people were described as those who do not take to being supervised very well. This is certainly true. Idea generators and champions have a great deal of ownership of their ideas. They gain their satisfaction by having "done it their way." The intrinsic satisfaction comes from ownership and autonomy. However, idea people also need help, advice, and sounding boards. The successful sponsor learns how to manage these people the same way a producer or publisher learns to handle the egos of stars and writers. The style was best described by a successful sponsor:

> It's a lot like teaching your kids to ride a bike. You're there. You walk along behind. If the kid takes off he or she never knows that they could have been helped. If they stagger a little, you lend a helping hand, undetected, preferably. If they fall, you catch them. If they do something stupid, you take the bike away until they're ready.

This style is quite different than the hands-on, directive style of an operating organization.

Of course, the best way to learn it is to have been personally managed that way and seen it practiced in an innovating organization. This reinforces the value of experience in an innovation organization.

More than the idea generators, the sponsors need to understand the logic of innovation and have experienced the management of innovation. As for any activity, the managers need to have an intuitive feel for the task and its nuances. Managers who are only experienced in operations will not have developed the managerial style, understanding, and intuitive feel that is necessary to manage innovations because the logic of operations is counter-intuitive to the logic of innovations. This means that some of the idea generators and champions who have experienced innovation should become managers as well as individual contributors. The president in the example scenario was the inventor of the first generation product and, therefore, understood the long agonizing process of developing a business idea. Perhaps this is why it is rare to find an R&D unit that is managed by someone who did not come through the ranks of R&D.

The best idea sponsors and idea reservations managers are people who have experienced innovation early in their careers and are comfortable with it. They will have been exposed to risks, uncertainty, parallel experiments, repeated failures (which lead to learning), coupling as opposed to assembly-line thinking, long time-frames, and personal control systems based on people and ideas rather than numbers and budget variances. Other managers who have already developed their intuition and style in operations have difficulty in switching to the innovating organization late in their careers. These sponsor and reservation managers can then be developed or recruited from the outside.

Sponsors and reservation managers need to be idea generators themselves. Ideas tend to come from two sources. The first is at low levels or the organization where the problem gap is experienced. The idea generator who offers a solu-

591

tion is the one who experience the problem and goes to a sponsor for testing and development. One problem with these ideas is that they are partial since they come from a specialist whose view can be parochial and local. But sponsors are at the crossroads of many partial ideas. They may get a larger vision of the emerging situation as a result. These idea sponsors can generate a business idea themselves or blend several partial ideas into a business idea. These sponsors and reservation managers at the crossroads of idea flows are an important second source on new ideas. Therefore, they should be selected and trained for idea generation.

Another skill the sponsors and, especially, reservation managers need is deal making and brokering. Once an idea has emerged, a reservation manager may have to argue for the release of key people, space, resources, charters, pro-

duction time, or a customer contact. These deals all need to be made through persuasion. In that sense it is no different than project or product management roles. But people vary in their ability to cut a deal and bargain. Those who can should be selected. Those who have the other idea management skills can be trained in negotiating and bargaining.

And finally, the sponsors and reservation managers need to be generalists with general business skills. Again, this skill is needed to recognize a business idea and to shape partial ideas into business ideas. They need to coach idea generators in specialties in which the idea generator is not schooled. Most successful research managers are those with business skills who can see the business significance in the good ideas that come from scientists.

In summary, the sponsors and reservation

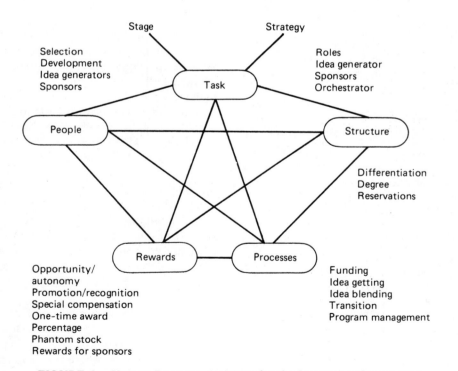

FIGURE 6. *Human Resource Activities for the Innovating Organization*

managers who manage the idea development process should also be recruited, selected, and developed. The skills that these people need relate to their style, experience, idea-generating ability, deal-making ability, and generalist business acumen. These skills can either be selected or developed. Since some of the attributes of successful idea generators and idea sponsors can be identified, the innovating organization should staff and develop according to these criteria. In so doing, the organization improves its odds at generating and developing new business ideas.

CONCLUSION

The innovating organization that has just been described is one that recognizes and formalizes the roles, processes, rewards, and people practices that naturally lead to innovations. The point emphasized throughout is that by purposely designing these roles and processes, the organization is more likely to generate innovations. This purposely designed organization is needed to overcome the obstacles to innovation. Innovation is destructive to many established groups and will be resisted. Innovation is also contrary to current business operations and will be ignored. These obstacles and others are more likely to be overcome with an organization designed to innovate.

Managers have tried to overcome these obstacles by creating good policies but by themselves will not generate innovations. The message is that a consistent set of policies concerning structure, process, rewards, and people is needed. The characteristics of the innovating organization are illustrated in Figure 6. It is the combination of idea people, reservations for them, sponsors to supervise them, funding for ideas, and rewards for success that increase the odds in favor of innovation. Simply implementing one or two of these practices will result in failure and will teach people that such practices do not work. A consistent combination of these practices will ensure an innovating organization.

NOTES

1. The Luddites were a band of British workmen who joined in riots between 1811 and 1816 for the destruction of machinery under the belief that its introduction reduced wages and increased unemployment.
2. See also Galbraith (1977) and Nadler and Tushman (1977).
3. Throughout the paper, the term ''innovation'' is used to mean either a substantive or process idea *that is brought to market*. This typically requires the coordinated involvement of two or more individuals.
4. The politics of innovation are well documented in such case studies as A. Pettigrew, *The Politics of Organizational Decision-Making*. London: Tavistock, 1973; see also Pfeffer and Salancik (1977).
5. Many papers discuss the impact of corporate culture on the organization. The importance of innovation in turbulent environments speaks to the design of an ''overlay'' on the human resource system and corporate culture of most organizations to foster innovation.
6. For a detailed discussion of the research on equity in organizations, see J. S. Adams (1965).

DATE DUE

The Library Store   #47-0103